TAKING FLIGHT

Inventing the Aerial Age
from Antiquity through
the First World War

TAKING
FLIGHT

RICHARD P. HALLION

OXFORD
UNIVERSITY PRESS
2003

OXFORD
UNIVERSITY PRESS

Oxford   New York
Auckland Bangkok Buenos Aires Cape Town Chennai
Dar es Salaam Delhi Hong Kong Istanbul Karachi Kolkata
Kuala Lumpur Madrid Melbourne Mexico City Mumbai Nairobi
São Paulo Shanghai Taipei Tokyo Toronto

Copyright © 2003 by Richard P. Hallion

Published by Oxford University Press, Inc.
198 Madison Avenue, New York, New York 10016

www.oup.com

Oxford is a registered trademark of Oxford University Press

Library of Congress Cataloging-in-Publication Data
Hallion, Richard.
Taking flight : inventing the aerial age from antiquity through the
First World War / by Richard P. Hallion.
p. cm.
Includes index.
ISBN 0-19-516035-5
1. Aeronautics—History.
I. Title.
TL515.H22 2003
629.13'009—dc21
2002030821

Book design and composition by Mark McGarry, Texas Type & Book Works
Set in Monotype Dante

10 9 8 7 6 5 4 3 2 1

Printed in the United States of America
on acid-free paper

To Christine

"I offer to your ladyship nothing of mine, either because it is already yours, or because I find nothing in my writings worthy of you: but I have a great desire that these verses, into what part of the world soever they may travel, may carry your name in the front, for the honour [that] will accrue to them. . . ."

from Étienne de La Boétie, to the Comtesse De Guissen,
in Michel de Montaigne, *Essays*, Book I, n. 28 (1580)

CONTENTS

Dear Friends, I have a wonderful story to tell you—a story that, in some respects, outrivals the Arabian Nights fables—a story, too, with a moral that I think many of the younger ones need, and perhaps some of the older ones too if they will heed it. God in His great mercy has permitted me to be, at least somewhat, instrumental in ushering in and introducing to the great wide world an invention that may outrank electric cars, the automobiles, and all other methods of travel, and one which may fairly take a place beside the telephone and wireless telegraphy. Am I claiming a good deal? Well, I will tell my story, and you shall be the judge.

—Amos I. Root, "Our Homes,"
Gleanings in Bee Culture (1 Jan. 1905)

INTRODUCTION:

From Myth to Machine

The late Mel Kranzberg, a great, energetic, feisty, opinionated, and iconoclastic historian who helped define and evolve the entire field of technology studies, used to caution new graduate students and veteran professors alike that the first question any study or essay they wrote had to answer is "So what?" As the one hundredth anniversary of Kitty Hawk beckons, it certainly isn't as if the story hasn't been told before. Forests have already fallen before the pens, typewriters, and word processors of authors extolling the heroic era of early aviation. An elemental search in February 2002 of available resources on early aviation pioneers revealed not quite 530,000 citations, mentions, and references.[1]

For example, it is already common knowledge that

—Though the dream of flight dated to antiquity, virtually nothing of significance was accomplished until the end of the nineteenth century.
—The crushing anti-intellectualism of the medieval Church, combined with the notorious superstitions and prejudices of the Middle Ages, stifled virtually all useful scientific and technological inquiry, including flight, which church fathers equated with witchcraft and heresy. Indeed, contemporaneous Islamic, Chinese, and Mogul societies manifested far more accepting and positive intellectual climates than the Christendom of medieval Europe. Only after the Reformation and the onset of the Scientific Revolution did Europeans make their first significant advances toward flight.
—The Wright brothers, untutored and working in isolation, drawing only upon their own skills, single-handedly invented the airplane, making possible every other plane that has flown to this day. Self-taught bicycle makers, they shrewdly used the simple "Yankee engineering" approach of the practical craftsman.
—The Wrights taught the world to fly, and their success led to many others expropriating their ideas, which robbed the brothers of the fruits of their labor. Europe (France in particular) had possessed little understanding of what path to

take until the brothers made their trips of 1908 and 1909—the first foreign tours of any airplane and its designers. Only after this eye-opening exposure did Continental aviation flourish, as Europe's aviators abandoned their own outlandish concepts, seized upon those of the Wrights, and then made their own copies and embellishments of the brothers' work.

—Tragically, the death of Wilbur Wright in 1912 rendered moot what future course Wright technology might have taken, for with his death, the boldly innovative and pathbreaking research of the two brothers came to an abrupt end. No other American or European possessed their insight, and their departure thus constituted a blessing for their rivals, particularly the Europeans, who subsequently dominated the aviation field through the First World War and into the 1920s.

—The invention of the airplane, prior to 1914, generated little interest in either its commercial or military exploitation; aviation was largely the stuff of sport and adventure, not part and parcel of national rivalries and arms races. Not surprisingly, then, when the airplane did go to war in 1914, it proved but a romantic and exciting sideshow to the crucial struggle on the ground and at sea: despite the glamour and adventurous appeal of wartime aviation, the airplane had virtually no influence on the outcome.

So with so much already known about early flight, why another book? In part because *every one* of the preceding statements is *false*.

First of all, the quest for flight involved far more than the drive to build the first airplane. By the Middle Ages, humanity already had a significant grasp on working the air via sails, kites, windmills, helicopter toys, flue turbines in kitchens, and rockets. Vigorous debates pondered the nature of the atmosphere, and numerous manuscripts and paintings appeared that depicted the act of flying or flying implements and vehicles. Balloon concepts appeared in the seventeenth century, and the balloon itself in the eighteenth. The late eighteenth and then the nineteenth centuries witnessed the balloon applied to both war and science, and the first experiments with steerable airships. Extraordinary work defining the requirements and essential shape of the practical airplane took place at the beginning of the nineteenth century, and even more detailed work thereafter, principally in England, France, and Germany, culminated in the glider experiments of the 1890s.

In contrast to popular myth, the medieval church was a vigorous intellectual body that championed the building of schools and universities, supported scientific inquiry and the adaptation and integration of knowledge from other societies (including both China and the Islamic world), and encouraged its priests and church leaders to study broadly in classical literature, mathematics, and the sciences. The Judeo-Christian tradition strongly endorsed flight, which it depicted prominently in church art, and medieval churchmen themselves were enthusiastic students and experimenters with flight and related scientific and technological matters. Indeed, Christendom proved far more supportive of flight (and all science and technology) after the twelfth century than other societies; by the time of the Scientific Revolution five centuries later, Islamic,

Chinese, and Mogul societies were already following, not leading, that of the West, which ensured that flight would ultimately be a product of a western, not eastern, sensibility. Finally, though the Scientific Revolution encouraged an experimentalist mindset and a rootedness of scientific work in hypothesis, observation, and measurement, the invention of flight was far more a product of a craft and technological tradition. Science came far later to flight than technology.

Let it be clearly understood that the Wrights, and no one else, invented the airplane. But they did not invent it in isolation. They were well aware of all previous work, sought out information and advice, relied (sometimes to their sorrow) on the work of others, and kept abreast of developments in America and abroad, even polishing their language skills in French and German so as to be able to understand the latest in European thought. Far from being "cut and try" craftsmen, the Wrights were highly trained and gifted proto-engineers who kept meticulous records, constantly assessed and evaluated their work, and creatively blended ground and in-flight research. They were masters at integrating various technologies into a synthesized, successful whole. They developed the world's first successful airplane capable of a powered, sustained, and controlled flight, but the design they chose differed radically from the mainstream path that world aircraft design would follow after 1905. There were elements of a Greek tragedy about the Wrights, for though they knew how to make—and did make—the first airplane, they did not know how to make its successors.

Most assuredly, the Wrights did not *teach the world to fly, for by the time the Wrights demonstrated their aircraft in public (in 1908 and 1909), the* French *were already flying basic designs by Blériot, Farman, and Levavasseur that would place them well ahead of the United States within two years.* And the Wrights were not the first to demonstrate an airplane overseas: before Wilbur flew in Europe, French airmen had already flown abroad, in Belgium, Italy—and even the United States. Instead, what the Wrights taught was something else: how to fly *better.* Though it is true the Wrights emphasized controllability, their views on this were not unique, with one important exception: they realized, from the outset of their work, the basic "three-dimensionality" of flight that differentiated it from merely "driving" through the sky. The Wrights recognized, better than others, that an airplane had to be controlled in banking and rolling flight, particularly to make turns.

Control is what really separated the work of the brothers from others'. In fact, the nature of their design gave them no option but to do so. The airplane configuration the brothers developed was essentially unique to them—a "tail-first" biplane demanding extraordinary piloting skills, for it was totally unstable in all three axes of flight: pitch (nose up–nose down), roll (wing up–wing down), and yaw (nose left–nose right). Excellent controllability was mandatory, not optional, if the Wrights were to fly safely, for their design was unforgiving of error, something that, a century later, would confound numerous enthusiasts trying to fabricate "authentic" flying replicas. Also, it had a very complex system of levers governing the flight controls, nothing so simple as the European-style "stick" or "wheel" and rudder pedal controls that proliferated by the time of the First World War. Thus, though successful in achieving the world's first powered, sustained, and controlled flight, the Wright Flyer was neither a commercial success nor an inspiration for similar kinds of airplanes built by others. The Europeans and other American pioneers examined the Wright's approach, recognized the importance of controllability in roll, adopted simplified joystick or control-wheel design approaches, and, most significantly, wisely chose the inherently stable philosophy for their own indigenous aircraft, which subsequently dominated world aviation by 1911.

The death of Wilbur Wright robbed American aviation of its brightest and most insightful and tenacious researcher, but by that time the work of the brothers was already in eclipse. As European aviation moved rapidly into the era of the streamlined monoplane and biplane, the American government dithered over its role (if any) in supporting aviation research and industry, an enervating patent suit increasingly dominated American aviation, and the brothers' configurations continued to emphasize incremental refinement to what had been the basic "practical" Flyer of 1905: wheels instead of skids and a catapult, an aft horizontal tail as a concession to stability, minor variations in design geometry and layout, changes to the control system, etc. But overall, even as late as 1914, the Wright company continued to emphasize the chain-driven "pusher" layout, a hopelessly outdated design approach at a time when the newest European aircraft were already routinely approaching and even exceeding 100 miles per hour, and when Russia's Igor Sikorsky was demonstrating enclosed cabin multi-engine biplane transports capable of flying hundreds of miles with a cargo of passengers—or bombs. In sum, Europe raced past the United States because of better ideas, better organization, and stronger national leadership—not because of the death of Wilbur Wright and the withdrawal of his brother Orville from an active role in the industry.

Both the airship and the airplane were integral to the big-power arms buildup prior to the First World War and the subject of much discussion and thought in professional military circles. By the summer of 1914, Europe's armies had been exercising military airplanes at their annual maneuvers for four years, and the airplane had been blooded in combat as early as 1911, when Italy dispatched an air expeditionary force to Tripoli that bombed, reconnoitered, and spotted for naval and army gunfire support. Airplanes likewise figured prominently in the Balkan wars prior to Sarajevo. No clear doctrinal understanding or structure existed for the employment of nascent air power in any of the European nations or the United States, but as the Great War drew increasingly close, it was generally accepted that the airplane would be employed for reconnaissance, artillery spotting, and bombardment in any future conflict.

Within a month of the outbreak of the First World War, the airplane had already demonstrated its transformational qualities in the battles of Tannenberg and the Marne. These two battles—among the most significant in world history—irrevocably altered the outcome of the First World War and, indeed, the twentieth century. That they did so was due largely to the use of the airplane as a reconnaissance system. By the middle of the war, the obvious value of reconnaissance and the utility of the airplane for artillery spotting and bombardment had spawned any number of military missions and given rise, as well, to the fighter. By war's end the air services were firmly established as full-fledged partners of their respective armies and navies, and indeed, Great Britain, in the face of the world's first sustained strategic bombing campaign, had gone so far as to create the world's first independent air arm, the Royal Air Force. Far from being a sideshow, land-and-sea-based air attack, air defense, air observation, and air superiority were intrinsic to combined-arms military operations from Palestine to the Western Front and the Balkans as well. Thus, within less than a decade of its creation, the military airplane had demonstrated its power to transform battles and strategy and significantly influence the war's outcome. Transforming the civil world would follow.

History at its heart is the working and actions of people through time. Also, history is the process and pursuit of definition; it is, as William Green has written, "what we make of the past. It is our means, however feeble, of imposing rational order upon chaos. As our needs, our perceptions, and our priorities change, so must our history. Even if the data of the past were to remain the same—which it does not—the information we would attempt to derive from it would change. . . . History is not a pursuit of perfection. It is a pursuit of meaning."[2]

Speaking to the school of law at Yale University in April 1931, Cornell's great intellectual historian Carl L. Becker stated, "The 'new history' is an old story. Since history is not an objective reality, but only an imaginative reconstruction of vanished events, the pattern that appears useful and agreeable to one generation is not entirely so to the next."[3] In the first of that same series of talks, he traced the evolution of natural philosophy into modern science and commented that the result of pursuing the scientific method "has been astounding. It is needless to say that we live in a machine age, that the art of inventing is the greatest of our inventions, or that within a brief space of fifty years the outward conditions of life have been transformed."[3]

The vantage point of a century after the invention of the airplane offers a valuable opportunity to reconsider how flight began, in a far broader and larger context than previously. Basically, the invention of flight represented the culmination of centuries of thought and desire. The balloon gave humanity its first experience aloft, but at the mercy of the winds. Its successor, the steerable airship, had more practicality but still any number of limitations that worked against it. But the airplane truly launched the aerial age. Its subsequent impact over a century has been extraordinary, across a range of purposes, chiefly for commerce and military affairs. (If nothing else, that would be reason enough to write yet another tome).

It is time to reassess and reexamine the early history of flight, address commonly held beliefs, determine what was and was not accomplished by early pioneers, trace the "transfer" of experiment and practice into what might be called the "operational art" of aviation, and analyze its impact on the course of subsequent history. I believe there were seven distinct phases to the invention of flight, and I have organized this work around them: the "prehistory" of human flight from antiquity to the Enlightenment, a period largely of dreams and desires but also some significant technical work; the era of the dominance of the balloon and the first airships, from the late eighteenth century to the beginning of the twentieth; early interest and work on the airplane, from the end of the eighteenth century to just before the success of the Wrights at Kitty Hawk; the triumphant development of the airplane, the fulfillment of work by four major figures (the German Lilienthal, America's Chanute, and America's two Wright brothers) whose own work was leavened by the experience and example (good and bad) of others; the resurgence of European aeronautics between 1905 and the end of 1909; the international expansion and maturation of flight and its incorporation into the military, from 1910 to Sarajevo, a period coinciding as well with the steep decline of America's aviation fortunes; and finally, what might be considered the transfer of prophecy into practice, as the airplane (and flight in general) came to play an ever more important role in world affairs.

Any historian stands on the shoulders of those who have gone before—my acknowledgments offer testimony to my own ample debts—and there is already an excellent and rich body of scholarship covering narrow aspects of the story, with some fine survey works that sweep more broadly across the entire history of flight from antiquity through the end of the Second World War. But it is surprising, with so much having been written and with only a century having passed, how many myths (such as those listed above), misunderstandings, and questionable assumptions and interpretations continue to influence our thought about the invention of flight and particularly its evolution over the first two decades of practical aviation.

This book is an attempt at integrating and interpreting the early international history of flight, both *aerostatic* (lighter than air balloons and airships) and *aerodynamic* (heavier than air airplanes), within the context of prevailing social, cultural, technological, scientific, political, and military history, and then taking it through the first 15 years—arguably aviation's most critical years—of the twentieth century. Since that time aviation has become pervasive and deserving of its own detailed subsequent examination.

But there is as well another, more emotional, reason underlying this work. That flight has had such an impact upon the modern world is due to its invention by a number of remarkable people. For centuries inventing flight occupied (and in some cases bedazzled) some of the best minds in the history of technology, as well as a host of unknown would-be inventors and occasional cranks. Today the visitor who at Malmesbury Abbey feels the cold sting of a sharpening wind out of the southwest, who walks the grounds of Versailles, or the Tuileries, or the Mall in Washington, who lands at Templehof or College Park, who skirts the Indiana shoreline of Lake Michigan, who crosses Salisbury Plain near Larkhill or visits Farnborough, Chalais-Meudon, Johannisthal, Hammondsport, the Outer Banks of the Carolinas, Rheims, Pau, North Island at San Diego, or any of dozens of other readily accessible sites, sees where these people made their contributions, experienced their successes (and sometimes more frequent failures), and flew in triumph or, too often, crashed and died. The models, kites, balloons, gliders, and airplanes they flew are readily on view in a wide range of excellent museums in Europe and America. Some are themselves located at historic aviation sites: Hendon, north of London, is home to the Royal Air Force Museum; Le Bourget, north of Paris, boasts the Musée de l'Air et de l'Espace; Wright-Patterson Air Force Base, east of Dayton, has the Air Force Museum, to name a few.

Seeing the places, seeing the machines, one cannot help but be moved at the effort so many made over so many years to achieve what is now simply and casually taken for granted by the modern traveler, headphones in place and drink in hand, idly watching a movie or reading a novel while flying at 10 miles per minute at altitudes over 35,000 feet. (Unless, of course, one belongs to that unhappy class of fearful flyers who once focused their anxious gazes to check if the wings were staying on, but who now, after 9/11/2001 [all too understandably], eye their fellow passengers and perhaps their shoes with nervous stares.)

Flight was an international achievement born of the attitudes, technological outlook, and previous accomplishments of a largely European-rooted culture (including that of the United States) that was at once exploratory and optimistic, and that displayed increasing mastery over nature via ever more complex machines and equipment. It was likewise an achievement that demanded rigorous analysis, keen insight, very hard work, physical courage, and an unflinching willingness to subject oneself to frequent criticism, ridicule, and even derision, knowing—and accepting—that one was working "outside the mainstream" of conventional scientific and popular wisdom.

It is the story of that achievement and the individuals who made it possible that I have sought to capture in this work. Finally, the opinions and views expressed in this work should not be construed as representing the views or positions of any person or organization, governmental or private, other than myself.

Richard P. Hallion
March 2002

PART ONE

PREPARING THE WAY:
FROM ANTIQUITY TO THE
ENLIGHTENMENT

CHAPTER ONE

Of Dreams and Desires

In the winter of 328 B.C., passing through the rugged mountains of Sogdiana, deep in Central Asia, Alexander the Great and his Macedonian army approached the Rock of Arimazes, an impregnable fortress looming over icy, treacherous perpendicular cliffs, accessible only by a steep and easily defended trail. Alexander had no expectation of successfully storming the fortress, save for his own growing reputation, and so he offered free and safe passage to its guardians if they would surrender. But the Bactrian leader Oxyartes and his garrison, secure in their mountain fastness, contemptuously rejected the generous offer and replied that they would capitulate only if winged soldiers landed on the heights. Fuming, Alexander resorted to subterfuge: he offered tremendous rewards for volunteers who would climb the cliffs at night. A total of 300 men responded. That night they made their way to the base of the most foreboding (and hence least guarded) cliff and slowly began to climb, using tent pegs and ropes. Though 30 fell to their deaths, sunrise the next morning witnessed the others perched *above* the fortress, derisively waving winglike white scarves at the astonished garrison. Unsure whether the men *had* flown to their perch, Oxyartes quickly assented to Alexander's next call for surrender. His attitude before—and reaction after—Alexander's brave volunteers ascended the windy, ice-encrusted heights of Arimazes indicates just how miraculous humans considered flight to be before the age of practical aviation. Nothing succeeds quite like success: Alexander subsequently married Roxana, the defeated king's daughter, and Oxyartes himself became a strong ally of the young warrior king.[1]

From the dawn of time people around the globe have expressed the dream of flight, emphasizing the incredible and depicting aerial powers as an element of religion, mythology, or war.[2] The Egyptians worshipped Horus, the sky-god falcon, son of Isis and Osiris and victorious over the evil god Set.[3] The peoples of Asia Minor venerated various flying deities, such as the winged Hurrian goddess Shaushka (Ishtar) and the sacred double-headed eagle of Hittite tradition. In addition there was the winged sun disk, another incarnation of Horus, that,

Icarus on the rocks, shaken not stirring. Celestin Nanteuil, 1845. Courtesy New York Public Library (NYPL)

transplanted from Egypt, appeared as a royal and divine symbol in Hittite and Assyrian society.[4] The angels of Judeo-Christian tradition carried this association of flight and divinity further still.[5]

The story of Daedalus and Icarus and their ill-fated escape from Crete on wings made of wax-glued feathers is the best-known example of flight in Western mythology. Daedalus, forced to escape from Crete after affronting King Minos, constructed a pair of wings with feathers secured in place by wax for his son Icarus and himself. He cautioned Icarus not to fly too close to the sun, but the impetuous youth, "rejoiced by the lift of his great sweeping wings," ignored the warning. He flew higher and higher until the sun melted the wax, loosening the feathers, and he tumbled from the sky into the sea. The grieving Daedalus retrieved the corpse, buried it on Icaria, and then flew on to Italy.[6]

Tales likewise abound from Africa, Asia, and the Americas. The ancient Ugandan king Nakivingi used the first "stealth bomber": a flying warrior, Kibaga, who could apparently cloak himself in invisibility. Thus hidden, he would locate the foe, direct Nakivingi's ground forces, and also hurl rocks down on his enemies. Eventually enemy archers killed him by shooting arrows toward the sound of his flapping wings.[7] Chinese folklore credits the emperor Shun as having made the first Asiatic flight about the year 2230 B.C. as a journey of necessity: his jealous parents trapped him on top of a granary and set fire to it, thus compelling him either (depending on the various versions of the story) to don a pair of hastily made wings or to use two large Chinese reed hats as an emergency parachute.[8] The Vedic writings of ancient India, particularly secular Sanskrit texts, describe mechanical winged flying machines (called *vimanas*) constructed of light woods and using heated mercury vapors for propulsion, some of which are attributed to foreigners *(yavanas),* as well as other, more mystical and magical creations.[9] South American cultures depicted winged humans, shaped religious and communal sites (notably Machu Picchu) in the form of the condor, and created a lore of feathered, flying humans. Local Peruvian myth has it that the ruins of towers (called *chullpas*) built by Colla tribesmen were the launch sites of actual flying attempts by these primitive bird-imitative men.[10]

In North America various Native American peoples looked to flying beings for protection from demonic or monstrous forces. They accorded the eagle and falcon particular respect, the former (because of its strong flying powers and ability to soar to high altitudes) as a consort and familiar of the Great Spirit, and the latter (because of its speed) as a messenger between the worlds of the human and the divine. Mojave tribes worshipped Mastamho, a warrior hero who protected and shaped the culture of these desert people and then transformed himself into an eagle before flying away into the heavens. Sioux legend held that the *Wakinyan Tanka* (Great Thunderbird) of the Dakotas saved humans from the Unktehi, a family of evil, river-dwelling monsters. Observing the Unktehi threatening the Sioux people, the Great Thunderbird rallied its fellow Thunderbirds (eagles) and eaglets, and they dove down, landed, and attacked the Unktehi at close quarters on the ground. But the Unktehi fought back viciously and inflicted serious losses.

6

TAKING FLIGHT

Alarmed, the Great Thunderbird ordered his cohorts to climb back into the sky, where they destroyed the Unktehi from the safety of high altitude by hurling precisely aimed flaming lightning bolts—a tale appropriate to the modern era, with its emphasis on avoiding the close and costly fight, striking from a distance, and using precision long-range air power! The eagle and Thunderbird, held in sacred respect throughout Native American society even today, are commemorated in Hopi carvings (the popular *Kwahu katsina*) and in the elaborately costumed and intricate eagle dances of the Rio Grande pueblos. Indeed, the legend of the Thunderbird is recalled most vividly in the bold colors and marking scheme of the United States Air Force's aerial demonstration team of the same name.[11]

The Chinese Emperor Shun escapes from his burning tower by using two large reed hats as "parachutes." Hallion Collection (HC)

Depictions of fanciful aerial creatures and combats abound in artistic carvings and friezework of the ancient world, particularly from Anatolia and Asia Minor, most notably in surviving works from the height of Assyrian power. Taken from the palace at Nimrud and dating to the time of the Assyrian king Ashurnasirpal, approximately 865–860 B.C., they show scenes of the king riding into battle accompanied by a winged deity on a hovering disk who watches protectively from above (and sometimes shoots arrows of his own at the foe), as well as other scenes of royal personages accompanied by flying beings or escorted by flying guardians, such as human-headed winged lions.[12]

It is logical to suppose that not all of these various myths, legends, and stories are merely the products of imaginative creation. For example, it is only a step from dancing in an eagle costume, complete with feathered wings, to leaping in one and attempting to fly (probably, alas, with tragic or at least painful results), as perhaps Peruvian tribesmen did. Some of these global accounts—particularly the story of Daedalus and Icarus—must stem from actual flying attempts, using either models or crude full-size wings that are, regretfully, otherwise lost to history. In any case, whether the roots are real, imagined, or (as seems likely) a mix, these stories furnished a supportive climate for others who followed to imagine flight, conduct their own experimentation, or propose various schemes for flying machines. This essentially nonscientific perspective thus played an important role in making humanity increasingly "air minded" and the idea of flight increasingly acceptable.

It would be nice to find evidence that humanity first thought of flight and flying to link lands and peoples in commerce and harmony. Alas, such is not the case. Even though the sheer pleasure of confronting the technical challenge of flight impelled some of the most interesting and influential of pioneers, from the earliest times thoughts of conflict and warfare dominated the quest to fly and the myths and legends surrounding it. People intuitively recognized that the exploitation of flight and the vantage point of height would furnish both basic knowledge of the opponent and positional advantage for subsequent exploitation (as with Alexander before the Rock of Arimazes).

Gradually mythic desire gave way to actual attempts at real flight. Aeronautical devices already existed as implements of hunting or war: the sling, spear, bow and arrow, throwing stick, and boomerang. The boomerang was the most sophisticated of all these weapons. First invented by Australia's early peoples, it actually functioned like a small helicopter, rotating and lifting as it moved through the air and (because of the unequal size of its two wings) following a curving flight path back to its point of origin. It appeared elsewhere as well and figured in the warfare of the ancient Near East. Thus by biblical times all of these "missile systems" were widely used in combat. The sling is immortalized in the account of David and Goliath, and Egyptian reliefs depict Semitic tribesmen carrying spears, bows, and boomerangs. The spear-thrower and archer, coupled with the charioteer for maneuver, quickly came to dominate ancient tactics; for example, archers and spear-throwers were an integral part of Assyria's war-winning shock tactics. Striking from a distance, archers could have profound influence on the outcome of a battle. Israel lost King Ahab to an archer at Ramoth-gilead, which sent his army into a panic and brought his previously highly successful campaign against the Arameans to a desultory close. The death of King Josiah, killed near Megiddo by an unknown Egyptian archer, set the stage for the subsequent fall of Judah.[13]

The Chinese kite appeared possibly as early as the second century B.C., for a legend about Han Xin, a general of the early Han Dynasty, credits him with using a kite to measure the distance to a palace by measuring the length of the kite string and then calculating the length of the ground track to the building. Like-

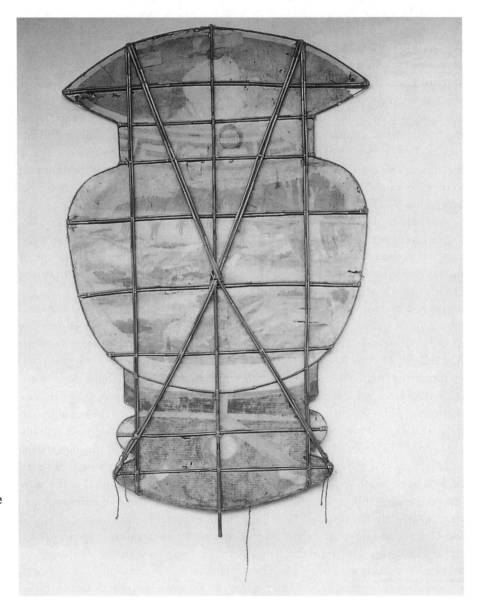

The underside of a 19th-century Chinese kite, showing its bamboo construction; the structure may be taken as typical for earlier designs dating to the kite's first appearance. National Air and Space Museum, Smithsonian Institution (NASM)

wise kites were used to carry fishing lines a good distance from shore or from small boats.[14] By the sixth century A.D., Chinese armies used kites for signaling purposes. In 549 Kien-wen, the future Emperor Wu, used a kite to send for help during the siege of T'ai, as did a Chinese general, Chang Pe'i, two centuries later during the siege of Lin-ming; in both cases enemy forces attempted to down the kites with arrows.[15]

Though it is not a lifting surface in the classic sense of the wing, the invention of the kite was notable, for it was an implement that used the air and demonstrated that air could be "worked" to a purpose. It is uncertain the degree to which the Chinese may have experimented with actual human-lifting kites. Accounts from the mid-sixth century A.D. tell of kite-wearing political prisoners coerced into leaping from a high tower outside the city of Yeh (near Lin-chang) before the emperor Kao Yang. Ostensibly a Buddhist rite of liberation, in reality this practice constituted a cruel means of perverse pleasure for the emperor and his entourage. One prisoner, Yuan Huang-T'ou, managed to ride an owl-shaped kite safely to earth (presumably because of its ample wing area) but then was immediately reincarcerated and eventually starved to death; it is likely this unfortunate wretch was the first individual in world history to make a safe descent to earth using a form of winged vehicle. Early in the Middle Ages, the traveler Marco Polo noted the occasional Asian use of human-lifting kites raised from ships at sea as an invocation to the spirits for a prosperous and safe voyage.[16] Europeans seem to have contemplated more practical uses. In 1326, in his *De nobilitatibus, sapientiis, et prudentiis regum* (The Noble, Wise, and Prudent Monarch)

Walter de Milemete's 1326 depiction of knights flying a bomb-laden kite from his *De nobilitatibus, sapientiis, et prudentiis regum* (The Noble, Wise, and Prudent Monarch). The Library, Christ Church, Oxford

Walter de Milemete, a *clericus* (king's clerk), depicted a group of young men flying a kite: a bucolic and satisfying scene, until one notices that the men are knights and the kite is carrying a black powder–filled firebomb over the walls of a city, beyond the reach of its defenders.[17]

Hellenic and Hellenistic Avian Influences: Archytas' Dove and the Sakkara Bird

Two unique artifacts, one lost, one found, offer clear evidence that ancient societies studied and copied birds with a view to understanding why—and perhaps emulating how—they flew. The first is the legendary flying dove of Archytas. Exactly what it was or how it worked is unknown, but around 400 B.C., Archytas, an experimentally minded mathematician, politician, seven-time governor of Tarentum (now Taranto), a friend of Plato (though they disagreed about the use of logic versus the use of plotting instruments) and disciple of Pythagoras, constructed some sort of wooden artificial dove that allegedly could fly via "hidden and enclosed air."[18] Perhaps it was a free-flying model, much like the hand-launched gliders that children throw about today; more likely it was fixed to some sort of pivoted whirling arm and intended for entertainment. In the latter case, it might have had some plumbing to vent a steam jet produced by superheated water, anticipating Heron of Alexandria's famous spinning boiler.[19] If so, Archytas' dove would not only supplant Heron's boiler as the world's first known reaction machine, but would also constitute the first attempt to apply reaction—that is, jet—propulsion to a winged configuration, nearly two millennia in advance of the Italian Giovanni da Fontana's much better known 1420 illustration of a rocket-powered model bird.[20] Unfortunately neither the model nor a description accurate enough to enable a precise understanding of what Archytas accomplished exists today, and Archytas himself met a sad fate, drowned off Tarentum in a shipwreck. But there are so many corroborative accounts regarding this episode that it cannot be doubted that this interesting man, at the dawn of European technological and scientific thought, created some sort of mechanical representation of a bird that others like him regarded with favor and respect, perhaps even as far as India, where it may have inspired at least some Sanskrit legends of *yavana*-built *vimanas* and *dkdsa-yantras* (sky machines).[21]

The second artifact is the so-called Sakkara bird of Hellenistic Egypt, which dates to the third century B.C. in the period of the Ptolomaic dynasties shortly before Cleopatra. Though it was discovered among the tomb artifacts of Pa-di-Imen in 1898, two millennia later, its true significance remained unknown until it was "rediscovered" in 1969 amid collections of bird carvings at the Egyptian National Museum in Cairo by Khalil Messiha, a doctor with an interest in bird flight. Subsequently, thanks to Farouk El-Baz of the Smithsonian Institution, curators placed an exact copy of this model on exhibit in the National Air and Space Museum in 1980.[22] Unlike purely decorative and painted birds, this carefully shaped and carved sycamore model, reminiscent of a falcon, portrayed a flying bird with a centered head, carefully executed wing, streamlined body, and prominent tail. Its fully extended wings, spanning seven inches, clearly have an airfoil (that is, cambered) cross-section. The streamlined body ends in a vertical fin, shaped as if the bird had twisted its tail feathers. All this suggests that the model had some different purpose than mere decoration, serving perhaps as a weather van to point in the direction of the relative wind. Its connection to Pa-di-Imen is unclear but suggestive of a personal interest in birdflight. Perhaps Pa-di-Imen carved the bird, but in any case the tomb preparers obviously considered it special enough to be included among the significant artifacts left to accompany Pa-di-Imen into the afterlife. Far too heavy and unstable itself to fly, it possibly inspired lighter and inherently stable glider toys for children, though this cannot be proven (reputedly Messiha's brother carved a copy out of light balsa wood—a wood unavailable to early Egyptians—and succeeded in making it glide a short distance). But in the absence of corroboratory evidence from its own time, this ancient artifact must regretfully be considered a singularity, despite some extravagant claims put forth for its design, purpose, and influence. It reminds us both of early humanity's insight into flight and of the tremendous creativity and inquisitiveness of Hellenistic Egyptian society.[23]

Islam, Christendom, and the Consciousness of Flight

In the ninth century A.D., the Moorish physician and "rather bad poet" (in historian Lynn White's words) Abu'l-Quasim 'Abbas b. Firnas attempted to fly in Cordoba, Spain. Using feathered wings, he leapt from a high spot and apparently glided for some distance, though he severely injured his back upon landing.[24] Nearly 800 years later, the historian Al-Maqqari attributed the injuries to Ibn Firnas' failure to attach some sort of tail surfaces. This is a perceptive judgment, since such surfaces could have enabled him to achieve a stabilized glide (as they do with a bird or a conventional airplane), offsetting the natural tendency of a wing to pitch over due to the forward-leaning angle of its lifting vector. But further details of this flight are lacking. It is unlikely that Ibn Firnas' wings were cambered—curved—like a bird's. Instead they probably resembled a cloak-parachute rather than a real wing. Thus it is in all likelihood more accurate to envision him sinking earthwards at a high—though fortunately not terminal—rate of descent rather than gently settling downwards in a true glide. In any case Al-Maqqari's analysis seems to have made no impression upon subsequent Islamic tower jumpers, two of whom (in Khorosan and Constantinople) subsequently made their own fatal impression upon aviation history while emulating Ibn Firnas' approach to flight. These examples indicate an early Islamic interest in flight, but the Islamic world did not go beyond this, despite considerable scientific and technical strengths. As will be discussed subsequently, the intellectual imperatives of Islamic society soon turned inwards and increasingly away from science and technology and began a gradual decline, so that by the late Middle Ages Islamic science and technology would follow, not lead, that of Christendom.[25]

At the end of the first millennium, embattled Christian Europe had finally achieved a measure of stability, peace, and opportunity. This came via the conversion or defeat of three people over a 40-year period of violent conflict and bloodshed: the Vikings, the Magyars, and the Moors. Between 974 A.D. and the year 1000, no less than ten major regional rulers from the North Cape south to the straits of Gibraltar and southeast from Scandinavia to the Black Sea converted to Christianity and in turn imposed religious orthodoxy upon their peoples. The most notable of these were Norway's Olaf Trygvesson, Russia's Vladimir I, King Stephan of Hungary, and Sancho the Great of Spain. As a result, as James Reston has noted, "Christian Europe had become a reality. It became a community of nations, with a continental view. . . . Hope and excitement about the future was the mood."[26] Thanks to these three victories—the first two outright, and the last a most important "holding action," Europe had the opportunity to indulge once again an interest in the larger world. Its population slowly increased, universities appeared, and so too did great cathedrals, flamboyantly showcasing the boldness of the Romanesque style, none more so than Chartres, the greatest of them all. In France alone during the twelfth century, workers constructed over 80 cathedrals, 500 abbeys, and no less than 10,000 churches.[27]

Popular wisdom holds that dogma-obsessed churchmen had little appreciation and very great suspicion of nonecclesiastical explanations of the physical world. Thus they retarded Europe by holding it in an unenlightened and superstitious thrall, the Age of Faith, until supplanted, over half a millennium later, by the seventeenth century's Age of Reason, characterized by broad inquiry and discourse. As with many such simplistic portrayals, the reality was quite different.[28] Both reason and faith have always existed uneasily between the twin extremes of materialism and dogma, and fanaticism in either direction then and now has generated extraordinary misery, be it the religious wars of the Middle Ages (and their more recent terrorist manifestations) or the "rational" science-and-technology-driven wars of the twentieth century.

But far from being the backward period referred to in the self-congratulatory writings of the eighteenth and nineteenth century's natural philosophers and scientists, the oft-maligned Middle Ages themselves set the stage for the subsequent enshrinement of reason within the Western European Judeo-Christian context. It was in that time that logic and empiricism came to characterize teachings in theology, philosophy, and science via that great European (and particularly French) institution, the university. "The use of reason in a self-conscious manner," historian Edward Grant has written, "began in the twelfth century and has continued, without interruption, to the present. The Middle Ages was itself an Age of Reason and marks the real beginnings of the intense, self-conscious use of reason in the West."[29]

The church had constituted a particularly bright spot in the dark period of instability afflicting western Europe from the decline of Rome through the tenth century. Then monasteries and monks were virtually the sole possessors and keepers of records and learning at a time when plunderers threatened the total destruction of Western civilization's cultural and intellectual heritage.[30] Truly, as Winston Churchill wrote, "The contrast is startling between the secular annals of these generations, with the meagre and tedious records of forays and slaughter, and the brilliant achievements of the English Church. The greatest scholar in Christendom was a Northumbrian monk. The most popular stylist was a West Saxon abbot. . . . The revival of learning in the Empire of Charlemagne was directed by Alcuin of York."[31]

The seat of learning was the cathedral school, which offered far more than just a religious education, for (in contrast to popular myth) priests and monks showed great interest in cosmology, medicine, the arts, natural science, and technology (indeed, the Cistercians even ran small factories at their monasteries, some powered by waterwheels). The schools offered courses in law, medicine, and administration as well. France alone had no fewer than six such institutions, at Chartres, Laon, Liège, Orléans, Paris, and Reims. Out of this climate sprang the first of Europe's great universities. The first two, those of Bologna and Paris, emerged by the end of the twelfth century. Over the thirteenth century, Europeans built new universities at the rate of one every 11 years. During the fourteenth century, the pace accelerated to one every eight years. By the early fifteenth century, Europe had a total of 29 universities in France, Italy, England, Scotland, Spain, Portugal, Germany, Poland, and Hungary—with new ones opening at the rate of one every six years.[32]

To the medieval monk, work was worship, both an ethos and a curiosity consistent with the growing and changing characterization of God away from a benign and cerebral creator to, instead, a master craftsman who physically and mechanistically created the universe.[33] Not surprisingly, then monks complemented their prayers and devotions with more worldly studies. As early as the sixth century, the archbishop Isadore of Seville wrote two widely read encyclopedic works of general scientific and social knowledge. A century later the Venerable Bede (remembered today primarily for his history of the early English church), expanding upon Isadore's work, wrote books on time, the calendar, and natural philosophy. Alcuin of York, slightly later, created a school for Charlemagne's court that taught various disciplines, including astronomy, to prepare future clergy and laymen for leadership roles in the Carolingian Empire. In the tenth century, Gerbert of Aurillac, the future Pope Sylvester II, studied and taught mathematics (even venturing to Spain to gain the latest insight into Moorish practices and technique) and astronomy and wrote a treatise on logic.[34]

Paganism in the days of Greece and Rome had emphasized an animistic world requiring the supplication and placation of multiple spirits just to meet the ordinary requirements of day-to-day existence. The ancient world "was a world of anthropomorphic deities interfering in human affairs and using humans as pawns in their own plots and intrigues," historian David Lindberg has written. "This was inevitably a capricious world, in which nothing could be safely predicted because of the boundless possibilities of divine intervention."[35] Then, in the fourth century A.D., came the collapse of paganism in the face of the Judeo-Christian revolution; at once the climate changed to one that encouraged a basic inquisitiveness into the processes of nature. "The Christian smashing of animism," Lynn White noted, "liberated artisans and peasants for matter-of-fact exploitation of their natural environment."[36] All this offered a highly supportive theological attitude towards flying, travel, and experiment.

In the Judeo-Christian tradition, God is a creature of the air, a theme that is repeated and elaborated to an extraordinary degree. Among His other attributes, He is surrounded by angels, whose principal characteristic is the ability to fly. His Heavenly host are locked in mortal combat with a foe—one of their own, but (literally) fallen from grace—who is likewise an angel, surrounded by other perverse angels such as himself.[37] Indeed, angels run the machinery of the universe that God has created.[38] God does not hesitate to intervene from the air to help those who believe in Him. Angels use their flying ability to rescue believers in danger of persecution or torment.[39] Believers are encouraged to think and pray in terms of flight and freedom, and in contemplation they use the attributes of flight.[40] Passages from scripture reveal this tendency: "Behold, the Lord rideth upon a swift cloud";[41] indeed, He "maketh the clouds His chariot."[42] "He parted the heavens and came down, a dark cloud under His feet. Mounted on a cherub He flew, borne along on the wings of the wind. . . . He let fly His arrows and scattered them; shot His lightening bolts and dispersed them."[43] The true believer yearned, "If only I had wings like a dove, that I might fly away and find rest."[44] But no matter how much one might worry, one could take comfort that the Lord "will shelter you with pinions, spread wings that you may take refuge," and command the angels, His flying beings, "to guard you in all your ways."[45] Indeed, the Lord would raise His followers "up on eagle's wings."[46] Finally, at the world's end believers "will be caught up together with them in the clouds to meet the Lord in the air."[47] Also, this is a faith that encourages experimentation: "Test everything," stated St. Paul; "retain what is good."[48] This latter sentiment is remarkable and captures the essence of the flight-testing and flight-research process even today.[49]

In view of these sentiments, then, it is not surprising that Christian religious art in this period took on a distinctly aeronautically friendly flair when dealing with one of the central tenets of Christian belief, the ascension of Christ into Heaven. Christian scholars such as Bede distinguished between movement through the air (the *caelum aereum,* or "sky of the birds"), and the vault of Heaven (the *caelum aethereum*). Increasingly at the end of the first millennium of Christianity, scholars went to great lengths to define the relationship between Christ and the sky, showing Him moving dynamically through the air, climbing through the sky on His way heavenwards rather than merely floating serenely or levitating majestically above the earth. In short, Christ is *physically working* upon the air to move through it, and the air in turn exhibits its own physical effects. Portrayals are replete of windblown apostles, and in some cases (such as an image in a psalter from Bury St. Edmunds now within the Vatican collections) only Christ's feet are depicted at the very top of a painting, as the apostles crane their heads and gesture in amazement. This "image of the disappearing Christ," the distinguished art historian Meyer Schapiro concluded nearly 60 years ago, reflected a critical change in religious and social thought, applying an "essentially empirical attitude to the supernatural."[50]

But there was also an equivalent change in the depiction of angels: no longer were they stylized creatures, floating placidly or hovering with vestigial wings. Portrayals of winged supernatural beings peppered the artistic history of the ancient world: various good and bad Hurrian, Hittite, and Assyrian deities; Iranian depictions of fantastical winged animals; the Great Frieze at Pergamum; and (perhaps most memorably) the evocative (if fragmented) Nike of Samothrace, one of the best-known sculptures in the entire history of artistic representation. This work, commemorating a naval victory, depicted winged Victory floating down to land, with perfectly proportioned, fully spread, fully fledged wings correctly positioned for a high-lift, near-vertical descent.[51]

Adoring Angel by Michelozzo di Bartelommeo (1396–1472), a marble relief in the collection of the Victoria and Albert Museum; note the fully cambered, fledged, and muscular wings. V&A Picture Library

But aside from the fabulous Nike sculpture, virtually all other early portrayals of wings had, at best, been immature (indeed often vestigial) and merely evocative of flight rather than indicating actual potentiality or possibility. Now that all changed, even as European artistic depiction itself changed, toward "more realistic human figures . . . moving more fluidly, and placed in increasingly realistic settings."[52] Increasingly from the beginning of the fifteenth century, artists, sculptors, and wood-carvers depicted angel wings with ever more exacting and precise detail, even showing the inherent lift-producing camber (curvature) of the wing and faithfully depicting the skeletal structure, musculature, and plumage, all rendered to an appropriate scale and proportionate size. In short, these are athletic angels that have to *work* at flying, and the wing is so fascinating to the artist that often its detailing is far more comprehensive and careful than the depiction of the rest of the figure. This form of depiction first appeared in northern France, Italy (influenced by English psalter art), and later in the Netherlands and Germany and is particularly evident in the works of artists Michelozzo di Bartelommeo, Petras Christus, Bartolomeo di Giovanni Corradini (Fra Carnevale), Simone Martini, Gerard David, and Andrea Della Robbia.[53]

This kind of art reflected a society rapidly extending its mastery over the air. Examples of this surprising sophistication include ever more complex sails enabling far more maneuverable, faster, and genuine oceangoing boats; windmills (invented in the coastal regions of the North Sea at the end of the twelfth century) for irrigation and flour production; powder rockets (from China); string-pulled helicopter toys; and by the fifteenth century A.D., gear-driven kitchen spits rotated by a fan placed in the hot rising gas stream off a cooking fire, essentially a hot-air turbine. Walter de Milemete even depicted the use of a windmill to hurl bees' nests into a besieged (*bee*sieged?) fortress, an early example of "aerobiological warfare," though it seems likely this was a wish, not a weapon.[54] In a broader sense, it represented what Edward Grant has described as " 'the culture of poking around,' or the irrepressible urge to probe into many things."[55]

Brother Eilmer, the Flying Monk of Malmesbury

In the first decade of the eleventh century, this "poking around" culture encouraged one significant attempt at actual flight. Brother Eilmer, a young Benedictine monk of Malmesbury Abbey, like Ibn Firnas before him, felt confident enough to actually build a crude pair of wings and attempt a short but very public gliding flight from an Abbey tower, perhaps inspired and encouraged by the ever-present jackdaws that circle its walls. The Abbey was no backwater but represented a regional pinnacle of the English Church. Founded by the Celtic monk Maildulph, who had built a small hermit's shelter on the site, the Abbey became noted in later years for the quality of its monks: one, Aldhelm, in Churchill's words, "was the most popular writer in Europe."[56] Further, it was the founding center of the kind of "disappearing Christ" art then beginning to appear in religious psalter prayer art. Thus that Eilmer could undertake such an attempt is itself a strong indication that his flight, at least on some level, had the official sanctioning of his Church superiors.

The twelfth-century monk-historian William of Malmesbury, in his *De gestis regum Anglorum* (The History of the Kings of England) credited Eilmer with "an attempt of singular temerity," noting that "he had by some contrivance fastened wings to his hands and feet, in order that, looking upon the fable as true, he might fly like Daedalus, and collecting the air, on a summit of the tower, had flown for more than a furlong; but agitated by the violence of the wind and a current of air, as well as by the consciousness of his rash attempt, he fell and broke his legs, and was lame ever after. He used to relate as the cause of his failure that he had forgotten to provide himself with a tail."[57]

To cover a furlong—approximately 600 feet—Eilmer needed a stable glide at a relatively flat angle of attack (giving him a glide ratio of at least 4:1, that is, over four feet forward for every one foot in descent), with his head and chest well forward. This suggests that the wings were fairly far aft on his body, otherwise, with the center of lift far forward (and perhaps forward of his own center of gravity), he would have quickly stalled and fallen to his death. The wings themselves were probably of ash or willow-wand construction, covered with a stretched and tied light cloth, with midspan hand grips under each wing, and perhaps attached with pivots to a bow brace across the back of the shoulders. Otherwise it is difficult to see how he could have kept two separate, disconnected left and right wings rigidly in place during the glide. This braced configuration also might have given him crude cambered (curved) wings and thus improved their lifting characteristics. Air pressure against the wings probably forced his arms up and back which furnished a stabilizing dihedral and also effectively swept the wings and helped to keep his center of gravity forward, ahead of the center of lift. This providentially did two things—it gave him the inherent pitch stability of a sweptwing tailless airplane and likewise kept him from flapping: that would have led to disaster, as he would have tumbled fatally out of control like the unfortunate Islamic tower jumpers of Khorosan and Constantinople.

Western Wiltshire is notorious for gusty days, a near-constant, damp, moisture-laden wind blowing cold and forcefully out of the southwest, particularly in the late winter. Being bird-imitative, Eilmer probably launched into this wind, undoubtedly after uttering a last hopeful *Pater noster,* leaping with outstretched wings from a watchtower. Probably he intended to cross the protective city wall, pass over a steep embankment separating the River Avon from the hilltop town and Abbey, and then land gently in an open field now known as St. Aldhelm's Meadow. Any other direction had obstructions or would have forced him to fly without the benefit of the wind. As he leapt, he would have fallen nose down, rapidly building up speed but also lift and thus flattening out and beginning a steady glide. Also, he would have gained another measure of lift from the accelerated gusty airflow streaming over the river's embankment, akin to a modern hang glider ridge-soaring along a hillside. If the measure of a furlong is accurate—and anything less than this, in view of the height of his launching point, would imply a very high and potentially fatal sink rate—he succeeded in passing over the city wall but then landed heavily on the eastern bank of the river, near a mill. The whole flight would have taken between 12 and 15 seconds, and as he descended, he would have soon realized that if he did not quickly increase his angle of attack, he would land headfirst. But he had no means of doing so easily. At some point, probably as he passed over the city wall, he instinctively raised his head and shoulders higher and higher, perhaps in a vain attempt to reach the river. This would have increased his angle of attack but also the retarding force of drag, killing both his speed and lift and increasing his sink rate. As speed rapidly dropped (and rate of descent just as rapidly increased), he desperately attempted to flap, and now he lacked the dynamic pressure against his arms and under the wing that had before providentially prevented him from doing so. Perhaps the wind dropped as well. For whatever combination of reasons, he immediately lost all lift, stalling and falling to earth, fortunately by now from low altitude (certainly no more than 15 or 20 feet), and breaking his legs.

In any case, and like Ibn Firnas before him, Eilmer possessed extraordinary courage—the total altitude from top of tower to landing site was approximately 150 feet—and the fact that he survived "merely" with broken legs is itself evidence that the outcome was due far more to his planning and design than to mere luck. His thoughtful comment on how a tail might have prevented the accident indicates that on some basic level he understood how a horizontal tail balances the lifting action of the wing and also prevents uncontrolled pitching motions.[58] A tail would have stabilized him, and if he had had a separate structure connecting the wings and tail to his body (like Lilienthal not quite a millennium later), he might have been able to control the glide by shifting his body weight. Eilmer therefore anticipated not only the modern hang glider but the engineering test pilot as well. It is thus agreeable to note that one of the world's premier flight test training schools, the Empire Test Pilots' School, is located a relatively short distance away from the site of his brave attempt, at Boscombe Down, and has a wonderfully appropriate motto: "Learn to test, test to learn." The Abbey possesses a stained-glass window of recent vintage commemorating the monk, but the wings shown are clearly suspect, derived from da Vinci's later depictions of mechanical wing-flapping ornithopters and not reflective of William of Malmesbury's account. Sadly, a cozy pub called the Flying Monk is gone, replaced by a supermarket.[59]

Unlike that of Ibn Firnas, who dropped quickly from view, Eilmer's career seems not to have suffered in the least. His fellow monks regarded him with respect, and his fame as an early aviator spread across England, France, and even Italy. Before William the Conqueror's invasion of England, Eilmer, then an old man in his eighties and not far from death, allegedly became the first individual to see the comet which "foretold" the Norman conquest, gloomily crying, "Thou art come! A matter of lamentation to many a mother art thou come; I have seen thee long since; but I now behold thee much more terrible, threatening to hurl destruction on this country."[60] Ironically, it is because of this "distinction" that he was mentioned in William of Malmesbury's history, which then went on to relate the story of his flight. Otherwise we might not know of him, which would be a tragedy, as he was the first of many churchmen of the medieval era and later to make a serious contribution to the study and development of flight.

The Rocket and the Helicopter: The First Powered Flying Machines

Two milestone early flying vehicles appeared in the thirteenth and fourteenth centuries, the first powered flight craft of any kind: the black-powder rocket and the drawstring helicopter. They differed greatly in intent and how they flew: the first was a weapon of war, the second a child's toy. One flew ballistically (i.e., like a projectile), and the other aerodynamically (i.e., using powered lift). Both of these anticipated much later developments, the one leading to the modern ballistic missile and space launch vehicle, and the other to the modern helicopter. In both cases, sadly, we have no idea who actually developed the first of these; we only have the roughest approximation of time and place, namely China for the rocket and medieval Europe for the helicopter.

In view of the story of Alexander and the Rock of Arimazes, it is wonderfully ironic that the history of the rocket seems to have its roots in Sogdiana as well. Not quite a thousand years after Alexander's men climbed the heights of Oxyartes' fortress, Chih Fa-Lin, a Buddhist monk from Sogdiana, journeyed to China, introducing knowledge of saltpeter (potassium nitrate), a substance used in metalworking and crude chemical processing. Somewhat later, certainly by the middle of the ninth century A.D., Chinese experimenters, apparently by accident, stumbled across the composition of black powder—a mix of saltpeter, sulfur, and charcoal—while producing potassium sulfate. That the Chinese invented both *huo yao,* the "fire chemical" better known as black powder and the rocket is well known.[61] Exactly how the rocket evolved is not.

Traditional explanations suggested a straightforward thirteenth-century progression from the invention of black-powder explosives to the derivation of a black-powder mix containing an inhibitor so that the explosive force would detonate more slowly—a rapid "whoosh" as opposed to a violent "bang!", so to speak.[62] Thus one could package the mixture in a bamboo tube open at the back end, affix a stabilizing stick and a pointed nosecap, and *voila!* one had the rocket. In fact, as the research of Joseph Needham has shown, the story is much more complex, nearly a half millenium earlier in origin, and firmly rooted in Chinese military technology and defensive strategy.

Most likely Chinese chemists developed black powder by the year 850. Unquestionably they used relatively slow-burning ("whoosh") black-powder mixes as both ignition and projecting sources for naphtha-spraying flamethrower weapons by the early tenth century. Further, they employed the blasting force of black powder itself in a variety of grenades and explosive parcels called *huo p'ao.* By 950 this had led to *huo ch'iang* (fire lances): pole-mounted, handheld bamboo-tube flamethrowers propelled by *huo yao*. The operator, holding the lance before him, would wait until his opponent approached to within ten paces, then ignite the *huo yao*, bracing himself against the recoil as a horrific blast of burning naphtha and explosive powder shot forward from the tube, enveloping and incinerating the hapless foe.[63]

These fire lances branched in two ways: first to larger-bore fixed and later wheeled weapons that were then used to project quantities of small rubble along with their Greek fire–like flame and then, eventually, special cannonballs. In short, they first evolved into the *pot-de-fer*, then the bombard, the ancestor of the modern cannon. Thanks perhaps to representatives of the Catholic Church and Chinese court who together sought to offset the rising tide of Islam, knowledge of this development eventually reached Europe, being first depicted by de Milemete in his *De nobilitatibus*; the bombard-cannon revolutionized European society and brought a speedy end to feudalism.[64] The second branch led to the rocket, the *huo chien*. In the late 1100s, someone whose identity is unfortunately unknown took a *huo ch'iang*, turned it around on its pole (perhaps, one imagines, sticking the pole in the ground), ignited the weapon, and watched as it took off in a blast of smoke and flame. At that moment the rocket became a reality and the first chemically powered flying machine in history, demonstrating flight via the power of jet thrust.

The first recorded use of rockets is in 1232 A.D., during the Mongol siege of K'ai-feng in today's Honan province, the capitol of the Chin emperor. The desperate Chinese defenders dropped and hurled *huo p'ao* grenades and bombs from the heights of the city walls onto attacking Mongols, sprayed them with *huo ch'iang* flamethrowers, and launched *huo chien* rockets at them as well. It bought time, but K'ai-feng nevertheless fell a year later, and the Chin state a year after that; by 1279 the Mongols and their allies, having extinguished the Sung state as well, controlled all of China. But in contrast to the ill-fated Chin and Sung states, Chinese rocketry prospered, if nevertheless under new management. During the Ming and early Ch'ing dynasties (1368–1650), Chinese rocketeers developed and placed into service two-stage black-powder rockets that at their apogee (the highest point in flight) would disgorge a cloud of arrows to descend on the enemy. They also developed massed mobile batteries of boxed rocket launchers capable of firing up to 50 rockets at a time, anticipating the Russian *Katyusha* (Stalin's organ) of the Second World War, or more precisely NATO's box-based Multiple Launch Rocket System of the present day.[65] This represented the peak of Chinese rocket science, for like Islamic society slightly earlier, China became fatally introspective. No further significant work would take place on rocketry in China until the late 1950s, when Qian Xuesen, the architect of the subsequent Chinese missile and space program, would introduce Western rocket technology back into the land of the rocket's birth.[66]

Knowledge of black powder and rocketry migrated quickly to Europe and the Middle East, perhaps assisted by Church missions to the Chinese court as well as visitations to the West by Chinese experts themselves. About 1248 the English

Franciscan monk Roger Bacon published a recipe for black powder, though concerned about too widely disseminating such information, he wrote both obliquely and in code. Several years later the German Dominican monk Albertus Magnus published his own recipe for rocket propulsion, which he called *ignis volans* (flying fire). But Christendom wasn't alone in learning the secret of the *huo chien*. In 1248 Mongol and Arab armies came into conflict, the Arabs suffering under showers of rockets. Within a few years, the military scholar Hassan er-Rammah wrote a textbook on warfare and tactics, including sections on how to make black powder and "Chinese arrows" (*alsichem alkhatai*; that is, rockets). Islamic armies quickly had their own rockets, using them against Valencia in 1288 "with frightening results."[67] So the secret had spread, though Arab armies never made the investment in rocketry that European and Asian armies did.

Rockets quickly appeared in European armies and navies and remained in service until the early 1500s, when replaced by smooth-bore cannons that—first introduced about 1313—had finally matured in accuracy, power, and range. Early rockets remained in naval service somewhat longer, as their incendiary effect could be disastrous against an opponent's sails and tarred rigging. Eventually here too they gave way to cannons. Relegated then exclusively to entertainment and celebrations, rockets would not reappear in European armies until painfully rediscovered by British forces battling Tipu Sultan in India at the end of the eighteenth century. The "Tiger of Mysore" had a 5,000-soldier rocket corps, and their rockets, fired by the thousands, panicked British cavalry horses, demoralized troops, and in one case detonated some ammunition supply carts, leading to a major British defeat in 1792. In 1799 more imaginative tactics and unremitting artillery fire directed against his fortress at Seringapatam ultimately defeated Tipu Sultan, who died in the fighting.[68]

In 1803, perhaps inspired by Tipu's example, the Irish revolutionary Robert Emmet built some black-powder rockets and test-fired them, noting that one "went off like a thunderbolt, throwing flames and fire behind it as it advanced."[69] Emmet and two assistants manufactured a quantity to be used in a revolt in Dublin, but a premature explosion in their cache on Patrick Street alerted authorities to the scheme. Emmet went to the gallows, and the principal assistant to jail, but the other met a more pleasant fate.[70] In 1804 artillerist Sir William Congreve, his interest perhaps kindled by Emmet's failed attempt but certainly reflecting lessons from the Mysore campaign, studied examples of the Indian rockets. He refined their design, adopting European manufacturing standards reflecting the technology of the early Industrial Revolution, and allegedly even hired the unfortunate Emmet's other assistant to work with him at Woolwich Arsenal on rocket development! In widespread military service with the British Army and Royal Navy by the time of the Napoleonic wars, black-powder Congreve rockets proved surprisingly effective, burning out large portions of Boulogne, Danzig, and Copenhagen (the latter unfortunate city hit with no less than 25,000 of them in a single night). Used in the War of 1812, they played a significant psychological role in shattering and routing American defenders at Bladensburg, Maryland, setting the stage for the sacking of Washington. At Baltimore they so impressed Francis Scott Key that he immortalized them in the words "the rocket's red glare" of the future American national anthem.[71]

Congreve's rockets eventually served with many European armies, and even with the American army. After his death in 1828, his stick-stabilized rockets quickly gave way to more accurate spin-stabilized ones developed by William Hale, used subsequently in a variety of British colonial wars and employed in 1846 by the United States Army against Vera Cruz in the war with Mexico.[72] Then the introduction of still-more-accurate and longer-ranged rifled artillery once again led to their disappearance as weapons, though they saw extensive use for throwing lifesaving lines to ships in distress. Eventually the introduction of far more powerful propellants and refined design brought about their return to combat during the Second World War.[73]

The drawstring helicopter had a less dramatic history but equally great influence upon the future. It was not the first rotary-wing "vehicle." Centuries before, Australian native peoples had invented the boomerang, probably casually discovered by a Neolithic hunter who threw a bent hunting stick that suddenly seemed to fly away and then curved back towards the thrower. Inspection would have revealed that the ends of the stick were twisted in opposite directions. Today we would recognize this as a crude propeller or "rotor"; when thrown, it would move forward through the air, spinning about a vertical axis and producing aerodynamic lift at the same time, causing it to rise as well. Now a hunter could throw a club at prey, knock it out or kill it, and the club would return to the thrower—most helpful if one misses on the first try! That unknown individual persevered in duplicating the shape of that throwing stick, and over time the shape grew thinner and more winglike. Also, hunters discovered that if they varied the span—had one wing longer than the other—it would generate more pronounced circling characteristics. They also discovered the basics of the airfoil, curving the top of the wood surface while leaving the underside flat, and giving it a twist, an angle-of-attack. Was all this recognized? Yes, in an intuitive way, but not in any sort of way that conceived other purposes, such as flight; still, those first hunters who conceptualized and used the boomerang as a tool were remarkable individuals and worthy of great respect.

Invented several millennia later, the helicopter had a different origin. Robert Temple has noted that as early as the fourth century A.D., Chinese children played with "bamboo dragonflies," which seem to have used a crude rotor that, when rapidly spun, would climb into the air. The helicopter toy appeared in Europe a millennium later in the early 1300s, in religious art. It constituted the first "powered" aerodynamically flying vehicle in history and consisted of a windmill-like set of four angled blades (the "rotor" in modern helicopter terminology) attached to a dowel nestled in a spindle. The child wrapped a string around the dowel, grasped the spindle, and then quickly yanked the string, spinning the rotor and sending it flying vertically into the air. The long dowel shaft would act as a bobweight stabilizer so that the rotor, as it decelerated through the point where it could not longer propel itself through the air, would autorotate gently to earth, like a powerless helicopter today. The earliest depictions of such devices are in religious art of the time, crudely in the case of a Flemish psalter circa 1325 and then in startling prominence and detail in a painting ca. 1460 depicting the Virgin and Christ Child, together with Saint Benoît, in which the Christ Child is holding such a toy.[74]

It is difficult to exaggerate the historical significance and influence of both of these devices. If the kite demonstrated passive flight—the flight of the windblown piece of paper or cloth, so to speak—the rocket demonstrated flight via propulsive jet thrust, and the drawstring helicopter toy demonstrated powered, aerodynamic lifting flight.[75] Both of these are genuine milestone developments, two of the six forms of flight.[76] After their appearance no one could doubt the reality of mechanical flight—the problems from this point on would be ones of *scale* and *concept refinement:* sufficient power to lift a piloted version and means of controlling its flight through the air. These are no small challenges, but the sadly anonymous inventors of both of these remarkable devices had already answered the larger and most important issue: humanity could build a craft to rise under power off the surface of the earth and fly through the air. We do not know the precise time or exactly where each of these first appeared, but within a generation both were popular across Asia and Europe and depicted in works of art, even religious ones. They spawned later and more sophisticated derivatives. The black-powder rocket led directly to subsequent solid-fuel rockets, down to the present day. The crude drawstring helicopter led to more sophisticated helicopter toys, such as those of the Frenchmen Launoy and Bienvenu, Sir George Cayley, and Alphonse Pénaud, becoming the most common of aeronautical playthings prior to the twentieth century. And one of these later models, presented by a clergyman returning from a business trip, would inspire two young children to make their own mark on flight: Wilbur and Orville Wright.

CHAPTER TWO

Conflicting Ideas and Societies

On Tuesday, May 29, 1453, 1,023 years of Byzantine rule came to an abrupt and exceedingly violent end as the army of the Ottoman Turkish sultan Mehmed II swept through a breach in the walls of Constantinople. Six weeks of unceasing bombardment from a giant bronze cannon (built by one Urban, a turncoat Christian gunner from Hungary or Wallachia) hurling 30-inch-diameter, 1,500-pound stone shot, assisted by smaller cannon, had shattered defenses hitherto considered impregnable. Soldiers of the Ottoman Empire—"created by slaughter and maintained by terror," in David Hackett Fischer's memorable phrase—poured into the city; its defenders withered before their merciless assault, the last of the Palaeologi emperors, Constantine XI Dragases, courageously falling in battle with his troops.[1]

If the collapse of Constantinople did not necessarily surprise the Christian world, it at least shocked it by its suddenness, due to the dramatic power of artillery, a form of warfare that all too soon would bring the age of feudalism itself to an end. The fall had numerous results, one of which was an intellectual migration from eastern to western Europe and a consequent reinvigoration of western European thought and society, particularly of mathematics, science, and technology. In part this manifested itself in the Renaissance era's fanciful machine art. Full of gears, pulleys, cranks, and levers, this folio art strongly emphasized mechanical solutions for a variety of practical and impractical problems and purposes, inculcating a profound receptivity to technological change. Though intended primarily for entertainment (in much the same way as individuals read speculative fiction today), it anticipated the general progression of European technical and mechanistic thought from the Renaissance era to the scientific and industrial eras that followed.

Of Birds and Ornithopters

The most remarkable of these artists was Leonardo da Vinci, born in Florence one year before Mehmed II's gunners tore apart Constantinople's walls, who "painted a few superb pictures and modeled one colossal statue" but spent "the greater part of his time and energy . . . observing the world around him, and in filling some twenty notebooks with the results of his observations."[2] Despite a lack of formal education, he was a voracious reader and student of previous poly-maths such as himself, including the Roman architect Vitruvius, the thirteenth-century French architect Villard de Honnecourt, and the fourteenth-century German military engineer Konrad Keyser of *Eichstätt*. Leonardo's notebooks reveal a keen observer of the natural environment, not surprising for a man who wrote, "A bird is an instrument working according to mathematical law, which instrument it is within the capacity of man to reproduce with all its movements."[3] But his clinical detachment had a soft side: Giorgio Vasari, the great Renaissance biographer, reported he would stop at market stalls selling live birds, purchase them, and then "let them fly off into the air, giving them back their lost free-dom."[4] His interest in birds apparently dated to a dream in infancy wherein a hawk flew down, striking at Leonardo's mouth with its tail feathers. Whatever the source of his inspiration, he studied in great detail their motion and that of insects as well, noting that they changed the position of their wings to climb and dive and that they pivoted their tails as rudders to turn left or right. He thus understood, if imperfectly, that they altered their flight path by varying the posi-tion of their lifting surfaces: the principle would be the same over 450 years later for the Wrights when they invented the airplane.[5]

Da Vinci ornithopter concept, showing its avian influence; the inner portion of the wing is fixed and the outer portion pivoted, so that it can flap. Sci-ence & Society Picture Library, Science Museum (SSPL)

Leonardo had little doubt that skilled artisans could fashion a mechanical bird and that it would "bring eternal glory to the nest where it was born."[6] (He further thought the first airplane would fly from the slopes of Monte Ceccri above Fiesole.) He generated ingenious schemes for human-powered ornithopters (flapping-wing aircraft), helicopters, parachutes, and streamlined and finned projectiles, as well as undertook pioneering studies in conceptual aerodynamics.[7] Additionally, Vasari tantalizingly recorded that during a trip to Rome, in association with Duke Giuliano de' Medici, he constructed some flying models shaped like animals using a soft, malleable wax, and launched using some sort of enclosed or vented air. Some have suggested these were kites, others that he created balloonlike toys that flew so long as air escaped from them, and others still that he actually flew very small hot air balloons. In fact, exactly what form these models took is, alas, unknown: Vasari was far more interested in Leonardo the man than in his technology.[8]

Sadly, realistic appraisal by those who did understand his work reveals that his ornithopter and helicopter designs, meticulous, detailed, and fascinating as they are, must be judged wholly impossible. He underestimated the power required for flight and misunderstood how a wing produces lift, believing wrongly that "the wind acts under the bird after the manner of a wedge which lifts up a weight."[9] His helicopter rotor was shaped like a screw, for he envisioned it "boring" its way through the air, and not as the rotating wing that it actually is (though, in fairness, such confusion afflicted twentieth-century Britons as well, hence the term "airscrew" for propeller!). Further, his very attention to birds and insects undermined his achieving a deeper and more fundamental understanding of flight. As one historian (while acknowledging Leonardo's undoubted "astonishing ingenuity") stated, "Only once, in the case of the proto-helicopter which he pursued no further, did it occur to him to depart from the example provided by living creatures."[10]

These schemes and his extensive writings demonstrated that conceptions of flight were not limited to hopeless dreamers but rather included thoughtful, gifted, and influential members of society and the world of the mind as well. But much of Leonardo's work remained unknown for centuries, partially as a result of his own great secretiveness and partly because the individual to whom he entrusted his papers, Francesco Melzi, unfortunately entrusted them after his own death to his son Orazio, who cared nothing for them and who bears direct responsibility for the scattering and loss of so much of Leonardo's materials.[11]

It is not surprising that humanity looked to the example of birds when contemplating flight.[12] But it is surprising how this "bird template issue" played a largely *negative* role in the history of flight. For centuries, certainly from Leonardo onward, flying enthusiasts considered absolute emulation of the bird as critical to any success in flight. Indeed, this belief manifested itself in many complex and ingenious (if sometimes bizarre) schemes to mimic the flapping of birds' wings. In fact, too slavish copying of the bird proved more an indication of a paucity of creative thought than a tribute to penetrating insight, for no such mere brute-force and bird-imitative approach to flying could possibly succeed. Even admitting these individuals lacked the wisdom of contemporary retrospective insight, one must conclude their attempts consumed far too much energy and thought that they could have better applied in other directions. Worse, their overemphasis upon the flapping of a bird's wing likely *retarded* the evolution of flight, for it mis-led a number of pioneers, starting with Leonardo, into thinking that the wing "pushed" against the air and as a consequence the bird rebounded upwards.[13]

In sum, the most important questions demanding study were far less the physiological mechanisms of wing articulation and far more the fundamental aerodynamic processes of how wings produced lift and how birds soared and maneuvered.[14] Thus strict duplication of the bird's mechanical flapping proved a false path, not least of all because of basic physiological concerns. Body size is critically related to virtually all biological functions and shows a surprising uniformity and ubiquity in mathematical relationships applicable across wholly different species.[15] The smaller the animal, the higher its heart rate, and the smaller its percentage of body mass taken up by its skeleton. These differences also are seen in disparate heart rates: a hummingbird, for example, has a resting heart rate of approximately 700 beats per minute, while a resting human has a heart rate of approximately 70 beats per minute.[16] When their size and relatively less dense and lighter internal (or external) skeletal structure

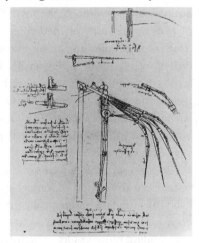

Da Vinci drawing of a mechanical flapping wing, using cranks and pulleys. It is unclear whether he ever attempted to actually build such a contrivance. Air Force Museum Archives (AFMA)

(as a percentage of body mass) is taken into consideration, smaller creatures typically exhibit higher power-to-weight advantages than larger species. Any school-child, for example, is aware of the tremendous mechanical advantage an ant possesses over a human.

By extension, all this clearly works against human-powered flight, especially something so demanding and tiring as flapping large wings that generate significant lift and drag forces. One only need to imagine, for example, the challenge of physically flapping a sail attached to a light frame of spars to see the problems inherent in this approach. Nevertheless, reputable researchers would not abandon their hopes of human-powered wing-flapping flight until after the publication of mathematician Giovanni Alphonso Borelli's *De motu animalium* (The Movement of Animals) in 1680, a year after his death from pleurisy on the last day of 1679. Borelli, a professor at the Universities of Florence and Pisa, had wide-ranging interests across many fields, including volcanology, physics, mathematics, astronomy, and zoology, and was an outspoken follower of Galileo. Also, he was "the best mind and the driving spirit" of the Accademia del Cimento, the Academy of Experiment, whose motto was *provando e riprovando* (test and retest).[17] Brilliant if tempestuous, Borelli's reputation attracted a young professor of medicine at Pisa,

Marcello Malpighi, who was making his own mark as the first to undertake microscopic anatomical research. The two mutually benefited from their association; of them Daniel Boorstin wrote, "Had it not been for Malpighi, the talented Borelli might have remained only a respectable disciple of Galileo and Kepler, who had traced the motions of the moons of Jupiter. Had it not been for Borelli, Malpighi might have remained only another expounder of 'theoretical medicine.'"[18]

In an era when most medical research emphasized the "big picture" via studying the entire anatomical system, Malpighi introduced Borelli to the complexity of human anatomy at its most basic and seemingly chaotic level, that of muscles and skeletal structure working together. Fascinated, Borelli set to work analyzing animals and humans as little machines. If Malpighi and his microscopes did for anatomy what Galileo and his telescope had done for astronomy, Borelli made an equivalent contribution, being the first to apply the coldly rational principles of physics to the study of medicine. He had a particular interest in flight, and so he undertook detailed and comprehensive analysis of how a bird's wing behaved as it did. Borelli's pioneering mathematical analysis of muscle performance and strength, published a year after his death, demonstrated that humans simply lacked the muscle power to operate an ornithopter—i.e., a wing-flapping—craft. As Borelli himself wrote, "Est impossibile, ut homines propriis viribus artificiose volare possint": "It is impossible that men should be able to fly artificially, by their very own strength."[19]

Borelli's work may have sounded the death knell for human-powered ornithopters, but the notion of a mechanical ornithopter showed surprising persistence even into the late nineteenth century, reflecting yet again the obsessive desire to copy exactly the fluttering flight of birds. Even the late-nineteenth-century German gliding pioneer Otto Lilienthal fell prey to the ornithopter's lure, though he sensibly rejected human power in favor of mechanical power. Lilienthal might have been overly susceptible to the ornithopter precisely because he had studied bird flight so closely, even publishing a book suggestively entitled *Bird Flight as the Basis of the Flying Art*.[20] Though he adopted a fixed-wing configuration for his gliders, he continued to believe a successful powered airplane could make use of the ornithopter approach. He advocated small birdlike "feathers" on the wing tips for propulsion at a time when virtually all other pioneers recognized the necessity of using rotating propellers. It is ironic that, had he lived, Lilienthal's crowning attempt at powered flight would have undoubtedly met with failure.[21]

Not quite three centuries later, of course, using sophisticated materials, advanced knowledge, design acumen unavailable to the pioneers of flight, and superbly conditioned athlete-pilots, humanity *would* successfully fly by muscle power, as demonstrated by Paul MacCready's wonderfully imaginative *Gossamer Condor* and Channel-crossing *Gossamer Albatross* of the late 1970s. But this does not detract one whit from Borelli's analysis, for he was considering the problem of human-powered flight as applied to *ornithopter*-type craft, and these latter were highly sophisticated *fixed-wing* designs. Overall, Borelli's judgments are as sound today as when he penned them near the end of the seventeenth century. Truly, as the late Charles Gibbs-Smith, the greatest of historians tracing the early history of flight, wrote in some wonderment, "The ornithopter tradition died hard."[22]

The Search for Alternative Solutions:
Lana de Terzi and Gusmão Envision Aerostatics

Borelli's judgment brought the gavel down on the first era of attempting winged flight, the era of the human-powered ornithopter. After his sobering work, practical flight would have to follow a different path than that of muscle-driven concepts—and in the absence of a reasonable "prime mover" to propel a mechanical flying vehicle, this essentially doomed any expectation of powered winged flight for the next 200 years. But it did not mean the total deferral of all flight.

The seventeenth century constituted a great period of inquiry into the air and the behavior of gases. In 1643 Evangelista Torricelli, like Borelli a follower of Galileo, invented the barometer to demonstrate air pressure (only later would the connection between air pressure and weather make the barometer of more value than merely a laboratory curiosity). Then in 1654 the German Otto von Guericke demonstrated the strength of a vacuum. Von Guericke served as burgomeister of Magdeburg, and the powerful Hohenzollern elector of Brandenburg, Frederick William, supported his scientific studies. Interested in pneumatics, he had experimented with crude air pumps made from sealed wooden casks, finally refining a metal design that could extract the air from a large bronze sphere formed in two hemispheres. As the Imperial Diet at Ratisbon looked on, a team of eight horses harnessed to each hemisphere could not overcome the external air pressure effectively locking the two hemispheres of the internally evacuated sphere together.[23]

Centuries earlier, Archimedes of Syracuse had recognized that a solid lighter than a fluid will, if placed in the fluid, displace an amount of the fluid equal to the weight of the solid, and further, that if the solid is forcibly immersed in the fluid, it will be driven upwards by a force equal to the difference between its weight and the weight of the fluid that is displaced. In the fourteenth century, the natural philosopher and theologian Nicole Oresme explored the possibility of building a ship that could "float" on the "surface" of the atmosphere if filled with the pure "aether" that Aristotle believed constituted the heavens. (Aether, also called "quintessence," was an imaginary element central to Aristotelian natural philosophy.) Oresme's proposition was not a physical experiment, but rather an exercise in logic—what is termed a "thought experiment" —for at the time, the experimental method was still unknown, awaiting its own discovery over 200 years in the future.[24]

Now, not quite 300 years after Oresme and fully 1,800 years after Archimedes, these propositions, plus the work of von Guericke, would inspire a Jesuit mathematics professor, Francesco Lana de Terzi, at the University of Ferrara to conceptualize the balloon, launching the aerostatics revolution. Born into a well-to-do noble family in Brescia in 1631, he had a long face, with fine features and penetrating eyes, though overall a tranquil, thoughtful expression. He entered the Jesuit order in 1647, showing an extraordinary ability in mathematics and the sciences and founding the *Accademia Brixiensis,* the Brescia Academy, an early scientific society. He determined to write a monumental survey of science based on experimental evidence rather than the hodgepodge of experiment, philosophical rumination, and outright folk myths that passed for scientific knowledge at the time. He finished three impressive volumes, the last of which was published after he died at the age of 56, greatly mourned by both the religious and secular scientific communities. In 1670 he published an extraction of this larger work, proposing the construction of a small *nave volante*—an "aerial ship" using four fully evacuated thin copper spheres as lifting balloons, and a sail to catch the wind and propel it through the air.[25]

While utterly impractical in hindsight (the atmospheric air pressure would immediately flatten his spheres), his basic notion—using a balloonlike craft to fly—was sound and inspired a great deal of comment and thought. As for himself, Lana de Terzi wanted to build a small demonstration model, but being a pious cleric, he remained steadfast to a vow of poverty he had taken that "prevented my expending 100 ducats, which sum at least would be required to satisfy so laudable a curiosity" though he hoped if others tried, they would let him know the results of their experiments.[26] In fact he had little expectation that such a craft would ever exist, for despite its practicality (in his view), he felt it would fly in the face of God's harmony and order, since "no city would be proof against surprise, as the ship could at any time be steered over its squares. . . . Iron weights could be hurled to wreck ships at sea, or they could be set on fire by fireballs and bombs; not ships alone, but houses, fortresses, and cities could be thus destroyed, with the certainty that the airship could come to no harm as the missiles could be hurled from a vast height."[27]

So Lana de Terzi conceptualized the modern balloon as well as a disturbingly accurate prediction of twentieth-century air war, even if his concepts lacked the insight to attain reality. But in fact there were more practical efforts as well, and even a common Asiatic and European folk experience. The Chinese of the second century B.C. recognized that an evacuated eggshell, if heated, would rise into the air. In similar fashion an eighteenth century rural French kitchen trick involved taking an egg, carefully piercing the shell and extracting the yolk, sealing the hole with wax, and then placing it on a hot stove where, after a few seconds, it would rise quickly to the ceiling as the air inside heated up.[28]

The first person to actually fly a small test balloon was the young Brazilian-born priest Bartolomeu Lourenço de Gusmão. Born in 1685 in Santos, in the Portuguese province of São Paulo, Brazil, he had resided in Portugal since the age of 20. He was one of 12 children born to a prison doctor and his wife, Francisco and Marie Alvares Lourenço. Father Alexandre Gusmão, a priest who taught at the local school, recognized Bartolomeu's abilities and subsequently proved so helpful to the young student's education that to honor him the family added the surname Gusmão to Bartolomeu's name. He attended the Baia Seminary, designed a

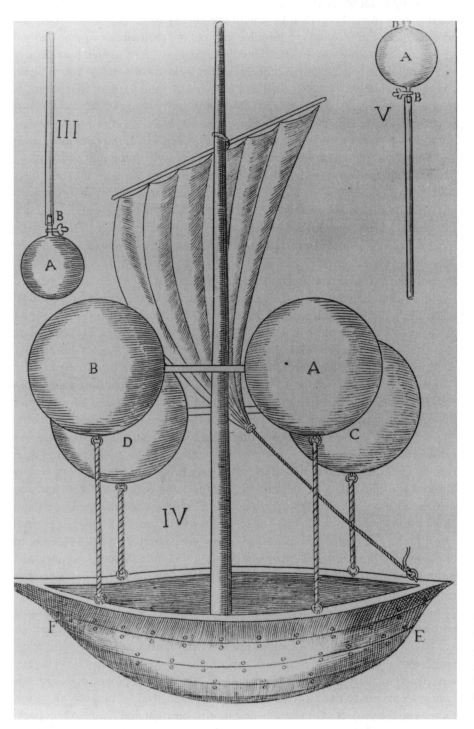

Francesco Lana de Terzi's concept for a *nave volante,* a vacuum balloon-ship, from his *Prodromo* of 1670. AFMA

novel pump to lift water 300 feet, and then, his education complete, sailed for Portugal in 1705. After his arrival he joined the faculty of Coimbra University for advanced study in theology, philosophy, science, and mathematics. As he washed up one day, a passing soap bubble floating through the air triggered his curiosity and eventual interest in flight. It is likely he already knew of Lana de Terzi's work, and the soap bubble merely goaded him further into thinking how to replicate it. In any case he began designing a possible flying craft, which he dubbed the *Passarola* (great bird), intended as a strategic transport for Portugal's far-flung empire but also as a means of mapping the earth more precisely to improve navigation and safety.[29] A variety of drawings from the time imply that the *Passarola* was a heavier-than-air craft, blending features of a parawing, airplane, and bird. Precisely how his design looked is unknown and the subject of debate among historians of early flight. But in any case, of course, it never actually appeared as a full-size machine. Far more likely, the drawings are intended to represent the inhabited gondola attached to a balloon, the entire construct—balloon and gondola—being the *Passarola*.[30]

Early in 1709, he had written to the king of Portugal, offering to construct this flying machine. Under most circumstances, such a letter would at best have received a polite discouragement from a court official and perhaps a private note to Gusmão's ecclesiastical superiors—"Please see that the good father doesn't bother His Majesty again." But the young priest had friends in court: his brother Alexandre was a highly regarded court official, and during a brief trip to Spain, Gusmão himself had met and so impressed Princess Isabel, the future Empress of Austria, that she had commended him to the Portuguese king, John V. Most importantly, John V was not the typical aloof aristocrat of his day. Then only twenty years old and king for only three, he had an engaging personality and exhibited tremendous interest in the arts, sciences, and humanities. More than this, he used the gold and diamonds from Portugal's Brazilian colony to endow libraries and educational establishments and fund the work of scientists and academics, a becoming philanthropy that would earn him the affectionate title of "John the Magnanimous." Perhaps he recognized in Gusmão a somewhat kindred spirit, for he encouraged the priest, granting him a charter on April 19, 1709, to construct an "instrument to move in the air," giving him financial support, and promising him as well a distinguished professorship in mathematics at Coimbra University.[31]

Gusmão set to work at the estate of the Duke de Aveiro. After experimenting with several approaches and spending a goodly sum of money, the young priest, age 23, was ready for his first demonstrations. On August 3, apparently before few witnesses, he attempted to fly a small paper balloon with an earthen bowl brazier attached to it, but it caught fire before takeoff. Word of this potentially disastrous failure seems not to have spread, probably due to the lack of notable witnesses. Otherwise the project might have been canceled outright and Gusmão sent packing in disgrace and derision. Undoubtedly, then, the young cleric must have been more than a little nervous when five days later, on August 8, 1709, he tried again, this time before a far larger and more important audience including King John V, Queen Maria Anna, the Infante Francisco, the papal nuncio (and future Pope Innocent III) Cardinal Conte, and numerous members of the court and diplomatic corps. But all went well. The balloon, consisting of paper covering a light wood frame, with an attached brazier burning "certain materials" that filled it with hot smoke, rose rapidly towards the ceiling, allegedly alarming courtiers into grabbing it before it set fire to the ornate furnishings of the palace. After this exercise and several additional trials, including one from a courtyard of the palace, the Lisbon citizenry dubbed him *voador* (the flying man), and word of the proposed *Passarola* spread around Europe.[32]

As early as June 1709, possibly because of his friendship with Princess Isabel, or because Queen Maria Anna of Portugal was the sister of the Archduke Leopold II of Austria, a brief description of the *Passarola* appeared in the Viennese newspaper *Wienisches Diarium*. Six months after Gusmão's first experiments, an English account of the *Passarola* appeared under the headline[33]

> The Description of a FLYING SHIP, lately Invented, in which one may Travel
> Two Hundred Miles in Twenty Four Hours, carry Orders to Generals in
> remote Countries, as also Letters, Recruits, Provisions, Ammunition and
> Money; supply besieg'd Places with all Necessaries, and transport Merchandise
> through the Air.

But despite rumors and hearsay, there is no reliable evidence that Gusmão proceeded to a larger human-carrying craft, as did the later Montgolfier brothers.

Why didn't he? The conventional excuse is that he fell afoul of the Portuguese Inquisition, and perhaps it is true, though it is far from certain. European society still bobbed and heaved in the roiling wake following the Reformation and Counter-Reformation and a succession of brutal wars reflecting religious, national, and ethnic differences. Persecution flourished as champions of all camps sought to impose their own orthodoxies. Portugal had helped trigger the great age of exploration. But then it watched in confusion and envy as other nations had swept to a level of power and influence well beyond its leaders' imaginings. Such unsettled conditions encouraged political, social, cultural, and religious turmoil, as well as a resurgence of the waning Inquisition. Then the enlightened John V experienced declining health, forcing him to leave much of the government functions in the hands of far less competent administrators.[34]

Allegedly the tribunal of the Inquisition expressed curiosity about Gusmão's work. One account states the tribunal saw his craft as the work of demons, another that Gusmão simply experienced "an unjustified panic." In any case the priest burned all his papers and fled the country for Spain, having "annihilated himself as a historical figure."[35] That the Inquisition was active at this time is beyond doubt; that it investigated his work is far from clear. If indeed it did, it is odd that he would willingly have chosen to flee to Spain, akin to leaping from a frying pan directly into the fire. From the 1580s onwards, Spain, the original seat of the Inquisition, had been particularly suspicious and hostile toward Portuguese arriving in their country, believing them undesirables (of many stripes) on the run. Both smart and well-placed, Gusmão would have known this; perhaps he planned to simply pass through to another country, such as Austria, where he had friends in court, including the empress. But if so, why did he tarry in such a hostile land? Perhaps he *had* panicked or suffered a nervous breakdown or some other loss of purpose. Whatever the case, "he died, poor and forgotten, in a hospital in Toledo," in 1724, at the young age of 39.[36]

Gusmão came closer to human flight than any of his predecessors. All he faced after his successful trial in the Palace of the Indies was the question of scale. It is difficult to assess his place in aviation history: certainly he is a tragic figure, his work arrested just as he might have taken it much further. In any case the success that attached itself to the Montgolfiers at the end of the century eluded this fascinating clergyman. Otherwise the birthplace of human flight might well have been Lisbon, not Paris. Of his accomplishment there can be no doubt: Gusmão, like the unknown inventors of the black-powder rocket and helicopter before him (and Alphonse Pénaud with the powered airplane after him) deserves all credit for demonstrating another of the six basic forms of flight: flight via a lifting gas. These two individuals, Lana de Terzi offering only theory and Gusmão practical demonstration, anticipated the balloon revolution triggered by the Montgolfiers and J. A. C. Charles at the end of the eighteenth century. In the short term, then, heavier-than-air winged studies (governed by *aerodynamics*)[37] declined after Borelli in favor of lighter-than-air balloon studies (governed by *aerostatics*).[38]

Pursuing the aerostatic alternative (which, in effect, deferred work on winged, heavier-than-air flight aviation until advances in propulsion made this more attractive aerodynamic solution possible) constituted one of the most momentous decisions in the history of flight. It represented as significant a choice as the decision by Russia and the United States in the 1950s to abandon winged flight into space in favor of more easily and readily achievable ballistically lobbed, blunt-body capsules. And like that later choice, the decision to opt for ballooning versus a winged approach essentially was a decision to fly first at the expense of losing nearly all control of where one's craft would go. The free balloon operated utterly at the mercy of any breeze, so that its passengers had little idea, and no control over, where the balloon would ultimately fly. (Indeed, in more recent times, the general public has witnessed this with the many fruitless attempts that preceded successful balloon flights across the United States, the oceans, and ultimately around the globe.) They only really controlled when it could land, by dumping gas and terminating the flight. Not quite two centuries later, a different lack of control attended spaceflight: the ballistic rocket, once launched, committed its crew of astronauts or cosmonauts to a single orbital plane with a mathematically predictable track. Thus they knew precisely where they would go, but they couldn't change the course after launch (the "next Tuesday at 10:33 GMT we'll be over the Caspian Sea" syndrome)—though, like ballooning, they could control the duration of the flight by deciding when to reenter the atmosphere and land.

Why Europe?

By 1780, then, three of the six forms of possible flight had been demonstrated, albeit in immature or only model form: *flight via direct jet thrust* (the rocket), *flight by rotating wings* (the drawstring helicopter, and earlier, in more primitive fashion, the boomerang), and *flight by enclosed gas* (the balloon). The remaining three were *stable winged gliding flight, winged flight under power,* and *powered, sustained, and controlled flight by inhabited airships and aircraft.* Only a little over two decades remained before Sir George Cayley would accomplish the first of these in 1804, and roughly a century before Alphonse Pénaud would achieve the second in 1871. The third would be achieved by Charles Renard and Arthur Krebs in an airship in 1884 and the Wright brothers in an airplane in 1903.

Of the pre-nineteenth-century accomplishments, one (the rocket) came from Asia, one (the boomerang-helicopter) independently from the Pacific, Asia, and Europe, and the other (the small hot-air balloon) from Europe. Approaching the end of the eighteenth century, no one could reasonably doubt that if the remaining three were solved, a European would solve them, for no other society was remotely in the position to seriously address these challenges. Certainly no one would have predicted that if humanity itself took to the air, it would be some society other than European. The triumph of flight inquiry over the last 400 years had been exclusively a European one.

Perhaps no question of all those that can be asked about the early invention of flight is more perplexing or intriguing than *why* Europe predominated. An easy answer one could offer is the Scientific Revolution and the Industrial Revolution that followed, but that answer, in fact, does not really correspond to the historical reality of these developments, which were at once far less clear cut, sequential, and abrupt than the term "revolution" would imply.[39] All three flight demonstrations took place independently of these two great movements, indeed, for all practical purposes, before them. The rocket dated to ancient China, the helicopter toy (a more sophisticated concept than the boomerang) to China and medieval Europe, the hot-air balloon to the Baroque era. Also, the early-eighteenth-century Portuguese court where Gusmão demonstrated his hot-air model was hardly a center of the scientific revolution like France or England, despite the enthusiastic patronage of John V.

The cause, then, must lie elsewhere—and it does, in the decline of non-European science and technology simultaneously with their explosive growth in the West.

Undoubtedly both Islamic and Chinese science declined from internal, not external, factors, chiefly the debilitating confluence of world views and religious imperatives that worked together to minimize further expansion of science and technology. Ironically, at the time when the first sustained interest in aviation occurred—about the time of Ibn Firnas, the first *huo ch'iang* fire lances, and Eilmer of Malmesbury—European science and technology were neither as established nor as advanced as that of the rising Islamic empire, China, and even, to a lesser degree, as that of India's Mogul empire. The kite, the rocket, black powder, complex machinery, sophisticated mathematics, magnetic compasses, mechanical astronomical clocks, the accumulated wisdom of ancient scholars—all this was in the hands of non-Europeans. Yet by the end of the seventeenth century, all this had reversed. Islam, China, and India were in decline, while robust organizations such as Europe's universities and, more particularly, the specialized scientific societies—Rome's Accademia dei Lincei, Florence's Accademia del Cimento, and Brescia's Accademia Brixiensis; the University of Rostock's Societas Erneutica; Sweden's Accademia Reale; Britain's Royal Society; and France's Académie Royale des Sciences—clearly spoke to the intellectual depth and vigor attending European science and technology, soon to wed in the spectacular developments of the Industrial Revolution.[40]

As luck would have it, the decline of non-European science and technology occurred precisely at the time when the generally supportive Judeo-Christian philosophy, the increasing rationality and empiricism accompanying the rise of European universities, and rising secular commercial interests drove Europe in exactly the *opposite* direction. Instead Europe moved onwards towards the intellectual fervor and relative stability of the Renaissance and subsequently on to the heady times of scientific and technological revolutions eventually emphasizing progressive (and, indeed, inevitable) evolution via a rigorous experimental method. And this took place *despite* a series of natural disasters destroying crops and grain that triggered widespread social upheaval and a nearly total collapse of European medieval civilization.[41] Clearly Europe possessed a surprising resiliency at this time that enabled it to absorb these various blows (including frontier invasions, civil wars, rampant lawlessness and criminality, and the Black Plague at home), and not merely survive, but actually prosper.

Although many factors played a role, the central key was its rootedness in the Judeo-Christian tradition. "It might be argued," A. Rupert Hall observed, "that Christianity was less 'other-worldly' than Buddhism, less socially rigid than Hinduism, more practical than Islam."[42] It might also be noted that, unlike other creeds, there was an inherent self-confidence within the Judeo-Christian tradition that permitted the relatively free examination and even exploitation of good ideas from other societies without fear of the core belief structure being "tainted" by such exposure (witness, for example, Gerbert of Aurillac's willingness to study Islamic mathematics—and he a future Pope).[43] In contrast, over time Islamic and Chinese society showed an ever-increasing introspection, an "inner-centeredness" leading to a fatal loss of inertia manifested by a growing lack of interest, concern, and curiosity, and eventually suspicion and (indeed) outright hostility towards the "outside" world. For its part Mogul society in India (talk of *vimanas* and *yavanas* aside) withered under the effects of rigid caste and taboo systems that stifled change and ensured orthodoxy at the expense of societal progress and even basic public health.[44]

Greek thought, spread during the Hellenistic era across southwest Asia and the Middle East, formed the roots of subsequent Islamic accomplishments in science, medicine, astronomy, and mathematics. Muhammad and his first followers had concentrated virtually exclusively on spreading his doctrine across the Arabian peninsula by conversion or the sword. Their immediate successors, the Umayyads, consolidated these gains, sweeping in just over a century from central Arabia to the Pyrenees, the Atlas Mountains, the frontiers of modern Afghanistan, and the edge of the Caucasus, building an empire more vast than Alexander the Great's. In 749 the 'Abbasid caliphs rose to power, launching a 500-year golden age of Islamic intellectual thought. The 'Abbasids were more receptive than the Umayyads to separating matters of faith from matters of the world and state, encouraging an energetic group of freethinkers established by Wasil Ibn Ata, the *Mu'tazilites* (dissenters). These challenged the existing orthodoxy, beginning a systematic translation of ancient works into Arabic, and established learning centers and libraries throughout the Islamic world, seeking to reconcile the already-proliferating sects of Islamic thought with the physical world and emphasizing argument rooted in reason.[45] But despite this promising beginning, as David Lindberg has noted, "science was far from central to Islamic culture, and there were forces within Islam tending to marginalize the foreign sciences . . . *Greek learning never found a secure institutional home in Islam as it was eventually to do in the universities of medieval Christendom."*[46] (emphasis added)

This tension boiled over in the late tenth century when, in Cordoba, extremist religious leaders held a book-burning of foreign texts; finally, in the twelfth century, the Persian cleric Imam Al-Ghazali preached a return to a fundamentalist view of the world that "championed revelation over reason, predestination over free will."[47] Muslim philosophers had expanded upon earlier Greek and Hindu work to derive algebra (from *al-jabr*—the reduction), but this Al-Ghazali scorned as "an intoxicant of the mind that weakened faith"; instead he sought to creatively blend Islamic religious law with mysticism.[48] A century later another advocate of a purer Islam, Ahmad ibn Taymiyya, "condemned all Islamic developments since the time of the Prophet as inauthentic."[49] Within a century the result was a turning away from rationalism and, within another hundred years, a complete and ultimately disastrous reversal of Muslim thought. "Caught in the viselike grip of orthodoxy," Pakistani physicist and historian of science Pervez Hoodbhoy has succinctly written, "Islam choked."[50]

Hand in hand with this was a corrosive xenophobia triggered by growing fears of heresy, subversion, and apostasy if outside contact persisted, ironic for a religious movement which had as its central credo the obligation of every believer to journey to Mecca as an act of faith and obeisance. "Imitation of anything alien," Howard Turner has written, "was to be scorned."[51] In its place came a debilitating decline into rote knowledge, with little or no new or original effort. From its very origins, Islamic theology stressed what might be called the "stand-alone" or "self-contained" nature of the Koran, which essentially held all other teachings or sources of knowledge superfluous to its own divine revelation.[52] A good example of this is found in a well-known story from Ibn Khaldun about the fall of Persia to Muslim forces. The local Muslim commander sent back for instructions on how to deal with a large library his forces had captured; the instruction came back to destroy the collection. If it conflicted with the teachings of Islam, its destruction would prevent the introduction of heresy; if it did not, Allah had nevertheless furnished better guidance than it would contain, rendering it superfluous.[53] Again, this stood in marked contrast to the medieval Judeo-Christian tradition, which had little problem complementing its own religious texts (particular the Bible) with a variety of incorporated secular works, including those from Greece, Rome, and, for that matter, the Islamic world.

Daniel Boorstin aptly captured this seeming paradox of an expansionist yet inward-looking society: "Since Muhammad himself was the climax of history, there was, of course, no place for the idea of progress. . . . The earth was not a scene of man's journey toward the City of God, but an arena for conquest by the Prophet's faith."[54] Ultimately such inner-centered thinking endangered the preservation of Islam's own intellectual accomplishments so that, ironically, it would be Christian scholars and educators after the fourteenth century who would translate, preserve, and disseminate the work of Islamic scientists, mathematicians, astronomers, and doctors, even as that work was lost in the lands of its birth.[55]

Pervasive religious orthodoxy increasingly influenced social and political affairs as well; by the time the Ottoman Empire collapsed for good in 1922, fully 62 percent—13 of 21 Sultans who ruled the empire after 1612—would be deposed on grounds of not being faithful to Islam's holy laws.[56] Only in the twentieth century, as the Ottoman Empire tottered towards the grave, would Muslim nationalists awaken to the modern world around them and seek to modernize their societies to emulate the West's success. But at best they enjoyed only mixed results. Turkey's charismatic Ataturk, the boldest, most remarkable, and most gifted of these individuals, enjoyed the greatest success, overcoming the prevailing orthodoxy and radically reshaping and redirecting Turkish society.[57] But others could not: Iran's ill-fated Mohammad Reza Pahlavi fell from power, Egypt's Anwar Sadat fell to assassins' bullets. At worst, attempts at modernization withered, replaced by religious extremism. It is instructive to note that Afghanistan's late-twentieth-century Taliban explicitly forbade kite flying as offending their own interpretation of the Islamic faith: a society that cannot condone kite flying is hardly likely to condone the flying experiments that must proceed building a practical airplane as well.[58]

Slightly later than Islam, China witnessed an equivalent turning within. Although Needham concluded, "The simple fact is that scientific and technological progress in China went on at a slow and steady rate, which was totally overtaken by the exponential rise in the West after the birth of modern science at the Renaissance," China's problems were far less a matter of keeping pace and dissimilar rates of development, and far more a matter of conflicting cultural values.[59] Despite the record of aggressive Chinese scientific and technological development, the China of the Ming dynasty rapidly turned its back on the technological advances of its predecessors. Instead the inward-turning society moved increasingly out of step with the rapidly accelerating outward-looking Europeans. With the "Great Withdrawal," Chinese maritime exploration, characterized by huge fleets exploring the Indian Ocean coastline as far as Africa, came to an abrupt halt, stopped dead in the water after 1433 by imperial decrees banning sea voyages (and eventually the construction of multimasted ships). In four decades the size of the Chinese fleet fell from a peak of 400 vessels to just 140 craft.[60]

Quenching China's intellectual fires brought a vibrant intellectual life stretching back approximately 1,500 years to a surprisingly rapid end. When, just 150 years after the Great Withdrawal, Matteo Ricci, a young Jesuit missionary, journeyed to Chao-ch'ing, he found the Chinese he met "grossly ignorant of what the world in general is like," even on questions of basic geography.[61] A century after Ricci's observations, in the late 1700s, England attempted to open relations with the Chinese court, sending a number of technological items (and even a balloon!) to the emperor. The response indicated just how detached China's leadership had become not only from the European world, but also from their own country's impressive history in science and technology: "We have never valued ingenious articles," the emperor replied contemptuously, "nor do we have the slightest need of your country's manufactures."[62] It was exactly this self-centered and appallingly ignorant attitude, developed over many centuries, that doomed Chinese science and technology. From being "fully equipped with the technology, the intelligence, and the national resources to become discoverers," Daniel Boorstin has rightly judged, "the Chinese doomed themselves to be the discovered."[63]

Overall, for both Islamic and Chinese societies, increasingly poor leadership coupled with loss of will and focus proved quickly fatal. The critical problem for both Ming China and the Ottoman Empire was "the defects of being centralized, despotic, and severely orthodox in [their] attitude towards initiative, dissent, and commerce."[64] Two centuries after Islam's victory over Constantinople, the defeat of Kara Mustapha before Vienna ended the Turkish threat to middle and western Europe.[65] By the mid-nineteenth century, imperial China could not prevent European intervention in its affairs. Both old systems would stagger into the twentieth century before undergoing final collapse within approximately a decade of one another.

The decline of the East and the rise of the West are no better exemplified than in the story of the clock. Lewis Mumford considered the invention of the mechanical clock as the birth of "modern technics." "The clock," he wrote, "not the steam engine, is the key machine of the modern industrial age."[66] Indeed, in its complexity and brilliance alike it constituted the computer of its day. Nowhere was there a greater contrast between the West and the East than in their respective concepts of time after the fourteenth century, a concept of seminal importance to science and particularly technology, including the technology of flight. China had pioneered in the development of the astronomical clock, with the eleventh century's great clock of Su Sung being the most advanced scientific machine of its time. But by the late fourteenth century, China had so wrenchingly turned away from mechanical time that this remarkable multistory "laboratory-machine" had totally disappeared. When over two centuries later Jesuit missionaries brought European clocks to China, they were in effect *reintroducing* the clock to its homeland![67] (By that time—the sixteenth century—the Islamic world was itself increasingly relying upon European time pieces to set the time for daily and evening prayers more precisely than sundials or water clocks rooted in Babylonian and Egyptian antiquity. Outside of cities, however, travelers already acquainted with the regularity and reliability of a clock or watch were often rudely awakened from deep sleep by well-meaning natives acting on wildly inaccurate "guesstimates.")[68]

At the same time as this Chinese (and Islamic) decline was taking place the fourteenth century marked an explosive period in the European development of clocks and complex clockwork machinery, typified by the extraordinary astronomical clock of Giovanni da Dondi. By a fascinating coincidence, this remarkable physician, astronomer, and mechanician completed his instrument just as Su Sung's machine fell apart (or was destroyed). The supportive attitude of the Christian church towards clocks—after all, clocks beckoned the faithful to prayer—encouraged a mechanistic view of the universe. This in turn encouraged further scientific and technological inquiry, as well as an attitude towards time management and business that, as medievalist Jean Gimpel has noted, led to an increasing belief that "time is money."[69] But the same could not be said of the Eastern world, where the notion of "eternal time" mitigated against individuals daring to subdivide it for their own purposes, and where, after Su Sung's short-lived success, the concept of mechanically divided time fell into disrepute.

In sum, at the very moment that both the Islamic and Chinese societies were at the apex of their power, European technological hegemony began its progression toward the mechanistic world of the eighteenth, nineteenth, and twentieth centuries. Central to this success was a supportive religious and intellectual tradition and culture that permeated European society and life at virtually every level. Accompanying this tradition was an increasingly sophisticated scientific and technological perspective characterized by a willingness to invent, experiment, innovate, and look to knowledge for practical benefit. Accordingly flight would be a product of Western, not Eastern or Near Eastern, civilization.

Science, Technology, and Inventing Flight

By the mid-eighteenth century, on the eve of human flight, European scientific thought was in full flower. Surely, it may be assumed, science had tremendous benefit on the quest to fly, along with technology. But did it? The answer is a hedge, a mixed "yes and no," or perhaps a "yes, but. . . ." Today the expression "science and technology" constitutes, in effect, a single word, the two perceived as inextricably linked by an implied causality: science "leads" or "enables" technology (one never hears "technology and science"). But the relationship is subtler, with contradictions and curiosities. While the invention of flight involved both science and technology, it involved them in very different ways and to very different effect.

The balloon and the airplane constituted the two great machines of the atmospheric flight revolution. The balloon was the more "scientific" as well as the simpler to achieve, and because it was easier, it appeared first. The airplane was more "technological" and difficult to accomplish, demanded a more interdisciplinary and industrial approach, and thus took over a century longer. The balloon sprang from the seventeenth and eighteenth centuries, the product of Archimedes' mechanics and Anglo-French chemistry (the ever more comprehensive understanding of the behavior and extraction of gases). The airplane was a creation of the nineteenth century more than the twentieth, an integration of multiple areas of inquiry: practical, experimentally based aerodynamics, structural engineering, and internal-combustion propulsion. By far the invention of the airplane possessed the greater significance for the future. It had the ability to exploit movement through the air with extraordinary freedom, speed, and effect, something the balloon could not do.

Scientists were always far more skeptical (and sometimes downright damning) about the value and possibility of inventing the airplane than were technologists, and their skepticism extended later to other fields, such as the jet engine, developing large rockets, flying into space, atomic energy, the value of weather satellites, etc., as well.[70] Each of these developments, while not easy to accomplish, proved not only achievable, but of great and lasting significance. Why were technologists so much more perceptive on the ultimate value and attainability of these creations? At least in part, it may have to do with a differing philosophical mindset between the scientist and the engineer, a difference between one emphasizing "scientific" difficulty and complexity (i.e., problems) and one that is trained to assess "technological" challenges, and look for utility and opportunities (i.e., solutions).

The roots of this mindset run deep. In the *Republic* Plato pronounced, "The object of science is knowledge."[71] Knowing and the search for the idealized Form are all; there is no compulsion for the mechanical or practical. Aristotle, though creator of "a philosophical system overwhelming in power and scope," carried this opposition further, stressing the logic of explanation at the expense of observation.[72] By the time of Galileo, Aristotelianism had so firmly rooted itself in Western science that, as one historian has noted, "Physics was simply the 'science of nature' and almost totally devoid of mathematics."[73] The English philosopher of science Francis Bacon, in his *Novum Organum*, overturned Platonic and Aristotelian thought, stating, "The real and legitimate goal of the sciences is the endowment of human life with new inventions."[74] Bacon anticipated today's mechanized and industrial world; though his reputation has waxed and waned, Jacques Barzun's careful judgment is irrefutable: "In sober history Bacon remains a hero."[75] It was Bacon, and subsequently the Newtonian revolution, that replaced the contemplative approach to science with that of the researcher employing an experimental method rooted in observation and measurement. In 1840, with the increasingly anachronistic character of the expression "natural philosopher" readily apparent, William Whewell coined the word *scientist*. The attitude of this new generation of inquisitive experimentalists was well captured by the nineteenth century's father of organic chemistry, Justus von Liebig, who stated, "The determination of the causes of a phenomenon is the first requisite to its explanation. These causes must be sought out and established through observation."[76]

To most people, even today, technology is "merely" applied science, and science thus "leads" technology. History seems to support this: the *Scientific* Revolution of the seventeenth and early eighteenth centuries preceded the *Industrial* Revolution of the mid-eighteenth and nineteenth centuries. It was as well a weltanschauung that suited most scientists. In 1881, less than a quarter century before Kitty Hawk, the British biologist Thomas Henry Huxley, the first and arguably the greatest of that distinguished clan, stated that "improving" the "arts and manufactures" required a thorough grounding in the principles and factual methods of physics and chemistry, "which is [and by implication could only be] given by long-continued and well-directed *purely scientific training* in the physical and the chemical laboratory."[77] Implicit within his reasoning is the unquestioned assumption that the scientist is an enlightened pathbreaker and the craftsman-engineer is a dependent follower. This attitude itself echoed a "class consciousness" dating to antiquity and the middle ages. Then, as Kendall Birr noted, "Science was the product of a literate, educated aristocracy; technology belonged to the lower and middle classes."[78] Plato felt the craft trades suitable employment for criminals and banished traitors; Aristotle considered craftsmen unworthy of full citizenship; even Archimedes (despite his own remarkable feats in defending Syracuse) thought engineering "sordid and ignoble": seventeen centuries later Leonardo da Vinci would himself suffer the sting of this prejudice by being considered "merely a manual worker, a technician."[79] Over many centuries, then, popular perception of the scientist as more of an exemplar of the best of society than the utility-oriented technologist steadily grew.

But in reality the historical relationship between science and technology has been far more complex, with science *more* dependent upon technology and technology *less* dependent upon science than is generally believed. Rapid technological growth clearly characterized society by the sixteenth century, and indeed, even in the medieval period earlier, derailing any attempt to speak of sequential periods of "scientific" and "industrial" revolutions. Science does not automatically "lead" technology; the relationship, as Arnold Toynbee famously noted, is more like that of a pair of equally proficient dance partners who "know their steps and have an ear for the rhythm of the music" even as they switch lead at any time.[80] In the nineteenth century, as Edwin Layton has noted, technologists would become the "mirror image" of the scientist as they shed the pure craft tradition and became adept at the ways and processes of experimentally and mathematically based inquiry as they pursued their goal of making something.[81] Ironically, by the mid-nineteenth century science itself had become far more dependent upon technology for its own functioning, a situation leading one commentator to note, "It then became apparent that the only questions science can ask *are those allowed by its instruments,* and the lofty art of speculative thought, which had stimulated knowledge since the time of Aristotle, was banished to the realm of philosophy."[82]

Inventing the airplane fit naturally within the optimistic engineering impulse of Britain's Victorian and America's post-Hamiltonian age, which held no definable problem as absolutely beyond solution. It was above all a product of technology more than science, for the individuals most successful in pursuing winged, powered flight were neither the natural philosophers of the Baroque era nor the scientists of the post-Newtonian period, but engineers and craftsmen, that is, *technologists*. While they used at least some of the tools of the scientist, such as the calculus or the experimental method, their tradition at root was far more the tradition of the artisan and craftsman (particularly the boat-maker and military engineer). Thus, as examined subsequently, aviation's pioneers looked more to the results of actual physical experimentation than to the contemplative processes of scientific thought, and therefore the accomplishment of flight would constitute almost purely a technological, not scientific, feat.[83]

As the eighteenth century neared its end, then, much had already been accomplished, but much, too, remained to be done. Obviously flights of models and small-scale demonstrators could not substitute for the flight of full-size human-carrying machines. Further, it is doubtful that many at all—even the most learned—fully appreciated the magnitude of accomplishment that these demonstrations represented. Nevertheless, these demonstrations had laid the basic groundwork for further development. Taken together, they offered tremendous proof and encouraging confidence that individuals could meet the challenge of human flight, and with a variety of possible solutions. The time had come for humans to go aloft.

PART TWO

ETHEREAL FLIGHT:
INVENTING THE BALLOON
AND AIRSHIP, 1782–1900

CHAPTER THREE

The Astonishing Year

The reality of practical human flight dates only to 1783, when two brothers and a scientist, Frenchmen all, invented the practical human-carrying balloon. With that invention, which set the stage for all that followed, humanity at last could leave the earth and gaze down upon it. This caused a sensation: balloons immediately became a staple of public entertainment, scientific research, and military observation, the latter the first practical use to which individuals applied the aerostatic revolution. Technology is replete with examples of contemporaneous developments that appeared within at most a few years of each other. Only rarely do revolutionary systems and technologies appear within the same year, but such is true of the balloon: the practical balloon constituted the dual invention in 1783 of the papermaking brothers Joseph and Étienne Montgolfier and scientist Jacques Alexandre César Charles.

In view of the tremendous interest in science and learning within France in the eighteenth century, it is perhaps not surprising that ballooning first appeared in that tremendously contradictory nation. It was at once a nation where the most advanced thinking vied with the most abject poverty and where societal pressures were already building that would would tear it apart in a paroxysm of violence and terror. France produced two notable inventions toward the end of the eighteenth century—one, the balloon, speaking to the best impulses of society and winning deserved fame, and the other, the guillotine, speaking to the worst of society's behavior and winning deserved notoriety. The history of the balloon is by far the more pleasant to relate.

Two Brothers from Annonay

Joseph and Étienne Montgolfier, the two inventors of the hot-air balloon, echo Arthur Miller's desperate salesmen "way out there in the blue, riding on a smile and a shoeshine."[1] Two middle-aged businessmen casting about for financial success but always just a step away from business collapse because of their own inept decisions and ill-advised efforts at innovation that antagonized their prickly work force, they became interested in aerostatics as a byproduct of their interests in paper production, mill power, and the invention of the steam engine. The steam engine revolutionized science, as scientists and mechanicians alike scrambled to find better ways to calculate engine efficiencies and thereby develop better and more economically productive engines. From this impetus sprang the field of thermodynamics, the science of relationship between heat and energy, of critical importance to future aeronautics.[2] A cousin had made Joseph, the principal force behind the brothers' work, aware of recent developments in gaseous chemistry, triggering a determination to undertake his own research on the relationship between heat and energy as part of a broader interest in heat engines, including possibly making a steam engine.[3]

Years later Joseph related that he first conceived of the balloon one chilly, dark evening in early November 1782, as he rested in a study at the University of Avignon, ostensibly studying law but in reality recovering from his most recent business failure, which had for a while put him in a debtor's prison. As a cozy fire warmed the small room, he idly examined a wall print showing the futile Spanish siege of British Gibraltar. Suddenly he had an inspiration: if a fire carried particles and ash up a flue, might not this rising flux of heat be captured and thereby a vessel constructed to carry soldiers over the earth and down onto a besieged fortress? On November 4 Joseph, adept with his hands, made a cubelike balloon of taffeta stretched over a light wood frame, filled it with smoke, and set it free . . . and as with the good friar Gusmão's model flown before the Portuguese court 73 years before and the egg balloons of French kitchens (of both of which Joseph apparently knew nothing), this oddly shaped taffeta balloon quickly rose to the ceiling. Immediately he wrote to his brother Étienne, ordering more taffeta and some cordage, and promising, "You will see one of the most astonishing sights in the world."[4]

For Étienne the call could not have come too soon. Locked in an increasingly acrimonious dispute with both his workforce and fellow manufacturers from an ill-fated labor management experiment, he was ready for a change. Together with Joseph he experimented with more complex taffeta balloons, one of which, launched on December 14, 1782, apparently rose to about 300 meters, approximately 1,000 feet, in full view of startled citizenry, coming to earth nearly a mile away. Ever and understandably concerned about potential benefits the brothers sought official recognition of their primacy in aerostatics, writing to a minor member of the French Académie Royale des Sciences (founded over a century before in 1666 to serve the public good) and requesting a formal demonstration before this august body.[5] They stressed that the balloon might be useful for a variety of tasks, including experiments on electricity in clouds (an allusion to the famous kite experiment of Benjamin Franklin in June 1752) and even transporting troops and bombing fortifications.[6]

But the official ignored them, and so they continued with experimentation on their own, using the time to abandon the slab-sided and leaky taffeta design for a rounded, more classic shape using less-porous paper backing under the linen envelope. On June 4, 1783, they demonstrated a much larger balloon, fully 35 feet in diameter, flying it from the Place des Cordeliers (the marketplace of Annonay) before an assembly of clerics from the Estates of Vivarais, itself a peculiar quasi-public, quasi-religious regional government dating to the Middle Ages. As one onlooker recollected later: "Imagine the general astonishment when the inventors announced that, as soon as [the balloon] should be filled with gas (which they had a simple means of making), it would rise of itself to the clouds. . . . Such an experiment appeared so incredible to those who were present that all doubted of its success."[7] And a spectacular success it was: filled from a smoking brazier, the balloon rapidly soared to an altitude of about 3,000 feet and then descended gently, drifting with the wind for nearly two miles, before the astonished eyes of citizens and civil and church officials, who readily made official note of the brothers' accomplishment. Now it was time to go to Paris, where the brothers hoped to duplicate their success, thus winning royal support for their experiments—and perhaps for a spinoff fulfilling some sort of military or commercial need.[8]

The Battle of the Balloons (I): Montgolfière versus Charlière—the First Trials

At this point a curious "balloon race" began, pitting the craft tradition of the Montgolfiers against the physicists and chemists of the French and British scientific establishment. In midsummer 1783 the Académie Royale received an official government request for its views on press reports of the Montgolfier experiments. This put it in the position of having to comment on the feasibility of their work at the same time that some of the Académie's own members were pursuing a scientifically similar but technologically much different path towards their own balloons. Like the Montgolfiers they recognized that one could fly by creating a balloon filled with a lifting gas. But unlike the two brothers, they believed in using a cold lifting gas, namely the 17-year-old discovery, hydrogen.

In 1766 the noted British chemist Henry Cavendish had first isolated hydrogen, then called "inflammable air," and two other researchers, Joseph Black and Tiberius Cavallo (the latter an Italian residing in England), had demonstrated that it could be used as a lifting gas. Cavallo, in fact, had filled soap bubbles with hydrogen, observing them climb upwards. The Montgolfiers had known all this but shrewdly recognized that they lacked the resources in far Annonay to afford hydrogen in anything like the quantities they would have needed, so they pressed on with their own hot-air concept. But money was far less a problem for the Paris scientific establishment and particularly for the most popular public scientist of all, J. A. C. Charles, a close friend of the American Minister to France, Benjamin Franklin. Like Cavallo, Charles had undertaken his own experiments with hydrogen-filled soap bubbles. Now, building on the growing Anglo-French scientific research base, the Académie's already strong tradition of excellence (a tradition filled with the brightest names of the French Enlightenment, including Jean A. N. de Condorcet, Jean Le Rond d'Alembert, Denis Diderot, and Antoine-Laurent Lavoisier), and the example of the Montgolfiers' own progress, Charles determined to use hydrogen as a lifting gas for a balloon of his own.[9]

Aided by a fundraising subscription started by an enthusiastic supporter, Charles set to work with a small team of assistants, including the brothers Jean and Noël Robert, building a 12-foot-diameter spherical balloon (appropriately named the *Globe*). Made of taffeta, it was backed with a rubberized covering, latex having been brought back from South America in 1736 by the French scientist C. M. de la Condamine. He had made a report to the Académie, which analyzed the substance, recognized its value—flexibility and imperviousness to moisture—and promptly dubbed it *caoutchouc,* after the Indian expression "tree that weeps."[10] Much smaller than the Montgolfiers' balloons, the little *Globe* could nevertheless demonstrate a powerful performance due to the lifting power of its hydrogen gas, only a tenth as dense as air. Construction proceeded swiftly, and Charles scheduled his trial launch of this unmanned aerostat for August 27. Using hydrogen necessitated creating some practical means of generating the gas, and the Robert brothers, after experimenting with a complicated device of their own design, settled for simply taking an oak cask, filling it with iron filings, and then pouring sulphuric acid (then called "oil of vitriol") over them. Inflation began on August 23 in a small courtyard off the Place des Victoires but had to be suspended and restarted on the twenty-fourth due to operator errors. Thereafter the process worked remarkably well, though it created serious hazards, from the nearly 500 pounds of caustic acid, the vapors produced by the chemical reaction of the filings and acid, and the tremendous heat generated by the process—a heat that threatened to detonate the rapidly filling balloon. Fortunately nothing of the sort occurred, and Charles and his assistants safely moved the *Globe* by night through the narrow, tree-lined streets of Paris and across the Seine to its launch site on the Champ de Mars, about 100 yards in front of the present-day École Militaire, the French military academy. (This is also close to the location of the present-day Eiffel tower, of course not yet then a feature of the Parisian skyline.)[11]

Despite increasingly threatening weather, crowds gathered along the Champ de Mars early on the morning of August 27, becoming loudly restive as the day wore on and a heavy rain began to fall. At five o'clock a cannon sounded, and the red-and-blue-striped *Globe* suddenly leapt aloft, the wind catching it and spiriting it across the city amid low-scudding clouds. An observer noted: "The idea that a body leaving the earth was traveling in space was so sublime, and appeared to differ so greatly from ordinary laws, that all the spectators were overwhelmed with enthusiasm. The satisfaction was so great that ladies in the latest fashions allowed themselves to be drenched with rain to avoid losing sight of the globe for an instant. The Balloon, after remaining in the atmosphere three-quarters of an hour, fell in a field near Gonesse, a village 15 miles from the Champ de Mars. The descent was imputed to a tear in the silk."[12]

Charles and the Robert brothers had won the race to introduce Paris, a city that had already seen many things, to the most remarkable image of the eighteenth century: a balloon floating sedately above a city. In the audience were two onlookers who fully appreciated the significance of the moment: the ever-inquisitive Benjamin Franklin and a teenage John Quincy Adams, a future American president who in later life would play the decisive role in the creation of the Smithsonian Institution. But the image of the tiny *Globe* racing the wind across the sky was not an image everyone understood and accepted: one person turned to Franklin and asked skeptically, "Of what possible use is it?" The distinguished American scientist, diplomat, and statesman snapped, "À quoi sert un enfant qui vient de naître?" (What is the use of a newborn babe?)[13]

Recognizing this, the Paris authorities had issued a proclamation to ensure the safety of the balloon, explaining that "any one who shall see in the sky such a globe, which resembles 'la lune obscurcie,' should be aware that, far from being an alarming phenomenon, it is only a machine that cannot possibly cause any harm, and which will some day prove serviceable to the wants of society."[14] But all to no avail! When the balloon burst (due to expansion of the gas in the upper atmosphere), it fell to earth outside Ecouen, near Gonesse. Today, both are close to the present-day site of Le Bourget, France's most historic airport (where Charles Lindbergh landed after his solo crossing of the North Atlantic in 1927, and home as well to the world's oldest and best-known airshow, the Salon de L'Aéronautique, and the sprawling terminals of the Aéroport Charles de Gaulle (through which pass millions of visitors to France each year). Then both Ecouen and Gonesse were small, rural hamlets of Paris. Peasants, farmers, and gentry alike, fearing the *Globe* to be an ungodly work, attacked the fabric with knives, pitchforks and even muskets, dragging the "carcass" to Gonesse, then assaulting it some more, an indication of just how unsophisticated life could be but a few miles beyond the Seine. Parisian papers lost no time in deriding their country cousins. The *Mercure de France* sarcastically described the struggle with the hissing, deflating balloon: "The creature, shaking and bounding, dodged the first blows. Finally, however, it received a mortal wound, and collapsed with a long sigh. Then a shout of victory arose, and a new valor reanimated the victors. The bravest, like another Don Quixote, approached the dying beast, and with a trembling hand plunged his knife into its breast."[15]

And what of the Montgolfiers? Étienne and his assistants had watched Charles's flight with a mixture of admiration and envy, and it drove them to redouble their own efforts at an even more impressive balloon than the brothers had flown in Annonay. In their borrowed works at the Reveillon wallpaper factory in the Faubourg Saint-Antoine, they created a 70-foot-tall balloon, azure with gold trim, and on the evening of September 11, during a prelaunch trial, it lifted eight men off the ground "and would have borne them aloft if others had not jumped for the ropes."[16] The next day echoed the afternoon of Charles's flight: rainy, gusty, miserable. The *Montgolfière's* pretty decoration disintegrated under the rain, and the balloon wound up a mass of soaking fabric littering the ground. Disappointed but not disillusioned, Étienne determined to do better.

In less than a week they turned out a new balloon, the *Martial,* featuring a varnished taffeta envelope. On September 19, at Versailles, they launched it. Present as witnesses were the ill-fated Louis XVI and his queen, Marie Antoinette; the two-year-old dauphin; and an audience of at least 100,000 Parisians, including two notable English visitors, William Pitt and William Wilberforce, two young members of the House of Commons, then in their early 20s and visiting France to learn the language. After an inspection by the keenly interested king, the *Martial,* resplendent in azure and gold, leapt aloft, lifting a basket with a sheep, a duck, and a rooster. Someone had named the sheep *Montauciel* (climb to the sky), but neither the duck nor the rooster—presumably considered lesser animals—received any appellation of their own; for the rooster, injury soon followed insult. Nearly upset immediately after launch by strong winds, the balloon survived the near disaster and drifted along for over two and a half miles before coming down in the forest of Vaucresson, eight minutes after liftoff, its animals dazed but safe, though (depending on the account) the sheep had kicked or trampled the rooster. The

The prolonged death of the *Globe* at the hands of the rural citizenry of Gonesse, as gleefully depicted by Parisian sophisticates who ridiculed their country cousins for thinking it was a living creature and then attacking it. SSPL

ALLARME GÉNÉRALE DES HABITANS DE GONESSE occasionnée par la chûte du Ballon Aérostatique de M.ʳ de Montgolfier le 27 Août 1783,
Ce Ballon de 38 pieds de circonférence, fait en taffetas enduit de gomme élastique, et plein d'air inflammable tiré du fer au moyen de l'acide vitriolique, s'éleva de lui même au Champ de Mars à Paris le 27 Août 1783 à 5 heures du soir en présence de plus de 300 mille personnes. La pluie abondante qui survint dans l'instant où on l'abandonna, ne l'empécha pas de s'élever avec un mouvement accéléré, jusqu'au delà des nues. On présume qu'il fut porté à plus de vingt mille pieds de hauteur où il creva par la réaction du Gaz inflammable sur l'air atmosphérique. Trois quarts d'heure après il tomba près de Gonesse à 10 milles du Champ de Mars. Les Habitans accoururent en foule, et deux Moines leur ayant assuré que c'étoit la peau d'un animal tout-à fait monstrueux, ils l'assaillirent à coups de pierres, de fourches et de fléaux. Le Curé fut obligé de se transporter près du Ballon pour rassurer ces paroisiens épouvantés. Enfin ils attachèrent à la queue d'un cheval, l'instrument de la plus belle expérience physique qui ait jamais été faite, et le traînèrent à plus de mille toises à travers champs.

subsequent fate of these hardy animal-aeronauts is unknown; unlike the "space chimps" of the 1960s, they did not retire to an honored old age and a Lenin-like stuffing for exhibit in some museum. Rather it is probable they soon graced some-one's table, probably that of the Montgolfiers themselves and—who knows?—per-haps even at the celebratory dinner that night to honor their flight. If so, it was an unkind end.[17]

The Battle of the Balloons (II): Humanity Aloft

All Paris now settled down for the ultimate race: who would put a manned bal-loon into the air first? Both teams had demonstrated persistency, insight, and excellence. But the laurels went to the Montgolfiers, a pleasant enough result in view of their family history and the long and uncompromising struggle they had put up to be first. They built a very large balloon with an internal volume of 56,000 cubic feet, as gaily decorated as a Fabergé egg: royal blue with gold trim showing the twelve signs of the Zodiac, the king's initials, the head of Minerva in a radiant sun, and *beaucoup* banding and entwined filigree, including a repetitive pattern of fleur-de-lis. If nothing else, as a decorative design the Montgolfier's bal-loon made history, for in the entire record of humanity and the decorative arts, their creation undoubtedly—and still today—must be judged the most spectacu-larly decorated vehicle ever to exist. Unlike many of the royal men-of-war and ceremonial barges and galleys created by England, France, Spain, and the Venet-ian state, it managed to be beautiful and memorable without being gaudy and grotesque.[18]

The team finished in mid-October and then undertook various tests with the balloon filled by a burning brazier and tethered to the ground. Étienne himself tested the balloon, rising with it as it climbed unsteadily to the top of its tether. But modestly he made nothing of this brave excursion, and thus history records the first man to rise in any balloon to be 26-year-old Jean François Pilâtre de Rozier, *un physicien autodidacte:* a popular lecturer in physics and chemistry, firmly bourgeois in family background (though under royal patronage), gifted, brave, and ultimately, fatally adventurous. On October 15, 1783, before representatives of the Académie Royale, he hesitantly rose on the tethered balloon to a height of approximately fifty feet, making two other tethered flights on the seventeenth and nineteenth. He experimented on the latter ascent with a small heater burning straw and wool to keep the air inside the balloon warm and thus prolong his test. He also carried André Giroud de Vilette and then François Laurent (the Marquis d'Arlandes, an infantry captain), lifting them to a height of over 300 feet.[19]

The Montgolfier team moved the balloon to the Château de la Muette in the Bois de Boulogne, the home of the sickly dauphin of France, under the care of the duc and duchesse de Polignac, one of France's most distinguished and power-ful families. There, from inside the sheltering walls of the stately chateau, Pilâtre de Rozier and the marquis d'Arlandes became the first humans to fly, completely separated from the earth, on Friday, November 21, 1783. That day dawned breezy, and indeed, a sudden gust sent the balloon lurching, tearing its fabric; quick-thinking ground handlers prevented the balloon envelope from catching fire—an unthinkable disaster that would have doomed the Montgolfiers' efforts to be the first to fly. Crowds had begun gathering early and now were sharply divided between those mocking the aeronauts and those shouting sympathetically and offering good wishes. Amid hoots and jeers from cynics and rowdies, several women stepped forward to help sew the rips closed. At 1:54 P.M., de Rozier and d'Arlandes cast off, their blue and gold balloon rising swiftly aloft. Among observers watching the ascent were members of an official body appointed to certify the success or failure of the attempt, including Benjamin Franklin, representing the Académie Royale.

The chief of the observer team, the Duc de Polignac, wrote that the balloon lifted off "in a most majestic fashion and when it reached about 250 feet above the ground, the intrepid travelers, taking off their hats, bowed to the spectators. At that moment, one experienced a feeling of fear mingled with admiration. Soon the aerial navigators were lost from view, but the machine, floating on the horizon and displaying a most beautiful shape, climbed to at least 3,000 feet at which height it was still visible; it crossed the Seine below the gate of la Conférence and, passing between the École Militaire and the Hôtel des Invalides, it was borne to a position where it could be seen by all Paris. When the travelers were satisfied with this experiment, not wishing to make a longer journey, they agreed to descend; but realizing that the wind was bearing them down upon the houses of the Rue de Seve [Sèvres], in the Faubourg Saint-Germain, they retained their calm and, increasing the production of gas, rose once more and continued on their way through the sky until they passed over the outskirts of Paris. They made a gentle descent into a field beyond the new boulevard, opposite the Croulebarge mill, without suffering the slightest discomfort, with two-thirds of their supplies still intact; so they could, if they had wanted to, have journeyed three times as far. Their voyage had taken them to 20 to 25 minutes over a distance of four to five thousand fathoms."[20]

Despite the apparent tranquillity of the journey, a letter from the marquis d'Arlandes revealed that the two aeronauts had experienced some bad moments, particularly as the balloon briefly paused over the Seine, dropping lower and lower towards its surface. De Rozier broke d'Arlandes out of a momentary sight-seeing reverie by exclaiming, "If you look at the river in that fashion you will be likely to bathe in it soon. Some fire, my dear friend, some fire!"[21] So d'Arlandes added some straw and wool to the brazier, and the balloon climbed again, continuing its journey. As it descended to land, it seemed it might collide with three large windmills at Butte-aux-Cailles, but it passed between them, landing heavily as its gas had cooled. De Rozier and d'Arlandes quickly pulled the collapsing fabric away from the still-smoldering brazier and stamped out any burning embers, and the arrival of civil authorities prevented its destruction from a growing crowd seeking souvenirs. Thus passed the first human flight in the history of the world, accomplished one year and seventeen days after Joseph had first sent his little taffeta balloon aloft in his room at the University of Avignon.

All attention now turned to Charles. A hydrogen balloon promised greater flight duration as well as greater lifting power, and onlookers were not disappointed when, on December 1, Charles took to the air in his *Charlière*. Preparations for the flight had not gone smoothly: while a new form of multibarrel hydrogen gas generator had proven a success, the tremendous volume of hydrogen gas

The *Montgolfière* of de Rozier and d'Arlandes, looking like a flying Fabergé egg, as depicted in a 1785 engraving, intended to acquaint the viewer with the dimensions and technical characteristics of the balloon.
SSPL

required to fill the 26-foot-diameter balloon—some 9,200 cubic feet—proved so difficult to produce that the launch date slipped from November 29 to December 1. By early afternoon, despite an early morning fog, the meteorological conditions bettered anything witnessed on previous flying days, still and cool with the barest hint of a breeze. An immense and increasingly restless crowd filled and surrounded the beautiful Jardin des Tuileries, from which sprouted the Charlière like some gigantic exotic mushroom, rising before the Tuileries palace. Charles and the Robert brothers had taken advantage of the weeks of preparation to design a much more sophisticated balloon than that of the Montgolfiers. It had a pressure-relieving dump valve to prevent the gas from uncontrollable expansion that would burst the envelope, and a pattern of fishnet-like netting surrounded the upper hemisphere of the balloon, both to reinforce it and to form an attachment point for support ropes holding the ornate crew gondola—no simple basket—suspended below the balloon. Spying Étienne Montgolfier in the audience, Charles approached his rival and gave him a small green balloon to release to find the wind direction, graciously remarking, "It is for you, monsieur, to show us the way to the skies."[22] The two pioneers noted the little balloon's flight, and then, accompanied by Noël Robert (the younger brother), Charles, ever the scientist, mounted the gondola with a set of instruments, including a barometer, thermometer, and notepaper. At 1:30 the yellow and ocher balloon lifted off, as Charles, ever so gallant, toasted the crowd with a freshly poured glass of champagne.[23]

The balloon rose almost vertically to a height of nearly 2,000 feet. "Nothing," Charles wrote later, "can compare with the joy that filled me as I flew away from the surface of the earth. It was not a pleasure, it was blissful delight. . . . [A] majestic spectacle unfolded before our eyes. Wherever we turned our gaze, we saw the heads of people, above us a sky free from cloud and in the distance the most allur-

J. A. C. Charles and Noël Robert aloft in their *Charlière*. SSPL

ing view in the world. I would have like to have shouted to the last of my critics: 'Look now, poor devil, see what is destroyed when the progress of science is obstructed!'"[24]

The tiny green pilot balloon Montgolfier and Charles had launched had briefly drifted northeast before turning over the city and then racing east-southeast, landing near the Château de Vincennes near la Pisotte. But after launch, Charles and Robert's balloon meandered northwest, passing south of Montmartre, crossing the Seine north of Clichy, and again north of Argenteuil, and continuing over Franconville, hooking northeast toward Eau Bonne, and then resuming its northwesterly progression to Taverny, Bessancourt, and Villiers Adam. It crossed the river Oise north of l'Isle Adam, passed south of Jouy, and then descended and landed near Nesle, after a flight of approximately 25 miles. Though it bumped along the ground, the balloon had survived in remarkable condition, and with its gas envelope intact and still full. The timely arrival of authorities led by the galloping Duc de Chartres and the Duc de Fitz James (who had raced all the way from the Tuileries) prevented any further damage by souvenir collectors, and Charles realized that he could continue to fly if he jettisoned some weight and flew alone.[25]

So Robert left to enjoy the enthusiastic huzzas of onlookers, and Charles took again to the air, the balloon climbing to 9,000 feet within ten minutes. He took numerous measurements, noting: "My fingers were benumbed by the cold, so that I could not hold my pen. I was now stationary as to rising and falling, and moved only in a horizontal direction. I rose up in the middle of the car to contemplate the scenery around me. When I left the earth, the sun had set on the valleys; he now rose for me alone; he presently disappeared, and I had the pleasure of seeing him set twice on the same day."[26] Suddenly he felt a "violent pain in my right ear and jaw," the first case in history of aviation medicine of ear pain caused by an abrupt change in pressure and expansion of the air within his inner ear. So, suffering from the cold and the intense pain, he valved off gas and returned back to earth, descending into the darkening twilight of the lower atmosphere and landing approximately an hour after his second liftoff, in the wooded countryside near le Lay.[27] When one thinks that the first human flight had only occurred ten days before, his solo ascent, in an open basket suspended under a thin experimental balloon filled with impure gas, constituted a flight of extraordinary boldness: among all his many virtues, courage undoubtedly predominated.

Consequences

Not quite a month later "the Astonishing Year" came to an end—and what a year it had been! At the beginning human flight was unknown, the stuff of the wildest speculation. At the end of the year, hundreds of thousands of people had seen balloons fly, ascend thousands of feet in the air, and cross miles of countryside. Truly, as the British historian Walter Raleigh wrote, "society went balloon-mad."[28]

Balloon motifs decorated furniture and clothing; images of the aeronauts adorned pendants and jewelry; elegant crystal chandeliers and clocks took on balloon shapes; and dinnerware reflected the personalities, events, and paraphernalia of the new balloon era.[29]

Ballooning and the balloonists dominated all conversation. Horace Walpole, no great fan of the new art, wrote to Sir Horace Mann after the de Rozier–d'Arlandes flight, "Do not wonder that we do not entirely attend to the things of earth: fashion has ascended to a higher element. All our views are directed to the air. *Balloons* occupy senators, philosophers, ladies, everybody." Walpole predicted, wrongly, that after the first accidents, it would be "adieu to air-balloons."[30] The balloon quickly became symbol, simile, and metaphor. When the German poet Goethe memorialized Voltaire, he wrote, "One could compare him to a *Luftballon,* which always swings airily over everywhere."[31] The philosopher Frédéric-Melchior Grimm noted: "Never has a soap bubble held the attention of a group of children in the way that the air-balloon has been, for a month now, holding the attention of the town and the court. Among all our circles of friends, at all our meals, in the ante-chambers of our lovely women, as in the academic schools, all one hears is talk of experiments, atmospheric air, inflammable gas [hydrogen gas], flying cars, journeys in the sky."[32] Writing to the French general Louis Le Bèque Du Portail, future president of the United States George Washington expressed his own amazement at this new invention, noting: "I have only newspaper accts. of the Air Balloons, to which I do not know what credence to give; as the tales related of them are marvellous, & lead us to expect that our friends at Paris, in a little time, will come flying thro' the air, instead of ploughing the Ocean to get to America."[33]

More importantly, humans had gazed down on the earth, forever altering their perception of the world. It constituted the transformation of perspective, the beginning of a three-dimensional appreciation unobtainable by viewers confined to a two-dimensional surface world. When de Rozier saw all Paris before him, and when Charles saw a double sunset, their experiences anticipated those of rocket pilots 170 years later who climbed high enough to see the curvature of the earth, cosmonauts and astronauts a decade further who marveled at a sunrise and sunset on every orbit, or the crew of Apollo 8 who in December 1968 first gazed back at the frail Earth suspended—as bright and gleaming as the most elegant Montgolfière or Charlière—against the blackness of space.

Within another year, the ballooning craze swept to other lands. In February 1784, outside of Milan, Paolo Andreani ascended in a Montgolfière, accompanied by Agostino and Carlo Gerli. On June 4, 1784, the first female aeronaut, Élisabeth Thible, flew over Lyons in *la Gustave* (a Montgolfière named after Sweden's King Gustave III, who observed the flight), singing operatic arias with her companion, M. Fleurant, as she did so.[34] Perhaps due to Franklin's unspoken influence, ballooning spread across the Atlantic before it spread across the Channel. On June 24, 1784, seven months after Pilâtre de Rozier and the marquis d'Arlandes wafted skywards, 13-year-old Edward Warren volunteered to go aloft in a balloon designed by lawyer Peter Carnes. The young lad subsequently ascended over Baltimore (as the *Maryland Journal and Baltimore Advertiser* reported) "and behaved with the steady Fortitude of an *old Voyager*," gravely doffing his hat to the enthusiastic crowds below, in the first human flight in the western hemisphere.[35] Two months later, on August 27, Scotsman James Tytler, a failed surgeon and apothecary turned encyclopedia editor, ascended in a Montgolfière over Comely Gardens, Edinburgh, becoming the first Briton to take to the air and anticipating the much better known two-hour-and-fifteen-minute ascent over London on September 15 by Vincenzo Lunardi, the young (and dashing) Tuscan secretary to the Neapolitan ambassador to England, by nearly a month.[36]

On September 18, 1784, Britain's great essayist and prolific man of letters Samuel Johnson complained to Sir Joshua Reynolds about the burst of letters he received on ballooning and the Lunardi flight. "I have three letters this day, all about the balloon. I could have been content with one. Do not write about the balloon, whatever else you may think proper to say."[37] Johnson, curious about many things, had made a near-miraculous recovery from a severe stroke but nevertheless knew he had not long to live, and thus did not wish to waste more time than necessary on any one thing, particularly something he viewed as skeptically as the balloon. Although he recognized "the first experiment, however, was bold and deserved applause and reward,"[38] he nevertheless wrote to one admirer: "In amusement, mere amusement, I am afraid it must end, for I do not find that its course can be directed so as that it should serve any purposes of communication; and it can give no new intelligence of the state of the air at different heights, till they have ascended above the height of mountains, which they seem never likely to do."[39]

But which balloonists would do. Quickly, very quickly, aeronauts extended their reach into the upper atmosphere and across borders. On January 7, 1785, less than a month after Johnson's death, Jean Pierre Blanchard and Dr. John Jeffries crossed the Straits of Dover from England to France, nearly ditching in the Channel until they jettisoned all possible weight, barely remaining airborne and then landing heavily in the forest of Guînes, near Calais, after the first international aerial voyage.[40] Within two decades balloonists had reached altitudes of over 23,000 feet, higher than all but the very highest of mountains. By the middle of the nineteenth century, using primitive oxygen breathing apparatus, British and French balloonists would be on the verge of ascending into the stratosphere.

Nothing so became the first aeronauts as those heady days in 1783. Both the Montgolfiers and Charles received due recognition and honors, the Montgolfiers being accorded the title *savant* by the Académie Royale, though Charles's design approach received stronger scientific endorsement as a more practical approach to flight. In January 1784 Joseph Montgolfier took to the air with de Rozier and five passengers in a huge hot-air balloon, *la Flesselles,* ascending from Lyons and reaching a height of 3,280 feet. This constituted the peak of the brothers' efforts, for though they continued to work on the periphery of aerostatics and aviation, in the future the Montgolfiers would be more revered as pioneers than as individuals with a continuing impact on future ballooning; indeed, much of their later work addressed other technical issues. Charles never flew again after his epochal first flight, perhaps because of the memory of that earache—or perhaps because nothing could ever match that first breathtaking moment as he beheld all of Paris before and below him and watched the sun set twice.

Destiny held a crueler fate for Pilâtre de Rozier. The young aeronaut had ambitious plans for more advanced and sophisticated aerostats, including a concept for a mixed hot-air and hydrogen vehicle, which he called an Aéro-Montgolfière, consisting of two separate balloons linked together by a cord network, the Charlière riding above a cylindrical Montgolfière like a gigantic golf ball perched on a thick tee. He had wanted to be the first to cross the Dover straits, but after Blanchard and Jeffries he determined to be the first to cross from France to England. Against the advice of others, including Étienne Montgolfier, he built his mixed lifting-gas balloon, and together with Pierre Romain, took off from the Pas de Calais on June 15, 1785. For a while all was well. Then, before the horrified gaze of onlookers, including Susan Dyer, de Rozier's English fiancée, a bright flame exploded around the upper balloon, wrapping the Charlière in a mass of flames. The unstable Montgolfière sank earthwards, rocking violently and casting the luckless aeronauts out of their gondola and onto the rocky shore below. De Rozier died instantly, of massive chest injuries, and Romain immediately afterwards. Tragically, overcome with shock and grief, young Miss Dyer collapsed and died herself eight days later, in a convent at Boulogne.[41] The deaths shocked all of France. In particular, de Rozier had been a popular figure, and not just with the nobility and bourgeoisie: none other than the bloodthirsty agitator Jean-Paul Marat, then living in London and editing a radical newsletter, "mourned that 'all hearts are stricken with grief.'"[42] The news reached across the Atlantic, where future president Thomas Jefferson wrote to Abigail Adams, "This will damp for a while the ardor of the Phaetons of our race who are endeavoring to learn us the way to heaven on wings of our own."[43] In fact it did not, for the balloon revolution had captured the human imagination to an extent even Jefferson would have found astonishing. De Rozier and Romain were not the first casualties in the history of flight, but they were the first after flight became a reality.[44] As such, their tragic deaths served as a grim warning that the air, even more than the sea, would always be utterly unforgiving of any error or misjudgment.

CHAPTER FOUR

Exploiting the Balloon

Despite occasional skeptics, few doubted that the balloon had some sort of potential, but exactly what that use might be was open to debate. After its invention the hot-air balloon, the Montgolfière, served primarily as entertainment for state functions or for the wealthy. So too did the cold-gas hydrogen Charlière, and scientists recognized that it offered them a unique way to study the earth and the atmosphere. But the hydrogen balloon had, thanks to its sealed envelope, another potential use as well: as a military observation system. André Giroud de Vilette, who had accompanied de Rozier on one of his tethered flights on October 17, 1783, reflected prophetically afterwards: "I was convinced that this apparatus, costing but little, could be made very useful to an army for discovering the positions of its enemy, his movements, his advances, and his dispositions, and that this information could be conveyed to the troops operating the machine."[1] An English publication a month after Vilette's flight endorsed the Frenchman's views, noting, "A general in the day of battle would derive singular advantage by going up in one of these machines; he would have a bird's-eye view of not only everything that was doing in his own, but in the enemy's army."[2]

Some observers had more bellicose ideas. Benjamin Franklin, American minister to France, noted in a letter to John Ingenhausz in January 1784, "It will be impossible for the most potent of [sovereigns] to guard his dominions. Five thousand balloons, capable of raising two men each, could not cost more than five ships of the line, and where is there a prince who could afford to cover his country with troops for its defense as that 10,000 men descending from the clouds might not in many places do an infinite amount of damage before a force could be brought together to repel them?"[3]

Writing to a cousin from the banks of the Severn River at Annapolis the following April, his countryman (and future president) Thomas Jefferson noted that balloons could soon be furnishing rapid transportation as well as "conveying intelligence into a besieged place, or perhaps enterprising on it, reconnoitering an army, etc."[4] To Francis Hopkinson, Jefferson penned, "This discovery seems to threaten the prostration of fortified works unless they can be closed above, the destruction of fleets and what not. . . . Inland countries may now become *maritime* states unless you chuse [*sic*] rather to call them *aerial* ones."[5] That same year a French author (his name regretfully unknown) published a book provocatively entitled *L'art de la guerre changée par l'usage de machines aérostatiques,* an ambitious tactics and organizational manual emphasizing the value of the balloon in observation, reconnaissance, and early warning. Another publication at the same time, by the Englishman Thomas Martyn, proposed employing balloons as night signaling systems, using multicolored fireworks.[6]

Not everyone viewed the military balloon as favorably as these writers, however. Samuel Johnson's contemporary Horace Walpole wrote to Sir Horace Mann, "I hope these new mechanic meteors will prove only playthings for the learned and the idle, and not be converted into new engines of destruction to the human race, as is so often the case of refinements or discoveries in science."[7] The poet William Cowper, in a wild-eyed frenzy, forecast the rise of anarchy and offered up a suitably radical "solution": "Were I an absolute legislator, I would, therefore, make it death for a man to be convicted of flying, the moment he could be caught; and to bring him down from his altitude by a bullet sent through his head or his carriage, should be no murder . . . [and therefore] the world would go on quietly, and if it enjoyed less liberty, would at least be more secure."[8]

Balloon "Close Air Support," as envisioned by German enthusiast Johann Martin Will, who saw it as the natural outgrowth of the invention of flying machines. AFMA

Professor Charles's Invention Goes to War

The balloon got its chance at war as a result of the French Revolution of 1789. By the late summer of 1793, enemies both at home and abroad beset the revolutionary government. Facing imminent disaster, the Comité de Salut Public (Committee on Public Safety) appointed a new minister of war, Lazare Carnot, and proclaimed in desperation the *levée en masse,* establishing the first modern citizen-based conscription army.[9] Quiet, shrewd, personally courageous, politically somewhat moderate, and immensely bright, Carnot had been a career engineering officer, a graduate of the École des Ponts et Chaussées (the School of Bridges and Highways). Always fascinated with technology, in January 1784 he had presented a paper on ballooning to the French Académie Royale, publishing it later that year as well.[10] Not surprisingly, then, he welcomed suggestions from balloon enthusiasts as to how this new invention could be turned to the service of Mars, even as some of those who had most eagerly supported the new revolution in aerostatics fell victim to the increasingly horrific Jacobin Terror. In 1784, at the request of the Académie Royale, Antoine-Laurent Lavoisier, working with Lieutenant Jean-Baptiste Meusnier, had determined the most efficient means to produce large quantities of hydrogen gas, undertaking experiments that subsequently earned him recognition as the father of modern chemistry.[11] His reward, a decade later, was a trip to the guillotine.

Louis Bernard Guyton de Morveau, an academic and balloon experimenter, proposed that Carnot might well find balloons useful for reconnaissance and observation. Joseph Montgolfier, co-inventor of the first balloon, thought his creation a fine instrument to bomb rebellious cities unpersuaded of the worth of the French Revolution, later enthusiastically drawing up a proposed plan of how one could lay waste to the city of Toulon by balloon attack. Encouraged by this ferment, the Committee moved swiftly. On order of Choderlos de Laclos (better known to history as the author of *Liaisons dangereuses*), workers transformed a portion of the Château de Meudon (the former home of the French dauphin, which, surmounting a broad plateau, reputedly commanded the finest vista in all of France), into a balloon factory. Then, on October 25, 1793, the Committee ordered chemist Jean Marie-Joseph Coutelle, a man possessed of a bleak and severe visage, to supervise the immediate building of a balloon for delivery to General Jean Baptiste Jourdan's Army of the North, the Armée de Sambre-et-Meuse. Armed with a letter of introduction from Carnot, Coutelle immediately left for Jourdan's headquarters to discuss future balloon operations.

Instead of welcoming the news, Jourdan, once a silk merchant's apprentice but now one of France's rising generals, dismissed Coutelle, treating him as a mere messenger. Another official rebuked the Committee in writing, noting "a battalion is needed more at the front than a balloon." But Carnot, the Committee, and Coutelle fortunately persisted, and balloon construction went ahead. Coutelle supervised establishment of a hydrogen-gas production facility using the Lavoisier-Meusnier process, with a hot furnace heating iron tubes in which metal filings were placed and then decomposing hydrogen from live steam; in 15 hours this plant could produce enough hydrogen to fill a balloon.[12] He refined the process of cutting sections of fabric that could be glued together to form a balloon, as well as the process for coating them with varnish to prevent the loss of gas after inflation. Eventually the Meudon factory built a dozen distinctively named balloons—*l'Agile, le Céleste, l'Emule, l'Entreprenant, l'Hercule, l'Industrieux, l'Intrépide, le Martial, le Précurseur, le Svelte, le Telemaque,* and *le Vétéran.*[13]

In April 1794, with the war situation still quite desperate, the Committee of Public Safety established the world's first organized aerial combat unit, the Première Compagnie d'Aérostiers. It consisted of 20 men under the command of Coutelle (newly commissioned as a captain), assisted by a lieutenant, two sergeants, and two corporals, with its own distinctive blue uniform. The Committee intended for this unit to undertake reconnaissance and observation, signaling, and the dropping of propaganda leaflets that would blow into enemy lines, using its balloon, aptly named *l'Entreprenant* (the Enterprise).[14] This time, perhaps because of a change of heart, Jourdan accepted the Première Compagnie into his army. Or perhaps he did so because of a concern that further failure to support the Committee's wishes might, in the age of "Monsieur Guillotine," have disastrous personal consequences—as it had for other obstructionist generals. So the Première Compagnie set off to war for "l'observation des marches et mouvements des ennemis."[15]

Subsequent operations overcame whatever remaining reservations General Jourdan may still have harbored about the military utility of balloons. *L'Entreprenant* and Coutelle went to war on June 2, 1794, at Maubeuge, raised over the besieged fortress to the accompaniment of cheers and a gun salute from the garrison. The scientist-turned world's-first-aerial-warrior, accompanied by an observer, spotted the location of Austrian and Dutch forces, and on his fifth ascent, narrowly avoided disaster when "straddled" by two cannonballs, one missing the top of the envelope and another grazing the bottom of the balloon basket—the first "flak" in history. The balloon company next transported their unwieldy charge from Maubeuge to French lines outside Charleroi on June 23. There Jourdan's adjutant, General Antoine Morelot, carried aloft by Coutelle to study enemy lines and dispositions, confirmed that the city's garrison was near to collapse, and in fact it surrendered the next day.[16]

The climactic battle of Fleurus on June 26, 1794, "the decisive French victory of the Revolutionary wars,"[17] marked the first use of an aerial vehicle in military history as a "command and control system."[18] On the day of the battle, Coutelle and Morelot remained aloft for approximately nine hours, and at one point Jourdan himself took to the skies. The general dropped signal messages in small bags weighted with sand and attached by rings to the balloon's retaining cables to be picked up and carried to French headquarters. Although accounts differ, according to Guyton de Morveau, Jourdan used them to plan his disposition of forces, and the Danish historian Lennart Ege has concluded that "practically all movements of the French troops were directed exclusively from the air, and as a result, the Austrians suffered a resounding defeat."[19] At the end of the day, the French revolution was secure, for the Austro-Dutch forces, though retiring in good order, had clearly lost, leaving 8,000 dead on the battlefield. One observer claimed that the battle showed that an army fighting without balloon observation was like a duelist fighting with a blindfold. For his part, Coutelle noted after the battle, "I was able to distinguish the corps of infantry and cavalry, the parks of artillery, their movements, and in general, the massed troops." Just days before Fleurus, the Committee of Public Safety had felt sufficiently confident in its balloon company to order the raising of a second. Now, its views vindicated by victory (always the greatest of military endorsements), the Committee further directed the establishment of a permanent aeronautical training base at Meudon, the École Nationale Aérostatique, the first of its kind in history, under the direction of Nicolas Conté. After Fleurus the grateful Jourdan changed the Army of the North's official letterhead to show not only his troops in battle, but also "a large observation balloon and its crew."[20]

Something of the innocence of those early days of flight, and perhaps the lingering of a spirit of chivalry that, alas, would all too quickly disappear from modern warfare, can be found in a subsequent sortie that Coutelle flew against the Austrians. He rose in extremely gusty weather, and his ground party had the greatest difficulty in keeping the *l'Entreprenant* under control, as the balloon bobbed and pitched. Concerned for his safety, believing that "he ought not to perish through circumstances alien to warfare," some *Austrian* officers advanced under a flag of truce and invited Coutelle to visit their headquarters! Coutelle, as gracious as they, declined the offer, but instead gave the visiting Austrians a complete briefing on his balloon and how it operated. The Austrians then returned to their own lines, and the war resumed.[21]

Fleurus represented the high point of French military aerostatics, for three events quickly conspired to, so to speak, puncture the balloon. First, the revolutionary government overextended itself, and Jourdan eventually met defeat at the hands of the Austrians at the battle of Würzburg. His balloon company fell into captivity together with their balloon *l'Hercule;* the museum-minded Austrians promptly put it on exhibit in Vienna, where it remains to this day.[22] Then, an administrative change placed the Deuxième Compagnie under the command of a general who lacked any appreciation for what it might do, and who in fact ultimately asked that it be removed from service. Despite this, Coutelle and Conté persuaded Napoléon to take the newly released Premiere Compagnie (freed by treaty after a year of captivity in Austrian hands) with him when he sailed for Egypt with Admiral François-Paul Brueys's fleet in May 1798, though there is no evidence that he ever had more than a passing interest in military ballooning, aside from public ceremony and celebration. The company and its equipment and provisions embarked on the *le Patriote* and the warship *l'Orient. Le Patriote* ran aground and sank off Alexandria on July 4, taking the balloon with it, and the following August 1, Admiral Horatio Nelson attacked Brueys at Aboukir bay, killing the hapless French admiral and sinking or burning 11 of 13 French ships of the line, virtually destroying Napoléon's naval support. Also, Nelson's bold attack accounted for *l'Orient* and all the balloonists' supporting equipment, before the Premiere Compagnie had any opportunity to serve in the campaign. After these reverses, early the next year the French government disbanded both balloon companies, and in 1802 the balloon school closed as well. French military aerostatics would not revive for another half century.[23]

So after the French revolution the balloon rapidly disappeared from military life, in that puzzling way whereby revolutionary military advances tend, more often than not, to be ignored or suppressed once a conflict is over, in favor of continuing to live with the normative existing doctrines and technologies. Despite the occasional appearance of small unmanned balloons as carriers of propaganda messages, ballooning made virtually no military impact until the American Civil War, being essentially exclusively relegated as an element of urban entertainment or scientific inquiry rather than an enabler of military force. Some suggested its use in France or Britain's colonial wars, in the American war against the Seminole Indians, or against the fortress of Vera Cruz during the Mexican War, all to no avail. In 1848, in a demonstration at Berlin, the English balloonist Henry Coxwell dropped small bombs from a balloon, and the next year, in July 1849, during the siege of Venice, the Austrians launched 100 small Montgolfiére-style balloons armed with time fuses and bombs upwind of the city, in hopes that the bombs would devastate the city, and they also launched others from the deck of the side-wheel steamer *Vulcano,* the first use of offensive "air power" from the sea. But despite remarkably thorough preparations (including the use of meteorological observations and trial pilot balloons to evaluate course and wind effects), this first attempt at "strategic bombing" failed, as contrary winds blew the balloons in all directions, including back over the *Vulcano.* The Austrians abandoned further attempts because of the risk to themselves.[24]

The Civil War

Throughout the early and mid-nineteenth century, ballooning had been popular entertainment in the United States. By 1859 more than 3,000 balloon ascensions had carried more than 8,000 Americans aloft. Thus it is not surprising that in the hectic early years of the American Civil War the balloon experienced a military renaissance, as balloonists served as observers for the Union army. That they did owed less to perceptive military planning than to the patriotic motives and ceaseless self-promotion of the balloonists themselves, particularly John Wise, John La Mountain, and Thaddeus S. C. Lowe, and the particularly strong patronage of President Abraham Lincoln and the first secretary of the Smithsonian Institution, Joseph Henry. Henry had closely followed ballooning and in fact had reviewed Lowe's plans (which remained unfulfilled) to fly a balloon across the Atlantic. In June 1861 Henry arranged for Lowe to demonstrate his balloon to Washington officials, including President Lincoln, during which demonstration Lowe telegraphed a message to the president while floating 1,000 feet over the White House.[25] Quite impressed, Henry subsequently wrote to the secretary of war: "From experiments made here for the first time it is conclusively proved that telegrams can be sent with ease and certainty between the balloon and the quarters of the commanding officer. . . . From all the facts I have observed and the information I have gathered I am sure that important information may be obtained in regard to the topography of the country and to the position and movements of an enemy."[26]

Lowe and his balloon *Union* made their first ascension with General George "Little Mac" McClellan's forces on August 30, 1861. Thereafter the balloonists showed considerable ingenuity in using their craft. Lowe and La Mountain also operated balloons off small "aircraft carriers," the collier *George Washington Parke Custis* and the transport *Fanny* (the birth of ship-based naval aviation, albeit with balloons). La Mountain made one ascension to 2,000 feet on August 3, 1861, while anchored off Sewell's Point in Hampton Roads, the first time a manned balloon ever operated from a naval vessel. He spotted and sketched Confederate fortifications and artillery sites on the point and looked as well (unsuccessfully) for evidence of the rumored Confederate reconstruction of the scuttled USS *Merrimac*. As the "ironclad" CSS *Virginia*, it would soon to have its own date with destiny and Swedish engineer John Ericsson's revolutionary USS *Monitor*. *Fanny* eventually fell to Confederate gunboats, being captured and subsequently used by the South; the *George Washington Parke Custis* served with distinction in the Potomac and

Professor Thaddeus Lowe's balloon gas generators on what is now the Washington Mall; note the unfinished U.S. Capitol in background. National Archives and Records Administration (NARA)

York rivers. In August 1862 it sailed with two gunboats, a sloop, and a tug, forming what might be considered the first "carrier battle group," to observe the bombardment of a Confederate fort.[27]

Following up on his White House experiments, Lowe ran a telegraph line from the ground headquarters to a sending key fitted in his balloon gondola. In one case Lowe's timely observations and telegraphed messages probably saved the Union army from a serious defeat at the battle of Fair Oaks, Virginia, when Confederate forces threatened to overwhelm Union defenders.[28] Afterwards Major General A. W. Greeley, the chief of the Army Signal Corps, stated, "It may be safely claimed that the Union army was saved from destruction at the battle of Fair Oaks, May 31 and June 1, 1862, by the frequent and accurate reports of Professor Lowe."[29] By this time Lowe commanded a force of no less than seven balloons (the *Constitution, Eagle, Excelsior, Intrepid, Union, United States,* and *Washington*) and a dozen or so aeronauts.[30]

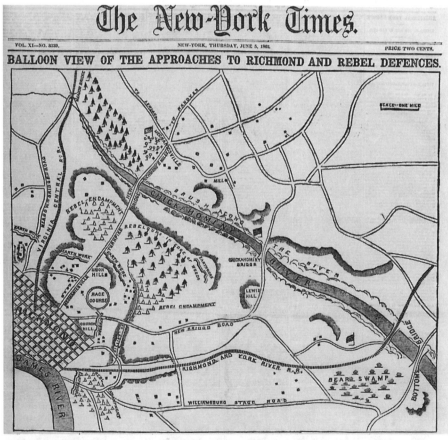

Drawn from balloon observation, this map of Richmond's defenses bears startling resemblance to radar imagery of Iraqi forces leaving Kuwait City in February 1991. From the *New York Times,* June 5, 1862.
NYPL

Confederate military leaders and ordinary soldiers alike quickly recognized the asymmetric advantage that balloon observation gave to the North. Indeed, even as their own government failed to sufficiently support the South's woefully inadequate efforts to develop their own balloon corps, Confederate commanders went to great lengths to attempt offsetting Union balloon reconnaissance, including intensive artillery barrages of balloon launch sites, igniting false campfires to offset night reconnaissance sorties, and building wooden decoy weapons called "Quaker cannon" to deceive prying eyes.[31] All of this took effort in manpower and man-hours that could have been far more profitably applied to other tasks.

Thus the Confederates were surprised when Union balloons disappeared from the sky. "I have not seen a balloon since [General George] Meade took command of that army," Confederate Captain James Pass perceptively wrote to his brother in late 1863; "I think he must not think so much of them as [General Joseph] Hooker did."[32] After the war General E. Porter Alexander remarked, "I have never understood why the enemy abandoned the use of military balloons early in 1863 after having used them extensively up to that time. Even if the observer never saw anything, his balloons would have been worth all they cost [us] trying to keep our movements out of sight."[33] General James Longstreet reflected that during the Peninsular campaign, "the Federals had been using balloons in examining our positions, and we watched with envious eyes their beautiful observations as they floated high up in the air, well out of range of our guns."[34] Ironically, the Union military leadership's own lack of appreciation had played a far greater role than any Confederate effort in dooming the North's balloon corps. Senior Union commanders such as General Henry Halleck tended to minimize the value of balloon reconnaissance, and rifts, disagreements, and acrimony often characterized relations between the balloonists themselves, and between military officers and the balloonists. All this hurt the program, and eventually Lowe resigned in frustration: the North's balloon corps disbanded before Gettysburg.[35]

But the balloonists had their supporters, and if too few to reverse the decline of Union aerostatics, they were nevertheless of distinguished rank, such as General Ambrose Burnside and particularly General George McClellan. McClellan almost always supported his aeronauts, though with one curious exception. During the Peninsula campaign in the spring of 1862, Major General Fitz-John Porter had a close call with disaster while on an observation flight. During preflight gassing, some sulphuric acid had spilled on the tether rope,

Lowe ascends to observe the Battle of Seven Pines (Fair Oaks) in the *Intrepid,* 1862, in this photograph by Mathew Brady. NARA

weakening it, and it broke after launch, sending the balloon into free flight. The break almost delivered him into the hands of the Confederates: he actually over-flew their lines amid a storm of shot and shell before a providential breeze blew him safely back over his own, where he quickly valved off gas and descended to earth. McClellan wrote his wife that the incident had given him "a terrible scare," and added, "You may rest assured of one thing: you won't catch me in the con-founded balloon nor will I allow any other Generals to go up in it!"[36] In fact this was either a snap opinion quickly rescinded or simply a ruse to reassure his wife he wouldn't take chances—for just eight days later McClellan himself ascended before the respectful (if wondering) eyes of Union troops, one of at least two occasions when he personally went balloon reconnoitering.[37]

Others venturing aloft were the mercurial and murderous General Daniel Sickles and a young and dashing cavalryman, Lieutenant George Armstrong Custer. A bold and promising staff officer fated for a lonely and merciless death amidst the overwhelming massacre of his regiment at Little Big Horn, Custer fre-quently ascended by day and night to study the progression of the Peninsula cam-paign through the eyes of a professional military officer, not those of a militarily untrained civilian aeronaut. If initially apprehensive (he regarded the balloon as "a wild and untamable animal"), he soon came to appreciate its unique vantage point and perspective.[38] But these were the exceptions. Shabbily treated, balloon-ing and balloonists disappeared from the Union army, remembered only years later in the occasional scholarly work or in children's literature.[39]

In retrospect, one of the greatest lessons of the Civil War—one unfortunately relearned over a half century later, after the invention of the airplane—was that education of senior army officers in the value of aerial observation was of even greater importance than furnishing an adequate organizational structure and logistical support for the system itself. It is interesting to contemplate how differ-ent things might have been at Gettysburg if Lee—even accepting the other defi-ciencies in Confederate planning and tactics at that decisive battle—had possessed a balloon corps and faced a Union army that had just shut down its own balloon establishment. But such was not to be. Of one fact there can be no doubt: the Civil War would not be the last time that armies showed less respect and apprecia-tion for their air arm than an enemy did.

The French Revival and the Siege of Paris

French ballooning, despite being militarily moribund since Napoléon's ill-starred Egyptian campaign, retained a tremendous vitality for public exhibition and scientific purposes, thanks in large measure to a remarkable man known by the mysterious name "Nadar," Gaspard Félix Tournachon. A flamboyant society pho-tographer and balloonist possessing a brilliant flare for publicity and sense of the-ater, he was a close friend of the poet Baudelaire, the writers George Sand and Jules Verne (who patterned the fictional character Ardan on Tournachon), and the artist Daumier. His brother Adrien Tournachon was a well-known painter. Nadar had pioneered stereoscopic aerial photography—taking overlapping images to map portions of Paris, an important step on the road to modern photomapping and photographic reconnaissance before, in 1863, unveiling a huge balloon, appropriately named *le Géant*. Nadar himself had just turned 43.[40]

Launched from the Champ de Mars where, 80 years before, Parisians had first witnessed a balloon rise from the earth, *le Géant* featured a two-level cabin complete with a captain's cabin, toilet, storeroom, and photography studio and printing press, and could carry up to 12 passengers. But despite all of this, it was not a great success. Indeed, on its second flight, it crashed heavily in Germany, barely avoiding an onrushing locomotive and then exploding. "It must be considered a miracle," Ege writes drily, "that everybody remained alive, but all were more or less badly injured."[41] Despite this disaster, Nadar rebuilt the gondola of *le Géant*, together with a new balloon envelope, and continued his flights. At the Great Exhibition, the festive high point of the Second Empire, held on Paris's Champ de Mars in 1867, Nadar took upwards of a dozen passengers aloft at a time in the reconstituted *le Géant* and another huge double-deck tethered balloon, the *Céleste*. Once aloft, they could feast on cold chicken and wine while overlooking the exhibitions and *la ville lumière*. Nadar played a tremendous role in making ballooning and aviation popular across France (promoting what in the twentieth century would be called "air-mindedness" and the "gospel of aviation,") and reviving French military aerostatics. Happily, in view of his interest in flight, he lived to witness Louis Blériot's epochal journey across the Dover straits in 1909 before dying the next year at age 90.[42]

It is not surprising, then, that ballooning played a major role in the Franco-Prussian War of 1870–71, specifically the siege of Paris. In 1870 Prussia and the other German states shattered the Second Empire of Louis-Napoléon, France's pretentious but ill-skilled emperor, after he had intemperately declared war on them over a dispute involving the Spanish throne.[43] After a series of military disasters, on September 1, bedridden by a kidney stone the size of a quail's egg, Louis-Napoléon surrendered at Sedan lest his remaining forces be pounded to pieces by German artillery. But the real war was just beginning. Despite being surrounded by German forces, Paris revolted and patriots announced a new provisional government for France from the steps of the Hôtel de Ville.

Not to be outdone, Nadar (with two balloonist friends) stepped to the fore, proposing to the French general Louis Trochu that the military incorporate balloons in the defense of Paris, that the fiery mayor of Montmartre, Georges Clemenceau, install a company of balloonists in his *arrondissement,* and—most usefully—that the minister of posts establish a balloon postal service to overfly Prussian lines. The balloon post seized the imagination: authorities quickly launched a thorough search throughout the city for any old balloon that could be patched and placed in service. The first flight got under way at eight o'clock on the morning of September 23, when Nadar's friend Jules Duruof ordered "Lâchez tout!" (Let go!), groundsmen dropped lines, and the balloon *Neptune*, carrying a small quantity of letters and messages, rose into the air accompanied by impassioned cries of "Vive la France, -vive la République!", passing over the enemy lines before the startled eyes of enemy troops and landing 11 hours later on the grounds of the Château de Cracouville outside Evreux, over 60 miles away.[44]

Thus inspired, the French minister of the interior, the nervous yet courageous young radical republican Léon Gambetta, escaped in the swaying balloon *l'Armand Barbès* from the City of Lights on October 7. He was the first government official of any country to take to the air, accompanied by a second balloon, the *George-Sand,* the latter carrying two American arms merchants, both rising from the Place St.-Pierre amid an even more emotional ceremony, a huge crowd including author Victor Hugo and Clemenceau, and draped French and American flags.[45] Landing outside Montdidier, Gambetta rallied a citizen army that returned to battle. Of his brave voyage, Horne has rightly stated, "From a man embarking on this kind of balloon journey in 1870, probably at least as much real courage was demanded as from a [Yuri] Gagarin, a [Alexsei] Leonov, or a [John] Glenn in the 1960s; and for the balloonists there were no helping hands or batteries of computers on earth, ready to guide them down, no flotillas standing by to pick them out of the sea, and only in the matter of 're-entry' did they have more control over their flight than the astronauts."[46]

A single victory followed, at Coulmiers; then German military superiority again showed. Besieged, Paris sank from civilization: its famous trees and gardens vanished for firewood or food, and desperate hunger reduced citizens to eating dogs, cats, and rats. After increasingly ferocious fighting and draconian German reprisals, the provisional government agreed to an armistice at the end of January 1871. Paris then sank into the bitterness of the Commune that followed, replete with a violent reimposition of order upon the Parisian revolutionaries. By mid-1871 Europe had returned to peace, however violent its imposition. Germany had unified on the back of a prostrate France, seizing two French provinces and imposing heavy reparations on its former adversary.[47]

Amid this carnage and horror, the balloons had been an undoubted (and even ennobling) triumph. Assembled in two railway stations, the Gare du Nord and the Gare d'Orléans, and then launched from hills and open plazas, approximately 66 balloon flights carried 102 passengers and approximately 11 tons of dispatches, including 1.5 million letters, out of Paris. A total of 58 of the 66—88 percent—were successful, while six were captured and two were lost at sea. Also, the balloons carried the first "microdot" communications: photographer René Dagron developed a microscopic photographic reproduction process that permitted 2,000 characters (either letters or digits) to be stored on a film about one-fourth the size of a playing card. Their frustratingly easy passage over Prussian lines caused Otto von Bismarck to order the world's first high-angle antiaircraft gun from armaments manufacturer Alfred Krupp.[48] Again, as Alistair Horne noted, "the balloons of Paris were to constitute probably the most illustrious single episode of the Siege, . . . the zenith of [civilization's] resourcefulness in adversity."[49]

If the United States did not remain steadfast to the balloon after 1863, other nations certainly did, not only because of their own previous experience, but because many of their attachés and observers had witnessed firsthand the use of balloons in the American Civil War and then followed France's exploits in the siege. They recognized, as one wrote, that "no method is better suited to viewing quickly the terrain of an unknown, enemy-occupied territory."[50]

Between 1794 and 1897, 17 nations created balloon services in their armies, across Europe, the Americas, and Asia. Balloons accompanied British troops to South Africa and the Boer War, French colonial forces relied on balloons for observation in North Africa, Tonkin, and Madagascar, and after the turn of the century, Russian and Japanese balloons flew in the Russo-Japanese war and the siege of Port Arthur.[51] Alarmed by this foreign interest, the U.S. Army attempted to revitalize its balloon program in 1890, with attendant organizational and material problems. Nevertheless, the service fielded an observation balloon in Cuba, where despite being taken under tremendous fire, its observers so successfully directed artillery down onto Spanish trench positions that it "may have been the determining factor in the capture of San Juan Hill."[52] When the twentieth century began, then, military ballooning had at last achieved the ubiquitous accept-

The Parseval-Sigsfeld *Drachenballon* of 1898, a tethered "kite balloon" that went on to subsequent extensive use.
AFMA

ance that early prophets such as André Giroud de Vilette had anticipated over a century before, in the first balloons bobbing over Paris. The next stage would belong to streamlined (and hence more wind stable) tethered observation balloons, typified by the German Parseval-Sigsfeld *Drachenballon* and its French equivalent, the *Caquot*; both would see extensive service in the First World War.

Trials and Tragedy:
Scientific Ballooning to the End of the Nineteenth Century

Just before Christmas 1783, the *Académie Royale des Sciences* issued a report on the relative merits of the Montgolfière and Charlière balloons. While they praised both types and deliberately avoided picking a winner, there was little doubt but that the Academy considered the Charlière the better balloon for scientific purposes because of the greater lifting power of hydrogen compared with heated air. The Academy's assumptions were generally correct: hot-air balloons proved popular at public exhibitions (and continue so today), but for scientific purposes the cold gas hydrogen (and later helium) balloon dominated, from the very beginning of scientific ballooning all the way through the use of so-called superballoons operating in excess of 100,000 feet today.[53]

Scientific ballooning had really began with the ascent of J. A. C. Charles on December 1, 1783, for he had taken a collection of instruments and a notepad on which to record data. Aeronaut Jean Pierre Blanchard and physician John Jeffries in London on November 30, 1784, approached scientific ballooning a bit more systematically. Riding a Montgolfière to 9,000 feet, Jeffries measured temperature, humidity, and pressure using a thermometer, hygrometer, and barometer that he had carried aloft while his trusty pilot, concerned more about his reputation, dropped armloads of promotional broadsheets that fluttered down over the city. Curiously, little was done after this for almost the next two decades, with one very notable exception. On October 22, 1797, Jacques Garnerin rose over Paris's Parc de Monceau in a parachute-equipped gondola, suspended under a green and orange balloon. At an altitude of approximately 2,300 feet, he severed the attachment lines and safely completed a shuttlecock-like descent to earth. Thus, after centuries of drawings and thought, was born the parachute, in a flight of remarkable courage and faith.[54] But overall, experimental ballooning remained quiescent until Étienne-Gaspard Robertson, a French physicist, and M. Lhoest went aloft over Hamburg in a Charlière on June 18, 1803, to study static electricity. They reached approximately 24,000 feet of altitude in the balloon *l'Entreprenant*—most probably the very same balloon used at Fleurus, as scientists employed at least one other war-surplus balloon for high-altitude flights. Robertson very quickly encountered what would be the greatest danger to scientific ballooning in the nineteenth and early twentieth century: open-gondola flight in an increasingly oxygen-poor environment. Indeed, it is not surprising that scientific ballooning very quickly ran into trouble, as these heroic if all too frequently foolhardy individuals were operating in conditions more suited to the pressurized cabin (and even pressurized flying suit) environment of the post-1935 world.[55]

Robertson and his colleague Lhoest noted what are now recognized classic textbook symptoms of anoxia, that is, deprivation of oxygen to the brain: "Our state was that of indifference; there the physicist is no longer sensitive to the glory and the passion of discoveries; the very danger which results from the slightest negligence in this journey hardly interests him. . . . We could hardly ward off sleep."[56] Despite this experience, Robertson continued his ascensions, and on January 30, 1804, at the invitation of the Russian Academy of Sciences in St. Petersburg, flew an academician, one Sacharof, on an over-three-hour evening flight. During the journey, the first balloon ascension in Russia, the excited academician threw a number of items overboard (including his coat) in an effort to make the balloon rise even higher. He also undertook a variety of experiments that seem oddly foolish even by the primitive standards of the time: shouting and then listening through an ear trumpet for an echo off the ground, dropping empty bottles in the Neva and watching the expanding wave circles, and the like. But he was the first Russian aeronaut, and in his own way the predecessor of the many aeronauts, aviators, and cosmonauts that would follow, not least of whom would be Dmitri Mendeleyev, the organizer of the periodic table of atomic weights and an enthusiastic balloonist as well.[57]

Back in France Robertson's flight had launched a sharp exchange in the Académie des Sciences (the provocative word *Royale* having understandably been dropped after 1789!) over data relating to earth magnetism, and during the next two months, the noted physicist and chemist Joseph-Louis Gay-Lussac and mathematician, astronomer, and mineralogist Jean Baptiste Biot ascended twice at the request of the Académie to make their own measurements of magnetism and the composition of the upper atmosphere. On the second of these flights, Gay-Lussac reached over 23,000 feet. But realizing it was pressing its luck, the Académie abandoned further high altitude investigations, for it recognized the risks to its scientists was simply too great. As Maurice Daumas rightly judged, "The audacity of the aeronauts won them more admiration than the results of their experiments."[58]

Anoxia is insidious, as any aircrew member who has ever taken altitude-chamber training knows: the passage from clarity to befuddlement to stupor, and finally to a life-threatening unconsciousness, is so gradual as to imperil even the most experienced airman. The cold environment of the open balloon gondola, or later the open-cockpit airplane, added its own physically taxing and endangering aspect, not least because it could distract one from the recognition of anoxia onset. In retrospect these flights were so personally dangerous (from the standpoint of cold as well as of oxygen deprivation) as to anticipate the early days of atomic-weapons research, when scientists would push small amounts of fissionable material together by hand to access criticality, at great risk to themselves. Today aircrews operating in excess of 10,000 feet of altitude are required to don oxygen masks, and Robertson, Lhoest, Gay-Lussac, and Biot were at over double that altitude, almost as high as the very tallest Himalayan peaks. And as will be seen, even the provision of oxygen was not enough to spare some early aeronauts.

In 1850 the French briefly resumed altitude flying, but no higher than approximately 20,000 feet, still a quite risky height, especially if a befuddled aircrew should accidentally drop more ballast than they should, or fail to valve off gas if the sun was heating and expanding a balloon, thus possibly carrying them to even higher and fatal altitudes. It now fell to the British to take the balloon higher, and into very dangerous circumstances. Henry Coxwell, the most famous British aeronaut of his day, and meteorologist James Glaisher of the Royal Observatory at Greenwich made three ascents, the third of which, on September 5, 1862, reached over 25,000 feet—just how much higher is the subject of debate. Both crew members passed out as the balloon kept climbing, with Coxwell pulling the dump valve with his teeth (his hands were too frostbitten to function) just before passing out himself, and Glaisher subsequently estimating that the balloon must have reached 37,000 feet. Subsequent analysis by aeromedical experts suggests

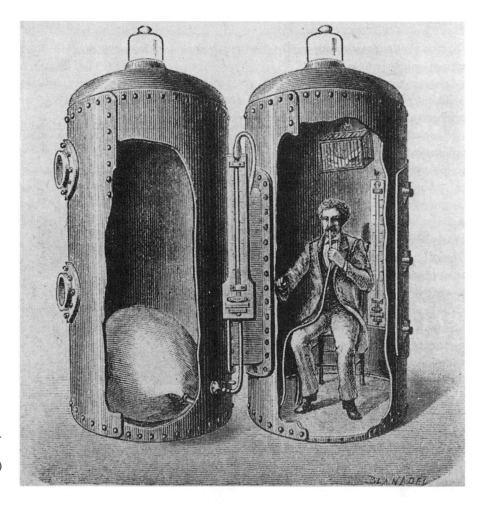

Paul Bert's altitude chamber, used to study the effects of breathing oxygen as a means of overcoming anoxia. Ciba Symposia (1943) (cs)

that they were at least 10,000 feet lower than this anticipated altitude, if for no other reason than that they survived the flight. Glaisher and Coxwell made additional ascents, totaling 28 in all, between 1862 and 1866, but none was as perilous as this.[59]

The next stage in scientific ballooning belonged to France. In the early 1870s, the physician and physiologist Paul Bert, holder of the chair of general physiology at the Sorbonne and credited posthumously as the "Father of Aviation Medicine," created the first altitude chamber, consisting of two chambers large enough to house animal or human subjects and capable of being evacuated by an air pump (venting into a converted boiler) to an altitude equivalency of 36,000 feet, though most of his tests involved lower "altitudes." In this chamber Bert first experimented with using bags of oxygenated air sucked through a rubber tube to relieve the symptoms of anoxia, and he conducted similar experiments on two colleagues, Joseph Crocé-Spinelli and Théodore Sivel. On March 22, 1874, these two flew the balloon *Étoile Polaire* to over 24,000 feet, assisted by portable bags of an oxygen-nitrogen mix, which they sucked through rubber tubes. For reasons that defy common sense, Crocé-Spinelli and Sivel now determined to outdo Glaisher and Coxwell's already legendary ascent and take along a third crew member, Gaston Tissandier (one of the most famous of Parisian balloonists during the Prussian siege), as well. Bert, when apprised of their plans, was aghast, for they planned to take at best a minimal amount of oxygen, intending (foolishly) to husband it until needed, not recognizing that the value of oxygen at altitude is in its *continuous,* not *intermittent,* use. Despite his warnings they pressed on in their desires to break the British "record" with an eagerness and recklessness worthy of Icarus himself.[60]

On April 15, 1875, the three men lifted off from Paris at 11:35 A.M. in the balloon *le Zénith.* They quickly reached 23,500 feet as Tissandier noted his two colleagues were already sleepy. Two hours after launch, *le Zénith* reached over 26,000 feet, with Tissandier by now so oxygen deprived that he lacked the ability to grasp the oxygen tube. Later he recalled, "One becomes indifferent, one thinks neither of the perilous situation nor of any danger; one rises and is happy to rise."[61] So he passed out, vaguely awakening over the next half hour or so to note both Crocé-Spinelli and Sivel lying unconscious in the bottom of the gondola, and finally to shouts of "Throw out some ballast, we are descending!" as a revived Crocé-Spinelli, still obviously enthusiastically pursuing an altitude record, tried to climb even higher. It was the last chance to avoid tragedy, and what Crocé-Spinelli did next doomed himself and Sivel. Tissandier drowsily observed Crocé-Spinelli pitching equipment overboard, and again the balloon began to climb. Then Tissandier passed out for the second time. *Le Zénith* rose up to over 28,000 feet (as measured by a barometer) while Crocé-Spinelli and Sivel died. Tissandier, who must have been blessed with the most extraordinary constitution, dozed onwards, awakening in the lower atmosphere at 3:30 P.M. to the horrific sight of his dead companions. The balloon descended gently to land a half hour later near the village of Ciron, 155 miles southwest of Paris.[62]

The *Zénith* disaster was so preventable as to baffle any examiner. Twenty-twenty hindsight is an occupational hazard for historians, but nevertheless, it is truly inexplicable that Crocé-Spinelli and Sivel essentially missed *all* the important lessons that they should have learned from their time in Bert's pressure chamber, chief of which were first, carry enough oxygen, and second, have the discipline to use it *all* the time when exceeding lower altitudes. Indeed, not carrying enough oxygen caused them to be far too miserly in using it when they needed to. Precisely because anoxia onset is so gradual, they did not use their carefully husbanded reserves when they should have. Or perhaps, like Tissandier, when they realized they needed it, they lacked the strength to grab the lifesaving tubes and breath it in. In any case they paid the supreme price for enthusiastic folly, for as aeromedical historian and physician Douglas Robinson has written, "The three oxygen bags were largely full when le Zénith landed 155 miles from Paris at 4 P.M."[63]

After *le Zénith,* the higher altitudes remained off limits to the unwary for nearly a quarter century, much as Mt. Everest remained inviolate after the death of George Mallory until Edmund Hillary and Tenzing Norgay successfully assaulted it in 1953. At the end of the century, German balloonists reached 30,000 feet, and then, on July 31, 1901, Professors Reinhard Süring and Artur Berson ascended from Templehof to nearly 35,000 feet in the balloon *Preussen,* a voyage eerily reminiscent of Coxwell and Glaisher's nightmarish journey. Despite having a supply of oxygen, both aeronauts passed out because of the inefficiency of their handheld oxygen tubes, and because at altitudes above 30,000 feet, blood oxygenation levels drop even if one is using 100 percent oxygen and a tight (and thus highly efficient) mask. (This too is something readily observable in a modern altitude chamber.) Süring and Berson had extraordinary good luck, for otherwise they could easily have perished. Based on the Süring and Berson experience, attendees at an international meteorological conference held in Paris in 1896 agreed to employ unmanned instrumented balloons for high-altitude observations rather than risk human lives.[64] Further, Austrian physiologist Hermann von Schrötter rightly recommended all future high-altitude balloons use a sealed gondola, and in fact this would become the standard for all subsequent high altitude exploration, with one notable and tragic exception. In 1927, operating in ignorance of the von Schrötter conclusions, U.S. Army Air Corps Captain Hawthorne Gray perished after reaching 42,470 feet in an open gondola balloon. He exhausted his oxygen supply, possibly from incipient anoxia or from a failure to appreciate how close he

The *Zénith* shortly before its crew succumbed to anoxia, killing Théodore Sivil and Joseph Crocé-Spinelli. As the balloon ascends, Sivil (at left) releases even more ballast, Gaston Tissandier (center) reads the barometer, and Crocé-Spinelli (right) takes a whiff of oxygen. cs

was to oxygen deprivation, thanks to not having reliable time references: his clock had frozen (which he knew), and a dropped oxygen cylinder had severed his radio antenna. Again, a highly enthusiastic attitude had led to terrible tragedy at high altitude.[65]

One final example of scientific ballooning from the nineteenth century is worth noting: the ill-fated effort by the Swedish polar explorer Saloman August Andrée to reach the North Pole by air in 1897. As early as 1784, future president Thomas Jefferson had suggested a polar balloon flight, writing to his cousin that the balloon seemed eminently suited for "the discovery of the Pole which is but one day's journey in a balloon, from where the ice has hitherto stopped adventures."[66] Supported by the Swedish Academy of Sciences, Andrée constructed a 160,000-cubic-foot hydrogen balloon, the Örnen (Eagle), with a cane and wood basket sufficient to allow three scientists to travel in reasonable comfort and efficiency. Andrée estimated that the balloon had an endurance of up to 30 days aloft, though others suggested a more reasonable 15. He recognized the risks and determined that only single men should go on the flight. Leaky seams plagued the attempt and caused one potential crewmember to resign, a prudent move. But in July 1897, Andrée, Knut Fraenkel (an engineering officer secretly engaged to be married), and physicist Nils Strindberg sailed to Danes Island off the northwest tip of Spitzbergen. From here on July 11, at the urging of Fraenkel and Strindberg, a seemingly reluctant Andrée took to the air, by which time his balloon was losing upwards of 100 pounds of lift per day thanks to hydrogen leakage. Ignoring the previous miserable history of attempts to guide balloons with sails and ropes, he had planned to steer the balloon via guide ropes trailed on the surface and connected to sails. But at launch the guide ropes detached, so that in effect the Örnen was a free balloon from virtually the moment of liftoff. At this point he should have abandoned the voyage, but he pressed on. The Örnen briefly touched the sea because of strong downdraft, rebounded into the air, rising to approximately 2,000 feet, and then drifted out of view. And that was the last the world knew of the Örnen and the Andrée party for the next 33 years.[67]

In 1930 a pair of Norwegian walrus hunters from the sealer Braatvag landed on White Island off the eastern coast of Spitzbergen. In short order they discovered utensils, a small folding boat bearing the inscription Andrée Polar Expedition 1897, and the bodies of Andrée and Strindberg; the crew of another sealer, the Isbjörn, recovered Frankel's body several weeks later. All were taken to Tromsø, Norway, and thence to Stockholm on the Swedish gunboat Svensksund for an appropriately reverential burial. (Frankel's former sweetheart, long married to an Englishman, gave instructions that upon her death her heart was to be removed and interred with her long-lost first love, which must have been as disconcerting to her husband as it was touching to those who knew of her wishes.)[68] The sealers likewise recovered Andrée's diary and a film canister that, when developed, yielded 30 poignant photographs of the expedition and its disintegration into disaster. Andrée's diary revealed that from the outset the balloon had the gravest difficulty remaining aloft, sustaining repeated impacts with the ice. It finally landed a good 65 hours after liftoff, heavily weighted down by the notorious icy fog of the arctic, 376 miles northeast of Danes Island and still almost 500 miles from the North Pole. The team stayed put for a week and then took off afoot for Franz Josef Land, still functioning as a scientific party, but increasingly sick. Days turned into weeks, and finally into 2 1/2 months. During that time the team members, now extremely ill, hauled their instrument-filled boat, pushing and pulling it over ice crevasses, crossing floes and hummocks, and doing so in a virtually continuous, enervating, enveloping icy fog corrosive to both health and spirits. At last they came to White Island, and here, sometime after October 17, 1897, they died.

Pioneer Arctic aviator John Grierson, no stranger to courage and accomplishment himself, has written: "In the annals of the Arctic, there have been many stories of endurance in the face of great hardships, but Andrée's courage was quite outstanding."[69] The party perished from a number of causes: poor equipment (especially poor clothing and a leaky balloon), poor concept (the idea of steering the balloon via guide ropes and sails was theoretically ingenious but impractical), underestimation of the difficulties involved, and the demanding physical environment (particularly the ice fog, which coated the balloon and its rigging and dragged it down). Even then they might have walked out, for their teamwork, spirit, and endurance were extraordinary.

But here fate played a particularly cruel trick. In 1949, curious about the symptoms experienced by the party and recorded in Andrée's diary, the Danish physician Adam Tryde received permission to study samples taken from the skin of a polar bear shot by Andrée and subsequently used as a sleeping bag. As Tryde suspected, the results indicated an infestation of *Trichinella spiralis,* the parasitic worm causing trichinosis, a common ailment in bears. Had the party been able to thoroughly cook the bears they shot for survival, they would have avoided this seriously debilitating disease. But they could not, and so this became, in all likelihood, the primary cause of their deaths. Grierson's judgment on the Andrée party might as well be a closing judgment on nineteenth-century scientific ballooning: "This was where the factor of craziness came in, that combination of ambition, vanity and bravery which drives man on to the most utter recklessness, to take risks which if weighed carefully would prove disaster inevitable. And all because he has set his course towards a certain goal, the attainment of which seems more valuable than life itself."[70]

CHAPTER FIVE

The Quest for Steerable Flight

In September 1784, just after Lunardi's London flight, Samuel Johnson, near to death, had seen with total clarity the weakness of the free balloon. "We now know," he wrote, "a method of mounting into the air, and, I think, are not likely to know more. The vehicles can serve no use till we can guide them."[1] Undoubtedly the balloon had two very serious deficits: first, its inability to move against the wind, and from a military standpoint, its large size and potentially explosive vulnerability. Highly visible and bobbing almost insultingly close to the enemy, balloons attracted a great deal of hostile artillery and mortar fire, as experiences from the French Revolution, the Civil War, the siege of Paris, and Cuba clearly demonstrated. Ironically, the vast majority of this fire came nowhere near the balloon itself, but instead fell to earth in the midst of troops congregating around the balloon launch site, often inflicting high casualties. Not surprisingly, fixed balloons were never popular with their ground warfare comrades, who viewed them as artillery magnets.[2]

But lack of maneuverability constituted the balloon's greatest weakness, particularly its inability to navigate against the wind, something dramatically illustrated during the siege of Paris in the Franco-Prussian War. Though many balloons had flown *from* Paris, not a single attempt to fly a balloon *to* Paris had succeeded, and the ones flown from the city had wound up scattered across Europe: six in Belgium, four in Holland, two in Germany, one in Norway (!), and two, sadly, swept out to sea. "Chemists and scientists share but one idea," one Parisian wrote, "to control the direction of balloons."[3]

Proponents of steerable airships had put forth various schemes of rudders and propulsion as far back as the days of the Montgolfiers. The brilliant French military engineer (and future general) Lieutenant Jean-Baptiste Meusnier—who earlier had plotted the flight path of the *Globe* as it flew across Paris from the Champ de Mars in August 1783, working also with Lavoisier to improve the rate of hydrogen production—had early recognized that a steerable balloon would have to be streamlined and would require specialized maintenance and support facilities. His concept for an ellipsoidal airship anticipated early blimps,[4] but as yet no means to power such a craft existed. General Pierre Lissarrague, the noted French aviation historian and director of France's Musée de l'Air et de l'Espace, quite rightly credited Meusnier with making the "first rational study" of an airship, for this gifted officer gave to the world the essential shape of all future airships.[5] But Meusnier fell in battle in 1793, and what other work he might have done to further the cause of aviation thus remains an unanswerable question. His design remains today as a tribute to his vision and a commentary on the lack of available technology to transform that vision into a reality, even as it served at the time as an inspiration to others that followed.

Precursors

By the middle of the nineteenth century, the steam engine offered some hope, and small clockwork-driven and steam models showed that powered, streamlined airships could fly. In 1834 an Englishman, Thomas Monck Mason, had exhibited a spindle-shaped 13-foot clockwork model airship at the Lowther Arcade in London, followed a decade later by France's Le Berrier with another, which he demonstrated along the Champs-Elysées. (Le Berrier, a physician by training, had earlier flown with the Comte de Lennox, a colorful and ardent admirer of Napoleon. In 1832 the Comte, his wife, and Le Berrier had flown a dirigible balloon from Montmartre; the balloon had large oars, and more by luck than planning, they man-

Model of the Giffard
Airship, Science
Museum, London.
SSPL

aged to reach the Vendôme column, where the Comte placed a laurel wreath crown on the statue of Napoléon at the top of the column.)[6]

Le Berrier's model, and Pierre Jullien's later 23-foot-long clockwork model *le Précurseur* of 1850 (powered by two spring-driven propellers) had great influence, for they inspired a young and highly successful French steam engine designer, Henri Giffard (who had worked with Jullien), to build a blimplike airship 144 feet long, powered by a three horsepower steam engine of his own design driving an 11-foot-diameter, three-bladed propeller that rotated at 110 revolutions per minute. Prudently, he went to great trouble to ensure that the coke-burning boiler was shielded by wire gaze so no burning particles could escape, and that the exhaust ejected downwards, blended with venting steam. Giffard subsequently flew it from the Paris Hippodrome to Elancourt, near Trappes, on September 24, 1852, the first flight of a steerable airship in aviation history. He averaged six miles per hour—about the same speed as a horse-drawn wagon—while nattily attired in a frock coat and top hat. Over several flights he demonstrated this obviously underpowered craft could maneuver, but it lacked the power to fly against the wind and eventually burst during a descent, fortunately without injury to its brave creator. Giffard thus became both the first to fly a mechanically powered contrivance and the first to pilot a guided aerial vehicle. Three years he later he experimented unsuccessfully with a larger craft, nearly losing his life in the process. Giffard planned a truly gigantic steam-powered airship of Jules Verne proportions, having an overall length of 600 meters (nearly 1,969 feet) and a capacity of no less than 220,000 cubic meters (7,769,200 cubic feet), which would have been nearly three times longer than the largest airships ever subsequently built. But he could not secure funding for such a monster, and so he abandoned airships, turning his attention instead to building larger and larger tethered passenger balloons, with which he hoped to raise funds to finance studies in heavier-than-air flight. His balloons culminated in *le Captif,* which could carry over 50 passengers at a time, and which flew no less than 35,000 passengers during the 1878 Paris World's Fair. Sadly, failing eyesight brought his further work to an end, and he "became disconsolate, pined away with pain and grief, and in 1882 ended his life by taking chloroform" at the relatively young age of 57.[7]

Less than a year after Giffard's pioneering flight, an American, Rufus Porter (best known as the founder of the journal *Scientific American*) demonstrated a 22-foot-long, streamlined, steam-powered airship model in a meeting hall in Washington, D.C., to enthusiastic audiences, including members of the United States Senate. Porter had been working on the airship concept for over 30 years, having earlier patented an extremely advanced and streamlined airship design in 1820 with a spindle-shaped passenger and crew cabin suspended from an equally spindle-shaped balloon envelope. Porter's efforts to raise enough funds for a full-size machine that could possibly fly coast-to-coast (hauling would-be miners to the California gold rush) failed miserably.[8] But two other American ventures of the 1860s anticipated the advent of the practical airship. The first and by far the more intriguing of these involved no form of propulsion whatsoever, and were it not so well documented, might seem a fantastic fiction.

New Yorker Dr. Soloman Andrews, a graduate physician and son of a minister, believed the secret to flight lay in exploiting gravity. One could use the lifting power of hydrogen to rise into the air and then blend the use of ballast and gas shifting to achieve forward motion. As odd as this seems, he achieved surprising results. In 1862 after brief service in the Union army, he left to develop an airship that he hoped would be far more effective as a reconnaissance system than the tethered balloons he had witnessed in action. Out of this came a mysterious craft named the *Aereon,* with triple side-by-side streamlined airship envelopes housing multicellular gas balloonets, sliding ballast weights (later removed as unnecessary), a suspended basket control car, and a rudder. It had a length of 80 feet, and each envelope had a diameter of 13 feet, giving it a span of approximately 40 feet. On June 1, 1862, at Perth Amboy, New Jersey, he made a short flight both with and against a gusting wind, successfully maneuvering the powerless craft to land back on the spot from which he had taken off. Another flight in August took the *Aereon* to 1,000 feet, and before numerous witnesses he maneuvered the craft with abandon. At the end of the day in the grand finale, Andrews tied off the rudder at an acute angle, removed the basket, and then released the airship, which circled upwards through a cloud deck at speeds estimated at 120 miles per hour. It disappeared, never to be seen again.[9]

On the strength of this demonstration, Andrews succeeded in getting an interview with president Abraham Lincoln, who listened politely and understandably requested letters of confirmation from responsible citizens that the *Aereon* had performed as Andrews said. Andrews had no difficulty in furnishing these, and in due course Congress invited the inventor-physician to brief the members of the House and Senate military committees on his work. Demonstration of a small flying model in the basement of the Congress in 1864 went so well that Congress asked Lincoln's secretary of war, Edward M. Stanton, to form a special investigatory committee. As constituted, it included three of the most notable names in American science and engineering: Joseph Henry, the secretary of the Smithsonian Institution, Alexander Dallas Bache, the superintendent of the U.S. Coast Survey, and Major J. C. Woodruff of the Army Corps of Engineers. Though these three gave but a lukewarm endorsement of Andrews's work, they did recognize that his practical demonstrations offset what was at first a seemingly absurd idea, and closed by recommending construction of a second human-carrying *Aereon* funded by the War Department.[10]

Such was not to be. For reasons that are unclear, Stanton (always a very secretive and forbidding personality) ignored the recommendation. The end of the Civil War likewise ended any hope of further governmental support. Next Andrews attempted to secure private support, scraping together enough funding to build another airship, the *Aereon II*. He flew it twice in 1866, demonstrating the classic up-and-down undulating flight pattern he had shown four years before with the original *Aereon*. Despite crowd-pleasing performances, in the chancy postwar economic circumstances of 1866, money failed to follow, and Andrews, like Porter and others both before and after him, gave up.[11] What can one make of this program? Was it really as potentially successful as it seemed, or was it all a chimera? If nothing else, the many endorsements that Andrews received from a number of prominent eye-witnesses indicate that Andrews certainly achieved a degree of airship control and maneuverability never seen prior to his activities, and, for that matter, never seen afterwards by any lighter-than-air craft but only by a powered airship. The *Aereon*'s configuration may have given it significant lifting capabilities simply from its aero-dynamic shape, as well as generating accelerated flows in the channels between the balloon envelopes, thus reducing its drag even further and enabling it to move at fairly high speeds. Further, what Andrews suggested—the combination of using a lifting gas and then gravity for acceleration—is not that far removed from contemporary notions of so-called energy maneuverability both employed in air combat between opposing fighters and postulated for advanced winged spacecraft returning to earth as well. One must conclude that, as a genuine pioneer, Andrews deserved both greater success and more attention than he enjoyed.

Compared to Andrews the second American venture of the 1860s was much more prosaic, but it too had its exotic elements: the *Avitor* of Frederick Marriott, an expatriate Englishman turned San Francisco banker and newspaper mogul. Early in his life Marriott had enthusiastically supported the work of William Henson and John Stringfellow on their so-called aerial steam carriage, then became discouraged with their lack of progress, emigrated to the United States (surviving shipwreck on the way), and settled in California. Like Porter and Andrews, he hoped to establish a coast-to-coast "aerial steam navigation company," and to make it a reality, he proposed building a craft blending the characteristics of an airplane and an airship. Accordingly, his *Avitor* featured a graceful swept delta wing running from the nose of the airship to a point halfway along its length. Superimposed in the trailing edges of the wing were propellers driven by a steam engine buried in the middle of the airship envelope. Though the precise dimensions of this airship are unknown (estimates running from a low of 28 feet to a high of 97), it did complete two unmanned, tethered, powered flights at San Jose in July 1869 before enthusiastic witnesses. Alas, as Marriott vainly sought funding for further development, a fire destroyed the prototype. The *Avitor* died, and he returned to pure heavier-than-air concepts like Henson and Stringfellow's, without success. Marriott and his efforts at flight are essentially unknown, save for a few devotees, and in particular an evocative replica of his *Avitor* airship on display at the Stanley Hiller Museum, fittingly near San Francisco International Airport in California.[12]

Europe offered numerous examples of its own crude attempts at powered airships. In 1871, during the war, the French government issued a desperate contract worth 40,000 francs to the well-known naval engineer Henri Dupuy de Lôme, who designed a crude streamlined airship with a rudder, a hand-powered, four-bladed propeller—and (perhaps reflecting his trade) an auxiliary sail. As French balloonist and balloon historian Charles Dollfus subsequently wrote, "Because of an inexplicable regression, Dupuy de Lôme discarded steam and constructed his propeller nine meters [29.5 feet (!)] in diameter, so that eight men had to turn it with manual cranks. An 'alcohol motor,' he quipped as he treated his crew to an encouraging round of rum!"[13] De Lôme's airship, a sort of flying galley, did not fly until 1872, and then, not surprisingly, only at a very low speed and in the absence of winds. Nevertheless, on February 2 the well-fueled crew lifted off from Fort Neuf at Vincennes, and then powered and steered the craft to the town of Mondécourt, averaging six miles per hour. Though the flight gained great attention (not least because of the "alcohol motor"), sober analysis clearly indicated the need for a reliable mechanical propulsion system, as well as far better aerodynamic design.[14]

As if in deliberate contrast to de Lôme's effort, that same year the Austrian Paul Haenlein flew another small airship, using an early Lenoir internal combustion engine. Over a decade later, the French brothers Gaston and Albert Tissandier flew another airship using electric power in October 1883, making a short journey from Auteuil, a suburb of Paris, to Saint-Germain, following it with another flight the next year after having modified the design to incorporate a more efficient rudder. But in fact these were no more successful than any of their predecessors, with the exception of de Lôme's weird craft. But the next year, 1884, marked a milestone in dirigible design, with the appearance of Renard and Krebs's la France, a craft so superior to all before it that the Tissandier brothers abandoned any further effort to refine their own design.[15]

The First Successful Airship: The Renards, Krebs, and la France

The story of la France begins in 1877, when the French government reactivated the old research establishment at Chalais Meudon, on the site of the original École Nationale Aérostatique, closed after the fiasco of Napoléon's Egyptian balloon force, a resurgence brought about by the prominence of ballooning in the recent Franco-Prussian war. In 1878 Captain Charles Renard, an energetic and far-sighted graduate of the École Polytechnique who had been decorated at the age of 23 with the Légion d'Honneur, began a series of studies on possible lightweight powerplants for aerostatic applications, in turn examining steam, compressed air, and electrical approaches. Together with a fellow engineering officer, La Haye, Renard sought airship research and development funding from the French army's engineering corps. But it was refused on the not unreasonable grounds that all previous attempts to develop useful dirigibles had failed. Dismayed but not disheartened, La Haye and Renard promptly went outside army circles, approaching politician Léon Gambetta, who readers will recall had escaped by balloon from Paris to rally the rest of the nation to resistance. Since the war Gambetta had become president of the Chamber of Deputies' budget committee, and soon, in November 1881, would be prime minister of France. A genial if radical visionary with wide-ranging interests (not least of which was ballooning) whose power matched his largesse, Gambetta watched as Renard demonstrated a small flying model, quickly assenting to Renard's plea and granting 400,000 francs from a personal account for the effort.[16] Young La Haye, the instigator of the meeting, was quickly posted to a regiment at Montargis, seemingly as payment for his audacity. In his place stepped Captain Arthur Krebs, a graduate of the École St.-Cyr and a career infantry officer.[17]

In 1881 Paris hosted a major international exhibition on electricity and the burgeoning electrical industry. Inspired, like the Tissandiers, by this new form of energy, Renard and Krebs began studies the next year for an electrically powered airship. By 1883 they had designed a streamlined, 165-foot-long craft, having a single large 23-foot-diameter propeller at the front of a 108-foot-long control car suspended beneath the pointed and tapered envelope. The design, early American aeronautical pioneer Albert Zahm subsequently concluded, reflected "uncommon good judgment and excellent scientific method."[18] A true team effort, it employed an 8.5-horsepower electric motor designed by Krebs but driven by a lightweight battery array conceived by Renard, and also had both an elevator and a fore-and-aft sliding weight that could shift the vehicle's center of gravity for raising or lowering the nose. Construction began in 1883. Patriotically (if grandiosely) named *la France,* Renard and Krebs's airship first flew from Chalais Meudon on August 9, 1884. The inventors piloted it on a circular 23-minute flight around Villacoublay at a maximum speed of nearly 15 miles per hour, the first time in the history of flight that a flying machine had taken off and returned to the same spot, winning recognition from the Académie des Sciences for their "brilliant demonstration."[19]

This constituted an accomplishment of truly momentous significance, for Renard and Krebs had demonstrated the *first completely controlled, powered flight of any sort* from the moment of takeoff to the moment of landing, in all of human history. Sadly, Gambetta did not live to see the success of Renard and Krebs's airship, for he had succumbed to appendicitis and general ill health in December 1882 at the young age of 44. Modifications to the propulsion system increased its power and enabled carrying a third passenger. So Renard and Krebs undertook a further six flights over the next year, overflying portions of Paris and carrying passengers including the actress Gaby Morlay (the first woman to fly in an airship) and a certain M. Duté-Poitevin, a civilian aeronaut attached to the Chalais Meudon establishment. While not a frequent sight, la *France* became more familiar, visible to thousands during its short flights, typically elliptical or figure-eight courses from Meudon north to Paris, crossing the Seine and passing over Billancourt towards the Bois de Boulogne.[20]

The public and official reception of la *France* encouraged Renaud's hopes that he could build a larger airship powered by a 100-horsepower internal combustion engine. But these dreams proved ill founded, despite his having constructed in 1890 an experimental four-cylinder double-acting engine giving the same propulsive characteristics as an engine having eight cylinders. Further development ceased in the face of rising technical problems, declining official interest, and lack of additional funding, thanks largely to a broad-based antimilitary feeling that swept through France coincident with the Dreyfus affair. Renard remained a fixture at the Établissement Militaire de Chalais Meudon over the next two decades,

Renard and Krebs's *la France*; the small size of the figures next to the airship give a dramatic indication of its size. Musée de l'Air et de l'Espace (MAE)

becoming chief of French military ballooning in 1888 and working in concert with his younger brother Paul, an army captain who replaced Krebs in 1885, following the latter's reassignment to other duties. Krebs eventually left the army for a brighter future, becoming the *directeur général* of the Société des Anciens Établissements Panhard & Levassor (a pioneer manufacturer of aero engines and automobiles). For almost 20 years after *la France* the brothers studied a variety of problems involving airships, propulsion (including railway propulsion), helicopters, and aerodynamics, always holding to the dream of building an even larger and more powerful airship to be named the *Général Meusnier,* honoring the father of the streamlined blimp concept. But governmental obstruction and lack of finances, together with greater technical challenges, always thwarted their work.[21]

Certainly some resentment must have built as the brothers saw outsiders advance more easily onwards, particularly as the celebrated Santos-Dumont, heir to a coffee fortune, routinely flew over Paris in his small airships (less sophisticated, except for their petroleum engines, than *la France*) to tremendous public and official acclaim, and Henri Juillot embarked on the first of his very influential military blimps sponsored by a family of sugar manufacturers! In 1904, for unexplained reasons, a leading member of the Académie des Sciences rejected then-colonel Charles Renard's candidacy for membership. This extraordinary rebuff made no sense, for Renard clearly was France's most accomplished aeronautical researcher at the time, a polymath equally at home in many different technical fields and an expert in virtually all of them. Together with the lack of progress towards building a larger airship, the Académie's decision delivered the final blow: fatally depressed, Renard committed suicide in April 1905.[22]

After this shattering tragedy, his brother Paul, by now promoted to the rank of *commandant* (major), eventually left the army for the civilian world. It is sad that, after having done so much to make the airship a reality, Charles Renard met such an end. In 1908, at the Premier Salon de l'Aéronautique held at the Grand Palais in Paris (the first occurrence of what has become the splendid Paris Air Show), the organizing Commission Aérienne posthumously honored Renard and his work, exhibiting a comprehensive sampling of his research with a commemorative program including a memorial essay by his brother. A year later the French government authorized purchase of a new airship, the *Colonel Renard*. Various patriotic organizations such as the Ligue Nationale Aérienne unveiled plaques and memorials. But nothing could undo the tragedy, nor compensate for the acute blow to French and, indeed, world aviation that his death caused.[23] At Renard's funeral, the physicist Arsène d'Arsonval concluded his eulogy with, "His name must be preserved from oblivion or, worse yet, ingratitude."[24] Regretfully, over time, as with Giffard earlier, *la France,* the Renards, and Krebs have passed into near obscurity, largely unrecognized today for their truly momentous work. It is unfortunate, for they profoundly influenced airship developments far beyond the shores of France, particularly in the Third Republic's archrival, Imperial Germany.[25]

Small Airships . . .

The advent of the practical internal combustion engine transformed both airship and airplane studies, but for the former the mix of a flame-producing engine and hydrogen envelope promised trouble. In 1888 Friedrich Wölfert, a German clergyman-balloonist, flew a crude airship with a Daimler engine at Caanstadt, the first application of a petrol-powered engine to a flight vehicle. The Daimler engine, designed before the era of sparkplug ignition, used a small platinum tube heated to incandescence and kept glowing by an open gas flame on the outside of the engine, an incredibly risky propulsion choice for a hydrogen airship. By a miracle he avoided disaster, and after this machine proved unsuccessful, he foolishly attempted to build an even larger airship, again using the risky Daimler with its open-flame ignition system. On June 12, 1897, while Wölfert ascended with his mechanic from the Prussian army's balloon center at Tempelhof Field, the engine's ignition system ignited a hydrogen-air mix venting from the envelope. Horrified witnesses saw a small flame dart from the engine through the air to the envelope, and then a searing fire engulfed the control car and envelope, incinerating its crew in a gigantic ball of blazing hydrogen, a frightful spectre settling slowly in the Berlin sky until it crashed, a smoking pyre, in the midst of what is now Tempelhof airport. Wölfert and his mechanic had earned the grim distinction of being the first of more than 750 individuals who would lose their lives in airship accidents.[26]

The next stage in the development of airships belonged to one of aviation's most eccentric, charming, and altogether appealing characters, whose happy-go-lucky exterior sadly hid a complex, depressive, and ultimately tragic personality: Alberto Santos-Dumont, a dapper, fastidious, adventurous, and tiny expatriate

Franco Brazilian playboy living in Paris. Born in 1873 on a remote farm in the state of Minas Gerais, Santos arrived in Paris in 1892, armed with a bequest from his father Henri (a wealthy planter known as the Brazilian "Coffee King"), dreams of airships from reading Jules Verne, and the inspiration of Henri Giffard's pioneering work. Very quickly he took to the air in conventional balloons, buying one made to his own specifications and named, appropriately, *Brasil*.[27]

Santos made his first airship in 1898, using a nonrigid, blimplike approach and a form and appearance not different in many respects from that used by Renard and Krebs, except for the addition of a 3.5 horsepower petrol engine à la Wölfert's earlier machine. But unlike the unfortunate German, Santos located the gas release valves in the stern of the balloon envelope and modified the engine exhaust so that it vented downwards. If Santos lacked a big engineering vision or goal for the future of airships, he more than made up for it with his energy, enthusiasm, and newsworthy behavior. In several years he built over a dozen small airships, flying them routinely from his base at Neuilly-Saint-James around Paris. His favorite was the *Number 9*, which he called "the Little Runabout": Parisians became used to seeing it "parked" in front of his home on the corner of the Rue Washington and the Champs-Elysées while its owner had a morning coffee, or moored along the Bois de Boulogne as Santos stopped off like any *boulevardier* to sip an *apéritif* at a café, or floating above his favorite restaurant, *la Cascade*, as the quirky Brazilian took his lunch.[28]

Santos-Dumont (center right) briefing Smithsonian Institution Secretary Samuel Langley (center left, back to camera) on his airships, at St. Cloud, a suburb of Paris, on September 21, 1900.
AFMA

In addition, he accomplished some spectacular feats. In 1900 Henry Deutsch de la Meurthe, a wealthy financier, offered a prize of 100,000 francs to the individual who could fly from the headquarters of the Aéro-Club de France at St. Cloud to the Eiffel Tower and back, a distance of 11 kilometers (just less than 7 miles) in 30 minutes or less. De la Meurthe eventually added another 25,000 francs to the prize, and with interest it totaled 129,000 francs when Santos took up the challenge. It was a rich purse: in American terms it was then equivalent to $25,800, an amount, a century later, worth roughly $516,000.[29] On October 19,

Santos circling the Tour Eiffel on October 19, 1901. AFMA

1901, Santos won the prize in a nail-biter of a flight that had at its very end a crisis Hollywood could not better: his engine quit less than a third of a mile from St. Cloud, forcing him to walk out on the keel of his balloon—without a safety line or parachute—and make repairs. He finished just in time to cross the finish line 40 seconds too late—but de la Meurthe believed he deserved the prize anyway, and after a review of the flight, the Aéro-club agreed. Characteristically generous to a fault, he split the award: 54,000 francs to his mechanics, and 75,000 francs to the Paris police to be distributed among the city's nearly 4,000 registered beggars. The Brazilian government made up for his generosity by awarding the dapper little airman an identical prize, plus a large gold medal.[30]

Like many quirky individuals, Santos had his share of eccentricities, one of which was deep superstition that manifested itself in a fear of the number eight: he never flew on the eighth day of a month, and his airships went straight from *Number 7* to *Number 9*. Overall Santos possessed tremendous good fortune, for on a number of his flights he had problems and some outright crashes. But even these had a zany, madcap quality to them: crashing into a tree on the Rothschild estate and being greeted by a butler with snacks and refreshments; crashing into the side of the Hôtel Trocadéro across from the Palais de Chaillot and being rescued from a window ledge by the Paris fire department; stopping an incipient engine fire by beating out the flames with his straw hat.[31] Such antics made him all the rage of both French and Brazilian society. In Brazil popular songwriter Eduardo das Neves penned a special ballad, *"A Conquista do Ar!"* ("The Conquering of the Air!"), including the words, "A new star shines in the sky: / Santos-Dumont is there!"[32] As John Toland wrote, "Everyone was Santos-Dumont conscious. Drinks and babies were named after him. His picture graced thousands of French postcards. If a hostess could inveigle him for a weekend, her entire season was a success."[33]

Though he did not himself develop a military airship, preferring to see his creation as one for commerce and pleasure, Santos's work greatly influenced French military aerostatics, and he was not oblivious to the airship's military potential. In his autobiography he compared the airship to the submarine, observing, "Thus, very curiously, the twentieth century airship must become from the beginning the great enemy of that other twentieth century marvel—the submarine boat—and not only its enemy but its master."[34] And he was right: during the First World War, Allied blimps markedly reduced merchant vessel sinkings from German U-boats by forcing them to submerge and ultimately driving them to seek safer operating areas. U-boats only sank three merchant ships from convoys or formations escorted by aircraft or airships.[35]

Encouraged and informed by Santos's experience, Henri Julliot, the chief engineer of the brothers Paul and Pierre Lebaudy's airship company, designed a semi-rigid airship approximately two-thirds greater in size than Santos's small blimps. First flown in 1902, this craft, the *Lebaudy I* (also called *le Jaune* because of its overall yellow color, the result of lead chromate coating applied to its rubberized cotton envelope as a means of protecting it from deterioration), became the antecedent of all subsequent French blimps. The Lebaudy-Julliot team built a number of successful airships before Julliot, at the age of 59, emigrated to the United States in 1915 to direct the Goodrich company's airship division and continue with the design of small airships and balloons. Additionally, some of Santos's experience can be found in the small military airships flown in Britain, France, and the United States, and, as well, in the *America,* journalist Walter Wellman's ambitious airship, with which he unsuccessfully attempted to reach the North Pole in 1906 and 1909, and, in 1910, to cross the Atlantic (he ditched at sea alongside the British steamer *Trent,* which rescued all the crew and even a stowaway cat).[36]

Overall then, Santos inaugurated the era of the practical and reliable little blimp, anticipating both its routine military use and its commercial use in advertising and entertainment. Entranced with the airplane, he eventually gave up his airships to pursue heavier-than-air aviation, a pattern Nadar and Giffard had followed as well. But even if he had not done so, his place in aviation history would be secure, if for nothing but the image of carefree pleasure that he had attached to flight thanks to his own extraordinary example. Sadly, Santos was not to enjoy the happiness he had given so many, for unfortunately he developed multiple sclerosis and also serious mental illness. Declining health soon forced his retirement from aviation altogether, his last known flight as a pilot being in November 1909. The First World War triggered increasing melancholia, as he held himself responsible for the violence of air warfare; accordingly, he destroyed many of his personal papers and documents tracing his role in aeronautics, to the everlasting loss of aviation history. As time went on, he assumed culpability as well for other aviation disasters, particularly the loss of the British airship *R 101* in 1930. In 1931, severely depressed and having already attempted suicide once, he sailed back to Brazil on the liner *Cap Arcona,* accompanied by his nephew. As the ship entered Rio harbor, the *Santos Dumont,* a Junkers seaplane carrying some of Brazil's most prominent and accomplished citizens, roared overhead in salute, then turned to land. Before his horrified gaze, it hooked a wingtip in the water, cartwheeled, and broke up, disappearing beneath the water in a spray of mist and killing all on board. Santos called off all ceremonies and went out himself in a small boat to search for the accident victims. The next year revolution broke out in São Paulo; the knowledge that Brazilian was bombing Brazilian constituted the final straw, and this mentally tormented and physically sick pioneer hanged himself on July 23, 1932, at the age of 59, his death so shocking the nation that it led to a cease-fire and eventual restoration of peace.[37]

Understandably, Santos is revered in Brazil, as visitors quickly realize when they arrive at Rio de Janeiro's international airport, named in his honor. Paris has less visible signs of his presence, but they are there. Today tourists on their way to the Arc de Triomphe pass right under the balcony of his old residence at 114 Champs-Elysées—which, fittingly, houses an airline ticket office! Santos, one imagines, would be pleased.[38]

. . . and Large

On August 19, 1863, two young Germans stood in a swaying balloon basket high over St. Paul, Minnesota, looking over the countryside below. Former Union army balloonist John Steiner and his passenger, a young military engineer, discussed the problem of steering. Steiner casually informed his fellow countryman that the solution could be a long, thin balloon with a big rudder.[39] The passenger, Premierleutnant Ferdinand Adolf August Heinrich Graf von Zeppelin, on leave from the army of the king of Württemberg so that he might observe the Civil War, added this to the many things he had noted on his trip to America. A phlegmatic Swabian of mixed German-French parentage, the 25-year-old von Zeppelin had little formal training in engineering, but a strong interest in technology nevertheless. He coupled this with an insatiable curiosity and personal courage. Already he had requested to go to America to study the Civil War and received a pass from President Abraham Lincoln granting him full access to Union forces. He had survived combat against Jeb Stuart's cavalry (just avoiding capture thanks to a fast horse), and though he missed the battle of Gettysburg, he took a long, meandering journey through the Midwest and the upper reaches of the Mississippi before reaching St. Paul. This journey held far more import for the future of aviation than anything he might have seen at Gettysburg, for as fate would have it, Steiner had his balloon tethered across the street from von Zeppelin's hotel. Two days later he and the aeronaut were floating 700 feet above ground, discussing the future of ballooning.[40]

Von Zeppelin quickly returned to Württemberg but kept Steiner's idea in mind.[41] Subsequently he served in both the Austro-Prussian War of 1866 (where he fought on the losing side) and the Franco-Prussian War five years later, which unified Germany into a single nation (where, as a brigade staff officer, he barely avoided capture by French troops). Coupled with his Civil War experience, it can be seen that whatever other strengths he may have possessed, von Zeppelin had an uncanny knack for getting into trouble, though he possessed the good luck to get out of it quickly enough. After he was detailed to the diplomatic corps and then, as a newly appointed general, assigned command in 1890 of the thirtieth Kavalleriebrigade—a *Prussian* cavalry brigade—his luck finally ran out. In the new German state, Prussia held position of first among equals. Von Zeppelin, a dedicated Württemberger who had fought against Prussia a quarter century before, could not curb his outspokenness in criticizing the growing pervasiveness of Prussian influence on Germany's military, even in print. Not surprisingly, he incurred the personal wrath of the greatest Prussian of all, the mercurial and insecure Kaiser Wilhelm II, a man given to wearing an ornate *pickelhaube* (spiked helmet) incongruously sporting a winged dove of peace—wings fully spread—wearing its own tiny little crown.[42]

Von Zeppelin's "particularist ideas" (as the Kaiser termed alleged separatist tendencies) brought his further military career to an abrupt halt. Cashiered over an alleged failure to lead his division well during some maneuvers that fall, von Zeppelin retired from the army virtually immediately, with the retirement rank of lieutenant general. But if his military career came to an end, his departure freed him to pursue his true passion, designing a steerable airship. Out of that fateful conversation with Steiner would be born the rigid airship, which would comprise fully 75 percent of the production models that von Zeppelin and his company would build, so linking his name with the type as to make "Zeppelin" more of a generic appellation, in fact, than, the broader-meaning word "dirigible."[43]

Von Zeppelin had aged well, with a piercing, distinguished look and a full brush mustache, and his position as a retired general officer in status-conscious and military-friendly Germany counted for a great deal. The count's interest in airships had received a powerful boost in 1874 when he read a reprint of a German postal official's lecture given by the German postmaster-general, Heinrich von Stephan, on the prospects of global airship delivery of mail; then, a decade later, came word of Renard and Krebs's flight. Anxious at France's vigorous pursuit of aviation, von Zeppelin began campaigning for a rigid airship "air cruiser," noting in one letter, "You will realize how we Germans must hurry up, if we are not to be left behind."[44]

Von Zeppelin's ideas at this time were nowhere as refined as those reflected in the first dirigibles with which Germany went to war in 1914. Instead he thought in terms of an aerial balloon train: a streamlined "locomotive" balloon pulling coupled cylindrical balloon "wagons." In one respect von Zeppelin had very good insight: he believed a rigid airship should be able to fly without resorting to routine dropping of ballast and jettisoning of gas, and thus recommended that it combine lift via gas with aerodynamic lift generated by its body shape and perhaps "planes" (wings). His ideas might have remained just another unfulfilled dream but for the advent of the practical internal combustion engine, and the fortuitous advice he received from several sources.

Ferdinand Graf von Zeppelin, the retired German general who invented the large rigid airship. AFMA

The precise influences upon von Zeppelin's thinking are uncertain, but a number of individuals in Germany were thinking and writing on airship topics at the time that he undertook his own research. One possible influence was an impetuous 27-year-old former law student, Hermann Ganswindt. In 1883 he registered a proposed airship design with the patent office in Berlin. What made his work interesting was his bold advocacy for very large airships—recognizing that volumetric efficiency increases by a cube law: that is, doubling the dimensions of an airship increases its volume eightfold; enlarging an airship ten times increases its volume a thousandfold. Ganswindt sent his patent and some supporting papers to the German general staff but received a pro-forma rejection on the grounds of no available money and no perceived need. He followed this with a book that did draw the attention of the German crown prince, the future Kaiser Friedrich III, who asked for a war ministry review: again the answer came down negative. Ganswindt turned his attention to other pursuits, earned the nickname the German Edison, and eventually dabbled in helicopter and rocket design, with no greater success than he had enjoyed as an advocate of large, rigid airships.[45]

Von Zeppelin wisely recognized that he lacked the technical expertise to bring his vision to a successful conclusion on his own, so he hired professional engineers to assist him, dismissing the first virtually immediately because the man lacked the fullest faith in the Count's optimistic vision. The successor, Theodore Kober, did produce a "Zeppelin air train" design (grandiosely named the *Deutschland*) that had some of the elements von Zeppelin would later incorporate in his airships. Von Zeppelin next wrote to the German general staff requesting an official review of his proposals, noting that an airship could furnish vital rapid and wide-ranging reconnaissance, aerial supply, and "bombardment of enemy fortresses or troop concentrations."[46] In 1894, at the request of the king of Württemberg, the growing attention focused on von Zeppelin's ideas caused the Kaiser to appoint a panel to review the count's work.

Hermann von Helmholtz, the aging director of Berlin's Physikalische-Technische Reichsanstalt (the Physical-Technical Institute, comparable to Britain's National Physical Laboratory or America's Bureau of Standards) and promulgator of the law of the conservation of energy, served as panel chairman. Nearly four decades earlier, he had studied vorticity in fluid flows, a problem of seminal importance to twentieth-century aerodynamics and aircraft design. Von Helmholtz influenced the entire field of vortex studies, as subsequently pursued by such notables as Lord Kelvin, Martin Kutta, Nikolai Joukovsky, Ludwig Prandtl, and Theodore von Kármán. Ironically, he had left the field for what he considered other more important areas of research, some of which in reality constituted terrible blind alleys.[47] The panel met in March 1894 and submitted its report to the Kriegsministerium the following July, by which time its aging and ailing chairman had already died, though he lived long enough to sign the final document. Its seven members—scientists, engineers, academicians, and military balloonists—rendered a mixed verdict. They recommended against governmental financial support, but some sympathetic members privately offered helpful ideas and suggestions, particularly on the proposed form and structure of the airship.[48] In retrospect it is hard to fault their conclusion, for the Kober proposal clearly needed a great deal of work.

Disappointed if undaunted, von Zeppelin appealed the decision; the war ministry reconstituted the Helmholtz commission, and it ruled as it had originally, this time making much of von Zeppelin's optimistic performance predictions. So von Zeppelin remained on his own, lashing out at his critics. Always testy, the count eventually challenged one to a duel, and only the intervention of the Kaiser prevented the count from following through on his threat. It particularly galled von Zeppelin that the Helmholtz commission, called at his request, favorably evaluated a proposal for an all-metal airship (including its gas envelope) submitted by rival inventor David Schwarz. While not advocating expending government funds, it did endorse Schwarz's design as practicable and recommended that

Schwarz have use of the balloon development facilities at Templehof—which he eventually did. The unfortunate Schwarz, who had been trying in vain for years to influence various governments in his ideas, died in January 1897, collapsing after receiving a telegram informing him of the government's interest in his studies! Thus he never saw his airship fly, which might have been just as well, as it crashed (fortunately without injury) at the end of what had been a thoroughly disastrous first-and-last flight later that year, as the Kaiser himself looked on.[49]

Von Zeppelin scraped enough money together—800,000 marks (then approximately $200,000, and a century later equivalent to roughly $4,000,000), including 300,000 marks of his own money—to proceed with construction of a much better concept.[50] It is uncertain to what degree he incorporated some ideas of his critics, for their criticism obviously stung him so deeply that he could not bear to acknowledge any assistance that they might have offered. Construction began in June 1898 and took the next two years. Technicians completed the first of his signature cigar-shaped Luftschiff Zeppelin designs, the LZ-1 (for Luftschiff Zeppelin-1), incorporating novel structural ideas and the latest internal-combustion propulsion technology, in June 1900, housing it in a long floating shed moored on Lake Constance. The LZ-1 had a length of 420 feet, making it roughly three times longer than any previous airship ever flown, and had a diameter of over 38 feet. Powered by two Daimler 14-horsepower engines driving multibladed propellers, the LZ-1 had a very weak structure fabricated entirely from an aluminum-zinc alloy formed into girders and 24-sided polygon frames, the entire framework braced by wire.[51] A total of 17 gas cells contained almost 400,000 cubic feet of the explosive hydrogen gas. While it lacked a horizontal tail with a pivoting elevator for nose-up or nose-down pitch control, von Zeppelin had installed a moveable 220-pound (100 kilogram weight hanging below the dirigible like a necklace that

The LZ-1 lifts off from Lake Constance on July 2, 1900.
NASM

could be winched fore-and-aft as needed for longitudinal trim, and it also had rudders for directional control.

On the evening of July 2, 1900, a ground crew maneuvered the LZ-1 out of its floating shed, the soft light reflecting off the surface of the lake and shimmering along the flanks of the gigantic airship. An awkward and uncomfortable exchange briefly threatened the Wagnerian majesty of the moment: von Zeppelin's construction superintendent, one Kübler (perhaps rightly having second thoughts about the design's structure), refused to go aboard, on the pretext that the count had not provided insurance coverage in the event of an accident! This career-ending move earned a frosty and dismissive stare from von Zeppelin, who immediately invited a physicist friend along in the unfortunate Kübler's place. The scientist quickly accepted, and after a brief prayer von Zeppelin, his friend, a journalist, and two crewmen—five persons in all—boarded the airship. At 8:03 P.M. von Zeppelin ordered the groundcrew to release the ship; the LZ-1 lifted off in a nose-high attitude. For the next 18 minutes the first of the Z-Schiffe floated majestically over the lake, though onlookers had little idea of the problems von Zeppelin and his crew faced on board: the understrength structure flexed and distorted under load, the shifting pitch-control weight stuck, requiring emergency ballast drops and engine reversing to keep the Zeppelin from nosing into the water, and one of its engines sputtered to a halt. Facing rising winds, von Zeppelin prudently ended this first excursion aloft, "landing" on the lake and having a small boat tow the LZ-1 back to its floating hangar.[52]

Given the spotty subsequent history of airship accidents related to structural problems, von Zeppelin and his crew were lucky fellows. Any fracturing member or snapping wire might have torn the gas cells and, striking a spark, replicated the disaster that had befallen Wölfert and his mechanic above Berlin three years before. Fortunately the LZ-1 returned safely to its floating hangar: von Zeppelin thus won the race to develop the world's first large rigid airship, even though an official governmental report on the flight would be less than enthusiastic, and even though he would sensibly ground the LZ-1 after only two more flights the following October. While the *Frankfurter Zeitung* stated the flight "proved conclusively that a dirigible balloon is of practically no value," the noted African explorer and journalist Eugen Wolff, aboard as an official observer, subsequently wrote in more balanced fashion, "What this short flight will lead to is not completely clear. But one thing it did show—dirigible flight is a reality."[53] So as the new century dawned, von Zeppelin and his creation faced an uncertain future. Over the next decade he would struggle for funds and support even as his conviction grew more strongly that the rigid airship constituted the key to Germany's aeronautical supremacy and as his new engineer, the reserved but undoubtedly accomplished Ludwig Dürr, gave his airships the reliable and safer structures they required.[54] In the days after the LZ-1's first flight no one could predict the rigid airship's future course. But there could be no doubt that more would be heard from the aging general and his large dirigibles.

PART THREE

WINGED FLIGHT:
EARLY CONCEPTIONS OF THE
AIRPLANE, 1792–1903

CHAPTER SIX

Sir George Cayley
and the Birth of Aeronautics

Achieving human flight required mastery of multiple disciplines, none more important or significant than aerodynamics—the study of airflow—for any flying machine would, by necessity, operate while completely shrouded in a wrapping of rapidly moving, turbulent, and viscous air.[1] Leonardo da Vinci was the first individual to study aerodynamics with human flight in mind. He pioneered both conceptual aerodynamics and hydrodynamics, for he recognized the similarities between the flow of water and of air. "In order to give the true science of the movement of the birds in the air," he wrote, "it is necessary first to give the science of the winds, and this we shall prove by means of the movements of the water." He noted subsequently, "All the movements of the wind resemble those of the water."[2] So he sketched the flow around objects in a stream, showing how that flow separated into eddies (vortices) and turbulence, and noted as well that the air disturbed by a racing horse on a dusty road, after having "moved a very short distance . . . turns back with an eddying movement and thereby consumes its impetus."[3] He postulated theories of how a wing produces lift (though he incorrectly believed that the downward stroke of a bird's wing compressed the air, missing that in fact it was the region of low pressure *above* a wing that essentially draws the wing upwards). He also concluded that air resistance of a body is directly proportional to the area of the body and produced quite practical sketches for streamlined artillery shells, some with stabilizing fins, anticipating artillery developments over four centuries in the future.[4]

Undoubtedly impressive for its time, Leonardo's work marked the first era in aerodynamics, depending on observation and insight rather than mathematical analysis, experiment, and measurement. His approach was consistent with the times, which emphasized observation and reasoned explanation, not the positing and testing of a hypothesis.[5] It is possible that had his drawings not disappeared for three centuries, later researchers would have appreciated the problem of flow separation off wings and vortex formation much sooner than they did. But sadly, as discussed previously, through bad conservation his drawings vanished, so that after his death, interest in studying fluid flow explicitly for applications to flying machines would have to wait 300 years, even as a number of notable individuals studied fluid flow for a variety of other purposes.

Aerodynamics before Sir George

The roots of modern mathematically based aerodynamics date to the seventeenth and eighteenth centuries, when numerous individuals studied fluid flow for naval ship design, hydraulics, and ballistics, marking the second stage in the growth and development of aerodynamics. These studies eventually led to greater understanding and appreciation of flow around airplanes as well when interpreted by air-minded individuals, though not so dramatically as to greatly influence the development of the first flying machines (indeed, in two notable cases, the "sine-squared law" and Smeaton's constant, they actually *hindered* progress, at least to some degree, as explained subsequently).

This second stage witnessed the determination of the basic governing relationships in fluid mechanics, beginning with calculating the resistance of a shape moving through a fluid and the velocity and pressure changes within a fluid, and measuring the speed of a flow. France's Edme Mariotte, Holland's Christiaan Huygens, and England's Sir Isaac Newton each enunciated the so-called velocity-squared law, that the force or resistance on a body increases as the square of the velocity of the body.[6] The Dutch-Swiss polymath Daniel Bernoulli derived the concept behind what is now commonly called the Bernoulli principle (somewhat misleadingly, since he was never so clear in expressing it) that as the velocity of a fluid increases, the pressure within the fluid decreases. Finally, the Swiss mathematician Leonhard Euler demonstrated that pressure could vary from point to point within a fluid and derived the modern Bernoulli equation[7] and the equations that bear his name for the study of compressible and incompressible inviscid flows (idealized flows ignoring the real-world effects of friction and heating).

Interpretation of one of Newton's propositions in his landmark *Principia Mathematica* indicated that in calculating the resistance of a plate set in a flow, one had to square the sine of the angle formed by the plate and the relative flow.[8] Fortunately this concept, the so-called Newtonian sine-squared law proved incorrect: the resistance force acting on the plate is proportional to the *sine* of the angle, not the *square of the sine* of the angle. Squaring the sine implied drastic increases in drag as the angle of attack increased. If true, this would have demanded construction of totally impractical flying machines having enormous wings that could furnish the requisite lift for an airplane only while operating at minimal angles of attack. Hence it would have called into question whether a successful airplane could ever be built. After further examining Newton's work, later researchers fortunately recognized the error, realizing that wings could operate quite well at modest angles of incidence, and Francis Wenham experimentally disproved this bogus "law" in his first wind-tunnel tests. Nevertheless, it continued to haunt aeronautics even into the early twentieth century, used by ill-meaning critics to assert flight's "impossibility."⁹

Significant advances beyond the purely theoretical required developing increasingly specialized testing tools, marking the third stage in the evolution of aerodynamics. The first significant experimentalist in the field of fluid flow was the Frenchman Henri Pitot. In 1732 he connected an L-shaped tube to a pressure gauge to measure the speed of flow in a fluid. Pitot demonstrated his device by measuring the flow of the River Seine, discovering that, contrary to popular belief, the speed of a river decreased at lower depths, rather than increased. Pitot had no apparent interest in aviation and died in 1771, but he left his instrument and his name to the modern pitot tube, which is a standard airspeed-measuring device on air-planes from the lowliest glider to the faster jet fighter. After Pitot the English military engineer Benjamin Robins (who died in 1751, rightly hailed as the "father of ballistics") made the second major contribution to early aerodynamic testing. He employed a falling weight to drive a whirling-arm test rig to make measurements of air resistance. Also, he built a novel ballistic test rig using a cannon firing projectiles into a large pendulum and then measuring the resulting change in deflection of the pendulum to calculate the velocity of the test projectile. His success with this machine led to even larger ones used as standard research and measurement tools throughout the era of classic cannonball artillery testing.¹⁰

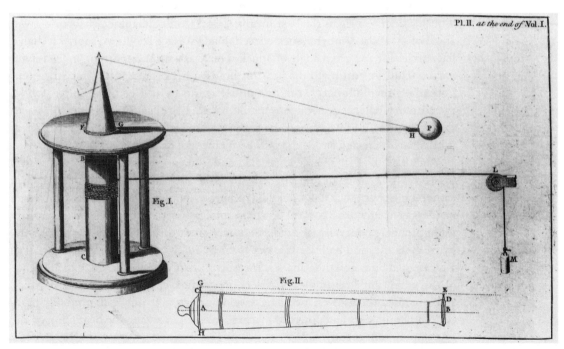

Benjamin Robins's whirling arm, the predecessor of the wind tunnel. The falling weight M rotates the arm and, hence, the test model located at the end of the arm, at P. SSPL

From the standpoint of early aviation, whirling arms had the greatest influence. They proved very popular for research and lasted well into the twentieth century, but they had a serious limitation overcome by the wind tunnel. The rig would spin a model placed at the tip of the arm at high speed while instruments measured various values such as lift and drag. But very quickly disturbed air would begin swirl around with the arm, prohibiting accurate measurements of the true flow conditions.[11] Robins validated the Mariotte-Huygens-Newton velocity-squared law, demonstrated that objects with the same frontal area but dissimilar shapes had different overall drag values, determined that spinning objects experience path-distorting side forces, and even made the first detection of transonic drag rise, whereby the velocity-squared relationship changes to a velocity-cubed relationship as a body approaches the speed of sound.[12]

Robins's work anticipated that of his brilliant countryman John Smeaton, the first individual to use the title "civil engineer" (to distinguish his work from military engineering). Smeaton is best known for building the famed Eddystone Lighthouse, one of the most demanding construction undertakings of all time, for it involved erecting a towering stone structure on a dangerous exposed ledge constantly whipped by wind and waves.[13] In 1759 Smeaton had received a Gold Medal from the Royal Society for a paper he presented on water and wind mills. As part of his research on the latter, he conducted a series of whirling-arm experiments assessing the performance of variously shaped windmill blades. Smeaton had sought some means of testing windmill blades, noting that "the wind itself is too uncertain . . . We must have recourse to an artificial wind," and settling upon a whirling arm test rig as the best means.[14] Smeaton determined that for a given angle of attack, a cambered (i.e., curved) blade surface produced more lift than a flat surface for any given angle of attack. This was a most important, indeed seminal, conclusion, cutting to the heart of how a wing produces lift. But Smeaton's potentially revolutionary work on camber seems to have escaped notice, while, most unfortunately, an erroneous mathematical construct of his (Smeaton's constant) most assuredly did not. The latter plagued early aeronautical researchers until finally corrected at the end of the nineteenth century.[15]

Again, none of these individuals had undertaken any of their work in support of studying flight or developing any sort of flying machine: as Professor John Anderson has noted, "The discipline of aerodynamics . . . developed quite independently of any drive toward practical applications."[16] For the most part, early flight pioneers generally ignored essentially all of this theoretical aerodynamic, hydrodynamic, and ballistic work in favor of relying on those experimentalists who studied birds and then actually measured aerodynamic effects. In the absence of the wind tunnel, they used a variety of test rigs, chiefly whirling arms. Many experimented themselves, including developing actual flying craft, primarily models, but later gliders and powered machines as well, marking the beginning of the fourth period in aerodynamics evolution. The first and greatest of all such early pioneers and experimentalists prior to the Wrights emerged at the end of the eighteenth century, a truly towering personality whose influence is felt to the present day: Sir George Cayley. Almost single-handedly he created aeronautics, first in Great Britain and then, by his influence, in other European countries and America as well.

The Country Gentleman as Aeronautical Researcher

Cayley is universally and correctly acknowledged as the first conceptualizer of the practical airplane, the Father of Aerial Navigation, but beyond this he really is the father of aeronautics as well.[17] No less than Wilbur Wright, speaking in 1909, remarked that "Cayley carried the science of flying to a point which it had never reached before and which it scarcely reached again during the last century."[18] Three years later his brother Orville wrote: "Cayley was a remarkable man. He knew more of the principles of aeronautics than any of his predecessors, and as much as any that followed him up to the end of the nineteenth century. His published work is remarkably free from error and was a most important contribution to the science."[19] Indeed, two of the earliest and very finest of aviation historians, Charles Dollfus and Henri Bouché, called Cayley "le véritable inventeur de l'aéro-plane, l'un des plus puissants génies de l'histoire de l'aviation" (The true inventor of the airplane, one of the most powerful geniuses of aviation history).[20] These are broad claims, but they stand up under historical examination. Had Cayley not lacked a proper engine to power his concepts, Brompton Hall might today be regarded as Kitty Hawk is now.

A portrait of Cayley at the National Portrait Gallery in London, executed by Henry Perronet Briggs when Cayley was well into his sixties, reveals an individual of better-than-average appearance, aging gracefully, with pointed features, thoughtful and appraising eyes, an intelligent and tranquil demeanor, and yet a set to the jaw indicative of a strong will and purposeful nature.[21] It is hard to imagine that this Yorkshire baronet, an isolated country gentleman lacking formal education, could have had such a profound influence on the history of flight, but so it was to be. He was a total aeronautical enthusiast, whose vision of flight embraced heavier-than-air gliders, helicopters, and airplanes, and lighter-than-air balloons and airships. But beyond this he had far broader interests in science, technology, and education that manifested themselves in various socially responsible ways, including improving Covent Garden's acoustics and helping found both the British Association for the Advancement of Science and an early technical institute, the

An 1840 portrait of Sir George Cayley by Henry Perronet Briggs. Courtesy of the National Portrait Gallery, London (NPG)

Regent Street Polytechnic. "His range of inventive imagination," historian Paul Johnson has rightly judged, "was astonishing."[22]

Born at Brompton Hall just after Christmas in 1773 into a moderately prosperous Yorkshire family whose aristocratic roots dated to the Norman invasion, young Cayley's early years shaped his questing and questioning nature. His father was the fifth baronet since the creation of the family title in 1661, and though not exceedingly rich, the Cayleys had few wants. His mother, a Unitarian, exerted a powerful influence on his education, and though the precise details of his early schooling are unclear, Cayley came under the tutelage of two leading Nonconformists of the day, George Walker (a fellow of the Royal Society and president of

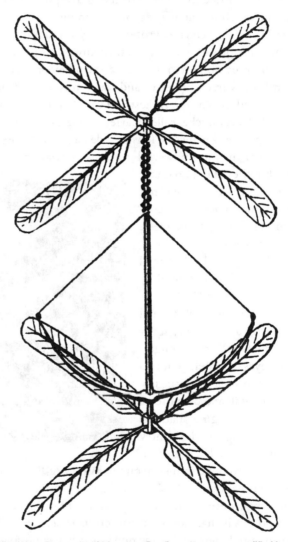

The bow-string *hélicoptère* of Launoy and Bienvenu, first flown in 1784, as modified by Cayley. Their helicopter, using two contra-rotating coaxial rotors, became both a popular amusement and demonstrator of powered, rotary-wing flight. Chanute, *Progress in Flying Machines* (1894)

the Literary and Philosophical Society of Manchester) and George Cadogan Morgan. His father died when Cayley was but 19, and the young man, now the sixth baronet, shortly thereafter married Walker's daughter Sarah, the beginning of a fruitful marriage that continued to his death.[23] From all of these influences, Cayley grew up as an individual with strong feelings for liberty, a belief that one had an obligation to benefit the larger society, and a curiosity about virtually all technical fields as well as about agriculture, the source of the family's wealth. In politics an active Whig (he served as president of the York Whig Club), he also took command of a corps of volunteers during the Napoleonic era, when it seemed France might try to invade England.[24]

Cayley apparently first expressed an interest in aviation in 1792, when still under the tutelage of Morgan at Southgate. Somehow he came into contact with a flying helicopter model, a derivative of the original drawstring helicopter toys of the middle ages, but more refined. In 1784 two Parisians, Launoy and Bienvenu, had flown a model helicopter having two small contra-rotating rotors powered by a taut bowstring. In 1796, after study, Cayley replaced their twin two-bladed rotors with twin four-bladed rotors (which he termed "flyers"), the individual blades, imaginatively enough, being bird feathers—stuck in two wine corks! (Perhaps this offers proof both on the extent that some pioneers would go in emulating the birds, and possibly on the congenial source of Cayley's inspiration.) Cayley likewise employed a small whalebone drawstring bow (acting like a bow drill) to store the energy needed for flight. Cayley never forgot this introduction to flight, and years later, in his eighties, he still would write to individuals describing how to make one. But more importantly, Cayley recognized that the little model helicopter demonstrated a large truth, namely, that a bigger vehicle incorporating larger rotors could fly and carry a man.[25] Thus intrigued and reinforced in his growing interest by the proliferation of ballooning after the 1780s, Cayley embarked on his own aeronautical research.

Cayley and His Work

Cayley worked in four primary periods. First, after being interested in flight from his exposure to helicopter toys and the public ferment over ballooning, Cayley devoted the first period of his aeronautical work, from 1799 to 1810, to the study of mechanical flight by airplanes and studies of finned projectiles for artillery. Then, from 1810 to roughly 1820, he devoted more attention to airships and airship design. During the next two decades he published little on aviation at all, but undertook work in other areas, including conceptualizing the modern tracked vehicle (what he called the "universal railway") and pursuing his political life. In the last period, from 1840 until his death in 1857, he resumed his aeronautical studies on both airships and aircraft, and also on artillery shells, vertical-takeoff-and-landing convertiplanes, and model helicopters.

Cayley's most notable contributions come from the first period of his research when, unlike any of his theoretical or experimental predecessors, he undertook his own work explicitly for the purpose of developing an actual flying machine. He recognized winged aviation as a balancing act among the four forces of flight: one had to use *power* to overcome *drag* so that wings could produce *lift* to overcome *gravity,* or as he put it (in the most often quoted of any statement he ever enunciated), "to make a surface support a given weight by the application of power to the resistance of the air."[26] Thus, unlike all his predecessors and even some of those who succeeded him, Cayley distinguished between the problem of *sustaining* a plane in the air via the lifting power of its wings and *propelling* a plane through the air via the power of its engine.[27]

Accordingly he blended theoretical study with practical experimentation, using a whirling arm, as had others before him, but also model helicopters, gliders, and actual human-carrying craft. Thus he was the first heavier-than-air pioneer to take his experiments into the air and in so doing created a pattern followed by subsequent pioneers. As Peter Jakab of the Smithsonian Institution stated, "Cayley established a methodology for flight research that consisted of a thorough examination of aerodynamics followed by the construction of aircraft to test the results of that research. Virtually all experimenters who were making genuine progress in aeronautics toward the end of the nineteenth century worked in this way."[28]

Cayley's contributions are all the more impressive when one realizes that he had little benefit—and in fact inherited some misleading information—from previous researchers. As one historian of aerodynamics has concluded, "The thinking and work of George Cayley . . . were carried out in an intellectual atmosphere of dawning enlightenment in regard to aerodynamics, but that atmosphere was too rarefied to have provided Cayley with many useful, practical tools . . . Cayley was on his own."[29] So too, it must be noted, were his successors: as late as 1879 the Aeronautical Society of Great Britain (later the Royal Aeronautical Society) noted in frustration, "Mathematics up to the present day has been quite useless to us in regard to flying."[30]

If he had done nothing else, Cayley significantly advanced aerodynamics simply by recognizing and reporting two of the key erroneous assumptions afflicting the field at the time. He detected both the error of the so-called sine-squared law derived from Newton's *Principia Mathematica,* which, if accurate, would have made winged flight virtually an impossibility, and the too-high value of Smeaton's constant, relating to the drag experienced by a flat plate moving through the air.[31] Unfortunately, would-be critics of flight ignored Cayley's work and continued for much of the nineteenth century to invoke Newton and point to "his law" (even though Newton never stated such) as proof that flying was an impossibility.[32] But again thanks to Cayley's timely intervention, it is likely this misconception caused no significant delay in the evolution of aircraft development: it seems not to have hindered other pioneers, and after examining the issue, the great aerodynamicist Theodore von Kármán stated, "Personally I do not believe that Newton's influence was really catastrophic."[33] The same, regretfully, was not true of the Smeaton miscalculation. Here Cayley criticized Smeaton's earlier figure indirectly, comparing Smeaton's results to his own calculation for how fast an airstream had to hit a flat plate having a surface area of one square foot in order to generate a resistance (drag) force of one pound. Smeaton stated 21 feet per second, and Cayley, using experimental measurements from his whirling arm, concluded the correct figure to be almost 24 feet per second. This revised the constant downwards from 0.00492 to 0.0038—still high, but more reasonable. Thus obliquely stated, his (semi)correction passed largely unnoticed at the time, and Smeaton's misconception continued to plague subsequent researchers to the end of the nineteenth century, including such greats and near greats as Francis Wenham, Hiram Maxim, and Otto Lilienthal.[34]

But Cayley's contributions went far beyond merely correcting previous work. In 1799 Cayley first recognized that lift, thrust, and drag were separate forces related to the problem of flight, each requiring careful approaches to solve or overcome. In 1800 he postulated the shape of the modern airplane: a body, or fuselage, with a cockpit for the crew, a fixed wing—a notable departure from his predecessors—and cruciform tail surfaces. Cayley's design is crude by the standards of later aircraft, but his correct insight into the problem of flight is clearly evident. All he failed to recognize was the value of having a broad, or high-aspect-ratio, wing for greater lift. He undertook the first studies of streamlining, based on examinations of the cross-sections of trout, producing drawings eerily anticipating the high-speed airfoils (wing cross-sections) of the 1940s and recognizing that the same shape could benefit the development of a streamlined airship. Cayley likewise recognized the value of dihedral, or angling a wing upwards to furnish greater lateral and directional stability. In 1804 he built the first of several whirling-arm test rigs, evaluating a series of wing configurations at varying angles of attack. Though whirling arms had been used by other researchers for various purposes, Cayley has the distinction of being the first to use one for the direct purpose of flight-related aerodynamic testing. The tests experimentally con-

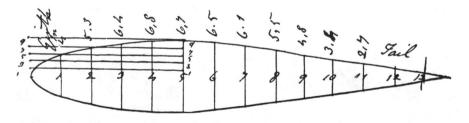

Sir George Cayley's sectional drawing of a solid of least resistance, based on the trout, and showing his appreciation of streamlining in nature. Cayley measured and thus quantified the relationship between cross-sectional area and body length, anticipating the 20th-century aerodynamic concept of "fineness ratio." SSPL

firmed the benefits of wing camber (curvature, like a bird's wing), specifically that a cambered wing shape would produce more lift for a given angle of attack than a flat plate. Also, they revealed the errors of the Newton "sine-squared law," and the Smeaton constant.[35]

What separates Cayley most completely from his predecessors, making him the first of the modern pioneers, is his emphasis on blending ground and flight research. In 1804 he constructed a small, five-foot-long glider to test his concepts, it having a kitelike wing set at a modest angle of incidence (i.e., angle of attack) above a streamlined dowel fuselage, and an adjustable cruciform tail, as well as a balancing weight that he could move back and forth to vary the location of the center of gravity (and hence the location of the center of pressure on the wing). The glider flew well in trials over hilly ground at his Brompton Hall estate outside Scarborough. Cayley recalled, "It was beautiful to see this noble white bird sail majestically from the top of a hill to any given point of the plain below it with perfect steadiness and safety, according to the set of the rudder, merely by its own weight, descending in an angle of about eight degrees with the horizon."[36] With this test, date unfortunately unknown, Cayley achieved a genuine milestone: for the first time, a winged craft had smoothly journeyed through the air, demonstrating another of the six forms of flight: *stable winged gliding flight.* The implications were clear: a larger vehicle could carry a person, and thus encouraged, Cayley constructed a much larger glider in 1809, flying a small boy "of about ten years of age" over a few yards! The name of this child-aviator is, alas, lost to history: that he flew is a tribute both to this young lad's courage as well as to the extraordinary singlemindedness of Cayley's quest.[37]

That same year he published his monumental, three-part *On Aerial Navigation.* One of the seminal texts in the history of aviation, which looked at the problem of flight from both a scientific and technological perspective, including a detailed examination of the requirements of flying machines.[38] Cayley explored a number of technical issues and illustrated his essay with drawings of bow-driven helicopters, parachutes, the forces acting upon a bird, and a variety of wings, one of which eerily anticipates the triangular (delta) parawing of the 1950s.[39] Then, for reasons that are obscure but might possibly reflect his frustration at the lack of a suitable "prime mover," he largely left the study of heavier-than-air machines

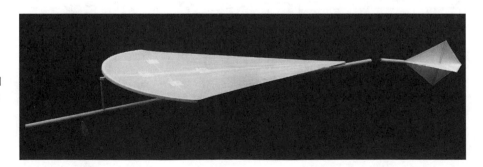

Full-size replica of Cayley's model glider of 1804, the first airplane in world history, on display in the collections of London's Science Museum. SSPL

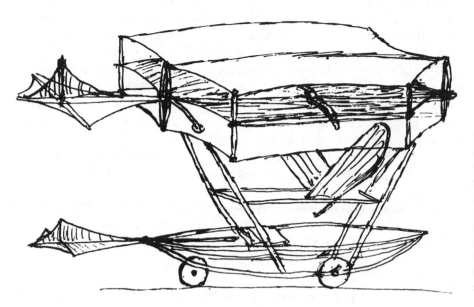

Cayley's triplane child glider sketch from 1849, with a wheeled undercarriage, and oar-like propulsive "flappers." Note the odd (if functional) wing layout with stabilizing tail surfaces.
SSPL

(except for making some small kite-gliders) and spent the next three decades studying the problems of lighter-than-air flight. He returned to writing about gliders in 1843 (encouraged, perhaps, by the renewal of interest in aviation accompanying Henson and Stringfellow's work), flew another anonymous child in 1849 in a glider that had a three-wing triplane layout, and capped his career in flight research by flying his coachman, also nameless (but possibly a groom named John Appleby), across a small valley in 1853. Cayley's granddaughter, Dora Thompson, recalled years later that the coachman subsequently said, "Please, Sir George, I wish to give notice. I was hired to drive, and not to fly!"[40] (In 1971 the distinguished British test and soaring pilot John Sproule built an exact replica of this glider using Cayley's drawings as a reference, and Derek Piggott flew it at Brompton Dale. It exhibited generally good flying characteristics and, in his words, constituted "splendid proof of Sir George Cayley's aeronautical theories.")[41]

Cayley's Other Interests and Influence

Cayley expressed a great deal of interest in two forms of air vehicles not often associated with him, namely airships and rotary-wing convertiplanes. In addition, he did significant work in the study of streamlined and finned artillery projectiles, the first such work since that of Leonardo over three centuries earlier. Perhaps because of the propulsion problems and also because of the immense lifting power of a gaseous approach, he gradually switched allegiances from the airplane to the airship (though he had an aversion to the hydrogen airship, preferring instead the Montgolfière approach). In 1816–17 he published a series of essays on airships, stating: "Balloon floatage offers the most ready, efficient and safe means of aerial navigation. . . . Elongated balloons of large dimensions, offer greater facilities for transporting men and goods through the air, than mechanical means [i.e., aircraft] alone. . . . When the invention is realized, it will abundantly supply the increasing locomotive wants of mankind."[42] In 1843 he went a step further, writing, "Mechanical flight seems more adapted for use on a much smaller scale, and for less remote distances; serving, perhaps, the same purpose that a boat does to a ship, each being essential to the other."[43]

Cayley's pronouncements on airships and his apparent turning away from heavier-than-air flight received wide attention. The next year the New York *Sun* trumpeted

ASTOUNDING NEWS BY EXPRESS VIA NORFOLK!
THE ATLANTIC CROSSED IN THREE DAYS!

Inspired by news accounts of Cayley, William Henson, and John Stringfellow (discussed subsequently), Edgar Allan Poe, then a brilliant if desperately poor American writer, had sold the newspaper a fabrication, announcing "the most stupendous, the most interesting, and the most important undertaking ever accomplished or even attempted by man."[44] His story claimed the Atlantic had been crossed by a nonstop balloon designed in part according to Cayley's principles, with an ellipsoidal—that is, blimp—shape. Poe's "Balloon Hoax" was widely accepted as true and helped launch his career as a writer of dark and complex fiction.

In fact Cayley was still very much a believer in the heavier-than-air flying machine. That same year, acting on the idea of inventor Robert Taylor, Cayley expanded the younger man's ideas and unveiled plans for what is clearly the antecedent of the modern convertiplane: a craft having a fuselage flanked by two sets of lifting rotors, and twin pusher propellers for forward flight. He planned that this craft would take off vertically, then the propellers would accelerate it in forward flight, after which the rotors could slowly come to a halt and act as two sets of parasol-like circular wings. This too, of course, remained just a paper study, but it is indicative of the catholic nature of Cayley's aeronautical interests.[45]

Finally, Cayley had a pervasive influence on subsequent aviation through another of his ideas—the rubber band-powered model airplane, which he conceived in 1853 at the age of 80. Although made a reality by the French pioneer Alphonse Pénaud in 1871, the originating insight came from across the Channel. Rubber cord, Cayley decided, would be a better, lighter, more powerful, and longer-lasting form of propulsion for models, since it offered the flexibility necessary to stretch and wind and furnish many seconds worth of power. Thus Cayley originated the concept behind the literally millions of model airplanes built since that time that have given pleasure, insight, and inspiration to generations of future aviators and aviation professionals.[46]

Cayley had tremendous influence over subsequent pioneers, and his work is most immediately evident in the conception of William Henson and John Stringfellow for the *Ariel,* a steam-powered "Aerial Steam Carriage." Conceived by Henson and Stringfellow after they had studied Cayley's work, and unveiled in April 1843, the Aerial Steam Carriage had many of the design features of a modern airplane. It featured a broad rectangular cambered wing constructed of numerous parallel ribs affixed to spanwise spars, a fuselage for passengers and crew, a large and efficient birdlike tail section consisting of a broad elevator for pitch control and a rudder for directional control, a steam engine driving two pusher propellers, and a tricycle landing gear. Model tests were inconclusive at best, but a publicity campaign that included running illustrations of it in the *Illustrated London News* and France's *L'Illustration* was a tremendous success.[47]

Cayley followed their concept, though critical of their overoptimistic expectations of success. In particular, over time Cayley had grown fond of the triplane, or three-wing, configuration, and he was convinced that Henson and Stringfellow's broad-wing design was doomed to failure, not least because the wing was so thin in relation to its span. Cayley always emphasized designs having what is termed a low aspect ratio, that is, they tended to be short in overall *wingspan* (width) and relatively long in *chord* (the distance from the leading edge to the trailing edge of the wing).[48] This is curious, as Cayley seems to have intuitively recognized what later pioneers experimentally confirmed, namely, that a cambered (curved) airfoil (wing cross section) produces the greatest portion of its lift well forward on the wing, which favors the design of very broad-span wings having a higher aspect ratio (if not thickness) such as that Henson and Stringfellow had selected. Despite his misgivings, he nevertheless wrote to Henson in 1846, "I like your zeal."[49]

In reality Henson and Stringfellow's aircraft could not be built at the time. But it constituted a popular and broadly accepted vision of flight possessing as much romantic force and appeal for aviation as, over a century later, the paintings of Chesley Bonestell had for spaceflight. In this regard it was a very important tech-

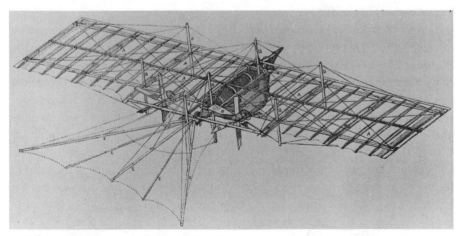

Henson and Stringfellow's proposed Aerial Steam Carriage drew international attention, as evidenced by this technical drawing from France's *L'Illustration* in 1843. AFMA

nological think piece, for it rationally integrated all of the essential elements of a successful airplane—structures, propulsion, aerodynamics, and controls—into a single integrated (and highly influential) design study.

British to the core (his official biographer judged him "almost fanatically patriotic"), Cayley could not understand why his native country hesitated to support aggressive research in aeronautics via government or private action.[50] In 1843, after the failure of the latest of his several attempts to establish national societies for "aerial navigation," Cayley wrote (with evident bitterness and exasperation), "I think it a national disgrace in these enlightened locomotive times not to realize by public subscription the proper scientific experiments, necessarily too expensive for any private purse, which would secure to this country the glory of being the first to establish the dry navigation of the universal ocean of the terrestrial atmosphere."[51]

Cayley was not alone in his prophecy: at the same time Alfred Lord Tennyson's brooding and tempestuous poem "Locksley Hall" presciently forecast what flight could accomplish both commercially and military:

> For I dipt into the future, far as human eye could see,
> Saw the Vision of the world, and all the wonder that would be;
>
> Saw the heavens fill with commerce, argosies of magic sails,
> Pilots of the purple twilight dropping down with costly bales;
>
> Heard the heavens fill with shouting, and there rain'd a ghastly dew
> From the nations' airy navies grappling in the central blue.[52]

Within a century after Tennyson penned these lines, the world's nations would have already had two wars and an interwar's experience with both the "ghastly dew" of grappling "airy navies," and "heavens fill[ed] with commerce," and Britain would have secured its national salvation through a three-month battle fought entirely in the air.[53]

Cayley contributed so much to aviation in the over half century of his active research after 1799 that one cannot help but view him somewhat as Moses and the Promised Land. As Moses pointed the way yet failed to reach it, so too did Cayley. And as Moses had to deal with recalcitrant and unenlightened followers, so too did this latter-day prophet—including members of his own family. His own son so disapproved of his father's interest in aviation that he made no effort to preserve any of Cayley's gliders, which gradually fell to bits, though one soldiered on briefly—as a roost for the manor's chickens![54] In 1907 Victor Tatin, one of the major figures of early French aeronautics, wrote, "In chronological order, one finds at the head of the inventors of the airplane is Sir George Cayley; a man of genius who lived at the beginning of the last century, having conceived the airplane more or less completely . . . Cayley's magisterial work passed unnoticed in France and was little known even in England."[55] Today, astonishingly, the only memorial in Great Britain to his work is a small, simple plaque at Brompton Hall, now a school.[56]

Just several decades separated Cayley from the opportunity to invent and demonstrate the first powered airplane himself. Unfortunately he lacked the one technological item that might well have made all the difference to him: a simple, lightweight, yet high-power propulsion system, something that caused him to conceptualize engines of his own, fueled by gunpowder or electricity, or "inflammable air." In view of his accomplishments, it is hard to imagine that he would have failed to succeed, had circumstances for his building such a craft existed. Nevertheless, Cayley at the time of his death was, one can assume, properly confident and serene in both the contributions that he had made to the field and the inevitability of their ultimate success. He passed away peacefully at age 84 in 1857, already recognized within the aeronautical community (if not more broadly) as the Father of Aerial Navigation, having left one of the more eloquent and memorable pronouncements in aviation: "An uninterrupted navigable ocean that comes to the threshold of every man's door ought not to be neglected as a source of human gratification and advantage."[57]

The Way Forward

Sir George Cayley is one of those bridging figures occasionally found in technology (but more often found in the political world) who link eras, crossing seemingly without effort from one to the other—in this case from thinking about flight to doing flight, from theory to practice. As one who undertook work of lasting—indeed seminal—importance, his influence extended far beyond England and his own time to pioneers such as his own countrymen Francis Wenham and Horatio Phillips, to France and Alphonse Pénaud, and eventually to the United States and the Wright brothers.[58]

In time the kind of supportive national aeronautical societies that Cayley advocated did appear. Five years before his death, French enthusiasts had created the Sociéte Aerostatique et Météorologique de France, which, as its name implied, concerned primarily ballooning and the study of weather. Less than nine years after Cayley's death, six men gathered one cold January day in 1866 at Argyll Lodge, Campden Hill, and formed the most important aeronautical organization created prior to the twentieth century's tremendous proliferation of governmentally supported research establishments: the Aeronautical Society of Great Britain.[59]

The Aeronautical Society constituted a quintessentially Victorian institution: the creation of upper-class gentlemen and nobles possessing a passionate curiosity about flight, a special sense of responsibility for the future of the realm as well as a desire to use their time and resources well, and a belief they had a special obligation to work for society's benefit. The duke of Argyll, a young patrician, easy on the eyes, with a straightforward, thoughtful nature, served as president, and the duke of Sutherland and Lord Richard Grosvenor served as vice presidents. It is perhaps natural, in a more cynical age characterized both by "big S" and "big T" government-supported science and technology and a "little d" democratic suspicion about the motives of the well-to-do, to smile somewhat at the thought of these Anglo-Saxon men of privilege forming "a Society for the purpose of increasing by experiments our knowledge of Aeronautics and for other purposes incidental thereto."[60] But, in fact, they formed an organization that shaped the future course of British aeronautical research through the invention of the airplane, influenced aviation around the world, served as a quasi-governmental and industrial body during the heyday of British aviation in the first half century after 1900, and is still one of the most respected and authoritative bodies of its kind.

From the outset the Aeronautical Society emphasized heavier-than-air flight over ballooning, itself a notable departure; indeed, the duke of Argyll considered the balloon but a toy, a distraction on the way to the true mechanical flying machine. Francis Herbert Wenham, an imposing, bearded marine engineer, was the most notable of the founders of the Aeronautical Society and, fittingly, the only one of them to survive long enough to witness the birth of the airplane at the hands of the Wright brothers.[62] Wenham delivered the Society's first public lecture (on "Aerial Locomotion and the Laws by which Heavy Bodies Impelled through Air are Sustained") in June 1866. The next year, at the Crystal Palace, Sydenham, the Society sponsored the world's first exhibition of aeronautical machinery, including small engines, models, drawings, and kites. Wenham had noticed that the best flying birds were ones with broad yet narrow wings and, intrigued, undertook a series of whirling arm experiments on wings having various degrees of span. He quickly discovered that his hunch was in fact correct, and from this he concluded that the greater portion of lift produced by a wing is produced near the leading edge of the wing. Thus, for most efficient flight a wing should be broad in span. Wenham's conclusion reflected the reality of how airplanes would develop: why bombers, transports, and sailplanes would have long, narrow wings, and why speedy fighters would have much shorter ones. He had, in short, discovered a basic characteristic of wing design: for maximum lift a wing should have the highest practicable aspect ratio.[63]

Creating "an Artificial Wind": Wenham, Phillips, and the First Wind Tunnels

But what Wenham did next gave aeronautics the tool with which it would break most future barriers blocking the fullest understanding of aerodynamics. In 1871 the Aeronautical Society sought a means by which it could derive "data on which a true science of aeronautics can be founded," creating a subscription fund supporting the creation of some new means of research.[64] Wenham conceived taking a large fan and blowing air around a model suspended in a square wooden trunk open at the ends. This brilliant insight led directly to that most important of all aeronautical research tools, the wind tunnel. Wenham and the research committee of the Aeronautical Society arranged for John Browning at the Penn's Marine

Engineering Works at Greenwich to build an apparatus 10 feet long and 18 inches square (sadly, no drawings or photographs of the tunnel exist), using a fan driven by a steam engine, with a small balance and springs to measure the lift and drag of wing shapes under test.

Wenham began his research with the tunnel—the world's first—about 1871 and unveiled his device publicly the next year. He had tested a series of "planes" (flat surfaces) at various angles of attack from 15 degrees to 60 degrees. Although the tunnel only had a maximum airspeed of 40 miles per hour, even at this lower speed he could clearly see the benefits of a wide-span as opposed to a short-span wing. The wider the wing, the higher the ratio of lift produced to drag encountered (commonly called the lift-to-drag ratio). Further, the lift produced came from the portion of the wing closest to the wing's leading edge—within about the first 25 percent of the fore-and-aft length of the chord, or within what is most commonly called the "quarter chord." Finally, the lift-to-drag values for a wing operating at a low angle of attack clearly demonstrated the fallacy of the so-called sine-squared law, a most important result.[65]

Wenham and Browning's tunnel could not produce much more useful information than this, but this is certainly enough to place it within the very highest reaches of important scientific instruments and tools developed over the entire length of human history. With the invention of the tunnel, as crude as it was, researchers now had the ability to test experimentally a variety of wing shapes while varying thickness, span, and aspect ratios, and then to compile tables of data that could be used by designers and inventors. In future years the tunnel would become to the aerodynamicist and the designer what the telescope was to the astronomer and the microscope was to a biologist: the absolutely critical professional instrument.

Wenham's model wings all consisted of flat surfaces—surfaces lacking the camber or curvature of a bird's wing, or that of a modern airplane. Even so, when tested in his crude tunnel, the wings displayed a lift-to-drag ratio (a measure of aerodynamic efficiency) of about 5. (In contrast, a sailplane may have a lift-to-drag ratio of about 50). Early in the 1880s, after looking at Wenham's data, as well as results of subsequent testing by other individuals using a large whirling arm, a young experimenter, Horatio Phillips, became convinced he could obtain better results using different wing sections and a new concept for a wind tunnel. His timing came at precisely the right moment, for the Aeronautical Society, having started with such promise, had entered technological doldrums exacerbated, unfortunately, by a personality feud between members that led to an exodus of many, including Wenham, who resigned in 1882. (He rejoined with an honorary membership in 1899 after the reorganization of the society by Captain Baden F. S. Baden-Powell, the brother of Robert Baden-Powell, the founder of the Boy Scouts.) Had Phillips not rejuvenated the Society's research program, it is possible that it would not have survived. But as it was, it did survive, thanks largely to the interest engendered by Phillips's work.

Phillips built his own tunnel, placing a steam injector fed from a large boiler downstream of the tunnel's test section. When opened, the injector released hot steam at high pressure into the exit area of the tunnel, expanding and creating a region of low pressure that in turn drew air through the entrance of the tunnel, and hence streaming around the test model. The quality of airflow through this "injector tunnel" was more uniform than in Wenham's original design, and indeed, it anticipated injector tunnels 60 years in the future designed to test models at supersonic speeds. But where Phillips made very significant contributions of more immediate application was in his testing of a series of airfoils (wing cross sections) having various degrees of camber (curvature). Whereas Wenham had obtained lift-to-drag ratios on the order of 5, Phillips routinely reached better than 10, the first quantitative proof that birdlike cambered airfoils were overwhelmingly better than kitelike flat plates. Until Phillips experimentally demonstrated this, many continued to believe, Leonardo-like, that a wing produced lift primarily because of air impacting the lower surface of an inclined wing. After Phillips, what might be termed the impact model of lift rapidly disappeared, and camber, in various forms, was king. Phillips recognized this, patenting a family of airfoils having pronounced camber. Above all, however, he firmly believed that

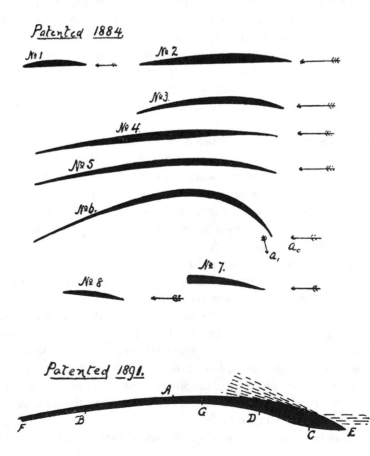

Phillips's cambered airfoil concepts, which he conceived and then wind-tunnel tested to assess their lift and drag characteristics. These anticipated many of the airfoil shapes used on early pioneer airplanes. Chanute, *Progress in Flying Machines* (1894)

the higher the aspect ratio, the better. He carried this to an extreme in 1893, constructing a tethered airplane test rig having a virtual Venetian blind for a wing: no less than 50 wings, one above the other, each having a span of 19 feet and a chord of only 1.5 inches, giving it the extraordinary aspect ratio of 152. Run around a circular track, this rig produced a lifting force of nearly 400 pounds at 40 miles per hour, proving the value of camber, though otherwise it was a completely impractical configuration.[66]

By the mid-1880s then, British aeronautics had made real and substantial gains, having evolved into an empirically based scientific process blending specialized ground research tools and methodologies with creative flight testing of models and technology demonstrators. Thanks to Cayley the configuration of the airplane had been fixed and the countervailing interrelationship between lift, gravity, drag, and power clearly appreciated if not completely understood. Thanks to Henson and Stringfellow, a very influential configuration integrating all the essential design elements for a successful airplane had appeared (their Aerial Steam Carriage), to a generally enthusiastic reception. Thanks to the duke of Argyll and a group of like-minded colleagues, a society existed for the encouragement of reputable experimentation and the exchange of reliable information. Thanks to Wenham the wind tunnel, the chief investigative tool that aerodynamicists and designers would rely upon for future research and development, was a reality. Thanks to Phillips the process of refining the tunnel into an even more useful tool had begun, and the first significant information demonstrating the quantifiable advantages of wing curvature had been assembled. Overseas, in Germany, a propulsion revolution promised to furnish the long-awaited prime mover that, unfortunately, Cayley had lacked. The next stage would certainly be the construction of actual flying machines—and *despite all of the above,* all available evidence suggested that the first country to do so would be . . . France!

CHAPTER SEVEN

The Frustrated Hopes of French Aeronautics

On Friday, August 18, 1871, a small group of young Frenchmen met in the midst of Paris's Jardin des Tuileries. It was not a propitious time, not an obviously auspicious day, and at that time not even a beautiful or evocative location. Less than a year before, France had experienced the full fury of *la Débâcle*, France's shattering defeat in the Franco-Prussian War. August 18 constituted the first anniversary of one of the most frustrating battles, Gravelotte–Saint Privat. There the indecision and timidity of France's generals had betrayed the extraordinary courage of her soldiers and thereby given victory to a foe whose attacks had been largely shattered by determined French defenders. The collapse at Sedan and the heroism of the siege had been followed by a new revolt in Paris in March 1871, as radicals created a militant Commune dedicated equally to fighting against both the terms of the armistice and the new government, which they considered dominated by monarchists of *l'ancien regime*. As government forces built up their strength to intervene, Parisian fought Parisian within the city's own *arrondissements*, displaying a savagery astonishing and horrifying even by the standards of civil war. The *communards* murdered hostages and burned public buildings including the Hôtel de Ville and the Tuileries palace. For its part, at the end of May the new French government ruthlessly restored order: over 20,000 of the *communards* perished, many executed in Père-Lachaise Cemetery. France, shattered to its core by the war and the Commune, understandably harbored a growing fury at its losses and the rise of the new German state. For their part the European and Russian left had a mythic revolution to inspire both Marx and Lenin, give to the world the terms *communist* and *communism,* and anticipate the even more ominous Russian revolutions of 1905 and 1917 that followed.[1]

For now, however, these young men, the self-styled Société Générale de Navigation Aérienne, were turning their attention back to other pursuits. They had gathered in the bleak setting of the once-beautiful Tuileries, surrounded by still-gutted and ruined buildings bordering the Louvre, to witness an aeronautical experiment. In their midst hobbled a young 21-year-old with a pronounced limp, making his way with difficulty, using crutches: Alphonse Pénaud. The son of a distinguished admiral who had commanded a French task force that (together with British vessels) boldly bombarded the Baltic Russian fortress of Sveaborg during the Crimean War, Pénaud had a degenerative hip condition that prevented him from following the naval career he had desired all his young life. But flight fascinated him too, and today he had a small wood and cloth model, an *aéroplane* he called the *planophore,* that he wished to demonstrate. It consisted of a wooden dowel 50 centimeters (20 inches) long, surmounted by an elegant tapered and cambered wing spanning 45 centimeters (18 inches), with a small diamond-shaped horizontal tail affixed to the back. The tips of the wing and the horizontal tail featured dihedral—they were angled upwards as a means of imparting some lateral and directional stability—and he had angled the tail surfaces slightly nose down to help the model maintain its longitudinal trim.

Several years earlier, while improving upon George Cayley's helicopter (and thus bringing this Gaullic invention full circle, from Paris to England and back to Paris), Pénaud had rediscovered rubber cords as a perfect lightweight powerplant. For his *hélicoptère* Pénaud strung rubber cord between two contra-rotating propellers; the cord, when twisted, stored enough potential energy to propel the little model about 30 feet into the air. Pénaud's little *hélicoptère* became a much-copied instant sensation. But the young Frenchman had bigger plans. He had his sights set on nothing less than developing a full-size airplane, and achieving that goal would require a number of technological demonstrations. To Pénaud a practical

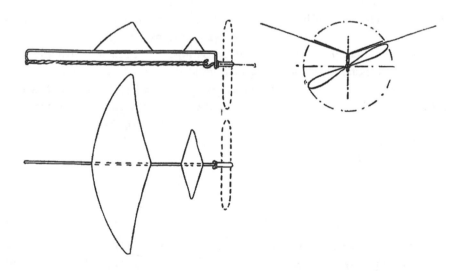

Pénaud's *planophore* as depicted in a 1910 drawing by F. W. Lanchester, based on Pénaud's crude 1871 drawing in *L'aéronaute.* This little rubbercord-powered model, flown in the Tuileries in August 1871, marked the beginning of the practical achievement of heavier-than-air flight. Lanchester, *Aerodonetics* (1910).

airplane would have to incorporate a high degree of inherent stability—the ability to fly in such fashion that a pilot did not need to manipulate the controls constantly to keep it on a steady course. Experimentation had led him to develop a configuration that he believed would work, and now he was ready to demonstrate it to the public. For his winged model, he used cord attached to a hook at the nose and running the approximately 20-inches length of the fuselage to a pusher propeller 21 centimeters (8 inches) in diameter at the back of the plane.

That morning in the Tuileries, his compatriots watched, intrigued, as Pénaud slowly turned the propeller through 240 revolutions, winding the rubber cord tighter and tighter. Then he held the model level at head height, let go of the propeller, and as it immediately began spinning with a slight buzzing sound, he launched the model horizontally in the air. As he wrote later, "For an instant it started to drop, but then, as its speed picked up, it flew straight away and described a regular movement, maintaining a height of 7 or 8 feet, covering a course of 40 meters [approximately 131 feet] in 11 seconds."[2] It had followed a slightly curving path, flying several gentle circles from the propeller's torque until the rubber bands fully unwound and, its power exhausted, it smoothly glided to earth. Stunned, the onlookers quickly measured the distance. The first significant powered flight of a heavier-than-air flying machine was history, and young Pénaud was the talk of the aeronautical world.[3]

Pénaud is one of the giants of the early days of aviation, a figure ranking with Cayley earlier in the nineteenth century, Henson and Stringfellow at midcentury, and such notables as Octave Chanute and Otto Lilienthal at its end. And rightly so, for what he achieved that August day in 1871 was no less than the answer to the question "Can an airplane fly?," a question that dated to the very dawn of interest in mechanical flight. As a result his Tuileries flight marked the beginning of the practical achievement of heavier-than-air flight, for Pénaud demonstrated almost all of the essential elements of the modern airplane, particularly the all-important one of flight under power.[4] Critics could no longer doubt that an airplane *could* fly; rather, the issue would be one of *scale,* involving two critical questions: *Can an airplane be built with an engine of sufficient power to lift a human aloft?* and *Can the operator control it?* Of these two questions, the second proved the more challenging and more important. But both of these questions dominated serious flight research until the Wrights dramatically answered them affirmatively above the dunes of Kitty Hawk on December 17, 1903.

The French Crucible

In view of the tremendous aeronautical ferment in France before and after the Franco-Prussian War, the really puzzling question is why *weren't* French aviators the first to develop a successful and influential airplane? It certainly wasn't for lack of trying. French scientists, engineers, and craftsmen possessed a deserved worldwide reputation for excellence. Most recently they had created the Suez canal, a feat of immense geopolitical and economic importance, once considered impossible but made practicable thanks to brilliant civil engineering and gigantic French steam dredges. France had pioneered ballooning and after the mid-nineteenth century had total unsurpassed dominance in aviation—indeed, a Frenchman, Gabriel de La Landelle, had created the term *aviation* in 1862, following up the next year with *aviateur.* Giffard had demonstrated his steerable balloon, de Lôme and Tissandier were working on their own ideas, and in slightly over a decade Renard and Krebs would follow with their even more advanced concept. Individuals such as Pénaud clearly understood the basic requirements for an airplane, and others such as Clément Ader were eager to go beyond models and develop full-size powered craft.

The record of experimentation and study spoke for the dynamism of the French aeronautical climate. In 1857, inspired by the soaring albatross, a French sea captain, Jean-Marie Le Bris, constructed a crude glider and made two hops, breaking a leg upon landing from the second. Prudently, Le Bris apparently continued his later studies with pilotless gliders (though this did not save him from dying violently, murdered in 1872).[5] In 1860 Pierre Hugon and Étienne Lenoir invented the first crude internal combustion engines, which promised an era of smaller, more compact, and yet more powerful engines suitable for aviation applications. Finally, there was a tremendous tradition of inquiry and communication.

In 1862 Nadar (the photographer-balloonist Gaspard Félix Tournachon) had joined with his friend Jules Verne to create the Société pour la Recherche de la Navigation Aérienne, a year later following with the awkwardly named Société d'Encouragement pour la Navigation Aérienne au Moyens d'Appareils plus Lourds que l'Air (Society for the Encouragement of Aerial Navigation by Heavier-than-Air Vehicles) and the even more grandiose Compagnie Générale Aérostatique et de l'Autolocomotion Aérienne (Aerostatics and Air Transit Company). Apparently quickly recognizing the potential dangers of having too many small and fragmented organizations, he regrouped with the more manageable Société Générale de Navigation Aérienne, covering both aerostatics and heavier-than-air flight, and dropped the overly ambitious notion of an aerial transit company. In 1864 Nadar began publication of *L'aéronaute: Moniteur de la Société générale de navigation aérienne.* Though it died after five issues, Abel Hureau de Villeneuve, who had become secretary-general of the by-now-yet-again-renamed Société Français de Navigation Aérienne, revived *L'aéronaute* four years later, successfully continuing publication of what was arguably the most important aeronautical journal of the early days of aviation until 1912. Also in 1864, Henri Philippe Ferdinand Comte d'Esterno published his milestone *Du vol des oiseaux,* the first analysis of bird flight distinguishing soaring, as opposed to flapping, flight. He also released drawings of an elegant and graceful glider which, save for the lack of a vertical fin above the tail (it had a rudder in front of the pilot), would have looked completely in place on the slopes of the Wasserkuppe in the 1920s during the golden age of German soaring.[6]

All of this spoke to a vibrancy in French aeronautics that promised much. After that exciting day in the Tuileries, Pénaud continued his model studies, building an imaginative rubber-powered model ornithopter, which like his helicopter became a popular toy. He lectured and wrote widely and contributed numerous papers on a variety of topics to professional societies and especially to the French aviation journal *L'aéronaute* and the *Journal de physique*. As Octave Chanute, one of the very greatest of all pioneers, stated tellingly (and somewhat tongue in cheek), "He was one of the few men who have taken up the subject in his youth, for it is a singular fact that most of the scientific students of this inchoate research are now men of middle age, perhaps past the dread of being considered mentally unsound, but no longer with the ardor and the daring of youth."[7]

But he also worked steadfastly towards his goal of a full-size machine. Finally, five years after the *planophore*, he released his vision, executed in association with Paul Gauchot. In February 1876 the two men patented a design for an inherently stable steam-powered, full-size airplane. A large, externally braced flying wing, it resembled nothing so much as a big moth. Designed as an amphibian, with retractable wheels so it could operate from land and a boat hull permitting it to operate off water, it incorporated a number of features found in the successful aircraft of the mid-twentieth century. These included two propellers located on the leading edge of the wing, an enclosed cabin and cockpit (with a fighter-style clear bubble canopy), instruments for the pilot's reference (including a barometer to measure height above ground, a level to assist in maintaining attitude, and a compass), moveable elevators on the trailing edge of the wing for pitch control, and a fixed vertical fin for directional stability that had attached to it a moveable rudder for yaw (directional) control. The Pénaud-Gauchot design possessed a Gaulic elegance of line going beyond Henson and Stringfellow's pioneering *Ariel* of midcen-

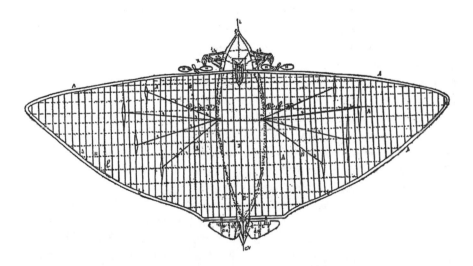

The Pénaud-Gauchot airplane, though not consciously intended to, resembled nothing so much as a large moth. It reflected the emphasis many early pioneers placed upon lift, though it had numerous interesting features for its time. From *L'aéronaute* (1877)

tury, with a slight dihedral to the wing and, as with his earlier model, graceful upswept wingtips to provide inherent stability. Its well-thought-out external bracing anticipated the design of early European monoplanes such as the Blériot, Béchereau's Monocoque Deperdussin, and the various Morane-Saulnier designs. Further, the two developers had undertaken a comprehensive performance analysis that indicated a depth of insight and study beyond most of the early pioneers.[8]

One can see clear potential for development in this airplane, though it had some flaws as well. The thin wing section reflected prevailing thought—once again the dominance of the bird influence—that a wing must have a thin airfoil cross section. In the pre–metal airplane era, this demanded external bracing and also reduced its available lifting power. The propellers are small and immature in design, and no existing power plant had the ability to propel it into the air. More seriously, it lacked any provision for roll control for turns or banking flight, and the elevator for pitch control and the rudder were undersized as well. But it obviously offered a superb starting point for a serious flying machine.

Sadly, however, Pénaud would never refine this design. Photographs show a neatly bearded, thoughtful young man, probably quiet and sensitive, perhaps too much so. His proposal for a full-size airplane did not receive the universal admiration he might have expected, and after his successes early in the decade, he was plagued by declining health and poor finances. He turned to Henri Giffard for help, but for whatever reason the airship pioneer, seriously ill himself, chose not to offer any support. The Franco-American pioneer Octave Chanute, writing two decades later, noted that "M. Pénaud was criticized, decried, misrepresented, and all sorts of obstacles arose to prevent the testing of his project."[9] Writing a century later, historian Charles Gibbs-Smith concluded he was the victim of "mischievous, and probably jealous, criticism and denigration."[10] And so in 1880, increasingly crippled and disheartened, he put drawings of all his inventions into "un petit cercueil"—a small coffin!—and then committed suicide at the age of 30. "The name of Alphonse Pénaud," rightly mourned L'aéronaute, "will always be inscribed among those making the very greatest advancements in aviation."[11] Two years later the depressed and ailing Giffard followed him into self-induced oblivion.

With Pénaud's death, France arguably lost its best chance to follow its success with the balloon and airship and be the first nation to succeed in flying a successful airplane, a tragic loss to French—indeed, world—aviation. Had he lived, he would have been at the height of his creative powers precisely at the point where the work of other pioneers and the beneficial development of the internal combustion engine came into confluence. There can be little doubt the aeronautical world would have heard more from this profoundly gifted, yet equally tragic, young man.

After Pénaud: Tatin and Goupil

Pénaud's death broke the pace of French aeronautical research and, in retrospect, cost France at least a decade in development, and perhaps much more. Afterwards

French aviation went into a quiescent mode for the better part of a decade, with French researchers content to reexamine birdflight (Louis Mouillard published his great reference, *L'empire de l'air,* the year after Pénaud's death),[12] build more flying models, and conceptualize more flying machines. But the kind of keen insight that young Pénaud had possessed—the ability to integrate a diverse set of technologies into a single design—was sadly missing. Nevertheless, with Pénaud gone, three individuals rose to prominence in his place: Victor Tatin, Alexandre Goupil, and Clément Ader.

Neither of the first two men dramatically influenced the future of aviation, though each did some interesting work. Tatin, a model builder destined to live well into the twentieth century and thus to play a major role in some of the leading controversies surrounding the question of who actually flew first, assumed the Pénaud mantle. Like many, he began with ornithopters, experimenting with rubber band–powered models having wings of varying span.[13] Fortunately this represented only a phase, and in 1879 he built and flew an impressive compressed-air-powered model spanning over 7 feet and having a single wing, a swept-back, birdlike, horizontal tail, twin propellers on the leading edge of the wing, and a streamlined body (formed by the compressed-air cylinder): clearly a surprisingly modern monoplane configuration. After some early tests, Tatin took his model to the military research establishment at Chalais-Meudon, where he tethered it to a pole and then let it take off from a circular track. The tests proved the craft could fly, as did later tests with the model suspended from a cable, but on nearly every flight it damaged its landing gear and propellers. Reporting on his activities in the journal *L'aéronaute* in September 1880, Tatin optimistically concluded, "These experiments would seem to prove that there is no fundamental impossibility preventing construction of large flying machines, and that possibly even at this time these machines could be used for aerial navigation."[14] But such would have to be for someone else to pursue for, as he pessimistically concluded, "practical experiments being of necessity quite expensive, I must, I regret, forego further undertaking."[15] Despite this pronouncement, late in his life, when greatly respected as the most distinguished spokesman on French aviation, he collaborated with some notable French pioneers. In 1911 he achieved a modest success at age 68 with a highly streamlined design, the Paulhan-Tatin Aéro-torpille (aerial torpedo), just two years before his death.[16]

His countryman Alexandre Goupil is a different matter. In 1883 Goupil actually built an airplane (sans engine), curved to resemble a bird, with a deep body or fuselage capable of containing the crew and engine, and a monoplane wing having pronounced camber. This ran counter to most existing design practice, and Goupil deserves recognition for appreciating the value of such a layout. The Goupil aircraft had a broad wing of 27 square meters (almost 292 square feet), and in December 1883, when Goupil tested it in a light breeze (tethered to the ground so that it could not rise higher than two feet), it nevertheless briefly lifted off while carrying two men. Subsequent winds blew so strongly that an insufficiently braced wing folded up, fortunately without resulting in injury to anyone. But the most notable technical attribute of the Goupil machine was—for the time—its sophisticated control system. In addition to a birdlike moveable horizontal tail for pitch control, Goupil added two other little elevators, one on each side of the fuselage, located forward and below the wings, to act as assists for the tail. But in addition they could operate differentially (i.e., one nose up, the other nose down) to roll the airplane about its longitudinal axis—in other words, to function as what are now termed *elevons,* combining the purposes of an *elev*ator for pitch control and an aile*ron* for roll control. Though Goupil did not conceptualize their use in conjunction with a rudder to control turning, as did the Wrights later, he nevertheless clearly recognized their value in imparting roll control to an airplane. Following his 1883 trials, Goupil abandoned further experiments, though he wrote a notable work, *La locomotion aérienne,* summarizing his work and ideas.[17]

Birds, Bats, and Clément Ader

The third French pioneer, Clément Agnès Ader, is one of the most controversial figures in the entire history of aviation, hailed by a few as the true inventor of the airplane, held by many as yet another who toiled in misguided fashion, and scorned by some as an individual who knowingly claimed success in the face of abject failure.[18] Unlike his predecessors Ader showed little interest in either model building or gliding as intermediate steps towards a powered machine even though he could have been a veritable French Lilienthal. Perhaps this is because, as a trained electrical engineer, he believed he had the necessary technical background to go directly to a full-size machine.

Ader came from an old and hardworking family in southern France. His grandfather had fought for Napoléon, being taken captive in 1815 and held for a time by the British aboard a prison barge at Plymouth. Young Ader was born in 1841 in Muret, a small village in the Haute-Garonne, the foothills of the Pyrenees, not far from Toulouse and the ancient city of Carcassonne, on the wild and dangerous Garonne River. Tales from his grandfather filled him with a fierce and abiding patriotism that adversity and personal experience strengthened even further. The son of a carpenter, he showed a marked technical aptitude and graduated from the École Industrielle of the Institution Assiot in Toulouse, a specialized school created by Félix Assiot (the son of the institution's founder, the noted French educator Louis Assiot) to train prospective engineers. Ader worked first for a railway company but then left to work on his own, designing a family of popular racing *vélocipèdes* (protobicycles using direct pedaling of a large front wheel rather than the gear-and-chain-driven technique of the classic later bicycle). Such was his success that he established the Véloces-Caoutchouc Clément Ader, producing (as he termed them) "très-élégant" bicycles, the "vainqueurs dans toutes les courses" (the victors in any race).[19]

The Franco-Prussian War encouraged Ader's long-standing interest in flight. As a boy Ader had "studied" natural flight, exhibiting an oddly disturbing curios-

ity. Using sticky paper, he would catch mayflies, tie fine thread around the unfortunate insects, and then observe their attempts to fly. He also watched the flight
of sparrows. Now, as an adult, the shocking French defeat in 1870 led him to conclude that France could best offset future German military land power only if it
developed an actual aerial army to attack with impunity from above.[20] (Ironically,
though his actual attempts to develop aircraft were anything but successful, Ader
always had a very perceptive and futuristic view of what aviation would mean to
international security and military affairs, once writing, "Military aviation shall
become all powerful, and control the destiny of nations").[21]

So he set to work. Ader, had he possessed a different outlook—in particular,
had he capitalized on the work of Pénaud, Gauchot, and Goupil—might have
secured the Holy Grail of powered flight for France, for he was an undoubtedly
energetic and enthusiastic developer. A year after Pénaud, he conceived an
ornithopter-like craft spanning 26 feet, which he proposed to flap using his own
power. When this, of course, failed miserably, he had no choice but to look to
fixed-wing and mechanically propelled solutions.[22] At this point he had a unique
opportunity to anticipate the extraordinarily influential work of Otto Lilienthal, a
full two decades before that German gliding pioneer began his work, for his tentative designs for a *planeur en plumes d'oie,* as the name implies, clearly reveal a shoul-
der-mounted glider with a gooselike wing configuration; that is, a Lilienthal-like
hang glider that the operator would strap himself to. But despite some tentative
experiments, Ader did not follow through and refine the glider as a interim (if
most important) step to moving on to larger self-propelled craft. Instead, he
turned away from aviation for the better part of the next decade, devoting himself
to electrical engineering and the new field of the telephone, and filing numerous
patents. (Eventually, over his lifetime, he would secure more than 58 French and
foreign patents, not counting additions, for a variety of devices.) In this he was
tremendously successful, securing both wealth and position, receiving the Prix
Vaillant from the Academy of Sciences and also membership in the prestigious
and exclusive Légion d'Honneur, the latter conferred in 1881. It was then, possibly
because of his newfound financial security and the inspiration of Louis Mouillard's *L'empire de l'air,* published that same year, that he returned to aviation, this
time with greater ambition and confidence.[23]

As a mature adult, Ader continued looking to the natural world for inspiration,
having moved on from insects to studying eagles, other large birds, and bats.
Again these studies had a Charles Addams quality to them: he would drug large
birds with a chloroformed mouse set out as bait, cage them, and then, while they
still were under sedation, gently move their wings and study their articulation,
keeping them as well to study their attempts at flight. From July through October
1882, at the age of 41, he journeyed first to Strasbourg to study storks and then
traveled to Algeria to study soaring vultures, leaving the relative security of Constantine on the coast, disguising himself as a native and journeying deep in the
desert with two Arab guides to observe them in their natural habitat, and meeting
and speaking as well with Mouillard.[24] But it was the bat that made the greatest

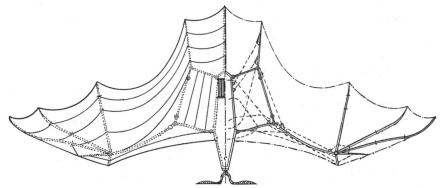

Fig. 1. — Surfaces sustentatrices. — Ailes pour petites vitesses. — (Échelle : 12ᵐⁱᵐ/1. par mètre.)

(Propulseur en projection diagonale comme ci-dessous.)

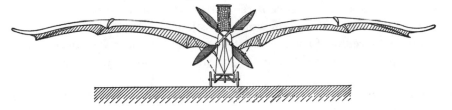

Fig. 2. — Aéroplane. — Élévation de face. — (Échelle : 12ᵐᵐ/1, par mètre.)

A technical drawing of Ader's *Éole* clearly reveals its creator's interest in both birds and bats. From *Revue de l'aéronautique* (1893)

impression upon him, and he chose its configuration, including the bone structure of its wing, as the pattern for the structure of his own flying machine. Thus inspired, he went beyond all those before him by being the first to actually construct a full-size airplane—the steam-powered *Éole* (for Aeolus, the Greek god of the winds)—and attempt to fly.[25]

Ader had hired two assistants in 1885, Éloi Vallier and Louis Espinosa, and working together, the team completed the *Éole* in 1890, working out of quarters on Paris's Rue Pajou. It has a Gothic look about it, as if out of some odd Verne fantasy. In shape the *Éole* has a batlike drooping wing spanning over 50 feet and a crude, four-bladed tractor propeller (crafted to copy the feathers of a bird but looking like nothing so much as some odd and exotic flower) affixed to its nose and connected to the engine. Ader did not incorporate an elevator for pitch control (as had Pénaud), hoping instead to climb or descend by adding or subtracting power (while this can work to some degree, it is on the whole an outlandish idea, more suited as a last resort in an emergency than as a primary means of control from the outset of a flight). Finally, the pilot sat behind the boiler, had essentially no forward vision, and a huge and ungainly condenser stuck straight up from the top of the engine, destroying any hope of smooth aerodynamic flow over the top of the body. (Indeed, this condenser shape virtually guaranteed it would function much as a modern speed-and-lift-killing air brake extended from the back of a fighter such as an F-15.) This airplane—the first in history, though certainly unsuccessful—featured a lightweight 20-horsepower steam engine of his own design, powerful enough (producing one horsepower per ten pounds of engine weight, a remarkable figure for the day) to propel it off level ground. Therefore, despite the lack of success he shared with all pre-Wright predecessors, Ader is due all credit for inventing the first significant powered airplane.[26]

Believing the airplane destined for military use, Ader always worked in great secrecy. When Octave Chanute sought information on Ader's efforts for his survey of aviation, *Progress in Flying Machines,* Ader declined, and Chanute could only report, "The details are being kept secret, as the inventor states that he believes that it is destined to play an important part in the national defense of his country."[27] Accordingly, when the *Éole* neared the flight, Ader's friend, the influential banker Gustave Péreire, arranged for him to use the secluded grounds of his mother's estate, the Château d'Armainvilliers. (The banker came from a family already connected to the periphery of ~~French~~ aeronautics: three other relatives—Emile, Issac, and Eugène Péreire—had bankrolled one of Nadar's earlier ventures, the Société de Photographie Artistique, in 1856.) Ader supervised the clearing and leveling of an unobstructed stretch of carriage way measuring 200 meters, approximately 700 feet, in length—short but sufficient, Ader believed, for his tests.

Ader's flight attempt with this craft at Armainvilliers, on October 9, 1890, constituted the first legitimate attempt in the history of the world to fly a powered human-carrying airplane. It demonstrated as well his undoubted courage, if not his design acumen or common sense. That day, as a small group of onlookers watched, Ader managed to accelerate to liftoff speed and skim the earth at a height of about a foot for about 50 meters (165 feet) in a machine that had essentially no forward vision and no flight control system. As with a modern airplane prior to its first flight, Ader initially made a series of high-speed taxi runs, feeling the aircraft lighten and then reducing power. He sent Espinosa and Vallier to the midpoint of the runway and began his attempt, recollecting later: "I advanced at high speed; the jolting of the wheels on the ground stopped almost at once, and for a few seconds I was suspended in a state of indefinable joy. But the end of the runway was very near and did not allow for more; I stopped the engine straight away and the *Éole* touched ground again, 50 meters further on."[28] No photograph of this flight attempt (or other Ader flight attempts) exists, and the only visual portrayal indeed, the only press account at all of the flight was an engraving that appeared in the French magazine *L'Illustration* nine months later.[29]

Ader's attempt proved he possessed great luck, for if the *Éole* had actually climbed into the air, even to a few dozen feet, it is extremely doubtful he could have returned safely. Far more likely, the *Éole* would have stalled and then pitched down, plunging vertically to earth and killing or seriously injuring its designer. Fortunately it never got high enough, nor fast enough, to threaten its creator's life. Three criteria characterize a successful heavier-than-air airplane flight: it must be *powered, sustained,* and *controlled.* Ader met the first of these criteria, came close but still missed the second, and definitely failed the third. It is unclear whether the *Éole* ever flew again, for Ader, after a silence of 16 years, claimed it made another flight of 100 meters in September 1891 at the military proving ground at Satory, being wrecked in a collision with some carts placed near the takeoff track. As intriguing as it is, there is no other evidence corroborating this much-after-the-fact claim.[30] In any case, nothing of the *Éole* survives to be seen today.

"L'affaire Ader": *Attempting the World's First Military Airplane*

Although financially secure, Ader's experimentation had cost him a great deal of money, and he recognized a need to secure other sources of funding to continue his experimentation. He wished to build a larger and more advanced airplane, the *Avion II*—after the Latin *avis* for (bird)—for the French military, giving it the name *Zéphyr*. Accordingly, in hope of securing support, he temporarily abandoned his secrecy and put the *Éole* on exhibit in the Paris Pavilion off the Champs-Elysées in a bid for publicity. Its display drew a great deal of welcome attention, not at least from one unusual visitor: the French president and minister of war, Charles-Louis de Freycinet, who visited the display pavilion on Saturday, October 17, 1891, accompanied by General Mensier, the director of French army engineering.[31]

De Freycinet, "who was for a whole generation to run up and down the corridors of the Third Republic like a little white mouse," ultimately worked in 12 separate governments, including serving as a member of nine ministries and four terms as *président du Conseil*.[32] Of unprepossessing appearance and mannerisms, he was an engeretic technocrat par excellence and a trained civil engineer who had graduated from the prestigious École Polytechnique. Military prefect for the Tarn-et-Garonne *département* at the beginning of the Fanco-Prussian War, he made his reputation brilliantly assisting Gambetta in raising citizen armies. Elected to the senate after the war, he received appointment as France's minister of public works, where he had gained further attention by his *"plan Freycinet,"* championing dramatic improvements to France's postwar transportation infrastructure. Over the next decade, his career rose and fell more frequently than a balloon. In 1888 he became France's first civilian minister of war since 1848, instituting widespread reforms, including establishing a general staff and a supreme war council. Now de Freycinet was entranced by Ader's work. "This is a scout and aerial destroyer, and its testing must continue under the auspices of *le département de la Guerre* for national defense," de Freycinet intoned, encouraging the would-be aviator to think of military applications and suggesting discussion of possible official support. If nothing else, this would be sufficient to earn this essentially colorless bureaucrat a place in the history books: de Freycinet was the first civil servant of any nation to recognize the potential of the military airplane and to put support toward developing one. Ader leapt at the opportunity.[33]

Thus, thanks to the French military, Ader's work now took a different direction, and he abandoned the single-engine *Avion II-Zéphyr* in favor of a more militant design, the twin-engine *Avion III*, which he tentatively called the *Aquilon*. After protracted negotiations, on February 3, 1892, Ader and de Freycinet signed a war ministry contract stipulating development of an airplane capable of carrying one or two passengers or a 75-kilogram (165-pound) quantity of explosives in addition to the pilot, all at a speed of approximately 35 miles per hour, at an altitude of roughly 1,000 feet. This constituted the first military research and development contract ever awarded for a heavier-than-air flying machine, and the performance demanded by this contract would not be attained by an airplane until the Wilbur Wright demonstrated the Military Flyer at Ft. Myer, Virginia, in the summer of 1908, 16 years later.[34] Supported with 550,000 francs of government money (then approximately $110,000 and a century later roughly $2.2 million), he moved into a large works on the Rue Jasmin, a small residential neighborhood in the sixteenth *arrondissement* off the Avenue Mozart, between the Seine and the Bois de Boulogne. There, with Vallier and Espinosa, he set to work on his new design, again under conditions of great secrecy.[35]

The absence of hard evidence encouraged sensational rumors. In response to a query from Chanute for information on Ader, Smithsonian secretary Samuel P. Langley implied fraud, claiming that an informant had indicated Ader was a "sharp" man using airplane schemes as a means of making money off investors.[36] In fact, however misguided, Ader *was* sincere, and very much in the real airplane business. The *Avion III-Aquilon* appeared in 1897. Larger than the original *Éole,* it featured two small 20 horsepower steam engines driving twin tractor propellers, and most notably a large rudder behind the cabin. But it also retained his odd notions on design and flight control: as with the earlier airplane, the pilot sat firmly in the rear of the vehicle with essentially no forward view, the drag-producing and lift-killing condenser still dominated the frontal aspect of the machine, the propellers (which in design copied the complex feathers of birds) had overlapping arcs of rotation, and the flight control system was even more convoluted and impractical than on his earlier vehicle. Though its primary structure was wood, it also incorporated aluminum, brass, and steel, and a silk covering. It had a very narrow-track landing gear of two wheels and a tailwheel, undoubtedly making it prone to upset.[37]

Ader did not complete his airplane until July 1897, by which time a whole new set of circumstances existed in the French government. De Freycinet had left, forced to resign from office in January 1893 after being implicated (though never charged or convicted) in a widespread bribery scandal involving France's disastrous attempt to build a canal across the isthmus of Panama, an attempt abandoned in 1889 after costing 1.5 billion francs (then approximately $300 million, equivalent to over $6 billion a century later) and over 20,000 lives.[38] (Ever resilient, he would return to government within the decade.) Then, the next year, a French secret agent had discovered missing French military papers in the wastebasket of the German embassy. Who had delivered them to the Germans? A bizarre investigation motivated more by anti-Semitism than the search for truth fingered a young staff officer: Captain Alfred Dreyfus. Charges, countercharges, and disgraceful behavior by those seeking to pin blame on Dreyfus (even as they knew the identity of the probable real suspect, the son of a prominent French general) tore at the war ministry and led to increasingly partisan and public exchanges between *dreyfusards* and *anti-dreyfusards*.[39]

So when Ader notified the ministry that he had completed the plane and requested arrangements for official trials, it had much on its mind. After several weeks, he received instructions to transfer the *Avion III* to the military grounds at Satory, near Versailles. Satory served as a camp, an engineering school, a maneuver area, and an artillery training center. Some indication of how important the ministry considered these tests can be seen in the urgency with which the ministry reacted when it learned that the grounds at Satory had to be prepared for the trials. It immediately ordered the governor of all military forces in Paris to acquire manpower from the French army's engineer corps and have these men work under Ader's direction. Ultimately numbering 45 persons, the team began laying out the grounds in August and did not finish until the morning of the first tests. What Ader directed now seems utterly bizarre: a circular racetrack-like runway measuring approximately 40 meters (130 feet) in width, having a diameter of approximately 475 meters (over 1,500 feet) and a circumference of 1,500 meters (nearly 5,000 feet), located in the midst of the artillery training grounds. Why he chose to employ such a runway is itself curious, as a flat straightaway would have been far more appropriate and, further, would have given him the benefit of a constant run into the wind. As it was, during his "takeoff roll" he would encounter a headwind, a crosswind, a tailwind, a crosswind, a headwind, etc., until liftoff—and also the track was far from level: it varied in height, the southeast portion of the circle being as much as 7 meters (23 feet) lower than the northeast portion.[40]

The *Avion III* arrived at Satory in the early fall of 1897. Preliminary ground testing impressed the committee members with the ingenuity of the design as a mechanical contrivance. For example, the two engines, taken together, weighed a total of 257 pounds yet produced 40 horsepower, a very respectable 6.4 pounds per horsepower. Overall the airplane weighed approximately 880 pounds, and its batlike wing spanned nearly 56 feet.[41] After final adjustments Ader made initial running trials. On Tuesday, October 12, late in the afternoon, he taxied the *Avion III* around the track at a speed of about 15 miles per hour. The next day's weather proved so foul that Ader deferred testing to the following day, Thursday, October 14. That day started out equally miserable, but finally, as evening approached, the weather moderated somewhat, and at 5:15 P.M. Ader, for reasons that are difficult to fathom, started the two steam engines and taxied to the circular takeoff track. With the two propellers whirring and the steam

Ader's *Avion III,* as exhibited at the Musée des Arts et Métiers, Paris. Hallion photograph

engines percolating away, Ader made his takeoff run witnessed by two French generals and a lieutenant as well as two mechanical engineering professors from the École Polytechnique.[42]

The results were unambiguous failure: unlike the earlier *Éole,* the *Avion III* could not gain the air. General Mensier's official report to the war ministry makes it clear that Ader's machine accelerated enough that the tail wheel rose, for its track disappeared. But the other wheels remained firmly grounded. Things rapidly got worse, and Ader and his airplane nearly came completely to grief when contrary winds blew it off the course. Ader was in a bind: moving fast enough to produce sufficient lift to raise the tail (and hence the tailwheel) off the ground, but still slow enough that the rudder itself was aerodynamically ineffective. In short, he was out of control; Mensier suggested subsequently that Ader could have used differential propeller thrust to steer, but it is difficult to see how Ader would have had the time or even the opportunity to do so, even had he retained the presence of mind to try. Thus, as the winds blew the *Avion III* off the track, he prudently shut down power as it skidded and rocked to a stop. Mensier detailed the failures, noting that the *Avion III* was seriously damaged, with the left wingtip bent, the landing gear partially wrecked, both propellers destroyed, and with possible engine damage as well. Nevertheless, he concluded somewhat positively that "the tests, though prematurely interrupted, have shown results of great importance, and though the final results are hard to foresee, it would seem advisable to continue the trials."[43]

However, the minister of war, General Mercier, had something far more important to worry about than *l'affaire Ader:* the growing *affaire Dreyfus.* For over three years Mercier had spearheaded a ruthless campaign against the ex-captain, and though Dreyfus now languished—largely at Mercier's insistence—in brutal solitary confinement on Devil's Island, increasingly his own army as well as the larger French society recognized that an injustice had taken place. Already a rising tide of *dreyfusards* prepared to do public and legal battle with Mercier and his fellow *anti-dreyfusards,* and 1898 promised to be a key year in the struggle.[44] With these stakes one can imagine how Mercier must have viewed General Mensier's cautious recommendation to spend further time and resources on something as odd as an unguided, steam-powered, mechanical bat. On January 31, 1898, he rejected both the recommendation and Ader's request for repair funds.[45] The dismal conclusion to the Ader trials escaped foreign notice, and indeed, ten months after Mercier's decision the Aeronautical Society of Great Britain's editors were still optimistically informing members that "the inventor is only awaiting the order of the minister of war to make another start, and we may hear that the problem of aerial navigation has been solved."[46]

So far as the ministry of war was concerned, Ader could wait forever. The inventor fought over the next year to secure official support to continue the trials, even if it meant foregoing additional governmental support. In October 1898 de Freycinet returned to office as minister of war, and in a last-ditch appeal for help, Ader wrote to him the following February, but to no avial: the minister refused to reverse previous ministry actions, grounding the *Avion III* for good.[47] Ironically, just five months later, in early July 1899, Samuel Langley visited Ader's workshop on the Rue Jasmin. By now well aware of Ader's sincerity and in fact wanting his help, Langley had a desperate need of information on how to power his own *Great Aerodrome*, then under construction, and had become convinced Ader's undoubtedly excellent lightweight steam engine technology could help him. Ader and Langley talked at length, and Ader graciously ran up the *Avion III*'s engines, as Langley walked all about, even foolishly approaching the front of the spinning propellers. Ader confided to Langley that he had spent more than 1,250,000 francs (then approximately $250,000 equivalent, a century later, to approximately $5 million) of his own and government money, that the French government had withdrawn all support after "the failure of No. 3 to fly in a trial last year." So well did the two men get along that Langley returned for another visit at the end of August. As much as he liked Ader personally, Langley had a totally different professional view of the *Avion III*. Although he found it "an ingenious and exquisite imitation of the bat on enormous scale," the Smithsonian Secretary was unimpressed with Ader's airplane, observing, "The 'Avion' is the work . . . of a naturalist with a hobby and unlimited means to gratify it . . . The 'Avion' is simply a gigantic bat, plus steam engine and propellers . . . It seemed to me that the 'Avion,' as constructed, had no chance of moving in the air for a single minute without disaster."[48]

So Langley returned to America and his own appointment with a cruel destiny. As for Ader, he turned from aviation back to telephones, and also to automobiles, founding Automobiles et Moteurs Ader; not a great success, his cars were good and serviceable. In 1902 Ader offered his surviving artifacts to Paris's *Conservatoire des Arts et Métiers* (now the *Musée National des Techniques, Conservatoire National des Arts et Métiers*), and the museum's curators took the *Avion III* and the engine of the abortive *Avion II* into their collections. (Both are prominently displayed, far better displayed, in fact, that the Musée's most significant—and arguably Europe's most historic—aircraft, Louis Blériot's channel-crossing monoplane of 1909.)[49] Then Ader destroyed much of his remaining papers and the remaining artifacts and vacated his workshop on the Rue Jasmin. But that did not mark the end of the Ader matter. Like a resting volcano, it lay dormant even as pressures grew beneath the surface: the growing reputation of the Wrights, the first tentative hops of Alberto Santos-Dumont in his awkward *14-bis* box-kite biplane, criticism from Ader's fellow countrymen. The eruption would come a decade after the Satory debacle, generating tremendous confusion over Ader's real role in aviation's early development, confusion that exists to the present day.

The Tragedy of Early French Aviation

What can one say of French aeronautics prior to the turn of the century? The answer, sadly, must be that rarely in the history of technology has greater opportunity or technical acumen been squandered so wantonly. French researchers had every opportunity to ensure that their country would be first to fly a successful airplane: the legacy of having been first in the balloon and airship field, a coterie of gifted and hardworking individuals; insightful experiments, a supportive national climate, pioneering work on internal combustion engines, a government willing to fund experimentation, a strong aeronautical infrastructure character- ized by vibrant societies, discussion, and even a national laboratory (at Chalais-Meudon); and a strong cultural and historical tradition of doing science and engineering well. They were well aware of foreign work and followed it closely.[50]

Also, of course, were the two strong chances; first, the brilliance of Pénaud and Gauchot, and second, the energetic Ader. But all this was for naught. Small-minded critics demoralized and depressed the ailing Pénaud to the point of sui- cide, and Ader's blindness to all but his own approach accomplished the rest. Devastating in their combined impact, these two factors held the key to France's failure to emulate the success of the Montgolfiers and Charles a century before. At least, unlike de Lesseps's (*père et fils*) ill-fated efforts to emulate the family suc- cess with Suez and span Panama with a canal, no one had died, save for the tragic Pénaud.

Of the two, the wasted years of Ader's experimentation are the more frustrat- ing, for with his energy and resources, he could very likely have achieved a suc- cessful first flight if he had taken a proper approach. So much wasted to such little effect! Though he deserves great credit for having developed the first significant powered airplane, for his profound insights into the future uses of aircraft in war (which anticipated those of the great theorists of air warfare and thus are by far his greatest contributions to both aeronautical and military history), for his per- sonal courage, and for his great enthusiasm, any further assessment of his efforts finds him wanting. He wasted tremendous amounts of money, and in the end never flew: the *Éole* hopped, the *Avion III* careened and crashed. Even if one could accept the claims of those who argue that the *Avion III* got airborne on that dismal mid-October evening in 1897, they would only be crediting Ader with duplicating his *Éole* experience: an uncontrolled, pell-mell skipping across the ground that was neither sustained nor controlled, and certainly not a flight.

Indeed, by any reasonable measure, neither the *Éole* nor the *Avion III could* have flown, as even Langley, for all his technical naïveté, summarized in his notes after having called on Ader and seen his contraption. In 1911, while in France, Wilbur Wright visited the *Conservatoire des Arts et Métiers*, privately confiding to his brother Orville, "I went down to see the Ader machine and got a ladder and examined it in detail. There was no adjustment in flight in this machine except to throw the wings forward and backward by means of a nut working on a screw, about 20 or 30 turns of which would be required to make any serious change in the position of the wings. The wings are not fitted with enough ribs to give them any shape or supporting power. The whole machine is most ridiculous."[51]

In short, Ader was lucky to survive his own experiments. He failed because he simply did not understand some very basic issues: the importance of clean aero- dynamic design, having a logical structural layout, and most seriously, the importance of control. He had the failure of Samuel Langley about him, but to an even more limiting and destructive degree: exquisite engineering and workmanship (particularly in propulsion) in service of terribly flawed basic ideas. Both men emphasized power and lift over the importance of control and first rooting one's work in glider research (which characterized such pioneers as Lilienthal and the Wrights). But Ader, recalling the Middle Ages, recast nature in wood and metal, exemplified by his propeller and wing design. The *Éole* and *Avion III* had propellers painstakingly fabricated from individual pieces of bamboo, cork, and paper cut, bent, shaped, and then attached to a spar so that each blade resembled a huge feather and quill—a concept so weird, so obsessive in its copying of the bird, as to be grotesque, as any visitor to the *Conservatoire des Arts et Métiers* can attest. The wing copied the radiating bone pattern of a bat's wing, with (as Wilbur Wright noted) insufficient ribbing to maintain the airfoil shape necessary to ensure uniform lifting characteristics across the span of the wing. Wright elaborated on his criticism of the Ader approach, noting that he had "attempted to solve the problem of human flight by a slavish imitation of nature, and had met with disastrous failure."[52]

Finally, Ader did not pay sufficient consideration to what others had accomplished before him, whether his fellow countrymen (du Temple, Pénaud, Renard, Gauchot, Tatin, and Goupil), British (Cayley, Henson, and Stringfellow, Wenham, and Phillips), German (Lilienthal), or American (Langley). If Pénaud's weakness was his sensitivity and insecurity in the face of criticism, Ader's was the utter opposite: such total confidence in his own vision as to limit his receptivity to the ideas and influences of others. He neglected to build on the work of Pénaud and Gauchot, and this was his worst error. More than any other factor, this cost France over a decade of work and, ultimately, any chance to be first in the air. Wilbur Wright recognized this when he wrote, shortly before his own death, that Ader "deserved great credit for the persistence and energy with which he carried on experiments for a great number of years, but unfortunately he did not succeed himself in solving the problem nor in making his labors useful to others. Consequently his work contributed nothing to the final success."[53]

In sum, the prize for constructing the first successful airplane was in a very real sense France's to lose—and lost it was. Though Britain put the world on the path to practical aeronautics, the tremendously energetic experimentation and thought in France created a logical expectation that France would duplicate its earlier success in ballooning and airships with success in heavier-than-air airplanes a century later. Pénaud's death removed the greatest and most perceptive of French researchers. Even so, France still had every chance to be first, for Ader possessed tremendous energy and the personal resources and influence to secure official support for his designs. But the bankruptcy of his vision cost the time and effort needed to secure the prize of winged, powered flight, ultimately dooming France to follow, not lead, the heavier-than-air revolution. The next phase in the invention of the airplane would belong to others.

CHAPTER EIGHT

The Anglo-American School
of Power and Lift

In the early hours of September 2, 1898, a British, Egyptian, and Sudanese army under the command of General Sir Herbert Kitchener anxiously awaited battle on the outskirts of Khartoum, scene of a bloody siege 13 years previously during which General Charles "Chinese" Gordon had died fighting, overwhelmed by the Mahdi's dervishes. Gordon's death in that teeming Nile river city had transformed him into the greatest hero-martyr of the Victorian age, an exemplar of the nobility and sacrifice expected of Britain's martial sons.[1] Now the Queen's forces had returned to the Sudan, implacably bent on avenging his death, destroying his enemies, and offsetting a rising French and Russian influence in Africa that bid to destabilize the region and perhaps even sever Egypt's vital lifeline if ambitious French plans for a Nile dam ever came to fruition.

Between Kitchener's 20,000 men and Khartoum stood over 60,000 devout *ansars*, followers of the Khalifa Abdullah bin Muhammed, on camel and horseback and foot, armed with rifles, muskets, spears, and swords. The day before, advancing over the hot desert bordering the Nile, Kitchener's scouts had noted horsemen in a distance and, further yet, a vague mass covering miles of hillside that they at first took for scrub brush. But then, as young subaltern Winston S. Churchill later reported, "The whole side of the hill seemed to move. Between the masses horsemen galloped continually; before them many patrols dotted the plain; above them waved hundreds of banners, and the sun, glinting on many thousand hostile spear-points, spread a sparkling cloud."[2]

Kitchener's men had found the Khalifa's army. The British Tommy had experienced the fury of these dervish warriors before. Though the average infantryman called them "fuzzy wuzzies" on account of their bushy hair, he said it with a soldier's respect rather than a civilian's derision, for he knew well the *ansars* would fight unto death. At the battle of Abu Tulayh, before Khartoum fell, they had even achieved the seemingly impossible—breaking a British square, the same hardened, four-sided formation of disciplined rifle-and-bayonet-toting infantry that had withstood the strongest attacks Napoléon's crack cavalry and Imperial Guard could dish out at Waterloo. No less than poet Rudyard Kipling, the Homer of the British Empire, immortalized the dervish warriors' accomplishment in verse.[3]

Now, after a night of preparation and taking position before the army of the Khalifa threw itself with reckless abandon on the British force, Kitchener and his commanders could see the serried rows of *ansar* infantry and cavalry stretching for five miles across the plain of Omdurman. The first mass attacks came shortly after dawn, and thereafter for hours the Khalifa's warriors charged ceaselessly in waves of soldiers and cavalry. Armed with rifles, spears, and swords, they had the advantage of numbers if not technology, and they hoped to sweep over the much smaller if better-equipped British, as King Cetewayo's Zulu warriors had over Lord Chelmsford's Twenty-fourth Foot at Isandhlwana not quite a generation before.[4] But over the crash and crack of Kitchener's vastly outnumbered rifles and artillery, over the war cries and ululations of the Khalifa's warriors, came another sound, an urgent and persistent *tack-tack-tack!*—the sound of rapid-fire Maxim machine guns. Artillery took a toll of the *ansars* at a distance, rifles at medium ranges, but at closer ranges, as Churchill recalled, "the Maxim guns pulsated feverishly."[5] They worked a terrible execution, dropping attackers in piles upon the hot desert plain. The battle would end with 11,000 *ansar* dead and another 16,000 wounded, while Kitchener's force lost but 48 killed in turn, one of the most lopsided military victories in all history. Khartoum fell the next day, and shortly, thanks to the poet-historian Hilaire Belloc, English schoolchildren would learn another bit of doggerel: "Whatever happens, we have got / The Maxim Gun, and they have not."[6] The Maxim gun ushered in the age of firepower-dominant, technology-driven war. The carnage it wrought in colonial conflicts only hinted of the even more terrible carnage it would wreak in the Russo-Japanese war a few years later and, more frightful still, on the Western Front less than two decades in the future.[7]

The man who made this weapon was an émigré American inventor living in England, Hiram Stevens Maxim, born in Maine in 1840, the inventive and inquisitive son of an inventive father.[8] Imposingly bearded, intelligent, shrewd, energetic, strong-willed, and with an enormous talent (and appetite) for self-promotion, Maxim had grown up in New England, learning his mechanical skills both from his father and through an apprenticeship to a carriage maker. Maxim had a complex relationship with his assertive and equally inventive brother Hudson. But these weren't the mutually supportive Wright brothers. Over time, sadly, both men grew apart, then estranged (as each saw himself a rival to the other), and finally tied only by blood and bitter enmity, leading to a total rupture in relations and the making of much misery for both. Tall and powerfully built, Maxim had the physique of a boxer—which he was—and an aggressive temperament to match. But it was seasoned with compassion and a sense of justice: as a young man, he once posed as a crippled derelict to lure three toughs who preyed on the elderly into a confrontation, then beat all of them senseless. He had wide-ranging interests and made a number of inventions—literally including the proverbial "better mousetrap"—before joining the electrical industry and discovering a new method of evenly coating a bulb filament with carbon.

Always interested in guns, he came up with the idea of a rapid-fire weapon using belted ammunition that would utilize the force of recoil to automatically load a cartridge, fire the bullet, and then eject the spent cartridge casing.[9] Surprisingly, his ideas received a cool reception from the American military, wedded to the older and more established hand-cranked rotating Gatling gun. But the British War Office expressed strong interest, and so he moved to England in the early 1880s, establishing the Maxim Gun Company, Ltd., and developing the Maxim gun, which made his name a virtual household word by 1884. Maxim and his style fit in well with the social culture of Victorian England, and he found the island nation so agreeable that he eventually took out British citizenship in 1900, receiving in turn a knighthood from Queen Victoria the following year for his services to the empire. But Sir Hiram Maxim was more than an expatriate American munitions czar who made good. First among all his interests, he had a fascination with flight, putting a great amount of his personal wealth and energy into aviation research in the late 1880s and 1890s.

Maxim: The Businessman as Airplane Inventor

Some indication of both Maxim's ego, personality, and perception of flight can be found in a letter he wrote to the editor of the *New York Times* in November 1890: "I would say that among the large number of societies to which I belong in England, the Aeronautical Society is one, and need I say that I am the most active member? At the present moment experiments are being conducted by me . . . with a view of finding out exactly what the supporting power of a plane [i.e., a wing] is when driven through the air at a slight angle from the horizontal. For this purpose I have constructed a very elaborate apparatus, provided with a great number of instruments . . . I have been experimenting with motors and have succeeded in making them so that they will develop 1 horsepower for every 6 lbs . . . I think I can assert that within a very few years some one . . . will have made a machine which can be guided through the air, will travel with considerable velocity, and will be sufficiently under control to be used for military purposes. . . . As I am the only man who has ever tried the experiments in a thorough manner with delicate and accurate apparatus, the data which I shall be able to furnish will be of much greater value to experimenters hereafter than all that has ever been published before."[10]

Indeed, both his hopes and enthusiasm were sincere. When Maxim was a youth of 16, his own father had proposed constructing a machine "of the *Hélicoptère* type, having two screws both on the same axis," triggering his son's first interest in flight.[11] Maxim himself captivated the Aeronautical Society with the grandiosity of his experiments, and he did approach the study of flight in a careful, methodical, and scientific way. In 1887 "several wealthy gentlemen" asked him if a flying machine could be built. Maxim confidently replied that "it would require my undivided attention for five years and might cost £100,000"[12] (an

Hiram Maxim poses with one of his light-weight steam engines in the early 1890s. Jarrett Collection (JC)

amount then approximately equal to $500,000, equivalent to $10 million a century later. Years later he rightly concluded, "I was altogether too ambitious").[13] He rented Baldwyns Park in Kent, where, assisted by "two very skillful American mechanics," he built a test site including both a large hangar and a huge whirling arm to test wing shapes up to 80 miles per hour around a circle measuring 1,000 feet in circumference. From the outset Maxim thought big, seeing in size an ability to better give an airplane inherent stability. He designed a huge 8,000-pound biplane test rig, having no less than 4,000 square feet of wing area, to run along an 1,800-foot railway track. He had no intention of flying this craft, which was not in any sense a true airplane: while it ran on conventional railroad track, an outer series of raised rails prevented it from rising more than two feet into the air. Maxim's rig, then, really approximated a laboratory tool more closely than an airplane, for its entire purpose was measurement of lift and propeller thrust, not the achievement of flight itself.[14]

Maxim's attention to engineering detail and rigorous measurement resulted in his rig having a number of notable features. Unlike other pioneers he preferred steel-tube construction to wood or aluminum, and he carefully designed two high-performance 180-horsepower steam engines, each turning a huge pusher propeller spanning 17 feet in diameter. He undertook exhaustive trials of his own and other designs to find the best shape for his propellers, and as a result, unlike the vast majority of early aero propellers, they had relatively high efficiency, though not so good as the Wrights' work later. Though Maxim clearly empha-

Maxim's test rig on its running track at Baldwyns Park, Kent, England, before its famous July 1894 test run, when it briefly became airborne. JC

sized lift and propulsion above all else, he was not as blind to the importance of control as some have alleged. The rig had a workable control system consisting of both front and rear elevators (though no rudder, as he believed one could use differential engine power to go left or right) and dihedral on the outer wing panels to impart inherent stability. He even planned a self-correcting "gyrostat," a gyroscopic wheel connected to the two elevators, a primitive form of stability-augmentation system and, indeed, a forerunner of the autopilot.[15]

Because of Maxim's prominence, his experiments gained a tremendous amount of attention. Baldwyns Park became a popular spot for visits, particularly by journalists, members of the engineering community such as the Aeronautical Society, and scientists including Lords Rayleigh and Kelvin. Lucky visitors would have an opportunity to see Maxim, long white beard flowing in the breeze, undertaking a trial run. Accompanied by a two-man test crew, he would increase power to a predetermined level of propeller thrust, release restraining ropes, and then ride the rig as it accelerated down the track, propellers thrumming, all to the background of the hissing and gurgling steam engines. As it neared the end of the track, a network of ropes and windlasses would bring it to a stop. Sometimes important visitors rode along themselves: on one test Maxim transported the Prince of Wales, the future King George V, escorted by Admiral of the Fleet Sir Edmund Commerell. While the admiral urged caution, the young Prince George countered with "Let her go for all she's worth!"[16] And Maxim did, giving the future monarch an exciting (if firmly grounded) ride; undoubtedly this exhilarating experience had a positive influence on the Prince, for as king he consistently supported aeronautical causes.

Maxim's most memorable test run came on July 31, 1894. That day he ran the boilers up to maximum pressure, and under a full head of steam, the rig accelerated so rapidly down the track that it threw its crew off balance. After a run of approximately 600 feet, at a little over 40 miles per hour, the rig rose completely off the support rails, buckling some of the structure supporting its outrigger wheels against the restraining guardrails and fracturing the guardrails themselves. "I found myself floating in the air," Maxim recalled, "with the feeling of being in a boat."[17] Maxim was well on his way to flying freely. Then some wreckage fouled one of the propellers even as Maxim, afraid of making an uncontrolled ascent, abruptly cut power; the test rig descended gently to a halt, damaged but intact.

Maxim and the rig never flew again; even by his standards, the costs of experimentation had been high. He had put £20,000 (equivalent to approximately $2 million in 2001) of his own money into the rig and associated research, but he could not secure further funds from others. Then came a series of blows. First the owners of Baldwyns Park sold the land to the London county council for development as a mental institution, forcing him to vacate. For a while Maxim attempted to continue his work, moving his hangar from the park to a company firing range near Eynsford. He persuaded Percy Pilcher, a brilliant young aviation researcher of immense talent, to leave a secure position at Glasgow University and become

Putting on the Ritz: Maxim (lounging lion like, center) hosting visiting scientists and engineers at Baldwyns Park, where they had the opportunity to examine his test rig; note the size of the propeller and the gargantuan dimensions of the entire machine. SSPL

his assistant. In 1896 he built the largest wind tunnel in the world (it would remain so until 1910), 12 feet long with a 3-foot-by-3-foot cross section, powered by a 100 horsepower steam engine producing a 50-mile per hour airflow. Perceptively, he used a grid of vertical, horizontal, and diagonal slats to straighten the airflow before it reached the test section (beyond the exhaust end of the tunnel), anticipating later practice. The next year he submitted a patent application for a twin-rotor helicopter (to be powered by a four-cylinder engine burning acetylene gas), an indication that his interests in aviation remained broad and diverse.[18]

But that same year, now at age 57, he sustained a second blow. For over a decade, Maxim's gun company had suffered financial woes, not least because of Maxim's distracted leadership, both from his interest in aviation and also from an increasingly acrimonious relationship with his brother (and former partner) Hudson. Indeed, the next year Hudson, apparently possessed of jealousy, envy, and a belief that Hiram Maxim had capitalized on his own work without giving due credit, instigated charges of bigamy against his brother that went to trial in the United States. In the highly charged Victorian era, the lurid charges generated tremendous publicity on both sides of the Atlantic, but the court, after examining them, concluded they were utterly groundless. This constituted the final rupture between the two men, and they never had any subsequent contact. Also, it fractured the larger Maxim clan and furnished a distraction to him from his work and other activities. So Vickers took over Maxim's gun company, keeping the Maxim name on the company masthead but little else. The new management, evidently looking askance at his fixation with flying, asked Maxim to remove his hangar from the firing range. Pilcher and Maxim amicably went separate ways, the former to a tragic death in 1899 eerily echoing that of his mentor, the German glider pioneer Otto Lilienthal, and the latter retiring from aviation for the next 13 years.[19]

Like Ader and, indeed, many older men, Maxim in his later years sought to claim credit and influence far beyond what he actually deserved, and this annoying self-congratulatory quality, as with Ader, has perhaps understandably caused the majority of aviation historians to minimize his work, occasionally in very harsh terms.[20] And in truth his contemporaries did not look to Maxim as an exemplar of how to conduct aeronautical research. But neither is it correct to see him as merely a rich, self-indulgent, and self-important dilettante, for aspects of his work were copied, his activities received considerable foreign attention, and his propeller research proved of value to other researchers.[21] In 1911 Wilbur Wright considered him one of "six very remarkable men who in the last decade of the nineteenth century raised studies relating to flying to a point never before attained. Lilienthal, Chanute, Langley, Maxim, Ader, and Hargrave formed by far the strongest group of workers in the field that the world has seen."[22]

Among his positive qualities, Maxim staunchly advocated refined propeller design based on careful measurement of performance at a time when others—including the great Otto Lilienthal—still retained faith in odd combinations of featherlike flapper vanes or viewed the propeller as little more than two flat paddles set at differing angles. Neither did Maxwell fail to appreciate the attractiveness of the internal combustion engine and the necessity of adequate control.

Trapped by circumstances (as was Ader) to live with a highly refined steam propulsion system (as internal combustion technology was not yet so advanced as to be able to solve his propulsion challenges), Maxim went on (like Ader) to develop a truly ingenious and powerful lightweight steam engine, but one altogether far more powerful than any attempted elsewhere, Ader's included. Unlike Langley later, he appreciated the importance of a rugged and well-thought-out structure; unlike Ader he recognized the complexity of control, if not fully appreciating its application to an airplane, particularly the necessity of blending wing roll and rudder action to make a turn. But if his ideas on control were immature, they were nevertheless extensive, anticipating the development of the autopilot and feedback-controlled stability augmentation systems such as are now commonplace. His work, in short, constituted completely respectable research at a time when many, many others had not the slightest idea of how to proceed towards the goal of a successful airplane.

Maxim possessed other significant qualities as well. He had a genuine appreciation for the aeronautical environment, particularly the aerodynamics of soaring flight, and the value of flying at high altitudes to gain range and speed. In 1908 his impromptu testimony on the future of high-altitude flight before a subcommittee of Britain's Committee of Imperial Defence revealed a "profound and remarkably clear thinker" whose words "would not bring discredit to a leading aerodynamicist even today," in the 1974-era words of the distinguished British engineer and Royal Aircraft Establishment administrator Percy B. Walker.[23] He never failed to excite his audiences, and if controversial, he nevertheless gave aviation a great stamp of respectability, the stamp of a recognized authority of national stature, an individual of real and significant technical accomplishment. Thus one can presume that had he been in a position to continue his testing, he might well have come around to a more practical, less gargantuan, approach to "manflight," and that a successful aircraft might have resulted from his efforts, possibly along the lines of the Voisin or Farman machines that appeared in France in the 1907–1909 time period. In that respect one must feel sympathy for this man whose work was terminated so prematurely by circumstances largely beyond his control. He was, as others have noted, virtually compulsively inventive, and one indication of how many interests he had can be seen from the amount of space he himself devoted to aeronautics in his autobiography, entitled simply *My Life*. Aeronautics occupied just three pages out of the book's total of 322, constituting a mere 1 *percent* of the entire work. He died in 1916, remembered not so much for his aviation interests as for his deadly machine gun, buried even as the descendants of that weapon grimly added to the daily slaughter of the Great War.[24]

Langley: *The Scientist as Airplane Inventor*

On Tuesday, December 8, 1903, shortly after 4:30 P.M., a group of men conferred uneasily aboard a houseboat moored in the Potomac River off Arsenal Point, the southern shore of the city of Washington, formed by the confluence of the

Potomac and Anacostia rivers.[25] A strange and unfamiliar framework of wood and rail perched on the houseboat. But resting on top of it sat an even stranger contraption, a machine unlike any seen in previous human history, resembling nothing so much as a large kite with two broad and upswept wings, one set behind the other. The equal-span wings sprouted from a long body containing a radical new 50-horsepower gasoline engine connected by gears and shafts to two huge pusher propellers mounted on the trailing edge of its front wings. The machine's operator sat nervously in a small enclosure shaped like a boat located under the front wing. This was the Langley Aerodrome A, better known to those present as the *Great Aerodrome,* developed by none other than the distinguished Secretary of the Smithsonian Institution, Dr. Samuel Pierpont Langley. A world-famous (and largely self-taught) astronomer already rich in honorary degrees and other distinctions, the near-septuagenarian Langley and his "assistant in charge of experiments," Charles Manly, a bespectacled Cornell-educated engineer, were about to perform on history's stage.[26] And what a stage: to the north, in the not-too-far distance, stood the slim shaft of the Washington Monument; further east the pale dome of the Capitol. The dark maroon plinth and striking architecture of the Smithsonian Institution's gothic castle poked skyward from mid-Mall, as the equally distinctive weather vane on its turreted tower turned abruptly and uneasily, pointing around the horizon. Closer still sat the brooding shape of the Army's Engineer School on the dreary point itself: once the district penitentiary and the site of the trial and execution of the Lincoln assassins, reputedly haunted by the ghost of Mary Surratt, unjustly convicted of the crime. It was a scene at once fraught with expectation and the natural drama that attends great events.

Certainly the development history of the *Great Aerodrome* was anything but a whim of happenstance. It sprang from two impulses, the "technological push" of Samuel Langley, and the "requirements pull" of President William McKinley and a host of other senior military and governmental officials. Langley had become addicted to solving the problem of flight after attending a lecture on aeronautics in 1886.[27] The next year he became the third Secretary of the Smithsonian upon the death of Spencer Baird. Following extensive research using specialized whirling-table and whirling-arm test rigs and over 30 rubber band–powered models, he built a series of larger and generally successful steam-powered models, launched from a small houseboat conveniently moored midchannel in the lower Potomac, 33 miles downriver from Washington, near Widewater, Virginia, south of Quantico and Chopawamsic Creek. These models he dubbed *Aerodromes,* after the Greek *aerodromoi,* in the mistaken thought that his fractured Greek meant "air runners." In fact he had created a word that could only mean a place where aircraft could operate, i.e., an airfield—the first, unfortunately, of his many misapprehensions about flight.

As Wilbur Wright noted in a 1910 letter to Charles D. Walcott, who had succeeded Langley as Secretary of the Smithsonian after Langley's death, "Langley was ill-fated in that he had been especially criticized by his enemies for things which were deserving of highest praise, and especially praised by his friends for things which were unfortunate lapses from scientific accuracy."[28] Nowhere was this truer than with regard to the so-called Langley's law. As a result of his research using test rigs, Langley believed he had proven that "mechanical flight" was an immediate possibility. One reason, he concluded, was because of a general law he thought he had discovered: the faster an airplane could fly, the less power would be required to sustain it in flight. This counterintuitive principle, called "Langley's law" by aeronautical publicist James Means, sprang from the incomplete and misleading tests Langley made using his whirling-table and whirling-arm test apparatus.[29]

Langley conducted all of his experiments at velocities less than 45 miles per hour, quickly discovering a "paradoxical" result: the drag of his design actually declined as speed increased. The implication seemed clear: an airplane would need less, not more, power the faster it flew. In fact, though counterintuitive, the test data was accurate enough, as far as it went. Below about 50 miles per hour, the "drag due to lift," the drag induced by the lifting action of the wing, steadily declined. But had he continued his tests beyond this point, he would have quickly found a steadily increasing rise in "parasite" drag, the drag induced by the resistance of the air to the wing passing through it as velocity increases. At the velocities at which Langley tested his wing shapes, parasite drag was far less significant than drag due to lift, and as a result, he reached the wrong conclusion. Beyond 50 miles per hour he would have immediately recognized the fallacy of his thought, as parasite drag quickly predominated. Langley, in short, had not conducted his experiments over a sufficiently broad speed range, and as a result his limited data led him to a fundamentally erroneous conclusion. It is a tale offering a cautionary warning to researchers across many fields to the present day—and for the future as well.[30]

Nor was Wright the only one to catch Langley in an error. On an 1894 trip to Oxford, thanks to an invitation from Hiram Maxim, Langley presented some of his research results at a meeting of the British Association for the Advancement of Science. But the session proved a mixed blessing, for while it gave Langley the chance to showcase his work, it also presented Lord Kelvin, Britain's most distinguished scientist and a critic of heavier-than-air flying machine research, with a perfect opportunity to point out some computational errors in Langley's mathematics. Lord Rayleigh, cautiously optimistic about flight (he was one of the first to work in the field of fluid dynamics and would be named chairman of Britain's Advisory Committee for Aeronautics, created in 1909), muted further criticism, coming to Langley's defense and suggesting that Langley's flying experiments would furnish the real test of his ideas.[31]

Not surprisingly, then, the prospect of Langley's Widewater flight trials attracted a great deal of attention. As they approached, the Secretary had his own doubts, noting that "the disappointments experienced in the preceding years prevented any great feeling of confidence that the trials which were now to be made would be entirely successful."[32] In the early afternoon of May 6, 1896, Langley launched one small Aerodrome, the *No. 6*, which—in a strange augury of yet another day seven years and five months in the future—snagged the launching mechanism and promptly crashed. Undaunted but undoubtedly unnerved, Langley prepared another aircraft for flight. Launched at 3:05 P.M., *Aerodrome No. 5*, an ambitious model spanning over 13 feet, with the same length, and powered by a one horsepower steam engine having a single cylinder and a boiler heated by a gasoline burner, performed beautifully.[33]

As Langley wrote subsequently, "Immediately after leaving the launching track, the aerodrome slowly descended three or four feet, but immediately began to rise, its midrod [nose boom] pointing upward at an increasing angle until it made about ten degrees with the horizon and then remained remarkably constant at this angle through the flight. Shortly after leaving the launching track the aerodrome began to circle to the right and moved around with great steadiness, traversing a spiral path. . . . The aerodrome made two complete turns and started on the third one. During the first two turns the machine was constantly and steadily ascending, and at the end of the second turn it had reached a height variously estimated by the different observers at from 70 to 100 feet. When at this height, and after the lapses of one minute and twenty seconds, the propellers were seen to be moving perceptibly slower and the machine began to descend slowly, at the same time moving forward and changing the angle of inclination of the midrod until the bow pointed slightly downward. It finally touched the water to the south of

Langley's steam-powered *Aerodrome No. 5* is catapulted from its houseboat at Widewater, Virginia, 3:05 P.M., on May 6, 1896, beginning one of the most significant model flights ever made. AFMA

the houseboat, . . . the time the machine was in the air having been one minute and thirty seconds from the moment of launching. The distance actually traversed, as estimated by plotting its curved path on the coast survey chart and then measuring this path, was approximately 3300 feet."[34]

The flights constituted the most impressive in aviation up to that point and were witnessed by telephone pioneer Alexander Graham Bell. A Langley friend and an aviation enthusiast, experimenter, and financial supporter of the Smithsonian secretary's work, Bell noted the "remarkable steadiness" of the flights and how "softly and gently" the little Aerodrome returned to land once its engine had run out of steam.[35] This, historian J. H. Parkin concluded, "convinced Bell that the age of the flying machine was at hand and encouraged and stimulated him to continue his experiments in his laboratory at *Beinn Bhreagh* [Nova Scotia] in the hope of contributing to its attainment."[36]

But more than this, it likewise saved Langley's reputation and kept his hopes alive, for had he not succeeded this day, his work might have ended then and there. Another flight on November 28 proved equally successful, the little Aerodrome flying almost a mile. And yet . . . and yet. One can suggest that had Langley ended his work after this success he undoubtedly would have faced a far kinder fate than what lay in store, even if he would have been criticized for not pressing onwards. As Octave Chanute mournfully remarked at a memorial service after Langley's death in 1906, "It would have been far better for Mr. Langley's happiness and reputation if he had terminated his experiments with the demonstration, in 1896, that artificial flight was possible."[37] But even if he had wished to quit, events far beyond Washington were occurring that would impel him towards a cold date with destiny in December 1903.

Langley and the Military

The interest of the burgeoning military community on the eve of the Spanish-American War furnished a most important impulse behind the *Great Aerodrome*, for without that interest Langley might never have received the funding necessary to build the large craft at all. A member of Washington's prestigious Cosmos Club, Langley moved in influential circles, routinely meeting and socializing with senior government members of various agencies and the military, some of whom followed his work. His closest friend was Dr. Charles Walcott, then the director of the U.S. Geological Survey and himself a future Secretary of the Smithsonian; another was Bell; and Langley also knew the energetic young Assistant Secretary of the Navy, Theodore Roosevelt, whose acid-tongued daughter Alice referred to the bearded professor as "Mr. Laggle."[38]

At this point, having flown a succession of small steam-powered Aerodromes, he needed at least $50,000 to pursue a full-size man-carrying machine, no small sum in 1898 (for it is equivalent to approximately $1,000,000 today, in 2001). Then came a strange turn in his fortunes. In the late 1890s, a growing crisis had erupted between the Spanish government and the citizens of its Cuban colony, marked by guerrilla attacks, counterattacks, repression, and much controversy. In January 1898, as world attention focused increasingly on Cuba and the rapidly deteriorating state of American-Spanish relations, the Navy sent the nine-year-old ironclad battleship USS *Maine* to Havana harbor to protect American interests. One month later, on the night of February 15, while anchored quietly in harbor, it mysteriously exploded. Amid American suspicious that the Spanish had destroyed it with a mine, a growing chorus of private and public voices called for war with Spain.[39]

On March 21, 1898, with war fever in the air, Charles Walcott met with his old friend Langley, telling him that President McKinley should be made aware of the state of the scientist's work and that a professional board should be established to review it. Though he had some reservations, Langley assented. Thereafter things moved very rapidly—so rapidly as to constitute, by the standards of the present day, an extraordinary comment on the pace and efficiency of government decision making at that time: a time bereft of electronic mail, multiple intervening levels of highly structured Department of Defense, Joint Staff, and Executive Branch bureaucracies, expansive service acquisition directorates, overly protective staffs clustered around key decisionmakers whose calendars are established weeks in advance, and huge Congressional staffs claiming "oversight." Walcott contacted the White House. The President requested photographs of the smaller Aerodromes in flight, subsequently met with Walcott, and then recommended that Walcott contact the Secretary of War, George Mickeljohn. Walcott did so, and the Secretary agreed to form a review panel in conjunction with the Navy. On March 25 Walcott met with the exuberant and always confident Theodore Roosevelt, an individual with a long-standing interest in military technology.[40]

Roosevelt, who knew Langley from the Cosmos Club, understood the military implications of an observation platform that could fly rapidly over an enemy and return to base. He immediately wrote to Navy Secretary John Davis Long, "Mr. Walcott, Director of the Geological Survey, has just been in to see me, having seen the President. He has shown me some interesting photographs of Professor Langley's flying machine. The machine has worked. It seems to me worth while for this government to try whether it will not work on a large enough scale to be of use in the event of war. . . . I think this is well worth doing."[41]

Long quickly endorsed the idea of a joint Army-Navy board to begin evaluation of Langley's work. The board, composed of two members from each service plus Walcott and Bell, met over one week and then issued a favorable report on April 29, 1898 (days after the outbreak of the war). With this endorsement Langley had little difficulty securing two grants totaling $50,000 from the War Department's Bureau of Ordnance and Fortification. The *Washington Post* announced the first of the grants on November 11, 1898; this money constituted the first American military research and development funding ever set aside for a heavier-than-air flying machine.

Thus enriched, Langley purchased materials and hired a young Cornell University engineering student, Charles Manly, as his chief assistant. The scientist and

Manly, aided by a small team that eventually grew to ten people, set busily to work, in space located behind the Smithsonian castle, already a cherished Washington landmark less than a half century after its construction. Bits and pieces of the fabric-covered machine came together, magnificently built and worked, and then, at last, came final assembly. In contrast to his smaller models, the full-size machine had an extremely powerful and well-thought-out 52-horsepower gasoline engine from the collaboration of Stephen Balzer and Manly.[42] Langley had worried about how to power the large machine, and in the summer of 1899 had assembled a comprehensive list of question to ask Clément Ader when he visited the Frenchman at his workshop, including whether Ader would be willing to build an engine for him or let him use Ader's designs.[43] But in any case Langley did not have to rely on Ader's work, having instead the talents of Balzer and Manly to draw upon. But this was the sole admirable element of his design.

Manly and Langley stand on the house-boat under the *Great Aerodrome*'s control car in 1903; note the stopwatch on Manly's "flight suit." NASM

Though as a young man he had worked briefly as a civil engineer, Langley was out of his depth dealing with the complex technology of flight. He had missed that one could not simply linearly "scale up" a full-size machine from his smaller models without drastically redesigning its basic structure. Thus no amount of beautiful and costly workmanship could overcome the inherent flaws in the design, chief of which was a weak and understrength structure. It was in fact frail beyond imagining, and a wire plucked or a wing spar jostled would set the entire structure aquiver.[44] Ominously, a quarter-scale, powered model of his full-size Aerodrome proved a disappointment when tested in August 1901, unable to maintain even level flight after launch. Further, he had no concept whatsoever of how important controllability would be once a machine took to the air. Indeed, had the *Great Aerodrome* by some miracle survived its launch, it is doubtful its pilot could have exerted any effective control, for the plane possessed but a single large pivoting tail and a tiny rudder underneath the fuselage. Finally, incredible as it seems, the *Great Aerodrome* lacked any landing gear whatsoever, its creators not thinking beyond simply splashing down in the Potomac at the end of a flight! Since Manly's "cockpit" was little more than an open shell, it is doubtful he could have survived an impact with any sort of velocity without sustaining serious injury.

Langley, Manly, and the rest of the team finished too late in 1902 to fly before winter set in, so the *Great Aerodrome* had to wait months until the warm summer of 1903 before undergoing a series of ground tests and engine runs in preparation for its first flight. During the course of these, a propeller disintegrated, damaging the machine; repairs took weeks, but then, finally, all was ready. On the morning of Wednesday, October 7, 1903, assisted by two tugs, Manly had set forth from the Washington waterfront full of hope and expectation, bound for the lower Potomac. Strangely, Langley remained ashore, claiming pressing business kept him in town.[45] It had taken the Langley team five years of hard effort to reach this point, and Langley's own research with test rigs and flying models went back over a decade further, for a total of 17 years. They had exhausted $73,000 in research monies: $50,000 from the U.S. Army, $10,000 from telephone inventor Alexander Graham Bell and the will of Dr. Jerome Kidder, a prominent physician, and $13,000 from the Smithsonian's own Hodgkins Fund, equivalent to approximately $1,460,000 a century later.

That day Manly, the prospective pilot, ran up the engine, as a crewman on the houseboat fired two signal rockets into the air, announcing the imminent takeoff. Tugboat horns sounded in reply, the houseboat's big spring catapult fired, and the *Great Aerodrome,* with a "roaring, grinding noise," raced down the launching track. Then disaster! A pin in the launching mechanism snagged the front bracing strut, hooking the *Great Aerodrome* as expertly as a fisherman gaffing a flapping flounder; the plane, as a *Washington Post* reporter George Rothwell Brown bluntly wrote, "simply slid into the water like a handful of mortar."[46] Manly, wet but otherwise unhurt, clambered aboard a boat.

Critics had a field day. The *Post's* headline the next morning read,

BUZZARD A WRECK
LANGLEY'S HOPES DASHED

Two days later subscribers to the *New York Times* awoke to read, "The ridiculous fiasco which attended the attempt at aerial navigation in the Langley flying machines [*sic*] was not unexpected. . . . It might be assumed that the flying machine which will really fly might be evolved by the combined and continuous efforts of mathematicians and mechanicians in from one million to ten million years. . . . No doubt the problem has attractions for those it interests, but to the ordinary man it would seem as if effort might be employed more profitably."[47]

Such journalistic judgments meshed nicely with the generally pessimistic views of professional scientists and engineers. In December 1896, after Otto Lilienthal, the most influential and best known of pre-Wright pioneers, died in a gliding accident, Lord Kelvin had stated witheringly, "I have not the smallest molecule of faith in aerial navigation other than ballooning, or of expectation of good results from any of the trials we hear of."[48] Two years later, apparently concerned that Dr. Alexander Graham Bell might irretrievably damage his reputation as a scientist and inventor, Kelvin unsuccessfully urged Bell's wife to persuade her husband to give up his flying experiments, which Kelvin believed "could only lead to disappointment if carried on with any expectation of leading to a useful flying machine."[49] Then, a little less than two years before Langley's very public failure, the chief engineer of the U.S. Navy, Rear Admiral George W. Melville, boldly wrote that any hopes of a successful flying machine were "wholly unwarranted, if not absurd," explaining, "Outside of the proven impossible, there probably can be found no better example of the speculative tendency carrying man to the verge of the chimerical than in his attempts to imitate the birds, or no field where so much inventive seed has been sown with so little return as in the attempts of man to fly successfully through the air."[50]

Now, after Manly's splash, Simon Newcomb, a frequent and well-known critic of flight, rose with pen in hand yet again to defend the scientific status quo. Both Newcomb and Langley were distinguished astronomers, and virtual contemporaries: Newcomb was just a year younger, having been born in 1835 to Langley's 1834. He had directed the Naval Observatory, served as superintendent of the prestigious *Nautical Almanac*, taught mathematics at the Naval Academy, helped create the Lick Observatory, and held a professorship at Johns Hopkins University, establishing a deserved (and indeed exemplary) reputation for extraordinary accomplishment. But here the resemblance ended, for he certainly didn't share the Smithsonian Secretary's faith in flight. Rather, he pompously wrote, "There are many problems which have fascinated mankind ever since civilization began which we have made little or no advance in solving. . . . May not our mechanicians, in like manner, be ultimately forced to admit that aerial flight is one of that great class of problems with which man can never cope, and give up all attempts to grapple with it?"[51]

In retrospect it is curious how vehement Newcomb was in his criticisms of Langley. Did some other motivation drove him, perhaps an envy or jealousy or resentment against the aging scientist? Had he himself hoped, perhaps, to be the Secretary of the Smithsonian, the biggest scientific plum in the United States at the end of the nineteenth century? His virulent and eventually irrational antagonism towards all things aeronautical (particularly after the success of the Wrights and other pioneers) might well have had its roots in some personal problem with Langley and not just the optimistic audacity of the Smithsonian Secretary's research. In any case, amid this rising criticism, the Langley team returned the water-soaked remains of the *Great Aerodrome* to the Smithsonian and set about repairing it. Two months later they tried again, but this time closer to the city, off Arsenal Point.

Tuesday, December 8, 1903, had dawned grey and cold. Weather conditions fluctuated during the day but improved in the early afternoon, and shortly after 2:30 P.M., two tugs pulled the houseboat from its anchorage along the Washington waterfront and began towing it towards Arsenal Point, a journey of at most 20 minutes. No sooner had the houseboat anchored than the weather turned for the worse. Scudding clouds and occasional squalling gulls rode a shifting and bitter wind that whipped the river's surface under an ever-darkening sky. The gusting air, "shifting its direction most abruptly and disconcertingly,"[52] rocked the ungainly and bluff-sided vessel, ruffling the hair of observers, chilling them to the bone, accentuating the bleakness of the ice-filled river, and warning of an even

The *Great Aerodrome* on its launching track, as its houseboat rocks gently in the Potomac River. NASM

colder winter to come. Around the houseboat moved tugboats and other small craft, filled with onlookers, including reporters from the *Washington Post* and Washington's *Evening Star.*

Langley and Manly faced a serious question: with the rapidly changing weather conditions, should they attempt to fly? Already the houseboat rocked uneasily, its anchor chains alternately tautening and creaking, as the uncertain winds pushed it about. The two men hurriedly conferred; any delay now might mean a flight pushed off well into the new year, past winter. Neither wanted a repetition of the delay that afflicted the *Great Aerodrome* the previous year. So both agreed this dwindling day seemed their last, best chance. Determined, Manly mounted the little control car, and at 4:45 P.M., under a darkening sky already so dim as to prevent most photography, tried again. The engine roared, shafts whirred, propellers beat the air, the *Great Aerodrome* quivered expectantly, and then the catapult released. Again it raced down the short 70 foot track. Unimpeded by snagging bits of houseboat, it gained speed, the wings producing more and more lift, until finally the too-frail structure could withstand no more, twisting violently under rapidly fluctuating aeroelastic loads.[53] With a loud crack, the aft wing's spar abruptly failed, and the aft wings folded and buckled upward like a flapping pigeon's. Manly "felt an extreme swaying motion immediately followed by a tremendous jerk which caused the machine to quiver all over."[54] The lift from the remaining front wings pitched the mortally wounded *Great Aerodrome* nose up as its propellers desperately thrashed the air and its pilot vainly deflected the tail to try to restore it to level flight. It paused momentarily, Manly hanging precariously, caught between the deadly props and yet dangling in front of the clattering engine. Then it fell tail first before the horrified yet fascinated eyes of spectators, sinking beneath the ice-filled Potomac waters with a barely heard splash.

"The next few moments," Manly recalled, "were most intense."[55] Again Providence looked out for the airman, for despite a projection that caught his cork-lined canvas jacket, he managed, by "exerting all the strength he could muster," to rip it in two. Then he swam clear of the remaining mess of wires, struts, and cloth-covered wings (any one of which could have snagged and trapped him again like a Chesapeake crab in a pot), coming up under blocks of ice and having to dive again to swim to open water. Assisted by one of the houseboat workers, a Mr. Hewitt, who "heroically plunged in" to help him, Manly clambered aboard the houseboat, where crewmen cut his frozen clothes from his shivering body as others plied the shaking, cursing, disheartened man with whiskey.[56]

As twilight set over the Potomac, it was as well the twilight—indeed the Götterdämmerung—of Langley and his ambitions, and twilight of the American military's first attempt to build a heavier-than-air flying machine. His failures had been profound, his larger machine doomed to meet a watery end before it even flew, but he deserved a far kinder fate. A cold midnight had struck on the Potomac before the houseboat and its tangled cargo of wreckage, tied to the stern of the boat, reached dockside. The next day the wreckage returned to the Smithsonian, though, strangely, history was not yet done with this bizarre-looking vehicle: it would return to the air, in highly modified form, as the prime exhibit in a bitter lawsuit over a decade later.[57]

Aftermath

So ended what had been, to that time, the most ambitious and publicized effort to seek the Holy Grail of powered flight. The critics, already energized by the first Langley failure, now raised their chorus to a louder and more strident pitch. Popular and professional sentiment alike mirrored the acid-penned Ambrose Bierce, who in his epitaph for Langley's efforts sarcastically noted, "I don't know how much larger Professor Langley's machine is than his flying model was—about large enough, I think, to require an atmosphere a little denser than the intelligence of one scientist and not quite so dense as that of two."[58]

After the Arsenal Point fiasco, an understandably chastened Federal government refused to make any further appropriations for the Langley effort, and what little military ardor for heavier-than-air flight as had existed noticeably cooled. The final War Department report on the *Great Aerodrome* dishearteningly concluded: "The claim that an engine-driven man-carrying Aerodrome has been constructed lacks the proof which actual flight alone can give. . . . We are still far from the ultimate goal, and it would seem as if years of constant work and study by experts, together with the expenditure of thousands of dollars, would still be necessary before we can hope to produce an apparatus of practical utility."[59] Predictably, Congressional response was quick and damning, chiding the War Department for supporting the project and ridiculing Langley for his obsession with flight. Congressman Gilbert Hitchcock of Nebraska stated, "The only thing [Langley] ever made fly was Government money."[60] Congressman James Robinson of Indiana railed, "Here is $100,000 of the people's money wasted on this scientific aerial navigation experiment because some man, perchance a professor wandering in his dreams, was able to impress the [military] that his aerial scheme had some utility."[61] It is hardly surprising, then, that as one historian has noted, "the War Department, ever conscious of the need for Congressional appropriations, came to distrust all inventors of heavier-than-air devices."[62] The editors of the journal *Popular Science* took it upon themselves to lecture Langley in a tone worthy of a schoolmaster addressing a particularly stupid child: "The Secretary of the Smithsonian Institution should be the representative of American science and should be extremely careful not to do anything that may lend itself to an interpretation that will bring injury on the scientific work of the Government or of the country [particularly by working] in a field where success is doubtful and where failure is likely to bring discredit, however undeserved, on scientific work."[63]

So popular and professional opinion alike consigned Langley to history's dustbin, and, sadly, the aging Langley did not long outlast the failure, dying in 1906. Certainly many read into the Langley-Manly accident that the entire cause of heavier-than-air flight was fatally flawed, for behind this catastrophic event extended a long trail of unfulfilled dreams and desires, a list of notable failures stretching back over a millennium to the tower jumpers of antiquity. Major figures from the two communities considered most qualified to judge the practicality of flight—the scientific and military communities—had united in pronouncing the cause of heavier-than-air flight an impossibility in terms just short of being overtly contemptuous. Now Langley had seemingly confirmed Kelvin's, Melville's, Newcomb's, and Bierce's damning judgments. In short, those in Europe and America who had applied the latest in advanced nineteenth-century technology to the problem of flight had met with the same equally dismal failure as the most untutored mystics and primitives of antiquity or the Dark Ages, who sought to fly by chance, magic, or faith.

Too few held more charitable views. "By the death of Professor S. P. Langley," Britain's Aeronautical Society noted after his passing in 1906, "aeronautics has not only lost one of its most steadfast workers, but one who, by his elucidation of some of its most difficult problems, did more than any other man has done to show that human flight was no chimera, but a scientific possibility."[64] "Langley was a man who possessed the capabilities to make real accomplishments in flight technology," German army officer and aeronautical commentator Hermann Moedebeck wrote. "Fate ensured that conclusive success eluded him. Though he went without victory he became yet another martyr to our ideal aspirations. His work and his name will never be forgotten by us. Honor his memory!"[65]

But it is a letter Wilbur Wright wrote to Octave Chanute in November 1906, not quite three years after the first successful airplane flight at Kitty Hawk, that best sums up Langley's place in aviation history. "The knowledge," Wright wrote, "that the head of the most prominent scientific institution of America believed in the possibility of human flight was one of the influences that led us to undertake the preliminary investigation that preceded our active work. He recommended to us the books which enabled us to form sane ideas at the outset. It was a helping hand at a critical time and we shall always be grateful. Of his actual work, his successes and his failures, it is perhaps too soon to make an accurate estimate, but entirely aside from this he advanced the art greatly by his missionary work and the inspiration of his example. He possessed mental and moral qualities of the kind that influence history. When scientists in general considered it discreditable to work in the field of aeronautics he possessed both the discernment to discover possibilities there and the moral courage to subject himself to the ridicule of the public and the apologies of his friends. He deserves more credit for this than he has yet received. I think his treatment by the newspapers and many of his professed friends most shameful. His work deserved neither abuse nor apology."[66]

PART FOUR

THE AIRMEN TRIUMPHANT:
LILIENTHAL, CHANUTE, AND
THE WRIGHTS, 1891–1905

CHAPTER NINE

The Lilienthal Legacy

At noon on Sunday, August 9, 1896—a beautiful, high summer day on the Gollenberg, in the Stöllner hills near Rathenow—a stocky, muscular 48-year-old Pomeranian engineer stood upwards in a kitelike glider with a batlike wing, gazing down at the plain below him, grasping firmly onto handholds on wooden support bars running beneath his arms. He gauged the breeze—strong but tolerable—and then began to run, holding the glider slightly nose high and leaping into the air. For about 15 seconds—15 long seconds—he sailed down in a gentle descent, buffeted by occasional sharp gusts and swinging his legs to shift body weight and thereby control the glider's movements. After landing and taking a half hour to lug the glider back to the top of the hill—no easy task, as the hills rose over 250 feet above the surrounding terrain—he attempted another flight. Again he ran lightly down the slope and then into the air. But then, as his timekeeper and other witnesses watched in alarm, a sudden building gust stopped the glider in midair, as its nose rose higher and higher. The athletic pilot swung his body as far forward as he could, but the nose continued to rise nearly vertically and then, as suddenly as it sprang up, the gust stopped. Fully stalled, the glider abruptly rolled right and pitched down, sideslipping into the ground from a height of about 50 feet. "I already knew," remembered mechanic Paul Beylich sadly, "what came next."[1] Under the crumpled glider lay the unfortunate airman, his spine fractured by the fall. Beylich and his comrades rushed the seriously injured pilot to the Bergmann Clinic in Berlin, but to no avail. Semiconscious, he lingered through the night, and died at about 6 A.M. the next morning, after muttering "Opfer müssen gebracht werden" (sacrifices must be made). So passed Otto Lilienthal, the Winged Prussian, the greatest of all pre-Wright airmen and the father of the hang glider.[2]

As the outstanding flying practitioner of the nineteenth century, Otto Lilienthal occupies a unique place in the history of aviation. Fittingly, Lilienthal, who would do so much to revolutionize aviation, was himself born in the revolutionary year of 1848 into a family possessed of a strong revolutionary tradition. When

Europe and Berlin exploded against monarchical rule in 1848, his father Gustav left his pregnant young wife to participate in the *Barrikadenkämpfe,* the street fighting against the monarchist forces. But as across the rest of Europe, the Berlin revolution quickly died (though it inspired Karl Marx to write his *Communist Manifesto*), as the largely idealistic impulses of the barricade fighters collapsed amid an absolutist restoration of monarchy and a turning away from popular sovereignty. Disheartened, Gustav took to drink and gambling and died when Otto was a teenager, leaving the family utterly destitute. Young Lilienthal, one of only three of the family's five children who survived infancy, possessed a strong work ethic, solid (if late-blooming) academic performance, a love of all things mechanical and musical, the physically tough and conditioned physique of a gymnast, and undoubted courage.

There can be no doubt that among his siblings Otto assumed the role of protector and leader: photographs show a energetic, curly-haired child with an uplifted chin and a confident, eager, and indeed, defiant expression, while his brother and sister are more reserved and withdrawn. His mother, a voice teacher, strongly supported his interests and education, and later his pursuit of aviation, and he returned the favor: he loved music, played many instruments, sang with a pleasant tenor voice, and was a member of Berlin's Singakademie. Additionally, he was a fine artist and sculptor, producing sensitive and detailed images of homes, towns, children, and nature. Lilienthal held various apprenticeships and attended several technical schools before graduating in 1870 as a trained mechanical engineer from Berlin's Gewerbe Akademie (today the Technical University of Berlin), having studied machine design and construction from Franz Reuleaux, who served both as teacher and mentor to the young student. Because of his student status, Lilienthal was eligible to serve voluntarily in the military for only one year as opposed to the standard two or three, so when war with France broke out, he volunteered immediately as a lowly *Soldat* in a fusilier regiment of the Prussian Guards, participating in the siege of Paris. He returned to civilian life after the war, working for two large Berlin machine shops. By now he had grown into a strikingly good-looking young man, neatly and fashionably bearded, clear-eyed and with a determined and indeed resolute expression. In 1878, like his father before him, he married a gifted woman musician, Agnes Fischer, and their first child, also named Otto, was born the next year. Then, in 1880, he opened his own shop, "bringing it to a flourishing condition by his energy and inventive powers," and subsequently winning state awards for his design of marine steam signals for nautical applications.[3]

Proving an apple doesn't fall far from the tree, he, like his father, possessed a strong sense of social criticism. He associated with activist Moritz von Egidy and participated in Berlin's often provocative *Volkstheater* movement. Germany already had a strong theatrical tradition dating to Goethe and Schiller when in the late 1870s Otto Brahm arrived in Berlin, the center of liberal and, indeed, radical thought. Inspired by Émile Zola, Brahm introduced "naturalist" theater, which emphasizing maudlin realism, yet was more nuanced than productions from

the class-conscious and more radical
Social Democrats. In the 1890s young
Max Reinhardt joined Brahm in
Berlin; he rejected both naturalist and
Social Democrat theater, emphasizing
cabaret productions offering more
escapist joy and less reinforcing misery. Lilienthal's tastes and work blended the naturalists' high-minded tone,
the Social Democrats' passion, and
Reinhardt's light-entertainment influence. In 1892 he formed a partnership
with theater director Marx Samst and
actor Max Oeser, appearing in a variety of plays and revues in Berlin's
Ostend-Theater. In 1894 he tried
his own hand at writing, scripting
a provocative stage piece entitled

Otto Lilienthal, the
greatest flight
researcher before
the Wrights, pho-
tographed shortly
before his death in
1896. NASM

Gewerbeschwindel (commercial fraud), later performed elsewhere under the no-
less-lurid title *Moderne Raubritter* (modern robber barons). Though Prussia's ruling conservatives generally considered both naturalist and Social Democrat
theater anathema, the play passed the state censor for, as Walter Laqueur has
noted, "Wilhelmian Germany was a permissive country to an almost bewildering
degree [and] censorship was applied only in extreme cases of *lèse-majesté* and
blasphemy."[4] But aviation, not social reform, constituted Lilienthal's true life's
interest.

The Making of an Airman

As children Lilienthal and his younger brother Gustav had experimented with
crude wings attached to their arms, inspired by the flight of storks. Like the
Wrights later, both brothers were content in their own company, though (unlike
the Wrights) they were otherwise quite social, outgoing, and at ease in the presence of strangers. Gustav, satisfied to work in the shadow of his more famous
older brother, recalled they never found another who shared their fanatical interest
in flight, and so they were happy to work alone.[5] In the 1860s to 1880s, both alone
and in concert with Gustav, Otto Lilienthal studied bird flight; built and tested an
experimental tethered ornithopter test rig, the so-called *Schlagflügelapparat;* joined
the *Deutschen Verein zur Förderung der Luftschiffahrt* (the German Society for the
Advancement of Airship Travel) and soon won election to membership on its
Technischen Kommission; experimented with whirling arms; flew paper models;
published a notable treatise (at his own expense) entitled *Der Vogelflug als Grundlage
der Fliegerkunst (Bird Flight as the Basis of the Flying Art)*[6]; and then, in 1891, began an

aggressive program of flight research using piloted gliders of his own design, beginning with a short glide of 25 meters (approximately 80 feet).[7]

To Lilienthal, actually flying was everything. In an article written for James Means's *Aeronautical Annual* and published the same year as his death, he stated: "One can get a proper insight into the practice of flying only by actual flying experiments. . . . It is in the air itself that we have to develop our knowledge. . . . The only way which leads us to a quick development in human flight is a systematic and energetic practice in actual flying experiments."[8] This was the credo, shared with others such as England's Percy Pilcher, France's Ferdinand Ferber, America's Octave Chanute, and the Wright brothers, that separated the genuine *airmen* who emerged at the end of the nineteenth century from their predecessors who thought almost exclusively in terms of lift and power.

Lilienthal's various gliders show both the range and the evolution of his thinking about aircraft design. At first, in 1890, he had consciously copied the shape of the seagull to produce a design echoing Ferdinand d'Esterno, having a broad and elegant wing such as characterized some of the first German sailplanes built after the First World War. Rightly rejecting this concept as impractical (though its overall wing shape offered a good departure point for his thinking), he next turned to smaller and more angular designs, each named after its test location or its purpose (such as flying in gusty weather) or configuration, for example, whether small (*klein*) or large (*gross*), or whether a monoplane (*Eindecker*) or biplane (*Doppeldecker*). (Indeed, he introduced these two words for monoplane and biplane into the German language).[9]

First came the Derwitz-Apparat of 1891, with which he made his initial flights, and then Südende-Apparat of the following year. With the Maihöhe-Rhinow-Apprat of 1893 he achieved the basic shape for all his subsequent gliders, and thereafter came a succession of derivatives and developments: the Kleiner Schlagflügelapparat, Grosser Eindecker, Modell Stöllen, Seilers Apparat, Sturmflügelmodell, Normal-Segelapparat; the Vorflügelapparat, Kleine Doppeldecker, Grosser Doppeldecker, Kippflügelapparat, Grosser Schlagflügelapparat; and the Gelenkflügelapparat. Each differed in span, aspect ratio, use of single or double wings, and planform, but overall each relied upon the airman's own shifting body weight for control. These gliders and other designs—some 18 over five years, including multiple copies of the Normal-Segelapparat—bespeak Lilienthal's feverish pace of work, his total devotion to his craft, and also his stature as a pioneer. While others toiled unsuccessfully attempting to build just one kind of basic design (for example, Ader or Maxim or Langley), Lilienthal was a veritable "skunk works" and centralized production shop and flight-test branch rolled into one.[10]

Lilienthal's major contribution came in his demonstrations of repeated flying. Five years after Lilienthal's death and two years away from his own success with his brother Orville at Kitty Hawk, Wilbur Wright stated perceptively that Lilienthal had been "the first man who really comprehended that balancing [i.e., controlling] was the *first* instead of the *last* of the great problems in connection with human flight. He began where others left off, and thus saved the many thousands of dollars that it had theretofore been customary to spend in building and fitting expensive engines to machines which were uncontrollable when tried."[11]

Lilienthal had started flying off a springboard at his house in the Berlin suburb of Gross-Lichterfelde but eventually had a small artificial hill raised in Lichterfelde from construction rubble. It amounted to no small expense, the engineer paying about 3,000 marks (then approximately $750, and now about $15,000) for its erection. It rose to a height of 15 meters (approximately 50 feet) with a base diameter of 70 meters (approximately 230 feet) and constituted a not inconsiderable achievement and measure of his devotion to flight testing.[12] During his flights in the Rhinow hills, while watched by a group of schoolchildren and their teachers, Lilienthal suffered one bad accident, eerily similar to his final, fatal crash. As the glider pitched up to a higher and higher angle of attack, he desperately attempted to move his weight forward to bring the center of gravity forward, but could not do so. "I gripped tight hold," he reported later, "seeing nothing but the blue sky and little white clouds above me, and so awaited the moment when the apparatus would capsize backwards, possibly ending my sailing attempts forever. Suddenly, however, the apparatus stopped in its ascent, and going backwards again in a downward direction, described a short circle and steered with the rear part again upwards, owing to the horizontal tail which had an upward slant; then the machine turned bottom upwards and rushed with me vertically towards the earth from a height of about 65 feet. With my senses quite clear, my arms and my head forward, still holding the apparatus firmly with my hands, I fell towards a greenward; a shock, a crash, and I lay with the apparatus on the ground."[13] In short, the glider had pitched up, stalled, slid tailfirst through the bottom half of a loop, stopped, tumbled or rolled inverted, and dived into the ground. Lilienthal owed his life to a so-called *Prellbügel*, a willow-wood rebounding hoop thought up by his brother Gustav, that he had fortuitously installed to protect him, which the accident had "broken to splinters." Tragically, the glider that killed him did not have such a hoop, for Lilienthal had neglected to bring it: a terrible oversight for which he paid a fatal price, for the machine otherwise suffered relatively little damage.[14]

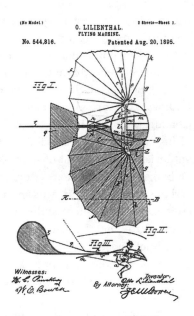

Lilienthal's glider configuration, from the American patent for his Normal-Segelapparat. U.S. Patent Office (USPO)

With Lilienthal's death European aviation entered a steep decline almost as precipitous as that which killed the German master. If not as cataclysmic as his mechanic Beylich recalled ("My master lay with a broken spine against the earth, and his death the next day signified as well the death of all aviation"),[15] it certainly specifically redirected German aviation for the next decade away from winged flight and towards the total embracing of lighter-than-air-balloons, blimps, and ultimately Zeppelins, as well as shocking the world aeronautical community more generally, particularly in France and England.[16] Outside of Germany nothing of lasting significance came of his European disciples, and the most gifted and energetic of them, Percy Pilcher, died on October 2, 1899, after sustaining injuries after his own hang glider (inspired by Lilienthal) broke up in flight.[17] With his death Europe had missed its moment of opportunity, and as surely as the earth rotates, that moment now passed to the United States.

Lilienthal's Influence: An Assessment

Undoubtedly Lilienthal powerfully influenced popular perceptions of flight, not least by his repetitive flights, which featured prominently in European and American news accounts illustrated by dramatic photographs of him aloft. His background as a person of accomplishment—as with Ader, Maxim, and Langley—greatly enhanced the reputability of aviation research, though his own work was far more advanced and perceptive than that of these other three. (He certainly recognized this: after Hiram Maxim belittled his work as akin to that of a mere parachutist, or at best a "flying squirrel," he sharply retorted that Maxim's major accomplishment "has only been to show us 'how not to do it.'")[18] His gliders and flight testing philosophy influenced a number of other international pioneers, including his fellow countryman Alois Wolfmüller, England's Percy Pilcher and Dr. T. J. Bennett, Ireland's George Francis Fitzgerald, Imperial Russia's Nikolai Joukovsky, France's Ferdinand Ferber, Argentina's Pablo Suarez, and Octave Chanute, Augustus Herring, and the Wrights in America. He even produced nine of his 1894 so-called Normal-Segelapparat (standard soaring apparatus) for other enthusiasts, selling eight of them, including two in America, one to Fitzgerald in Dublin, one to Bennett at Oxford (who flew it briefly and then gave it to Pilcher), and one to Joukovsky in Moscow, making it both the world's first production aircraft, and the first successfully exported one as well.[19] In total, by the time of his death, Otto Lilienthal had made approximately 2,000 glides. But his flying times were brief. Indeed, Wilbur Wright later remarked, "We figured that Lilienthal in five years of time had spent only about five hours in actual gliding through the air. The wonder was not that he had done so little, but that he had accomplished so much."[20]

Lilienthal's death hardened preexisting attitudes towards flight. Believers such as America's Octave Chanute saw him as a martyr—particularly in light of his dramatic last words—"who probably would have accomplished final success if he had lived."[21] On the other hand, critics saw him as one more casualty of a lost cause. One cold Scottish Tuesday morning four months after Lilienthal's death, Lord Kelvin took up his pen and some university letterhead and in a scrawling, dismis-

Lilienthal in flight, 1895; note the potential difficulties and awkwardness of shifting body weight for control, which greatly contributed to his fatal glider accident in 1896.
SSPL

sive hand famously wrote a quick note to Baden F. S. Baden-Powell of the Aeronautical Society of Great Britain:[2]

Dec 8/96
THE UNIVERSITY
GLASGOW

Dear Baden-Powell:

I am afraid I am not in the flight [*sic*] for "aerial navigation." I was greatly interested in your work with kites; but I have not the smallest molecule of faith in aerial navigation other than ballooning or of expectations of good results from any of the trials we hear of. So you will understand that I would not care to be a member of the aëronautical society.

Yours truly,
Kelvin

Both views were wrong. Flight certainly wasn't a lost cause, as the Wrights would show a little over seven years later. But neither could Lilienthal have flown before the Wrights, unless he dramatically reexamined his work, reconsidered his aircraft configurations, and drastically reshaped his philosophy on propulsion and control. Three problems stood between him and final success.

First, his most important legacy—comprehensive tables of aerodynamic coefficients (values for the lift and drag of various wing cross sections that he developed) unfortunately proved misleading. While they possessed a quantified, measured, authoritative appearance, they lacked the accuracy other researchers required to build their own successful aircraft.[23] To be fair, Lilienthal certainly tried to ensure that his work was as reliable as he could make it within the limitations of the instrumentation he possessed, and he never exaggerated or oversold the significance of his research. But on the whole he was a far better flight researcher than aerodynamicist; as John Anderson has written, "Lilienthal was correct in the broadest sense, but not in the details."[24]

His tables illustrate this. While impressive upon initial examination (for his was the first-ever plotting of lift and drag values for various angles of attack, that is, the angle of inclination of the wing with respect to the oncoming air), they contained flaws introduced by his reliance upon a whirling arm (which quickly caused the air to rotate around with it, making accurate measurements impossible) instead of a wind tunnel. As a result they could furnish little more than a generalized appreciation that a curved airfoil wing cross section would be better than an inclined flat one—something already known through the work of Horatio Phillips. Further, Phillips studied more efficient airfoil shapes having their point of maximum curvature far forward of the wing centerline, rather than the simple shallow-arc-of-a-circle shapes Lilienthal emphasized, which had their point of maximum curvature exactly at the wing centerline, halfway back along the chord (the distance between the front and rear of the wing). Oddly, Lilienthal's theoretical work and his actual design practice clashed: patent drawings clearly reveal his gliders featured wing cross sections resembling a bird's—that is, like Phillips's, not like a circular arc. Lilienthal's tabulated data certainly misled the Wrights later, as will be seen.[25]

Second, Lilienthal had little appreciation for flight control beyond shifting body weight. As an accomplished athlete, he could do this readily enough, remarking that he was like an "aerial gymnast swinging from trapeze to trapeze."[26] But it was totally unsatisfactory for any powered machine and, as he himself tragically proved, shifting body weight could not substitute for a genuine flight control system during an emergency. Indeed, even in normal operation it proved unsettling: after Augustus Herring, William Avery, and Paul Butusov had test-flown a Lilienthal glider (built from plans) over a week in June 1896, Octave Chanute damningly concluded, "It was realized from the first that the machine was difficult to handle. . . . The operator was compelled to shift his weight constantly, like a tight-rope dancer without a pole, in order to bring the center of gravity directly under the center of pressure and to avoid being upset. . . . Lilienthal was an expert in its use, . . . but it is due to those who may desire to repeat such experiments to state here plainly that we found it cranky and uncertain in its action and requiring great practice. . . . It was finally decided, on the twenty-ninth of June, to discard it, and it was accordingly broken up."[27]

Exactly six weeks later, Lilienthal died. (There are some tantalizing indications that over the winter of 1895–1896 his brother Gustav, every bit as involved as his better-known flying brother in the engineering of the gliders, recommended finding ways to increase the controllability of the gliders, but exactly to what extent is unknown.)[28] So as with many other pioneers, controllability was—and would have continued to be—his most serious challenge. The real puzzle is why, *70 years after* Lilienthal's death, some individuals and manufacturers would persist in using shifting body weight to control hang gliders during the hang gliding renaissance of the late 1960s onwards, with often fatal or crippling results.[29]

Third, Lilienthal always showed a surprising tendency to copy the bird, even to the extent of advocating powered ornithopter-type approaches. Accordingly, although aware of it, he rejected the propeller in favor of six birdlike "flappers" located on the outer wing panels. This alone doomed him to failure had he attempted to fly a powered craft. Presumably in time he would have come around to accepting the inevitability of propeller-driven propulsion, but probably not soon enough to have been first to complete a powered, sustained, and controlled flight. This constituted the only seriously retrograde aspect of his work—but it was an inexplicable choice for such a gifted and insightful individual to have made.

In conclusion, as tremendously accomplished as Lilienthal was, as insightful his recognition that success at flight demanded creative flight testing, history must judge that he pursued a path of development that ultimately would have led to failure, as with Ader, Maxim, and Langley. Only by changing significant aspects of his approach could he have attained his own Kitty Hawk–like success, and there is no indication—in fact, quite the opposite—that he was open to such change. He died at the height of his reputation, no small mercy if one thinks of the derision cast at the unfortunate Langley, but tragically the accident almost shattered the close-knit family, contributing to the early death in 1916 of his eldest son, who never fully recovered from the shock of his father's sudden demise.

Berliners have well remembered their pioneer airman, who, if not native born, nevertheless came to call the imperial *Hauptstadt* his home. Fittingly, today most travelers to the capital of reunified Germany land at Berlin-Tegel, the *Flughafen Otto Lilienthal*. If among the relatively few arriving at Berlin-Tempelhof, they may catch a glimpse of *Lilienthalstrasse*, skirting the eastern edge of the terminal complex. If so moved, they can journey a little ways to the *Lilienthalpark* in Gross-Lichterfelde. There they can climb up the same hill from which he flew so many of his flights, a site dedicated in his honor in June 1914, and once on the top they can look over the park while resting on the benches of the *Lilienthal-Gedenkstätte*, a memorial raised in 1932 by the *Wissenschaftliche Gesellschaft für Luftfahrt* (Scientific Society for Aviation). In 1933 Germans voted Adolf Hitler into power; in the Nazi era, party and air ministry propagandists virtually at once portrayed Lilienthal as a *heroischen Vorkämpfer*, a "heroic front-fighter" *gefallen* in the cause of flight, linking by word and image his work in the Kaiser's Germany to the "progressive" Nazi cause, particularly to the pervasive youth gliding movement which enthusiasts had started in the 1920s. The Nazi-established Association for Aviation Research (*Vereinigung für Luftfahrtforschung*) renamed itself the Lilienthal Society for Aviation Research (*Lilienthal-Gesellschaft für Luftfahrtforschung*) in 1936, and as such remodeled the entire locale, giving the grounds a Speer-like neoclassical look.[30]

With all this, it is pleasant to note that in his personal life Otto Lilienthal was about as far removed as one could be from the Nazi ethos. He was liberal in politics, tolerant of others, open to all who saw and visited him, supportive of the less fortunate, moderate in temperament, socially concerned, a patron of art and culture for the everyday citizen, optimistic about the future of humanity, and dedicated to flight as a means of reducing nationalism, linking peoples together, and ending the spectre of war by negating the value of armies, fleets, and fortresses. He was, in short, a good person. Finally, nothing can take away Lilienthal's chief claim to fame: he had the courage to try his ideas out routinely in the only laboratory that really mattered, the sky, and not once or twice or a dozen or so times, but thousands of times, without exaggerating his work or accomplishment. A most remarkable man, he eagerly put his life on the line to further the cause of flight; tragically, flight in turn took the cruelest advantage of his faith and trust.

Octave Chanute and the Transferring of Aeronautics from Europe to America

Over 16 years before Lilienthal plunged from the sky, on the evening of the first of March 1880, a group of New York's most powerful and influential citizens gathered in the main dining room of Delmonico's, the already-legendary New York restaurant, to attend a fete for a living legend, France's Ferdinand de Lesseps. The man famous for joining the Mediterranean and Red Seas at Suez had just arrived from Panama, where he hoped to duplicate the earlier feat. That night, beneath draped American and French flags, he sat as guest of honor while an almost equally distinguished group of speakers extolled his reputation and his plans for a canal joining the Atlantic and Pacific Oceans. Sitting at one of the main tables was another native son of France, arguably the most accomplished American engineer of his day: the 48-year-old chief engineer of the Erie Railway, Octave Chanute.[31]

With a fashionable goatee betraying his Parisian roots, Chanute had the dapper appearance of a middle-aged and genial *boulevardier*. Born in 1832, the son of a history professor at the Collège Royale de France, he emigrated with his parents to the United States at age six, where his father assumed the vice presidency of Jefferson College in Louisiana. Though he considered himself American, young Chanute grew up in an intellectually oriented household so European in outlook that a pronounced Gaulic accent would forever tinge his English. Gifted in mathematics, he chose a career in engineering while still a teenager, subsequently joining a railway survey crew and learning engineering firsthand. He eventually rose to the very top of his profession, earning a fortune while working with a series of railroad companies, as a noted bridge builder, and as the architect and chief engineer of the Union Stock Yards in Chicago and Kansas City. His colleagues recognized his professional accomplishments by installing him as president of the

American Society of Civil Engineers. That night in Delmonico's, he was among his peers—men of power and influence who controlled the industrial, political, and financial future of America. But Chanute harbored a dark secret, something he feared that if learned could hurt his reputation: he had accumulated a wealth of material on early flying attempts, paths taken, and configurations chosen. He was in fact a closet aerophile, had been since taking a trip to France with his wife and children in 1875 that had exposed him to the work of Pénaud, Wenham, and others, and in few more years, he hoped, he might be able to come out in the open.

Octave Chanute, the most distinguished American civil engineer of his time, and a notable patron and student of flight.
AFMA

Happily such was the case. In 1883, financially secure beyond the imaginings of youth, he could afford to enter semiretirement. He picked and chose subsequent engineering projects with great care, moving to Chicago before the end of the decade and founding a firm specializing in preservation of wooden structures and timber. Only when in his late 50s, so distinguished, accomplished, and professionally secure as to no longer fear ridicule for advocating and discussing aviation, did he now devote his full attention to flight. And he did so with the characteristic energy and enthusiasm he had brought to his career as a practicing engineer. He became a virtual one-man aeronautical information clearinghouse and also bankrolled a number of individuals studying aviation. He tried to arrange for Maxim and Lilienthal to come to America, the former to resume his work and the latter to make an American tour. He communicated widely and publicized the work of numerous pioneers, from the well known like Lilienthal to the unknown like Australia's notable-if-isolated kitemaker, Lawrence Hargrave. Upon Chanute's death in 1910, Wilbur Wright would state: "No one was too humble to receive a share of his time. In patience and goodness of heart he has rarely been surpassed. Few men were more universally respected and loved."[32]

In 1891 he wrote the first of a series of articles for *American Engineer and Railroad Journal,* which he would pull together and publish as a book three years later. He also sponsored professional meetings, most notably a four-day international Conference on Aerial Navigation held in Chicago on August 1–4, 1894, that drew together most of the major names in American aviation, and some international figures as well.[33]

The international conference had started as an idea by Albert Francis Zahm, a young and gifted graduate student from Ohio holding degrees in physics and engineering from Notre Dame and Sibley College (where he got to know Charles Manly) who would eventually receive his doctorate from Johns Hopkins University in Baltimore. The son of an Alsatian logger and brother of a priest who was himself a scientist and expedition companion of Theodore Roosevelt's, Zahm was an avid model builder and experimenter. He represented the increasing scientific and technical professionalism of aeronautical researchers, in contrast to the craftsmen and tinkerers of previous times. He would soon build the first significant wind tunnel in the United States, become a confidant of Samuel Langley and later Smithsonian Secretary Charles Walcott, run a Navy aerodynamics laboratory, and eventually hold the Daniel Guggenheim Chair in Aeronautics at the U.S. Library of Congress, where he would supervise the acquisition and assembling of the nation's finest single collection of aeronautical reference materials and papers. Although once on friendly terms with the Wrights, as an enthusiastic supporter of Glenn Curtiss in the Wright-Curtiss patent controversy, he earned a reputation as an unabashed critic of the brothers and their work. If this has caused him to be criticized harshly by some, it should not obscure his very real contributions to early American flight and in particular to the creation, during the First World War, of the National Advisory Committee for Aeronautics (NACA), the greatest aeronautical research organization ever to exist and the predecessor of today's National Aeronautics and Space Administration (NASA).[34]

Zahm conceived holding an international conference on aeronautics to coincide with the Columbian Exposition in Chicago. Chanute served as chairman of a 12-person committee (including a future president of the Massachusetts Institute of Technology, Samuel W. Stratton) and Zahm was secretary. Held in the Windy

Albert F. Zahm as a young graduate; the young physicist would establish the first aeronautical research laboratory in the United States, at the Catholic University of America, Washington, D.C. Archives of The University of Notre Dame (AUND)

City over the first four days of August 1893, the conference was a huge success. It brought together a truly international collection of speakers and enthusiasts, who presented 35 papers on topics ranging from meteorology to bird flight. Some papers—such as one on the advantages of beating wings for propulsion—were hardly the stuff of the future, while at least one other—a paper on the merits of gas turbines for aircraft propulsion—might have revolutionized aviation at a far earlier stage had greater attention been paid to them. But it was the range of speakers, paper presenters, and attendees that drew the most attention, for it included individuals such as England's Francis Wenham, the Smithsonian's Samuel Langley, Australia's Lawrence Hargrave, Egypt's Louis Mouillard, America's Edward Huffaker and John Montgomery, and of course Chanute and Zahm themselves. As well were individuals not working per se in aeronautics but interested in the subject, most notably John P. Holland (soon to invent the practical submarine and equally enthusiastic about flight), F. A. Pratt (inventor of the revolutionary Lincoln milling machine and cofounder of Pratt and Whitney, which would become a major manufacturer of aircraft engines by the mid-twentieth century), and Thomas Edison (the popular Wizard of Menlo Park, best known for inventing the carbon-filament electric lightbulb). Chanute supervised the collection of papers and arranged for the publication of the conference proceedings as well, the following year.[35]

Chanute clearly enunciated his own thoughts on flight in his address at the opening of the conference. Flight to this point, he said, "has hitherto been associated with failure," its advocates viewed "as eccentric—to speak plainly, as 'cranks.'" But the record of ballooning and airship development, and now increasingly that of winged aviation, held great promise, even if the precise commercial and military potential of such craft could not yet be clearly seen. Most significantly, Chanute emphasized the importance of seeking integrated solutions to the problem of flight. "It is a mistake," he wrote, "to suppose that the problem of aviation is a single problem. In point of fact, it involves many problems, each to be separately solved, and these solutions then to be combined. These problems pertain to the motor, to the propelling instrument, to the form, extent, texture, and construction of the sustaining surfaces, to the maintenance of the equipoise [i.e., stability], to the methods of getting under way, of steering the apparatus in the air, and of alighting safely. They each constitute one problem, involving one or more solutions, to be subsequently combined."[36]

Chanute's own book, *Progress in Flying Machines,* appeared shortly after the conference concluded. It appeared but a year before another notable compilation, the first of Bostonian James Means's three-volume *Aeronautical Annuals.* Like Chanute Means was wealthy and had a fascination with flight and a keen appreciation for significant work, but unlike Chanute, Means himself was a businessman, not an engineer or technologist, and he was younger by over 20 years. Strikingly good-looking with a distinguished, reserved air, James Means was the epitome of the successful Yankee entrepreneur. Descended from old Massachusetts Bay pioneer stock—his father was a Congregationalist minister in Dorchester—he had attended local schools, the Phillips Academy at Andover, and the Massachusetts Institute of Technology, before leaving school to start a wildly successful shoe-manufacturing business. Selling cheaply manufactured but very high quality shoes at a low price proved so profitable that he was able to retire to pursue his own interests at the age of 40 in 1893. And chief among his interests was flight, an interest triggered in 1879 when as a 26-year-old he watched soaring gulls from the deck of a paddle-wheel steamship, the SS *Constitution,* slowly making its way from Panama to San Francisco on its last voyage before going to a breaker's yard.[37]

Means wrote widely and perceptively on aviation himself, even anticipating the era of precision-guided aerial munitions and cruise missiles 50 years before their appearance in rudimentary form in the midst of the Second World War, and not quite 100 years before their deadly effectiveness would shock observers worldwide during the Persian Gulf War.[38] He was far less successful as an inventor. But where Means shone was—like Chanute—as an aerial clearinghouse. Together Chanute and Means assembled a tremendous aeronautical database for the use of other researchers. Chanute's *Progress* and Means's *Annuals* have been likened (not without justification) to the Old and New Testaments of the Bible: the former constituting the historical record and the latter the state of current work.[39] In particular Means's *Annuals* contained a wealth of readings and insights, including material from Cayley, Wenham, Maxim, Lilienthal, Herring, Chanute, and others, patiently assembled by Means working in his library at his house at 196 Beacon Street, Boston. He ceased issuing the *Annuals* after 1897 because he received too little good material and the cost of publication was becoming excessive. But he followed aviation assiduously, journeying to Ft. Myer in 1908 to watch Orville Wright demonstrate the first Military Flyer, to France in 1909 to the Reims international air meet (the world's first such event), and the Harvard-Boston air meet of 1910, among others. Following a final European tour in 1912, his health worsened, and he ceased active participation in aviation, though he watched (in some shock and sadness, as he hoped "that man having attained the blessing of flight would have the wisdom to refrain from using it for self-destruction") as the airplane became a deadly weapon in the First World War. He died in 1920 at the age of 67.[40]

Into the Air: Chanute and the Birth of American Flight Testing

Like Lilienthal before him, Chanute clearly came from the "airman" school of aeronautical pioneer. In 1895 Chanute turned away from merely reading and writing about aircraft to actually designing them, working with Augustus Herring, a well-to-do Georgian who experimented with copies of Lilienthal gliders. For the briefest period, Herring left to assist Samuel Langley, but as both were opinionated and uncompromising sorts, he quickly returned to Chanute's team. At first Chanute had looked at simply improving upon Lilienthal's work, going so far as to file a patent application for a derivative of his Normal-Segelapparat. (The Patent Office granted it nine months after Lilienthal's death.) It bore an obvious similarity to Lilienthal's design but differed in two important respects: it had pivoting wings for preserving balance, and (since the pilot thus no longer needed to shift his weight for control) a small seat so that he could get the mechanical advantage to move the wings.[41] But Chanute had a more practical structural outlook than any of the other pre-Wright pioneers who attempted actual aircraft, including Lilienthal, and after reconsidering, quickly abandoned Lilienthal's design concept. Since prevailing thought emphasized very thin wing sections and a birdlike planform (the shape of the wing when seen from above), a major challenge for all these individuals was furnishing sufficient rigidity and strength and ensuring that it retained its airfoil shape and overall planform without distorting under the loads it experienced in flight. For example, Lilienthal chose multiple wing spars of varying length radiating from a tall central post (somewhat in the fashion of an open umbrella) with wires connected from the top and bottom of the post to the ends of each spar.[42] Chanute took a very different approach, favoring multiwing designs having stacked wings one above the other, based on his experience building bridges, where the interconnected wings and struts acted like a reinforcing truss.

Trusses were something Chanute knew a great deal about. The introduction of iron had revolutionized building and bridge construction in the nineteenth century. In the early 1840s, building upon the earlier wooden truss designs of William Howe, Caleb Pratt and his son Thomas patented a new design for an iron truss bridge that used regularly spaced vertical posts under compression connecting upper and lower deck frames. Within each "bay" formed by the posts, a pair of diagonals held in tension imparted further rigidity and stability to the structure. The geometrically clean and logical Pratt truss enabled straightforward calculation of loads and load distributions and quickly became one of two dominant bridge forms in America, the other being a design by Squire Whipple a few years later that emphasized a closer spacing of vertical posts and diagonals running across two bays, not just one.[43]

When Chanute began building his own glider he adopted a "multiwing" planform, using the Howe truss as the key structural concept. Though not as extreme as Horatio Phillips' Venetian-blind approach, Chanute's glider nevertheless had no fewer than 12 separate wings (which Chanute called "aerocurves") arranged in six pairs. This machine, informally called the *Katydid* because it resembled a giant insect, had these wings ingeniously pivoted where they joined the main frame (there was no "body" or "fuselage" per se) so that if a gust hit the glider, the wings would be blown backwards a foot or two until wires with restraining springs prevented their further movement. Thus the wing could automatically compensate for changes to the center of pressure without requiring extraordinary—and perhaps futile—body movement by the pilot. In late June 1896, together with carpenter William Avery, Paul Butusov (an émigré Russian sailor), and Dr. James Rickets (a young surgeon), Chanute and Herring set up a camp on the shores of Lake Michigan near Miller, Indiana, at the first American flight test center. They began a series of gliding trials, first with Herring's Lilienthal glider copy, and then with several of Chanute's own multiwing designs.[44]

But Chanute's *Katydid* trials did not go well, as the multiple wings and profusion of bracing struts and wires created a great deal of retarding drag, and the automatic wing pivoting feature proved less useful than hoped. The Chanute team made extensive changes, primarily reducing the number of wings and trying different tail configurations. But problems persisted, and ultimately they returned to Chicago to make more changes; flight testing after returning to Lake Michigan resulted in even more problems . . . so *Katydid* undoubtedly was a troubled design. But another concept offered great promise: a Chanute-Herring collaboration, a "three-surface" glider—that is, a triplane—with non-pivoting rigid wings trussed together to provide the necessary strength and rigidity.[45]

The Chanute-Herring glider skimming the Michigan dunes as Chanute's test team run excitedly alongside; note the initial triplane configuration.

This glider proved an important design for several reasons. First, it had a very simple, uncomplicated, straight-line structure (anticipating the design of the Wrights' own aircraft a half decade hence) in contrast to virtually all previous gliders (by Chanute, Lilienthal, and others), which had generally adopted the curvaceous lines of birds or bats. Second, in contrast to *Katydid*'s awkward multiplane design, it had just three wings, superposed one above the other, rectangular in planform and equivalent in span and chord. Chanute and Herring cut away the center section of the lower wing so that the pilot could fit into the machine, his legs, like Lilienthal's, dangling free so that he could control the craft by shifting his body around. Finally, the glider featured a tail boom ending in a Herring-designed, self-adjusting, spring-loaded cruciform tail (which Chanute called a "combined horizontal and vertical rudder") to give the craft automatic and self-restoring stability, no matter what the wind conditions. In short, it was a crisp, clean, logically thought-out, and altogether practical craft that at once signaled Chanute and Herring's mastery of design, even beyond that of the venerated Lilienthal, and certainly beyond any of his predecessors.[46]

Chanute had to delay trials of this craft, for a violent storm (possibly a tornado; at least Chanute thought so) wrecked his little camp early in the morning of Friday, August 21, 1896, and caused much damage. Repairs to the camp and the gliders occupied the next week; on Saturday, August 29, Avery and Herring began testing this glider, not quite three weeks after Lilienthal's demise. While it flew very well, when banking or inclining close to the ground the lower wing tended to strike the surface. Trials to date had clearly shown the glider had excellent lifting characteristics, so Chanute simply removed the lower wing. The result was a "two-surface" machine—that is, a biplane—now perfectly Pratt-trussed: the essential shape of the early airplane.

Best of all, it flew superbly, gliding over 350 feet in 14 seconds with a reasonably good gliding descent of 5.75:1; that is, nearly six feet forward for every one foot in vertical descent. It had none of the skittish and potentially fatal quirkiness of the Lilienthal type. As Chanute recalled, "During the next 14 days scores and scores of glides were made with this machine, whenever the wind served. It was found steady, easy to handle before starting, and under good control when under way—a motion of the operator's body of not over two inches proving as effective as a motion of five or more inches in the Lilienthal machine."[47]

Thus, thanks to a fortuitous series of circumstances—his background as a bridge builder and his knowledge of truss design, the problems with the *Katydid*, Herring's influence, the beguiling simplicity of the alternative triplane approach, the problems with snagging the lower wing against the ground—Chanute gave the Pratt-trussed biplane configuration to aviation. It was a pivotal moment in the history of aircraft design, ranking with Henson and Stringfellow's postulation of the Aerial Steam Carriage over a half century earlier and Cayley's even more distant derivation of the modern airplane shape. It ushered in an era of strong, light, straightforward, uncomplicated (and easily analyzed) rectangular structures that quickly superseded the convoluted curves and framing of older attempts such as those by Ader and Lilienthal. Chanute, in short, had taken both glider experimentation and structural design to a new level, contributions of seminal importance.[48]

August 1896 must thus be seen as a month of mixed happenings. It started with the shocking loss of Lilienthal, proving that winged flight would be every bit as unforgiving as ballooning before it. Then Chanute had his near-disastrous windstorm. But by the end of the month, although largely unrecognized at the time, a torch had passed from Europe to America: the old bird-or-bat-imitative concepts of what aircraft should be were being surpassed by a new simplified and regularized approach to flight consistent with the rapidly industrializing nature of American society and the no-holds-barred, full-steam-ahead character of the burgeoning pre-Progressive Era. Sad as it had been, in some ways Lilienthal's death had been an attention-getting catalyst. All that was needed now were individuals motivated by his sacrifice to take aviation to its next stage. And fortunately two such people existed: Wilbur and Orville Wright.

CHAPTER TEN

Enter the Wrights

When Lilienthal died, an unsuspecting Orville Wright was incubating typhoid fever and about to enter a six-week delirium that would bring him near death. While Orville lay sick, his brother Wilbur thought of Lilienthal's fatal crash. The brothers had followed Lilienthal's work at a distance via newspaper accounts, and when Orville at last began a slow recovery, he and Wilbur pondered the problem of flight.

If the Montgolfiers were the stuff of Arthur Miller, the Wrights were the stuff of Sinclair Lewis and Hamlin Garland, seasoned with healthy dashes of Thornton Wilder and the Brontë sisters: solidly Midwestern products rooted in mainstream, small-town, agrarian-oriented WASP culture. Their father, Milton Wright, an unbending, inflexible, and contentious bishop in the Church of the United Brethren in Christ, came from old Puritan English and Dutch stock and had married a shy and studious woman, Susan Koerner, of German-Swiss roots; from this union came seven children, five of whom, four brothers and a sister, survived into adulthood. Of the children, Wilbur, born in 1867, Orville, born in 1871, and Katharine, born in 1874, formed a natural and mutually supportive team.[1]

Thanks to a rigid upbringing (coming from a family that often settled disputations with formal courtlike proceedings and judgments), both brothers had an inflexible view of family, friendships, and business relationships that bordered on—and sometimes crossed over into—obsession, stubbornness, and suspicion. Unlike some of their siblings, they evinced little interest in leaving the family home, in part reflecting the economic depression of the 1890s, but perhaps also exacerbated by their father's unsettled (if nevertheless successful) nature: he made 12 moves in 25 years. Despite this uprootedness, Wilbur apparently had a relatively normal childhood until struck by a flung bat at age 17. This event turned him into a semi-invalid for several years and prevented his going to Yale, his parents' dream. It is uncertain how much this stemmed from actual injury as opposed to unreasoning concern over his health that never really left him. His younger brother Orville (known as "Bubbo" to the family), who was so shy as never to be able—even as an aged and venerated adult—to make the slightest remarks before an audience, left high school before graduation. But it is a mistake to assume that they were uneducated: both read voraciously across the fields of science, literature, the arts, history, and philosophy. They possessed profound scientific insight, a sure grasp of mathematics, and excellent analytical skills, and clarity, style, and grace mark their writings.

Neither brother had an extensive social life. They certainly did not form any noticeable emotional attachments. Some who knew the brothers recalled that Wilbur seemed discomfited in the presence of young women, while Orville took virtually no notice of them. Perhaps they simply reflected the generally patriarchal times in which they lived, but to an exaggerated degree, thanks to their rural upbringing. When Colonel John Capper, a senior British engineering officer, visited the brothers in Dayton in 1904, Wilbur felt moved to note that his wife was "an unusually bright woman," as if discussing a particularly smart racehorse.[2] Yet ironically, their own Oberlin-educated sister Katharine was one such woman herself, and she shared with them (at least at first) their lack of interest in leaving the family, marrying, and settling down. It was to her that the work-obsessed brothers turned for emotional support, Orville most of all, something sadly evidenced by the irrational bitterness he exhibited when, to his surprise, Katharine married late in life. Convinced she had willfully and irretrievably broken a family pact, thus leaving him on his own (his brother Wilbur having died in 1912), Bubbo had nothing further to do with her, ignored her pathetic pleas for a reconciliation, and later, only with the greatest difficulty could bring himself to be at her bedside as she died.[3]

The brothers inherited a tremendous work ethic and the ability to focus on problems virtually to the exclusion of all else. Orville determined while still in high school to become a printer and, confident of his choice, willingly left before the end of his senior year. The two brothers made a success of a small printing operation, proving mechanically adept and insightful in making much of their own equipment. Then, in 1892, in response to a bicycling craze sweeping the Midwest, both became

The Wright brothers, Wilbur (left) and Orville on the back porch of their home in Dayton, Ohio, sitting with dapper composure, in June 1909. U.S. Air Force Aeronautical Systems Center History Office (ASCHO)

involved in a YMCA-sponsored racing league, proved their skills as mechanics, and then—at Wilbur's suggestion—opened a bicycle shop. By 1896 they had branched into making their own bicycles, fabricating their production machinery and even a one-cylinder internal combustion engine used to power the works, and Orville thought about possibly branching into making automobiles as well. But Wilbur scoffed at the idea, and they continued on with a secure income from their bicycle manufacturing and secondarily from their print shop. If this was all they had ever done with their lives, working with bicycles and a print shop, their father Milton Wright could have taken comfort in having raised two principled, self-reliant, and commercially successful young men. But the brothers would now take their lives in a very different direction.[4]

In 1878, succumbing to one of his frequent spasms of wanderlust, Milton Wright had moved his young family to Cedar Rapids, Iowa. Church business frequently took him out of town, and as an attentive and loving parent, he always brought gifts back from his trips. Late that summer, returning from one such journey, he called 11-year-old Wilbur and seven-year-old Orville to his side, and then, as they watched his closed hands expectantly, he opened his hands wide. As the delighted (if startled) brothers watched, the hidden toy leapt upwards, whirring its way to the ceiling, where it briefly bobbed and bounced, as if struggling to drill its way onwards to freedom. Little did he know it, but Milton Wright had just opened the eyes of his two youngest sons to the potential of flight, courtesy of one of Alphonse Pénaud's flying toys. Years later Orville would recall, "Our first interest in flight began when we were children. Father brought home to us a small toy actuated by a rubber spring which would lift itself into the air. We built a number of copies of this toy, which flew successfully."[5] Attempts to scale up the little helicopters failed, for the young boys did not understand what as adults they would: doubling the size of a model requires an eight-fold increase in its power. So they gradually turned to other pursuits. But in the back of their minds, a seed continued to germinate, first breaking the earth in 1896, when they learned of the death of Otto Lilienthal.

The brothers had followed news of Lilienthal, a legacy of their childhood interest, and now his death galvanized them to action. Clearly Lilienthal had lost control of his glider, and thus, they concluded, body shifting must be an inferior and potentially fatal means of attempting to exert mastery over a flying machine. So as Orville subsequently recalled, "We at once set to work to devise a more efficient means of maintaining the equilibrium."[6] Despite this recollection events actually moved more slowly than he remembered, for only in the spring of 1899 did the brothers seek to expand their knowledge when on May 30 Wilbur Wright wrote to the secretary of the Smithsonian Institution.

Richard Rathbun: The Unsung Bureaucrat

On the morning of Friday, June 2, 1899, Mr. Richard Rathbun sat at his desk in the gothic Smithsonian Castle, peered through his spectacles, and scanned the letter that had just arrived from Ohio. "I have been interested in the problem of mechanical and human flight," Wilbur Wright began, "ever since as a boy I constructed a number of bats of various sizes after the style of Cayley's and Pénaud's machines." The author went on to explain his ultimate faith in human flight and announced his intention "to begin a systematic study of the subject in preparation for practical work." Then, somewhat defensively, he concluded, "I am an enthusiast, but not a crank in the sense that I have some pet theories as to the proper construction of a flying machine. I wish to avail myself of all that is already known and then if possible add my mite to help on the future worker who will attain final success."[7]

For many traditional bureaucrats approaching the end of a work week, Wright's words would have earned the letter a quick drop in a wastebasket, its author dismissed as another deluded hayseed, like the fictional Darius Green of John Townsend Trowbridge's then-30-year-old but still popular poem.[8] But dual-hatted as both the Smithsonian Assistant Secretary and as director of its National Museum, Richard Rathbun had a very different reputation: energetic, an able administrator, self-made, and one of the most accomplished men in American science. Age 47, lean, with a bushy mustache and round spectacles, Rathbun had attended public schools in Buffalo, New York, leaving at age 15 to work with a construction firm, though he studied paleontology on the side. Made curator of paleontology for the Buffalo Society of Natural Sciences at age 19, he attracted the attention of Cornell University professor Charles Hartt, a former student of the Swiss-born Harvard naturalist Louis Agassiz. Hartt convinced Rathbun to enter Cornell, where he excelled, also venturing to Cambridge and taking a lecture course from Agassiz shortly before that eminent scientist died. Rathbun subsequently did notable fieldwork in Brazil, assembling a collection of Devonian and Cretaceous fossils. He developed a great interest in sea life (colleagues named a genus of fish and a genus of starfish, *Rathbunella* and *Rathbunaster,* after him) and worked for various governmental commissions on fisheries issues, including settling disputes with Canada and negotiating the fur seal trade with Imperial Russia. He joined the Smithsonian in 1897, and less than a year later, Langley appointed him both Assistant Secretary and director of the National Museum.[9]

To his very great credit, Rathbun neither pitched the letter nor fobbed it off on some junior staff assistant to draft up a negative reply. Instead, with a few quick pen strokes, he directed his staff to assemble some materials for him to send Mr. Wright—the most decisive and influential action ever undertaken by any Smithsonian administrator in the entire history of the Institution, both before and after that day. He certainly could not have realized the significance of what he had done. Perhaps as an end-of-week treat he left to lunch at the Cosmos Club with other faithful members like himself. If so, one wonders if they asked how his day was going, and what he replied: certainly not that he had played a major role in inventing the airplane and influencing the future transformation of the entire world.

Three weeks later the Wrights received the package of reading materials assembled by Rathbun's staff, including suggestions referencing virtually every significant text then existing on flight: Octave Chanute's *Progress in Flying Machines;* James Means's three *Aeronautical Annuals* for 1895, 1896, and 1897; Samuel Langley's *Story of Experiments in Mechanical Flight* and *Experiments in Aerodynamics;* E. C. Huffaker's *On Soaring Flight;* Louis-Pierre Mouillard's *Empire of the Air;* and Otto Lilienthal's *The Problem of Flying* and *Practical Experiments in Soaring.* With this the Wrights had the basis for their own future work. They subsequently credited these works with giving them "good understanding of the nature of the problem of flying" and in particular noted that Mouillard's and Lilienthal's writings "infected us with their own unquenchable enthusiasm and transformed idle curiosity into the active zeal of workers."[10]

It is rather astonishing that historians have for the most part ignored Rathbun's actions or simply mentioned them in passing, for what he did was in its own bureaucratic fashion an act of critical decisiveness. He literally controlled the future course of aviation, for with the Wrights just beginning their work, any significant discouragement might have derailed their research, if not forever, then at least for some extended period of time. It is unclear if Rathbun himself ever recollected Wilbur Wright's letter and his small if vital role in instigating the brothers' work. In fact he probably did not, for it obviously escaped others: mention of the Wrights or their correspondence is absent from Rathbun's own obituaries or the recollections of others who knew him. Rathbun died suddenly at the age of 66 on Tuesday, July 16, 1918, having lived long enough to get used to the sight of growing numbers of airplanes flying over the nation's capital, and apparently not knowing his own key role in making it all possible. Shocked at the news, the Smithsonian staff gathered that day with regent Henry White to express "their profound sorrow at the loss of a sincere friend, an executive officer of marked ability, and one whose administration has had a wide influence upon the scientific institutions of the nation." If only they had known, they might have concluded, "and a key figure in launching the Wright revolution that created the first successful airplane."[11]

"Annihilating" Time and Space

The onset of the twentieth century found the United States in the midst of a profound transformation. Popular attitudes toward technology and industrialization, rising economic strength, and industrial and technological development already anticipated the ebullient national self-confidence and expansive view that would characterize "the American Century." Already Yankee engineers, builders, entrepreneurs, and inventors occupied positions in an American pantheon of heroes even more exalted than Industrial Revolution–era Britain's. In just a half century, the number of patents issued annually to American inventors had gone from a trickle to a flood, from fewer than 700 in 1846 (the year Congress established the Smithsonian Institution) to more than 22,000 per year by the end of the century. The Centennial International Exhibition in Philadelphia in 1876, powered by the mighty Corliss steam engine (stark, massive, unadorned with false embellishments, and supremely redolent of power, endurance, and strength), had virtually signaled the birth of this new, post–Civil War America, a nation rich in resources, confidence, enthusiasm, and energy.[12] In the 1890s even before the Spanish-American War signaled its rise to world power, America outstripped Europe in many key production and industrialization indicators, including coal, iron, and steel production. "During the century after 1870," Thomas

Parke Hughes has written, "Americans created the modern technological nation; this was the American genesis."[13]

A number of profound changes rapidly affecting transportation and technological change accompanied this transformation. Water, wind, animal, and human power as "prime movers" had given way to the power of the steam engine, electricity, and then, at the end of the nineteenth century, the steam turbine and the internal combustion, petroleum-fueled engine. Humanity entered the nineteenth century moving at about 6 miles per hour—the speed of a horse-drawn coach. It entered the twentieth moving at 60 miles per hour—a whole order of magnitude—the speed of a steam locomotive, and a new invention, the automobile, had already appeared in practical form in Germany, France, England, and America. "American civilization," Daniel Boorstin has written, "grew by getting people out to the edges and by getting people and messages back and forth across the verges. . . . This yen for the verges gave a newly dominating significance to technologies of transportation."[14]

Also, the unprecedented rate of change led some to predict even more astonishing developments in the future. At the end of December 1901, Henry Litchfield West made one such New Year's prediction in a remarkable *Washington Post* article: "If only the same proportion of increase is maintained, the year 2000 will see a distance of 600 miles covered in an hour—the journey from Washington to Chicago occupying only 70 or 80 minutes. This seems incredible, but is not more marvelous than it would have seemed in 1800 to suggest that the 40 miles between Washington and Baltimore could be traveled in 40 minutes."[15] West was on to something: he was correct in his prophecy, for the year 2000 did witness routine 600-miles-per-hour transportation via the jet airliner. West went further in his end-of-year message to the *Post*'s readers. "The limitations imposed by the attraction of gravitation upon land and by the frictional resistance of an almost solid mass of water at sea suggest that, after all, the great discoveries of the coming century, in the matter of transportation, will be in the navigation of the air. . . . The time is not far distant when aerial cars will ply between great centers of population, arriving and departing upon fixed schedules and carrying their human cargoes. . . . Aerial navigation seems to be the only method now apparent by which time and space can be more completely annihilated than it is at present."[16]

The British science fiction author and futurist H. G. Wells had only a slightly less optimistic view of the future: "Few people, I fancy," he wrote the next year, "who know of the work of Langley, Lilienthal, Pilcher, Maxim, and Chanute but will be inclined to believe that long before the year A.D. 2000, *and very probably before 1950*, a successful aeroplane will have soared and come home safe and sound."[17] Less than two years later, the most expensive, elaborate, publicized, and humiliating failure to fly was history. The broken and water-soaked remains of the *Great Aerodrome* lay sodden and dripping in the halls of the Smithsonian. "Knowledgeable" spokesmen thundered against the foolishness of flying machines. And most people could be forgiven for possessing little of Henry Litchfield West's soaring optimism, or even H. G. Wells's more cautious tone, regarding the future of "aerial navigation."

History loves strange twists of fate, and one of the most surprising occurred a mere nine days after Langley's machine tumbled into the Potomac. Since mid-1900, Wilbur and Orville Wright had flown a succession of ever-more-complex gliders, and following refinement of their ideas on aerodynamics and controls, they turned to making a powered machine. On December 17, 1903, another cold and windswept winter day, the revolution occurred: the world's first four powered, sustained, and controlled heavier-than-air flights, at Kill Devil Hill, Kitty Hawk, North Carolina.

The Wrights as Engineers

In 1923 Charles-Edouard Jenneret-Gris wrote, "The airplane mobilized invention, intelligence and daring: *imagination* and *cold reason*. It is the same spirit that built the Parthenon."[18] Coming as it did at a time when most airplanes remained frail craft of wood and wire, possessing only modest performance, such a statement might well have smacked of exaggeration. But this was no ordinary spokesman: he was the Swiss architect Le Corbusier, the leading exponent of the modern movement, challenging accepted doctrines and arguing for a new style blending engineering aesthetics and architecture.[19] To him the new technology of flight symbolized the liberating force required by a new architectural style, one combining grace, simplicity of line, and the advanced structural design possible with twentieth century engineering. A decade later, in a book provocatively entitled *L'avion accuse* . . . (The airplane indicts), he wrote that the airplane "carries our hearts above mediocre things. . . . [It] has given us the bird's-eye view." It is, he concluded, the "symbol of the New Age. . . . The airplane arouses our energies and our faith."[20]

Le Corbusier was not alone in his almost mystical view of the airplane, its invention, and its inventors. The French aviator-philosopher Antoine de Saint-Exupéry considered designing an airplane less a matter of engineering than a matter of art, akin to creating a great sculpture. "Have you looked at a modern airplane?" he challenged his readers, "Have you ever thought that all of man's industrial efforts . . . invariably culminate in the production of a thing whose sole and guiding principle is the ultimate principle of simplicity? . . . Perfection is finally attained not when there is no longer anything to add, but when there is no longer anything to take away, when a body has been stripped down to its nakedness. . . . [The sculptor-designer] is not so much inventing or shaping . . . as delivering the image from its prison."[21]

If Le Corbusier's comments pointed to the significance of what the Wright brothers accomplished, "Saint-Ex" indicated the seminal root of their work: the Wrights had an extraordinary ability to cut to the heart of a design problem, find a solution, pursue it vigorously to completion, and then integrate it with solutions to other challenges, the whole comprising a successful airplane. This separated them from their predecessors who had unsuccessfully attempted powered flight, as well as from those whose philosophy anticipated the Wrights themselves, and even many of their successors. Where their predecessors and contemporaries chose complexity, the Wrights chose straightforward design. Where their predecessors slavishly emulated the lines of a bird or bat or engaged in convoluted constructions, the Wrights selected the purity of the straight line and the Pratt truss. Where their predecessors left only sporadic documentation, the Wrights generated voluminous correspondence, study papers, commentary, critique, and diaries. They were at heart technological minimalists, and through them and their influence it is understandable why Le Courbusier and other spokesmen and prophets of the modernist era (such as Saint-Exupéry, Norman Bel Geddes, and Richard Buckminster Fuller) found flight so congenial and downright seductive.[22]

The key Wright contributions to achieving flight were threefold. First and most importantly, the Wrights recognized that the most important problem was one of *control*. All else was secondary to this. It was not enough to get off the ground with lift and power, one had to be able to guide and steer the airplane and eventually return safely to earth. Second, they recognized the importance of *integrating diverse technologies* into a single, successful airframe. Third (to put it in somewhat modern terminology), they recognized that developing a successful airplane involved *progressive flight research and flight testing,* following an incremental path from theoretical understanding through ground-based research methods, then early flight trials with subscale "technology demonstrators," and finally with full-size piloted machines.

Wilbur Wright expressed this philosophy very well when he compared flying to riding a "fractious horse." Speaking in Chicago before the Western Society of Engineers in September 1901, he said, "There are two ways of learning how to ride a fractious horse: one is to get on him and learn by actual practice [and] the other is to sit on a fence and watch the beast. . . . It is very much the same in learning to ride a flying machine; if you are looking for perfect safety, you will do well to sit on a fence and watch the birds, but if you really wish to learn, you must mount a machine and become acquainted with its tricks by actual trial."[23] In short, the Wrights exemplified the airman's philosophy, the belief of the practitioner that actual experience must accompany theory.

Four challenges confronted anyone hoping to build a flying machine: designing and fabricating a suitable structure, powering the craft, ensuring it could generate sufficient lift to remain aloft, and giving it some means of control. Thanks to Chanute, structures did not pose a serious problem for the brothers. Likewise, thanks to a variety of pioneers (mostly German), propulsion no longer posed the problems that it had for would-be airmen from the time of Cayley through Ader and Maxim—though the requirement to build a light, powerful engine still demanded the highest possible engineering standards. But significant challenges remained. Since any successful flying machine must be capable of altering its flight path (climbing, circling, and flying against the wind), *control, stability,* and *lift* constituted the critical pacing technologies.

Control and Stability: The Anticipated and Unanticipated Challenges

In their single-minded emphasis upon mastering three dimensional movement, the Wrights clearly differed from all their predecessors. They recognized immediately that two basic schools of researchers existed: those emphasizing power and lift (such as Langley and Maxim) and those emphasizing soaring flight (such as Lilienthal, Mouillard, and Chanute). "Our sympathies," the brothers wrote in 1908, "were with the latter school."[24] Lilienthal's vain struggle to regain mastery over his glider as it pitched upwards caused the brothers to focus their work on *control*. In part they did this under the mistaken assumption that other problems, namely, how to design efficient wings and propellers, had already been resolved; they would soon learn otherwise.[25]

The Wrights immediately rejected the idea of using the Lilienthal-Pilcher-Chanute-Herring method of shifting body weight to control an airplane, recognizing that the pilot possessed a very limited range of motion and distance over which he could shift his weight; that the opposing forces operating against him increased dramatically as a function of machine size, angle of attack, and speed; and that, finally, the pilot would in any case quickly fatigue himself if flying for more than a few minutes at most.[26] Any machine would have to have moveable control surfaces, not an operator as a living bobweight. Indeed, the Wrights were the first pioneers to appreciate fully that an airplane moves—and thus must be controlled—in *climbing and descending* flight (nose-up or nose-down longitudinal pitching motion controlled by elevator inputs), *yawing* flight (nose-left or nose-right directional motion controlled by rudder inputs), and *banking* flight (wing up–wing down lateral motion controlled by wing warping [then] or aileron or spoiler [now] inputs). All other motions are derivations or combinations of these.

Roll control (or "lateral balance," as the Wrights termed it) constituted the most critical of all controllability challenges. Ironically, when the brothers first began working, they thought it would be far easier to achieve than longitudinal (pitch) control.[27] Researchers had long recognized the need for a moveable rudder for directional (yaw) control and an elevator for longitudinal (pitch) control, but very few had considered the problem of lateral (roll) control. The Wrights focused on this and initially came to believe that if the machine had roll control, it might not require a moveable rudder at all, but merely a fixed vertical fin. (This, of course, was a mistake, rectified in their final glider of 1902–1903). It is likely that the brothers seized upon roll because of their background as bicycle makers. During a turn a bicycle banks into the turn, so that such a motion seemed completely natural to the brothers, in contrast to other aeronautical experimenters who envisioned airplanes making rudder-controlled flat turns similar to an automobile operating on a two-dimensional surface.

The concept of how to achieve control in roll seems to have first occurred to Orville Wright, who realized that if one could vary the lifting characteristics of the wings, the change in lift would cause one wing to rise and the other to descend, thus rolling the plane about its longitudinal axis. He sketched a wing having a fixed center portion but with the outer portions free to be pivoted about long shafts running spanwise from wingtip to wingtip.[28] Structural problems pre-vented pursuing this design, but then, in July 1899, Wilbur Wright conceived of a more structurally sound means of changing the lifting properties of the wing via "wing warping." The older brother took a "small pasteboard box" and demon-strated how one could twist it so that the top and bottom surfaces—representing the top and bottom wings of a flying machine—would flex. Slightly over two decades later, Orville recalled, "From this it was apparent that the wings of a machine of the Chanute double-deck type, with the fore-and-aft trussing removed, could be warped in like manner so that in flying the wings on the right and left sides could be warped so as to present their surface to the air at different angles of incidence and thus secure unequal lifts on the two sides."[29] The two brothers immediately built a biplane kite spanning five feet, having a Chanute-like two-bay Pratt-truss layout, with two sets of control cords running to the wingtips and attached at the tops and bottoms of the front support struts. As Dayton schoolchildren nearing the end of their summer vacation watched, the two brothers controlled the kite handily. The next step, they decided, would be a man-carrying machine, built according to the values of Lilienthal's tables. In Novem-ber 1899 they wrote to the U.S. Weather Bureau for information on places with suitable winds, thinking of testing their glider near Chicago, like Chanute. Then, on May 13, 1900, Wilbur wrote his first letter to Chanute.

The letter began with some hesitancy, almost a shyness. But very quickly the tone changes to one of surprising confidence, followed by the setting forth of a plan of action. "For some years I have been afflicted with the belief that flight is possible to man," he stated. "My disease has increased in severity and I feel that it will soon cost me an increased amount of money if not my life. I have been trying to arrange my affairs in such a way that I can devote my entire time for a few months to experiment in this field."[30] For his part Chanute sent an encouraging reply and offered to meet with Wright any time he might visit Chicago. Thus began an extraordinary correspondence that would last until Chanute's death in 1910: he soon became the brothers' closest professional friend and confidant. Other letters followed, and emboldened, Wilbur sent one on August 10 that undoubtedly stirred the old engineer: "It is my intention to begin shortly the con-struction of a full-size glider," the Daytonian began provocatively, before asking how to procure quality wood and varnish. Chanute responded four days later, sending a recipe for varnish, an address for a suitable Chicago lumber company, and some practical advice: the brothers should select "sapwood, clear, straight-grained, and thoroughly seasoned."[31]

After receiving Chanute's reply in mid-August, the brothers had set to work, rapidly building the glider, which followed the general configuration of their 1899 kite, but of course much larger. The glider reflected their thoughts of what a piloted airplane should be. The pilot would lie on, rather than hang from, the lower wing, assuming a prone position to reduce frontal resistance, and operating a "horizontal rudder" (as the brothers termed what is now more properly called an elevator) located ahead of the wing. At first glance this made perfect sense. This "tail-first" or "canard" configuration accomplished two things. First, it gave it much more refined and gentle behavior during a stall—the condition whereby a wing ceases to produce lift, typically at low speed and at a high angle of attack, as with Lilienthal's fatal accident. Most conventional "wing-first" designs dive after a stall, for the wing loses lift, the airplane drops nose down, and the tail stabilizes it in a dive. The pilot must wait to recover until the wing is going fast enough to produce lift and the tail surfaces are going fast enough to enable a pullout. Although all this only takes seconds at most, if the airplane is close to the surface—as with Lilienthal—the result can be a catastrophic plunge into the ground. But a "tail-first" canard configuration has totally different characteristics. The little canard surfaces stall while the main wing is still producing some lift. The airplane typically develops a modest sink rate, but not the headlong dive of a more conventional design. Dropping the nose slightly and accelerating beyond stall speed quickly restores control. And the brothers' choice had a second benefit as well: in the event of a crash, the front structure of the elevator and its supports would absorb much of the force, acting like a super-size *Prellbügel*. Subsequent experience with other Wright designs gave the brothers the opportunity to demonstrate both advantages.[32]

But they learned as well about the canard's surprising *dis*advantage, a byproduct of serious weaknesses in the general study of aviation at the end of the nineteenth century: the lack of understanding of the basic mechanics of flight. In bluntly stated terms, the two brothers had no appreciation for the subtleties of aircraft motions—but then no other early pioneers did either. Early pioneers recognized *translational* motions, those referring to the four forces of flight: *lift*, produced by the wing; *weight*, the gravity-imposed burden of flight; *thrust*, generated by the engine's power driving the propeller; and *drag*, the resistance produced by the airplane's moving through the air. They knew that flight involved a balancing act between the four forces: lift had to equal weight, thrust had to equal drag, and steady, stable "equilibrium" flight demanded that the center of pressure (the lifting point acting on the wing) should correspond with the airplane's center of gravity. But they did not appreciate how this changed for an airplane in real-world flight, where the airplane is buffeted by winds and gusts, and maneuvering as well. Gusts and maneuvers, even simple climbs and dives, introduce *rotational* torques and motions (called moments) that act upon an airplane, and these demanded a far more sophisticated approach to stability and control, namely, the recognition that an airplane has a *neutral point,* and as a result (depending on its design) either stable or unstable flying characteristics. Had they known the implications of this, it is likely they would have rejected the canard configuration outright, for it caused a serious stability problem that more than offset its perceived advantages.[33]

The Wrights cannot be faulted for not understanding this concept, which aerodynamicists would first comprehend more than three decades after the brothers began their work—over two full decades after their triumph at Kitty Hawk. Every lifting surface has a so-called aerodynamic center where the lift and the drag forces act upon a single point. It is normally located at approximately the quarter chord (that is, one-fourth of the distance between the leading and trailing edges). The rotational moment acting about this point is called the pitching moment.

Now, if one applies the notion of the aerodynamic center to the *entire* aircraft, by considering the forces and moments acting on *all* its lifting surfaces—that is, the wings and tail (or canard) surfaces—one derives an overall single aerodynamic center for the entire aircraft—and that is the neutral point. An aircraft with both its center of gravity and the wing's aerodynamic center ahead of its neutral point is inherently stable. If, for example, it raises its nose, its lift increases, and the pitching moment becomes negative, tending to restore the aircraft to its original position, that is, a state of equilibrium. This is the configuration of the classic "wing forward, tail aft" airplane.[34]

But the canard—"wing aft, tail forward"—airplane has its aerodynamic center *behind* the neutral point, and typically its center of gravity as well; as such it is inherently unstable. Its stability can only be maintained by the pilot deliberately holding ("fixing") the controls firmly to prevent it from going out of control, or by extraordinary ballasting of the nose with compensatory weights (thus bringing the center of gravity forward) to make it inherently stable, or in the modern era by an electronic flight control system that constantly deflects control surfaces to keep the airplane in trim. By innocently adopting the canard configuration because of what they perceived were its desirable stall and safety characteristics, the Wrights unknowingly also adopted an inherently unstable configuration, exacerbated by the mass distribution of the design they eventually produced, which had the pilot, wing cell (the upper and lower wings), and eventually fuel and engine as well all located very far aft. Thus, that their gliders and powered canard aircraft were all unstable wasn't the result of the brothers' deliberate choice but simply an accidental and natural outgrowth of their having selected the canard configuration in the first place. Ironically, the absence of any inherent stability demanded that the brothers absolutely master flight control technology, for they essentially had to work the controls constantly to keep their gliders and powered machines in trim and thus fly at all. It is again a measure of the brothers, their abilities, and their persistence, that they were able to confront these challenges and persevere.[35]

The Wrights Aloft: First Experiences

In 1524, while on his great voyage of discovery, the Italian "gentleman explorer" Giovanni da Verrazano had briefly anchored his vessel the *la Dauphine* off a windswept beach beneath some towering dunes halfway up the North American coast, naming the spot Arcadia. Shockingly, his French crew kidnapped a child to take back to France and, when confronted by a native who thrust a mysterious "burning stick" toward them, fired a musket in his direction (though mercifully without a ball) to scare him off. The poor native, presumably offering nothing more ominous than a smoldering peace pipe, stood aghast, likely the first to have learned that, indeed, smoking can be hazardous to one's health. Thus did Western technology first come to what is now Kitty Hawk, North Carolina.[36] Verrazano sailed onwards, explored the northeastern coast upwards to Maine, and returned to France. Two hundred years after Verrazano, Edward Moseley, surveyor general of the North Carolina colony and the "foremost lawyer in the province," mapped the entire area of the Carolina coast and Outer Banks, from Cape Roman to the Virginia border.[37]

In late September 1900, 376 years later, two new explorers trod the same beach, looking to use those winds to their own purpose. The Wright brothers had selected Kitty Hawk after studying data furnished by the U.S. Weather Bureau. The recorded winds were so favorable that the brothers banished thoughts of using the far closer Great Lakes coastline from their minds. With them they had their 17-foot-wingspan biplane glider. The Wrights made their first flight attempts in early October 1900, a year after Percy Pilcher's death and over four years after the death of Lilienthal. They found the glider "a rather docile thing," but to their discomfort likewise found that the tail-first configuration lacked the inherent stability they believed it would possess. In fact, the kite-glider flew with "much improved" stability if flown backwards, with the canard elevator behind the wing (that is, like a conventional biplane). At this point the brothers could have abandoned the canard and moved on, adopting configurations more like those seen with the European aircraft after 1907. But so concerned were the Wrights about avoiding a Lilienthal-type accident that as Orville recalled years later, "we retained the elevator in front for many years because it absolutely prevented a nose dive."[38] So they chose to live with the canard's nagging instabilities and in fact eventually retained the canard configuration for too long, until 1911, by which time world aviation design had passed it and them far behind.

Despite the lack of stability, tests with an operator on board were highly encouraging; in particular the ease with which the brothers could control the glider in "fore-and-aft balance" (longitudinal control) "was a matter of great astonishment to us." Wilbur Wright wrote to Chanute, "Although in appearance it was a dangerous practice we found it perfectly safe and comfortable . . . and the machine was not once injured although we sometimes landed at a rate of very nearly 30 miles per hour. The operators did not receive a single bruise. . . . The distance glided was between three and four hundred feet at an angle of one in six [i.e., one foot in descent for every six feet forward]."[39] Greatly encouraged, in late October the Wrights returned to Dayton and the business of running a bicycle shop, abandoning their first glider on the side of a Kitty Hawk sand dune. A local woman used its French sateen covering to make dresses for her two children, and a passing gale destroyed the remains of this historic machine nine months later. They had demonstrated practical longitudinal and lateral control and basic handling qualities and landings and had made some rudimentary measurements of lift and drag characteristics. The glider did not have a rudder or even a vertical fin, and much remained to be done—but much had been accomplished.

In July 1901 the brothers returned to Kitty Hawk with a new and much larger biplane glider, spanning 22 feet with a wing area of 290 square feet, and also with a forward elevator. Designed in complete accordance with Lilienthal's aerodynamic tables, it had his circular-arc airfoil section for its wings, featuring a thickness-chord ratio (the ratio of wing thickness to the length of the wing from its leading edge to its trailing edge) of 8.33 percent, that is, 1 in 12 (1 inch of thickness

The Wright 1901 glider at launch, poised in a steady wind: Wilbur is lying in the hip cradle; Bill Tate, a Wright friend and local government official, is holding the glider's right outboard forward wing strut; his half-brother Dan is holding the left outboard forward strut.
ASCHO

for every 12 inches in chord length). The earlier 1900 glider had much thinner wings, with a thickness-chord ratio of about 4.3 percent, a camber of 1 in 23. Not surprisingly, since lift loves a thick wing, the brothers discovered that the 1900 glider had disappointing lifting characteristics—but they also suspected, for the first time, that perhaps Lilienthal's data might be in error. In any case they were certain the 1901 machine would perform much better.[40]

But it didn't: in fact, the 1901 machine performed far *worse* than the 1900 glider, having a lifting capacity "scarcely one third of the calculated amount." The brothers concluded that they had several problems: the anemometer used to measure wind speed was off by 15 percent, Smeaton's coefficient of 0.005 must be off by "at least 20 percent," Lilienthal's lifting values by at least 50 percent, and finally, the biplane configuration itself must cause a slight but still significant reduction in lift over a single-wing monoplane having the same total wing area. Further, the front elevator hardly worked at all, requiring extreme inputs to achieve even basic longitudinal control.[41]

This last problem was the most serious, and in view of the pleasing results of the earlier 1900 glider, the most unexpected. From comments by two visiting guests working with Chanute and attempting to fly a glider of their own, the Wrights learned that the elevator problem might stem from a reversal of the center of pressure location on the wing's thicker airfoil at low angles of attack. As the angle of attack of the wing decreased, the center of pressure would move forward. But when the angle decreased to the point where the oncoming wind hit the leading edge of the wing—in other words, the top of the wing's upper surface—the center of pressure would reverse rapidly, moving towards the trailing edge of the wing. This, of course, generated a pronounced nose-down trim problem . . . and if the pilot corrected it by a large control surface input to the elevator, the angle of attack would increase and the center of pressure would reverse yet again, this time moving forward toward the leading edge . . . until the angle of attack increased still further, whereby the center of pressure would again move aft . . . so this back-and-forth center of pressure travel eventually would get the pilot into what is now termed a "pilot-induced oscillation" (PIO), and his efforts to control it might actually "pump" it and make it worse. Besides giving the glider an unseemly up-and-down hunting oscillation, the problem posed a serious danger of the pilot's losing control at low altitude and inadvertently diving abruptly into the ground. After thinking about what their guests said, the Wrights reduced the wing's camber from 1 in 12 to about 1 in 19, closer to the 1900's glider's airfoil shape. Thus modified, the glider flew better, more like the 1900 machine. On August 5 Chanute arrived for a week's stay, writing in his diary, "A number of excellent glides were made, Mr. Wilbur Wright showing good control of the machine in winds as high as 25 miles an hour. . . . Longest flight about 335 feet."[42] Then another problem cropped up.

With the longitudinal control problem apparently solved, Wilbur set out to try a turn using wing warping. The Wrights very ingeniously used a hip cradle that the pilot could slide from side to side. The cradle pulled cables that twisted the wings to generate a change in wing camber and hence vary the lifting characteristics between the right and left wing. When Wilbur tried a left turn, the glider obediently started to bank to the left. Then, as the left wing lowered, the turn suddenly *reversed* and the plane began rotating around to the right! He hastily managed to straighten out and land.

Something was seriously wrong, beyond their ability to resolve it at Kitty Hawk. Amid heavy rains mirroring their own disappointment and confusion, they broke camp at Kill Devil Hill on August 20 and returned by rail to Dayton, arriving home two days later. At least they could take comfort in having learned one important lesson from the 1901 glider: their ideas about longitudinal control and the lifesaving value of the front elevator worked. On their second day of testing, they had faced potential disaster: a mirror image of Lilienthal's fatal accident almost exactly five years before. As Wilbur Wright recalled, "In one glide the machine rose higher and higher till it lost all headway. This was the position from which Lilienthal had always found difficulty to extricate himself, as his machine then, in spite of his greatest exertions, manifested a tendency to dive downward almost vertically and strike the ground head on with frightful velocity. In this case a warning cry from the ground caused the operator to turn the rudder [i.e., elevator] to its full extent and also to move his body slightly forward. The machine then settled slowly to the ground, maintaining its horizontal position almost perfectly, and landed without any injury at all . . . Several glides later the same experience was repeated with the same result."[43]

But this was really the only good news: the Wrights left Kitty Hawk so discouraged that Wilbur confided his worst fear to Orville—man wouldn't fly "for fifty years."[44]

CHAPTER ELEVEN

"They Done It, They Done It, Damned If They Ain't Flew!"

As the fall of 1901 approached, the Wrights were in serious trouble. After the disappointment with the 1901 glider, lesser men might have walked away from the problem of flight. The Wrights themselves might have wasted time trying to rationalize all the data they had from Lilienthal, Chanute, and the rest of the relevant pioneers. But instead, again exemplifying the remarkable degree of self-confidence and perseverance that the brothers possessed, as Wilbur put it, "we cast it all aside, and decided to rely entirely upon our own investigations."[1] The next phase in the brothers' work involved comprehensive ground-based research. They built a special bicycle test rig equipped with a wheel balance placed on the front of the bike, and subsequently built a small wind tunnel and measuring balance à la Wenham, Browning, and Phillips.[2] The Wrights, in short, set out to develop their own aeronautical tables.

The result of that work, undertaken over a remarkable three-week period, radically reshaped their thought and guaranteed the success of their future ventures. They first evaluated approximately 200 different wing shapes, then settled on detailed testing of 38 shapes having different cambers and curvatures, a range of aspect ratios from perfect squares to long rectangles, and a variety of curved and elliptical shapes. They made lift and drag measurements, tested airfoil behavior at a variety of angles of attack, and evaluated the influence of multiplane configurations with the test wings mounted one above the other. Out of this work came the most reliable compilation of airfoil data assembled to that point in aviation history; more importantly, the Wrights now appreciated that the key to higher lift in their gliders was higher aspect ratio—one insight that Samuel Langley had appreciated for many years and that the brothers had seemingly missed or perhaps ignored in their general distrust of his approach to flight. In any case, by December 1901, the Wrights had assembled a set of data they could use with total confidence, and that was also reliable enough to extrapolate from. Only in two areas were their tests deficient: they made no measurements of center of pressure travel (which could have given them insight into pitching moments and canard instability), and they spent a great deal of effort determining the optimal lift characteristics of highly cambered airfoils, emphasizing lift at the expense of stability. But, again, in the absence of a broader understanding of flight mechanics, these deficiencies are understandable as well as forgivable.[3]

At this point, to the consternation of Chanute, the brothers briefly had to withdraw from their aeronautical research to look after personal affairs. It echoed, to a differing degree, the problems Maxim had encountered in Great

A replica of the Wright brothers' 1901 wind tunnel, key to their subsequent success.

NASM

Britain that derailed his own work: a mix of business and family problems. First, they were small businessmen, doing their aeronautical research on the side, with the 1902 biking season fast approaching. Second, their hot-headed father become involved in a nasty scrap in his church against a probable (but popular) forger, and needed Wilbur's keen financial eye and publishing skills for his defense. Not aware of the details, Chanute offered to help secure them a grant from Andrew Carnegie to make them independent, but the Wrights, always leery of being controlled by others, politely declined. Wilbur replied that while the older engineer's offer of assistance was "very much appreciated," he thought it likely that "Andrew is too hardheaded a Scotchman to become interested in such a visionary pursuit as flying."[4]

Rethinking Their Design

In due course Orville took care of planning and manufacturing for the 1902 spring and summer biking season, and Wilbur helped defend his father before the church, though without success: Bishop Milton's own conference would eventually expel him the following year.[5] But by early summer the brothers could turn their thoughts back to flying. They designed a new biplane glider, spanning 32 feet, weighing about 260 pounds and having, in addition to its elevator, a fixed, double-surface, nonmoving vertical fin, the latter intended to prevent the kind of turn-reversal they had experienced with the 1901 glider. Its wings were long, narrow rectangles, giving it an aspect ratio twice that of their earlier machines. The brothers completed assembly of the glider at midday on Friday, September 19, 1902, incorporating some of the 1901 glider's wing struts in its structure, and began test flying it that same afternoon. The flights revealed that as it glided down the slope of a dune, it lacked sufficient stability in a crosswind to prevent the gust from raising up a wing and upsetting the machine. Earlier, in tests of their original 1900 glider, the brothers had noticed the same problem and had related it to the flight of birds, and specifically whether a bird flew with *dihedral* (i.e., with its wings sweeping upwards at the tips: v), level wings (-) or *anhedral* (the wings sweeping down at the tips: ∧). Wilbur Wright had recorded in a notebook (illustrated with little drawings), "The buzzard which uses the dihedral angle finds greater difficulty to maintain equilibrium in strong winds than eagles and hawks which hold their wings level. . . . A buzzard soaring in the normal position [i.e., with dihedral] will be turned upward by a sudden gust. It immediately lowers its wings, much below its body [i.e., anhedral]."[6]

So in an attempt to enhance the glider's stability in gusts, they decided to re-rig the wings with a modest anhedral, trussing the wings spanwise so that they drooped noticeably at the tips when viewed from the front or the rear, four inches lower than in the center of the wing arch above the prone pilot. On Monday, September 22, they tried out the modification, operating the glider as a tethered kite and noting, "The machine flew beautifully," weathering crosswinds without upset.[7] But the next day, Orville crashed "while sailing along smoothly"; the glider abruptly rolled and yawed, then pitched upwards as Orville tried to return to wings-level flight. It promptly stalled and spun into the dunes, the hapless pilot winding up in "a heap of flying machine, cloth and sticks in a heap, with me in the center without a bruise or a scratch."[8] Although the brothers didn't recognize why, the anhedral aggravated the design's already marginal roll characteristics, generating what engineers now call a "spiral-mode instability" and contributing significantly to the tendency of the glider to tighten its turns and begin a spiraling descent into the ground. Repairs took a few days, and then the brothers returned to the air. By early October the Wrights knew they had licked the problem of lift—their glider was routinely flying in excess of 500 feet on each glide with perfect longitudinal control and gentle flying characteristics. A year before, Wilbur Wright had believed the solution to fly would not be found in the brothers' lifetime. Now he could confide to his father, "We now believe the flying problem is really nearing its solution."[9]

But the spiral-mode instability generated serious and continuing problems. The fixed, double-surface, vertical tail—looking like a little vertical biplane itself—did improve the glider's handling qualities, ending the rapid rotation (virtually a spin) the 1901 machine had encountered after turn reversal. However, now the glider would tighten its turn into a spiral, sliding (what is termed *sideslipping*) down the inside of the spiral and usually slamming into the ground in a process the Wrights called "well digging."[10] What caused this was a simple problem: as the glider turned, the lowered wing—the wing inside the turn—would slow, thus losing lift and naturally lowering even further. Since the Wrights were flying at most a few feet over the dunes (rarely higher than the wingspan of their gliders), the glider would thus occasionally strike the ground. In the mid-1950s, test pilots George Cooper and John Harper derived the so-called Cooper-Harper handling qualities rating scale, a ten-point scale relating aircraft characteristics to demands upon the pilot, now accepted worldwide as the best objective evaluation tool for assessing aircraft handling qualities. The Cooper-Harper scale asks three basic

Orville Wright being launched in the 1902 glider at Kill Devil Hill. United States Air Force (USAF)

questions about a new airplane: Is it satisfactory without improvement? Is adequate performance attainable with a tolerable pilot workload? Is it controllable? By these standards the 1902 glider would have undoubtedly failed all three and received a ten—improvement mandatory—meaning "control will be lost during some portion of required operation."[11] Something had to be done.

So the brothers next made their most important change since developing wing warping: they decided to change the fixed vertical tail into a moveable rudder, and they linked the rudder to the wing-warping controls so that whenever the pilot warped the wings, the rudder would pivot in the appropriate direction to assist in turning the glider. At the same time, they changed the vertical tail from a two-surface fixed tail to a single-surface moveable rudder.[12] Having thus modified the 1902 glider, the brothers flew it hundreds of times—375 flights in six days, including about 250 flights in just two days—gliding up to 622 feet at a time. These flights, still unavoidably at low altitudes, could not enable full assessment of turning performance, but the glider did perform much better in its shallow turns and banks, demonstrating that the moveable rudder linked to the wing-warping mechanism clearly improved controllability. The moveable rudder also compensated for the anhedral-aggravated spiral-mode instability, still unrecognized by the brothers; though it made the instability controllable, the rudder did not overcome it—that would come much later, in 1905.

But things were getting better, to the point where the Wrights could contemplate putting an engine on an airplane and powering their way into the air. They could do so because by now the Wrights had no superior in their airmanship or understanding in flight. On October 23 Orville said as much, writing to his sister Katharine: "The past five days have been the most satisfactory for gliding that we have had. . . . We have gained considerable proficiency in the handling of the machine now, so that we are able to take it out in any kind of weather. . . . We now hold all the records!"[13] As this letter reveals, the pace of the Wright brothers' flight research was nothing short of remarkable. They returned to Dayton on the

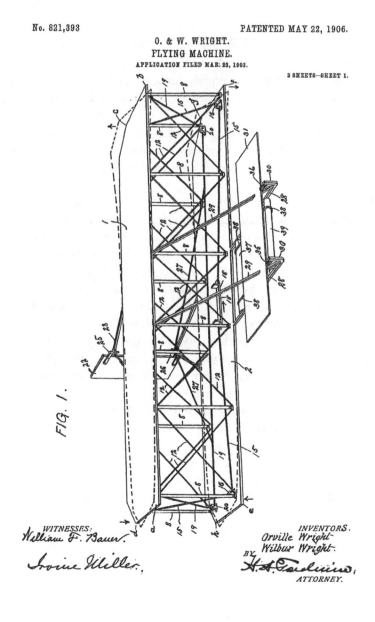

No. 821,393   PATENTED MAY 22, 1906.

O. & W. WRIGHT.
FLYING MACHINE.
APPLICATION FILED MAR. 23, 1903.

3 SHEETS—SHEET 1.

FIG. 1.

WITNESSES:
William F. Bauer.
Irvine Miller,

INVENTORS.
Orville Wright
Wilbur Wright.
BY
H. A. Toulmin,
ATTORNEY.

The Wrights' 1906 patent, detailing the design of their interconnected lateral (wing warping) and directional (pivoted rudder) control system. USPO

last day of October 1902, their spirits elevated far beyond where they had been the previous year. A year before, they had confronted perplexing and seemingly incomprehensible problems. Now, with the 1902 glider, they realized they had at last mastered aircraft design, and in light of this they promptly filed for a patent to protect their rights and secure recognition as the true inventors of the airplane.[14] However premature this may have seemed, however much more remained to be done, they knew they were ready for the final step: building a powered machine.

The Prime Mover

Early in the Roman Empire, technicians could have cut, framed, and assembled the basic structure of a wood-and-fabric airplane, and had they possessed the Wrights' insight, could have flown and controlled it—but a "prime mover" required the high-temperature materials, fuels, propeller design, and engines of the late Industrial Revolution. In the absence of this, even the most insightful pioneers—people such as Cayley—were reduced to seeking what in retrospect were bizarre or even laughable solutions, such as complex banks of oars, or moving wingtip featherlike paddles. The Wrights would have confronted the same problem, except for one thing: their work coincided with the development of the internal combustion, petroleum-fueled engine.

On August 29, 1859, Edwin L. Drake, a self-styled but commendably obstinate "colonel," struck oil in the small northwestern Pennsylvania community of Titusville, becoming the first oil driller and triggering the petroleum revolution. Out of that discovery came fuels for illumination, cooking, heating, and propulsion, as well as lubricants and waxes. But his discovery, as significant as it was, could not have had anywhere near the impact it ultimately did had it not been for the invention of specialized engines to burn petroleum distillates. That enabled the creation of modern mechanized transportation systems, typified by the automobile and the airplane. It was of particular importance to the invention of powered flight.[15]

Ironically, the prototypes of all such internal combustion engines appeared the very next year after Drake's discovery, in France. In 1860 two inventors, Pierre Hugon and Étienne Lenoir, independently developed the first modestly successful internal combustion engines in the world. Hugon's remained a technological curiosity, but Lenoir's entered production. Very crude, extremely noisy, and rough-running (to the point of alarming onlookers), this "double-acting" engine burned a mix of air and illuminating gas sucked into a piston and detonated, propelling the piston on its power stroke. Then another mix of air and gas entered behind the piston, detonated, and drove the piston back to its starting position.

In 1876 Nicolaus Otto, a salesman with a penchant for mechanical tinkering, built a model of the Lenoir engine and determined to smooth and refine its operation. By 1868, teamed with Eugen Langen, a shrewd businessman, he had produced a more powerful derivative; sales flourished, but the engine remained far from perfect: still huge, noisy, and producing insufficient energy to replace the established steam engine. Franz Reuleaux suggested that Otto compress the fuel-air mixture before detonating it. Otto accepted the suggestion, persisted in his work, and by 1876 had reached an important but counterintuitive insight: an engine would operate more efficiently if it employed four strokes instead of two in each operating cycle: an *intake* stroke, a *compression* stroke, a *power* stroke, and an *exhaust* stroke. He quickly built a demonstrator engine. First the piston pulled a partial vacuum in the cylinder drawing in a fuel-air mixture. Next the piston moved towards the top of the cylinder, compressing the fuel-air mix. Then an ignition flame detonated the mix, forcibly ramming the piston downwards. Finally the piston moved back to the top of the cylinder as the waste exhaust gases vented out of the engine. On the face of it, this seemed counterintuitive—if one wished to increase an engine's operating power and speed (and thereby its smoothness), it would seem important to *increase* the number of power strokes, not *reduce* them. But the all-important compression stroke was every bit as important to good engine performance as the one power stroke, and more than compensated for the "low" ratio of only one power stroke in every four.[16]

It was a breakthrough, even though Otto himself seems not to have fully appreciated just how much the four-stroke cycle revolutionized engine design. Otto's engine, while technologically similar to the modern piston automobile or airplane engine, still lacked refinement, and making it a practical propulsion system for motorized vehicles occupied almost the rest of the century. Four other Germans, Gottlieb Daimler (who had worked for Otto), Karl Benz, Wilhelm Maybach, and Rudolf Diesel played key roles in making the four-cycle engine a transportation success, particularly by reducing its weight, introducing carburation, a liquid fuel (gasoline), electrical ignition, and (in the case of Diesel) by abandoning conventional carburation and ignition in favor of high working internal pressures allowing use of crude, heavy fuels. Some measure of the progress these individuals made can be gathered from reviewing power-to-weight progression to the end of the century. Otto's first four-cycle engine produced three horsepower and weighed approximately 1,500 pounds per horsepower. The first automobile engines from Daimler, Benz, and Maybach furnished about one horsepower for 150 pounds of engine weight. Then, with continued refinement, in 1901 the first Mercedes automobile appeared, with a 35-horsepower engine weighing only 14 pounds per horsepower. Ironically, the engine makers themselves failed to make the connection between what they had achieved and the possible advent of the practical aircraft. Indeed, when Daimler, in a legal action, listed the possible uses for his engine, he enumerated all sorts of coaches, cars, trucks, trams, and boats, but didn't once list any sort of aerial application. But this rapid development removed the last propulsion barrier to the practical airship and airplane. Thus, when the Wrights needed a power plant, the technology base existed for them to make one.[17]

Final Preparations

So fortunately all the elements that would make a successful airplane—structures, aerodynamic understanding, controls, and propulsion—were readily at hand. After having returned to Dayton and caught up on work, the brothers sent out letters to the leading internal combustion engine manufacturers around the world, soliciting information on obtaining an engine producing at least 8 horsepower and weighing no more than 180 pounds. Most companies ignored the inquiry or sent at best dismissive or overly optimistic replies.[18] At worst the brothers found this an annoyance, for they had, after all, already designed and built the engine that powered their bicycle "factory." And they had an ace in the hole as well: a very gifted self-taught mechanic, Charles "Charlie" Taylor, a "young man of exemplary and industrious habits."[19] Born in Illinois in 1868 and raised in Nebraska, Taylor met the Wrights through his wife Henrietta, who knew their father. He moved to Dayton in 1896, set up a machine shop, and worked as a subcontractor for the brothers, making bicycle repairs and specialized parts. In 1901 he joined the Wrights full time, in part because the brothers needed someone to run their business while they undertook their flying experiments in North Carolina. So Taylor very much became a member of the Wright "team."[20]

The Wrights seem never to have thought about a twin-engine airplane, though they deliberately chose a twin-propeller approach. Like everything else about their work, practicality dominated. Here was where the superior mechanical skills of Taylor came into play, as he took charge of transforming the brothers' plans into a practicable and workable engine using a lathe and drill press. Concerned about vibration, the brothers chose a four-cylinder layout for their engine to achieve greater smoothness of operation, and, in a bid to keep weight low, opted for forming the crankcase and water jacket as a single one-piece aluminum casting. (Dayton possessed a number of small specialized machine shops, and thus finding a qualified local foundry to do the casting proved no difficulty.) It had a machined steel crankshaft connected to a heavy flywheel, with cast-iron cylinder barrels and pistons. Overall, it measured not quite 33 inches in length, 27 inches in width, and 16 inches in height, and with its flywheel-driven, ignition-sustaining magneto installed, weighed a total of 179 pounds. The Wrights and Taylor began construction of the engine in December 1902, a full year in advance of the first successful flight, and had it ready for testing in early February. On Friday, February 13, the engine fractured, requiring a new aluminum casting, which did not arrive until mid-April. Thereafter testing went smoothly, the Wrights bettering their estimated performance requirement of eight horsepower with an actual attainment of twelve horsepower at 1,090 revolutions per minute. Now they had their engine.[21]

But they recognized propulsion involved more than merely developing an engine. The power had to be transmitted to the propellers, and the propellers themselves had to be as efficient as possible. Here too the Wrights' directness and preference for the simple clearly showed. They chose a twin-propeller layout (for two propellers would act upon a greater quantity of air, enhancing performance), and located the propellers behind the wings, making them contra-rotating to cancel out each other's torque. Thus, when viewed from behind the airplane, the left propeller would rotate counterclockwise and the right one clockwise. The single engine would drive both; but rather than rely on some sort of complicated and heavy shafting and gearing arrangement, they chose a simple approach that reflected both their bicycle business and prevailing automotive practice: a chain drive using two bicycle-like sprocket chains running from the engine hub, one to each steel-tube propeller shaft. This chain-drive system was simple, effective, and low risk. Additionally, it enabled them to experiment with a wide range of speed ratios for their propellers, something that a direct-drive approach would have prevented, and that a cross-shafting approach would have made prohibitively difficult.[22]

As for the propellers, the Wrights recognized, as had few other pioneers, that a propeller is really a rotating wing with a twist, following a helical path through the air.[23] It generates a forward lift vector, in contrast to the popular image of an "airscrew" that somehow bores its way through the sky. Thus maximum propeller efficiency demanded the same kind of refined aerodynamics that the brothers had already demonstrated with their gliders. They quickly discovered that the existing literature on maritime propellers had no relevancy for the kind of propellers they needed for a flying machine. Therefore, in mid-December 1902 they began an aggressive program of research, eventually arriving at a long, elegant, high–aspect ratio propeller shape far superior to the fan, screw, angled flatplates, and "bird-feather" approaches taken by other would-be aviators. Shaping wooden propellers requires careful woodworking to ensure balance and match the lifting characteristics of the blades, for an unbalanced or dissimilar propeller can induce vibration and loads, destroying an engine or tearing it from its mount. Again their confidence showed, for the brothers did their own woodwork, bonding three laminations of spruce together and, after it thoroughly dried, hewing out the complex shape with a hatchet and drawshave, carefully varying the blades' angle of attack from 8 and a half degrees at the tip to 4 degrees near the root. Overall the propeller had a diameter of 8 and a half feet and a maximum blade width of 8 inches.[24]

Compared to the propulsion challenges, the airframe of the new airplane represented simply a larger extrapolation of the 1902 glider, but with reinforced ribs, landing skids, a 10-inch wing droop for stability (a mistaken continuation of the anhedral idea), a 1-in-20 airfoil camber, and a double-surface, not single-surface, rudder.[25] It spanned 40 feet, 4 inches, with a wing chord of 6 feet 6 inches, and had a total wing area of 510 square feet. The "horizontal rudder" (canard elevator) had an area of 28 square feet, and overall the machine had a length of 21 feet, 1 inch, and a maximum weight of 750 pounds, giving it the very low wing loading of 1.47 pounds per square foot. It still had the inherently unstable tendencies of its predecessors, and no wonder: fully 94 percent of the empty weight of the 1903 Flyer was bounded by the distance from the leading to the trailing edge of the wing, giving it an extreme-aft center of gravity location (well behind the neutral point). The pilot still lay prone in a hip cradle offset just to the left of the aircraft's centerline, and the engine counterbalanced him by being offset to the right. Here too the Wrights had given clear thought to safety, for they had no desire to risk the engine breaking loose in a crash and crushing or pinning the pilot, as might be the case if it were installed behind him. (To offset the heavy engine, which weighed an additional 34 pounds more than the pilot, the right wing had an additional four inches of wing span.) A small tank carrying a quarter gallon of gasoline was affixed to the top of the left inboard wing strut, feeding the engine by gravity, and the radiator ran vertically along the right inboard strut. The plane, which they called the Flyer, would rest on a small takeoff dolly or truck running along a 60-foot monorail launching track pointing into the wind. They finished the new craft over the summer of 1903 and then, in late September, left with it for Kitty Hawk.[26]

Triumph of "the Whopper Flying Machine"

Nature and chance still held surprises for the Wrights. A fire destroyed a railroad depot at Elizabeth City, North Carolina, together with a quantity of shipped goods, but fortunately not those of the Wrights, which had passed through a few days before. Then no sooner had they set up their camp and made a few refresher flights in the 1902 glider, than a 75-mile-per-hour gale blew through, driving five vessels ashore, threatening to tear apart their shed and all within, and forcing the brothers to take hammer and nails to the roof in the midst of howling wind and drenching rain. When the weather cleared, the brothers continued their "requal" flights in the glider, and assembling what they called "the whopper flying machine," finishing by November 5.[27]

The Wrights were in for one last bad scare, discovering they had underestimated the plane's weight by over 75 pounds. Could the engine haul the extra weight? Fortunately, tests at Kitty Hawk revealed they had also underestimated the performance of their propellers, which produced over 50 percent more thrust than they had anticipated. The two underestimates canceled each other out: the Flyer *would* fly. The last great challenge they faced was getting the propulsion system to work smoothly. Engine runs revealed irregular operation, loosening chain sprockets, and fracturing propeller shafts. They adjusted the gasoline feed to smooth out the engine and eventually cemented the sprocket nuts in place with tire cement, curing that problem, but the fracturing steel-tube propeller shafts proved more difficult to resolve. Eventually Orville returned to Dayton and made solid steel shafts, the single greatest reason why the Flyer could not attempt its first flight until mid-December.[28]

By the time Orville returned Langley had failed in his second flight attempt. When writing to the Smithsonian in 1899, Wilbur had stated his intention "to add my mite to help on the future worker who will attain final success."[29] Now there

The Wright's flight test encampment at Kitty Hawk with "The Whopper Flying Machine," newly completed, shortly before attempting its first flight. USAF

was no such false modesty. Coolly assessing Langley's first failure, Orville had written to Chanute, "I see that Langley has had his fling, and failed. It seems to be our turn to throw now, and I wonder what our luck will be."[30] Chanute visited the camp briefly in early November, pressing the brothers to test one of his variable-wing gliders and also mentioning the possibility of getting the Ader *Avion III* and having the brothers fly it. For all his expertise, Chanute clearly did not understand just how far advanced the brothers were over any of their predecessors or contemporaries; to him they were just two of many pursuing flight, all of whom seemingly had a relatively equivalent chance of success. For some time the brothers had humored Chanute and endured his assistants coming to Kitty Hawk and attempting to "help." But this distraction was frustrating, as they were concentrating with all their energy on getting off the first flight, deep in the midst of the fracturing propeller shaft problem, and their understandable frustration and tension boiled over in a sarcastic letter from Orville to his father and sister after a visit by Chanute in which the old enthusiast had recommended they work on Ader's *Avion III*: "[Chanute] seems to think we are pursued by a blind fate from which we are unable to escape. He has been trying to purchase the Ader machine built by the French government at an expense of $100,000.00 which he was intending to have us fix and *run* for him! He thinks we could do it! He doesn't seem to think our machines are so much superior as the manner in which we handle them. We are of just the reverse opinion."[31]

On December 12 the brothers installed the new solid steel propeller shafts. Two days later they made their first flight attempt. A coin toss decided in favor of Wilbur, and the brothers placed the launch track on a small incline, facing downhill. They started the engine, and the Flyer roared down the track and into the air. Wilbur overcontrolled the sensitive front elevator, and the unstable Flyer pitched up, stalled, and settled gently to earth 60 feet beyond the end of the launch rail not quite four seconds into its flight, though not gently enough to avoid breaking some of its front elevator supports. Any previous pioneer—and many afterwards— would have been happy to claim it as a first flight, but not the brothers, who had every confidence they could soar high over the dunes, perhaps as high as 1,000 feet. Repairs took the next two days. Even so, the brothers were confident and sent a message to their father concluding "success assured, keep quiet."[32]

The next flight attempt came on Thursday, December 17. Earlier in the week the weather had been warm, but the seventeenth dawned fiercely cold and windy, with a 27 mile-per-hour wind gusting across the hills from the north. The Wrights were in the same position Langley had been nine days before: winter was settling in, and they were running out of time to make a first flight before having to break camp and return to Dayton. But nothing was going to stop them now, and they pressed on. Volunteers from the Kill Devil Hill lifesaving station helped them take out the Flyer and lay out the sections of launch rail, this time on a *level* stretch of ground: an important distinction that would aid them in silencing other claimants for the "first flight" crown in years ahead. As his colleagues W. S. Dough, A. D. Etheridge, W. C. Brinkley, and Johnny Moore—a young boy from nearby Nags Head—watched the brothers, John T. Daniels set up a camera, perhaps little realizing that he would capture one of the most important images ever caught on film; at a distance, Captain S. J. Payne and Robert Wescott watched through spyglasses from the station.[33]

Orville carefully got on the machine and lay down in the hip cradle, his left hand holding a vertical control lever on his left that controlled the front elevator. With his right he started the engine by moving a small horizontal lever on the wing, rotating it horizontally like the hands of a clock from the one-o'clock "off" position to the twelve-o'clock position, which opened a fuel cock, priming the engine. Behind him Wilbur swung one of the propellers, and the engine fired. It settled down to a steady rasping putter, the chains racing with their characteristic clicking sound as they passed over the gear teeth, and the twin propellers thrummed like giant fans. Satisfied, at 10:35 A.M. Orville moved the starting lever to the eleven-o'clock position, breaking a frail cotton tie-down that tethered the Flyer to its launching rail. At once the Flyer began to move down the rail, supported by the little carrying truck and heading into the teeth of the wind. Wilbur ran alongside, steadying the right wing, and Orville carefully controlled the elevator with his left hand, steadying himself by holding on to the wing's leading edge with his right, and bracing the insteps of both his feet against footrests at the trailing edge of the lower wing.[34]

Orville wrote in his diary, "On slipping the rope the machine started off increasing in speed to probably seven or eight miles. The machine lifted from the

truck just as it was entering on the fourth rail [section]. Mr. Daniels took a picture just as it left the tracks. I found the control of the front rudder quite difficult on account of its being balanced too near the center and thus had a tendency to turn itself when started so that the rudder was turned too far on one side and then too far on the other. As a result the machine would rise suddenly to about ten feet and then as suddenly, on turning the rudder, dart for the ground. A sudden dart when out about 100 feet from the end of the tracks ended the flight. Time about 12 seconds (not known exactly as watch was not promptly stopped)."[35]

Daniels's photograph is one of the seminal images of the twentieth century and, indeed, one of the most remarkable documents (visual or otherwise) from all of human history. It shows a revolutionary moment: the Flyer has lifted off the launch track, Orville is struggling with the elevator (almost fully deflected), and Wilbur, excited, is running alongside. Wilbur made the next flight, then Orville his second, and finally, at noon, Wilbur flew for 852 feet in 59 seconds. Shortly

Orville Wright rises off the monorail launch track at 10:35 A.M., December 17, 1903, and climbs into the wind with the front elevator fully deflected as his brother Wilbur watches anxiously.
ASCHO

after, an errant wind gust rolled the machine over, breaking it up; it would never fly again. Orville Wright immediately sent another telegram home:

> Success four flights Thursday morning all against 21 mile wind started from level with engine power alone average speed through air thirty one miles longest 57 seconds inform press home Christmas.[36]

The world had changed forever, as young Johnny Moore realized: he ran down the beach after the last trial exuberantly shouting to another native, "They done it, they done it, damned if they ain't flew!"[37]

Afterwards

True to Orville's telegram, Bishop Wright contacted the press. Possibly reflecting the post-Langley climate, few newspapers actually covered the flight; those that did had the details wrong. On December 18 editor Keville Glennan (more well meaning than most post-Langley journalists) of the Norfolk *Virginian Pilot* ran a banner headline reading

FLYING MACHINE SOARS 3 MILES IN TEETH OF HIGH WIND OVER SANDHILLS AND WAVES AT KITTY HAWK ON CAROLINA COAST: NO BALLOON ATTACHED TO AID IT.[38]

Only five other newspapers picked the story up, but it did resonate in one North Carolina household: "Did you ever hear anything as foolish as that?" one Elizabeth City housewife asked her husband. The man, owner of the Kramer Brothers' lumber company, replied the Wrights had come by his shop, purchased lumber to build their camp, and overall had appeared to be "right sensible looking boys."[39]

Breakfasting *Washington Post* readers scanning the paper on December 19—a scant 11 days after Manly plunged into the frigid Potomac—caught an optimistically entitled small story on the front page:

SOARED LIKE AN EAGLE

> It is reported that a successful trial of a flying machine was made yesterday near Kitty Hawk, N.C. by Wilbur and Orville Wright, of Dayton, Ohio. It is stated that the machine flew for three miles in the face of a wind blowing at the registered velocity of 21 miles an hour, and then gracefully descended to earth at the spot selected by the man in the navigator's car as a suitable landing place. The machine has no balloon attachment, but gets its force from propellers worked by a small engine.[40]

The story made its way across the Atlantic, and before Christmas British readers of the *Daily Mail* noted a tantalizingly brief article that also happened to be one of the most accurate:

Messrs. Wilbur and Orville Wright of Ohio, yesterday successfully experimented with a flying machine at Kittyhawk, North Carolina. The machine has no balloon attachment, and derives its force from propellers worked by a small engine. In the face of a wind blowing 21 m.p.h. the machine flew three miles at the rate of eight miles an hour and landed at a point selected in advance. The idea of the box-kite was used in the construction of the airship.[41]

After this initial flurry of publicity, the flight largely disappeared from public accounts, in part because of its seeming improbability. By the end of the month, the Wrights themselves were beginning to evince a more cautious attitude reflective of their desire to keep key details of the machine a secret. When Octave Chanute inquired if the brothers would present the results of their work at the winter meeting of the American Association for the Advancement of Science in St. Louis, Wilbur Wright telegraphed a terse and to-the-point reply. "We are giving no pictures nor descriptions of machine or methods at present."[42]

Instead the Wrights concentrated on refining their airplane. They had gone from writing the Smithsonian for basic information to making the first flight in the extraordinarily short time of four and a half years; it would take them another two years to refine their design into a production-worthy machine. In 1904 the Wrights returned to the air with a new, more powerful Flyer at a new test site: Huffman Prairie, on the eastern outskirts of Dayton, an 87-acre field bordered by thin, low woods, conveniently located by Simms Station off the Dayton transit line. (Fittingly enough, their site is now part of Wright-Patterson Air Force Base, one of the premier aerospace research, development, acquisition, and logistical centers in the world.) Their rebuff to Chanute's inquiry at the end of December 1903 whether they would publicize their work now hardened into a steely reluctance to deal with the media. In May 1904, before beginning their Ohio flights, they ostensibly arranged to fly the plane before the press, though without permitting photographs. But on the appointed day, they never flew at all: the winds were too high, then too little, and finally they had engine trouble that prevented them from even running the plane down the track. The media, after hours of waiting impatiently, eventually left; the brothers rewarded those that returned the next day with a momentary and unimpressive 60-foot skimming flight marked by continuing engine problems. Perhaps the Wrights just had two days of particularly bad luck, but then, perhaps not. In any case, after this newspapers (understandably) generally left them alone, which suited the brothers just fine.[43]

Although convenient, Huffman Prairie had some drawbacks, forcing changes in the way the brothers tested their airplanes. Unlike North Carolina, Ohio around Dayton lacked the continuous strong winds off the ocean that made for good flying. Low winds meant that very often they could not take off, for a series of small hummocks dotting the prairie prevented laying out a launch track any longer than that which they had used at Kitty Hawk. To get around this restriction, they came up with a truly ingenious solution: they developed a simple gravity catapult, running a cable attached to a 1,600-pound weight from a 16-foot derricklike tower and connecting it through gears and pulleys to their Flyer. When dropped, it generated a 350-pound pull that accelerated the Flyer down the track, helping it reach flying speed in about 50 feet.[44]

With their new machine, the Wrights attempted to impart better longitudinal stability and also to demonstrate circling flight. At first they shifted the engine much further aft to produce an even-further-rearward shift in the center of gravity, in the terribly mistaken idea that this might improve stability. Of course it did not, and they quickly reverted to a more forward location, adding ballast to the canards as well. On September 20, 1904, they made the first circling flight by an airplane in aviation history: a "first" improbably reported in the quaintly titled agricultural journal *Gleanings in Bee Culture* by an author with the wonderfully rustic name of Amos Root, a Sunday-school teacher who ran a beekeepers' supply business.[45] The long-standing tendency to spiral during turns persisted, and with the moveable rudder removing one cause of the problem, at last the brothers recognized the culpability of the archlike anhedral wing trussing. They reduced the anhedral angle and performance improved. Thereafter, turning flights became commonplace, so much so that one local farmer, Amos Stauffer, watching them circle, remarked, "Well, the boys are at it again!"[46]

In 1905 the brothers built a new Flyer, using the engine and propellers from their 1904 machine, the rest of which they unceremoniously burned (it is a miracle, in view of the brothers' casual attitude towards their creations, that the 1903 machine survived—and it almost didn't, being damaged in a flood while in storage. They scrapped, abandoned, or destroyed all of their gliders, for example). The new Flyer looked generally like its predecessors but had a larger rudder, only slight anhedral (and even this was quickly abandoned), heavier weight, and small finlike gap fillers between the struts of its biplane front elevator to assist in preventing sideslip during turns. It had two important differences from its predecessors: the brothers disconnected the rudder from the warping mechanism, giving the Flyer independent directional control, like a modern airplane, and eventually they swapped the uncomfortable prone piloting position for two seats permitting the pilot and passenger to sit upright. With this machine the Wrights crossed the threshold from experimental to production flight test: the 1905 machine was a truly practical and reliable craft, as evidenced on October 5, 1905, when Wilbur Wright flew 24 miles in 38 minutes and 4 seconds, making at least 30 circuits of the field before witnesses.[47]

It had taken them over six years to reach this point, and roughly 150 flights, approximately one-third of which had ended prematurely, either in hard touchdowns or outright crashes. Their total "pilot in command" time, taken together and covering both brothers' flights in gliders and powered machines, amounted to less than six hours, only slightly longer than it takes to cross the United States from east to west, and as Caltech's Fred Culick has noted, less than that required just to solo a private pilot undergoing flight training today.[48] Throughout it all their engineering had been exemplary. Studying their work, Leonard Hobbs, himself a gifted designer, ably summarized their approach to problem solving: he concluded they made an "essentially perfect engineering achievement" using "available art and science to accomplish the desired end with a minimum expenditure of time, energy, and material [and a] constant striving for the utmost simplicity."[49]

The accomplishment they achieved reflected their hard work, not merely good fortune. If luck they had, it was the luck that accompanies those who take the greatest pains to assure their success, not the hoped-for luck of the dabbler or dilettante. But in retrospect their approach had been undeniably bold, perhaps far more so than even their staunchest advocates would recognize, culminating in a first flight in an inherently unstable, lightly loaded airplane on a gusty day with

Here Orville Wright is flying the 1905 Flyer over Huffman Prairie, east of Dayton, Ohio, on October 4, 1905, when it still had a prone piloting position. Later the brothers would modify it with seats for a pilot and passenger. It was the first Flyer with independent pitch, roll, and yaw control.
ASCHO

winds well over 20 miles an hour! Some measure of the boldness and risk of their approach can be seen in how difficult it has been to replicate and fly the actual 1903 machines since that time: many have attempted to do so but found they have had to make extraordinary and often quite visible modifications to ensure the kind of safety desired by modern aviators.

In 2000, at the request of the American Institute of Aeronautics and Astronautics (AIAA), a group of student test pilots and flight-test engineers at the Air Force Flight Test Center undertook a class project to assess and recommend desired safety and handling qualities requirements for a replica of the 1903 Flyer sponsored by the AIAA. Intended to be flown on the hundredth anniversary of Orville Wright's first flight, the replica already had several significant safety-enhancing differences from the original, including a larger canard elevator located further forward (to increase pitch damping), ballast (to improve stability by shifting the center of gravity further forward), a different airfoil cross section with less camber (to reduce pitching moment), reduced anhedral and perhaps even dihedral (to eliminate spiral mode instability), and a larger vertical tail located further aft (for added directional stability). Despite these modifications from the original design, after reviewing the program and then undertaking complex ground analysis and in-flight simulations using a sophisticated variable-stability research airplane, the test-center team suggested additional changes: a pitch stability augmentation system, no flying in crosswinds, landings over a wide area to avoid the necessity of making large-input rolls, and finally, a ground-based simulator to prepare for the "first flight" of the replica.[50] Clearly, in view of the unforgiving nature of the 1903 design, their extremely rapid mastery of flying itself, the complexities of operating its rudimentary control system, and the general lack of success of those trying to strictly emulate their design years later, the Wright brothers were superlative pilots by the standards of any era, then or now.

Overall the Wrights had set the conditions for a transformation of the world: at the end of the twentieth century, Bill Gates, the founder of Microsoft, would credit the Wrights with developing the first "World Wide Web": "The Wrights created one of the greatest cultural forces since the invention of writing, for their invention effectively became the World Wide Web of that era, bringing people, languages, ideas and values together."[51] In short, the success at Kitty Hawk created the conditions that have in turn spawned the complex, challenging, and fast-paced global village that constitutes the world of the present day.

But in 1905 the brothers were not concerned about such weighty matters. Convinced they had fully exploited their original concept for an airplane and concerned about possibly letting the secrets of their success out for others to copy before they had fully secured their rights, the two brothers now refrained from flying for almost the next three years, using the time to refine their thought and pursue the business of aviation sales. Chief among their concerns were, first, securing their patent rights and, second, securing purchase negotiations with both the American and foreign governments. As their airplane went from experimental to developmental, so too had the brothers evolved, from experimenters to entrepreneurs. They would find that role infinitely more challenging, and far less rewarding.

PART FIVE

EUROPE RESURGENT, 1905–1909

CHAPTER TWELVE

"L'affaire Wright"

On Saturday evening, October 14, 1905, delegates to the newly formed Fédération Aéronautique Internationale, just created by Comte Henri de La Vaulx, sat back in their chairs to enjoy their cognac, their cigars, and an after-dinner speech by Ernest Archdeacon. Archdeacon, a flamboyant and wealthy attorney-adventurer, possessed of good looks and impeccable dress, had a justly deserved reputation for taking chances, racing automobiles, motorcycles, and even balloons. But his abiding interest was flight: like Chanute and Means in America and Patrick Alexander in Great Britain, he corresponded widely with would-be aviators and aeronauts, and again like these, he was unstinting in his generosity in endowing prizes and supporting aeronautical causes. In 1898 he had helped found the Aéro-Club de France, of which de La Vaulx served as vice president. More recently, in partnership with the renowned Henry Deutsch de la Meurthe, he had created a 50,000-franc prize, the Prix Deutsch-Archdeacon, for the first aviator to fly a one-kilometer closed-circle flight. The prize was a substantial one, then worth $10,000, equivalent today to $200,000.

As he stood to speak, the delegates expected him to discuss some experiments he had made with a box kite–like glider. Instead he reported on something else: the rumors that the Wright brothers had perfected a powered, controllable airplane. "Whatever respect I have for the Wrights," Archdeacon said, "I find it impossible to accept as historically accurate the report of their recent tests, which have not been witnessed, and which they have kept deliberately shrouded in the most complete obscurity."[1] Archdeacon was no stranger to the Wrights and their work, but "respect" does not seem fitting to describe whatever feelings he had. He clearly did not consider the Wrights the equal of European (and especially French) aeronautical enthusiasts, and therefore one can imagine how he would have reacted had he known that, just nine days before his speech, the brothers had covered over 24 miles in a little over 38 minutes!

Concerns, Irritations, and Frustrations

If by 1905 Archdeacon did not care for the Wrights, in mid-1903 he certainly had accepted without question Chanute's reports of their gliding successes, even if he mistakenly thought, somehow, that they were pupils of the older man. He had seen the earliest garbled accounts of their flight at Kitty Hawk, and had heard of the brothers when Chanute visited France in spring of 1903, lecturing at the Aéro-Club, as well as from the Wright's French disciple (and Archdeacon's friend), the artillery captain Ferdinand Ferber. Both Archdeacon and Ferber were fiercely patriotic, and each warned, as early as mid-1903, that America might slip past France in the race for the first airplane. Reporting on Chanute's visit, Archdeacon had invoked the memory of the Montgolfiers, noting that France risked "the shame of allowing that ultimate discovery of aerial science to be realized abroad," while Ferber simply intoned, "The airplane must not be allowed to be perfected in America."[2]

The next year, on February 4, 1904, in a dinner speech before the Aéro-Club de France, that aging model maker, Victor Tatin, added his voice to the growing chorus. He gave a rousing speech warning of the threat to French aeronautical supremacy from abroad and condemned the "slavish copying" of American gliders (which he mistakenly thought were inferior to those of Lilienthal a decade before, an indication of just how out of touch he was with the latest state of Wright and even Chanute-inspired research). Building copies of American gliders, he railed, was as good as a "confession" of France's inability to match foreign advances. He concluded with an appeal to French pride: "Shall we, one day, read in history that aviation, born in France, only was achieved because of *American* work, and that only by slavishly copying them did the French obtain results? We certainly would find *that* glorious! Have not foreigners already fully exploited too many French inventions such as the steam engine, gaslight, steamships, and many others?"[3]

To Archdeacon, France's ultimate trump card was propulsion—the development and proliferation of light, powerful engines weighing less than 4.5 pounds per horsepower, while its most serious challenge was ensuring stability to prevent the pilot from "breaking his bones."[4] Like Ferber, Archdeacon attempted to copy the Wrights' gliders, working with a young and enthusiastic would-be aviator from Lyon recommended to him by both Colonel Charles Renard and Ferber: Gabriel Voisin.[5] But the information both Ferber and Archdeacon possessed about the Wrights' approach was incomplete, and their attempts at copying the Wrights resulted in craft that bore a superficial similarity, but lacked the all-important provisions for control—especially wing warping—that had made the Wrights a success. As they could not replicate the Wrights' performance, over time, the tone of Archdeacon and other French enthusiasts changed: no longer were the Wrights to be feared, rather they might well be *bluffeurs:* outright frauds.[6] And so, in March 1905, Archdeacon sent a blunt, challenging letter to the brothers, expressing his

The *Nulli Secundus II,* an outgrowth of an earlier British design, first flew in 1908 but made only three flights before being broken up, as it had little potential for military use. Turner Collection (ᴛᴄ)

"incredulity" at accounts of their successes and concluding sarcastically, "Please let me know if one may see you experiment in America; or if you would be disposed, should the occasion arise, to come and give us lessons in France."[7] How the Wrights, by now no strangers to circling flight, responded is not known, though they did reply. But to their friend Octave Chanute, they referred to Archdeacon's letter as "rather amusing," concluding that he and other experimenters "have much to learn."[8] In any case Archdeacon took his next shot at the FAI dinner.

Archdeacon's attitude echoed the increasing frustration affecting European aeronautics. In England, with Maxim and Pilcher removed from the scene, aerostatics reigned supreme, while in Germany after Lilienthal's death, the small airship and, increasingly, the Zeppelin held sway. In France nothing had come of Pénaud, Goupil, Tatin, and Ader, and efforts to copy Lilienthal and the Wrights by Ferber, Archdeacon, Esnault-Pelterie, and Voisin seemed doomed to failure. Renard had just committed suicide, and the only bright spot on the horizon was French aerostatics, courtesy of Juillot and the Lebaudys. Everywhere, then, aerostatics predominated. But what of heavier-than-air winged flight? Thanks to the prolific Octave Chanute, the Europeans learned of the Wright brothers even before their success at Kitty Hawk (though in no great detail).[9] One detects a tone almost of relief (as their failures to copy the Wrights' gliders multiplied) that "the Wrights must be bluffers!" But there is always that little echoing doubt in the mind answering, "but maybe not. . . ." For some the issue echoed older issues of class and status: the notion that two seemingly uneducated unknowns from that upstart collection of federated immigrants known as the United States could have accomplished quietly and quickly what had eluded some of the very best European minds smacked of rank fiction.

After Lilienthal's death and Maxim's and Ader's failure to fly, European aviation had entered a dormant state, roused but briefly by Percy Pilcher before his own death in 1899. Since then, only the enthusiastic airship exploits of Santos-

In contrast, France's collaboration between Juillot and the Lebaudys generated the *République,* a fine design for its time, shown here over Chalais-Meudon. Tragically, a fractured propeller caused it to crash fatally in 1909, after a year of Army service. TC

Dumont and von Zeppelin, the later airship work of the Lebaudys and the German Parseval, the glider research of French Army Captain Ferdinand Ferber, and continuing interest in flight by organizations such as Britain's Aeronautical Society and Royal Aero Club and France's Société François de Navigation Aérienne and Aéro-Club de France had kept it barely alive. At the time Archdeacon wrote to the Wrights, not a *single* European powered airplane even existed—and this at a time when the Wrights *already* had a machine that was fully controllable in three dimensions, capable of repeated reuse, and capable as well of flying in excess of 30 minutes at will—something no European aircraft would achieve for over *three years*.[10] After the ferment of the 1890s, then, *practical, technological* European aviation stagnated, clearly behind that of the United States save for periodic fits of activity dominated by lighter-than-air efforts.

It was frustrating, particularly since an explosion of wind-tunnel and laboratory building had catapulted European *science*-based (i.e., theoretically and empirically rooted) aeronautics well ahead of the Americans. Nothing demonstrated this more than new dedicated aeronautical laboratories rising across Europe, taking fullest advantage of the wind tunnel first pioneered by Wenham and Phillips. After their first two wind tunnels, Nikolai Joukovsky, a professor of mathematics at the Moscow Higher Technical School (MVTU), had followed with a third in 1891, triggering a veritable European tunnel frenzy comparable to the growth of lasers in the 1960s after the first crude laboratory demonstrations. Researchers built eight tunnels in Austria, Denmark, France, and England between 1893 and the turn of the century, including the world's first smoke tunnel (with thin tubes to produce stream lines revealing the flow around models, one of the basic analytical tools used by aircraft and automotive designers, and even architects). Then, in the early years of the twentieth century, this wave of tunnel-building spawned the first European aerodynamic laboratories in Russia, Italy, France, Germany, and England—but it did little if anything to immediately address the growing backwardness of European aeronautics.[11]

"Fliers or Liars": The Growing "l'affaire Wright"

In truth, through Europe's growing fixation on scientific aeronautics would pay large dividends in the future, in the near term Europe's would-be aviators needed more practical, technology-focused experience of the sort the Wrights had demonstrated. And despite the antipathy expressed by some towards the two brothers, European researchers increasingly sought information about what the two Americans had accomplished. Foreign interest in the Wrights had started early, thanks to the ever-voluble and exceedingly well-meaning Octave Chanute. In September 1902 Britain's Major Baden F. S. Baden-Powell (who at age 20 had been the youngest member accepted into the Aeronautical Society and subsequently, at age 40, its president in absentia while on active service in the Boer War) wrote to Octave Chanute, asking, "I hear that a Mr. Wright has been doing some good work in America. Do you know of any full account being published of his experiments?"[12] Then came Chanute's visit to France in the spring of 1903, kindling further interest, and the following year increasing news from the United States of the Wright's work led to a major essay in Britain's *The Aeronautical Journal*.[13] So it presumably came as no surprise to Chanute when on November 15, 1904, Wilbur Wright wrote to him that: "On the ninth [of November 1904] we went out to celebrate [President Theodore] Roosevelt's election by a long flight and went around four times in 5 min. 4 sec . . . . evidently a little over three miles. . . . Col. Capper stopped off at Dayton on his way East and spent a day with us. We were much pleased with him, and also Mrs. Capper, an unusually bright woman."[14]

The "Col. Capper" was none other than Colonel John Edward Capper, Royal Engineers, commandant and supervisor of His Majesty's Balloon Factory at Aldershot, England, and his visit to the brothers constituted the first indication that the Wrights' work was beginning to draw governmental interest abroad. This foreign attention all related to possible purchases of successful airplanes for military purposes, but none of the European nations nor the United States was willing to purchase airplanes on merely the promise of performance. And the Wrights, for their part, did not wish to give too much away by allowing inspection of their airplanes in advance of firm contracts. This standoff came to characterize the Wright search for contracts and the European attempt to secure the Wrights' services, to the mutual frustration of both sides.[15]

Certainly European work had so far led to little success. In England the great days of Maxim, Phillips, Pilcher, and others had ended, leaving only newer enthusiasts such as Samuel Franklin Cody actively working in the field. A colorful if illiterate expatriate American cowboy (born in Iowa in 1867), he was a crack shot and expert rider who organized popular Wild West shows. He had boldly changed his name from Cowdery to Cody in a successful bid to emulate the success of the well-known "Buffalo Bill" Cody, dressing like his "mentor" as well. Oddly, he had an even greater interest in flight, building on the work of Anglo-Australian Lawrence Hargrave but carrying it further, developing huge, winged, human-lifting box kites. These so impressed Britain's War Office that Capper hired him as a kite instructor at the Balloon Factory, in hopes that his work would eventually lead to a successful airplane. In Denmark, Jacob Christian Ellehammer built a crude monoplane, tethering it to a central pole in the midst of a circular track on the island of Lindholm in January 1906 and then skimming the earth like a huge U-control model airplane. He followed this with a semibiplane, testing it in similar fashion in September of that year, but neither machine ever achieved a true, free flight. Influenced by Victor Tatin, Trajan Vuia, an émigré Transylvanian engineer and lawyer living in France, had developed a crude and awkward-looking flying wing monoplane design echoing the gliders of Lilienthal (though without Lilienthal's understanding or insight), propelled by a modified steam engine fueled with carbonic acid. He unsuccessfully attempted to fly in 1906, and then, the following year, added an elevator, completing a series of eight brief, uncontrolled hops. In mid-1907, he unveiled a new machine of similar design, but despite two flight attempts it failed to better the performance of its predecessor. With a better engine and more refined propeller design, and with some suitable control system, Vuia might well have played an important role in European aviation—but then, that could have been the epitaph accorded many who worked in this time period. Vuia made no further contributions to aviation, but he had left one important mark: he updated a monoplane tradition dating as far back as Cayley and Pénaud, and this alone greatly influenced the course of subsequent French aircraft design, particularly the designs of Louis Blériot.[16]

Overall, France undoubtedly constituted the vibrant center of European aeronautics. There *l'affaire Wright* was rapidly heating up. Both the editor of the magazine *L'auto* and the Aéro-Club de France had gone so far as to have investigators, Robert Coquelle and Henry Weaver, visit Dayton, interview eyewitnesses, and assess whether the Wrights had in fact achieved as much as Chanute and the brothers themselves claimed, to the general bemusement of the brothers and presumably also the farmers scattered around Huffman Prairie. And the investigators reported that indeed they had: Weaver tersely replied, "Claims fully verified, particulars by mail," a message that "caused almost a riot among the members" of the Aéro-Club.[17]

At once the Wrights became the focus of major articles and speculation. So reputable were the reports that the journal *L'aérophile,* edited by the sympathetic Georges Besançon, in its first article on the state of the Wrights' research in December 1905 took the *bluffeur* issue head-on and turned it around, stating, "If any other *but* the brothers Wright announced these results, it would have been taken for a simple bluff."[18] The next month, *L'aérophile* went further still, with the venerable Victor Tatin—he of model fame and the generation of Pénaud, Gauchot, Goupil, and Ader—throwing in the towel. The Wrights, he wrote, had seized the glory of being first, "a glory forever lost to France." Further, it was "undeniable that a flying machine has been able to fly for extended time, and before numbers of witnesses." What remained now was something quite different—France had to rebuild its aeronautical competitiveness: "The native inventive genius of the French will restore to aviation the rapid progress which will return our country again to the position that it has but momentarily lost, of that I am certain; it is in France that fast, superior flying machines must be constructed, to match the automobiles which are already made; it is but a question of getting to work."[19]

But Besançon's and Tatin's acceptance was not good enough for others, and the Wrights would remain the subjects of acrimonious controversy for over another two years, until Wilbur Wright first flew in France. The controversy built over 1906, even as the evidence grew stronger of their accomplishments, particularly the publication of their patent covering their methods of lateral (roll) control, published in the January 1906 issue of *L'aérophile*.[20] Early the next month, the Paris edition of the *New York Herald* bluntly summed up the situation in an editorial that stated in part, "The Wrights have flown or they have not flown. They possess a machine or they do not possess one. They are in fact either fliers or liars."[21]

Clearly there was much thrashing about as France's would-be aviators struggled with the challenge of the Wrights, with French aviators having to learn much on their own. Alarmed, the Aéro-Club de France and the Commission Aéronautique de l'Académie des Sciences issued twin white papers in August 1906 on the state of French aviation, outlining a proposed way forwards. The first, entitled "Vers l'aviation," (Towards Aviation), served really as a foreword to the second and far more important document, "Pour le succès de l'aviation Français." Very much the work of Archdeacon, this document nevertheless grudgingly conceded there was "certainly some truth" in the reports surrounding the Wrights and their successes. It argued that there was still time for France to sweep ahead, that the Wright machine must still be a tentative aircraft at best, and that the way forward required a stimulus: an even larger prize than the 50,000-franc Prix Deutsch-Archdeacon, nothing less than a *500,000*-franc ($2 million today) Grand Prix d'Aviation.[22] But as many have found in the aerospace business since that time, merely throwing money at a problem hardly guarantees success. Then, barely a month later, even as all seemed hopeless, along came a saving event: the first tentative hop of a French-built airplane, one that could, in retrospect, serve to recover some of the honor and prestige already lost to the two bicycle-makers from midland America.

Santos to the Rescue, Archdeacon to the Attack, and Ader to the Barricades

The face-saving aviator wasn't an Ader, or a Ferber, or an Archdeacon, or any of the other rising stars (such as young Louis Blériot) of Gaulic flight. Instead it was that most remarkable and seemingly carefree of airmen, the irrepressible Alberto Santos-Dumont, he of the little airships. In 1904 Santos had visited the United States, attending the St. Louis Exposition, where Octave Chanute had hoped the Wrights would demonstrate their airplane. But the Wrights, after inspecting the grounds where flying would take place, concluded it was too unprepared and risky to attempt flying; also, they questioned the competition rules and so did not participate.[23] While at St. Louis, Santos had talked to Chanute, apparently learning of the Wrights' great successes. Over the next year he completed his personal transformation from aerostatics to winged flight, briefly (and abortively) dabbling with both a glider towed behind a motor boat and the design of a twin-rotor helicopter, then building two more airships (the *Numbers 13* and *14*). By the summer of 1906 he had constructed his first airplane, the oddly-named *14-bis*.

The *14-bis* owed its design to worlds beyond Europe, namely, the influence of the Wright brothers blended with that of the Anglo-Australian box-kite pioneer, Lawrence Hargrave. The Wright brothers' influence can be seen in its canard "tail-first" configuration, with front control surfaces intended to function as an elevator for pitch control and also a rudder for directional control. (As originally completed, it totally lacked any provision for lateral control such as the Wrights incorporated with wing warping). The box-kite influence came from the other side of the world. The Australian Hargrave, "an inventor of prime quality," in the words of Charles Gibbs-Smith, had invented the box kite in 1893, drawing on some earlier work of Francis Wenham, by combining the tandem-wing concept then being pursued by Samuel Langley and a few others with the rapidly emerging biplane concept.[24] The result was a rugged, strong lifting kite with "sidewalls" between the upper and lower surfaces and—more importantly, in the minds of European aviators—a great deal of inherent stability. Hargrave made a few brief attempts to fly his box kites as hang gliders à la Lilienthal, but after a succession of hard landings and near catastrophes decided prudently to remain on the ground. Hargrave lived too far from the aeronautical mainstream to enjoy success himself, though he traveled to America and Europe and gave presentations and left examples of his kites and models with other pioneers. The box kite dramatically influenced European aviation, so much so that many early aircraft were reflexively dubbed "box kites" by aviators, the press, and the public: the Voisin and early Farman biplanes all easily reveal their box kite heritage. But the first to employ it was Santos's *14-bis*.

Nothing Santos ever did was without its own quirkiness, and so it was with his first airplane. He had designated it the *14-bis* because he intended to launch it on its first trials from his *Number 14* airship, and so it became the "little 14" or the "14 encore." In looks it was a generally workmanlike and logically thought-out machine, with a fully covered narrow-but-deep fuselage, a box kite–like front canard elevator-rudder, and broad, high-aspect-ratio wings of pronounced dihedral with six characteristic box kite–like "side curtains" between the upper and lower wings separating the individual cellular wing bays. Altogether it spanned a little over 11 meters (almost 37 feet), with a length of almost 10 meters (nearly 32 feet) and a wing area of 52 square meters (560 square feet), and it had a 24-horsepower (later changed to a 50-horsepower) Antoinette engine driving a crude two-bladed pusher propeller; it had a tall nose skid just aft of the canard elevator-rudder, and a narrow-track, two-wheel undercarriage just under its wings. Oddly, the pilot stood, rather than sat, in a modified wicker balloon basket buried in the fuselage. In July 1906 Santos first experimented by suspending this machine from a pulley on a wire at his shop at Neuilly and towing it behind a donkey. Then, apparently encouraged by this "proof of concept" demonstration, he moved on as planned to suspending it from his airship, anticipating the later "flying aircraft carrier" airships of the 1920s and 1930s. But when he set about to actually fly, he operated it from the ground, first unsuccessfully at the polo grounds in the Bois de Boulogne, and then, after equipping it with a much more powerful engine, at Bagatelle.[25]

On Thursday, September 13, 1906, Santos hopped off the ground for a distance of 4 to 7 meters (between 13 and 23 feet). What is surprising is that he did not achieve better performance. He had a light, inherently stable airplane that had a fully loaded wing loading of only 1.18 pounds per square foot, compared to the Wrights' 1.47. (Both, of course, are extremely low figures.) The power loading offered greater advantages to Santos—13.2 pounds per horsepower versus the Wrights' 62.5 pounds per horsepower—for his engine had over four times the power of the Wrights' 1903 machine. His propeller design, however, was extremely crude—basically two small flat plates affixed to a pipe and set at an angle, and this undoubtedly deprived him of much of the benefits of higher power. Finally there are all those thousands of glides the Wrights made before their first flight. Undoubtedly, lacking that experience, Santos (despite his extensive balloon and airship time) was uncomfortable in the airplane, got behind what was happening as it started to move, and set down quickly and perhaps inadvertently. In any case he shattered his propeller (not surprising, given its location), bringing his first hop to an abrupt if nevertheless successful conclusion.[26]

After repairs, late on the chill, damp afternoon of October 23, before an expectant committee from the Aéro-Club de France, Santos started the engine and

Santos-Dumont and his *14-bis* airplane airborne at Bagatelle. "14 bis" referred to its place in his series of airships and aircraft.
MAE

began his takeoff run for a more ambitious flight. "The airplane ran for a few yards along the ground," one eyewitness reported. "Then, suddenly, it rose; steadily it flew for about 40 or 50 meters, and continued on a level keel for another 10 meters. As it advanced, however, the aeroplane became less stable, and after flying 60 meters it rocked visibly. Santos cut off his ignition at once, and his descent was distinctly abrupt. But what did a broken elevating plane and a couple of wheels matter in such an hour of victory? A power-driven machine had flown, and Santos-Dumont had flown it."[27] He had flown approximately 60 meters (almost 200 feet) at a height of about 3 meters (approximately 10 feet), winning the Coup Archdeacon, a silver trophy offered for a flight of 25 meters.[28]

Santos's two hops had fulfilled all of Archdeacon's and Ferber's expectations and resulted in a growing crescendo of public adulation. Archdeacon and the Aéro-Club arranged an award banquet at the Café de Paris on Saturday, November 10, and though pro-Wright as he undoubtedly was, Ferber nevertheless penned a glowing article for *L'aérophile,* provocatively writing, "I believe if the Wright brothers will not make a public trial, *they will lose not only their anticipated profits but as well the glory of being the first inventors.* . . . One salutes the triumphant, and the new era which opens before us."[29] (emphasis added) At the dinner, before a packed audience representing the cream of French aeronautics, past and present—Victor Tatin, Paul Tissandier, Deutsch de la Meurthe, Ferdinand Ferber, Charles de Lambert, Louis Blériot, Georges Besançon, and Robert Esnault-Pelterie, among others—Archdeacon went even further. He soaringly claimed that Santos had achieved "the first truly decisive experiment in aviation science," and then all but called the Wrights liars and frauds, saluting the diminutive Santos-Dumont for having achieved "not in secret, or before hypothetical and favorable witnesses, but in full daylight before a thousand people, a superb flight of more than 60 meters."[30]

But it was something else entirely that Archdeacon did that had the most profound consequences for subsequent aeronautical history: in his zeal to play up Santos's accomplishment, he launched a surprise attack against Clément Ader, retired but still smarting over the treatment of his *Avion III.* In a popular sporting magazine, Archdeacon claimed Ader had never flown back in 1890 with his *Éole.* Whatever else could be said of Ader, there was little doubt that he had skimmed the earth for 50 meters, and not giving the old man his due was at the least cruel and hurtful. Ader had the temperament of a twitchy old lion with chronic tooth problems, and Archdeacon's barb roused his full wrath. "The effect on the aging Ader," as historian Charles Gibbs-Smith subsequently wrote, "was to touch off a veritable explosion."[31] Indeed, Ader not only indignantly responded that he *had* flown the *Éole* in 1890, he staggeringly overplayed his hand, claiming a second and previously unknown flight in that craft the next year, and then further stating that his pride and joy, the sum of all his creative powers, the *Avion III,* had flown for no less than 300 meters that fateful day at Satory in 1897! Now on the defensive, Archdeacon shifted aim from the two American brothers to his fellow countryman. He attempted to counter Ader's defensive strike by getting the war ministry to release the still-restricted Mensier report. Ader must have truly been stung to the quick, for the stakes were enormous: if Archdeacon disproved Ader's claims, the aged pioneer's entire reputation would be in tatters. But now the Ader story took a really strange turn: for whatever reason, the war ministry refused to release the report. Thus Ader not only dodged his own bullet but also successfully planted the seeds of a story which grew unchallenged, like weeds in a garden, despite eventual release of the report four years later.

By that time the historical damage had been done, and the report had no significant impact. Monuments went up in Ader's name, testimonials were offered in his honor, the *Avion III* underwent enshrinement (taking pride of place at the world's first Salon de l'Aéronautique, held in the Grand Palais in December 1908) and exaggeration.[32] In 1911 General Pierre-Auguste Roques, the chief of French Army aviation, directed that Ader's term *avion* be henceforth the accepted word for an airplane, in honor of Ader. *Avion* thus supplanted *aéroplane* in the lexicon of French airmen, overturning a previous half century of tradition, even though the latter was in reality an authentically *French* word itself in origin, dating to J. Pline in the 1850s and used by Pénaud in the 1870s! Ader lived on: in 1911 he was again named an officer of the Légion d'Honneur this time for his aeronautical research. Then came the Great War and further legitimate luster, thanks to his genuinely prophetic works on air power and military aviation. Finally, in 1922, the president of the French republic elevated him still higher, making him a *commandeur* of the Légion d'Honneur, the first and foremost among French aviation pioneers! So Ader eventually wound up rich in honors before dying in May 1925 at the age of 84, justly vindicated for his genuine 1890 attempt and his contributions to air power thought, but questionably idolized for the *Avion III*.[33]

There is something bemusing in how Archdeacon unwittingly set the stage for enshrining Ader as *the* genuine hero of early French aviation above all others, including Alphonse Pénaud, Charles Renard, Louis Blériot, and even Santos-Dumont. Aviation historians passing through Charles de Gaulle's Terminal Two are invited to ponder this with a cup of coffee or something stronger at Chez Clément, a buffet restaurant replete with a graphic of its namesake laughing jauntily (in First World War era flying togs, no less) with his *Éole* climbing effortlessly skywards in the background.

Following his second flight, Santos-Dumont had grounded the *14-bis* to incorporate rudimentary ailerons for roll control, locating them between the upper and lower wings in the outermost wing cells, and controlling them via a body harness. On November 12 he made six brief hops, the last of which covered about 220 meters (722 feet) at a height of 6 meters (approximately 20 feet) and an airspeed of approximately 23 miles per hour, securing an Aéro-Club 1,500-franc prize for the first flight to reach 100 meters.[34] This flight electrified not only France, but all of Europe, particularly Great Britain. When the *Daily Mail,* Britain's most widely read newspaper (with an average daily circulation of more than 500,000 copies), reported the flight in a brief notice, Lord Northcliffe, the newspaper's founder, quickly intervened. Born Alfred Harmsworth, self-made, and Britain's first press magnate (indeed, one of the world's greatest), he informed his editors that the story was not that an airplane had flown over 700 feet, but that England was no longer an island. "Let me tell you," he roared into a telephone, "there will be no more sleeping safely behind the wooden walls of old England with the Channel as our safety moat. If war comes, the aerial chariots of the enemy will descend on British soil." (A decade later, they would, in the form of the first Zeppelin and Gotha bombers raiding British cities.) The next day the *Daily Mail* opined, "They are not mere dreamers who hold that the time is at hand when air power will be an even more important thing than sea power."[35]

Octave Chanute had followed Santos's progress through the years, and as the dapper aviator began his heavier-than-air experiments, the old engineer wrote to the Wrights to solicit their views. "We estimate that it is possible to jump about 250 feet, with a machine which has not made the first steps towards controllability," Wilbur replied dismissively on November 2. "If he has gone more than 300 feet he has really done something; less than that is nothing."[36] Less than two weeks later, with his November flight, Santos *had* "really done something." Even if not equivalent in duration nor distance to the brothers' own first flights at Kitty Hawk, Santos had salvaged Europe's—and particularly France's—honor in aeronautics, achieving at little cost and effort what others far better positioned to make their mark had failed to do; it was, in its own way, another deliciously ironic little moment.

The Roots of European Resurgence

It is perhaps not surprising that, given the early futile efforts of their European and American contemporaries, the Wrights had little regard for essentially all other would-be aviators. In response to a Chanute missive sent in early October 1906, Wilbur replied in a tone of supreme confidence, "We are convinced no one will be able to develop a practical flyer within five years. . . . [In fact] it is many times five years. We do not believe there is one chance in a hundred that anyone will have a machine of the least *practical* usefulness within five years."[37] In this conclusion the brothers were totally, absolutely wrong. In five years—1911—a number of airplanes from a variety of firms—the American Curtiss; the British Bristol; the Austrian Etrich; and the French Antoinette, Blériot, Breguet, Deperdussin, Farman, Morane-Saulnier, Nieuport, REP, and Voisin companies—would demonstrate not only equivalent but indeed *superior* performance to Wright aircraft of their same time period. In five years European airplanes would already be in military service and, indeed, off to war.

It is perhaps natural, in view of some of the press reaction to the European flights of Wilbur Wright, and also some of the comments of his fellow aviators, that the exposure to Wright practices has been generally credited with causing this transformation. But did it? In fact a review of European work—particularly French work—in the middle part of the decade clearly indicates that by the time the elder

Wright brother made his first flights in France, Europe's own aviators had *already* sown and nurtured the seeds of a resurgence that would soon sweep rapidly past the accumulated accomplishments of the Wrights and other American pioneers.

The European resurgence began well before Wilbur Wright arrived in France in the midsummer of 1908. The transformation started with the first hops of Santos-Dumont, steadily expanded over the years 1907 and 1908, and then exploded in multiple directions after that time, coincident with the first Wright flights in Europe. Developments in the United States and Canada, and eventually in Britain and Germany, picked up rapidly in this time period as well, typified by the first flights of F. W. "Casey" Baldwin, Glenn Curtiss, and John A. D. McCurdy under the auspices of Alexander Graham Bell's Aerial Experiment Association; early British gliding and powered trials by John Dunne, Samuel Cody, and Alliott Verdon Roe; and German-Austrian work by Professor Friedrich Ahlborn, Ignaz Etrich, Franz Wels, and Hans Grade. Much of this led directly to major new pre–First World War aircraft types having performance at least as good as their Wright contemporaries, particularly the Curtiss pusher family, Dunne's stable tailless flying wings, and the ubiquitous German *Taube* (dove).[38]

France took the greatest and most rapid strides. France had a number of would-be aviators, most a galaxy of lesser lights (as in other nations as well), but including a number of standouts who would rise to great prominence. Taken together, they constituted a "second generation" on the heels of the older pioneers, of whom only Tatin was still actively at work. The connections among these men were varied and complex, and as with their British and American contemporaries, they tended to communicate among themselves and follow each other's work and the work of others with tremendous interest. In this they had the advantage of a number of widely available and high-quality French aeronautical journals, reporting in detail anything of any significance whatsoever in the aviation field, particularly *L'aérophile,* the official house organ of the Aéro-Club. Together with a growing number of aviation societies and interest groups, this boded well for the future of French aeronautics, despite their lagging behind the Wrights and America.

Léon Levavasseur, Louis Blériot, the Voisin brothers, Robert Esnault-Pelterie, the Farman brothers, Louis Breguet, and Raymond Saulnier were among the more gifted French airplane enthusiasts. Interrelationships among all of them greatly stimulated their subsequent work. For example, Levavasseur built the engines Blériot, Voisin, and the Farmans used in their early airplanes; Blériot worked with Voisin and Levavasseur, adopted the aileron concept for roll control from Esnault-Pelterie, and later used an engine of REP's design as well; Saulnier had a major hand in designing Blériot's most famous airplane, the Model XI monoplane that crossed the Dover straits; the Farmans drew upon experience with Voisin to start their own design firms (working independently of each other until the First World War), and Breguet, having fiddled unsuccessfully with a powered helicopter, turned to fixed-wing aviation as the result of a chance conversation he had with Blériot and Gabriel Voisin.

Because of their subsequent influence, Levavasseur, Blériot, the Voisins, and the Farmans deserve special mention.

Léon Levavasseur, one of the least appreciated of early pioneers, first came to prominence by designing an important fuel-injected, eight-cylinder, V-type 24- (and later 16-cylinder 50-) horsepower engine, spawning the most significant family of European aero engines prior to the introduction of the Gnôme rotary engine by Louis and Laurent Séguin in 1909. Levavasseur's engines, in the words of Charles Gibbs-Smith, "virtually made European aviation viable."[39] The portly and bearded son of a naval officer (like Pénaud before him), Levavasseur had first studied at the École des Beaux-Arts before giving up art for naval architecture. A successful designer of small boats (perhaps in some small degree because he so looked the part, thanks to his fondness for yachting attire), Levavasseur made the acquaintance of Jules Gastambide. The owner of a powerplant in Algeria, Gastambide liked the gregarious Levavasseur and invited him in 1902 to join his family in a vacation on the Normandy coast. Like Lilienthal, Mouillard, Ader, and other avian-inspired pioneers, the 39-year-old Levavasseur was impressed by the soaring flight of the cormorants he saw patrolling the shallows as he walked along the beach. He remarked to Gastambide that he would develop a powerful lightweight engine to enable man to fly, informing Gastambide's young daughter Antoinette he would name it in her honor. Within two weeks he had a design and applied for a patent; by 1904 he had produced the first examples, initially trying them on a succession of highly successful speedboats.[40]

Confident they had a winner, Gastambide and Levavasseur next turned to aircraft engines, forming (in partnership with Louis Blériot) the Societé Antoinette in 1906, and then in time turning to designing airplanes as well. Levavasseur's first, reflecting the times and the influence of Santos-Dumont, was a pusher canard monoplane, such as Blériot had first tried. He abandoned this before completion, and embarked next on a broad-wing tractor monoplane with pronounced dihedral and a cruciform tail. While pretty, it lacked adequate provisions for control and was very much a "hopper" rather than a flyer. Levavasseur and Gastambide rebuilt it following a landing accident, incorporating crude ailerons in addition to its rudder and elevators, and named it the Antoinette II. Tested in the summer of 1909, it still made but brief hops, its greatest accomplishment being a circling flight of 1 minute and 36 seconds—the first circular flight by a piloted monoplane. But Levavasseur now had a suitable configuration to fully develop, one destined to become one of the most successful and influential of all early airplanes.[41]

Louis Blériot had taken a very different path to prominence. A graduate professional engineer from an old northern French family in Cambrai, Blériot had struggled hard during his time at Paris' École Centrale des Arts et Manufactures, finishing slightly below the middle of his class with a degree in metallurgy in 1895, at the age of 23. His graduation photographs show a lean, confident, and indeed, strikingly attired young man, neatly groomed and with a pointed and waxed mustache. Later in life, fuller in figure, more casual in dress, and concerned about financing his aviation experiments, he would take on more of a now-familiar mournful look, like a worried peasant dreading some nameless fate. After his graduation and brief mandatory military service, he had founded a company manufacturing acetylene automobile headlamps of his own design. Quite successful, he made a comfortable livelihood but turned to aviation in 1902, inspired by the stop-motion bird photography of physiologist Étienne Jules Marey. Blériot, like so many, started with the ornithopter and, indeed, built an unsuccessful flying model, providentially moving onwards to more practical concepts. In early June 1905, after watching early float glider experiments by Gabriel Voisin on the river Seine, he asked the young developer to build such a craft for him, the beginning of a brief partnership with Gabriel and his brother Charles, and marking as well the beginning of Blériot's own interest in airplanes.[42]

Les frères Voisin, destined to play major roles in French aviation history, bear a more than passing similarity to the Wrights: the elder brother furnished the main impetus to their work, and the younger was more of a supporter. Both also overemphasized the pusher configuration. Finally, in both cases, a brother died in 1912 from causes unrelated to flight. But in the case of the Wrights, it was the elder brother, Wilbur (from typhoid fever), and in the case of the Voisins, the younger brother, Charles, from an automobile accident. There was, as well, another significant difference: one has the impression from his autobiography that Gabriel Voisin's interests in aviation took a distant second place to his major enthusiasm in life, namely bedding as many *jeune femmes* as he could persuade; perhaps this is indeed why the firm of Voisin Frères never quite fulfilled its aeronautical promise. Gabriel credited his own interest in aviation to seeing Ader's *Avion III* on exhibit at the Paris Exhibition of 1900. Then a young 20-year-old architectural student in Lyon, he later recalled, "On that day I was overcome by an enthusiasm which I had never known before."[43] His enthusiasm led him to Charles Renard, and thence, in 1903, to Ferber and Archdeacon, and resulted in his piloting (with Ferber) a *faux* Wright-like glider sans wing warping commissioned by Archdeacon and tested before an exited crowd of adults and children on the dunes at Berck-sur-Mer in April 1904.[44] Archdeacon next commissioned a float glider that the elder Voisin tested (and that brought his work to Blériot's attention), this craft being the first flying machine of any sort to incorporate Hargrave's box-kite approach, which would become a characteristic of the Voisin brothers' future airplane designs. A month after meeting Blériot, Voisin had the young industrialist's glider ready, and on July 18 he took it out for a test, towed behind a speedboat designed by Levavasseur. As the glider lifted off, it became completely unstable, plunging into the Seine and nearly drowning Voisin, whom it trapped briefly underwater.[45]

After this near-disastrous experience, both Blériot and Voisin turned to powered craft, creating the world's first firm intended from its inception just to produce airplanes. But they had no success, in part due to Blériot's odd (and constantly changing) ideas regarding what constituted an ideal airplane shape: he then favored cylindrical wings placed one behind the other in ringlike fashion, later adapting at the behest of Voisin a tandem wing planform looking in profile from dead ahead like a flying ellipse. Blériot and Voisin tried out this idea with a second float biplane having a small engine, modified it after it failed to fly, tried and failed again, and modified it to take off from land, testing it at Bagatelle. It failed for the last time on the morning of November 12, 1906.

Thus it was that Blériot had the opportunity that afternoon to see Santos-Dumont make his flight of 220 meters. Captivated, he abandoned both his ring-wing kind of approach and his partnership with Voisin (though they parted amicably) and struck out on his own. In 1907 he assembled a small design team, which built a racy-looking canard pusher monoplane having wings covered by varnished paper. Blériot made three brief hops in it, all less than 20 feet, at Bagatelle in April 1907 before it finally crashed on a fourth, fortunately without injuring him. He next turned his attention to a tractor monoplane, that is, a monoplane having the engine in front. His friend and colleague Louis Peyret designed such a craft for him, dubbed the *Libellule* (dragonfly), influenced heavily by Peyret's admiration for Samuel Langley's *Great Aerodrome*. Both Peyret and Blériot hopped it off the ground at Issy-les-Moulineaux, destined to be the first genuine European airfield and now the site of the Paris heliport. The two men made a series of about a dozen hops in July and August 1907, again without great success. Perhaps most notably, it did incorporate rudimentary roll control via wingtip elevons (pivoted surfaces combining the function of elevators for pitch control and ailerons for roll control) that Blériot had adapted from fellow pioneer Robert Esnault-Pelterie. The *Libellule* did launch Blériot down the path of the robust tractor monoplane, and his next machine, the so-called Blériot VII monoplane, of 1907, clearly demonstrated his growing mastery of design and concept. It had completely enclosed fuselage and a well-thought-out wing and tail layout (the tail grouping consisting of a rudder and elevons). During tests at Issy in November and December, Blériot made a number of increasingly longer hops, two of these reaching 500 meters (approximately 1,650 feet), before the plane flipped over after a wheel ran into a hole, destroying it (but fortunately not injuring its aviator).[46]

If Blériot's accident had given him a greater appreciation for the importance of having a rugged landing gear—all his future designs would feature strong, redundant undercarriage members—he nevertheless now knew that, with the Model VII, he had, at last, a generalized configuration that he and others could use as the basis for more advanced designs.[47] His next aircraft, the Models XIII and IX of 1908, clearly show its influence, indicating that at last his long quest for a suitable configuration was at an end. Ahead lay further refinement leading to the epochal Model XI, with which he would fly from France to England in the summer of 1909, and which would be one of the most outstanding of all early airplanes, widely copied and widely flown in many countries.[48]

The Voisins took a different path, opting for the Wright-like pusher biplane, but with a box kite–like tail unit. In 1907 they had built two Chanute-type hang gliders (modifying them to incorporate their signature box-kite tail), one for Henry Farman (who, despite his name—which the French often spelled Henri—

was, like his brother Maurice, the French-born son of English parents, and a confirmed Francophile), and the other for Ferdinand Ferber. Then, later that year, they built the first of their powered biplanes, though it did not fly. Their second, built for the sculptor-aviator Léon Delagrange, and powered by a 50-horsepower Antoinette engine driving a pusher propeller, could only make brief hops, completing a flight of perhaps 80 meters at Bagatelle on March 30, 1907, piloted by Charles Voisin. Another, built for Henri Farman, became the first European airplane to fly longer than a minute, at Issy on November 9, 1907, winning the Coupe d'Aviation Archdeacon. Two months later, again at Issy on January 13–15, 1908, Farman completed a 1-kilometer circular flight and attained 1.5 kilometer in distance, winning the 50,000 franc Prix Deutsch-Archdeacon. While these accomplishments paled in comparison with those of the Wrights (who had preceded Farman in these achievements by four years), the Voisins (and Farman) were nevertheless well on their way to equaling their American predecessors, and shortly would.

Farman's flight excited the European imagination even more than had Santos-Dumont's of less than two years previously, and it seemed the Wrights were in full eclipse. Prior to turning to aviation, Farman (like other aeronautical pioneers such as Britain's Moore-Brabazon, C. S. Rolls, and Geoffrey de Havilland) had been an enthusiastic racing driver. Competing for the Panhard firm, he had earned respect as a skilled if unlucky driver on a number of tough racing courses and events, including Belgium's Circuit des Ardennes and the Gordon Bennett Trophy races. While racing in the Auvergne in 1905, his car skidded off the Clermont-Ferrand course and tumbled down a ravine, depositing him and his mechanic into the tress.[49] Farman abruptly (if understandably) turned to the then hardly safer field of aviation, and if not subsequently missed on the racing circuit, his change of allegiance had a major impact on future French aviation. With English parentage and French orientation, Farman appealed to national pride on both sides of the Dover straits. The *Times* of London hailed Farman's accomplishment as

> THE CONQUEST OF THE AIR
> SUCCESS OF AN ENGLISHMAN

(though Farman could only speak English with the greatest difficulty). In France the Aéro-Club threw yet another of its self-congratulatory banquets, and Archdeacon, ever-ready to take a shot at the Dayton brothers, boldly proclaimed, "It is Farman who has first and incontestably won mastery of the air in an airplane," effectively toppling Santos from the throne he himself had constructed for the little Brazilian aviator just 18 months previously.[50]

And so things went, as Levavasseur, Blériot, Voisin, Farman, and others worked, refined, and cross-fertilized their ideas. Some even flew abroad: Delagrange took his Voisin to Italy, flying in Rome, Milan, and Turin; in the latter city, on July 8, he had flown with a friend, an attractive young artist from Orléans, Thérèse Peltier, who thus became the first woman to ever fly in an airplane.[51] Farman flew in Ghent and then made the first transatlantic demonstration of an airplane, when he journeyed to America and flew at Brighton Beach, New York, in July and early August 1908 (though a poor flying ground, bad winds, and rain curtailed much of his flying and rendered what he did generally unimpressive).[52] Then Wilbur Wright made his first flight in France.

Hunaudières

Early 1908 marked a propitious time for the two Wrights. In January 1908, after years of back-and-forth wrangling by both sides, they had submitted a bid to the U.S. Army to furnish it with a military airplane. The next month the Army accepted, and a month later the brothers likewise secured a contract with a French syndicate headed by Lazare Weiller (and including Deutsch de la Meurthe) to purchase the Wrights' French patents and build Wright machines under license. Not having flown in the previous two and a half years, Wilbur and Orville prudently set out to Kitty Hawk to get back in practice, taking their 1905 Flyer—now modified to seat two people—with them. They made a number of flights, and on two of them carried the first passenger ever to fly in an airplane, their worker-mechanic Charlie Furnas.[53] The brothers hoped that they could jointly demonstrate their Flyer in France and then demonstrate the Military Flyer at Ft. Myer, Virginia (on a high bluff overlooking Washington), but Wilbur recognized as early as May that each would likely have to go on his own, Wilbur to France, and Orville to Ft. Myer.[54]

The elder Wright sailed for France on the *Touraine* on May 20, arriving in Paris nine days later. In 1907 the brothers had visited France in an unsuccessful attempt to sell their airplane to the French government, during which they had shipped a crated Flyer that had remained in storage ever since.[55] Now, in borrowed factory space at Le Mans, Wilbur worked to get it ready for flight. But overzealous French customs inspectors had badly repacked it following their inspections, resulting in broken framing, torn fabric, and other, more serious damage to the radiators and magneto. "I never saw such evidences of idiocy in my life," he complained to Orville, initially thinking his brother and Charlie Taylor responsible for the mess.[56] So Wright had much work to do before it was finally ready to take to the air at the beginning of August. Then he received a bad scalding from a radiator hose that separated during an engine test. But at last all was ready, and fully confident of his success, Wilbur Wright announced he would make his first demonstrations on Saturday, August 8 at the Hunaudières racecourse, five miles south of Le Mans, an announcement that brought out in full force the pro- and anti-Wright partisans, the fiery Archdeacon among them, as well as numerous journalists.

That day Wilbur Wright moved the Flyer out of its small shed at the racecourse, mounted it on its starting rail, and attached the catapult strap. In the early evening, at approximately 6:30 P.M., he started the engine, as an associate cautioned the crowd that the taking of photographs was strictly prohibited. There began the most remarkable demonstration of flying since the Montgolfiers and

Charles wafted over Paris in their gaily colored balloons 125 years previously. He released the catapult weight, and the clattering Flyer accelerated quickly, proceeding to take off "like an arrow from a crossbow." To the astonishment of those watching "le grand oiseau blanc," he immediately racked the Flyer into a steep fully controlled banking turn "at almost terrifying angles"; after two circles he rolled out wings-level, landing a minute and 45 seconds later "with the ease and grace of a wood pigeon."[57]

The Wright brothers' winning submission to the Signal Corps' specification of December 1907, requesting bids for a flying machine capable of carrying a crew of two at 40 mph. They bested 21 other proposals; evaluators earlier had rejected a further 19 as lacking in any merit. USAF

He made a further eight flights over the next five days, then moved to a more suitable site, the military camp at d'Auvours seven miles east of Le Mans, where through the end of the year he completed a further 104 flights, one of which lasted an extraordinary 2 hours, 20 minutes, and 23 seconds. On 60 occasions he took passengers, one of whom, Britain's Griffith Brewer, recalled nearly four years later: "I remember wondering whether we should really rise from the rail, and then a feeling of elation when the grass slipped away backwards and downwards and the machine seemed to be sitting on nothing. There was no sense of traveling except by the appearance of the earth moving backwards, and on look-

Wilbur Wright making a low pass in his Wright A in August 1908 during the French demonstrations; it had first been shipped to France (but not flown) over a year earlier, in the summer of 1907. TC

ing upwards it seemed that we were on a frame structure in a high wind, but without the sense of movement inherent in all other vehicles which are supported below on wheels or on water."[58]

The effect on European aviation was electric. Recognizing the significance of the brothers' gliding research to their ultimate success, and motivated not a little by national pride (for he noted as well the "deutsches Blut" of the brothers' partial German ancestry), Raimund Nimführ commented in *Illustrierte Aeronautische Mitteilungen,* "From Lilienthal through Chanute and on to the Wrights is a direct development path. The victory of the Wrights is as well the victory of the Lilienthal school."[59] An accompanying article on the Le Mans trials ended provocatively by asking "Und Deutschland?!" (and Germany?!).[60] Britain's Major B. F. S. Baden-Powell, he who had received Lord Kelvin's scathing rejection of membership in the Aeronautical Society a dozen years before and who had journeyed to France to see Wilbur Wright fly, stated melodramatically (if understandably), "That Wright is in possession of a power which controls the fate of nations is beyond dispute."[61] The French journal *L'aérophile,* always known for its support of the Wrights, graciously noted, "The ease with which the machine flies, and the dexterity of the aviator in his maneuvering has dissipated all doubts. None of the old Wright detractors can question today the previous achievements of these men who were truly the first to fly. . . . For *L'aérophile,* it is a matter of profound pride to have been the first, in 1903 and afterwards, to have made known the decisive importance of their work and hastened the dawn of their glory."[62]

The reactions of his fellow aviators offered the most significant commentary. "Blériot and [aviator Léon] Delagrange were so excited they could scarcely speak," Wilbur privately chortled to his brother Orville after his first flights, "and [airship enthusiast Henry] Kapferer could only gasp and not talk at all. . . . You never saw anything like the complete reversal of position that took place after two or three little flights of less than two minutes each."[63] "*Eh bien,*" Léon Delagrange muttered morosely, "we are beaten. We just don't exist," and his colleague and sometime airplane builder René Gasnier mournfully agreed: "Who can now doubt that the Wrights have done all they claimed?" he asked rhetorically. "We are as children compared with the Wrights."[64]

CHAPTER THIRTEEN

"The Flying Industry Is Already Born"

Given the intensity of the *bluffeur* controversy, after Wilbur Wright's extraordinary demonstrations at Hunaudières, d'Auvours, and later at Pau, partisans from both sides of *l'affaire Wright* exhibited remarkable graciousness. This surprised no one more than Wilbur Wright, who wrote Octave Chanute, "I have been received in France with a friendliness scarcely to be realized. I never hoped for such treatment."[1] Speaking before the Aéro-Club de France at—yes—yet again another banquet (but with a twist: this one honoring the brothers, on November 5, 1908), he expressed his gratitude: "If I had been born in your beautiful country and had grown up among you, I could not have expected a warmer welcome than has just been given me. When we did not know each other, we had no confidence in each other; today, when we are acquainted, it is otherwise: we believe in each other, and we are friends. . . . [As for the future] we see enough already to be certain that it will be magnificent. Only let us hurry and open the roads."[2] The sentiments were sincere, and his hosts across Europe reciprocated them.[3]

In the fall of 1908, Wilbur and Orville Wright could afford to be magnanimous. Feted, honored, proclaimed, acclaimed, the toast of European heads of state, the pride of America, the first national heroes of the new century, the Wrights seemingly had it all. While Wilbur had stormed France, Orville had been "working quietly, without causing any excitement"; then he too took to the air and took Washington as well.[4] On September 9 he had beaten his older brother to making the first flight exceeding an hour in duration. Daily, nearly 3,000 people gathered along the parade ground at Ft. Myer to see Bubbo Wright fly, sometimes solo, but also with passengers such as Major George O. Squier, future chief of the aviation branch of the U.S. Army's Signal Corps. Wright droned along in perfect control (though the basically unstable Flyer visibly bobbed and weaved slightly) on a racetrack pattern between Ft. Myer and Shooter's Hill, outside Alexandria, Virginia, about five miles away, paralleling the Potomac River.[5] It was proof positive the brothers had invented a completely successful airplane, the world's first, one capable of repeated reuse, and fraught with military possibilities.

But it had not come without a price. That evening as Wilbur spoke to the Aéro-Club, his brother Orville was fresh out of the hospital, recuperating at home from the world's first fatal airplane accident. On September 17, while the Flyer cruised at about 150 feet over the edge of the parade grounds, there was a sound like a pistol shot: spectators saw something flutter off the Flyer, which staggered, abruptly descended halfway to the earth, then pitched nose down and dove into the ground. A propeller blade had split, cut a bracing wire, and sent the Flyer plunging to earth. The crash seriously injured Orville and killed his passenger, Army trials observer Lieutenant Thomas Selfridge, scion of a distinguished naval family. (An uncle of the same name had fought gallantly during the epic Civil War battle between the hapless wooden USS *Cumberland* and the ironclad steam ram CSS *Virginia* and subsequently played a major role in the siting of the Panama Canal.) There was somewhat of a conflict of interest in having Selfridge fly the Wright machine, for he was a leading member of Alexander Graham Bell's Aerial Experiment Association. Selfridge had extensive design and flying experience with the AEA, having designed their first airplane, the *Red Wing,* and flown their second, the *White Wing,* aircraft that the Wrights believed infringed on their work. Ironically, had he lived, he would undoubtedly have been caught up in the about-to-explode Wright-Curtiss patent feud, which embittered all it touched. (As it was, distrust characterized the necessary interactions of the Wrights with Selfridge, which were formal and correct, though hardly warm.)[6]

"Old Meets New" (I): A cavalryman looks over the 1908 Military Flyer at Ft. Myer. Note the detail of the chain-drive, and the starboard propeller (which fatally fractured on September 17, leading to the death of Thomas Selfridge). U.S. ARMY

The Wright 1908 Flyer circling at Ft. Myer, Virginia: "Everyone of consequence in the social set of the Capital City [attended]," Frank Lahm later wrote," . . . making [for] quite an unusual social event." U.S. ARMY

Shocking as it was, all involved recognized that this was the kind of accident that could affect any mechanical system and that it did not reflect on the basic concept or principles underlying the Flyer's design; from his hospital bed, Orville promised he'd be back next year with a better airplane, and the Army had no problem accepting that offer. So Wilbur remained overseas, setting up a flying school at Point-Long, outside Pau, in the south of France at the base of the Pyrenees. (His first pupil was Paul Tissandier, the son of balloonist Gaston Tissandier, who had survived the *Zénith* catastrophe.) On the very last day of the year, Wright braved an icy mist to win the Coupe Michelin, a 20,000-franc prize established for the year's longest duration flight.[7] Eventually the slowly mending Orville and sister Katharine joined him in January 1909 as well. He flew before visiting kings Alfonso XIII of Spain and Edward VII of England and then took the Flyer to Italy at the behest of Giovanni Pirelli, flying before King Victor Emmanuel; the three Wrights remained in Europe until May 1909.

Before departing they stopped briefly in England for just two days. If French aviation was in its adolescence, British aviation was in its infancy. Not a single British airplane existed that could favorably compete with the Wrights', or even the various French Voisins, Blériots, or Antoinettes. Though quite a few differed with the brothers' design approach, Britain's aviators and airplane designers had never doubted the Wrights' success, and now, with the proof offered by the French flights, treated them like visiting royalty. Mutual good feelings especially flowed when, after official visits to the War Office, the Aero Club, and the Aeronautical Society in London, the brothers visited "Mussel Manor" (in reality an old farmhouse) at Shellbeach, a marshy flying field just established on the Isle of Sheppey. There they met with many of the leaders of British aeronautics, including the Short brothers (whom they already knew: balloon makers turning to aircraft production and destined to run one of Britain's major aircraft companies), Griffith Brewer (their British agent, who had flown with Wilbur in France), Charles Stuart Rolls (cofounder of the Rolls-Royce automotive empire), and J. T. C. Moore-Brabazon (a young Anglo-Irish aristocrat, later a pioneer in aerial reconnaissance who went on to a distinguished career in aviation and government service).

Moore-Brabazon had earlier piloted a Voisin at Camp de Châlons in late 1908, a feat which earned him French pilot's Brevet No. 40 and British Aviator's Certificate No. 1, issued by the Royal Aero Club. "We did a lot of flying down at Châlons," he recalled later, "and frequently made flights of about half a mile. Turning, and that kind of thing, was becoming a possibility, but no high flying was indulged in—30 to 40 feet being, I suppose, the utmost we achieved."[8] The weekend before he met the Wrights, he had made the first flights in England by a native Englishman in another Voisin, the infamous Farman-purchased machine. Named the *Bird of Passage,* it had nearly killed him when a gust threw the plane out of control. He tried to correct by rudder, the rudder control broke, and the machine pitched and rolled into the ground. "With the shock of impact," he recollected, "the engine left it moorings and came hurtling through the air from behind me—missing me by inches—and buried itself in the ground." He quickly untangled himself as his two little Irish terriers bounded up and anxiously began licking his face.[9]

Moore-Brabazon was lucky to escape with his life. Voisin was the last French pioneer of any significance to pick up on the value of wing warping and ailerons, and his pushers at this time had no form of lateral control whatsoever, as Moore-Brabazon's "startling and disconcerting" experience clearly indicates. But Britain's own pioneering aircraft designers at this time—John William Dunne and the American-born Samuel Cody (born Cowdery) of the Balloon Factory, independent inventor Alliott Verdon Roe, and Geoffrey de Havilland—made no provisions for it either. The Shorts had earlier arranged with the Wrights to build a small production run of Flyers, which had, by the standards of the day, superb lateral control, and the first of these would eventually fly before the end of 1909, together with the first indigenously developed Short airplane, also obviously drawn from the Wright experience. Not surprisingly, then, the Wrights' influence would be far more pronounced in British aviation than in the other European nations.

The Wrights had a very influential supporter who greatly stimulated British aviation prior to the First World War: Lord Northcliffe, Alfred Harmsworth, founder of the *Daily Mail.* Northcliffe established a variety of prizes for flying events in the early years of flight prior to the First World War and firmly believed in the future of the airplane at a time when many more pinned their hopes on the airship. He is caricatured (fondly) as a character played by the late Robert Morley in the finest of all aviation films, the 1960s' comedic *Those Magnificent Men in Their Flying Machines,* but the characterization is on the whole accurate. Northcliffe justly feared Britain would fall behind in aeronautics, a concern that lead him to urge a "Wake up, England!" campaign to make the country air minded; aviator Claude Grahame-White would lead a "circus" of airplanes emblazoned with the slogan around Britain in 1912. Critics of Northcliffe saw his efforts as promoted more by newspaper profits than by patriotism, but as Alfred Gollin has rightly judged, "there can be no doubt that he was keenly and genuinely alert to the dangers and the significance of the arrival of the air age for his country."[10]

In a world that they often saw as hostile, critical, and fraught with risk, the open, sincere, and unqualified admiration of Britain's aviators and aeronautical establishment for their accomplishments further bonded the brothers and their British counterparts. After all, it had not been the British who had alleged their work a "bluff" or challenged them to prove themselves "fliers or liars." Northcliffe's ever-growing respect and friendship for them and their sister, and also the conscientious efforts on their behalf by Griffith Brewer secured it further. All through the upcoming patent fight, Brewer would be a confidant, strong ally, sometime spy, and staunch defender. In time he would also be the strongest British keeper of their reputation and contributions (until the late Charles Harvard Gibbs-Smith, his worthy successor) via his establishment of the annual Wright Memorial Lecture at the Royal Aeronautical Society.[11]

So, generally satisfied with life, the Wrights returned in triumph to the United States, coursing across the North Atlantic at 24 knots on the sleek North German Lloyd Line's *Kronprinzessin Cecile,* a beautiful four-stack express steamer as evocative of the modern era as their own airplane. No one anticipated that, a mere half century later, businessmen returning from Europe would *fly* across the ocean over *20 times* faster thanks to jet-powered, all-metal, sweptwing descendants of the Wrights' frail cloth-and-wood biplane that would put the transatlantic passenger steamship out of business. The Wrights arrived to a tumultuous reception in New York harbor early on May 11, a preview of equally grand receptions in Dayton and Washington, D.C.[12] Trials of the new Military Flyer, protecting their patents, sales prospects for their machines, and a return to Europe already occupied their thoughts, and if they could not have spared greater time on their short British stay, at least it constituted a particularly bright highlight in what had been a very long and arduous trip.

The Spectre of Obsolescence: America's First Fliers and France's Fast Seconds

Focused on selling their airplane and protecting their rights, the brothers had little awareness that beyond the honors, beyond the public recognition, beyond their obvious mastery of the air lurked the spectre of imminent obsolescence. As he circled over Hunaudières on that Saturday evening of August 8, 1908, Wilbur Wright could not have known—indeed, could not have imagined—that he had just attained the apogee of American aeronautics, the highest point it would hold for nearly 40 years. Not until the late 1940s would American aeronautics again reign so supreme and so completely dominate the international scene.[13]

"We are as children compared to the Wrights," René Gasnier had complained, but children grow up even as adults age. French aviation was nascent, rife with varied possibilities. But the Wright Flyer, the world's first airplane design capable of powered, sustained, and controlled flights, had reached full maturity. It had been brilliant in its time, more than sufficient to fulfill the dream of ages—but its time was now past, roughly a half decade after it had first appeared. And the brothers really had nowhere to go unless they dramatically rethought their basic assumptions about airplane design—but time was running out, and their vision did not extend beyond the Flyer's basic concept. That concept—an unstable canard configuration, requiring full-time pilot control inputs, necessitating a catapult and launch rail for takeoff and skids for landing—simply did not match the needs and desires of the growing world aviation community. Whether Americans or Europeans (the only two national groups flying in 1909), community members increasingly favored a Cayley-Pénaud-Lilienthal-like "wing in front, tail in back" layout, inherent stability to ease the pilot's workload, and a simple wheeled undercarriage permitting operation anywhere a flat patch of land existed. The Wright machine was expensive as well—about $7,000 per airplane, as opposed to $4,000 for a new Curtiss Pusher, or as little as $2,400 for a Blériot XI monoplane. (In 2001, after almost a century of inflation, these would approximate $132,500 for a Wright Flyer, $75,700 for a Curtiss Pusher, or $45,400 for a Blériot.)[14]

The Wrights, it may be said, knew how to make the *first* airplane—but they did not know how to make the *second*. They could fiddle with the basic Flyer—add wheels instead of skids, play around with the structure, control system, and size of components, change engines and propellers—but at heart it was basically little more than their 1905 machine updated and refined. Already, with its instability, complex control system, demanding piloting workload, and inconvenient launch and landing system, it was in many ways the "wrong" airplane. In short, what the Wrights had to sell was steadily declining in value; already it—and they—represented the past, not the future, of aviation.

The Wrights inspired the French to action and their obvious mastery of flight goaded France's airmen to greater and more perceptive effort. But seeing Wilbur Wright turning effortlessly over the racecourse at Hunaudières and then examining the machine and its warping mechanism did not reveal some secret that "taught" the French to fly, for they were *already* flying. By mid-1908, *before* Wilbur Wright flew in Europe, the Antoinette, the Blériot, the Voisin, and the Farman had already flown and, indeed, had even flown in foreign skies, namely Belgium, Italy, and the United States.[15] What the Wright demonstrations taught was something else: how to fly *better*.

The French already knew the basics of aircraft design by mid-1908, as painful and unnecessarily long as their journey had been. As the Wrights had known, they recognized that any working airplane represented the successful integration of four main disciplines: aerodynamics, structures, propulsion, and controls. While much of their design work remained empirical—the "try what works" school— they nevertheless had access (if they chose) to advanced aerodynamic research, thanks to specialized and sophisticated laboratories unknown to the United States. They understood the structural requirements: no more for them the slavish copying of bird-and-bat-like forms like an Ader, no matter how much he might be venerated. They understood propulsion—by 1908 they actually had better and more powerful engines than the Wrights. French propeller design still seemed almost an afterthought of angled flat plates versus the Wrights' genuine rotating wings, something Lucien Chauvière would shortly redress by crafting a highly efficient (and beautiful as well) propeller for Louis Blériot.

They had been slowest in learning the importance of control in three dimensions, but by 1908 they already had planes flying with a solution (the pivoting aileron) that would eventually replace the Wrights' wing-warping approach over the next eight years and endure to the present day. What they lacked was the refinement of practice and experience of using the Wrights' proven (if ultimately more restrictive) wing-warping system. Seeing Wright easily pirouetting and steeply banking greatly accelerated their subsequent application of both wing warping and the aileron to existing and new designs. It was this lesson that most powerfully influenced the Europeans after August 1908. Indeed, so memorable was the evident Wright success with wing warping that two of the leading French pioneers, Levavasseur and Blériot, turned their backs on ailerons and adopted the wing-warping system, a curious result, for by the middle of the First World War, all new French—and European—aircraft had ailerons, even those of the Wright company.

Wright's flights thus constituted primarily a stimulus to those who thought about flying but as yet had not. Sir Geoffrey de Havilland, Britain's most notable aircraft pioneer, an individual whose career spanned from the era of the open-framework biplane to the turbojet fighter and airliner, recalled decades later that his "highest ambition" had been to get a job as a draftsman in an automobile design firm. The Wrights changed that: "The year 1908, when Wilbur Wright brought his machine to France . . . marked the turning point for me, away from cars and towards the heavier-than-air craft . . . [I] knew at once that . . . this was the machine to which I was prepared to give my life."[16]

Also, they were a goad to better performance by those who had gotten off the ground. They were a foretaste of *Sputnik* a half century later, which stunned Americans not by revealing that engineers could design a rocket booster and orbit a satellite, but that *Soviet* engineers could design a booster and orbit a satellite. And like *Sputnik,* it encouraged a "fast second" syndrome that would see European aviation sweep well beyond the United States within four years by 1912. Had Wilbur Wright never shown up at all in France, French aviation would have gone on much as it had, with perhaps some slowing of its pace. But his visit altered the dynamic of change and, despite the admiration of most French airmen and their fulsome public graciousness, profoundly reinforced their determination to restore France's lead in world aviation. "The exploits of Wilbur Wright at Camp d'Auvours have revealed to us a new extraordinary man," aviation commentator Baudry de Saunier wrote at the end of 1908. "But by this I do not say that Wilbur Wright has revealed to us, all of a sudden, the mechanical vehicle which is the definitive master of the air. *Far from it.*"[17]

By the summer of 1908 four different French aircraft developers had derived two different kinds of perfectly practical and stable airplanes: the monoplanes of Blériot and Levavasseur (one relatively small and racy, the other large and graceful) and the biplanes of Voisin and Farman (Voisin's a modified box-kite biplane, and Farman's a Voisin derivative). Farman would soon abandon the box-kite approach completely, following his severing of ties with the Voisins after they cheated him in a business transaction as incredible as it was unscrupulous.[18] Thus the French were on the "Wright" path, had gotten there by their own efforts, and

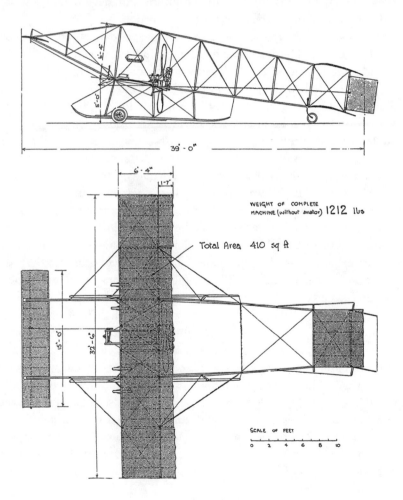

The design layout of Farman's biplane. A good basic design, it spawned numerous successors. From *Flight* (1909)

had not sacrificed their belief in inherent stability in the process. They had gained the practical experience and had closed the basic technology gap with the Wrights, even if they had not yet attained the kind of endurance or in-flight proficiency that characterized the Wrights' fully mature airplane and eight years of accumulated glider and powered-flying experience.

The First Aeronautical Salon

Any notions that French airmen and designers continued to lag fundamentally behind the United States were dispelled by a seminal event that occurred at the end of 1908: the Premier Salon de l'Aéronautique, held in the Grand Palais in Paris, across the Pont Alexandre III from the Invalides. The display, added to the annual Salon de l'Automobile, opened on Thursday, December 24, and was presided over by the President of the French Republic, Armand Fallières, and attended by Georges Clemenceau (the minister of the interior, of siege of Paris fame) and other dignitaries including the minister of war. It ran for the following five days, packing in huge crowds, upwards of 120,000 people per day, who streamed past "a fearful and wonderful birdlike structure [stretching] its uncanny wings in silent benediction over all who enter," Ader's ever-more-adored *Avion III*.[19]

The fully inflated Societé Astra blimp *Ville-de-Bordeaux,* with its odd inflated stabilizing fins, visually dominated the exhibit hall, looking like a plump knockwurst surrounded by four small cocktail sausages. Robert Esnault-Pelterie displayed an interesting monoplane with anhedral (negative dihedral, that is, the wings drooped towards the tips), and a bicycle-like landing gear and two outrigger wheels, one on each wingtip. Esnault-Pelterie would eventually make serviceable and reliable aircraft, but this wasn't one of them: it was extremely unstable. Eventually an accident tempered his enthusiasm for flying, and he turned away from aviation entirely to concentrate on spaceflight, becoming one of the first to use the word "astronautics" and to define the field itself.[20] Santos-Dumont had a new airplane on exhibit, "a small monoplane lacking any pretension," in the words of one journalist. Called the *Demoiselle,* it would become one of the most appealing and famous of early aircraft, the world's first light airplane.[21] The French firm representing the Wrights exhibited a full-size model of their Flyer, employing a guide who could speak Esperanto to shepherd international visitors around the display, though critics noticed the model was "une mauvaise copie," incorrect in structure and other details.[22] There were two experimental helicopters (actually more like vertical lift test rigs), one by Paul Cornu, and the other by brothers Louis and Jacques Breguet. Neither of these designs constituted a great success in aviation, and their principle value, as with roughly similar vehicles developed over the next decade by Jacob Ellehammer in Denmark, Raul Pescara in Spain, Igor Sikorsky in Russia, and Theodore von Kármán in Austro-Hungary, lay primarily in illustrating just how demanding solving vertical flight would be: it would take the next three decades.[23]

But the stars of the show were anything but fanciful. First was Henri Farman's Voisin-Farman biplane, newly outfitted with ailerons and winner of the Coupe d'Aviation Archdeacon and the Prix Deutsch-Archdeacon. It had flown in Belgium in late May, locals hailing its adventurous pilot as either "l'homme volant" or "de vliegende mensch," depending on their ethnic origins. Farman had taken it to America in July and August and most recently had flown 40 kilometers (approximately 25 miles) in 44 minutes, 31 seconds, on October 2, 1908, at Camp de Châlons. Then Léon Delagrange had his Voisin-Delagrange biplane on exhibit, which he had flown at Issy and also in Rome, Milan, and Turin. Levavasseur had his latest graceful Antoinette (successor to the modified Gastambide-Mengin I, which had completed the first circling flight by a monoplane on August 21, 1908, at Issy) prominently displayed; the type would become one of the most commonly seen designs at future European air meets.[24] Blériot had no less than four machines on exhibit: three monoplanes and a new pusher biplane, the latter a multiseat airplane inspired by the Wrights ("Wright modifé," one journal called it) that drew much attention at the show, but which he would never complete, wisely preferring to stick with monoplanes. Journalist Jacques Lorisson considered one of the new monoplanes, the Model XI, "a small marvel" built by "a remarkable man."[25] This last design, smaller than its predecessors, had a neat, trim, appearance and a strong, robust landing gear—he obviously remembered his hard landing that ruined the Model VII—with a centralized "cloche" flight control system (first tried on the bigger Model VIII) to control pitch and roll: the pilot pushed and pulled on a vertical stick surmounted by a fixed wheel to move control lines connected to the elevator, and moved the column right or left to move lines that warped the wings and banked the plane. His feet rested on a foot bar

"Old Meets New" (II): The graceful Antoinette startles a skittish cavalry horse at Camp de Châlons in 1909, possibly flown by Hubert Latham. TC

connected to wires to control the left-right movement of the rudder. Altogether it was a simple, straightforward system—and the direct ancestor of the modern joystick and rudder bar or rudder pedal combination.[26] Blériot would soon fly the Model XI, and to startling effect.

The diversity of exhibits, the wide range of firms exhibiting special wares and equipment, and the overwhelming public reception, particularly at a time around the Christmas holidays when most Parisians were content to remain at home with their families and friends, provided the Salon's major impact. Per day the aeronautical salon made *six times* the money the predecessor auto show had earned each day, even though the auto show, a Parisian fixture, had run twice as long as the aviation exhibition. The different kinds of configurations, the appear-

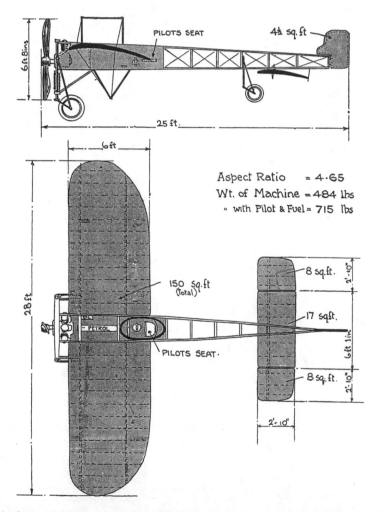

The design layout of Blériot's monoplane. Well thought out, with a monoplane configuration and possessing inherent stability, it represented a logical evolution beyond the first generation experimental airplanes and became the first widely produced airplane in aviation history. From *Flight* (1909)

ance of no less than three different kinds of monoplanes—the REP, the Antoinette, and the Blériot—spoke to the tremendous vibrancy, indeed the roiling ferment within the French aeronautical community. All this led to one inescapable conclusion succinctly framed by the reporters of Britain's newly launched *Flight* magazine: "Although these are the earliest of days, it is impossible to ignore the fact that the flying industry is already born."[27]

France, Europe, and the First Aerodynamic Laboratories

An industry demands a strong science and technology base, and coincident with the first aeronautical salon, Europe had developed just that: an important step in what was to become a rapid shift in aeronautics back across the Atlantic. In the first decade of the airplane, private, academic, industrial, and governmental aeronautical laboratories proliferated in Europe, making their appearance not only in France but across all of the Continent's major nations, and Russia as well. They sprang up even as America's only aeronautical laboratory, a tiny one-man shop set up by Albert Zahm at Catholic University in the District of Columbia, closed down for lack of funding.

The laboratory movement constituted a logical, indeed inevitable, next step after the major wave of European wind-tunnel construction in the 1890s, discussed earlier. It reflected not only concern over the Wrights and the American invention of the airplane but also the growing tension between the European nations and their increasing anxieties about possibly falling behind in what were becoming rapidly unfolding technological races involving such areas as mechanization, dreadnoughts, communications—and now aviation. Now France and four other nations—Russia, Italy, Germany, and England—moved well in advance of the United States in building a university-and industry-based laboratory infrastructure to support their growing national aeronautical efforts. If at first their efforts had little visible impact on practical aviation, they virtually guaranteed that within a decade new generations of foreign aircraft would incorporate the fruits of this research.

Again France moved quickest in this direction. Gustave Eiffel, of the famed Tour Eiffel and infamous de Lesseps bribery scandal, took French aviation beyond Renard's pioneering *Établissement Militaire de Chalais Meudon*. After the scandal forced him out of the construction field, Eiffel, always interested in flight, had turned to aeronautics. In a series of imaginative experiments, he measured the drag of objects falling from the second level of his famed Tour Eiffel, nearly 380 feet above the Champ de Mars, from which so many famed ballooning exploits had started. Dissatisfied with the limitations of such a test approach, he next constructed a laboratory at the base of the tower in 1905, unimaginatively called the Laboratoire du Champ de Mars. Although he added a proper wind tunnel in 1909, he moved to a larger laboratory, the Laboratoire Aérodynamique Eiffel, at Auteuil two years later. Eiffel's work anticipated the even more sophisticated Institut

Aérotechnique de l'Université de Paris (Aerotechnical Institute of the University of Paris), funded by Henry Deutsch de la Meurthe, which opened at St.-Cyr in 1910. It not only incorporated a wind tunnel, whirling arm, and other testing devices, but also had an open-air, three-quarter-mile, electric-powered track along which ran special test cars that could carry models and even full-size airplanes for brief test runs.[28]

In Russia, shortly after the turn of the century, Nikolai Joukovsky began studying the air circulation around a wing, assuming for ease of calculation a so-called two dimensional wing, that is, a wing of infinite span. Independently, intrigued as to why a curved surface creates lift and wishing to understand it on a mathematical level, the German mathematician Martin Kutta, inspired by the work of Lilienthal, did the same. Kutta and Joukovsky defined one of the great aerodynamic concepts, the Kutta-Joukovsky condition: air attempting to move from the lower surface of a wing around the sharp trailing edge to the upper surface forms a spanwise rotating vortex at the trailing edge. This creates a continuous "vortex sheet" streaming behind the wing and curling upwards and back on itself in a rolling cylinder or a horizontal, spanwise tornado. Kutta and Joukovsky's work stressed the necessity of understanding and visualizing the flow around a wing. Thus it is not surprising that Joukovsky clearly saw a need for expanded laboratory facilities in Russia. In 1904, at his urging, Dimitri Riabouchinsky built a genuine, full-fledged, experimental aerodynamic institute, l'Institut Aérodynamique de Koutchino, dedicated to the study of both pure and applied aerodynamics. Scion of a wealthy and distinguished family (his brother Vladimir became a noted art historian), Riabouchinsky had exhibited a flair for science early in life. Now he added a more modern tunnel than Joukovsky's, generously paying for the expansion from his own personal funds and building the institute on his father's estate. (In 1911 Riabouchinsky and others expanded its mandate, planning and then building a comprehensive hydrodynamic laboratory at the same institute.)[29]

In Italy, in 1903, as the Wrights returned to Kitty Hawk with their powered Flyer, Lieutenant Gaetano Crocco, an Italian military engineer, established an aerodynamics laboratory near Rome, equipped with a 1-meter-by-1-meter (approximately 3.28-feet-by-3.28-feet) wind tunnel of his own design. The Italian army used this tunnel for a series of propeller and airship model tests, the results of which benefited the first Italian airship, constructed in 1907. Crocco himself went on to a long and distinguished career in aeronautical research. Today he is noted primarily for his pioneering work in the field of airship stability (beginning the very next year after first building his tunnel), and his recognition of links between the fields of fluid mechanics and thermodynamics that led to the study of aerothermodynamics. (The latter is a subject of acute importance in high-temperature jet-and-rocket-engine research and supersonic and hypersonic aircraft design.) The great Hungarian aerodynamicist Theodore von Kármán called Crocco "a man of far-reaching vision," and indeed he was: in 1935, by then a general, he organized the Volta Congress on High Speeds in Aviation, a milestone international conference

that anticipated the supersonic revolution of the late 1940s and from which sprang the first discussion of swept wings for high-speed flight.[30]

It is ironic that the best known and ultimately most influential of all these early laboratories was an outgrowth of the Physikalischen Institut (Physical Institute) of the University of Göttingen, for its director, the renowned Bavarian engineer-turned-fluid-mechanician, Ludwig Prandtl, had no apparent interest in flight whatsoever when he took up his position in 1904. Prandtl arrived from the Technische Hochschule at Hanover, lured away by an academic headhunter determined to get the best possible people. The young Bavarian had a strong interest in materials and the flow of liquids, though not an interest in aerodynamics or flight—but the headhunter, Felix Klein, did. Largely through Klein's doing, and in conjunction with industry, Göttingen created an airship study institute in 1906, the Motorluftschiff-Studien Gesellschaft. This complemented the building of industrial laboratories sponsored by the Zeppelin, Parseval, and Siemens-Schuckert companies.[31]

The interior of the working room at the Koutchino Laboratory showing the equipment layout, as it appeared in 1914. Riabouchinsky, *Institut Aérodynamique de Koutchino, 1904–1914* (1914)

In the nineteenth century, France's Claude Navier and Britain's Sir George Stokes had set forth basic equations governing the *viscous*—the friction—effects that act on a moving fluid; later Osborne Reynolds took this further, studying turbulent flow in fluids and the point where fluids transitioned from smooth, "laminar" flows to disrupted ones.[32] In 1904 Prandtl postulated the existence of a boundary layer: a transitional layer where a fluid moved very slowly while just above it in the "free stream," the fluid moved more rapidly. Klein immediately realized the significance of the boundary layer and with his support, in 1908, Prandtl installed the world's first closed wind tunnel—the air flowed through a sealed tunnel circulating around and around, the prototype of the modern tunnel. Under Prandtl's leadership Göttingen subsequently played a major role in aerodynamic research. He himself made seminal contributions to understanding how a wing produces lift, the concept of induced drag, the mechanics of the boundary layer, airflow separation, turbulence, and vortex formation.[33]

Prandtl's work complemented that of the great British aerodynamicist Frederick W. Lanchester, the first to examine circulation around a wing of *finite* span—a three-dimensional, "real" wing. Like Kutta and Joukovsky, Lanchester recognized that the wing produces a "bound" vortex-like circulation flow field that forms around it, but also that this vortex must move outwards, streaming off the wing in a spanwise direction, until, finally only "attached" at the wing tips, it twists away from each tip in the form of a free trailing vortex, a kind of horizontal rolling tornado streaming behind each tip behind an airplane. Lanchester recognized these two wing vortices must contribute greatly to the overall drag of the wing, producing what aerodynamicists now term *induced drag*. This was a seminal discovery, unfortunately not as widely recognized as it should have been, in part because of his own convoluted method of expression: it was some years before Lanchester received the fullest appreciation of his contributions that he deserved. (The

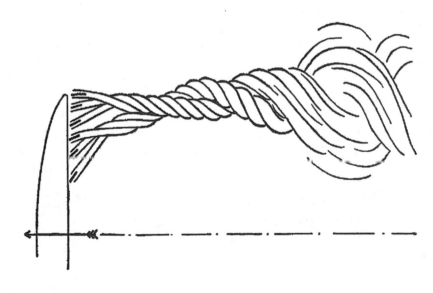

Lanchester's classic depiction of the "twisted rope" wing-tip vortices produced by the flow field around a wing. This is one of the seminal conceptual drawings in the history of aerodynamics. Lanchester, *Aerodynamics* (1907)

upswept wingtip "winglets" found on modern aircraft are designed precisely to minimize the effects of wingtip vortices).[34]

Despite its solid beginnings with Cayley, Wenham, and Phillips, Britain had lagged behind the other European nations in establishing its own laboratory tradition. In 1903 Thomas Stanton had built a vertical wind tunnel at the National Physical Laboratory in London, but only for the purpose of studying air loads and flow patterns around architectural structures. In 1905 John Fullerton, a brevet colonel in the Royal Engineers, drew up a plan for systematic tests of "flying machines," following this the next year with a recommendation that the British government form a professional committee to investigate aeronautics; but though his proposal received some senior-level endorsement, it quickly died outside military circles. Further action lagged for two years until in the autumn of 1908 Prime Minister Herbert Asquith, alarmed by foreign advances and clearly evident British stagnation, appointed a subcommittee of the Committee of Imperial Defence specifically to study aviation and its implications for British security. In mid-1909 (before Louis Blériot's dramatic flight across the Channel from France to England, Britain's secretary of state for war, Richard Haldane, successfully pressed for a permanent advisory body, subsequently established as the Advisory Committee for Aeronautics (ACA). Following its creation, Cambridge physicist Lord Rayleigh presided over the ACA, which constituted a department of the National Physical Laboratory; the NPL director, Dr. Richard Glazebrook, served as its chairman. (Its charge, "the scientific study of the problems of flight, with a view to their practical solution," constituted words that would also echo through and influence subsequent American aeronautics, for they would be copied exactly when the Congress established the National Advisory Committee for Aeronautics in 1915). Under Rayleigh and Glazebrook, the ACA moved quickly to develop its own tunnels and laboratory facilities.[35]

All of this—emerging aeronautical manufacturers and experimenters, the first aeronautical salon, the expansion of Europe's existing laboratories, and the beginning of new ones using, in many cases, industry and governmental funding—evidenced the increasing desire of French and other European and Russian enthusiasts, industrialists, and government officials to take charge of the aeronautical revolution. The Wrights had laid down a gauntlet, and the Europeans had taken it up. Just how rapidly Europe would master the airplane and flight would be evident not in a year or two, but in months. An intense competition on both sides of the Atlantic might have been expected. But across that ocean aviation was in hiatus, as both America's aviation community and its science and engineering establishment became distracted by other issues or simply went to sleep.

CHAPTER FOURTEEN

"The Age Of Flight Is the Age We Live In"

In the fall of 1908, Lord Northcliffe conceived of a dramatic flight to demonstrate the arrival of the air age and the vulnerability of Britain to attack from the air: a flight across the Dover straits, the English Channel to the British, la Manche to the French. He had earlier sought unsuccessfully to get Wilbur Wright to compete for a prize he offered for the first airplane flight between London and Manchester, but now, in early October, he established a public prize of £500, later increased in January 1909 to £1,000, for the first flight across the straits. Privately, he wanted Wilbur Wright to win. "The *Daily Mail* has offered a prize of $2,500 for a flight across the Channel, and has offered to privately give me $7,500 extra, $10,000 in all, if I will go for the prize and win it," Wilbur helpfully informed Orville, adding unnecessarily, "The latter is confidential." It was a significant amount of money: nearly $190,000, adjusted for 2001 inflation values. But his brother, recuperating from the Ft. Myer crash, quickly replied, "I do not like the idea of you attempting a Channel flight when I am not present. I haven't much faith in your motor running."[1] Rank showmanship had never been the Wrights' style, but this offer clearly had Wilbur intrigued. The timing was perfect—but on the other side of the Atlantic, Orville's long convalescence spoke to the risks in flying becoming more apparent every day, and also, it wouldn't do to have two Wright accidents. In the end, despite being easily able to accomplish the feat, Wilbur Wright backed off, and in so doing missed one of the most extraordinary opportunities ever presented to an inventor to show off his wares. The stage was now set for two of the most experienced French airmen, Hubert Latham and Louis Blériot, to compete for the prize.

The two men could not have been more different: then 26, Latham, a self-proclaimed "man of the world," was, like the Farman brothers, of English parentage, though born in Paris. Suave, good looking in a Dorian Gray sort of way, extremely wealthy, he spent his time traveling in search of excitement; eventually it would kill him, for he died in 1912, fatally gored by a wounded buffalo in the Sudan. He had taken to ballooning, and Jules Gastambide, Levavasseur's colleague, had introduced him to airplanes, then given him the opportunity to fly his latest creation, the beautiful, broad-winged Antoinette IV. Latham first flew the Antoinette IV in early 1909, and thereafter his name and that of Levavasseur's shapely airplane were inextricably linked forevermore: "Hubert Latham, c'est Antoinette," wrote *La revue de l'aviation;* "Antoinette, c'est Hubert Latham."[2] Blériot, plain-looking and much more a product of the entrepreneurial middle class, was an enthusiastic but worried businessman trying to further both his company and the aviation field. And at the end of 1908, he had his set of challenges: true, he had developed a basically excellent monoplane, refined into his latest (if still untested) Model XI. But as successful as his automobile headlight business had been, the costs of developing a succession of varied and challenging new designs had expended approximately 750,000 francs (equivalent to $150,000 at the time and $2.84 million almost a century later), calling into serious question whether he could continue his aeronautical work beyond 1909. Latham saw the Northcliffe prize as a nice trophy; Blériot saw it as the key to his financial survival, for it would bring welcome prestige and support to his future efforts.[3]

Crossing la Manche

In mid-1909, Latham and Levavasseur's Antoinette team set up their camp at Sangatte, near Calais; preparations for the flight were, for their time, as complex as those for a space launch in the early days of the American space program a half century later. The French navy assigned two destroyers for search and rescue duties, British small craft stood by as well, and the *Daily Mail* supported construction of a Marconi wireless station at the site to provide weather information. This last measure was extraordinary: the first linking of weather forecasting and radio to aviation. And also, it marked one of the first practical uses (as opposed to demonstrations) of wireless telegraphy. In 1894 Gugielmo Marconi, a young, well-to-do, privately tutored Italian savant, had conceived of the radio, building on Heinrich Hertz's earlier studies on low-frequency electromagnetic radiation. By the end of the year, he had transmitted signals 30 feet; by the end of 1896, he could reach nearly two miles. He broadcast 25 miles by the end of 1898 and in December 1901 received a signal sent across the Atlantic from Cornwall to Newfoundland. By the middle of the decade, experimental radio transmissions routinely reached ships at sea, and then, as mentioned above, in 1909 came the first efforts at linking electronic communications to aviation. It itself constituted a revolution that would, by the end of the twentieth century, witness an era of real-time communication and navigation, including navigation via specialized global positioning satellites.[4]

Latham damaged his airplane with a hard landing in stiff winds on July 13; six days later, after repairs, he attempted to fly the straits. But his engine quit a few miles off the French coast; Latham recalled, "I tried desperately to find the cause without any success," but the Antoinette IV glided down gently and splashed smoothly into the water "as the engine gave a final cough as if for one last effort."[5] Despite the gentle landing (Latham literally did not get his feet wet as he waited for the destroyer *Harpon*), the immersion severely damaged the plane, necessitating its going back to the shop. Levavasseur, rather than waste time on the IV, arranged to send the brand-new Antoinette VII, which looked similar but had wing-warping in place of the IV's ailerons, and a 60-horsepower engine. It arrived at Sangatte on July 22, highly favored to win the challenge. But by now there was a new airplane on scene: Blériot's Model XI. Blériot had first test-flown the XI on January 18 at Issy, flying it extensively from then until April. Unsatisfied with its handling and nose-heavy characteristics, he changed its first engine and a crude propeller (both built by Esnault-Pelterie) for a lighter engine built by the gifted but uncouth Allesandro Anzani, and a highly efficient and elegantly curved propeller from Lucien Chauvière. The modified machine flew beautifully. Blériot suffered a badly burned left foot during tests of another new monoplane, his two-seat Model XII, in early July. That did not prevent him from flying the Model XI southwest from the outskirts of Mondésir outside Etampes to Chevilly, just north of the forest of Orléans, on July 12, following the railroad line. For this he received a prize of 14,000 francs, his share (after deductions to Anzani and Chauvière for their contributions) coming to 9,000 francs.[6] The previous month, he had shared a 100,000 franc Osiris prize from the Institut de France with Gabriel Voisin. Coupled with a providential loan of 25,000 francs from a Haitian planter whose son's life had been saved by Blériot's wife, a series of other small prize awards, and a back order for 15 of the new Model XI monoplanes, Blériot felt more financially secure.[7] More importantly, he was confident he could fly the channel.

But there were some final scares. As noted earlier, plagued by dreadful ill luck, Blériot had suffered a bad burn when defective engine exhaust pipe shielding loosened during a flight of the Model XII. Then, on a subsequent flight, he suffered a second serious burn—before the first had fully healed—when the Model XI's Anzani engine backfired violently. The two burns necessitated an operation that left him limping in pain and under strict instructions to tend carefully to the injuries lest he experience possible infection, even gangrene. Despite this he pressed on, opting to use the proven XI instead of the newer XII, equipping it with a flotation bag in case engine failure forced him down at sea. He shipped the XI to Calais by train, picked out a small farm at Les Baraques as his starting field, and waited for the weather to break, while Latham and Levavasseur readied their replacement Antoinette VII and another French aviator—actually a Russian of French descent—Charles, Comte de Lambert, announced his intention to fly in a Wright biplane. Meantime, two journalist friends, Charles Fontaine and Marcel Marmier of *Le matin,* had journeyed to England, gone to the Dover cliffs, and noticed a gap—the Northfall meadow, next to Dover Castle—dipping down almost to the water. They realized this was a natural break in the cliffs for Blériot to land in, an important consideration in an era when a flight above 150 feet was considered high altitude, and when a pilot like Blériot could entrust his life to a plane with only a 25-horsepower engine. Fontaine sent a picture of the site, together with a note to Blériot, via the night cross-channel mail packet boat: when the pilot flew, the journalist would be at the gap, waving *le drapeau tricolore* to guide him in.[8]

The best of all possible worlds would have been a genuine race by all three airplanes, taking off at one single time. But it was instead a race of cunning, based on who read the weather more quickly and leapt to their plane. Over the night of July 24–25, the winds died, and by early morning on Sunday the twenty-fifth, the air was clear and still. Blériot's friend Alfred Leblanc, a balloonist and therefore particularly weather savvy, realized the moment had come, and it might not last. He woke the airman at 2:30 A.M. Blériot, nervous, dressed hurriedly, putting on overalls and a cork jacket and skipping breakfast. Together with Leblanc, he drove his worried wife to the quay where she boarded the French destroyer *Escopette* together with five journalists from *Le matin, Le figaro,* and the *Echo de Paris.* Then he and Leblanc made their way back to the field where Blériot's two mechanics, Colin and Mamet, were busily readying the plane. Anzani's mechanics had a less pleasant awakening from their reveries, as four blank revolver shots fired by their tyrannical boss blasted them into consciousness. Dutifully obedient, they set off to work on the engine.[9]

Alerted by a wireless message sent to Dover at 4:05, Fontaine and Marmier made their way to the gap, driving down country roads (their path, ironically, probably illuminated by a pair of Blériot headlamps). Still a half hour before dawn, before a growing crowd of reporters and locals, Blériot, limping and on crutches, got into the XI, its smoky, oil-throwing Anzani engine already running

As dawn breaks on July 25, 1909, Blériot stands in his plane as his mechanics position it for its attempted flight across the Channel.
MAE

A clearly anxious Blériot and his stoic weather advisor Leblanc (left) before takeoff. Earlier, Leblanc had correctly predicted the air at dawn would be still and clear, permitting the little airplane to fly safely. But its pilot realized just how daunting a trip across the Channel in such an underpowered airplane would be. MAE

raggedly in the dark. Barking furiously, an agitated dog leapt at the plane; the invisible, whirling propeller killed it instantly. Despite this ghastly accident (understandably alarming the superstitious), Blériot took off—still in the predawn darkness—at 4:15 for a final ten-minute proving flight around the field. After landing, mechanics topped off his gasoline tank and added additional castor oil lubricant to the engine, and he climbed back into the plane. "A little emotion seized me as I took my place in the machine," Blériot recollected. "Whether I would finish? Could I get to Dover?"[10] Then it was time. He put any doubts out of his mind and accelerated bumpily across the ground, his wheels leaving the French earth at 4:41, just as the first glimmering of the bright rising sun touched the ground. The little monoplane flew across the shore, passing left of the *Escopette* which was straining to keep up, its flogging engines making 23 knots, spewing vast quantities of black coal smoke so thick as to obscure the sun.

The rasping noise of the little three-cylinder Anzani awakened Latham from a deep sleep. Incredibly, Levavasseur and his team completely missed the significance of the falling winds during the night, despite a note from Latham the evening before telling them to wake him at 3:30 if the winds continued to drop!

Standing before his damaged craft, Blériot talks to countrymen Charles Fontaine and Marcel Marmier, as a crowd forms and Bobbies keep order. MAE

Stunned, he frantically dressed while the Antoinette team readied his plane—but then the winds rose again, as coastal France's traditionally fickle weather turned against them, and Levavasseur glumly concluded the Antoinette could not take off safely. Latham was out, heartbroken at the lost opportunity. The Comte de Lambert made no effort as well.[11]

So Blériot was alone over la Manche. The little airplane droned along at a bit over 40 miles per hour at a height of about 250 feet, in such tranquillity that it seemed he was in a balloon. Ten minutes after takeoff, Blériot hung between sea and sky, outside the sight of land, the destroyer *Escopette* left far behind, flying with perfect stability, the rasping Anzani a "marvel," the plane "docilely obedient to my thoughts." The winds remained calm, but without references or a compass, he wandered slightly in his flight path, jogging further to the north toward the North Sea, while below him the always-treacherous waters of the straits tossed and broke. A glimmering of dirty chalk white revealed the looming cliffs, a morning mist clinging and whipping around their crown. Now the winds returned with a vengeance, buffeting his plane about as he approached the shore. He pressed on, spotting three small *pacquebots,* and flew over them, hearing the sailors' "enthusiastic hurras." "Hélas!" he thought, "je ne parle pas anglais!"—so he could not ask which way to Dover. Concluding he had drifted north, he turned southwest along the cliff face, looking for the castle and the gap. On the ground a watchman on Dover's Promenade Pier saw the little plane "moving very rapidly," while several miles away a Coast Guard officer heard "a continual buzzing" from the rasping Anzani. Blériot passed by the imposing stonework of Dover Castle, looking anxiously. Suddenly he was upon them: there was Fontaine, "le brave garçon," eagerly waving the red-white-blue *tricolore*. Blériot turned into the gap over the meadow as the wind buffeted and frustrated the first of his landing attempts; he approached again and then cut his ignition at a height of about 60 feet. The little airplane dropped precipitously, landing heavily, damaging its undercarriage (despite its robust design) and fracturing its propeller.[12] It hadn't been an elegant arrival (none of Blériot's landings ever were), but it sufficed. He had crossed the channel in 37 minutes, landing at 5:18. Climbing stiffly from the cockpit, he set foot on English soil as Fontaine and Marmier rushed up and embraced him. "And Latham?" he asked nervously. "Latham's still at Sangatte," they replied, as British bobbies arrived to keep order. Back in France, Latham briefly stood teary-eyed by his Antoinette before immediately sending a congratulatory telegram to the new hero, an admirable action that led one journal to rightly hail him as "the unlucky rival of Blériot, but no less worthy than him of our admiration."[13] The plucky *Escopette,* bringing Blériot's wife and the five journalists, docked at Dover just over a half hour after the landing, at 5:50. That afternoon, *Le matin* trumpeted in a banner headline:

LE FRANÇAIS BLÉRIOT VIENT DE TRAVERSER
LA MANCHE EN AÉROPLANE

and all France went wild.

Northcliffe's desires to awaken Britain to the aerial age and its dangers could not have been better fulfilled. "England is no longer an island," the *Daily Mail* pronounced the next day, and one correspondent subsequently wrote, "Blériot did not get up in any blare of trumpets. In the cold, grey dawn of the morning, before the sun had warmed up things, before it had dissipated the dewdrops, he was in our country. It marks a new era in the world." Alan Cobham, who would do much to make England air minded, noted, "The day that Blériot flew the Channel marked the end of our insular safety, and the beginning of the time when Britain must seek another form of defence beside its ships."[14] Futurist and Fabian socialist H. G. Wells, a friend of British flying-wing experimenter John William Dunne and a confidant of Britain's secretary of state for war, Richard Haldane, fumed like a Jeremiah: "It has been raining warnings on us—never was a slacking, dull people so liberally served with warnings of what is in store for them. . . . In spite of our fleet, this is no longer . . . an inaccessible island."[15]

National security aside, all admired the man who had made the flight. Blériot basked in a warm glow of public adulation on both sides of the Channel, his plane first displayed at Selfridge's department store in London, then at the offices of *Le matin* in Paris, and finally enshrined in the Conservatoire des Arts et Métiers, where it hangs to this day.[16] The aviator himself was feted in both London and Paris: in London at Northcliffe's award dinner, he shared the spotlight with Sir Ernest Shackleton, the noted Antarctic explorer; in Paris, a crowd of 100,000 Parisians greeted him upon his arrival at the Gare du Nord.[17] "With verve, by the aerial way, planting the *tricolore* on the soil of Old England, Blériot has permanently advanced the cause of aviation," enthused one journal, adding, "The aviation impetus is a fact; the airplane has become an object of commerce. . . . It will progress at the pace of a giant."[18] "Yes," *L'aérophile* soaringly reported, "Blériot is certainly one of those men who do honor to mankind, one of the modern heroes, soldiers of science and progress, vanquishers of the hostile forces of nature, which they confound by their double superiority of character and intelligence."[19] Thanks to Blériot, the editor of *Flight* wrote, "the whole civilized world was made aware of the fact that the age of aerial locomotion by mechanical means is no longer of the distant future but is in very deed of this year in which we are living"; the flight caught the imagination of a certain young Italian firebrand, a self-confessed "fanatic for flight," who hailed Blériot's "Latin genius and courage"; thus did Benito Mussolini pass judgment on the Frenchman's heroic journey.[20] More important to Blériot, within two days of the flight he received orders for more than 100 of his little monoplanes, yet another reason that it is nice to record his triumph for, unlike Latham, Blériot *really* needed to win. (It is a measure of him that, after arriving at Dover and despite his lingering financial concerns, he generously offered to split the £1,000 *Daily Mail* prize with Latham if his rival managed to fly the Channel any time that Sunday.) Blériot's company, and the era of mass aircraft production, had arrived.

The Great Aviation Week at Reims

In June and July 1909, the Wrights returned to Ft. Myer with their new Military Flyer. This time they stayed together, Orville to fly, and Wilbur as technical advisor. The trials came off without serious incident, despite several minor landing scrapes and fractures of the machine's skids. The Wright airplane clearly was a reliable and easily maintained machine, and also it had duration, though its instabilities tended to afflict both pilot and passenger with airsickness. On one flight Orville remained aloft for an hour and 20 minutes, circling the parade ground 83 times at a height of 300 feet; even Orville and Wilbur must have been bored senseless after *that* particular excursion.[21] Not surprisingly, the plane had no difficulty meeting the contractual requirements set forth by the Army, particularly the one-hour endurance and the 40-mile per hour top speed requirements, both met with a two-person crew. On July 27 Orville took off at 6:35 P.M., accompanied by Lieutenant Frank Lahm, circling the field 79 1/2 times, remaining aloft over one hour and 12 minutes, meeting the one-hour endurance requirement. Then, on July 30, accompanied by Lieutenant Benjamin Foulois, Orville passed the speed test, averaging 42.58 miles per hour over a ten-mile out-and-back course between Ft. Myer and Alexandria; among those watching was the president of the United States, William Howard Taft.[22] Because they not only had met but exceeded the performance requirements, the Army paid the brothers an additional $5,000 over the $25,000 contract price (with inflation, equivalent in 2001 to $568,000). It accepted the airplane on August 2; now it had an airplane, the first military service in the world to possess the technology of the third dimension, even though it still had numerous uncertainties over the significance of what it had just bought. On August 10 Orville and Katharine again boarded the *Kronprinzessin Cecilie,* bound for Germany to demonstrate the Flyer before the royal family and senior officials.[23]

The big international aviation news in the late summer of 1909, however, was not the Wrights' Ft. Myer flights, or even Blériot, but la Grande Semaine d'Aviation de la Champagne (the Great Aviation Week of the Champagne), held in Reims, France from August 22 to 29.[24] The world's first international flying competition and air show, it promised 200,000 francs in prize money (then $40,000, and approximately $760,000 in 2001) for winning aviators. The contributors were a consortium of the region's most prominent champagne vintners, including Moët et Chandon, Veuve Clicquot-Ponsardin, Pommery et Greno, Heidsieck Monopole, G. H. Mumm, and Louis Roederer, as well as wealthy expatriate newspaper publisher James Gordon Bennett. A naval veteran of the Civil War (his service earned him the nickname "the Commodore"), Bennett had a nose for notable news, most famously sending reporter H. M. Stanley deep into Africa to find missionary-explorer David Livingstone. He lived well, maintaining a residence a few doors down from Santos-Dumont on the Champs-Elysées, a yacht, the curiously named *Lysistrata,* crewed by 100 men, and vacationing in then-exotic locales like Biarritz. But he had left the United States in social disgrace "after relieving himself while drunk in the fireplace of his fiancée's home" and then fighting an inconclusive duel with her outraged brother. He had an early fascination with automobiles, and then with flight in all its forms, establishing an international balloon competition in 1906, and now an aviation competition as well.[25]

The show offered a spectacular setting on the plain of Bétheny, three miles north of the old cathedral city: a large demonstration field and chalet grandstand of such imposing magnificence as to have been used by the French government for a military review in honor of Czar Nicholas II when he visited the country in 1901. Organized by a committee directed by the Marquis de Polignac (whose ancestor, 126 years previously, was the official representative at the first human flight in history, by Pilâtre de Rozier and the Marquis d'Arlandes from the grounds of the Polignac estate at the Château de la Muette), the Grande Semaine was at once elegant, exciting, and inspiring. High society flocked to enjoy a week of gourmet dining accompanied by the world's finest champagnes, formal-attire events, and people-watching; an estimated 500,000 visitors (150,000 on the last day alone) paid to watch the sputtering *aéroplanes* (as many as seven airborne at any one time) and their daring pilots; and government and military officials came as well to assess the state of the craft, and ponder the future possibilities of the air.[26] *La piste* (the course) resembled a lopsided hexagon 10 kilometers (6.2 miles) in length, with pylons at each of the six corners, centered near the intersection of two roads just southwest of Bétheny and the St. Étienne–Reims road. A huge sports-style scoreboard gave competition results, adding an air of athleticism and undoubtedly encouraging more than a few to gamble on this new form of locomotion.

Seven great prizes enticed the leading aviators of France and overseas as well:

the 100,000-franc Grand Prix de la Champagne et de la Ville de Reims for the greatest nonstop distance flown during the meet, the 20,000-franc Prix de la Vitesse for the fastest speed over a distance of 30 kilometers (18.64 miles), the 10,000-franc Prix des Passagers for the greatest number of passengers (pilot excluded) carried on a single lap of the course, the 10,000-franc Prix de l'Altitude for the highest flight above 50 meters (about 165 feet), the 10,000-franc Prix de Tour de Piste for the fastest single lap of the 10-kilometers (6.21-mile) course, the 25,000 franc Coupe d'Aviation Gordon Bennett for the fastest speed over a 20-kilometers (12.43-mile) course, and a variety of smaller prizes.[27]

The range of aircraft entered in the competition spoke to the intensity of the meet and the growing diversity in designs. The overall attendance, and the personalities both flying and on the ground, reflected its prestige as well. A total of 38 airplanes powered by 12 different kinds of engines appeared at Reims, 23 of which (15 biplanes and 8 monoplanes) eventually flew, representing nine different types. The biplanes included three French-built Wrights, three Farmans, six Voisins, and Curtiss's *Reims Racer*. All were pushers, except for an experimental tractor design by Louis Breguet. The monoplanes consisted of three comfortable Antoinettes (the IV, V, and VII), four sporty Blériots of two basic types (two XIs, the aileron-equipped XII, and its similar stablemate the new XIII), and an REP (the 2-bis), whose wing anhedral endowed it with a perpetually downcast look but little else; it would make but one brief unspectacular flight at Reims.

The half-million visitors saw a galaxy of already famous names: Louis Blériot and Hubert Latham attracted the greatest attention, but also Leon Delagrange, Ferdinand Ferber (flying under the assumed identity of "F. De Rue"), the Comte

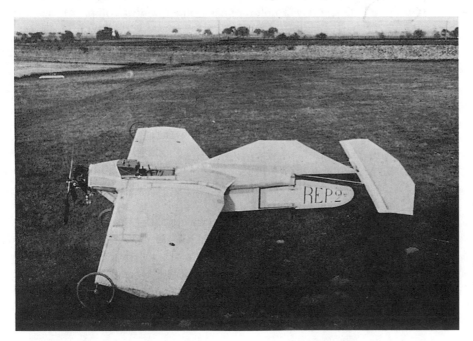

The REP 2-bis monoplane, despite its modern lines, was a disappointing (if technically interesting) French design, more "hopper" than "flyer." TC

de Lambert, Eugène Lefebvre, Louis Paulhan, and Paul Tissandier, as well as promising unknowns such as the Chilean pilot Sanchez Besa, Louis Breguet, Étienne Bunau-Varilla, Englishman George Cockburn, American Glenn Curtiss, Henry Fournier, Jean Gobrun, Maurice Guffroy, Henry Rougier, Swiss pilot Eugène Ruchonnet, and Roger Sommer. Surprisingly, there were some absences: although he had agreed to enter the competition with his delightful little *Demoiselle,* Santos-Dumont chose not to appear; the Wrights passed as well; and none of the British experimenters—Cody, Dunne, Roe—showed up. Looking on as these bold aviators showed off their talents were senior French military and political figures, including the genial and tranquil president of the republic, Armand Fallières; other guests included Roger Wallace, the chairman of the Aero Club of the United Kingdom; Cortland Bishop, president of the Aero Club of America; American ambassadors Robert Bacon and Henry White; former first lady Mrs. Theodore Roosevelt and her children Archie, Ethel, and Quentin; British army general Sir John French, and British politicians David Lloyd George, Richard Haldane, and Sir Henry Norman.

The week began inauspiciously as rains turned the grounds to mud and winds whipped up a drenching spray. "Anything more unpropitious than the weather conditions under which the Reims aviation meeting opened it would be difficult to imagine," *Flight*'s aviation correspondent wrote.[28] Despite this mess a few aviators attempted to fly, without any great success. First to actually get aloft was a Wright piloted by Paul Tissandier, which skimmed the ground for several hundred yards before landing; Latham turned in a similarly disappointing performance in his Antoinette IV, and even Blériot, fresh from his Channel-crossing triumph, managed only a short flight for about 1 1/2-miles. Piloting a French-built Wright, Eugène Lefebvre stayed aloft for nearly nine minutes, completing a single lap of the 10-kilometer (6.2-mile) course, an average speed of about 41 miles per hour, an excellent speed under the conditions.[29] Thereafter the weather improved steadily over the week, and the last day, Sunday, August 29, dawned hot and clear. By the end of the week, Latham had reached a height of 155 meters (508 feet) to win the altitude contest, Henri Farman had flown for three hours and fifteen minutes, covering 180 kilometers (approximately 112 miles) to win the Grand Prix, Blériot had secured the prize for the fastest speed over 10 kilometers (at 76.95 kilometers per hour, 47.75 miles per hour), Farman had won the passengers' prize by carrying two passengers around *la piste,* and Bunau-Varilla had flown 62 miles to win a mechanics' prize for his team. The new airship *Colonel Renard* won a lighter-than-air performance award, a nice tribute to its namesake's memory.

American Glenn Curtiss won two prizes for speed, the Prix de la Vitesse (for averaging 75 kilometers per hour, 46.63 miles per hour, over three 10-kilometers laps), and the Gordon Bennett trophy for averaging 75.7 kilometers per hour (47.02 miles per hour) over 20 kilometers. It had not been easy; Curtiss had faced construction deadlines and finished the *Reims Racer* barely in time, then, once in France, he had to race again to get to the flying meet in time to complete. James Gordon Bennett, like Northcliffe for the Wrights, hoped Curtiss would win but

Latham in the Antoinette IV about to take off from the plain of Bétheny at Reims on August 26; he set a distance record on the flight of 70 kilometers. SSPL

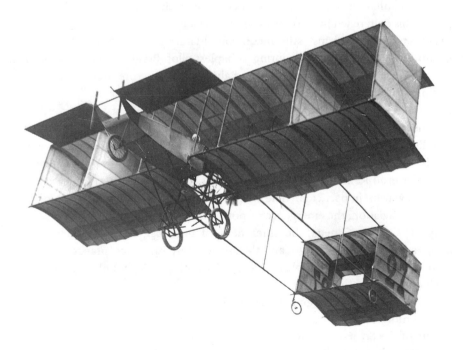

Bunau-Varilla and his Voisin passes over the crowd at Reims; the Voisin was a design lacking any form of lateral control and, as such, inferior to virtually all other aircraft in the meet. MAE

was privately aghast at how the intense American was struggling on a virtually shoestring budget. On Saturday, August 28, when Curtiss squared off against the best French and one English flier, spectator interest in the competition had reached fever pitch. All week Curtiss had carefully husbanded his engine, virtually babying the plane, though onlookers marveled at its quickness on takeoff: *Flight's* correspondent considered it "absolutely amazing," noting "sometimes it would be in midair in less than 50 yards."[30]

Now, as the first to fly the course that day, Curtiss went all out: he climbed as high as he could before crossing the starting line, and then flew full throttle in a constant gradual descent to get a little gravity assist, banking steeply into his turns. He averaged 47.02 miles per hour over the two-lap course, and his mark withstood later challenges from Cockburn's Farman, Latham's Antoinette, Lefebvre's Wright, and Blériot's latest Model XII. (The Model XII resembled his Model XI, but with an exaggerated vertical fin running almost the length of the upper fuselage, an odd staggered biplane-like horizontal tail, and a "rigid" wing, with small Curtiss-like ailerons perched off the lower sides of the fuselage.) It was a bravura performance, but the future would belong to the Europeans: Curtiss's flight was the last international speed competition America would win for the next 16 years, until 1925, when a later Curtiss product—the elegant R3C-2 racer, piloted by Jimmy Doolittle—took the Schneider Trophy.[31]

Reims was not without incident and its share of accidents, some funny and some not. Cockburn crashed his Farman into a haystack, ending Britain's chances for a prize. Another pilot came down in the crowd, fortunately without injuring anyone. Paulhan just avoided a midair collision with Delagrange, at the price of putting his own machine into the ground and badly damaging it. A passing breeze upset one of the Voisins—still uncontrolled laterally—and it tumbled into the ground, fortunately without injuring its hapless pilot. Breguet crashed his biplane, but some of its features—steel-tube and aluminum structure, tractor layout, and enclosed fuselage—would become standard elements of later machines. Blériot lived up to his disaster-prone reputation. He had two accidents, the second quite serious: on the last day, his Model XII sprang a fuel leak; he hastily landed, just as it spilled over his hot engine and ignited. He barely escaped as the plane went up in a billow of orange flame and black smoke, sustaining bad burns to one hand.[32]

But overall Reims was an extraordinary success for aviation in general and French aviation in particular. The week-long show highlighted three important aspects of aviation: the emergence of powerful lightweight aero engines, particularly the Gnôme Omega; the emergence of practical, successful airplanes of indigenous European design; and the surprisingly rapid acceptance of the airplane as a practical, accomplished reality by both public and official audiences. Each deserves brief comment.

While a number of engine designs had worked reasonably well, a new French aircraft motor, the Gnôme Omega, designed by half brothers Laurent and Louis Séguin of the Société des Moteurs Gnôme in Génévilliers, received its baptism at the meet and became the talk of the aviation world.[33] The simple and ingeniously designed seven-cylinder, 50-horsepower Gnôme, the most reliable of pre–Great War engines, constituted the first example of a second-generation aviation engine. It powered Farman's Grand Prix winning flight, as well as three other airplanes, two of which received lesser prizes. Somewhat breathlessly, Farman allegedly exclaimed, "It runs without a vibration, faultlessly; it blasts like thunder!"[34] Crafted from forged steel, creatively engineered to be as light and powerful as possible, and not merely extrapolated from automotive and maritime "best practices" (despite the brothers' background in both automobile and boat engine design), the Gnôme set a design standard that lasted over the next decade of flight. In Blériot's judgment it "enabled the industry to advance by leaps and bounds."[35]

Light but very powerful for its time, it weighed approximately 3.3 pounds per horsepower; in contrast, a contemporary 50-horsepower Antoinette engine weighed almost 7 pounds per horsepower. Spinning constituted its most distinctive feature: it rotated at 1,000 revolutions per minute, so that its cylinders, arranged like the spokes on a wagon wheel, would keep cool in an era when aircraft still operated well below 100 kilometers per hour (62 miles per hour). It was also a "backwards" engine, rotating around a fixed hollow crankshaft bolted to the airplane and acting also as the engine mount. The fuel-air mixture passed through the hollow crankshaft and thence to each cylinder; and the engine itself and the propeller were bolted solidly together, rotating as a single unit. The Gnôme revolutionized engine design and would in more powerful variants (including 9 cylinder and eventually two-row 14- and 18-cylinder combinations offering up to 200 horsepower) become one of the standard power plants for aircraft well into the First World War. Much studied and copied by other engine designers in other countries, such was the reputation of the Séguin brothers' engine that it was the first power plant ordered into production by the United States after it entered the First World War.[36]

The revolutionary Gnôme rotary engine, designed by half-brothers Laurent and Louis Séguin of the Société des Moteurs Gnôme in Génévilliers, gave early aviation its first lightweight, reliable, and powerful engine; this example is on exhibit at the Musée des arts et Métiers, Paris. Hallion photograph

Overall, before an international audience, French aircraft and airmen had generally matched or exceeded the performance of their foreign competitors, just three weeks shy of the third anniversary of Santos-Dumont's first hop in the *14-bis* off the ground at Bagatelle, and just a year since Wilbur Wright flew his "great white bird" at Hunaudières. The eight top prize earners were Farman (Fr 63,000), Latham (Fr 42,000), Curtiss (Fr 38,000), Paulhan (Fr 10,000), Tissandier (Fr 8,000),

Blériot (Fr 7,000), Lambert (Fr 5,000), and Lefebvre (Fr 2,000). Thus no fewer than seven of the eight (88 percent) were French, these seven having won 137,000 francs, fully 69 percent of the total prize money.[37] Henry Farman's pusher biplane constituted the star of the show, winning two firsts (the Grand Prix for its impressive 112-mile distance, and for the passenger competition), and a second (the altitude competition). Next came Curtiss—two firsts in speed, and a second. Third was the Antoinette: one first (the altitude prize), and two seconds, one of which was a very impressive almost-96-mile distance flight. Then in fourth came the Voisin, with a first, a second, and a third; and finally, in fifth place, Blériot with a first and a second. None of the French Wrights placed. Admittedly things might have been different had the Wrights competed, for they were the world's two most experienced airmen. In any case it is telling that *already* the technological gap between the Wrights and their European rivals was beginning to visibly widen. Clearly it calls into question yet again the conventional wisdom that European airmen were languishing in doldrums of inactivity and uncertainty until Wilbur Wright "showed" them how to fly in 1908.

In all aspects, then, Reims greatly influenced attitudes towards aviation. Indeed, even before the last airplane and airship flew over the plain of Bétheny, even before the last engine clattered to a stop, the editor of Britain's *Flight* magazine was moved to write: "The Reims meeting marks an epoch in the history of mechanical aerial locomotion. It is the first occasion on which a wide variety of machines has been brought together. . . . The result is that none who read can scoff any longer. *The age of flight is the age we live in*"[38] (emphasis added). But it was not just air enthusiasts who reached such conclusions: the mainstream press agreed as well, a remarkable turnaround in journalists' attitudes since the days of Langley. "After the events of 1908–09," Michael Paris has written, "the press was forced to take aeronautics seriously and many began to devote regular space to the subject and even appoint air correspondents."[39]

"Reims," Charles Gibbs-Smith rightly judged, "marked the true acceptance of the airplane as a practical vehicle, and as such was a major milestone in the world's history."[40] After Reims interest in flying grew so pervasive and dominant that a few months later the Automobile-Club de France canceled a Grand Prix competition for lack of public interest![41] In contrast, after Reims, air meets proliferated all across Europe, a forecast of even more numerous meets that would take place the following year. Reporters commented on the throngs that attended the meets despite the occasional blustery weather; officials examined airplanes. Even insurance underwriters looked more favorably on flying: *Flight* reported "underwriters are contemplating developing [a] special branch of the business for dealing with aviation," and indeed, Lloyds of London issued its first aviation policy a little over a year later, in 1911.[42]

Military officers, who heretofore had accepted aerostatics but been dubious about the value of the airplane, became far more enthusiastic over heavier-than-air flight. That fall, for example, the French war ministry released funds to purchase a Farman, a Blériot XI, and a Wright for operational test and evaluation.[43]

Indeed, it was perhaps in its military implications that Reims had its greatest impact, for the show clearly brought home to both Great Britain and Germany their relative inferiority to their Continental neighbor. David Lloyd George grumbled "Flying machines are no longer toys and dreams. They are an established fact. The possibilities of this new system of locomotion are infinite. I feel, as a 'Britisher,' rather ashamed that we are so completely out of it."[44] The German military attaché in Paris, Major Detlof von Winterfeldt, warned that Reims marked the emergence of aircraft for a variety of purposes, and "that the French have made in a relatively short time enormous progress in the field of aviation technology."[45]

French aviator G. Blondeau flying a Farman biplane in 1910 at Brooklands, an auto racing course southwest of London; in the foreground is an early simulator conceived to give students the feel of flight while on the ground. SSPL

Dénouement

France held a huge aeronautical salon at the Grand Palais a month after Reims, showcasing more than 30 French airplanes, and with 333 exhibitors, 318 of whom (fully 95 percent) were French themselves. Blériot's historic channel-crossing

Model XI occupied a special place of honor, and elsewhere in the exhibit area, visitors (100,000 in just the first two days) could stroll by a variety of his other designs, as well as a profusion of Antoinettes, Farmans, Voisins, aircraft inspired by these types, and Santos-Dumont's little *Demoiselle*. A lonely Wright Flyer was hidden, relegated to an upstairs loft, "tucked away in the most perfectly complete manner conceivable."[16] French aviation had come a long way from Santos-Dumont's unsteady hops at Bagatelle three years before, and the organizers of the salon clearly didn't think that visitors needed to be reminded of the Wrights with the fresh triumphs of Reims scant weeks in the past.

Even a rash of unfortunate accidents did little to dampen the spirits of the European aviation community, though they brought home to French aviators—as Selfridge's accident had to Americans—that heavier-than-air aviation and the new generation of small airships could be every bit as lethal as the older balloons. On September 7 Eugène Lefebvre fatally crashed a French-built Wright at Port-Aviation, the world's first specially built airfield, at Juvisy, south of Paris. The accident occurred just four months after it opened, while he was testing the airplane for a Wright client. On September 22 came a shocking loss: Ferdinand Ferber, the first Wright disciple in France, died at Boulogne-sur-Mer in a Voisin accident when he taxied into a ditch and the plane's engine broke loose and fell on him. For a while he seemed unharmed and even walked about, but he quickly collapsed and died from an internal hemorrhage. Then, just three days later, the airship *République* took off from its base at La Palisse en route for Paris; near the Château d'Avrilly, disaster struck; it shed a propeller blade, which sliced through

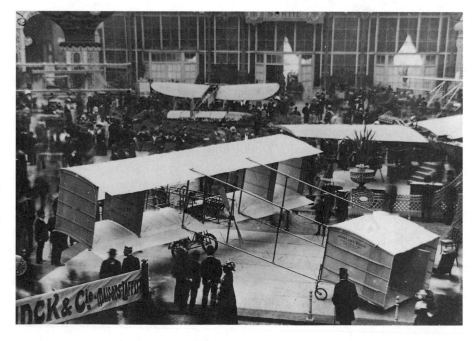

The aeronautical salon at the Grand Palais, 1909; in the foreground is a Voisin, to the right an Antoinette, in the middle (top) Blériot's Channel-crossing Model XI (fresh from its triumphant return to France) and, left (top) a Farman. NASM

the envelope, releasing so much hydrogen that the airship vented virtually its entire gas supply, plunging to earth at high speed and killing its crew of four.[47] Several years before, such accidents might have resulted in a tremendous outcry against aviation and its risks, but not in the wake of the Wright demonstrations, Blériot, and then Reims. *Flight* mourned the deaths of Selfridge and Lefebvre, but stressed "how mercifully small in relation to the progress made in flight has been the toll of human life," while *La revue aérienne* considered the fatalities a particularly heavy price demanded "for the safeguarding of air power."[48]

While Reims held the world's attention, Orville Wright went to Germany and had a notably successful visit, flying a Dayton-built-but-German-assembled Flyer from the Flugmaschine Wright GmbH (established months earlier by a group of prominent businessmen). He spent approximately a month overseas, flying before the Kaiser and his court; making a number of demonstration flights at Tempelhof and Potsdam before thousands of onlookers; flying the Kaiser's son, Crown Prince Friedrich Wilhelm (the first member of a royal family ever to take to the air, who gave Orville a monogrammed diamond-and-ruby stickpin as a souvenir); and even flying as a guest of Count von Zeppelin in the LZ-5 from Frankfurt to Mannheim (his sister Katharine flew in a smaller Parseval airship). On September 17 he flew before the Empress of Germany and her retinue, enthralling them. Mathilde Gräfin von Keller, the chief lady in waiting, found the experience "of unprecedented interest and excitement," particularly Wright's *Höhenflug* to 172 meters (approximately 565 feet), "though the [onlooker's] heart stands still at the shock!"[49] (She likewise noted "the poor Miss Wright," obviously anxious for her

Orville Wright flying before the Empress of Germany; this particular Wright machine is now exhibited at the Deutsches Museum, Munich. NASM

brother's safety: Katharine undoubtedly realized September 17 constituted the first anniversary of Bubbo's disastrous accident at Ft. Myer. Tempelhof crowds had a unique opportunity one day when Wright and Hubert Latham both demonstrated their airplanes back to back, quickly revealing the differences between the two design philosophies. Wright maneuvered with abandon, while Latham took his hands off the controls; onlookers mistook Latham waving his hands as a "typically Latin gesture," but in fact this was a perfect way to show to a technically minded viewer that the Antoinette was a more stable (and hence safer and more useful) machine requiring far less pilot workload than the tricky if agile Wright.[50]

But Tempelhof and Potsdam constituted the international swan song of the Wrights and their machine, for from that point onwards, they had nothing further to offer the world aviation community. Both European and American aviation were already moving away from their approach to flight, and they would make no further impact on the evolution of either. They had taken their brilliant basic design as far as it could go: the publication at the end of 1909 of the Wrights' latest patents in French and German journals added nothing of further significance to European aviators—they were already well along their own paths towards the planes of the First World War.[51] In any case the brothers themselves had moved by this time from experimental design and development into overt salesmanship and defending their patent rights. If their efforts in this regard would largely be a failure, that failure must not obscure their very real contribution to aviation: they invented the world's first successful airplane, the 1903 Flyer.

Also, 1909 might be seen as the year in which the *invention* of flight ended and the process of *continual refinement* began. By the end of that year, practical balloons, airships, and airplanes were flying in America and Europe, and the basic experimental era in the invention of flight was at an end. Indeed, on October 16, 1909, the ambitious Count von Zeppelin even founded an airship airline, DELAG (for Deutsche Luftschiffahrt Aktien Gesellschaft, the German Airship Travel Corporation), the first airline of any kind in aviation history. The future would witness technological refinement, practice, and the development of an infrastructure to support both commercial and military aviation, *but the airplane, airship, and balloon, as mechanical systems, had moved from dream, through theory, into experimentation, and on to routine production. Humanity could move, at will, through the air, in a purposeful way, between destinations of the airman's choosing.*

PART SIX

EXPANSION, INCORPORATION, MATURATION: BEGINNING THE AERIAL AGE, 1910–1914

CHAPTER FIFTEEN

Global Expansion

Within three years after 1909, aviation spread globally, went to war, and entered commercial service. Flight reached beyond western Europe and America, making a start in northern, southern, and eastern Europe, Russia, and Asia, though to markedly varying degrees. But it advanced rapidly enough that by mid-1911 the Fédération Aéronautique Internationale (FAI) established an international commission for aeronautical maps, working with established geographical and mapping bodies to develop common practices and standards. The commission met in Brussels in late May, with attendees from Austria, Belgium, England, France, and Germany, addressing issues including scale, notations, and generic symbols. By 1914 the FAI had affiliated seventeen national clubs and aero organizations, in America, Argentina, Austria, Belgium, Denmark, Egypt, France, Germany, Great Britain and Ireland, Holland, Hungary, Italy, Norway, Russia, Spain, Sweden, and Switzerland, an indication of both growing international interest and the burgeoning proficiency of the world's aviators.[1]

The path forward was neither foreordained nor easily accomplished, particularly in less-developed nations, and even in Western Europe considerable hesitancy and confusion existed. Britain lingered behind France, and Germany dallied as well, officials in both countries (but particularly Germany) taking copious amounts of time debating the relative merits of airships versus airplanes. Everywhere the French influence predominated: at the beginning of 1911, the FAI listed 353 pilots in France, compared to 57 in England, 46 in Germany, 32 in Italy, 27 in Belgium—and just 26 in the United States.[2] France's dominance extended to aircraft as well: only later would Germany, and then Britain, join France as a major prewar exporter of aviation technology. Italy followed developments abroad closely and, while encouraging its own indigenous pioneers (such as brothers Gianni and Federico Caproni and Agostino di Agostini), generally purchased French and then German aircraft. In 1908 Russian enthusiasts created an Imperial All-Russian Aero Club, which, like the Aéro-Club de France and Britain's Aeronautical Society and Royal Aero Club, quickly served as a vital center for aeronautics.

In 1909 a Wright Flyer flew in Russia, but like the Europeans, once exposed, the Russians turned to France, buying aircraft and airships and modeling their aviation industry, research establishment, and air service along French lines. Also, flight reached around the world, to Japan, China, and Southeast Asia.[3]

Aviation in Britain

By 1914 Britain had over 90 separate aeronautical clubs and societies scattered across England, Scotland, Wales, and Ireland, including three major national organizations, the Aeronautical Society, the Royal Aero Club, and the Aerial League of the British Empire, the latter an organization established to promote air-mindedness and national defense.[4] Despite this, British aviation was slow to mature, a situation highlighted by a simple data point: at the time that Cody and Roe were only hopping off the ground, the Wrights, Blériot, and Latham were all flying airplanes that could span the channel. After Reims, French aviation led, anticipated, inspired, and in some cases intimidated all of Europe: when Britain established its Royal Aircraft Factory in 1912, the factory designated new aircraft types it generated as F.E., S.E., or B.E. designs, for *Farman* Experimental, *Santos* Experimental, and *Blériot* Experimental, a tribute to the French designers whose approaches the factory wished to emulate with its own indigenous aircraft!

The Olympia Aero Show, Britain's first aeronautical exhibition in the post-Wright era, held in London in March 1909, included a display of 11 aircraft.[5] Though the Shorts had one of their Wright-inspired designs on exhibit, and another British inventor, Howard Wright (no relation to the brothers) had a Voisin-inspired machine displayed, neither Cody, Dunne, nor Roe sent their own crafts to the show. Handley Page showed a crescent-winged canard glider and the fuselage of a proposed airplane, both by French émigré landscape painter and bird enthusiast José Weiss. Of the eleven exhibits, eight were totally foreign in origin, and only three British. But even those represented foreign-inspired work: work by the Wrights, by Voisin, and by Weiss. Had Cody, Dunne, and Roe exhibited, in theory there would have been six British exhibits out of fourteen, a not-unreasonable 43 percent. But in truth, since Cody and Roe were themselves inspired by the Wrights and Goupy, only Dunne's tailless biplane would have been truly indigenous to the British Isles! Thus, strictly speaking, Olympia at best could only have shown *one* authentically British exhibit out of a potential 14 displays: fully 93 percent of the exhibits would have represented foreign work, or British work inspired by foreign predecessors. No wonder Lord Northcliffe believed it time to launch a "Wake up, England!" campaign.

Then came the Blériot flight and its attendant enthusiasm and alarm, all of which acted to accelerate the pace. Even so, numerous problems remained. Manufacturing, quality control, and supply delays kept the Short brothers from flying their first Wright copies until November 1909. Though they also developed a series of unremarkable Wright-inspired aircraft, the inherent limitations of

Wright's catapult-rail-and-derrick launch mechanism and the constant pilot effort needed to fly the basically unstable Wright machines quickly cooled their enthusiasm for the type. (Horace Short called the Wright airplane "a beast that needs some handling.")[6] Being more imitative than original at this point in their company's history, they turned in 1910 toward copying French and American innovators, adopting a Farman-Curtiss pusher approach, and finally, in 1912, to copying the Blériot monoplane.[7]

By establishing the Factory, Britain took a great step towards ending the "hobby shop" mentality that had previously afflicted British aviation. Cody, for all his genial common sense, energy, and inventive spirit, was not a Wilbur or Orville Wright. He could follow a blueprint, but unable to read and write, he could not do the kind of basic analysis the brothers had accomplished so readily. He and

Samuel Cody flies past the grandstand at the Doncaster racecourse during the rainy aviation meet of October 1909 in his large canard biplane. SSPL

Alliott Verdon Roe's triplane, the "Bull's-eye Avroplane," constructed in a crude "factory" he established in rented Great Eastern Railway arch-space at Lea Marshes. This marked the birth of what would eventually become one of Britain's major aircraft manufacturers, Avro. SSPL

Roe were adapters and craftsmen, not creators: what Sidney Hook called "eventful men," those who take advantage of circumstances provided by others, rather than "even-making men," those who make their own circumstances. (Sadly, he and a passenger died in 1913, thrown out of their airplane when one of his designs broke up in flight, due apparently to his underestimation of the loads it would experience.) Dunne *was* different: technically gifted, brilliantly creative, even driven. But his personality, working style, and fixation on a single configuration—the inherently stable tailless aircraft—was as obsessive as the Wrights'. It is ironic that he and the Wrights differed so much over the basic principles of stability, because under the skin they could have been triplets.[8]

Far more difficult to overcome were the vicious personality conflicts and debates over the conduct of aeronautical research and development and the government's role (if any) that afflicted British aviation. As a result Britain fell even further behind. A ruinous decision by a special joint Army-Navy subcommittee of the Committee of Imperial Defence in 1909 nearly destroyed military aviation altogether: in January 28, 1909, it boldly stated, "There appears to be no necessity for the Government to continue experiments in aeroplanes, provided that advantage is taken of private enterprise in this form of aviation."[9] The report went for review to the secretary of state for war, Richard Haldane. Haldane had earlier journeyed to Scotland to watch some of Dunne's experiments, being so unimpressed that he later told a colleague "aeroplanes would never fly"; he approved the conclusion with an abrupt "I agree on all points." The prime minister concurred, considering that "the recommendation that they be discontinued was a good one."[10] By this extraordinary action, Britain fell even further behind its continental neighbors; fortunately the CID reversed itself a year later.

Thus hobbled, British aviation would continue to proceed at an excessively cautious pace, as French aviation continued to race ahead. C. S. Rolls, a racing driver and auto entrepreneur turned balloonist and aviator, generously gave a Short-built Wright Flyer to the Royal Engineers, who took it on charge at Aldershot, but nothing came of this attempt to jump-start military aviation, and it never flew again. From an aristocratic family (his father was Lord Llangattock), "Charlie" Rolls had gained popular attention in England in June 1910 by flying a French-built Wright from Dover to Sangatte and back without landing, proof enough that the Wrights themselves could have crossed the Channel had they wished in 1908. In fact his association with aviation dated to the turn of the century, when he had helped found the Aero Club (later the Royal Aero Club) of Great Britain. Though he was an energetic (if impulsive) young man, Rolls's colleagues found him a challenging companion: stingy, crude, sarcastic, aloof, and dismissive of both friends and servants. Surprisingly, he also inspired intense devotion: Moore-Brabazon recalled that Rolls seemed "a rather lonely figure who had been starved of real love."[11]

Rolls died in a tragic crash at the Bournemouth air meet a little over a month after his daring Channel flight. Rolls had fitted an experimental rear elevator on his French Wright to the tail booms carrying the rudder, and during a landing competition at Bournemouth, he seriously misjudged his approach. Rather than prudently go around, he stuffed the nose down, diving steeply for the designated landing spot. With the earth approaching at an alarming rate, he reflexively deflected the elevators fully to climb away, overstressing the structure as the plane abruptly nosed upwards. The entire tail assembly collapsed with a loud crack, and with "appalling suddenness" the French Wright pitched over and dove headlong into the ground. Rolls died almost immediately, without regaining consciousness. His death shocked Britain's aeronautical community and added to growing disenchantment with the tricky Wright Flyers; *Flight* mourned the passing of one of aviation's "most brilliant supporters," and Moore-Brabazon recalled nearly five decades later that the accident "sickened me and my wife of aviation altogether, and I never flew again until the [First World] War."[12] What Rolls might have further accomplished for British aeronautics may only be conjectured, but in partnering with Henry Royce (creating one of the legendary automobile, and aviation engine, manufacturers), he had already prepared the ground for one extraordinary contribution: Rolls-Royce engines powered the fighters that saved England in 1940.

French manufacturers—Blériot, Farman, Deperdussin, Nieuport, REP, Morane—greatly influenced British airplane design and competed for British military contracts. For example, Sir George White, the chairman of the Bristol Tramways and Carriage Company, established the Bristol aircraft company, and after unsuccessfully attempting to license-build Voisin biplanes, turned to Voisin's great rival, Henry Farman, with much greater success. The Farman-inspired, Gnôme-powered, two-seat Bristol Boxkite (which actually bore no resemblance to a box kite whatsoever), first flown in July 1910, became Britain's first successful "export" aircraft, copies being sold to other European nations (including nine to Russia), as well as to the British government and private enthusiasts. French army aviation served as a model for other services as well: both Britain and Germany paid close attention to French military aviation developments, translating documents and reports issued by the French regarding aeronautical activities.[13]

The creation of the Royal Aircraft Factory induced some stability and overall strategic direction to British military aviation procurement, through not without controversy. From that point on, British aviation advanced, though it still had not caught up with France or Germany by the war's outbreak in 1914. To a great degree, Britain's perilous recovery reflected the tireless energy and single-minded efforts of Mervyn O'Gorman, who had replaced Colonel Capper at the still-quaintly-named Balloon Factory and who assembled an excellent design team of engineers and mechanicians working for him. A "witty Irishman of flamboyant courage" with an ever-present monocle and cigarette holder, this automotive engineer of wide experience was a master of working around bureaucracy, and threw himself wholeheartedly into his new duties as superintendent. O'Gorman, Geoffrey de Havilland recalled, "was a far-sighted and brilliant administrator. . . .

The British Army's S.E. I canard biplane at Aldershot, designed by Geoffrey de Havilland. Dangerously unstable, it spun and crashed, killing a British Army officer on a familiarization flight in August 1911. HC

He was utterly convinced of the superiority of the aeroplane over all forms of lighter-than-air craft, revealing this persuasion early on in his administration in April 1911 by changing the name from the Army Balloon Factory to the Army Aircraft Factory, and twelve months later to the Royal Aircraft Factory."[14]

Flight in the Vaterland

Germany viewed the dominance of the French with undisguised concern. In April 1912 the chief of the general staff, Generaloberst Helmuth von Moltke, warned the Prussian War Ministry, "The French have a perfect right to look upon their extraordinary superiority in [military aviation] with proud satisfaction. It needs no argument to show that in a war that superiority will be associated with all kinds of disadvantages for us."[15] The extraordinarily energetic Prince Heinrich of Prussia (the Kaiser's brother) started a popular air-mindedness campaign, the Deutscher Luftflottenverein (German Air Fleet Union). It raised more than nine million marks for German industry and research activities, an extraordinary sum then equivalent to $2,250,000, $41 million in 2001. Prince Heinrich, who served as *Grossadmiral* of Baltic naval forces, was an adventurous sort himself, fond of solo-sailing his own small boat around the Baltic, and also a fully trained pilot who had learned to fly in 1910. He bluntly warned of French aeronautical dominance, and increased patriotic enthusiasm for aviation. Thus, if Germany's military aviation still faced an uncertain future at the beginning of 1912, the nation's aviation industrial base was clearly expanding. Underpinned by a strong existing university-and-industry-based scientific research establishment and broad public support, this base guaranteed that German aeronautics would be increasingly competitive with that of its European neighbors in the months and years ahead.[16]

But the road ahead would be difficult. Germany had its own problems in developing aviation, but for different reasons than other nations. Here the airship held near-total sway after the death of Lilienthal, in a situation characterized by intense rivalries between the advocates of Zeppelin-like rigid airships and followers of the Bavarian blimp developer Major August von Parseval, himself inspired by the work of France's Renard, Krebs, and Santos-Dumont. Parseval had invented the so-called Drachenballon, a streamlined kite balloon tethered from the ground, then oversaw the design of Germany's first military blimp.[17] Von Zeppelin, still trying to make his own large rigids a success, saw the Parsevals and indeed any blimp as a distinct threat: Hugo Eckener recalled subsequently, "The feud between the 'rigids' and 'non-rigids' was conducted with a fierceness before which the Medieval antagonism of Guelph and Ghibelline pale into mere bickering!"[18]

It might be said that von Zeppelin made not only personal success of very public failure, but that he throve amid adversity. A disastrous accident to his fourth airship (fortunately without fatalities) nearly destroyed his hopes, but a spontaneous public subscription by sympathetic and, indeed, admiring German citizens, the so-called Miracle of Echterdingen, immediately put him back in business. He became an instant celebrity, and thousands turned out when his airships overflew towns and cities. The big gasbags, emerging symbols of a new, progressive, and vibrant Germany, had the power to stir emotions even in the most cynical and detached. Count Robert Zedlitz-Trützschler, a senior court official, noted, "Anyone who three months ago heard nearly every day that Count Zeppelin was the biggest fool in Germany, and is now told [by the Kaiser, no less] that he is the greatest German of the century, is prepared for any kind of change."[19] On the first of April 1909, writer Thomas Mann wrote his brother Heinrich of one such airship visit to Munich: "This morning, as I entered my room, the Zeppelin maneuvered over right in front of my window. The rooftops black with people, the whole city on its feet, great excitement." Mann concluded somewhat darkly and unwillingly, "Impressive nevertheless."[20] That same year von Zeppelin set up his airship airline, DELAG, and inspired the Swiss to follow suit with a Luzern-based airship airline of their own.[21] Zeppelin kitsch—including handbags, nutcrackers, dinner plates, and cigars—abounded, as with ballooning 125 years previously. Even the Kaiser, who had terminated von Zeppelin's military career many years before, became a firm friend and supporter. He invited the old count to court events (including the christening of the baby prince Hubertus Karl Wilhelm) and, as noted parenthetically above, prematurely if enthusiastically hailed him as "the greatest German of the twentieth century"![22]

Von Zeppelin's status and the public's and Kaiser's love of the airship masked some very real concerns that worked in favor of the airplane. First, the airship could not offer the flexibility, speed, maneuverability and ease of operation that a heavier-than-air machine, using aerodynamic lift as opposed to gas-dependent aerostatics, possessed. But safety constituted the major concern, particularly with passengers and crew nestled scant feet below a huge envelope filled with hydrogen. Between the creation of DELAG and the spring of 1911, Zeppelin lost no fewer than *four* airships (an average of one every four and a half months!): the army's LZ-5 (wrecked at Weilburg), and DELAG's LZ-6 (burned in its shed), LZ-7 *Deutschland* (crashed in the Teutoberger Wald), and LZ-8 (the so-called *ersatz Deutschland*, wrecked at Düsseldorf). Miraculously, von Zeppelin's luck held, for only one unfortunate mechanic perished in the course of all these disasters. But they clearly tarnished the image of the airship with the German General Staff and with the senior command of the High Seas Fleet. Even before the last of these, Generaloberst von Moltke had cautioned that artillery tests "revealed the great dangers which airships run from howitzers and antiaircraft guns," arguing instead for reliance on airplanes, and asked pointedly how heavy a weight of bombs could be dropped from airplanes and whether bombs could be used against airships. So despite von Zeppelin's public adulation and the eventual development of very advanced airships for naval service, the German military establishment had begun the first turning away from the rigid airship and increasingly toward the airplane, a combination of concern over safety, cost (a single Zeppelin cost as much as 30 Albatros biplanes), and alarm over the rapid progress of the French. In Germany as elsewhere, the future of military aviation lay with the airplane, not the airship.[23]

Germany's entry into the airplane field was almost as tortuous as the Zeppelin story. The first officially sponsored airplane, designed by W. Siegfried Hoffmann

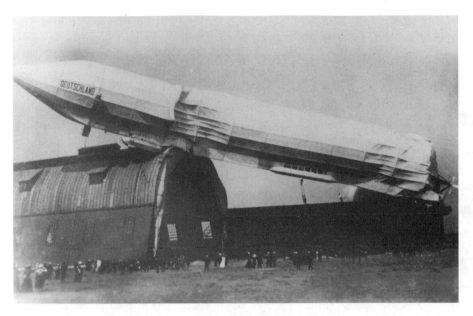

The *ersatz Deutsch-land*, DELAG's LZ-8, lies shattered and deflated across its hangar at Düsseldorf, after an encounter with high winds in May 1911; miracu-lously, its hydrogen did not ignite, and all passengers and crew survived, at the price of a perilous descent via fire ladders. AFMA

for the army, had proven as unsuccessful as Ader's *Avion III* or Langley's *Great Aerodrome*. First "flown" in 1910, it cost 42,000 marks, reached a height of ten feet, and then crashed. After a second, more serious accident, it reputedly ended its life as a chandelier in the officers' mess at Johannisthal.[24] Thereafter, like the other European governments, Germany looked first to the Wrights, then to the French, and finally to Teutonic firms. The result of this journey was a remarkably birdlike and attractive monoplane, the Etrich Taube (dove). Designed by the Austrian Ignaz "Igo" Etrich based on the studies of Professor Friedrich Ahlborn on the *Zanonia macrocarpa* winged seed, and subsequently mass-produced in Germany and elsewhere (even being exported widely abroad), the Taube (first flown in 1910) coupled gentle flying characteristics with excellent stability and safety. Well-harmonized controls, a rugged structure, and a powerful Austro-Daimler, and later Mercedes, 120-horsepower engine assured its success. German aviators flying Tauben rapidly began catching up to the achievements of their foreign contempo-raries, notably in a series of highly successful public air meets and events such as the Flugwoche held at Berlin-Johannisthal from June 4–11, 1911. Also, the Taube inspired other designers and manufacturers, whose own configurations resembled its sweeping, curvaceous lines, notably the elegant and deceptively delicate Alba-tros biplane of 1911.[25]

Italy, Scandinavia, Russia, and Asia

Across the smaller European nations, Russia, and Asia, the French (and subse-quently German) influence prevailed. Italy had undoubtedly benefited from creat-ing a strong aeronautical research establishment, but the same lighter-versus-

The Etrich-Ahlborn Taube, progenitor of one of the most significant and useful military airplanes at the outbreak of the Great War, with appreciative Austro-Hungarian officers. Note the extensive bracing, including the unusual spanwise trussing spar under each wing. HC

heavier-than-air debates that raged in other nations affected Italian aviation as well: fully 75 percent of its aeronautical budget in 1914 went to airships, not airplanes. Italy's airplane technology came primarily from adopting French and later German designs until it could produce its own aircraft and engines. Despite this, of all the European nations, Italy was quick to place the airplane into military service, having appropriated 10 million lire to purchase aircraft and material, and establishing an aviation section on October 28, 1910. (Less than a year later, it was the first to send the airplane into combat.) Holland acquired Farmans for its first military airplanes; only later would it develop its own indigenous aircraft industry. At first Sweden simply purchased Blériot, Farman, and Nieuport aircraft from France. Then, in 1913, Enoch Thulin and Oskar Ask founded Sweden's first aircraft company, the Aeroplanvarvet I Skåne, license-manufacturing copies of the Blériot. The next year Thulin reorganized the company and under his own name (but sponsored by industrialist Gustaf Dahlén) produced copies of French Morane-Saulnier monoplanes as well. Other Swedish firms produced copies of the Farman and Albatros biplanes. Out of this small beginning would eventually spring the Saab aircraft production concern, which, while small, is nevertheless one of the world's most sophisticated and consistently successful aerospace companies.[26]

Airplanes figured in Nordic "arms races" (albeit to a smaller extent) just as they did among the French, British, Germans, Italians, and Russians. Indeed, a provocative "aerial bombing" directly led to the creation of the Norwegian army and navy air services. In 1905 Norway had separated from Sweden, and in the

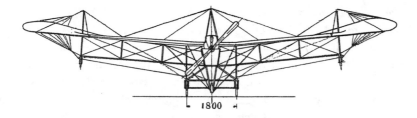

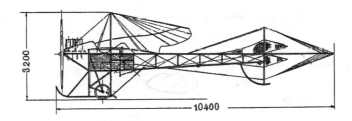

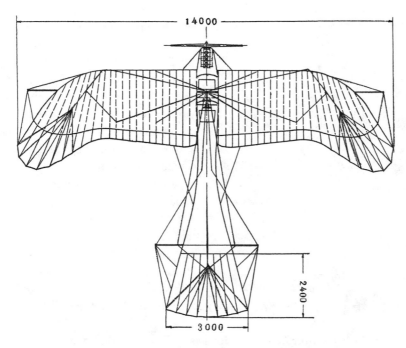

The Taube owed its design to both avian and botanical influences: the bird's shape, and the influence of the stable and gently falling *Zanonia* seed, something that even the plane's extensive external bracing and strutting could not hide. By 1911, Taube airplanes were already entering widespread service, in Germany, Austria-Hungary, and abroad. Adapted from *Flugsport* (1911)

uneasy months thereafter, being concerned about its security, purchased a teth-ered Parseval Drachenballon to maintain watch over Fredrikstens against any pos-sible Swedish massing of forces. In time the crisis passed, but then, in 1911, Sweden's leading aviator, Baron Carl Cederström, a noted practical joker, over-flew Kristiansten Fort at Trondheim in a Blériot monoplane and flippantly "bombed" it with lemons, and another Swedish aviator announced his intention to do the same to Norwegian naval headquarters. The officers of the Norwegian submarine *Knobben,* taking umbrage at this cheekiness, raised funds to send one of their number, Lieutenant Hans Fleischer Dons, to Germany to learn to fly and purchase a Rumpler Taube, and in May 1912 Norway created the Norsk Luft-seiladsforening (Air Voyage Association) and an associated fund drive. On June 1, accompanied by Captain Tank Neilsen, Dons completed the first flight of a Nor-wegian airplane, his Taube, appropriately named the *Start,* from Gannestadjondet to Øra. Acting amidst the publicity following this interest, the Norwegian parlia-ment, the Storting, appropriated Kr 12,000 to train pilots, and the government sent Captain Einar Sem-Jacobsen to France in the summer of 1912 to learn to fly and purchase two airplanes. The first of these, a Farman (oddly named *Gange-Rolv* after a ninth-century Norse chieftain who conquered Normandy, an ancestor of William the Conqueror), flew in the 1912 autumn army maneuvers at Elverum,

Aviator Maurice Chevillard aggres-sively demonstrating a Farman before a Norwegian audi-ence, 1913; his bold aerobatic perform-ances earned him recognition as a *"mesterflyver"* ("master flyer"). HC

where, according to the Norwegian army chief of staff, its airmen "made themselves useful by their boldness and their reporting."[27]

French aviation likewise influenced Czarist Russia, a polyglot nation of many contradictions and problems that had only risen to great power status after defeating Napoléon during his disastrous campaign of 1812. Russia entered the last half of the first decade of the new century in turmoil. It had experienced a humiliating defeat at the hands of the Japanese (including a dis-astrous naval battle at Tsushima straits that all but destroyed the Russian navy and heralded the rise of Japan as a major power). A popular revolution in 1905 promised a long-anticipated trans-formation of the Czarist government into a constitutional monarchy, but triggered bitter counterdemonstrations as well. A series of pogroms swept the land, "a methodical campaign of murder and robbery."[28] Only just entering the industrial revolution that had begun in western Europe roughly 150 years previ-ously, Russia lacked a robust broadly developed technological or scientific base. In

1899, belatedly recognizing the necessity of doing so and spurred by his aggressive finance minister Sergius Witte (who pushed hard for industrialization), the Czar had added a section to the state council for industry, science, and commerce. Nevertheless, its economy and society remained firmly agricultural and feudal (the primary export was grain), in great measure from resistance by large landowners and the burdensome bureaucracy that afflicted the imperial government. This occurred even though, ironically, the upper class of Russian society had strong traditions of pursuing higher learning: mathematics, medicine, and the natural sciences had always been strengths.[29]

Aviation would prove to be no exception to this rule. Whether the work of the French-oriented Institute Aérodynamique de Koutchino, or individual efforts of various Russians attempting to build an industry, those working in aeronautics showed keen appreciation of both technological requirements and the problems confronting the new and emerging aviation field. Some pursued very lofty goals. Koutchino's Riabouchinsky, for example, boldly wrote in March 1914 (just 11 years after the Wrights' success at Kitty Hawk): "The problem of aerodynamic flight is resolved, *but after the conquest of the air, another conquest—very much more difficult, and much grander in its scope—offers itself up to the ambitions of man: that of interplanetary space.*"[30] What they lacked was the necessary industrial base equivalent to that supporting aviation west of the Russian frontier, so they looked to France, and later Germany, for industrial support.

In 1909 the Grand Duke Alexander Mikhailovich, the second cousin and brother in law of the Czar and thus an unusually well-placed air enthusiast, had witnessed Blériot's flight across the channel; as a result, after he returned to Russia he organized a Committee for Strengthening the Air Fleet. Also subsequently he played the major role in organizing, training, and equipping the Czar's military aviation forces, largely on French and German models. Russian aviators engaged in the same kind of speed, distance, and endurance contests that attracted their western European and American contemporaries, supported by the creation in 1911 of the Vserossiiskiy vozdukhoplavatel'nyy soyuz (All-Russian Aeronautical Union) which sponsored such events, working with the government and other Russian aviation organizations. But of all the figures in Russian aviation, two men—one young and one older, both immensely gifted individuals—towered above the rest: Igor Ivanovich Sikorsky, the "pre-eminent Russian designer of the pre–World War I period," and his financial and industrial backer, the energetic and shrewd Mikhail Vladimirovich Shidlovskiy.[31]

Born in Kiev to Russian parents active in the medical field (his father was a professor of psychology and a physician, and his mother also a physician, though she did not practice), trained as a naval officer, and with a substantial background in engineering as well (from studying in Paris as well as Russia), Sikorsky had a strong interest in flight, thanks to both a childhood spent reading Verne and his education in France. Like Breguet and Cornu, he began in 1908 by attempting to build a successful helicopter, perceptively using a coaxial (i.e., one rotor perched above the other), contra-rotating (to overcome torque) approach. Despite such insights his design proved a failure. When his second such effort met the same fate as the first, he gave up, though he would eventually return to the field three decades later, with such success as to make his name synonymous with rotary-wing flight. Instead Sikorsky concentrated on developing his own flying skills and designing and building a series of small biplanes in a barn on his father's estate, each performing better than the last, and eventually culminating in the S-6 of 1911, which in a more fully developed model, the S-6A, won a 1912 Russian military competition. The S-6A marked Sikorsky's emergence as something more than just an airplane inventor, for it won even against foreign competition by French aircraft, then rightly accepted as the world's finest.[32]

Sikorsky's triumph with a homegrown product encouraged those who believed Russia had a bright aeronautical future. At first Russia had looked to the Wrights and Curtiss. But like other nations, the Russians turned quickly towards France after the cross-channel flight and Reims, purchasing quantities of French airplanes including Farmans, Nieuports, Moranes, and Deperdussins. The Russian aircraft industry began in 1910 at the Shchetinin works, at St. Petersburg, making copies of the Blériot, and thereafter it largely emulated the latest French design practices. Vladimir Alexandrovich Lebedev, a lawyer, champion bicycle racer, and French-trained aviator, established a flying school at Gatchina and, slightly later, the Peterburgskoye tovarishchestvo aviatsii (PTA, or Petersburg Aviation Association), manufacturing Farman copies and parts for other French airplanes, notably Nieuports and Deperdussins.[33] But Mikhail Shidlovskiy had bigger plans than merely expropriating foreign technology for Russia's purposes. Shidlovskiy, an energetic former naval officer and civil servant with wide-ranging interests in industry and finance, served as chairman of the Russo-Baltiiskiy Vagonnyy Zavod, the Russo-Baltic Wagon Company (R-BVZ), a railroad company headquartered in Riga, Latvia, then a part of the Czarist empire. The R-BVZ had already diversified into the automotive field, building a small but rugged automobile known, unimaginatively, as the Russo-Baltic. Shidlovskiy wanted to establish an aviation branch, saw Sikorsky as an ideal colleague in the venture, and succeeded in forming a partnership with the young designer and pilot.

Out of this came one of the most remarkable of all early airplanes built prior to the First World War, the Sikorsky *Russkiy vitaz* (Russian knight), more popularly called *le Grand,* the direct ancestor of all subsequent large multiengine airplanes. Constructed of ash, pine, and spruce, and powered by four 100-horsepower German-built Argus engines, this passenger biplane weighed

Igor Sikorsky, the father of the multi-engine passenger airplane; he began his aviation career interested in heli-copters, but abandoned them for the more practical (at the time) airplane. Later, in America, after a career of building large air-planes, he returned to his first love, inventing the first truly practical heli-copter, and enjoying such success as to make his name vir-tually synonymous with rotary-wing flight. New England Air Museum (NEAM)

The *Le Grand,* at St. Petersburg in 1913. The elegant glassed-in cabin and outside perch (complete with searchlight!) reflected the inspiration of Jules Verne's futuristic novels. Note the dual control wheels—an important and trend-setting innovation. NEAM

9,000 pounds, spanned 92 feet, had a length of over 62 feet, and could fly at 60 miles per hour. It featured dual controls for a pilot and copilot—a profoundly significant innovation—an enclosed cockpit and cabin (including a sofa, table, washroom, and closet), and an outdoor balcony ahead of the cockpit with a searchlight to pick out details on the ground. Piloted by Sikorsky and a crew of two, it completed its first flight on the late evening of May 26, 1913, at Korpusnoi Aerodrome at St. Petersburg. Thereafter it became a commonplace sight in the skies over the city and it set an endurance record of nearly two hours with eight people on board. The year 1913 constituted the three-hundredth anniversary of the Romanov dynasty, and at the request of Czar Nicholas II, Sikorsky flew it to Krasnoye Selo so the ill-fated monarch and Grand Duke Nicholas could both inspect it. Afterwards, he received a gold watch with the imperial eagle as a remembrance. Thus officially encouraged, Sikorsky embarked on an even larger military development, the *Il'ya Muromets,* named for a legendary Russian warrior.[34]

In 1910 aviation reached the Far East, birthplace of the kite and rocket. Japan looked to Europe, sending two officers to France and Germany, having them trained as pilots and then purchasing Farman, Blériot, and Grade aircraft, together with a Parseval airship, for delivery back to Japan. Captain Yoshitoshi Tokugawa flew a Farman at Tokyo on December 19, 1910, the first flight in Japan; thereafter Japanese aviation developed slowly, Tokugawa supervising the training of other pilots and the government forming a Military Aeroplane and Balloon Investigation Society. Even though in the last two years of its woefully inept imperial government, China purchased a Blériot and sent a royal prince to Germany to study both Zeppelin and Parseval airships.[35]

In contrast, Siam (now Thailand) took to the air with intense fervor. On December 10, slightly over a week before Tokugawa's Tokyo flight, French pilot Charles Van Den Born piloted another Farman from a racecourse at Saigon at the behest of the Société d'Aviation d'Extrême Orient, an aviation booster organization; it was the first flight in Southeast Asia. Van Den Born next went to Bangkok, and there, on January 30, 1911, he made the first flight in Siam and also flew the commander of military engineers, Prince Purachatra, the brother of the recently crowned Siamese monarch, King Vajiravudh. Siam occupied a tenuous and unenviable position, caught between the imperial ambitions of Britain and France. Keeping Siam independent demanded extraordinary diplomatic acumen and finesse and also a strong national military. Ironically, its best military officers attended European war colleges (the new king himself had been educated at Sandhurst), and Siam purchased weapons and equipment from both nations. Van Den Born also flew the king's other brother, Prince Chakrabongse, chief of staff of the Royal Siamese Army. The far-sighted Chakrabongse thus has the distinction of being the world's first army chief of staff to ever fly in an airplane. As a result of the royal interest and a subsequent European trip by the Siamese minister of war, three engineering officers were sent to France for aviation training, and the service acquired four Breguets and four Nieuports. The fully trained aviators returned to their homeland in November 1913, and the war ministry established an aviation section (later reorganized as a flying battalion) within the Royal Siamese Army. The first flight in Siam by a native pilot occurred on December 29, 1913, when Major Luang Arwut flew a Nieuport at the Bangkok Sports Club. (The king subsequently wrote, "I am delighted that we Thai are not bested by the Westerners; truly we can do whatever they can do.") The next year engineers began construction of the first Siamese airfield at Don Muang.[36]

Whither America? The Wright Patent Muddle

Less than ten years had passed since Orville Wright had first left the windswept sands of Kitty Hawk, yet already the United States, the birthplace of heavier-than-air flight, lagged alarmingly behind the latest foreign developments. To be sure, there were significant technical demonstrations: early bombing and gunnery trials using Wright and Curtiss pushers, the first flights from and to a ship, the first commercial airplane airline experiment, even an abortive attempt to cross the Atlantic by airship, and another to design an Atlantic-crossing seaplane. But increasingly, Americans saw more and more Europeans in newer and more advanced airplanes, flying in the United States and winning competitions against American airmen. Britain's charismatic Claude Grahame-White made the greatest impression. He came to America in 1910 and in the face of competition from both Orville Wright and Glenn Curtiss swept Boston's Belmont aviation meet, winning $60,000 in prizes (equivalent to nearly $1,136,000 in 2001). He flew a number of attractive society women and Mayor John "Honey Fitz" Fitzgerald (the grandfather of future president John F. Kennedy), invited President William Howard Taft aloft (the portly chief executive graciously declined), and then journeyed to Washington, D.C., where he landed on West Executive Avenue between

Louis Paulhan's Farman passes a balloon from the Los Angeles *Examiner* at the Dominguez Field air meet in 1910. He set a new altitude record, won an endurance prize, and made a cross-country flight totaling ninety miles. The Huntington Library (THL)

the White House and the State, War, and Navy Departments.[37] Overall, the gap between European and American aviation grew ever more pronounced in the decade ahead, despite steadily increasing numbers of individuals entering the aviation field, including two notable pioneers, Glenn Hammond Curtiss and Glenn Luther Martin.

Each greatly influenced the American aircraft industry. Curtiss became the second successful American planemaker after the Wrights. Shrewd, energetic, and intense, the lean and hawk-nosed Curtiss was both more adaptable to technological change and possessed an incomparably stronger business drive than the Wrights, quickly winning a larger market share for his company than the brothers would ever achieve once the airplane proved a commercial success. By 1916 fully 69 percent of America's 165 military aircraft purchased since 1909 would be Curtiss designs, and only 9 percent Wright machines (the other 22 percent represented a mix of miscellaneous types). In 1917, by which time he already had a main plant, three branch factories, and training schools in New York, Virginia, and California, he issued a slickly produced and illustrated catalog of his products offering "new worlds to conquer" for "those whose enthusiasm for outdoor sports has, successively, led them through motoring, motor boating, hydroplaning and ballooning."[38] By the end of 1918 and the massive orders accompanying America's entry into the First World War, Curtiss designs would account for nearly 99 *percent* of all American-built U.S. Army aircraft (5,139 of 5,206 airplanes ordered), with Wright or Wright-Martin aircraft representing only about two-thirds of 1 percent (34 airplanes).[39]

Curtiss had moved quickly to create the first American aeronautical firm, the Herring-Curtiss company, incorporated on February 19, 1909 (even predating the Wrights, who would not incorporate their own Wright Company until November 22 that year). His development of the "hydroaeroplane," both the floatplane and flying boat, gave the United States the only significant technological advantage it possessed over the European nations in the years between 1910 and 1914.[40] Well-publicized triumphs helped his efforts and gained him an international reputation. On the afternoon of Tuesday, February 23, 1909, a cold and bleak day, John A. D. McCurdy took off in the Curtiss-powered AEA *Silver Dart* before an audience of over 100 villagers, flying about a half mile above the frozen Bras d'Or lake at a height of up to 30 feet and then "landing without jar." It constituted the first airplane flight in Canada (and the first flight in the overseas British Empire). Martin, a young automobile garage and agency owner from Santa Ana, in the heart of Orange County by the sprawling Irvine ranch, began both the Golden State's aviation industry and a burgeoning empire, which, involving both an aviation school and a manufacturing plant, became a training ground for some of the greatest names in American aviation, all of whom would form major aircraft companies.[41]

But all that would be in the future: for almost the next *two decades,* until deep in the mid 1920s, during one of the most explosive periods of aviation's growth, America would trail well *behind* the European "fast seconds." A near-disastrous mix of inadequate governmental support and the industry's own self-inflicted wounds from the Wright patent controversy ensured that the birthplace of the airplane would lag behind all other advanced nations in its employment for commerce and war. Some of this represented a lingering effect of the embarrassing Langley failure of 1903 and perhaps also a reaction to the Selfridge Ft. Myer accident in 1908 (despite the successful trials of the Wright 1909 Military Flyer). (Indeed, as late as December 1914, some Congressmen would congratulate themselves for not having wasted money on supporting aviation!) However, the patent dispute must be considered the single greatest factor in directly damaging active American aeronautical industrial development over almost a full decade until

Wright Company demonstration pilots Arch Hoxsey and Ralph Johnstone, two superlative airman, were nicknamed "The Heavenly Twins." Hoxsey (who flew Theodore Roosevelt on one flight) is shown here being carried in triumph after setting a new American altitude record in 1910. THL

Wright accidents killed five of nine company exhibition pilots—56 percent. Johnstone perished during a spiral dive in November 1910, and six weeks later, a similar tragedy (shown here) claimed Hoxsey. Orville Wright eventually closed down the company's exhibition flying. THL

resolved by a cross-licensing agreement in the midst of the First World War. By 1914 the damage had been done, lasting so long as to lead philanthropists Daniel and Harry Guggenheim, in the 1920s, to create a great fund for aeronautical development that radically transformed—"cured" might be a better choice—American aviation, from education to airline operations, aviation law, aircraft design, and flight safety.[42]

To participants, suits between the Wrights, Glenn Curtiss, and other early aviators and aircraft developers involved more than just business, more than just principle: indeed, they virtually involved good and evil themselves. Curtiss's business success exasperated and infuriated the Wrights, and the brothers immediately sued once he attempted to secure commercial benefit from his aileron-equipped designs.[43] To them Curtiss and other pioneers who infringed upon their patent for personal gain were no better than thieves. The battle seesawed through American and international courts for years. While the Wrights won many cases, final success against Curtiss eluded them; meantime, to many in the public, the brothers increasingly appeared as competition-stifling monopolists. The financial stakes led to escalation and immediately affected American aviation.

The Wright's patent problems started with the voluble if well-meaning Octave Chanute. In early 1903 Chanute described the wing-warping principle to the Aéro-Club de France, the key factor alerting French researchers into the importance of roll control. A year later Robert Esnault-Pelterie translated these vague ideas into rudimentary ailerons, which he and other pioneers (including Blériot and Levavasseur) fitted to their aircraft *before* Wilbur Wright flew in Europe. Defendants seeking to circumvent the Wright's patents pointed to Chanute's talk, but also to earlier work by Goupil and Mouillard. The Wrights had learned *of* Goupil from Chanute at the end of August 1901, but by that time they were already well down the road to solving their controllability challenges, and thus they learned nothing *from* Goupil. The French pioneer deserves great credit, however, for his work, which did anticipate the modern aileron (and elevon), as well as the kind of pitch control system seen on more recent canard airplanes. As for Mouillard, Chanute stated in a 1909 letter, "When Wilbur Wright wrote to me in 1900, I sent him full details and a copy of Mouillard's patent . . . *His patent clearly covers the warping of wings.*"[44] (emphasis added) In fact this was not correct, the mistake likely attributable to Chanute's advancing age: the Wrights did not have access to the Mouillard patent until the very end of 1902, by which time they had already flown their wing-warping gliders and understood perfectly the significance of roll control.

American court decisions by Judge John R. Hazel and the legendary jurist Learned Hand went in the Wrights' favor. In January 1910 Judge Hazel issued an injunction against the Herring-Curtiss Company prohibiting the manufacture, sale, and exhibition of airplanes. "The decision," Curtiss biographer C. R. Roseberry subsequently wrote, "was a thunderclap in the aeronautical world."[45] The leading Wright biographer, Tom D. Crouch, noted that it "gave the Wright brothers an effective monopoly in the flying machine business in America."[46] But not for long: though the company folded due to legal circumstances, Curtiss was soon back in business with a new Curtiss Aeroplane and Motor Company, forcing the Wrights to return to the courts. Overseas the verdict was mixed, with a world-turned-upside-down quality. French courts might have been expected to be more sympathetic to the home team, but even there the arguments in favor of the brothers prevailed by a ruling in May 1911. The German patent office, where the Wrights expected to win, held that Chanute's disclosure to the Aéro-club invalidated the Wrights' case and ruled against the brothers, and the brothers lost an appeal to the German supreme court almost a year later as well.[47]

The case seesawed back and forth for several more years in a series of injunctions, judgments, and appeals, both overseas and in America, drawing partisans to both sides. Automobile entrepreneur Henry Ford weighed in for Curtiss, allegedly striding up to the aviator as he dined in New York's Brevoort Hotel and offering use of his lawyers. It was an impressive gesture, for his legal team, headed by W. Benton Crisp, had single-handedly won (against all expectations) a notable patent fight that threatened to put Ford out of business, defeating the very Judge Hazel who had ruled against Curtiss. But there was more to it than mere personalities. Ford detested patents as contrary to the best interests of both inventors and consumers, once remarking "They don't . . . stimulate invention. . . . But they do exploit the consumer and place a heavy burden on productive industry," even visiting Hammondsport to consult with Curtiss on the patent fight, disguising the real purpose of his visit by inspecting one of the manufacturer's new flying boats when he did so.[48] Amply staffed by skilled lawyers on all sides, the domestic and foreign lawsuits undoubtedly played a role in wearing down Wilbur Wright's

Glenn Curtiss (left) and Henry Ford, two businessmen whose products revolutionized mobility, at Lake Keuka with one of Curtiss's Model F flying boats, circa 1912–13. Inspecting the flying boat masked the real purpose of the meeting: to plan strategy to defeat the Wrights' patent suit. H C

health, something unforgivable to Orville. In February 1913 Hazel issued a final ruling, again in the Wrights' favor—and again Curtiss appealed: in January 1914 the U.S. Circuit Court of Appeals upheld the decision. Curtiss next announced he would build planes with a slightly different form of aileron control, triggering a new cycle of suits . . . but this time he had plans for using Langley's old *Great Aerodrome* to bolster his case.

Curtiss attempted to have the Wrights' suit dismissed, essentially by showing that the Langley aircraft *could* have successfully flown before theirs, except for bad luck. In January 1914 Charles Walcott, the Secretary of the Smithsonian, let his strong friendship with the late secretary cloud his judgment and concurred with a request by Glenn Curtiss for loan of the old Langley wreckage. Curtiss and his team, assisted by Albert Zahm, essentially built an entirely new airplane out of the original components and some of their own, redesigning, rerigging, and, ultimately, changing its power plant as well. The final result bore only a vague visual similarity to the 1903 machine. Yet even so it was hardly a success. In 1914 and 1915, he and his test pilots made short skipping flights off Lake Keuka, one of which ended remarkably like the original's final accident: the rear wings folded vertically, and it collapsed into the water, as one of the Wrights' relatives, sent to spy on Curtiss, looked on (presumably amused) in secret. The spy was Orville Wright's brother Lorin, who had traveled to Hammondsport and checked into a local hotel under the nom de plume W. L. Oren. Things turned ugly at one point, when he tried to take a roll of surreptitious photographs. Curtiss workers spotted him, and he was forced to give up his film. The Curtiss team, to avoid the image of bullying, immediately offered to replace it, even sending a young boy on a bicycle to a nearby store to purchase some, but Lorin refused to accept it.[49] Even the Aerodrome reconstruction was not enough for the tenacious Curtiss. The next year, 1916, Curtiss built a full-size aircraft based on Goupil's drawings, the so-called Goupil Duck. It apparently hopped off the ground on one occasion, but seems not otherwise to have flown.[50] Subsequent events overtook the case before such "evidence" could be presented.

In 1915, worn out and discouraged, Orville Wright finally decided to cut his losses. He put his company on the market, selling it quickly and for a tidy profit; the company itself struggled to maintain its competitiveness, eventually finding its future in engine, not airplane, manufacturing. In 1917 the patent suit wound down thanks to an agreement worked out by a new industrial organization, the Manufacturers Aircraft Association. Harry Bowers Mingle, the president of the Standard Aircraft Corporation, and representatives of various aircraft firms founded this direct antecedent of today's Aerospace Industries Association in early 1917. After the United States declared war on Germany in April 1917, resolving the lingering patent dispute took on new urgency. In just *two weeks,* a special committee of the association created a cross-license agreement "by which all patents, not only basic, but others of a more recent or minor character, were made available for use by all members," using as a model a previous agreement worked out in the automobile industry. The legal fight was over.[51]

Curtiss (left), Zahm (right), and Charles Manly (in the "cockpit") pose with the resurrected Langley Great Aerodrome as it is readied for its ignoble role in the Wright-Curtiss patent feud, in the spring of 1914. Note the floats and Curtiss-style flight control system, both missing from the original configuration when Manly attempted to fly it in 1903. AUND

In the face of France's rapid progress, the Wrights abandoned the troublesome canard configuration with the Model B. But though it generated spin-offs, the B failed to reverse the Wright decline. Here Harry Atwood is buzzing the White House in a Model B in 1911. Martin Luther King Memorial Library, Washington, DC

Calbraith Perry Rodgers crossed America in 1911 in the Wright model EX *Vin Fiz,* named for a soft drink. It took nearly *three months;* only the rudder and two wing struts remained of the original aircraft. Rodgers crashed and died four months later while trying to evade a flock of seagulls. NASM

One can understand and sympathize with the Wrights' feelings against Curtiss and other aviators who transgressed on their patent rights; but Henry Ford certainly had a point when he remarked to Curtiss that "Patents should be used to protect the inventor, not to hold back progress"; undoubtedly opening the "aviation war" (in *Flight*'s memorable phraseology) constituted a terrible moment in American aviation history, since it ultimately seriously hurt America's international aeronautical competitiveness.[52] The personal and psychic toll was excessive as well. The suits dominated the rest of Wilbur's short life and Orville's until he finally actively left aviation in the middle of the First World War. They effectively shattered the already strained friendship with Octave Chanute, as reviewing the increasingly acrimonious correspondence between the brothers and the old pioneer over 1910 clearly indicates (though the brothers were gracious in their tributes after his death). They shattered as well the relationship between Orville Wright and the Smithsonian. Eventually he sent the original Kitty Hawk Flyer on loan to London's Science Museum. It did not return to the United States until after his death—and then only after the Smithsonian issued what amounted to an abject apology for its actions in 1914 and afterwards in claiming Langley's Aero-drome had been the first airplane capable of flight. Likewise the demands on the brothers' time for courtroom depositions and preparations denied both of them any opportunity to contribute further in any significant way to aviation technol-ogy (though they seem to have had few ideas to advance in any case). The dispute distracted other aviators and manufacturers and split the military aviation com-munity into "Wright" and "Curtiss" factions. Neither side won, and it embittered both the brothers and Glenn Curtiss to an almost unimaginable degree.[53]

All of this took place against a background of aviators, businessmen, journal-ists, and political and military decisionmakers alike all dithering over the direction America should take in aeronautics, while European aviation forged boldly ahead, European airmen entered American air meets and won them, and the Wright approach to flight grew increasingly archaic. Afterwards both Orville Wright and Curtiss effectively left the aviation field. Orville returned to a career of general invention, and Curtiss took up real estate. It is one of history's true ironies that a merger over a decade later, in June 1929, would link both their names in what would become a major aeronautical powerhouse of mid-century, the Curtiss-Wright Corporation. One can only think how beneficial that might have been for American aeronautics had it occurred, say, in 1910, or after Wilbur's death in 1912 . . . but such was not to be.

CHAPTER SIXTEEN

The Loss of Innocence

In 1894 Octave Chanute had concluded his *Progress in Flying Machines* with the wish "that the advent of a successful flying machine, now only dimly foreseen and nevertheless thought to be possible, will bring nothing but good into the world; that it shall abridge distance, make all parts of the globe accessible, bring men into closer relation with each other, advance civilization, and hasten the promised era in which there shall be nothing but peace and good-will among all men."[1] Alas, such was not to be, for from the outset, virtually all aeronautical pioneers (and even Chanute, in the same book), recognized implicitly that an airplane would possess profound military significance—if for no other reason, because of its unique vantage point. At heart military dominance demands *height*. With height comes *view,* with view comes *awareness,* and with awareness comes the *ability to undertake decisive action.* Since earliest times, from the days of the scout perched on a horse on top of a hill, military leaders sought means of reaching across intervening terrain to learn about an enemy and his intentions, and if possible, to strike at him. Wellington, victorious over assorted armies at Seringapatam and Assaye in India, over various of Napoleon's marshals in Spain, and finally over Napoléon himself at Waterloo, famously remarked in 1845, "I have been passing my life in guessing what I might meet with beyond the next hill, or round the next corner."[2] Early aviators recognized that the vantage point conveyed by flight offered tremendous possibilities of assuaging the frustration Wellington had expressed.

Despite his lofty sentiments, a decade later, in December 1904, just a year after Kitty Hawk, Chanute had bizarrely suggested that the Wrights offer their services to Japan (then fighting Imperial Russia) for $100,000, "for a few months' work in reconnoitring [*sic*]," speculating that the Russians would hire Santos-Dumont to do the same in one of his dirigibles![3] The brothers made no reply, but wrote a few months later, "We stand ready to furnish a practical machine for use in war at once, that is, a machine capable of carrying two men and fuel for a 50-mile trip. We are only waiting to complete arrangements with some government. The

American government has apparently decided to permit foreign governments to take the lead in utilizing our invention for war purposes."[4] So the fathers of flight saw the airplane's military potential and sought to sell it essentially anywhere.

Visions of Future War

Prospects of air war alarmed both pacifists and futurists. As early as 1899, the Hague international conference on peace and disarmament had addressed the possibility of three-dimensional warfare—that of the submarine and dirigible balloon (no one forecast the heavier-than-air flying machine)—and Russia (the organizing force behind the conference) proposed a permanent ban on air-dropped weapons (though for economic reasons rather than issues of morality). The American delegation successfully lobbied for just a five-year ban, arguing that improvements in accuracy would prevent indiscriminate slaughter. The 1904 conference, suspended on account of the Russo-Japanese War, met in 1907; this time France opposed extending the ban, arguing that airships (again, no one predicted the winged bomber) should be treated with no greater restrictions than other forms of military power. Conferees agreed to submit the ban proposal to their respective governments, but eventually only Britain and the United States adopted it. There would be no restrictions on air warfare should it come (indeed, no further international legal action affecting air warfare would occur for another 70 years).[5]

If such prospects alarmed pacifists, the possibility of unrestricted aerial attack intrigued and excited others, who saw air warfare as inevitable and something for which nations needed to prepare. Some of these were authors closely focused on flight and its possible impacts; others were writing in the tradition of the *guerres imaginaires,* Europe's "imaginary wars" literature that had first appeared in the 1870s, looking at large geostrategic issues. In 1887 General Prinz Kraft zu Hohenlohe-Ingelfingen, commander of Prussia's Guards Artillery, writing on strategy, commented that military operations would likely remain unchanged unless "new inventions do not create new strategical means such as aeronautics might do."[6] In 1891 Hiram Maxim exuberantly wrote that military aviation would enable the virtual paralysis of an enemy nation.[7] Two years later Major John Fullerton, an India-born Royal Engineer with wide-ranging and distinguished combat service in Afghanistan and Burma, suggested in 1893 that aeronautics would work "as great a revolution in the art of war as the discovery of gunpowder," and that in future wars victory would go to the nation that possessed "command of the air."[8] (Later Fullerton would become an influential force in early British aeronautics. In 1905, then a retired colonel, he proposed a comprehensive national plan for British aeronautical research and development and, the following year, a proposal to establish a governmental committee to investigate aviation. Though the former remained unfulfilled, the latter eventually did come to fruition.)

Generally, the public's perception of future flight came from popular authors such as France's Jules Verne and "Capitaine Danrit" (the pen name of French army officer Émile Driant); Germany's Rudolf Martin; and England's Rudyard Kipling, "Herbert Strang" (the collaborative pen name of George Herbert Ely and James L'Estrange), E. Douglas Fawcett, and H. G. Wells. [9] Before and just after the fin de siècle, Verne had written two novels about Robur-le-conquérant, a mysterious, world-ranging aerial scientist-entrepreneur who skippered a huge and powerful airship, a veritable Clipper of the Clouds. If relatively benign at first, by the time of his second appearance he had evolved into a meglomaniacal menace roaming the skies in a combined submarine-automobile-airplane ominously named *le Terrible;* only nature itself, in the form of a powerful storm, could destroy him. [10] Slightly later Danrit-Driant wrote a series of "techno-thrillers." Immensely popular in France's belle époque this military officer-turned-novelist showcased how advanced technologies and the capabilities they furnished could play a critical role in ensuring eventual French military success in a series of perceptive and well-grounded stories of future conflict. [11] In 1907 Martin, a former official in the Kaiser's government, envisioned a powerful, air-minded Germany engaged in a series of defensive (if nevertheless expansionist) wars with rival airpower states and coalitions. [12]

In his story "With the Night Mail," England's Kipling predicted global air transport by the year 2000. Later, in the draft of a sequel, he foresaw world government via an international Aerial Board of Control using Anglo-Saxon air power to preserve global order and harmony "as easy as ABC," linking flying machines and radio communications under the benevolently despotic rubric "Transportation is Civilization." [13] (Later, in the 1930s, Wells would similarly advocate a one-world government by enlightened airmen in his *The Shape of Things to Come,* which, made into a successful Hollywood film, featured—approvingly—a new benignly fascistic order wedded to art-deco aesthetics with overtones of Italian *aeropittura* Futurism.) The Strang team echoed this, forecasting the possibilities of the airship for colonial "policing" and attacking threatening fleets. Their fellow countryman E. Douglas Fawcett took the opposite tack, writing of Hartmann, a mad anarchist, flying an airship appropriately named the *Attila,* destroying much of London. [14] The result of all of this literature was a widespread belief in both the future of war and the future role of some sort of air vehicles. In particular, as Michael Paris has noted "By 1914, then, a whole generation of young men had grown up in a literary climate which had taught them that a European war was inevitable and that the aeroplane was the ultimate weapon of the future." [15]

Most influential of all was British author (and flying enthusiast) H. G. Wells's sobering speculative novel of 1908, *The War in the Air,* which reached a truly international audience. Wells postulated a world fascinated with flight, but one in which nations were already secretly vying for control of the sky, with leading experimenters disappearing from view to work for their governments (he pointed to the Wrights, then taking their sabbatical). "I tell you, sir," a soldier warns a civilian, "there isn't a big power in Europe, or Asia, or America, or Africa, that hasn't got a least one or two flying machines hidden up its sleeve at the present time."[16] Suddenly, Germany launches a surprise attack with a fleet of airships; one by one, all the other major powers are drawn into conflict among themselves or with a variety of regional alliances—South American, Asian, among others— that are revealed to possess robust air-power forces developed in secret. The war goes global; eventually, as civilization collapses, flying itself disappears, and society returns to a surface existence, reduced to a new Dark Age of prefeudal struggle.

As Wells recognized somewhat melodramatically, both parts of Tennyson's "Locksley Hall" vision would be fulfilled. While the revolution in flight would immensely benefit world commerce and communication, twentieth-century air war promised the most devastating fulfillment of sudden, unanticipated global mechanized combat, even more than traditional conflict on land and sea. If from the outset aviation's pioneers generally recognized that the first and most productive market for the airplane would be the military, members of the military services themselves were increasingly interested in examining the suitability of the airplane for wartime operations. Doing so required partnering aviators and military officers to work together on technical demonstrations.

America and the First Demonstrations of Military Value

Ironically, despite the otherwise growing backwardness of American aviation after 1909, America's Army and Navy aviators excelled in such demonstrations. By 1910 Army aviators were undertaking significant frontier-pushing work (what today would be a blend of developmental and operational test and evaluation), even if the path forward was anything but easy, and they were far from being an "operational" force.

In October 1909, at an airfield at College Park, Maryland, Wilbur Wright had taught Lieutenants Frank Lahm and Frederic Humphreys to fly. (The Army had selected the College Park site because Fort Myer lacked the requisite space to safely train student pilots.) In the course of this instruction, Wright and Humphreys made a 42-minute night flight under bright moonlight on Friday, October 22, the first recorded night flight in aviation history, and a remarkable accomplishment in view of the unstable characteristics of the airplane and the lack of any sort of attitude reference instrumentation.[17] In 1910 the Army moved its aviation activities to Fort Sam Houston, Texas, temporarily leaving College Park, and Glenn Curtiss had begun a fruitful association with the service. In June he had dropped dummy bombs on a mockup of a battleship on the shores of Lake Keuka, and then, the next month, flew one of his pushers while his passenger, Lieutenant Jacob Fickel, fired a rifle from the air, putting two of four rounds into a 3-foot-by-5-foot target. In early 1911 Lieutenant Benjamin Foulois had several bad accidents in Texas while flying on maneuvers with local Army forces, and

The Signal Corps Aviation School at College Park, Maryland, established in 1909 because the available space at Ft. Myer was too small for safe instruction; visible are two Wright (left) and two Curtiss (right) aircraft. USAF

in May Lieutenant George Kelly died in the crash of a Curtiss airplane, the victim of excessive speed and misjudged height while flying a landing approach.[18]

After Kelly's accident the Army moved its test and training activities back to College Park, flying in the still air of the early morning and resuming in the afternoon, often continuing late into the evening. More Wright and Curtiss machines arrived, and new pilot candidates, including one officer with a perpetually pleasant (if quizzical) expression: Lieutenant Henry H. "Hap" Arnold, destined to be the chief of the Army Air Forces in World War Two, and the architect of the postwar United States Air Force. Accidents were all too common, some fatal. Before Arnold's first flights at Dayton, Wright test pilot Al Welsh pointed out the local undertaker and said "He comes out every day and drives back empty. Let's keep it that way."[19] Arnold would survive—but Welsh himself would plunge into the ground at College Park a year later, killing himself and a young officer in a particularly dangerous Wright machine, the Type C Speed Scout, after apparently misjudging his height while in a steep dive.[20]

Over the summer of 1911, the Army's College Park contingent took photographs and cross-country flights, and later that year, to much greater public attention, the first serious bombing trials. From the outset, and unlike other early air-power proponents, American airmen conceived of the aerial bomber as a means of conducting precision attacks against an enemy, a curiously prescient aspect of early American air-power doctrine that seems to have been a legacy of an earlier tradition of American military "marksmanship" dating to the frontiersman with his long rifle and, indeed, to the riflemen of the Revolutionary War itself.[21] On Friday, October 9, 1911, Lieutenant Thomas De Witte Milling took off from College Park in a Wright biplane, with Riley Scott, a former coast artillery officer who had developed an experimental bombsight. Milling and Scott circled back across the field at 400 feet and 40 miles per hour and dropped two 18-pound bombs, missing a 4-foot-by-5-foot target by 62 feet. A second flight under the same conditions reduced this error to 32 feet, and a third trial with another "bombardier," a certain Sergeant Idzorek, saw the "inexperienced" Signal Corps NCO miss by only 11 feet. Perhaps concentrated by this one-upmanship, Scott made a final flight with Milling and dropped both bombs within ten feet of the aim point (about the same accuracy as a modern laser-guided bomb dropped from 60 times the height and over 15 times the velocity). Milling promptly enthusiastically (if overoptimistically) predicted that "it will not be long before the army will be able to completely destroy any large fortress or fort in the world."[22] (Three weeks later an Italian pilot would heave four small bombs over the side of his Taube above a Libyan oasis, ushering in the era of aerial bombing.)

But, disturbingly, the Army General Staff proved less receptive to such demonstrations than their enthusiastic young aviators, the Signal Corps' own leadership (which tended to support the airmen), or indeed, the larger American public which (then and now) saw precision bombing as a means of preventing large casualties in the close fight on the ground. They rejected further developing Scott's bombsight, so the inventor immediately left for Paris and a French bomb dropping competition at Châlons sponsored by the Michelin company, the Aéro-cible Michelin. There he dropped 12 out of 15 test bombs (80 percent) within 30

Army student pilots at College Park flying Wright and Curtiss pushers could walk a few yards down the flightline and see civilian students training in a more advanced airplane than they themselves possessed: a Blériot of the National Aviation Company, a private flight-training academy. College Park Airport Museum

Curtiss (between front booms) acquaints an Army officer with the D-III pusher in 1911; note the ailerons for lateral (roll) control (mounted on the interplane struts between the wings), the simple control wheel and column, and the tricycle landing gear, all standard features of later designs. USAF

feet of an aim point—sufficient to win a $27,500 Michelin-sponsored prize.[23] Not being as penurious or shortsighted as Scott's countrymen, the French government promptly bought his bombsight, and, indeed, American mercenary pilot Bert Hall flew for the Bulgarians with a version of the Scott sight during the Balkan War of 1912.[24]

Months later, in the summer of 1912, Army aviators at College Park met with Lieutenant Colonel Isaac Lewis. Lewis had improved upon a lightweight drum-fed machine gun designed by Samuel McClean, and now persuaded the aviators to test it on a Wright biplane. On June 2 Captain Charles de Forest Chandler flew the test mission, with Milling acting as gunner, strafing some fishponds. As with the bombsight earlier, the Army again rejected this promising development, since it already had decided against armed airplanes, as its standard weapon, the heavier and more cumbersome clip-fed Benet-Mercier, could not be installed on Wright or Curtiss airplanes already in service! So for largely logistical convenience reasons the service rejected Lewis and his gun. The infuriated inventor, like

Maxim before him, soon departed for Europe. There he formed production partnerships with Belgian and British arms manufacturers, to the discomfiture of the American attaché in London—Major George Squier, who had earlier supervised the ill-fated 1908 Wright trials at Fort Myer. Meanwhile, perhaps inspired by press accounts of the American trials, in late July 1912, the first British airplane to mount a machine gun took to the air, Geoffrey de Havilland's F.E. 2, carrying a Vickers machine gun. That same year the French experimented with firing a 37-millimeter cannon from a Voisin, but the cannon imposed a dangerously high loading on the lightly built biplane; the service downgraded its expectations, undertaking further firing trials with conventional Hotchkiss machine guns. As in bombing and the exploitation of flight itself, here too Europe would move more rapidly than the Americans who had first accomplished the feat. When the various combatants' planes went to war in 1914, the Vickers, Lewis, Maxim, Spandau, Hotchkiss, etc., would be all too plentiful.[25]

The Birth of Maritime Aviation

Next to incorporating the airplane in armies, the prospect of aircraft in naval service elicited the most interest from military aviation proponents in France, Great Britain, and America. In 1909 Clément Ader had written perceptively on the need and, indeed, "indispensability" of "un bateau porte-avions"—an aircraft carrier; naval aviation figured prominently in his book *L'aviation militaire,* which included a detailed scenario of an enemy fleet attacking Brest and being destroyed by the combined attacks of *avions marins* and *avions terrestres.*[26] France's interest in naval aviation was not surprising as, next to Great Britain, it had the strongest of European naval traditions, and already an extremely robust emergent aircraft industry. What was surprising was the degree that Britain, which had risen to world status on the basis of sea power, initially tarried in marrying the airplane to the ship. In great measure, this stemmed from the debilitating effects of the CID subcommittee, which had generally dismissed as too speculative thoughts of aircraft and airships in warfare (though it noted the potential value of the naval airship for scouting forces).[27]

Maritime aviation began in France on March 28, 1910. That day Henri Fabre completed the world's first seaplane flight. Imbued with classic Gaulic verve Fabre, a young 27-year-old electrical engineering graduate of Paris's École Supérieure d'Électricité, had never previously flown in an airplane. Powered by a Gnôme engine, his *Hydravion* rose from the waters of la Mède harbor near Marseilles as its Chauvière propeller kicked up a fine spray. It skimmed the surface for about 500 meters (over 1,600 feet) before settling gently back down. The *Hydravion,* a canard pusher monoplane equipped with three broad hydrofoil-like floats, looked like a child's rubber band powered "stick and tissue" model. But if as impractical an airplane as Santos's *14-bis,* it nevertheless flew ten months before Glenn Curtiss's better-known and undoubtedly more useful Hydroaeroplane.

Fabre subsequently built some other inconsequential designs and eventually turned his full attention to simply manufacturing floats for other designers' airplanes. But his basic configuration influenced Voisin, who developed his own Fabre-float-equipped canards, of a cleaner biplane configuration. They would become France's first naval aircraft, operated from an aging destroyer modified as a seaplane tender, the *Foudre,* beginning in 1912, the same year that the French navy established the Service Aéronautique, the predecessor of today's carrier-equipped Aéronavale. *Foudre* itself was the first ship in history to be permanently modified for carrying aircraft.[28]

But it was the United States Navy that first explored military maritime applications, thanks to a particularly perceptive naval officer, Captain Washington Irving Chambers. Though naval observers had studied the early Wright military flights, the service's civilian secretary, Victor Metcalf, had concluded that the airplane "held no promise."[29] Chambers, responsible for handling all the service's correspondence relating to aviation, respectfully disagreed. He was an unlikely aviation advocate: a career engineering officer with no previous interest in flight, most

Captain Washington Irving Chambers, father of American naval aviation. U.S. Navy (USN)

recently serving as skipper of the battleship *Louisiana.* But the Navy's General Board, chaired by the sainted Admiral George Dewey, victor over the Spanish fleet at the battle of Manila Bay, had concluded airplanes might be useful for scouting, and that was good enough for Chambers. He would prove far more influential than aviation supporters could have hoped: he played a key role in getting the airplane on ships, and also in creating a pro–national laboratory climate that eventually spawned the National Advisory Committee for Aeronautics.

In late October 1910, seven months after Fabre's flight, Chambers asked Wilbur Wright if the brothers would be willing to fly a plane from a ship. Ever conservative, Wilbur demurred, stating it was too risky. But Curtiss test pilot Eugene Ely quickly agreed, volunteering to do so himself, even though he could not swim. Less than two weeks later, at 3:16 P.M. on Monday, November 14, 1910, Ely took off from a ramp hastily rigged on the forward deck of the cruiser *Birmingham* as it sat anchored off Old Point Comfort, Virginia, dropping precipitously off the bow, touching the water, and damaging his propeller; he staggered along to a landing on Willoughby Spit. Despite the near dunking in the Chesapeake, Navy officers were ecstatic, for the United States had scored an undoubted first. (It would be over a year later, on January 10, 1912, when Lieutenant Charles Sam-

On November 14, 1910, at 3:16 P.M., flying a modified Curtiss Pusher, Curtiss test pilot Eugene Ely launches from the cruiser U.S.S. Birmingham, the first flight in history of a plane from a ship. Ely was a man of remarkable daring, for he could not swim, feared the water, and took off in the face of an impending squall. USN

son would duplicate Ely's feat, flying a Short biplane off the Royal Navy battleship *Africa,* and over three years before French pilot René Caudron would complete the first shipboard takeoff in France, flying a Caudron amphibian off the deck of the *Foudre* while anchored off St. Raphaël.)[30]

Chambers next arranged for Ely to land back aboard a ship. On Wednesday, January 18, 1911, Ely took off from Tanforan, near San Bruno, California, and flew out to the armored cruiser *Pennsylvania,* anchored in the middle of San Francisco Bay, off Goat Island. In a fashion remarkably similar to how naval aircraft today approach, "break," and land on an aircraft carrier, he droned up the starboard side of the cruiser, "broke" to port, flew down the port side, turned, and then began his straight-in approach to land. Fifty feet off the stern he cut his engine; a sudden gust lifted the machine and he jammed the nose down, landing firmly on the "flight deck" erected on the stern. Hooks under the plane caught weighted lines stretched across the deck—the ancestor of the modern landing wires—and the plane came to an abrupt halt. Ely had completed the first "trap" in naval aviation history. Together with his wife and the captain, Ely was ushered below where, with other guests, all toasted the birth of naval aviation. Less than a year later, the personable young aviator perished during a flying exhibition in Georgia.[31]

Ely's "flattop" demonstration failed to impress George Meyer, the new Secretary of the Navy, who favored the Fabre approach, namely depositing a floatplane on the surface via a ship's crane and then letting it take off from the water; indeed, not until 1917 would an airplane again land on the deck of a ship, and then it would be a British, not American, vessel. To meet this objection, in January 1911, Glenn Curtiss introduced his Hydroaeroplane, a straightforward modification of the Curtiss pusher layout with a central pontoon and wingtip stabilizing floats replacing its wheeled undercarriage. From this quickly evolved his Triad (so called because it had wheels to operate off land, had floats to operate off water, and flew through the air). It became the Navy's first aircraft accepted for service. But Curtis next took the very significant step of progressing from a float seaplane to a genuine small flying boat—an aircraft having a boatlike hull for a fuselage (that is, its body) and small stabilizing wingtip floats. The first of these appeared in 1912, initially with a smooth unbroken hull bottom, until trials on Lake Keuka revealed hydrodynamic drag so great that the plane could not even leave the surface (The faster an unbroken hull moves along the water, the stronger the suction force holding it to the surface becomes). Curtiss perceptively "broke" the hull line by adding an abrupt step (now standard on virtually all sea- and floatplanes), and thus modified, his prototype proved a great success. The Navy immediately bought a number of these Curtiss flying boats, and the Army a few as well. (Indeed, one of these Curtiss boats would become the first American combat aircraft to see action, flying from the cruiser *Birmingham* [of Ely fame] on mine-spotting duties during the Vera Cruz contingency in April 1914). Flying mostly Curtiss pushers, naval aviators, starting with Lieutenant Theodore "Spuds" Ellyson (who had started his career as a submariner) duplicated the kind of trials

Glenn Curtiss demonstrates his Hydroaeroplane to Navy Lieutenant Theodore "Spuds" Ellyson (the first naval aviator) on the waters of Lake Keuka in 1911. USN

the Army's aviators were undertaking, including operating wireless sets from airplanes and directing gunfire.

On the eve of the First World War, Curtiss's interest in flying boats had led to his partnering with a remarkable British officer, John Porte, to build a twin-engine flying boat to cross the Atlantic in hopes of winning another *Daily Mail* competition, this one offering a prize of £10,000 for the first crossing of the North Atlantic by air.[32] Though the outbreak of the First World War prevented the Curtiss design, the *America,* from attempting the flight, this seaplane subsequently influenced the development of the most significant Allied maritime patrol airplanes of the First World War, the Curtiss H-16 "Large *America,*" and (via Porte) the British Felixstowe F.2A, protectors of ships, submarine hunters, and Zeppelin killers. Maritime aircraft, and seaplanes in particular, thus constituted the one bright spot in American aviation prior and during the First World War and set the stage for the U.S. Navy to succeed in making the first crossing of the Atlantic by air, in the Curtiss-built NC-4 flying boat of 1919.[33]

Airships: The Prewar "Wunderwaffen"

Ironically, in view of its subsequent abject failure in combat, the rigid airship—typified by von Zeppelin's dirigibles—received the greatest military respect and attention prior to 1914. "By far the most spectacular new invention to be adopted by armies between 1906 and 1908 was the dirigible airship," David Herrmann rightly concluded from his studies of Europe's prewar armament races.[34] Airships, both the smaller Santos-and-Lebaudy-inspired blimps and the larger rigids of Count von Zeppelin (and the rival Schütte-Lanz firm), dominated military thought in the early years of the century, perhaps not surprisingly at a time when airplanes seemed so frail, underpowered, and limited in range and height. Much like the theater ballistic missile of the present era, Germany's Zeppelins constituted the "weapons of mass destruction" of their time, engendered fear and concern in foreign countries, accelerated development of high-angle antiaircraft artillery, and even inspired counterstrategies aimed at eliminating them at the outset of a conflict. Coming on the heels of H. G. Wells's *War in the Air,* lurid speculative fiction turned the Zeppelin into an all-powerful city-destroyer. Accounts abounded in the British press in 1909 of phantom airships overflying England's east coast and mysterious aerial noises heard in the middle of the night, prompting official pronouncements, smirking in the German press, and strenuous denials from Count Zeppelin himself.[35]

In late February 1913, a new Zeppelin panic swept the British media, prompted by alleged nightly excursions of mysterious airships droning over the coast. Further "sightings" over a week triggered screaming headlines across Britain, none more shrill than Yorkshire's *Whitby Gazette:*

ENGLAND AT GERMANY'S MERCY

Though time eventually tempered the scare, sightings briefly proliferated so that, by the end of the month, "airships were seen everywhere—in Lancashire, above the West coasts, over the South . . . while Germany rocked from end to end with mirth."[36] The *Daily Mail*'s Lord Northcliffe promptly commissioned H. G. Wells to explore the topic of air warfare in three articles; he predicted a future world where Britain's battle fleet would encounter not dreadnoughts but submarines, torpedo boats, Zeppelins, and aircraft, what today would be called an asymmetric strategy.[37]

Indeed, the Zeppelin seemed a good deal. For approximately the price of one dreadnought battleship, von Zeppelin and the rival Schütte-Lanz airship works could build approximately 80 dirigibles, attractive as long-range scouting and bombing platforms.[38] Before 1914 one of the highest priorities of French and particularly British planners was countering the Zeppelin. Both nations mounted aggressive intelligence campaigns to learn as much as possible about these weapons and their employment. Britain even sent the Royal Aircraft Factory's Mervyn O'Gorman and a senior naval officer to Germany and Austria where, posing under assumed names as Americans, they flew on both a DELAG Zeppelin and a Parseval blimp!

European maritime aviation, prior to the naval airplane, had emphasized airships. Santos-Dumont had forecast their use for antisubmarine warfare, some in the German navy saw the airship as an aerial cruiser for long-range fleet reconnaissance, and the British government supported development of a naval airship largely from a sense that "if the Germans have it, it must be good." (It even contemplated ordering a German Zeppelin and did in fact order several Parsevals for the Royal Navy, one of which was actually delivered, and which flew Britain's first wartime aerial sortie in August 1914, patrolling the entrance of the river Thames).

Strongly supported by both the First and Second Sea Lords, Britain's legendary Admiral "Jackie" Fisher (the father of the turbine-powered big-gun dreadnought) and Admiral John Jellicoe (who had flown in the Zeppelin *Hansa* in 1913 with the blessing of Grand Admiral Tirpitz while on an official visit to Berlin), the Royal Navy set out to build its own airship. The British government spent approximately £70,000 (then equivalent to $350,000—$6,390,000 in 2001) on His Majesty's Airship No. 1, popularly known as the *Mayfly*. Three years in the making, it broke up in gusty winds upon leaving its Zeppelin-like floating shed on September 24, 1911, fortunately without killing anyone, thanks largely to a defective structural design and some ill-considered modifications after it had already been assembled.[39] Unlike the Royal Navy's First Sea Lord Fisher, Winston Churchill, the civilian First Lord at the Admiralty from 1911 to 1915 (when laid low after the Gallipoli fiasco), had a poor opinion of airships. "I rated the Zeppelin much lower as a weapon of war than almost anyone else," he wrote with characteristic insight and bluntness later. "I believed that this enormous bladder of combustible and explosive gas would prove to be easily destructible. I was sure the fighting aeroplane, rising lightly laden from its own base, armed with incendiary bullets, would harry, rout and burn these gaseous monsters."[40]

Coupled with the *Mayfly* accident, Churchill's understandable—and undeniably correct—attitude was a temporary death knell for British rigids, though after his departure the government sponsored development of others, based on captured plans relayed by the French and the actual example of a Zeppelin that had crash-landed in Britain without exploding. Britain's rigid naval airship program never bore worthwhile fruit, though it did lead to the first transatlantic airship flight, by the R 34 in 1919, itself a copy of a German design, the L-33. In contrast the Royal Navy's (and French navy's as well) investment in small coastal airships paid tremendous dividends in the bitter antisubmarine war to come. After the war Admiral Fisher wrote, "I had fully satisfied myself that small airships with a speed of 50 miles an hour would be of inestimable value against submarines and also for scouting purposes near the coast. *So they proved.*"[41]

But the Zeppelin—and fears of Zeppelin attack—would continue to demonstrate considerable psychological power to both its friends and its foes for some time yet. Ironically, for all of the fear of German airships, when war broke out, the German Army possessed only eleven (three of which were ex-DELAG passenger ships), and the Naval Airship Division possessed only one. Five others—three Army and two Navy ships—had been lost over the previous year in accidents. These included a disastrous in-flight explosion over Johannisthal in October 1913 that eerily echoed the Wölfert tragedy above nearby Tempelhof over 16 years before. Witnesses watching a steep ascent of the Navy's new L-2 saw a bright flame shoot between its forward engine gondola and the envelope, and then the entire airship burst into flame: poor design had led to entrapment of a hydrogen-air mix and then its detonation by the engine exhaust or ignition system. The furiously burning airship sank rapidly earthwards amid multiple explosions of bursting gas cells and fuel tanks, consumed so completely that finally only its glowing and smoking skeleton remained to fall from the sky. Not one of its crew of 28 survived, and the unfortunate designer was included among the dead. Zeppelin's string of good luck had at last run out, and though he remained a figure of great popular appeal, the L-2 disaster and his characteristic ill-tempered response to naval authorities (including an utterly inappropriate graveside harangue of Grossadmiral Alfred von Tirpitz himself during the official funeral services!) began a downward spiral in his fortunes that soon resulted in his being removed from any real future control over his company.[42]

Europe Exercises Its Military Aviation

In the increasingly unsettled and bellicose environment prior to the First World War, the European armies experimented with and exercised their growing air power forces. From observing aircraft at air meets and in rudimentary military maneuvers, perceptive military professionals recognized aeronautics would assume far greater importance than they previously had when restricted simply to tethered balloons. The first use was clearly reconnaissance, where an airplane with a crew of two could bring back information otherwise available only by a reconnaissance in force that would risk the lives of "several thousand men," and possibly antisubmarine patrol around fleets as well.[43] But such views of younger officers were hardly congruent with senior leadership.

In August 1910 French General Ferdinand Foch attended the Circuit de l'Est, a ten-day aerial tour sponsored by the French newspaper *Le matin,* watched the sputtering airplanes, and remarked dismissively, "L'aviation pour l'armée, c'est zéro."[44] These were damning words, for Foch (who would eventually rise to command all Allied armies by the end of the First World War) had a deserved reputation as one of France's most profound military thinkers, had directed the French Army Staff College (the École Supérieure de Guerre), and had written a highly regarded book on the principles of war.[45] Ironically, when France incorporated airplanes in its traditional September maneuvers the next month, the results were considerably different. France had established a small nucleus of an air arm as part of the army's artillery branch in November 1909, complementing the earlier purchase of some airplanes by the army engineers; the maneuvers held in Picardy in 1910 pitted aircraft versus airships. The airships couldn't fly because of extreme winds, but the airplanes flew consistently and well, and afterwards engineer General Pierre-Auguste Roques stated, "Airplanes are also as indispensable to armies as the cannons and the rifles," adding that it was a fact that could only be ignored at one's peril.[46] (A month after the maneuvers, Roques was named inspector of military aeronautics, though artillery aviation would continue as a separate entity for another two years.)

Maneuvers across the European nations in 1911, 1912, and 1913 reflected both the growing assurance of airmen in operating their craft and participating in war gaming and the wisdom of Roques' judgment.[47] In 1911, during maneuvers in India, an adventurous young British army captain, W. Sefton Brancker, had flown with Henri Jullerot, a visiting French pilot, successfully detecting "enemy" forces and delivering the information back to his commander, Major General Sir Douglas Haig, about an hour later.[48] Back in England the general participated in Britain's 1912 maneuvers, but as his biographer John Terraine has noted, they "were not a shining hour for Haig."[49] Despite his previous experience and a reputation as a thinker, Haig proved surprisingly blind to the value of the new arm and did not use his own aircraft wisely. Airplanes and a small airship detected and tracked Haig's attacking forces so well that his forces spent much of their time vainly trying to find concealment. The airship, outfitted with primitive wireless, sent signals to his opponent, General Sir James Grierson, who could maneuver his own troops freely. With such an information advantage, Grierson easily won, stating thereafter that "war is impossible without command of the air" and that aviation "has revolutionized the art of war."[50] Afterwards Major Frederick Sykes, a flying Hussar officer only recently promoted to major and command of Britain's Royal Flying Corps (the predecessor of today's Royal Air Force) after its establishment that same year, assembled the small RFC contingent at an afternoon parade,

With the B.E. 2, a machine of eminent practicality, British military aeronautics at last matched that of France's. In the aft (pilot's) cockpit is its designer and test pilot Geoffrey de Havilland; in the front (observer's) cockpit is Major Frederick Sykes, the first commander of the Royal Flying Corps. On August 12, 1912, they climbed to 10,560 feet in 45 minutes. British Aerospace (BA)

informing them that "any skepticism on the part of the general public as to our ability to do much has been almost entirely overcome."[51]

The 1912 French army maneuvers under General Joseph Joffre likewise showcased the importance of aerial reconnaissance: the Blue army commander, General Joseph Galliéni, met each evening with his aviators to review the day's work and plan his scheme of maneuver; the games ended with the Red army commander and his staff "riding carelessly into the enemy's ranks."[52] (Both Joffre and Galliéni would be heard from again, at the Marne.) That same year's *Kaisermanöver* taught Generaloberst von Moltke that Germany needed to acquire more reconnaissance and observation airplanes, because "officers controlling artillery fire will be very materially assisted by spotting and observations from aircraft."[53] (Based on their own maneuvers, Britain and France would reach the same conclusion the next year, noting as well that valuable reconnaissance observations could be made from altitudes of over 6,000 feet.) After the 1913 French maneuvers, Colonel Hirschauer, the chief of the French army's aeronautical branch, boldly stated, "Aviation without a doubt has revolutionized warfare. I am not predicting merely that there will be a revolution. There has been one. The recent maneuvers in France, German and England all proved it."[54]

Despite this and other developments reflecting the growing age of mechanization, European general staffs still largely embraced tactics and strategy reflecting nineteenth- or even eighteenth-century military values, overemphasizing manpower and the clash of armies, and undervaluing the growing importance of

France's Blériot monoplane was aviation's first great "export" success, with extensive foreign military service in both peace and war. Here is one at the British Army's military trials, held at Larkhill, in the midst of Salisbury Plain, in 1912. RAF Museum (RAFM)

technological supremacy.[55] In February 1913 Major Sykes of the Royal Flying Corps and General Sir John French, chief of the imperial general staff, lectured a combined meeting of the Aeronautical Society of Great Britain and the Royal United Services Institution. Sykes echoed Grierson's comment, "War is impossible without command of the air," but French (despite having attended the Reims meet in 1909) took a far different view. He remarked (a *rapporteur* noted) that "it was sometimes said that aviation would revolutionize warfare.... This, he thought, was absurd."[56] The next year, again despite what had happened to him in the 1912 war games, Haig cautioned students at the British army's staff college, "I hope none of you gentlemen so foolish as to think that aeroplanes will be usefully employed for reconnaissance from the air. There is only one way for a commander to get information by reconnaissance and that is by the use of cavalry."[57] (To their credit, Foch, French, and Haig changed after witnessing what airplanes could do in war, proving more flexible in using the airplane than their throwaway remarks would at first indicate. Unfortunately, many others would not.)

To War on Wings

By that time maneuvers were being overtaken by actual fighting experience, for long before the Western Front, Europe witnessed actual air war, and so too did the Americas. The first nation to take both the airplane and the blimp into combat

WAKE UP ENGLAND!

SECURE AERIAL SUPREMACY

SHOW YOUR PATRIOTISM

NATIONAL AVIATION FUND
of One Million Shillings

To provide Prizes and Awards of all kinds to Manufacturers, Inventors, and others with a view to fostering **AERIAL NAVIGATION THROUGH-OUT GREAT BRITAIN**, and encouraging the development of a **PURELY BRITISH AERONAUTICAL INDUSTRY**, and hastening the improvement of existing types of machines, in order to render them **SAFER** and more suitable to the conditions peculiar to these islands.

I am in entire sympathy with such a scheme, and shall be very glad to further it. I warmly congratulate your League on their forward policy, and I wish you every success in your patriotic undertaking. THOS. BOOR CROSBY
(Lord Mayor).

I sincerely trust Million Shilling Fund will be well supported and prove a great success. ROBERTS.

Hearty good wishes. Conquest of the air will produce a tremendous weapon for that nation which possesses the greatest number of efficient air-craft.
CHARLES BERESFORD (Admiral).

I believe the time has now arrived when a considerable sum of money can be spent advantageously in the different ways described in the scheme.
GENERAL RUCK.

Sincere good wishes in your great undertaking. F. E. SMITH.

I have, of course, every sympathy. CONAN DOYLE.

Will you help this great movement by subscribing, or by becoming a Local Honorary Secretary, or Honorary Treasurer, and distributing collecting cards?

Communicate at once with the Chairman :—

General H. T. Arbuthnot, C.B., R.A., 6, Coventry St., London, W.

SUPPORT BRITISH INDUSTRY

KINDLY MENTION "THE AEROPLANE" WHEN CORRESPONDING WITH ADVERTISERS.

The parlous state of British aviation in 1912 led to appeals for financial assistance to the burgeoning aeronautical industry; similar fund drives in Germany, France, and Russia matched the increasingly frantic pace of the pre-World War European arms races. From *The Aeroplane* (1912)

was Italy. In 1909 Guilio Douhet, an artillery captain serving on the general staff, perceptively argued that the airplane would not prove merely an auxiliary to armies and navies, but rather "as a third brother, younger but no less important, in the great warrior family."[58] While his views did not yet permeate the growing Italian air establishment, nor did they echo internationally (as they later would), they nevertheless reflected a rising interest in military aeronautics within the Italian army, which formed an aeronautical section in 1910. In late September 1911, Italy delivered an ultimatum to the Ottoman Turkish government, ostensibly over mistreatment of its nationals. In fact Italy had desires on Tripoli and Libya, desires strengthened by the ever-weakening decline of Turkish power in Libya, thanks to the Ottoman Empire's need to shift forces into the troublesome Balkans and other distant regions, whose restless people—Islamic people included—were fed up with centuries of corrupt, despotic, and exploitive rule. As expected, Turkey rejected the ultimatum, and Italy promptly invaded.

To assist its forces, Italy dispatched a small force of 11 pilots and 30 enlisted men on October 15, the Squadriglia di Tripoli, composed of nine airplanes: two Blériot, three Nieuport, and two Taube monoplanes, as well as two Farman biplanes. Three blimps soon followed as well. On October 23, 1911, Captain Carlos Piazza undertook the first combat aerial reconnaissance by an airplane, flying a Blériot from Tripoli to Aziza (four months later, he would add a camera to his airplane, inaugurating the era of photographic reconnaissance). Two days later Piazza and Captain Riccardo Moizo detected an approaching Turkish column; the army used the information to position itself and defeat the Turkish forces. Next Piazza and Second Lieutenant Giulio Gavotti directed the fall of naval artillery fire from the Italian warships *Carlo Alberto* and *Sardegna,* shelling enemy positions. The next week, on November 1, Gavotti dropped four small 2-kilogram Cipelli grenades from a Taube on the towns of Taguira and Ain Zara, ushering in the era of aerial bombing: Ain Zara experienced several more attacks from Gavotti and Piazza over the next few days. For their part, beginning in March 1912, the three airships flew bombing and photographic reconnaissance missions, both by day and by night, dropping approximately 330 bombs on 86 missions by the beginning of 1913. At the battle of Zanzur on June 8, 1912, timely airship bombing broke up a Turkish cavalry formation waiting to ambush Italian troops. Generally the Italians operated with little risk from enemy action, though two pilots were wounded by intense small-arms fire that eventually drove them to higher altitudes. Two airmen flew 80 missions apiece, but pilots found such sustained operations quickly fatiguing. Moizo earned the unhappy distinction of being the first airman captured in war when he force-landed his Nieuport after engine failure over Turkish territory; his captors treated him well and freed him in a prisoner exchange after the war. Just two years had passed since the U.S. Army accepted the first military airplane into service.[59]

Italy's air operations in Libya constituted only a footnote to the overall intervention, but it did attract great attention in the military community: the airplanes and airships had fulfilled multiple roles, supported the land battles and naval operations, and even undertaken strategic and tactical air attacks themselves. Also, the Libyan air war drew the attention of artists and intellectuals such as the aviation-minded Futurist poet Filippo Marinetti (who earlier had dedicated a play to Wilbur Wright) and artist Carlo Carrà. In 1912 Marinetti authored a book of impressions from the war, entitled *Zang Tumb Tumb*, "referring to the whistling and echoing sounds of speeding bullets and exploding bombs": 17 years later, he founded the *aeropittura* movement, dedicated to Futurist art employing aviation as its central theme.[60] Musings of the literati aside, Italy's experience undoubtedly encouraged future military use of the airplane and airship. After Libya, Britain's then-Captain Sykes (in Italy during the war, where it is likely—but not certain—that he learned of Douhet's theories of air warfare) wrote, "There can no longer be any doubt as to the value of aeroplanes in locating an enemy on land and obtaining information which could otherwise only be gained by force."[61] By the middle of the First World War, Italy would field multiengine, long-range, strategic bombers, the result of the collaboration of Gianni Caproni and Douhet, and Douhet himself would refine his thinking, eventually becoming one of the three major air-power theorists—indeed, prophets in the eyes of their followers—together with Britain's Hugh "Boom" Trenchard and America's William "Billy" Mitchell.

After Libya the airplane swiftly appeared in other conflicts as well. In late 1912, after Bulgaria, Greece, Montenegro, and Serbia formed the Balkan League, the Balkans erupted in war against the Ottoman Empire. French and German airplanes figured prominently, as did new kinds of twentieth-century warriors: the mercenary airman, motivated by idealism, profit, or a judicious mixture of both; and the airman, ostensibly detached from his country's military, but actually serving it in a covert role. French and Russian military airmen delivered airplanes and flew for the Greeks, Bulgarians, and Serbs, British mercenaries flew French and German airplanes for the Montenegrins and Bulgarians, and eastern European and Turkish pilots familiarized themselves with the new aerial weapon.[62] Bulgarian airmen bombed the Turkish fortress of Adrianople.[63] Greek airmen bombed Turkish troops, "creating a veritable panic."[64] Bulgarian pilots flew over the Black Sea coast, "scouting, dropping bombs, and generally making themselves unpleasant."[65] As in Libya earlier, chivalry still existed, at least to some degree: when Russian pilot Nicholas Kostin, flying for the Bulgarians, experienced engine failure over Adrianople, Ismail Pasha, the Turkish commandant, introduced him to his family and treated him more as an honored guest rather than the prisoner that he was.[66] In 1914 both France and Spain would take their nascent air arms to Morocco, using their airplanes both for reconnaissance and bombing against rebel forces.[67] By that time American and European mercenary pilots flying a mix of French- and American-built airplanes would have flown in combat on both sides of the Mexican revolution, scouting for both government and rebel forces and even bombing troops and towns using modified artillery shells dropped by hand. Air warfare, like the airplane itself, was rapidly proliferating around the globe.[68]

CHAPTER SEVENTEEN

Triumphs of Speed and Distance

In the last two years of peace, Europe consolidated its supremacy in world aviation, as France extended its own particular dominance over Europe. Reims had marked the passing of the "Can humans fly?" era of flight, and aviation's globalization and introduction into practical use quickly followed, at least partially answering the "But is it worth it?" question. Then, from 1912 through mid-1914, continuous refinement expanded the airplane's performance and broadened its potential uses, addressing the question of "What are the new opportunities?" In response, the practical streamlined airplane appeared, as did the practical multi-engine airplane, and significant advances occurred as well in structures and propulsion. Gone completely were the shaky pioneer days of 1906–1909, so far removed from the world of 1912–1914 as virtually to render that earlier period as quaint as the days of Cayley and Pénaud.

France owed its dominance of European and international aeronautics to the unabated and energetic expansion of its aviation industry, first evident at Reims. By 1912 French aircraft clearly constituted the "gold standard" of international design, holding all significant records. A review of all unrestricted international air competitions held between 1909 and 1914—that is, air competitions open to all entrants and not limited to, say, just French or British or German designs—demonstrates how rapidly French aviation predominated. Out of 14 competitions, French aircraft (flown by French or non-French airmen) won 11, a staggering 79 percent. French aviators or airmen flying French aircraft won the first German and British national air competitions. That proved *too* much: not surprisingly, both countries quickly limited their *national* competitions to entrants flying their own airplanes, not those originating in other countries.

The French success could be summed up in one word: *vitesse*—"speed." The James Gordon Bennett Aviation Cup offers one (but by no means unique) example. In 1909 Glenn Curtiss had won at Reims. When the competition was held in America the next year, Englishman Claude Graham-White took it, flying a Blériot. Then, since an Englishman had won, it moved to the UK. There, in 1911, it fell to a Nieuport flown by the American Charles Weymann. It moved back to the United States in 1912, where Jules Védrines, flying a Deperdussin Monocoque racer, won it. With the competition remaining in France the next year, his fellow countryman Maurice Prévost secured it, flying an even more advanced Deperdussin. Had the First World War not intervened, it is likely French airmen would have secured it yet again in 1914. So out of five competitions, French aircraft had won an impressive four.

But even more impressively, the trophy requirements had increased dramatically over time: the course lengthened from 12.4 miles (20 kilometers) in 1909 to 124 miles (200 kilometers) in 1913. Thus, in just five years, the Gordon Bennett competition had witnessed nearly a *tripling* of flight speeds over *ten times* the original course length, itself a significant commentary on French engine reliability as well, for the already ubiquitous Gnôme rotary powered every winning competitor after Curtiss first took the trophy at Reims. Indeed, the Deperdussin of 1913 had over a 22-*fold* increase in performance over the 1909 generation of French and American airplanes.[1]

The beautiful and influential Deperdussin Monocoque racer of 1912–1913 exemplified the extraordinary progress made by French aviation in the years between 1906 and the outbreak of the First World War. In many respects it reflected the natural evolution of French aviation, building on the monoplane tradition begun unsuccessfully with Ader in the 1890s but then flowering with the Antoinettes and Blériots of the 1908–1910 time period. Additionally, however, it reflected the more sure-footed design practices already appearing in aviation, namely, a tendency towards greater aerodynamic cleanliness (what would be termed streamlining in the post–First World War time period) typified by minimizing external bracing as much as possible and fully enclosing the fuselage (unlike the open-fuselage approach taken by Blériot or any of the Wright, Voisin, or Farman biplanes), as well as moving to greater structural efficiency.

The Triumph of the French

By 1911 the awkward Farmans and Voisins of the 1908–1910 time period were already giving way to a new aesthetic, and even the partially open-framework Blériot looked increasingly passé. The year 1911 marked a major departure in French aeronautics, as new developers burst upon the scene: Armand Deperdussin, Edouard de Niéport, Léon and Robert Morane, and Raymond Saulnier, all crafters of exquisite monoplanes. That year each of them—Deperdussin, Niéport, and the Moranes and Saulnier working together—introduced three highly successful designs that carried aircraft design to a level of performance, practicality, and reliability anticipating the aircraft revolution of the 1920s and 1930s leading to the modern airplane. Niéport developed a very neat and attractive monoplane, the Nieuport, which subsequently enjoyed great foreign sales success, though its creator died in a September 1911 crash at Chany while demonstrating it to the French

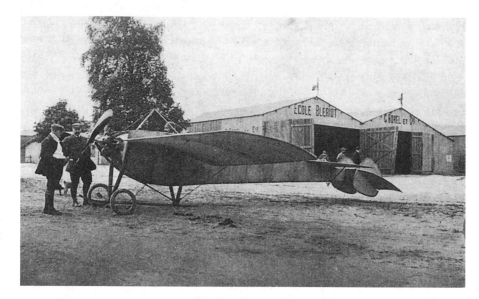

Edouard de Niéport in his first Niéport (subsequently Nieuport) monoplane, at Issy-les-Moulineaux. Hayward collection

military. (Tragically, his brother Charles, who took over the company following his brother's death, himself perished in a landing accident less than two years later.)[2] The Moranes and Saulnier developed robust, workmanlike, yet attractive designs that likewise saw widespread production both in France and overseas. But the most exciting and significant of all came from the Deperdussin firm.

Armand Deperdussin, a flamboyant if venal entrepreneur, led a life that with its peaks and valleys could have inspired an Aeschylus play. A wealthy, Belgian-born, middle-aged silk magnate and small-boat manufacturer who had started out as a cabaret singer, he entered the aviation field in 1909, largely as a publicity stunt, partnering with an extraordinarily gifted 29-year-old engineer, Louis Béchéreau, a graduate of the École des Arts et Métiers in Angers. The slight and sharp-featured Béchéreau, looking somewhat like Santos-Dumont, had previously joined with Clément Ader's nephew to establish a small company, the Société de Construction d'Appareils Aériens. Now Deperdussin's infusion of capital brought the businessman a measure of control, so that the next year the company was renamed as the Société pour les Appareils Deperdussin—SPAD, destined to be one of the most famous acronyms in all aviation history. Their first collaboration resulted in a trim monoplane having a conventional slab-sided framed fuselage structure of rectangular cross section, though the underside beneath the cockpit resembled a shallow rowboat or racing shell. Flown by Jules Védrines, it set a number of flying records. It competed in the 1911 French army airplane trials where it did very well against a strong field of competitors, coming in third (behind a Nieuport monoplane and a Breguet biplane) and winning a small production order. With these small successes, SPAD joined the leading French airplane manufacturers.[3]

By 1911 designers were beginning to recognize the importance of robust structures; indeed, French aviators were particularly aware of this, as a result of a series of spectacular accidents involving Blériots shedding their wings and thereby killing some of the best-known European aviators, including Léon Delagrange, Hubert Leblon, and the Peruvian Georges Chavez (killed after just having traversed the Alps from Switzerland to Italy). Cut-and-try strengthening of the Blériot's front wing spar, in the absence of strong empirical analysis, cured its problems, but the entire episode, and other accidents to other aircraft as well, indicated that structural design had to proceed hand in hand with refined aerodynamics and more powerful engines. The challenge was combining strength with the requisite lightness. Various possibilities existed. Louis Breguet made extensive use of metal in his biplanes, using steel-tube longerons and wing spars and aluminum wing ribbing. The German Hugo Junkers favored an all-metal pure flying wing approach. The Swiss Eugene Ruchonnet favored wooden shells. Out of this latter preference would come the most refined airplane to appear before the First World War and arguably one of the most refined airplanes to appear even in the first quarter century of flight: the Deperdussin Monocoque.[4]

The story of the Deperdussin Monocoque begins with Eugene Ruchonnet, a 35-year-old Swiss engineer, who had become interested in aviation after beginning his career as a boat designer. He flew at Reims, distinguished only by crash-landing an Antoinette, fortunately without injuring himself. By the next year, he was an accomplished pilot and became a flight instructor, but his real interest was building lightweight aircraft structures. And here he believed airmen could learn from boat builders, building the fuselage of an airplane like that of a boat, in layers of thin bonded wood strips wrapped over each other in a cross-hatched pattern to form a single lightweight shell, or *monocoque*. In 1911, at his small French aircraft works at La Vidamée near Senlis, he set to building such an airplane, a monoplane having the general appearance of a Deperdussin, but with a monocoque shell fuselage. It flew before the end of the year, and locals looked at the carefully formed fuselage with its pleasing streamlined shape and promptly nicknamed it Ruchonnet's Cigar. Around 5:30 on the afternoon of Friday, January 12, 1912, after completing several short flights, he took off and climbed slowly in the direction of the small community of St. Nicholas. Suddenly, from a height of about 300 feet, for unknown reasons (maybe simply a lift-destroying stall), the plane pitched over abruptly and dove headlong into the ground, killing him instantly. The well-liked Ruchonnet's tragic death shocked the Franco-Swiss aviation community, and the Club Suisse d'Aviation took up a collection to support his young widow and aged mother, both left nearly destitute by the accident.[5]

Ironically, the day after Ruchonnet's death, Deperdussin test pilot Jules Védrines, a tough, perpetually angry-looking, hard-bitten socialist from the Paris working class, exceeded the world's airspeed record at Pau, reaching 90 miles per hour (145 kilometers per hour) while flying a new Deperdussin design that incorporated, in partial form, Ruchonnet's ideas. How Béchéreau came to know of Ruchonnet's work is unclear, but it was perhaps through Deperdussin, in view of his shared nautical background with the young Swiss. In any case, in mid-1911, after the success of their 1910 design, Béchéreau and Dutch engineer Frederick Koolhoven determined to build a streamlined racer partly using the Ruchonnet monocoque technique, powered by a 100-horsepower Gnôme Double Omega rotary. They initially drew a slab-sided configuration but with a rounded and smooth laminated wooden shell for the top and bottom, sharply swept-back tail surfaces, and short monoplane wings featuring a minimum of external bracing. Its success at Pau led to its reengining with a more powerful, 140-horsepower Gnôme Double Lambda. On March 2, 1912, Védrines reached 168 kilometers per hour, the first flight faster than 100 miles per hour.[6]

Encouraged by this interim design, Béchéreau and Koolhoven next drew up a genuine monocoque shape over the early spring of 1912, a true "body of revolution" with a circular cross-section, projectile-shaped fuselage tapering to a sharp point, retaining the sharply swept-back tail surfaces, streamlining the ash-wood landing gear struts, and enclosing the 140-horsepower rotary in a tightly fitting aluminum engine cowling. A large, rounded spinner capped the propeller; everything about this plane, known as the Monocoque racer or simply Monocoque,

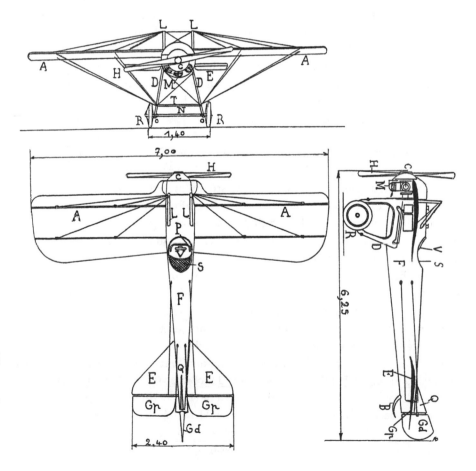

The design layout of the first Deperdussin Monocoque conceived by Louis Béchéreau and Frederick Koolhoven in mid-1911; this radical aircraft firmly placed French aeronautics ahead of every other nation. From *L'Aérophile* (1912)

bespoke streamlining and speed. It was as different from the era of Wright, Farman, Voisin, and Curtiss pushers as night from day.[7]

Unlike the built-up rib and stringer construction that had characterized most early airplanes, fitted together, wire-braced, and covered with stretched and doped fabric drawn tightly across the frames, the Monocoque's fuselage consisted of two half shells joined together. Under the direction of Deperdussin's shop foreman Henri Papa and his chief carpenter, the cabinetmaker André Herbemont, skilled wood craftsmen assembled a master form of the fuselage shape, one for each half. Next they set down a layer of thin tulipwood strips over the form, pinning and gluing these strips to a hickory framework. Two more layers of tulipwood were added over the first layer, each layer forming a crosshatch pattern with the one below, to counter any tendency of the fuselage to twist in flight. Then the workers removed the almost-completed section from the form, added internal bracing for the pilot's seat, other equipment, and the engine mounts. They assembled the other fuselage half in a manner similar to the first, joined the two together, and then covered the entire fuselage with fabric, varnishing it for smoothness and added strength. The result was a true monocoque: a streamlined shell having maximum internal volume, a beautiful aerodynamic form, exceptional structural strength, and low weight. During flight testing in the early summer of 1912, Védrines reached 106 miles per hour.[8]

The Deperdussin team got a chance to show what it could do on the morning of Monday, September 9, 1912. That day found the team at Clearing, Illinois, outside Chicago, readying the trim monoplane for the Gordon Bennett trophy race. For months rumors had circulated in the United States about the powerful new

Shape of planes to come: looking like a winged bullet, Védrines' Monocoque flashes past the cameraman, nine years after Kitty Hawk.

MAE

racer, and in anticipation of its arrival, both Glenn Curtiss and the Burgess company of Massachusetts had announced their intentions to defend the trophy. Curtiss stood no chance in any case, for his was nothing more than a standard open-framework pusher with a cut-down wingspan to reduce drag, fitted with a 75-horsepower engine, not all that different than the pusher with which he had won the original Gordon Bennett race at Reims three years before. The Burgess company proposed a copy of the previous year's winning Nieuport, but with a new 160-horsepower Gnôme Double Gamma, even bigger than the engine in the Deperdussin: in short, effectively a French airplane built in America. But come race day, neither was ready, nor even Weymann's Nieuport, the defending champion. Thus, not nine years after Kitty Hawk, an *American* team on *American* soil could not defend the Gordon Bennett trophy it had won the previous year in a French airplane against a newer and better French airplane, all because no suitable American airplane, or even an American extrapolated clone of a *French* airplane, existed. It was a sorry state of affairs.[9]

So it was that when Védrines walked out into the early morning sunshine and mounted his machine, he had no American opposition. It was a hot day, clear, with a slight breeze blowing off Lake Michigan. The big twin-row rotary coughed to life with the odd popping and whining sounds common to all rotaries, before giving way to a full-throated roar as a cloud of blue-grey smoke whipped away in the prop blast. Védrines's ground crew held the airplane back until he signaled release, and then it shot forward before the awed spectators. He averaged over 105 miles per hour along the 124-mile course; when he landed he put down on the far side of the field lest the enthusiastic onlookers strip the fabric from the plane. As it came to rest, French armaments producer and aviation enthusiast Jacques Schneider rushed up and emotionally draped the tired pilot in the French tricolor. The magazine *Aerial Age* caught the tone of the moment when it wrote, "Jules Védrines fulfilled all expectations. He came and flew and conquered."[10] It was Hunaudières all over, but in reverse. France would dominate the world's speed events for the next decade.

Later, his countryman Maurice Prévost flew the less-powerful 100-horsepower Monocoque to a very respectable 103 miles per hour while a much slower Hanriot racer flown by André Frey failed to finish. That afternoon Védrines took off again and set a new world's airspeed record of 108.18 miles per hour: it had been a revolutionary day, one that dramatically illustrated the superiority of French aeronautical technology. The only American airplane aloft that day had been an old Wright carrying a press photographer.[11] Indeed, the *latest* Wright airplane, just produced that year, the euphemistically named Wright Model D Speed Scout, retained the open-framework and chain-driven twin propellers of its predecessors and could attain but 67 miles per hour, just 64 percent of the performance of Bechereau's speedster. Nothing could have so dramatically illustrated the differences between French and American aviation than the juxtaposition of these two contemporaries. So Deperdussin secured a one-two knockout blow. By day's end the Aero Club of America was already arranging the packing and shipping of the Gordon

Bennett cup to the Aéro-Club de France. For his part, in response to a press question whether America could successfully compete the following year, the normally moody Védrines had some advice for his American colleagues. In a genial and atypically modest mood, he explained all the problems he had faced getting ready. "If America would fly in the Gordon Bennett race next year," he concluded, "let her start to work at once. *There is no time to lose.*"[12] (emphasis added)

Readying a Monocoque for flight at Chicago, September 1912. HC

La glorieuse année

Not without reason, French airmen referred to 1913 as "the Glorious Year." In April 1913 Prévost won Jacques Schneider's first trophy contest for seaplanes, piloting a float-equipped Monocoque. That same month Gustav Hamel flew himself and a British journalist in one of the new Blériot two-seat military Model XIs nonstop from Dover to Cologne, Germany. Alarmed that anyone just might pop over the Channel to look down on Britain's ports and forts the Home Secretary, "under the powers conferred upon him by the Aerial Navigation Acts, 1911 and 1913," immediately designated a series of prohibited areas, designated aerial ports of entry, established conditions of entry, and banned "foreign naval and military aircraft" from British skies "except on express invitation or permission of His

The Morane-Saulnier exhibit at the 1913 Paris Salon, replete with examples of this triumphant company's slab-sided speedsters. MAE

Majesty's Government."[13] Aviation was suddenly a great deal more bureaucratic, if understandably so.

By mid-1913 France's new Moranes, slab sided and less elegant than the Deperdussins (but surprisingly fast, still pleasing to both eye and the air, and easier and cheaper to build as well) had joined the Monocoques in wresting prizes and sweeping records across Europe. In 1912 company pilot Roland Garros had set a new altitude record of 5,610 meters (over 18,400 feet); it was a far cry from the "30 to 40 feet" Moore-Brabazon achieved in his Voisin at Châlons in 1908. Now a flood of records fell to the trim design. In June and July, Brindejonc des Moulinais covered 5,000 kilometers (3,100 miles) across Europe in his Morane. On September 20 Gustav Hamel, flying a special short-span version, won Britain's Aerial Derby; three days later Garros flew 730-kilometers (453 miles) across the Mediterranean from St. Raphaël to Bizerte. It took just short of eight hours and left him with but *seven minutes* of fuel remaining when he landed; only four years and two months separated Blériot's brief crossing of the channel from Garros's flight of even more breathtaking boldness. Then, at the end of the month, came the year's most anticipated event: the 1913 Gordon Bennett race, held at Reims.[14]

America did not compete that year: no other nation had an airplane that could either, so it was French airplane versus French airplane. That September 29 Maurice Prévost flew an even more powerful, refined, and streamlined short-span ver-

sion of the 1912 machine to almost 125 miles per hour, winning the cup and finishing ahead of three other competitors, two Deperdussins and a Ponnier monoplane, the latter a very fast machine but of conventional design. During the flight he had become the first pilot to exceed 200 kilometers per hour. Afterwards, his winning Deperdussin Monocoque was retired and placed on exhibit; it can be seen today by visitors to France's Musée de l'Air et de l'Espace at Le Bourget. Together with the Vuia, Farman, Blériots, Antoinette, Nieuport, and Moranes, it illustrates France's extraordinary six-year progression from inferiority to superiority, the most refined and impressive high-speed airplane of its time, and among the finest of all times as well. It was the apogee of the Deperdussin Monocoque's fortunes.

For his contributions to aeronautics, France awarded Armand Deperdussin membership in the Légion d'Honneur—but he received it in jail. Over the summer his financial empire had collapsed like an ill-conceived house of cards, amid a welter of sadly justifiable accusations of fraud, embezzlement, and financial manipulation. Time passed as the charges were investigated, with Deperdussin remaining in prison and French aviation continuing to advance. His company went on without him, being reorganized and taken over by Louis Blériot, who, following a horrific accident in Turkey, had at last given up flying for good, preferring to control a business through the ups and downs of the commercial world

Prévost's Deperdussin, the ultimate Monocoque, winner of the 1913 Gordon Bennett race (and the first aircraft to exceed 200 km/hr), now exhibited in the Musée de l'Air et de l'Espace, Le Bourget. Hallion photograph

than to continue to risk his life aloft. SPAD remained, with new words: Blériot renamed it the Société Provisoire des Aéroplanes Deperdussin, then it became the Société Anonyme pour l'Aviation et ses Dérivés. Béchéreau and Herbemont continued to furnish the engineering genius behind the company's later designs. A galaxy of French, British, Italian, and American airmen would fly the most famous of these, the SPAD VII and SPAD XIII fighters, which dominated the aircraft of the Central Powers from midwar onwards. Convicted in 1917 (but given a suspended sentence), Deperdussin lived to see victory, though he ended the war disgraced and shunned by old colleagues from his aviation days. Not even the debt France owed the company he founded could gain him rehabilitation and restoration of his reputation, and the postwar years were no kinder. On June 11, 1924, he shot himself while staying in a seedy Paris hotel, dying, like so many other French aviation pioneers, by his own hand. It is at least some small mercy that his name today is inextricably linked with one of the finest, most significant, and indeed, most beautiful airplanes ever built, though it is tragic that this association, of which he could be justly proud, proved insufficient to prevent him from taking his own life.[15]

. . . and Afterwards

If 1913 had been "the Glorious Year," many believed 1914 would be even more so, and it certainly started out on a promising note. At 10:00 A.M. on New Year's Day, January 1914, at Tampa Bay, Florida, pilot Antony "Tony" Jannus of the "St. Petersburg-Tampa Airboat Line" flew paying passenger A. C. Thiel, the mayor of St. Petersburg, in a Benoist XIV flying boat across the bay to St. Petersburg, inaugurating the first airline passenger service in the United States, and the first airplane airline in the world. The flying boat, similar to Curtiss's designs, covered the 22 miles between the two communities in 23 minutes, and the fare—anything but cheap—was $5.00 (equivalent to $86.05 in 2001). Jannus gamely kept at it for four profitless months before throwing in the towel, having carried 1,204 passengers in the little two-place plane.[16] In March Ginzo Nojima, a Japanese pilot trained in the United States, flew a Curtiss pusher named the *Junyo* (falcon) around Taiwan, where he "terrified the aborigines and contributed to uplifting the dignity and authority of the Japanese forces," as interesting as a commentary on Japan's attitudes towards the occupied indigenous Taiwanese as it is on the growth of Japanese aviation.[17]

In June 1914 American pilot Lawrence Sperry made one of the most significant of all early aviation demonstrations, flying an airplane equipped with a primitive gyroscopic stabilizer, the ancestor of the modern autopilot. Sperry's father Elmer, the father of modern feedback controls, looked more like a prosperous banker than a gifted inventor, but he held more than 350 patents. His handsome engineer son shared the father's passionate, and inquiring nature and was a pilot as well. In 1913, working with Glenn Curtiss and supported by the U.S. Navy, Sperry, then just 20, perfected a gyroscopic stabilizer. It consisted of two gyros, one vertical and one horizontal, that would keep an airplane from deviating in roll, pitch, or yaw, thus holding it to a steady course. Lieutenant Patrick Bellinger worked with young Sperry, the two flying upwards of 50 test flights in a modified Curtiss C-2 flying boat. By the end of 1913, they had refined its performance, and Sperry and Curtiss set their sights on winning a 50,000-franc ($172,100 in 2001) international safety competition in Paris, sponsored by the Aéro-Club de France and the French war ministry. In June 1914, at Bezons, France, Sperry put on a spectacular demonstration. As his French mechanic, Emile Cachin, bravely walked out on one wing, Sperry flew "hands off" with his hands raised above his head, with the autopilot fighting the unbalance and keeping the plane in level flight. The boldness and assurance of the demonstration staggered onlookers. That Sperry had won was but the most obvious and foregone conclusion. Additionally, it offered proof that while the United States might have lost the impetus in aeronautical development, it still clearly possessed a surprising vibrancy and creativity that augured well for its future. Sperry, having earned the nickname Gyro from his fellow airmen, next took the prize money and turned to coupling the gyro-stabilizer and a gyro steering mechanism to a bombsight. Later he turned to creating a primitive automatically stabilized cruise missile—proof yet again that early aviation was at once more complex and sophisticated in intent than the simple image of wood-and-fabric airplanes would indicate.[18]

Distance, endurance, and altitude records were made almost weekly over the spring and summer of 1914 as German airmen began to successfully contest the French for the first time in international aviation, thanks to the new generation of biplanes using a powerful new 100-horsepower Mercedes inline engine. At Johannisthal on June 28, flying a trim new Albatros, Werner Landmann remained aloft for nearly 22 hours, covering a distance of 1,900 kilometers (approximately 1,180 miles); his countryman Reinhold Boehm extended this two weeks later to just over a full day (and night): 24 hours, 12 minutes. In December 1913 the French pilot Georges Legagneux had piloted a straining Nieuport to a height of 6,120 meters (approximately 20,000 feet); in July the German airman Gino Linnekogel took a Rumpler biplane to 6,600 meters (nearly 22,000 feet), then witnessed his own record broken less than a week later by Heinrich Oelrich, who piloted a D. F. W. biplane to 7,850 meters (approximately 26,000 feet). A mere five years had passed since Louis Blériot had struggled to get over the windblown Dover cliffs in his little Anzani-powered monoplane, and not quite eight years since Santos-Dumont had first hopped off the ground at Bagatelle for a few seconds.[19]

With results like these, thoughts turned to crossing the Atlantic, and indeed, in 1913 the ever-enthusiastic Lord Northcliffe had offered up yet another *Daily Mail* prize, this one for £10,000 for the first airplane to span that ocean. In response Glenn Curtiss developed his large flying boat, the *America,* and over the summer of 1914 arrangements for the flight were well underway. But the Curtiss *America* was not the only significant large airplane in the world; Russia's Igor Sikorsky had just completed his latest four-engine biplane, the *Il'ya Muromets,* and was eager to try it out on a really significant long-distance flight. The opportunity presented itself in late June 1914.

Five months before, in January, Igor Sikorsky and Mikhail Shidlovskiy had completed their new craft. In contrast to the earlier *Russkiy vitaz*, the larger *Muromets* was "dual use": both a potential airliner and a warplane—in fact, the world's first multiengine strategic bomber. Other nations might have talked about airplanes bombing from the air, even dropped bombs from small aircraft—but the *Muromets* was the real thing, the harbinger of all long-range bombers and airliners developed since. By the standards of 1914, it was opulent: a separate pilot cockpit, a passenger cabin with heating courtesy of engine exhaust channeled through steel tubes, lighting via an airstream-driven generator, and complete furnishings including a lavatory, wicker chairs, and a private suite with a table, cabinet and bed, a small front balcony, and a larger balcony aft of the top wing. If needed, doors over the wings enabled mechanics to crawl out on the wing and service the four 100-horsepower German Argus engines in flight. As originally completed, it had one odd feature: Sikorsky had fitted it with an auxiliary wing located halfway between the biplane wings and the horizontal tail. Fortunately for the plane's looks, early test flights demonstrated such good handling qualities that he removed this line-disrupting excrescence. A second *Muromets* followed early in the year, with more powerful engines giving it an additional 130 horsepower. Flights of both planes drew tremendous attention, so Sikorsky set up a small waiting room that harbored some strange bedfellows: "At times we saw a Cabinet Member of the Imperial Government," Sikorsky recalled, "calmly and peacefully discussing flight impressions with some of the Leftist members of the Douma. A

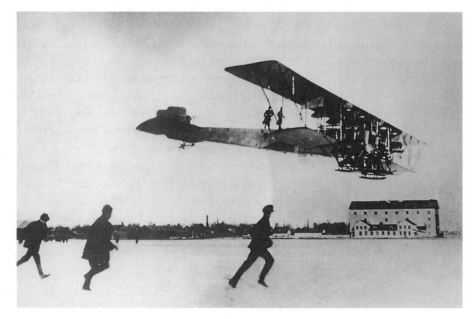

The ski-equipped *Il'ya Muromets* landing at Russia's Korpusnoi airfield, 1914 Note the passengers casually standing aft of the wing; obviously no concern about seat-backs and tray tables on *this* flight! NASM

person familiar with the state of mind in Russia at that time would have realized that this, unfortunately, was not the usual thing."[20]

On February 11, Sikorsky set a world record, carrying 16 passengers and a friendly dog aloft over St. Petersburg. But despite his success, naysayers persisted in questioning the capabilities of the large plane. (Years later Sikorsky commented, "I can see now that aerodynamic drag is much easier to take care of than other types of parasite resistance which often slow down progressive work").[21] Some said it wouldn't fly high; Sikorsky took the plane to nearly 7,000 feet with 12 people aboard. Others thought it couldn't fly far; Sikorsky determined to fly from St. Petersburg to Kiev, the city of his birth, a distance of 1,200 kilometers (approximately 750 miles).

The flight took off at 1:00 A.M. on June 30, 1914, with Sikorsky sharing piloting duties with copilot Staff Captain K. F. Prussis and pilot-navigator Lieutenant G. I. Lavrov. Mechanic Vladimir Panasiuk furnished technical support. Ever curious, after takeoff Sikorsky actually walked out on the lower wing in the predawn sky to see if a mechanic could in fact repair an engine in flight. "It was beautiful and interesting to watch from this point the huge body of the ship and the wide, yellow wings," he recalled later.[22] He hoped to make the flight in two hops, stopping at Orsha along the way. Shortly after nine o'clock, the crew sighted Orsha and landed in a field previously marked out for their use, to the acclaim of the local citizens. The Orsha stop came off without incident, and the *Muromets* returned to the air in midafternoon. The day was hot, and the heavily loaded plane staggered along at about 400 feet of altitude. Then, disaster struck. The right inboard engine fractured a fuel line, and the exhaust immediately ignited it, triggering a blowtorch of a flame jetting back 12 feet behind the engine, playing on the wing surface and wing struts. Without hesitation Lieutenant Lavrov and mechanic Panasiuk went out on the wing; the quick-thinking Lavrov leaned over the roaring jet of flame, reached down, and closed a fuel valve, shutting off the flow. Then the two men, using their greatcoats, smothered the flame. But they weren't out of the woods yet: the heavy and smoking *Muromets* now began a steady descent, incapable of remaining aloft on just the three remaining engines. Sikorsky put it down without damage in a small field; as he looked over the singed and blackened wing, the seriousness of the incident became clear. "Smiling and congratulating each other, we realized that this had been a narrow escape," the young inventor wrote later.[23]

Although they had the engine repaired in an hour, Sikorsky and the crew wisely decided to remain at the landing site, near the city of Scklov, and fly out early the next morning. The day began rainy and gloomy, but true to their plans the team left a little after 4:00 A.M., almost immediately entering cloud, enduring heavy rains, and being buffeted by gusts. They reached 3,000 feet but, buffeted and tossed, often descended well below this before fighting their way back aloft. These conditions were a prescription for disaster. Proper blind-flying instrumentation (the artificial horizon, precision altimeter, and gyro-compass) did not appear until 15 years later, thanks to the work of Paul Kollsman, Elmer Sperry, and the

Guggenheim Fund for the Promotion of Aeronautics. Until that time a pilot risked becoming quickly disoriented in cloud, particularly in buffeting conditions; even now it is a potentially killing condition for unskilled airmen. At some point the airplane "departed": it stalled and began spinning, a condition unrecognized by its pilot and crew. All Sikorsky noted was that the controls "appeared loose and the ship did not obey the ailerons."[24]

Like blind flying, spinning—then called the "spiral dive"—was a killer: in fact, usually the mechanism whereby a disoriented pilot flying in cloud fell to earth and died. Even in clear air, spins took a heavy toll of airmen: it had not been until August 1912 and the British military trials at Larkhill that the first glimmerings of understanding how one should recover from a spin appeared. Then Lieutenant Wilfred Parke of the Royal Navy had entered a spin as he spiraled earthwards in an experimental Avro cabin biplane. Instinctively he used the rudder against the spin to stop the rotation and then pulled back on the controls to recover into level flight. "Parke's Dive," one of the most dramatic of early flights, ended the killing and injuring streak of spins and caused a sensation among early aviators: but the word apparently hadn't got to Russia, for now Sikorsky found himself in a condition he didn't recognize and didn't understand.[25] Years later he could not recall precisely how he returned to controlled flight, except thinking that he must have instinctively understood he had to neutralize the controls—that is, center the controls, let the plane develop some speed in the resulting dive, and then recover into level flight. This he apparently did, as the big biplane returned to level flight after dropping more than 1,200 feet.[26] Sikorsky had been lucky beyond imagining.

Without any navigational aids beyond a simple magnetic compass, Sikorsky and the crew pressed on. The cloud and weather conditions continued to test their skills: they had planned to follow the general course of the Dnieper River, but the weather thwarted such a simple plan almost to the very end. Then the weather eased somewhat, and at an altitude of but 800 feet they at last spotted the Dnieper and managed to follow it for the better part of an hour, checking their position and ascertaining that they were midway between Orsha and Kiev. The long flight had consumed so much fuel that the plane had lightened considerably, dramatically improving its performance. So after conferring with the crew, Sikorsky decided to climb above the rain. Just above 5,000 feet they finally broke out into the clear, into a brilliant blue sky above puffy, white, sunlit clouds. It was a Jules Verne moment, one that Sikorsky must have recognized and desired ever since as a child he had avidly read *Robur-le-conquérant* with its imaginary open-air promenade above the clouds. Sikorsky turned the plane over to Prussis, had a cup of coffee, put on his greatcoat, and then stepped out on the upper bridge, keeping his position by holding the rails. "Only a few times in my life have I seen such a majestic and beautiful spectacle as I did then," he recalled later. "Our ship was gliding along a few hundred feet above a sparkling white surface. The air was calm and the plane seemed motionless with its huge yellow wings. . . . All around me there was a fairyland, formed by clouds."[27]

Cold finally forced Sikorsky indoors, where he rested in his cabin. Two hours after breaking out into the sunlit sky, Lavrov announced it was time to descend to Kiev. Sikorsky took over, and the plane plunged back into a gloomy, dark, and turbulent world of clouds. As the altimeter slowly unwound below 1,000 feet, the crew was uneasy: did the vaporous layer persist all the way to the ground? But then it began to thin and finally, at about 900 feet, they broke out, and there, dead ahead, were the domes of Kiev's famed cathedral. A little further off nestled Kurenev Aerodrome. Sikorsky throttled the four faithful Argus engines back and set up a straight-in gliding approach, engines and props ticking over slowly, landing on the muddy field without further ado, tired and worn, but understandably jubilant at having proven the practicality of the long-range airplane. The sudden appearance of the distinctive *Muromets* out of the clouds surprised the locals, who had not expected its arrival on such a stormy day: only one dignitary, the secretary of the Kiev Aeronautical Society, was there to greet them, wrapped in a coat against the damp. He did not offer the reception they might have expected; after only the briefest of perfunctory congratulations, he told them the latest news: the archduke Franz Ferdinand and his wife had been assassinated by Serbian terrorists in the little Balkan city of Sarajevo.[28]

PART SEVEN

TENNYSON FULFILLED:
PUTTING PROPHECY INTO PRACTICE,
1914 AND AFTERWARDS

CHAPTER EIGHTEEN

Into the Whirlwind

As a terrorist's bullets brought to a close that period in European history the French fittingly called la belle époque, Igor Sikorsky's flight ended as well the heady days of prewar aviation. At the beginning of the twentieth century, buoyant optimism characterized European society. In part the product of centuries of common historical experience and culture made manifest by the rise of influential nation states, it reflected those states' growing economic power. That power itself gave evidence of the increasing significance of science, technology, and industry. America—whose institutions, government, and values sprang from that European culture—shared the optimism, largely because of its own special circumstances as already the most powerful and unified nation in the western Hemisphere. The international pursuit of flight—both the long history antedating the balloon and its far shorter history since Kitty Hawk—exemplified this optimism as well, particularly in the hope of an unfolding harmonious future without limits.

The airplane—the "annihilator of time and space," the embodiment of speed, even more than the locomotive—promised, through shrinking distance and compressing time, to create a world of convenient travel. Thus Sikorsky's flight from St. Petersburg to Kiev had an innocence about it that captured at once the romance, the hope, and—yes—the naiveté of early flying. A young man reveling in his creation, he stood outside as his machine droned along above the clouds, drinking in the bright sky and sun, living the fictional adventures of his childhood, seeing the beauty of the cavernous vista around him, and like the world he was in, not thinking of the dark, turbulent storm hidden within all that beauty. Fellow aviators generally behaved the same. They flew in competitions, crossed frontiers, admired the vistas, flung their aircraft about with increasing abandon, seemingly oblivious that soon they would participate in a far more deadly international competition, crossing each other's frontiers, observing troop movements below, and flinging their aircraft about in desperate attempts to evade or destroy.

The Road to War

Their collective frolic collapsed one bright summer Sunday morning amid the cobbled streets of Sarajevo, nestled amid steep Balkan hills on the banks of the Miljacka river. Four years before, when the ill-fated Archduke Franz Ferdinand had ridden in the funeral cortège of England's Edward VII, an American newspaper had speculated (more by chance than insight) he was "destined to make history in southeastern Europe."[1] But no one could have predicted the awful role this good man would play. An extraordinary lack of security that led to a near-fatal bombing earlier in the day; the inexplicable (and suspicious) misdirection of the motorcade off Appel Quay, requiring it to reverse course so that the arch-duke's car halted directly in front of Gavrilo Princip; the assassin himself—a trained, fanatical 19-year-old Bosnian Serb gunman, "tiresome, ego, mare eyed, consumptive looking"[2]—all this culminated in two well-aimed shots from Prin-cip's Browning pistol that irretrievably shattered and reshaped not only European life but the entire course of subsequent world history.[3]

The deed done, 39 days passed before the world exploded into war. In that time multiple mistakes set Europe down a path to horrendous worldwide con-flict, but in truth, once the summer crisis of 1914 accelerated towards its dismal end, few were really surprised at the outbreak of war. In anticipation, one by one, aviators returned to their homelands, the military ones rejoining their units, the various national aviation magazines featured articles on lessons learned from aer-ial warfare over Tripoli and the Balkans, and popular newspapers and magazines opined about aerial bombing and Zeppelin attack. Some optimists still attempted to keep the prewar spirit alive. Exhibition pilots roamed Europe before being in many cases unceremoniously escorted to the nearest frontier. On July 30, 1914, the dashing Norwegian pilot Tryggve Gran flew a Blériot from Cruden Bay, Scotland, to Revtangen, Norway, in four hours and ten minutes. The first crossing of the treacherous and unforgiving North Sea, it constituted one of the most impressive of early long-distance flights and as such deserved great attention. But Gran and his nervy flight were at once swept from the front page by far more ominous breaking news: Imperial Germany's declaration of war on August 1 against Rus-sia; Gran himself soon volunteered for service with Britain's Royal Flying Corps.[4]

The tone of Europe's aviation magazines immediately shifted. Utterly gone was the casual goodwill, the sense of an international adventuring brotherhood and bonhomie of airmen shaped by five years of meetings and competitions; now came a harder, divisive, nationalist edge: Oskar Ursinus, editor of the German magazine *Flugsport* and soon to originate the Gotha long-range bomber, called upon *"Deutsche Flieger!"* to have but "one emotion in our hearts: revenge," appeal-ing a month later for *"Flieger an der Front!"* (aviators to the front!)[5] Across the North Sea, *The Aeroplane's* bloody-minded Charles G. Grey waxed equally belli-cose. "In the name of common sense, let us have at it," he exhorted, "and smash Germany thoroughly, once and for all."[6] Such sentiments mirrored those of the larger populations, who raced off to war with an extraordinary passion and eagerness, rallying by the thousands. There were some that realized the tragedy to come: "The lamps are going out all over Europe," Sir Edward Grey, Britain's foreign secretary, memorably said. "We shall not see them lit again in our lifetime."[7] In fact they went out all over the world, not just in Europe, and nearly a century later, we haven't seen them since. Today, deep in the age of modern terrorism, we are still the heirs to the disastrous echoes and reverberations, the monumental global consequences, of the "colossal, seismic charge of diabolic energy" loosed by Princip's pistol.[8]

In the spring of 1914, the airplane was a thing of wonder and hope, and even after war broke out, it briefly enthralled those who saw it: resting in a trench outside Antwerp, the poet Rupert Brooke took note of "a lovely glittering aeroplane" that passed overhead.[9] But by the fall of 1914, when an anonymous French *poilu* saw an artillery-spotting German Taube puttering over a road, it had become quite something else: "There," he bitterly exclaimed, "is that wretched bird which haunts us!"[10] In less than a year, the airplane had gone from a peacetime marvel, a symbol of the best of humanity, to a fearsome tool of war, a bringer of destruction and death. His lament could have served as a commentary upon the twentieth century, a century of uncommon scientific and technological promise and fulfillment, but also one in which both science and technology served the baser, as well as the more noble, of human instincts.

Within weeks of the opening of the First World War, the rasping reconnaissance airplanes wafting over the heads of grim-faced troops shaped and decisively influenced the two great battles that themselves shaped the nature and conduct of the rest of the war: the battles of Tannenberg and the Marne. It was the most dramatic form of confirmation that all those who had sought to create military air forces could have conceived. The German victory at Tannenberg in late August and the French-British victory at the Marne in early September transformed not only the course of the First World War, but also the history of the twentieth century. Their impact is felt even today in the twenty-first.

After the Franco-Prussian war, Otto von Bismarck had assiduously pursued a strategy of isolating France by trying not to antagonize other European powers. But in just two decades, two years after the accession of Wilhelm II as Kaiser in 1888, his policies and influence collapsed amid the new emperor's dreams of an expansionist state. In response to Germany's new bellicosity, France and Russia had joined in a secret alliance, tacitly recognizing Germany as the common probable enemy. Germany's rupture and subsequent naval rivalry with Britain in the early years of the new century added a new potential enemy. All this spelled acute anxiety for the German military as it contemplated a general European war. The spectre of getting caught in a prolonged, draining conflict on two fronts constituted its chief fear. In response, in 1906 the then-chief of the general staff, Alfred von Schlieffen, conceptualized a rapid thrust through neutral Belgium and Holland (virtually guaranteeing British entry into the war) and on into France, with an invading army heavily weighted on its right flank swinging around the line of French fortifications and fortresses defining the Franco-German border. The plan conceded that France would be able to hold its own against the German left flank, even advancing perhaps into German territory. But any success the French enjoyed against the German middle and left flank would come at the expense of a shattering blow from the German right flank, composed of no less than 90 percent of available German forces. The attack would steamroll over French forces, loop behind Paris, and curve back, rolling up the remaining French resistance in the middle of the country. All German resources could then turn and confront the Russians who, it was assumed (incorrectly), would be far slower to mobilize than the French. It was bold, insightful, and potentially deadly. But would it work?

The cautious Generaloberst von Moltke, the 66-year-old chief of the general staff, wasn't certain. Nicknamed *der Junge* to distinguish him from his more skillful uncle, who had crushed Austria in 1866 and France in 1871, von Moltke's temperament and interests suited him far more for the university or concert hall than the rigors of running a world war.[11] So he reduced the force disparity between the left and right wings of the German army from 9:1 to 1.5:1. The right wing, with five full armies, still had a large advantage in numbers, but nowhere near the overwhelming advantage it had possessed under the original von Schlieffen construct. That way, von Moltke hoped, the French attacks against the middle of the German front, held by two armies, would be far less effective. And he was right, to a point, thanks in large measure to his opponent's own planning. Colonel Loyzeaux de Grandmaison, the chief of the French Army's Operations Bureau ("a gaunt Peter the Hermit with flaming eyes," in Cyril Falls's evocative phrase), had promulgated an utterly foolish doctrine, the *attaque à outrance,* overwhelming attack, which doomed thousands by its disregard of both the enemy's intentions and firepower.[12] From the outset the French took horrendous casualties, starting with the Lorraine offensive that opened the war. Brightly clad infantry and cavalry, using nineteenth-century tactics and repeatedly thrown into battle in accordance with Grandmaison's loony theories, clashed with *Soldaten* wearing low-visibility *Feldgrau,* operating twentieth-century artillery, machine guns, and repeating rifles.[13] Regimental commanders lost up to 80 percent of their men, and casualties eventually reached 300,000, an average of a division per day for the entire month of August. "Altogether de Grandmaison's doctrine," Alistair Horne has written, "was to cost France the lives of hundreds of thousands of her best men; including that of the prophet himself, when fallen from grace."[14]

Tannenberg: Annihilation of an Army

But while the German center held firm against the French, the German high command watched with increasing disbelief as Russia mobilized with remarkable speed and then began a surprisingly rapid advance across the Prussian frontier (in what is now Poland), driving like a dagger aimed at the Prussian heartland. Two Russian armies, under generals Pavel Rennenkampf and Alexander Samsonov, clashed with German forces, and a spectre loomed of Germany, having underestimated Russia's response, being decisively defeated in the East.

Germany entered the war with decided advantages over the Russians, particularly in communications, logistics, and aviation. On paper both countries had roughly equivalent aviation strength: just eleven years after Kitty Hawk, and but six years after the appearance of the first military airplane at Fort Myer, Germany had 232 aircraft and 11 rigid airships, and Russia had 244 aircraft and 14 semirigid blimps. Both had their aviation forces divided into flying detachments attached to field units and fortresses. But maintenance, logistical, and basing problems; lack of standardization among types; and large numbers of obsolescent machines plagued the Russian air arm, and only four of its airships could fly. From the outset, then, the Russian army could not expect to receive the kind of support that German aviators would routinely furnish their own forces. In the campaign to follow, this would be one of the most distinctive differences between German and Russian operations.[15]

In contrast to the Czarist army, Germany's Eighth Army, charged with defense of East Prussia against Russian attack, had sufficient aviation forces available early in August 1914 to conduct productive routine reconnaissance operations. These consisted of four field flying detachments *(Feld-Flieger-Abteilungen)* of observation aircraft (typically Taube monoplanes or Albatros biplanes), one assigned to each

The aptly named Taube was Germany's most prevalent military airplane at the beginning of the First World War. Here a group of German officers and airmen pose with a line-up of production Tauben at Edmund Rumpler's manufacturing plant and flying school at Johannisthal. NASM

Fliegerschule: RUMPLER Luftfahrzeugbau,
Flugplatz - Johannisthal.

of the three *Armeekorps* and another to *8. Armee's* command headquarters; and four fortress flying detachments *(Festungs-Flieger-Abteilungen),* one each for Posen, Thorn, Graudenz, and Königsberg. These eight detachments should have furnished the army commander, General Max von Prittwitz, with a total of 48 airplanes, but the actual number was about 40. Probably a little less than 30 were available for service at any one time. Prittwitz did have three rigid airships he could call on (the Army Zeppelins Z IV and Z V and the army Shütte-Lanz airship SL II, this last a wooden-framed, not metal-framed, dirigible), based, respectively, in Königsberg, Posen, and Liegnitz.[16]

From the outset of the eastern campaign, German reconnaissance aircraft and airships did their best to maintain watch on Russian forces, "flying over the Russian columns before they left Poland."[17] Russian aircraft, in contrast, rarely appeared: the majority had been sent to Galicia, not East Prussia, and even those on hand were largely kept on the ground. General Nikolai Martos, the otherwise aggressive and perceptive commander of the Russian Fifteenth Corps attached to Samsonov's army (and taken prisoner in the battle), recollected afterwards, "I did not send our aeroplanes out, *keeping them for a more important moment.*"[18] What could have been "a more important moment" is hard to imagine. Worse, when they did fly, Russian commanders seemed unwilling to believe what their observers said, in part because of preconceptions of how any battle might unfold.[19] In contrast German forces immediately benefited from their access to air information. Reconnaissance flights over Russian territory began on August 2, and within a week a standardized system of patrol zones had been established for each flying detachment. Starting on August 10, the Z IV flew nightly reconnaissance missions from Königsberg northeast to Tilset, east to Insterburg and Gumbinnen, and due south as far as Mlawa, occasionally dropping streamer-stabilized artillery shells on Russian encampments. The Russians quickly learned to attempt concealment when German airmen were overhead, and the newness of aerial reconnaissance by airplane and airship itself guaranteed that it would not function smoothly. Airmen still had not developed the "eyes" to know what to look for when spotting for enemy troops, and in any case no process or system existed on the ground for the prompt exploitation of their discoveries.[20]

But despite all these limitations, by the middle of the month the airmen had made some notable contributions. They had spotted a growing gap between Rennenkampf's northern "Niemen" army (the Russian First Army) and Samsonov's southern "Narew" army (the Russian Second Army), a gap corroborated by communications intercepts that confirmed Rennenkampf had ordered a halt south of Gumbinnen. On the nineteenth, airmen spotted two Russian corps moving north from Goldap to reinforce Rennenkampf, then locked in battle with German forces. This timely information prevented a possible disaster, as cavalry patrols from a German reserve corps charged with protecting the flank against just such as attack had failed to detect this threat, and the corps commander had been on the verge of shifting his forces. Now, thanks to the airmen, he was able to engage and block the Russian maneuver. Overall the airmen were furnishing increasingly significant information on Russian locations and movements, enabling von Prit-twitz to develop a comprehensive picture of what he was facing—and he didn't like it. Rennenkampf's army had emerged victorious at Gumbinnen and now stood poised in the North, with Samsonov's army below, ever advancing onwards. The cautious von Prittwitz determined he had to fall far back to the Vistula River, well west of Gumbinnen and the Masurian Lakes region.[21]

Such a decision was anathema to the German high command. Even the hesitant and overly cautious von Moltke found this so disconcerting that he immediately sacked the aging von Prittwitz. In his place stepped an even older retired general, Paul von Hindenburg, partnered with a younger rising star as chief of staff, Erich von Ludendorff, already battle tested from the Western Front. Ludendorff moved to hold Rennenkampf in position and shifted the bulk of his own forces to confront Samsonov. In ignorance of this deployment, without meaningful air reconnaissance of his own, Samsonov blundered into German forces at Orlau on August 24, where German troops fought his Narew army to a halt, and then, over the five days from August 26 through 31, encircled and shattered it utterly at Tannenberg. During this time German airmen generally kept track of Russian units (particularly Rennenkampf's), and in several notable cases warned German ground commanders to the presence of Russian forces that had gone undetected by other means. Completely disorganized, Samsonov's Narew army disintegrated, with 33,000 dead, wounded, and missing. Thousands perished in marshy swamps and lakes south of Tannenberg, the Germans took a further 92,000 into captivity, and Samsonov himself committed a lonely nighttime suicide in the woods.[22]

The German victory at Tannenberg stemmed from a variety of causes, but certainly the combination of aerial reconnaissance and communications intercepts, when coupled to Russian battlefield ignorance and poor decision making, was most responsible for the von Hindenburg–von Ludendorff victory. Ironically, they had used a maneuver strategy very much like that von Schlieffen had envisioned in the west; as Roger Chickering has written, "Schlieffen's vision had materialized in the wrong theater."[23] Tannenberg set the stage for the collapse of Rennenkampf's own forces and his hasty (if prudent) retreat at the battle of the Masurian Lakes just a month later, with equivalent losses to those of the unfortunate Samsonov. But its psychological impacts were perhaps the greatest.

For the Germans the battle constituted not merely a deliverance but a triumph of staggering proportions, what some termed a latter-day Cannae. For Russia and its partners, Tannenberg was an unimaginable disaster. Its outcome shattered the Allies' faith in the Czarist government, and far worse, "instilled in the Russian high command and in the ranks of the army a lasting sense of inferiority."[24] It loosed a corrosive lack of confidence, so much so that in 1917, during the brief Kerensky ascendancy, the then-provisional government's war minister declared that from the moment of Tannenberg onwards, he had known the war was lost.[25]

After the battle von Hindenburg remarked to German air officer Major Wilhelm Siegert, "Ohne Flieger kein Tannenberg!" (without the airmen, no Tannenberg!), an indication of how firmly Tannenberg established the necessity and importance of aerial reconnaissance in the minds of German commanders, certainly the value of aerial reconnaissance for warning and defense, in view of the number of occasions when airman had warned their ground comrades of threatening or unexpected Russian movements.[26] General Ernst von Hoeppner, a career cavalry officer commanding the *Luftstreitkräfte*, the German army air service, noted at the war's outset that few officers anticipated that airplanes would possess military significance. But "the shining reconnaissance results of our airmen in the first weeks of the war resulted in a complete change in the perception of this new combat weapon. What in peace we could not have anticipated, had occurred: the *aviators had almost entirely replaced the cavalry as the means of long-range reconnaissance.*"[27] (emphasis added)

Decision on the Marne

If the United States' great weakness after the Wrights invented the airplane was not assiduously pursuing its further technological development with sufficient vigor, France's weakness had been overconfidence, the failure of the rabbit in its race with the tortoise. After its airmen and engineers mastered and exploited aviation technology with commendable speed, the French military's adaptation of the airplane started rapidly, but then, even as war fears grew, it slowed and then lagged significantly, primarily from bureaucratic inertia and a failure to appreciate how useful an airplane could be. As a result, in 1914 France went to war with 162 aircraft (of 14 different types) and six airships, less than 60 percent of the total number of German aircraft, and less than 60 percent of the total number of German airships. Worse, some of the areas that French airman had pioneered—such as controlling artillery fire from the air—had gone out of practice or become outmoded. At the outbreak of the war, France had a total of 24 *escadrilles* (each with an average of six aircraft, equivalent to the force structure of a German *Flieger-Abteilung*).[28]

German air power in the west consisted of 190 airplanes, five airships, and sixteen tethered kite balloons, Parseval's so-called Drachenballone. The summer of 1914 was one of the finest in Europe over the previous century, and so the aviators had generally good weather and long flying days to undertake reconnaissance. But unlike in the east, such did not translate into immediate operational success in the west. Any war quickly reveals organizational and command problems that need resolution. For German aviators, usually ignored in the daily operational orders streaming from army headquarters, that meant improving access and influence at higher command. Clearly they had to prove themselves useful to "win the right," as it were, to a place at the decision-making table. But opportunity did not come, thanks in part to the relatively short range of the Taube monoplane and Albatros biplane, which prevented very long-range reconnaissance.[29]

Such might have revealed the landing and deployment of the British Expeditionary Force (BEF) which, consisting of two corps and a cavalry division under the

command of Field Marshal Sir John French, began its embarkation on August 9. By August 20 the BEF had advanced to positions along the Sambre River, running southwest for slightly less than 25 miles between Maubeuge (itself located approximately 15 miles south of Mons, Belgium) to Le Cateau. In the middle of the month, the air component of the BEF, under the command of Brigadier General Sir David Henderson, flew to France, from Dover to Amiens, and thence on to Maubeuge. On the morning of Thursday, August 13, five years after Blériot had struggled to cross the Channel, five dozen airplanes began flying across without incident, the first time in history a military force had flown to war in another nation.

On the sixteenth, 120 years since Coutelle had risen with *l'Entreprenant* on the world's first aerial reconnaissance, aviation returned to Maubeuge, in the form of four Royal Flying Corps squadrons flying a mix of 60 clattering Blériots, Farmans, and B.E. 2s, the first of a force that would eventually expand to over 1,200 airplanes and over 60 squadrons less than four years later.[30] On August 19 the Royal Flying Corps flew its first sortie "in anger," an uneventful Blériot reconnaissance northeast of Mons. Over the next few days, twitchy French *poilus* took potshots at the British airplanes, which they mistook for German, and when British troops

Parseval-Sigsfeld tethered kite balloons, like those shown hangared here, inspired a more streamlined Allied equivalent, the Caquot, designed by French Army Captain Alfred Caquot. AFMA

arrived, they did the same. "We were rather sorry they came," wrote one British pilot of his countrymen, "because up till that moment we had only been fired on by the French."[31] Very quickly they painted huge Union Jacks, and later red-white-blue roundels (like the French but with the colors reversed from the outside to the center), on their wings.

The Germans moved quickly to exploit their initial success against the French, and, once aware of the presence of the BEF, to preempt the British as well. On August 23 Generaloberst Alexander von Kluck's First Army fell upon the BEF in a savage action at Mons. But the embattled British fought back with tenacity, inflicting heavy casualties on the attacking Germans (thanks largely to the "Tommies'" legendarily disciplined and accurate rapid-fire marksmanship) and then dug in for further fighting. Unfortunately a French army under General Charles Lanrezac, mauled on the Sambre over the previous two days in fighting against the German Second and Third Armies, abruptly withdrew, and the Allied retreat continued. Assuming that both the French and British forces had been decisively defeated, the three German armies pressed onwards to the southwest. But from August 25 through the twenty-ninth, both the embattled British and French forces continued to offer surprising resistance. At Le Cateau on the twenty-seventh, the BEF fought its biggest battle since Waterloo not quite a century before, successfully evading an attempt by von Kluck to envelop it. And it was now, for the first time, that Allied aerial reconnaissance proved its overwhelming worth.[32]

French and British air reconnaissance had started enthusiastically if not auspiciously. At Mons the Royal Flying Corps had detected a long column and correctly concluded it represented an enemy corps on the move (actually von Kluck's Sec-

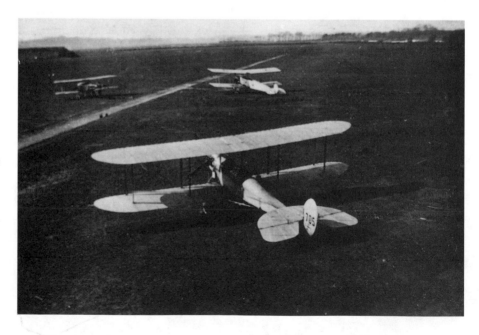

After having crossed the Channel en masse just five years after Blériot, Royal Aircraft Factory B.E. 2bs of No. 4 Squadron, Royal Flying Corps, at St. Omer, France, await their first reconnaissance missions, August 1914. RAFM

ond Corps), but Field Marshal French, perhaps on the advice of General Sir Henry Wilson, failed to act. Fortunately General Sir Douglas Haig, commander of the BEF's First Army Corps, was not as obtuse as his prewar maneuver experience and staff-college statements might have indicated, and so when a similar opportunity presented itself to him, he acted with commendable decisiveness. On August 28 RFC reconnaissance detected the Germans presenting an open flank to both Haig's corps and the French Fifth Army under Lanrezac: von Kluck had clearly lost track of the BEF. It was a moment of supreme importance, and with "the lesson of air reconnaissance at the 1912 maneuvers well digested" (as his biographer John Terraine has noted), Haig rose to it. He immediately urged the French general to attack, and Lanrezac did so at Guise. What might have been accomplished by a joint Anglo-French assault can only be conjectured, for Field Marshal French denied Haig permission to join in Lanrezac's attack. So on the twenty-ninth the French Fifth Army alone struck hard at the exposed flank of von Kluck's First Army, then stopped the German Second Army in its tracks; its nervous commander, Generaloberst Karl von Bülow, immediately asked von Kluck for help.[33]

By coincidence, two days before, Chief of the German General Staff von Moltke had altered the advance of the armies, directing that they march straight southwest towards Paris and the Marne valley, to force a decision and keep French units off balance and unable to reorganize. Under this scheme of maneuver, the First Army would still pass west of Paris, but just. The others would drive onwards, the Second to Paris, the Third towards Château-Thierry, the Fourth towards Reims and Epernay, and the Fifth towards Vitry. This completely undid von Schlieffen's plan. Further, von Moltke instructed von Kluck that the First Army's "task, above all, is to cover the right flank of the armies," essentially transforming it from an offensive to a defensive force.[34] Von Kluck and von Bülow had already contemplated shifting their line of advance eastwards, and growing communications delays and problems with the German high command in Berlin encouraged their go-it-alone tendencies. So when von Bülow called for help, von Kluck had every inclination to go to his assistance. On the thirtieth von Kluck shifted his line of march to the southeast, which would mean passing to the east of Paris, in accordance neither with the original von Schlieffen plan nor with von Moltke's own directive. (Informed of the change later, von Moltke gave it his own blessing, largely because to do otherwise would have generated utter chaos.)[35]

Thus British air reconnaissance had set the stage for the French victory at Guise, which itself set the stage for von Kluck's decision to change his line of march from west of Paris to east of the city. The Schlieffen plan was dead: between them von Moltke, von Kluck, and von Bülow had utterly destroyed it. The stage was now set for the battle of the Marne, wanting only for a requisite catalyst to trigger it. That too would come from the Allied airmen.

As August ended, General Joseph Joffre combined withdrawing forces together with his reserves into two new armies, the Sixth Army commanded by General Michel Maunoury, and the Ninth under General Foch. Paris seemed the target of the German thrust, and the military governor of Paris, General Joseph Galliéni, prepared his defenses. Old in years but young in temperament, Galliéni already had a reputation as "one of the rare generals that believe in aviation."[36] An engineer, he had extensive experience in France's colonial development, where he had first met Joffre. Before his retirement in the summer of 1914, he had commanded the Fifth Army, during which time he had held a controversial war game that pointed out many of the flaws in French operational thinking. The game had not made him popular among war planners, and its results were, unfortunately, ignored. But the August crisis had brought him back in service. Now temporarily commanding the Sixth Army as well as the city's military garrison, he activated a hastily drawn-together reconnaissance force, including civil as well as military airplanes, on August 30.[37]

His predisposition to accept the airmen's reports and seek their advice would prove providential very shortly. By the end of August, both German and Allied communications (via landlines, telephones, and primitive wireless) were breaking down. "Only the pilots," Correlli Barnett has written, "drifting over that noble landscape in their clattering kites, could really place in perspective the blind gropings and toilings of the millions of insect-men. One such primitive aircraft . . . was worth all the 20,000 splendid horsemen of a cavalry corps."[38]

On August 31, RFC air reconnaissance detected the first evidence of von Kluck's turn, and that night British headquarters sent out a message stating that German forces had shifted toward the southeast; the next day follow-on flights confirmed the change in direction. But what of Paris? The day after, Galliéni's hastily formed flight hit pay dirt. Designer-pilot Louis Breguet had volunteered his services, receiving the lofty rank of corporal. September 2 found him flying one of his own biplanes with an observer. They spotted elements of von Kluck's First Army crossing above Paris, to the southeast: Paris clearly was *not* the target of the German thrust. Breguet and his observer reported their finding to the intelligence chief of the Sixth Army. Incredibly, he promptly dismissed their report as unbelievable, even though he had, in addition, intercepts of German communications between von Moltke and von Kluck that confirmed the change in direction! For a full day, the information sat, until on September 3 multiple recce crews from the Paris garrison and the Sixth Army confirmed the sighting. This sufficiently emboldened the aviators to bypass the Sixth Army's recalcitrant intel staff and take their information direct to the liaison officers for Galliéni (who immediately realized von Kluck's flank was utterly vulnerable to attack by the Sixth Army) and Field Marshal French. Joffre and Galliéni now plotted their scheme of maneuver based on aerial reconnaissance from both the French and the British airmen.[39]

The subsequent story of the Marne is well known: von Kluck, driving his forces hard, pushed his army so far ahead as to leave his flank open to attack, and now the French and British seized the opportunity. For two days the battle raged furiously, while von Kluck attempted to continue his own thrust, in part because his fourth Reserve Corps, charged with responsibility for guarding the First Army's flank, lacked any reconnaissance aircraft of its own, and thus he had no appreciation for the increasingly precarious nature of his situation. With so many

Allied forces shifting position, it was inevitable that German airmen, even mis-used as they were, would eventually learn the true nature of the Allied threat. When they did, von Kluck immediately pivoted westward to confront the Sixth Army. Three more days of savage fighting followed, as the battle expanded to include the other German and French armies. If Allied reconnaissance aircraft had proven their use in preparing for the Joffre counteroffensive, German recon-naissance aircraft proved their worth in preventing total disaster to German forces. On the morning of September 9, a German reconnaissance pilot spotted five enemy columns directly threatening von Bülow's beleaguered Second Army. Already having discussed withdrawing with a staff officer sent from von Moltke's forward headquarters (whose arrival had been delayed by a spontaneous allied air attack that disrupted German transport), von Bülow needed little further urging. Less than an hour after the airman's report, he ordered a general retreat.[40] With von Bülow withdrawing, von Kluck had little choice but to follow. What followed was a rapid disengagement and race to establish new defensible positions.

So the Marne was history—a great strategic victory that saved France and utterly changed the nature of the war in the West. Von Moltke suffered a nervous breakdown, forcing the Kaiser to relieve him less than a week later. For a brief moment, the All Highest thought of bringing von Hindenburg, victor of Tannen-berg, back from the Eastern Front, but the situation was so critical that not even the few days it would take him to arrive were acceptable. Instead he appointed General Erich von Falkenhayn, another fatally flawed leader, who when facing his own tests would "bring heartbreaking tragedy to both France and Germany at Verdun."[41] Ahead lay four full years of horrific warfare and the deaths of a gener-ation of British, French, and German youth.

Key to the Allied success on the Marne was aerial information. Even as the bat-tle raged, Joffre realized how fortunate he was to have had reliable air reconnais-sance working for him. On September 5 he had gone to Melun, where he and his senior staff met with their British opposite numbers and he offered a status report on the campaign. As one participant recalled, he thanked the airmen of the Royal Flying Corps for their "prominent, in fact a vital part" in watching the shift in the German advance, noting that "he had been kept accurately and constantly informed of von Kluck's movements. To [the airmen] he owed the certainty which had enabled him to make his plans in good time."[42] For the airmen it had been a struggle. On September 10 Brigadier General Henderson, the commander of the RFC, wrote to his wife, "We went through a pretty tough time," mentioning as well that Joffre had sent a note to Field Marshal French thanking him for the "won-derful information obtained by the English Flying Corps."[43] For his part, in mid-October, French wrote to the War Office in London requesting expansion of the Royal Flying Corps to meet the army's reconnaissance and artillery spotting needs, noting that "since the beginning of operations it has been found that the calls on the services of the Royal Flying Corps have materially increased," because combat conditions "demands continuous and extended reconnaissance to an unforeseen degree."[44] "Unforeseen" to him, perhaps, but certainly not to the British and

French airmen who worked so assiduously before the war to give their two countries the capabilities their armies fortunately possessed in that decisive month.

Within the first six weeks of the war, then, the fruits of aerial reconnaissance dramatically shaped not only the history of the First World War, but also the history of the twentieth century, first at Tannenberg and then at the Marne. That impact is felt even today. Had Germany lost at Tannenberg, Russia probably would have forced an Eastern Front settlement of some sort, and the Czarist government would have continued on, basking in a triumph that would have, at once, offset the shame and humiliation of its defeat less than a decade before at the hands of the Japanese. What future course Russian discontent might have taken cannot be known, but the circumstances that directly triggered the Russian revolutions—first that of Kerensky, and then the expropriation of that revolution by the Bolsheviks under Lenin—would not have been present. Lenin probably would have remained in Zurich, known today, together with Trotsky and Stalin and all the rest, only to graduate students studying Russian radicals. On the other side of Europe, had France lost at the Marne, the Allied cause would have been lost. The French army, though prodigiously capable of taking casualties and rebuilding itself (as the rest of the war would indicate), simply would not have had the time to do so. With Paris in German hands, France, as well, probably would have had to reach a Western Front settlement, together with Britain. Coupled with its win at Tannenberg (and arguably even if it had still lost there), Germany would have become the dominant Continental player of the twentieth century. *Gefreiter* Hitler would have demobilized into a victorious, confident, and prosperous member of society, perhaps resuming his prewar existence as a minor painter, and hopefully remaining blessedly unknown to recorded world history.

But the course of events was very different, due to a surprising degree to an invention that had not even existed a decade before: the military airplane. Its crews, if not omnipotent, omniscient, and omnipresent, were nevertheless more nearly so than any of their predecessors at any previous time in history. Indeed, this noisy, frail, primitive device, not much more powerful than a powered hang glider or ultralight today, enabled them to observe, warn, and direct the movements of millions of men, influencing their fate and that of their nations with a facility worthy of the ancient deities.

CHAPTER NINETEEN

Grappling in the Central Blue

So by the end of the Marne, only a few weeks after the outbreak of the war, the airplane had already proven its value. It had passed from the dream of flight, from the innocence of research and development, to the reality of use, the reality of war. Commanders were already critically dependent upon its reconnaissance and observation for battlefield awareness and decision making—so dependent that they immediately recognized the necessity of controlling the air to prevent an enemy from access over their territory, leading within months to the introduction of the specialized fighter plane. It had fulfilled the expectations of those who thought it might influence military affairs, and in the years of the war yet to come before the Armistice in 1918, it would fulfill even more. "To the infant invention of aviation, the War proved to be a forcing-house of tropical intensity," David Lloyd George concluded perceptively in his postwar memoirs. "The development of aviation during the War had given this branch of the Service an importance beyond the conjecture of any military teacher before the War. *Supremacy in the air had become one of the essentials of victory.*"[1] (emphasis added)

Prewar skeptics and critics alike were converted. By mid-1915, at the battle of Neuve Chapelle, Haig (*"There is only one way for a commander to get information by reconnaissance and that is by the use of cavalry"*)[2] was berating artillery officers who ignored or minimized the value of aerial reconnaissance for their "early Victorian methods."[3] By late November 1916, Foch (*"L'aviation pour l'armée, c'est zéro"*)[4] would issue an order stating, "Only superiority in aviation permits the superiority in artillery that is indispensable for having superiority in the actual battle," adding in his own hand, "Victory in the air is the preliminary to victory on land, which is forfeit by itself."[5] Reflecting on military aviation in the Great War, Generalmajor Heinz Guderian, the great advocate of armored warfare and one of the key fathers of the *Blitzkrieg* notion of war, would write, "Aircraft became an offensive weapon of the first order, distinguished by their great speed, range, and effect on target. *If their initial development experienced a check when hostilities came to an end in*

1918, they had already shown their potential clearly enough to those who were on the receiving end."[6] (emphasis added)

The same wasn't true of the airship. Churchill was right: the "gaseous monsters" proved all too easy to destroy, whether German or Allied. In the first month of fighting, the German army lost four Zeppelins to antiaircraft fire: they had simply flown too low, French and Russian troops potting them as easily as shooting a cow. Then, on October 8, a fifth Zeppelin fell to a daring pilot who flew from Antwerp to Düsseldorf and bombed its shed, the first "strategic air attack" directed against an enemy's "weapons of mass destruction."[7] On January 19, 1915, amid daunting weather, the Zeppelin L-3 flew from Fuhlsbüttel across the North Sea to Great Yarmouth, dropping 13 small bombs over the small port, killing four, wounding 16, and causing £7,740 (approximately $666,000 in 2001 monies) in damage. Thereafter the airship went to war as a strategic bomber. For a while it instilled a mix of fear and wonder. Returning to his home in Hampstead late in the evening of September 8, 1915, novelist and poet D. H. Lawrence heard explosions and saw gun flashes as, nearly two miles overhead, a "golden Zeppelin" threaded its way among "a fragile incandescence of clouds": it was Kapitänleutnant Heinrich Mathy's L-13, which, having taken off from Hage, had crossed the North Sea, gone "feet dry" over the English coast well to the north, and then wended its way down from Cambridge to London. There Mathy scattered bombs across the city, killing 22 people and inflicting losses totaling £534,287 (approximately $46 million in 2001)—making it the costliest single air raid against England during the First World War—as London's primitive antiaircraft defenses banged away impotently.

To Lawrence, Mathy's airship displaced the moon as queen of the night. "I cannot get over it," he wrote to Lady Ottoline Morrell. "It seems the Zeppelin is in the zenith of the night, golden like the moon, having taken control of the sky; and the bursting shells are the lesser lights."[8] Similarly impressed, Grand Admiral Tirpitz nevertheless expressed some ambivalence, writing, "The English are now in terror of Zeppelins . . . but I am not in favor of 'frightfulness.' . . . The indiscriminate dropping of bombs is wrong; they are repulsive when they hit and kill an old lady and one gets used to them." (Then he muddled his moral high tone by adding absently, "If one could set fire to London in 30 places, then the repulsiveness would be lost sight of in the immensity of the effort").[9] Patriotic German schoolchildren enthusiastically sang: "Zeppelin, flieg / Hilf uns im Krieg / Fliege nach England / England wird abgebrannt / Zeppelin, flieg!" (Zeppelin, fly / Help us in the war / Fly against England / England will be all burned down / Zeppelin, fly!)[10]

Instead over 400 Zeppelin crewmen died in ghastly immolations as fighters firing newly developed explosive and incendiary ammunition transformed their airships into plummeting fireballs illuminating England's southeastern nights. Even the garrulous von Zeppelin, shortly before his death in 1917, turned away from his own creation, working instead on developing new large *Riesenflugzeug* (R-planes, "giant-aircraft"): multiengine biplane bombers, some eventually as large as a Second World War B-29. By then it was too late for the German Naval Airship Divi-

Possessing a menacing beauty, Zeppelins had numerous flaws: difficult to control, underpowered, vulnerable to weather, and filled with hydrogen which, if ignited, doomed their crews to a terrible death. Here is the 743-foot-long L-57; intended to fly to German East Africa, it broke up in a storm in a ground-handling accident on October 7, 1917, fortunately without the loss of any of its crewmen. AFMA

sion, 40 percent of whose crews died, an average of one airship and crew lost for every 11 missions. Mathy perished in 1916, leaping to his death as his blazing Zeppelin plunged to earth near Potters Bar, barely missing the fighter that shot it down.[11] The Zeppelin service started the war as a volunteer elite; not surprisingly, it ended the war composed largely from the unwillingly drafted. In August 1918 the division's much-respected (if imprudent) commander, Fregattenkapitän Peter Strasser, perished as his riddled Zeppelin, "a roaring furnace from end to end," fell into the North Sea.[12] (Ironically, the intercepting airplane had taken off from Great Yarmouth, victim of the first Zeppelin raid over Britain three years before.) Thereafter the division wisely ceased further raids by the discredited dirigibles. Having proven a failure at war, the Zeppelin's enthusiasts hoped it might have a better peacetime commercial future; alas, they would prove as horribly mistaken in this as in its potential for combat. Today, certainly among people younger than age 50, the word "Zeppelin" conjures more images of a rock group than the ill-fated creations of the old count. On the shores of Lake Constance, however, the torch of hope still burns even as a new experimental, high-technology, helium-filled Zeppelin—the first in over 60 years—has taken to the skies.[13]

On October 20, 1917, the L-49 met an even more dramatic fate. After being thoroughly riddled by five French Nieuports *without* being set ablaze, it settled to earth near Bourbonne-les-Bains. Meticulously examined, its design influenced later Allied airships, including the U.S. Navy's airship *Shenandoah*. AFMA

Each year of the war showcased new developments: 1914, the airplane as reconnaissance system; 1915, the fighter; 1916, the strategic bomber; 1917, the ground attacker; 1918, carrier-based aviation. On the Western Front, fighters battled for control of the air and attacked enemy bomber and reconnaissance aircraft, armored assault airplanes bombed and strafed front-line troops, and spotter aircraft working with artillery added to the misery of trench-bound ground forces. Airplanes cooperated with and fought against the first tanks. They dropped supplies to beleaguered troops and even inserted covert espionage and sabotage teams behind enemy lines. Strategic bombers built by Russia, Italy, Germany, and England raided targets hundreds of miles from their bases, including the cities of Vienna, London, Paris, Mannheim, and Cologne, while intercepting fighters, by day and night, sought to shoot them down. Specialized signals intelligence units connected by communications to airfields near the front monitored enemy communications and warned of incoming air attack.[14]

Aviation proliferated into all combat theaters, not just Europe and Russia. In the Far East, Japanese and German airplanes clashed at Tsingtao; in Africa, German reconnaissance airplanes tracked South African forces, setting the conditions of "information dominance" that led to victory at Sandfontein, and the British used aircraft to locate the German cruiser *Königsberg* and then direct the naval gunfire that eventually destroyed it; in Palestine, French seaplanes tracked Turkish movements, even at night; and in 1918 the combination of strategic air attacks against Turkish communications and direct attacks against Turkish forces in the open combined to destroy a Turkish army and speed the fall of Damascus and the eventual collapse of the Ottoman Empire.[15]

The Rise of the Fighter: The Birth of Air Superiority Warfare

Air fighting and bombing drew the greatest attention. With reconnaissance so critical, commanders now had to deny enemies access to their airspace. The result was the advent of the fighter airplane—here, too the French were first—initially a modified scouting airplane hastily equipped with a machine gun, but then, by early 1916, a specialized creation of its own optimized for the maneuvers, visibility, performance, and killing power required of air combat, equipped with machine guns and even rockets for igniting observation balloons, this last feature the ancestor of the complex air-to-air missile of the present day. By 1918 over 50 different fighter designs had entered squadron service with the various combatant air arms, and the fighter had already passed through no less than five separate technical generations. What had been a frail, modified sporting or observation airplane in 1915 was now, in 1918's fifth generation, an all-metal internally braced monoplane not unlike the airplanes of the early 1930s.[16]

Two different doctrines governed fighter operations: the Germans, favored by winds that blew towards their territory, believed in a defensive air strategy of "letting the customer come into the shop." It was a flawed short-range doctrine that emphasized an air blockade approach to warfare, tying fighter stations to front-line air-warning posts and then trying to intercept incoming Allied airplanes. On the other hand, the British and to a lesser extent the French believed in an offensive long-range air doctrine of aggressively seizing control of the enemy's own airspace. Though costly at first, by 1918 there was no doubt that this had been the far better doctrinal choice, akin to stopping an overflowing bathtub by turning off the tap rather than trying to mop up each little rivulet of water spilling onto the floor.

Fighter operations in the First World War taught that there is no substitute for control of the air. Securing control has to be the highest priority of an air arm. With control of the sky, all other operations—air, sea, and land—are made easier. Without that control all are compromised or rendered difficult at best and impossible at worst. In the Great War, air superiority was inextricably bound up in the quest for greater artillery dominance over the foe. In mid-1916, at the height of German air supremacy over the Western Front, a doctor serving with the Canadian Expeditionary Force captured this interdependence, noting, "Only the men who saw planes come over, hover about, and were in consequence heavily and accurately shelled shortly afterwards, realized what command of the air meant."[17] It is a lesson that has been reaffirmed since, in skies from Europe to the Pacific, to Korea, Vietnam, the Falklands, the Middle East, and on to the Balkans and Southwest Asia.

No. 85 Squadron's pilots and mechanics stand before their Royal Aircraft Factory S.E. 5a fighters in 1918. Fast, rugged, maneuverable, and forgiving (unlike its better known rival, the Sopwith Camel), the S.E. 5a was a favorite mount of Britain's leading fighter aces. AFMA

The French first introduced modified reconnaissance aircraft for air fighting, but it was the Germans, in 1915, who introduced the first practical fighter plane, the Fokker Eindecker (ironically based on a prewar French Morane design!) equipped with a synchronized forward-firing machine gun. Within weeks, in the hands of pilots such as Max Immelmann and Oswald Boelcke, it had savaged Allied reconnaissance airplanes, forcing the British and French to employ large numbers of armed escorts to fly with the lumbering observation planes so that they could safely return to base. Then, in 1916, the British and French countered with newer airplanes (typified by the

Rittmeister Manfred Freiherr von Richthofen, the notorious "Red Baron," shot down 80 airplanes in 21 months. By the time he died in 1918, he was uncomfortably aware the *Luftstreitkräfte* lived on borrowed time, thanks to deficient leadership, organization, training, and equipment. NARA

De Havilland D.H.2 and the Nieuport Bébé deployed in specialized fighter squadrons). Virtually immediately the shoe was on the other foot, as they swept the Fokker from the skies and established British and French air superiority over the Western Front, from Verdun to the Somme. At the end of the summer of 1916, the Germans introduced the superlative Albatros biplane fighter, with a Deperdussin-like monocoque wooden shell fuselage. The graceful Albatros dominated air warfare against lesser opponents until the end of April 1917, when newer generations of Allied fighters—the French SPAD, the British Camel, and S.E. 5—entered service. Thereafter the German air service remained entirely on the defensive. As early as mid-July 1917, the "Red Baron" himself, Manfred von Richthofen, depressingly wrote of the *"lausigen"* literally, lousy Albatros soldiering on against greater and greater odds, dismally concluding, "Nowadays, nobody wants to become a fighter pilot . . ."[18] Germany would not introduce a fighter airplane to match the Allies until the introduction of the Fokker D VII in mid-1918, following it a little later with the world's first all-metal monoplane fighter, the Junkers D I. But it was a case of too little too late (as with the German jets of the Second World War), and the Allies continued to dominate the German air service until the armistice in November.

The war produced a new warrior, the fighter pilot, epitomized by the "ace" who shot down five or more foes, often while flying a flamboyantly decorated airplane. The world's first fighter pilot was that master of the Morane, Roland Garros, flying in 1915, who shot down three German planes before himself being shot down while bombing a train, and then taken prisoner. Speaking of allied fighter pilots in words that could have applied to all, David Lloyd George evocatively extolled them as "the knighthood of the war."[19] Leading aces such as Germany's Manfred von Richthofen, France's Georges Guynemer, England's Mick Mannock,

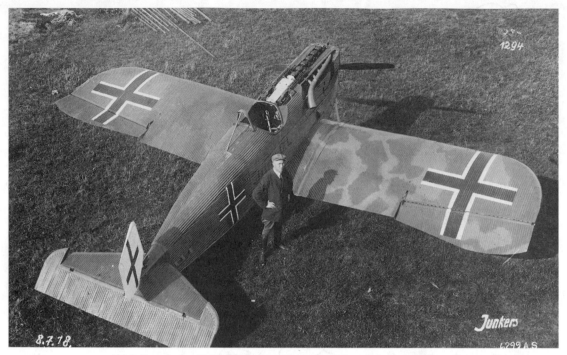

This is Hugo Junkers' J 9 (officially the D I fighter), an internally braced metal monoplane with a corrugated external skin: too late to help Germany, but an influential herald of the all-metal monoplane era—and produced less than fifteen years after Kitty Hawk. HC

Canada's Billy Bishop, Italy's Francesco Baracca, and America's Eddie Rickenbacker became public celebrities, their exploits and lives followed as avidly as those of sports figures and rock stars of a later era. Generaloberst Erich von Ludendorff considered von Richthofen (whose penchant for bright red airplanes earned him the nickname *der rote Kampfflieger*) worth two divisions in Germany's cause. They adorned newspapers, magazines, and posters; artists such as France's Henri Farré (the first—and one of the greatest—of all aviation artists) painted their portraits; journalists penned their biographies (and a few wrote their own).[20] Some of their images persist, modified into a new cultural context: von Richthofen's blood-red triplane is forever locked in combat with Snoopy's "Sopwith Camel" doghouse; Baracca's *cavallino rampante,* the rearing-horse insignia, now adorns Ferraris.

More than this, they became role models for others to emulate. Decades later American author William Faulkner recalled that by the middle of the war, "I had seen an aeroplane and my mind was filled with names: [Albert] Ball, [Max] Immelmann, and [Oswald] Boelcke, and [Georges] Guynemer, and [Billy] Bishop, and I was waiting, biding, until I would be old enough or free enough or anyway could get to France and become glorious and beribboned, too."[21] Faulkner subsequently went to Canada as an aviation cadet. Though the war ended before he earned his wings, aviation dominated much of his writing, and he flew occasionally until the Second World War.

But in an era of wooden structures, leaky engines, oil-and-fuel-soaked doped fabric, unprotected cockpits, engines, and fuel systems, and no parachutes, such fame extracted a terrible price. Among the very best pilots, von Richthofen, Guynemer, Mannock, Bishop, Baracca, and Rickenbacker claimed victory over 335 airplanes and their crews—but only two of the six, Bishop and Rickenbacker, lived long enough to survive the war. Four of the five airmen Faulkner recollected—Ball, Immelmann, Boelcke, and Guynemer—fell from the skies. Recklessness spelled death, even for the best. Von Richthofen became fixated on a fleeing Camel, followed it to low altitude, failed to check behind, and fell before the combined fire of another Camel and Allied infantry on the ground. Garros, the first fighter pilot of all, escaped from captivity in 1918, returned to the air, and foolishly persisted with lone-wolf patrols; a month before the Armistice, he fell in solitary combat against a dozen Fokkers. Some airmen met strange postwar fates: a leading German fighter ace perished at the hands of a Communist mob in 1920, strangled with the ribbon of his own *Pour le mérite,* the elegant and highly prized "Blue Max."

Pilots of lesser ability fell by the thousands. The Royal Flying Corps lowest combat loss rate was one airman killed or missing per 295 flight hours: at its worst, in early 1917, the loss rate was one airman killed or missing for every 92 flight hours. Combat loss rates averaged one airplane per 100 sorties; some measure of the extreme lethality of First World War air combat can be gained by comparing it to the Gulf War of 1991, where combat loss rates averaged only one airplane every 2,700 sorties.[22] "Oftentimes, during the war," Charles Nordhoff and James Norman Hall recalled a decade after the Armistice, "one heard with a shock of incredulity, 'They got Bill yesterday—he went down in flames in the Saint-Mihiel Salient'; or 'Harry's dead; crowned this morning on our side of the lines.' One thought of Bill's amiable eccentricities, or of some human and lovable weakness of Harry's, and it was hard to realize that one's friend—the incongruous and picturesque bundle of qualities that made a human individual—was gone. One shook one's head in bewilderment, and banished such reflections by murmuring the sadly overworked phrase: '*C'est la guerre.*'"[23]

In their exuberance, their acceptance of risk, their dogged heroism in the face of almost certain death if their planes were hit (their odds of surviving the war were worse, not better, than those of their colleagues in the trenches), and in their respect for each other and their adversaries, the "fighting scout" pilots of the Great War well earned the many accolades offered them in the postwar world. Robert Graves notes in his classic memoir of infantry service in the war that "At least one in three of my generation at school was killed . . . most of them in the infantry and flying corps. The average life of an infantry subaltern on the Western front was, at some stages of the war, only about three months. . . . The flying casualties were even higher." Indeed they were: in April 1917, RFC fighter pilots flying over the Somme had a life expectancy of about three *weeks*. Truly, as one of their number, Sir Robert Saundby, wrote decades later, "They were a gallant band of warriors."[24]

The Coming of the Bomber and the Advent of Strategic Air Attack

In 1916 the airplane proliferated as a strategic bomber. On August 30, 1914, a roving Taube pilot dropped several bombs accompanied by a derisive note on Paris, according it the dubious distinction of being the first capital city attacked by an airplane, not quite six years after Orville Wright unveiled the first military airplane at Fort Myer. On Christmas Eve 1914, a German dropped a small bomb that blew up in a garden near Dover Castle, within hearing distance from where Blériot had landed just five and a half years earlier. These insults anticipated the appearance of the specially designed strategic bomber the next year, first by the Russians and Italians, then, later in the war, by the Germans, and lastly the British. In mid-1915 Russia and Italy undertook the first long-range strategic air attacks, using bombers

A 1917 lineup of Caproni Ca 4 triplane bombers and crews of the *Corpo Aeronautica Militare,* with Gianni Caproni proudly standing in the foreground. AFMA

built by Sikorsky and Caproni. Equipped with over seventy *Muromets,* the Eskadra vozdushnykh korablei (squadron of flying ships) completed over 400 missions before the Russian revolution, including strikes on communications, enemy forces in the field, and railway targets, losing only one airplane to enemy action.[25] Italy's strategic bombing force constituted the fruits of a partnership between designer Gianni Caproni and the army's Guilio Douhet that generated over 800 three-engine triplane and biplane bombers of increasing utility and power. These routinely raided Austro-Hungarian targets, including attacks of up to 36 airplanes directed against Fiume, Innsbruck, Lubljana, Pola, Trento, and Vienna, and piloted by American airmen, formed the core of America's first strategic bomber efforts as well, after the United States entered the war.[26]

After the failure of the Zeppelin, Germany raided England with the Gotha, a *Grossflugzeug* capable of carrying 300-kilograms of bombs to London and protected by multiple defensive gun positions. The first Gotha, the odd-looking but weirdly attractive twin-engine G I *Kampfflugzeug* (battle plane) biplane of 1915 (it had its fuselage affixed to the upper wing and thus perched well above the lower), was a product of the prewar editor of *Flugsport,* the engineer-publicist Oskar Ursinius. Bloodthirsty and nationalistic, Ursinius was fond of posing in his ungainly creation in various warlike stances, typically wearing a uniform and grimly huddling behind a Spandau machine gun. The G I accomplished little aside from establishing the Gotha firm as a manufacturer of large airplanes; its subsequent designs were far more successful.[27]

Altogether, between 1917 and the end of the war, 52 raids by Gotha and later R-planes (the Zeppelin-Staaken "Giants," the count's final contribution to Teutonic *Schrecklichkeit*) dropped 73 tons of bombs, killing or injuring nearly 3,000 people

The angular and infamous Gotha bomber brought the air war to the heart of England. Here is a factory fresh Gotha G V in 1917, as posed for a German aircraft specifications book. AFMA

and inflicting nearly £1,450,000 (approximately $125 million in 2001) in damage. More serious still were delays to production by the intimidation of war workers: in one case production of .303 caliber cartridges at Woolwich briefly fell by 81 percent because only slightly over a quarter of the arsenal's employees showed up for their jobs. Overall, munitions production reductions in the London metropolitan area nearly reached 50 percent.[28]

Leaving "a deep resonant, snarling sound with an odd rhythm of its own: *Raum-m, raum-m, raum-m, raum-m*," German bombers ranged all over the fronts, "the hum of motors" (as future American secretary of war Henry Stimson put it) often "interrupted with the crash of bombs."[29] As allied air superiority steadily increased, their losses rose. One night in August 1918, amid blaring air raid sirens and exploding bombs, James Redding Rives, a young American ambulance driver at Beauvais, watched in awe as searchlights coned a five-engine Zeppelin-Staaken R-plane droning overhead. Antiaircraft guns fired noisily, expending hundreds of rounds in an impressive (if futile) fireworks display. Having already experienced several air raids (together with some unnerving near misses), Rives huddled for safety as the bombers unloaded their deadly cargo unhindered by Allied defenses. But then two British Camel night-fighters attacked the behemoth. 'I could see every time they hit him," Rives penciled in his diary, "and they soon shot him down. After they hit him several times his airoplain [*sic*] was set on fire by the explosions and he came falling through the air." Seven German airmen died (together with a luckless Tommy, killed when a bomb exploded as he and others examined the smoldering wreckage), earning the dubious distinction of having perished in the largest airplane shot down during the First World War.[30]

German air raids directly led to creation of the world's first independent air arm in April 1918, when Great Britain merged the Royal Flying Corps and Royal Naval Air Service into the Royal Air Force. Air power had gone from an experiment to a combat branch, and then to an independent combat arm, in less than a decade after the appearance of the military airplane. It is largely because of this "first" battle of Britain that the "second" Battle of Britain in 1940 resulted in a British victory, for the image of Gothas maneuvering over London lingered in defense planners' minds all through the 1920s and 1930s, encouraging their development of heavily armed fighters such as the Spitfire and Hurricane, radar, command and control facilities, and antiaircraft defenses. Further, the establishment of the Royal Air Force as an independent and coequal service with the British Army and Royal Navy freed it to be able to deploy its fighter forces in 1940 where they could do the most good—defending England—rather than frittering them away in the doomed battle of France in May and June of that fateful year. The surprising power the *Luftstreitkräfte* showed over London in the first Battle of Britain thus led to the defeat of the *Luftwaffe* against the RAF over London in the second.[31]

Soon Britain established its own independent bombing force, prodded by Mark Kerr, a Royal Navy admiral-aviator transferred to the RFC as a major general, and Major Lord Tiverton, a gifted staff officer and armament expert. Tiverton, a pre-

Britain's equivalent to the Gotha and the larger R-planes was the Handley-Page O/400, one of which is photographed here at Ellington Field, Texas, in 1919. Nicknamed the "Bloody Paralyser," it flew raids into Germany, over the Mediterranean, and Palestine, and served as well with the American forces. Ellington is now home to NASA's astronauts. AFMA

war barrister, delineated the basic structure and operational philosophy underpinning the subsequent campaign, stressing attacks against four geographical target sets (Cologne, Düsseldorf, Mannheim, and the Saar valley) housing Germany's key industrial base, particularly chemical plants.[32] Of him Kerr subsequently wrote, "He was one of those who had sufficient vision to understand the peril of the air when most people could not lift their eyes above the land and sea."[33]

But Independent Force's birth was neither easy nor quick. Personalities clashed violently, and strategy shifted from the initial goal of destroying key industries to shattering enemy morale. There was one particularly embarrassing moment when, thanks to a navigational error, one of the first bombers delivered to France landed behind German lines, presenting the *Luftstreitkräfte* Britain's newest and most impressive aerial weapon![34] Today the Force is best remembered for a series of 57 raids by twin-engine Handley Page 0/100 and 0/400 night bombers undertaken in 1918 at the direction of the charismatic Major General Sir Hugh "Boom" Trenchard. (Colorfully nicknamed for the timbre of his voice, not the sound of a bomb, and subsequently a Marshal of the Royal Air Force and the influential post-war Chief of Air Staff of the RAF, Trenchard left both an indelible stamp upon the RAF and air power doctrine, philosophy, and strategic bombing that rightfully resonates down to the present day). Among other targets the raids hit Coblenz, Cologne, Karlsruhe, Mainz, Mannheim, Saarbrucken, Stuttgart, and Thionville.[35]

Handley Pages also flew in the Middle East. On occasion they could have surprising effect. One bombed and sank a Turkish destroyer, the ill-fated *Yadighair-I-Milet,* the largest ship lost to air attack in the First World War. In mid-September 1918 another bombed a telephone exchange at the outset of General Sir Edmund Allenby's Palestine offensive, so disrupting communications that for days powerful Turkish forces remained in bivouac east of the Jordan, ignorant of the disaster unfolding west of the river. This one air strike profoundly helped Allenby's offensive, which resulted in Damascus falling less than two weeks later.[36]

At war's end Britain had an even larger bomber, the Handley Page V/1500, in flight testing. Britain's largest wartime airplane, it had a wingspan of 126 feet, greater than both the Wright brothers' first flight and the wingspan of any of Britain's Second World War bombers. Intended to fly from bases in East Anglia against Berlin with up to 6,600 pounds of bombs, it did not enter operational service until after the war, though it anticipated Bomber Command's nightly missions a quarter century later from East Anglia to pound Hitler's Third Reich. The V/1500 did eventually see combat, however, in 1919, during the Third Afghan War, when one, named *Old Carthusian,* flew from Risalpur across the Khyber Pass and Pathan Hills to Kabul. There it scored multiple hits on the stronghold of Amir Amanullah, before returning safely to Risalpur—where postflight inspection revealed such extensive termite damage and infestation that the wooden bomber was immediately (and permanently) grounded! The British commander in chief in India subsequently wrote, "There is little doubt that this raid was an important factor in producing a desire for peace at the headquarters of the Afghan Government."[37] Also, England and particularly the United States experimented with "drone" unmanned flying bombs, anticipating the infamous V-1 "buzz bomb" of the Second World War and the cruise missiles of more modern times.

Throughout the Great War, Allied strategic bombing efforts seem to have been more directed at enemy capabilities than merely targeting populations in the pursuit of destroying morale. Overall, Allied raids against German cities killed a total of 641, wounded a further 1,262, and inflicted over 200 million marks (equivalent to approximately $860 million in 2001) worth of damage, lost production, and other economic costs.[38] The low number of casualties and the greater economic damage makes an interesting comparison with the results of German raids on British targets, which inflicted far higher numbers of casualties, but at lower economic impact. It may reflect more focused Allied targeting directed against production, transportation, and distribution targets as opposed to merely dropping bombs on cities—anticipating, incidentally, the American approach to strategic bombing taken in the Second World War a quarter century later. Though strategic bombing was obviously not a decisive factor in the First World War, this level of result encouraged future development of independent air forces built around long-range bombers, promoted the thinking of three genuinely influential air power prophets (England's Boom Trenchard, America's Billy Mitchell, and Italy's Douhet), shaped the nature of both the Royal Air Force and the United States Army Air Corps in the interwar years, and created a kind of generic large multi-engine "dual-use" technology base that benefited both military and civilian aviation. After the war many converted bombers flew as crude commercial airlines until replaced by later and more suitable designs.[39]

Air Power over the Battlefield

The airplane contributed significantly to conventional land warfare during the First World War, in reconnaissance, artillery observation, and by direct attack of enemy fielded forces. As noted earlier, before the war armies had looked to the airplane to improve the accuracy of artillery. The outbreak of war gave this even greater urgency, for artillery quickly became the dominant arbiter of power. At the outbreak of the war, the British, French, and German armies variously stipulated between four and six cannons per 1,000 infantrymen; by the time of the spring offensives in 1918, the number had more than doubled, to between 11 and 13 artillery pieces per 1,000 infantry.[40] So improving the efficiency of artillery as a

Early aerial photographers employed hand-held cameras man-handled against the blowing slipstream of the aircraft, such as this Graflex demonstrated by a U.S. Army Air Service (USAAS) observer.
NARA

battlefield weapon became a major priority for all sides. Very quickly planners learned how to resolve distortion problems from aerial photographs taken at various angles and perspectives, joining them with improved mapping, and also incorporating real-time ranging observations from airborne artillery observers in aircraft (as well as captive balloons). This quickly increased the accuracy of both observed artillery fire and fire by predetermined map and position coordinates.

The outstanding artillerist of the war, Colonel Georg Bruchmüller—known as *der Durchbruchmüller* (Breakthrough Müller) to the German infantry, and considered the father of modern artillery doctrine and tactics—quickly adapted the air-

This cartoon (by W.J. Enright of the USAAS 9th Photo Section), shows the emphasis on speed: acquiring, developing, plotting and lettering, printing, finishing, and then delivering imagery to higher headquarters. Raymond John Jeffreys Collection, East Carolina University

plane to his novel ideas of rapid and overwhelming fire support for offensive operations. Bruchmüller emphasized temporarily overwhelming and thus neutralizing
enemy forces via unexpected whirlwind artillery assault. (Traditional extended
"artillery preparation" aimed at an enemy's total destruction but, as often,
because of its length, gave away the attacker's long-term intentions.) By 1918 he
had integrated aircraft observation and control into all his artillery fires, including
close support (to defend against enemy infantry attack), counterbattery (to neutralize enemy artillery), long range (to conduct strategic attacks against command centers, artillery dumps, assembly areas, etc.), and heavy (to destroy key
robust targets like bunkers and bridges). Recognizing what a later generation of
planners would refer to as reducing "sensor to shooter" times, he directed that if
aerial observation warranted it, artillery commanders could change previously
established fire support operations in the midst of battle. Germany's demonstrated success with such innovative control and tactics (particularly during the
opening of the spring offensive in 1918) influenced the other European armies as
well, so that by war's end the airplane was firmly positioned in the artillery support schemes of virtually all combatant nations. Both Britain and France honed
the liaison of their artillery and aviation units to a high degree, with dramatic
impact upon the success of their own combat operations in 1918; by the end of
the war, it would have been unthinkable to undertake any sort of ground operation without aerial artillery observation and fire control playing a key role.[41]

Direct air attack began virtually at the outset of the war, as individual pilots
dropped canisters of crude darts, grenades, and converted artillery shells on their
enemies. Towards the end of the battle of the Marne, for example, a single air
attack generated serious panic among withdrawing German troops (and incidentally contributed to the critical delay of a senior intelligence officer so that by the
time he finally met with on-scene commanders they had already decided to
retreat).[42] In the battle of the Somme in 1916, the Royal Flying Corps began
attacking German trenches (attacks the Germans termed *Strafen,* or "punish-
ment," the birth of the word *strafe*). By the middle of 1917, organized air attack
against enemy ground forces became commonplace as sporadic attacks evolved
into two specific kinds of systematic missions: "trench strafing" (what would
today be called "close air support" of friendly troops in contact with an enemy)
and "ground strafing" (what would today be considered "interdiction" attacks
directed as enemy forces in bivouac or on the move, but not yet in contact with
friendly forces). Such attacks were highly effective, particularly when they cooperated with the advance of Allied tanks, but came at the price of high casualties
from German fighters and ground fire. At the battle of Cambrai in the fall and
winter of 1917, fully 35 percent of British attack aircraft sent across the front failed
to return.[43]

Both the Allies and Germans made extensive use of fighters and specialized
ground-attack airplanes during the bitter fighting of 1918. The British favored
bomb-dropping fighters as ground attackers but found that they had to armor
them to withstand ground fire; the Germans preferred heavily armored specialized

Early air attack, like early aerial photography, saw airmen hand-dropping crude bombs, grenades, or converted artillery shells over the sides of their craft. Here a German aviator shows how it was done. NARA

As fighters became outmoded for the rigors of air-to-air combat, they were often applied to ground attack duties. Here is a Royal Aircraft Factory F.E. 2b used as a night attack airplane, with bomb racks under its wings and fuselage—and a standing open-air gunner up front. BA

ground attackers called *Schlachtflugzeug* (assault planes) organized into special attack squadrons. Again casualties soared: 91 dead or missing British aircrews in February 1918, 245 dead or missing a month later, all essentially across a 50 mile front. Fighters and bombers worked together to attack targets behind enemy lines; German *Schlachtflieger* struck at Allied troops and tanks, and Allied attackers struck at German bivouac areas, in attacks that sometimes involved hundreds of aircraft. Some of the most savage fighting accompanied Germany's last desperate attempts to secure victory in the summer of 1918. The French air officer General Marie Charles Duval imaginatively employed concentrated formations of rugged Breguet XIV bombers, each carrying dozens of antipersonnel bombs against German troop concentrations. One attack, on June 4, saw no less than 120 Breguets strike a ravine where German troops had taken shelter from Allied artillery, preventing an anticipated attack; another, a week later, witnessed 600 aircraft of various kinds assisting a major French counterattack by General Charles Mangin. The next month, in the Champagne, concentrated attacks by Duval's Breguets effectively shattered a German division before it entered combat. From merely an observer of troops, the airplane had become a merciless destroyer as well.[44]

The charismatic Brigadier General William "Billy" Mitchell, whose creative ideas on air power were tried and tempered over France, was the world's first joint force air component commander to run a coalition air war. He is pictured here after the war, at the Dayton air races in 1922. USAF, Air Combat Command History Office (ACCHO)

In the St. Mihiel offensive in September 1918, American Brigadier General Billy Mitchell oversaw the activities of all Allied airmen, functioning much like what today would be called a joint force air component commander, or JFACC. He controlled a total of nearly 1,500 French, British, Italian, and American aircraft, including no less than 700 fighters, applied to air to ground attack: the greatest concentration of air power yet seen in the war. By October 1918, John Eisenhower has written, "The airplane was no longer a novelty; it made a real difference whether one side or the other enjoyed air supremacy in a given sector."[45] In Palestine, British and Australian air attack devastated two Turkish armies, the Eighth (fatally caught in a defile on September 19) and, two days later, the Seventh, trapped along the Wadi el Far'a. The latter attack, a day-long series of ferocious assaults by no less than seven separate squadrons strafing and bombing, resulted in hundreds of dead, hundreds more wounded, several thousand prisoners (who raised a large white flag to the aircraft), and dozens of guns, trucks, and cars abandoned, as well as over 800 wagons. "The feeling of helplessness in the face of the enemy fliers instilled a paralysis in both officers and men," the German general Liman von Sanders wrote afterwards. "The columns of savaged artillery pieces, automobiles, and motor transport, together with shattered wagons, horses, and men, blocked the road in many places." Again, this was but a foretaste of what air attack against fielded forces would do in the future, from the Blitzkrieg and Normandy on to the 1967 Arab-Israeli war, the Gulf War of 1991, and even Afghanistan in 2001.[46]

Aviation at Sea

In August 1914 the warring powers possessed approximately 260 airplanes and 11 airships assigned to naval duty; by the end of the war, this had increased to almost 9,000 airplanes and nearly 450 airships, a measure of how significant air power at sea had become.[47] Naval aviation operations began at the onset of the war and continued to the very end; however, overall they did not have an equivalent impact upon naval warfare as air operations ashore had on land warfare, largely because all the warring powers failed to make the fullest use of the airplane and airship for reconnaissance. This is surprising, as before the war, naval aviation enthusiasts had clearly recognized the value of both types of machines as long-range scouts, and in the German navy (largely due to the influence of the air-and-sea-minded Prince Heinrich), planners anticipated using a full range of weaponry, including airships and aircraft, against blockading British forces should war come. Nevertheless, aviation in support of fleet action at sea played virtually no role in the war; at Dogger Bank, for example, a Zeppelin observed the fleet action, but the lack of good working doctrine prevented both the airship crew and fleet commanders from working effectively together. Otherwise, if they had, a crippled British battle cruiser might well have been sunk, a crippled German battle cruiser might have been saved, and Dogger Bank might have been a notable German victory rather than a German defeat. After Dogger Bank the German Navy attempted to use its naval Zeppelins to greater purpose. At Jutland Zeppelins supported the fleet's advance along the Danish coast, but weather prevented them from taking any part in the action during the day. With clearing weather they did observe some of the muddled night action, but again without effect. Dogger Bank and Jutland were the two battles where maritime aerial reconnaissance could clearly have made a major difference, but for both sides it was an opportunity lost. At Jutland the British possessed two seaplane carriers, but a signals mix-up resulted in one missing its chance to participate, while the other was too slow to simultaneously deploy its aircraft and steam with the fleet. Never again would major German and British fleet units clash on the open seas.[48]

Not surprisingly, because of its strong maritime history, the Royal Navy's aviation activities predominated; in contrast, at the outset of the war, the German naval leadership judged its own airships and airplanes as "of limited range and practically useless in bad weather," although a galaxy of senior German commanders recognized the potential value of aerial reconnaissance.[49] Operating from land bases, Royal Naval Air Service airplanes had raided Zeppelin sheds early in the war, and on Christmas Day 1914, the Royal Navy attempted a sea-launched raid, using three seaplane carriers in the North Sea. This triggered the world's first air-sea-land-and-subsurface battle, as two German Zeppelins and numerous German seaplanes attacked the three ships and a British submarine, and the British seaplanes attacked a Zeppelin base. Inconclusive in result, it nevertheless foreshadowed the great naval air battles of the Second World War.[50]

At the last prewar naval review on July 28, 1914 (the same day the Austro-Hungarian dual monarchy declared war on Serbia), Royal Navy pilot A. M. Longmore demonstrated dropping a torpedo from a Short 184 biplane. The next year, in August 1915, Short torpedo-dropping seaplanes operated from the tender *Ben-my-Chree* sank two Turkish merchant ships during the fighting at Gallipoli, the first ships ever sunk by aerial torpedo attack.[51] Britain's Grand Fleet commander, Admiral Sir David Beatty, was so impressed by the potential of torpedo aircraft to overfly German mine defenses and attack German ships in port that in September 1917 he put forth a "Most Secret" plan for attacking Germany's High Seas Fleet in harbor at dawn. It envisioned attacks by "not less than 121" Sopwith Cuckoo torpedo-carrying biplanes launched from modified merchant ships carrying "flying decks," accompanied by flying boats from shore bases acting as navigational pathfinders, bombers, and search-and-rescue aircraft.[52] Their lordships lacked

The *Ben-my-Chree,* a Manx steam packet (the name meant "Woman of my Heart") converted as a seaplane carrier, could carry up to six Short Type 184 torpedo planes, such as the one shown on its aft deck. Turkish coastal artillery sunk the vessel in 1917. Imperial War Museum (IWM)

both the resources and the will to do so, and after almost a year of dithering, Beatty exploded, in understandable anger, "In February 1918 the Admiralty informed me that by the end of July 100 torpedo-carrying aeroplanes would be available. On 18 July 1918 I am informed that instead of 100 the number will be 12. Actually there are three. As late as 18 July the Admiralty stated 36 pilots would be trained by the end of August. Actually there will be none."[53]

Despite such lack of vision, some progress was made: in July 1918 the Royal Navy undertook the first carrier air strike in history, sending a force of seven bomb-carrying Sopwith Camels from the carrier HMS *Furious* to attack the German airship sheds at Tondern. One shed "immediately burst into flames which rose to a great height," as two airships, the L 55 and L 60, blew apart; three fuel-starved Camels diverted in Denmark, two force-landed at sea, and two successfully returned to "trap" aboard ship.[54] The next month a Camel pilot flying from *Furious* shot down a Zeppelin, and the same day German seaplanes operating from shore bases attacked a British force of six torpedo boats with bombs and machine-gun fire, sinking three and forcing the crippled remainder ashore. All of these episodes afforded "a striking demonstration of the new dimension in naval

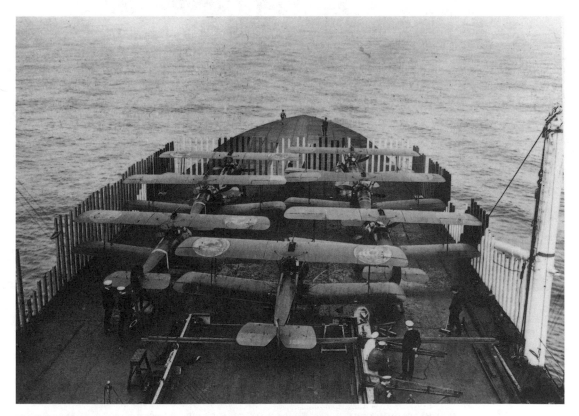

The flight deck of HMS *Furious,* showing the seven Sopwith Camels employed on the historic Tondern raid being readied for the attack—the first carrier air strike in naval aviation history. RAFM

A Camel flying off the flight deck of the *Furious.* IWM

warfare" and gave an indication of the serious depredations land-and-sea-based aircraft would inflict on seagoing traffic as well as shore targets in the Second World War.[55]

At sea Allied blimps, aircraft, and even towed observation kites kept watch for submarines with such success that such protected convoys only lost three ships to submarine attack. British blimps sighted nearly 50 lurking U-boats in time to alert potential victims, and French airships spotted 60 others; they detected and subsequently destroyed over 100 waiting mines as well.[56] In the Adriatic, Austrian seaplanes spotted and bombed a submerged French submarine, the *Foucault,* blowing it to the surface, where its crew fortunately escaped. Around the British isles, Allied maritime patrol planes—particularly the Curtiss "Large *America*" (named after his prewar design for crossing the Atlantic) and Curtiss-inspired Felixstowe boats—did sterling service, suppressing U-boats, flying convoy patrol, and coastal patrol, and even anti-Zeppelin operations. Flying boats attacked several U-boats, and one, a British-flown, American-built Curtiss, dropped two bombs on the UB-32, caught on the surface of the English Channel in September 1917; this time there were no survivors. At war's end one U-boat skipper remarked, "Aircraft are our worst enemy," anticipating the grim experiences of the Second World War when maritime patrol airplanes would prove the U-boat's deadliest foe.[57]

Aircraft operations even extended to commerce raiders. The SMS *Wolf,* the second commerce raider of that name and one of Imperial Germany's most successful sea-going predators, captured fourteen ships, and mined fourteen others

(eleven of which sank) in a cruise through the Atlantic, Indian Ocean, Pacific, and back again. Often times, the first warning a ship had of its presence was a roar as its Friedrichshafen seaplane, the *Wölfchen* ("Wolf cub"), swooped overhead, and prepared to strafe and bomb the bridge if the ship's captain attempted to radio a warning. "The plane was flying so low that it appeared to be just skimming the masts," one victim reported; "the observer could be clearly seen dangling a long pear-shaped bomb over the side."[58] As well it flew reconnaissance and scouting missions to guard its mothership. So valuable did the little *Wölfchen* prove that it was accorded the honor of circling the ship upon its triumphal return to Kiel in February 1918. Aircraft proved a feature of German raider operations in the Second World War as well.

Overall, air action directly or indirectly accounted for 41 vessels at sea or in harbor, consisting of 15 warships and naval craft (including three destroyers bombed or mined from the air), 14 merchant vessels (including 6 torpedoed by German or British airplanes), and 12 submarines (7 of which were bombed by German, British, French, or Austro-Hungarian airplanes and airships).[59] Thus, if unlike land-based aviation, naval aviation did not prove so dramatically significant during the First World War, it nevertheless made important contributions (such as convoy protection) and gave clear indication of its future potential. It established its basic roles and missions by the time of armistice, including coastal and antishipping patrol, antisubmarine attack, fleet air defense, and attacks against shore targets. Germany had even experimented with crude (if ambitious) wire-guided,

At war's end, HMS *Argus*, the world's first genuine flush-deck aircraft carrier, joined Britain's Grand Fleet. Here it is anchored in the Firth of Forth, with HMS *Furious* anchored off its port bow. Note the startling zebra-like dazzle deceptive camouflage. IWM

Zeppelin-launched, antishipping glide bombs and remotely controlled speedboat-like explosive vessels controlled into the side of Allied ships from airships and aircraft, one of which damaged a British monitor. These anticipated revolutionary guided robotic weapons it would, in fact, employ during the Second World War, beginning with the sinking of the Italian battleship *Roma* by a glide bomb in 1943. It should not be surprising, then, that no less a personage than Admiral Lord Fisher, whose name was synonymous with the emergence of the dreadnought battleship, remarked after the Armistice that "the prodigious and daily development of aircraft" had "utterly changed" naval warfare. "All you want," he pronounced with characteristic bluntness, "is the present naval side of the Air Force—that's the future navy."[60] In sum, the first glimmerings of Taranto, Pearl Harbor, Midway, and the convoy and antisubmarine air-sea battles of the Second World War are glimpsed in the naval aviation experience of the First World War.

Bombing and torpedo attack clearly threatened the primacy of the dreadnought and thereby established naval doctrines as well. In March 1921 America's charismatic and controversial air-power prophet, Billy Mitchell, dismissively compared the battleship to "the knights in the middle ages, encased in their heavy armor, in which they could scarcely move."[61] Four months later, flying twin-

SMS *Ostfriesland* mercilessly battered off the Virginia Capes by Mitchell's 2,000-lb. bomb-dropping Martin MB-2 bombers, 1921. ACCHO

engine Martin bombers not unlike the Gothas and Handley Pages, Mitchell's airmen would bomb and sink the captured German destroyer *G-102,* the cruiser
Frankfurt, and unforgettably, the dreadnought *Ostfriesland* (a Jutland veteran), cap-
ping this by sinking an aging American battleship as well, the USS *Alabama*—the
first ominous shaking of the complacency of big-ship partisans.[62]

One nation that took naval air power to heart was Japan, which always modeled its navy on that of Great Britain's; representatives contacted the British government and requested a technical mission to assist them in establishing a
Japanese naval air arm. In due course a British aviation mission arrived complete
with trainers, torpedo planes, and flying boats, established a training facility and
curriculum, supervised a weapons qualification program (including bombing and
torpedo dropping), and brought the Imperial Japanese Navy fully up to speed on
current naval air thinking. Japan launched its first carrier, the *Hosho,* in 1921, essentially contemporaneously with the United States (which commissioned its first
carrier, the USS *Langley,* in early 1922). Japan's naval airmen had learned their lessons well and were suitably grateful; as the British mission wound down, the
Japanese Navy did a mass formation flyover of a visiting British battleship while it
was still steaming two hours out from Yokohama. The next time Japanese planes
overflew a Royal Navy battleship was December 1941, off Malaya; they sank it (and
another as well) in just two hours, killing 840 British sailors.[63]

The Industrial Dimension

The First World War constituted a particular triumph for the newly emergent
international aircraft and aero-engine industry, which had to adjust to rapidly
changing needs and circumstances, advancing new technology, and constant pressures for more and better production. The belligerent nations produced well over
200,000 aircraft and nearly 250,000 engines during the First World War. Throughout France continued (and indeed, expanded) its aeronautical dominance over all
other countries: it manufactured 33 percent—fully one third—of *all* aircraft built
and 38 percent of *all* engines produced. Its aircraft production grew geometrically,
the fruit of an industry that had not even existed a decade before. In 1918 alone
France produced nearly 24,000 aircraft and 45,000 engines, funded with an annual
budget of *2.7 billion* francs (then approximately $540 million per annum, equiva-
lent to roughly *$9.3 billion* in 2001, allowing for inflationary growth). In total,
between the beginning of August 1914 and the end of December 1918, French
manufacturers produced 67,982 airplanes, exporting 16 percent to other nations,
including 4,881 to the United States. During that same time, French firms produced 92,386 engines, exporting 28,150 of them. (By comparison, Britain produced
55,093 aircraft and 41,034 engines, Germany 47,637 aircraft and 40,449 engines,
Italy 12,000 aircraft and 24,000 engines, and the United States 16,004 aircraft and
32,420 engines.)[64]

Some measure of both the rapid expansion of Allied air power and the equiva-

Large French production rates benefited all the Allies, as evidenced by these trim Nieuport fighters lined up for inspection at Issoudon, the USAAS's advanced flight training center. NARA

lent decline of that of the Central Powers can be seen in a comparative analysis of production and inventory figures for the respective sides via three tables, beginning with front-line combat air forces strengths as shown in table 1.[65]

Table 1

Total Aircraft in Service at Front, November 1918

Allied		*Central Powers*	
France	2,820	Germany	2,592
Great Britain	1,664	Austria-Hungary	717
Italy	614		
United States	270		
Belgium	160		
Total	5,528		3,309

Ratio 1.67:1

These figures, when compared to the overall production statistics enumerated earlier (over 200,000 aircraft and nearly 250,000 engines) indicate as well the "perishability" of airplanes from accident and combat loss, and also because of the relative immaturity of the technology. For example, the average fighter design went from introduction to combat to obsolescence in less than a year. Aircraft that were midwar winners (such as the V-strut Nieuport and Albatros) were virtual death traps by war's end. The analysis of production trends among the Big Four industrial combatants—Great Britain, France, the United States, and Germany— shown in Table 2 below gives a further indication of this quantitative disparity, particularly how it was rapidly accelerating by war's end.

Table 2
Big Four Aircraft (on Charge and Operational) vs. Available Aircrew

County	Aircraft on Charge	Operational Aircraft	Aircrew
Great Britain	22,098	14,000	24,000
France	13,100	12,000	16,000
United States	18,000	10,000	13,000
(Allies, total)	(53,198)	(36,000)	(53,000)
Germany	21,386	11,000	12,000

Ratio of Allied to German Operational Aircraft: 3.27:1
Ratio of Allied to German Available Airmen: 4.42:1

A comparison of operational aircraft available in 1914 and 1918 indicates just how explosively aviation grew in the war years. In August 1914 Great Britain, France, the United States, and Germany possessed a total of 530 aircraft; in 1918 that number had grown to 47,000 operational aircraft, an almost 90-fold increase. Table 2's figures need to be qualified in two respects. First, total aircraft on charge includes unserviceable or nonairworthy aircraft as well as those capable of operational flying. Hence the operational total is more indicative of actual combat force strength. Secondly, the vast majority of American aircraft were trainers, not combat types, and thus this is misleading as to actual Allied force structure advantages. Even with all American aircraft deducted, however, the Allies, at the time of the Armistice in November 1918, still possessed an overall operational strength advantage over Germany of nearly 2.4:1. Table 3 below shows the accelerating production advantage enjoyed by the Allies as the war reached its culminating point.

These figures indicate the tremendous industrial reserve possessed by the Allies: at this point in the war France, Great Britain, and the United States were producing, respectively, 16, 31, and 86 times more airplanes *per month* than they had possessed in toto at the beginning of the war. (By comparison Germany was down to a "mere" 7.5 times more airplanes built per month than it had possessed in 1914.)

Table 3

Big Four Monthly Production of Aircraft and Engines at War's End

County	Aircraft	Engines
Great Britain	3,500	4,000
France	2,650	4,500
United States	2,000	6,000
(Allies, total)	(8,150)	(14,500)
Germany	1,750	2,000

Ratio of Allied to German Monthly Aircraft Production: 4.66:1
Ratio of Allied to German Monthly Engine Production: 7.25:1

Overall, as this data indicates, in the Great War Germany was not only outfought but outproduced—as it would be a generation later as well. Doctrinal and acquisition failures—particularly the dominance of defensive, not offensive, thought in its fighter forces—ensured that after mid-1917 Germany's air arm was both quantitatively and qualitatively inferior to the that of the Allies. As a result losses rapidly increased, forcing shortcuts in training so that by war's end the average German fighter pilot was, like his *Luftwaffe* successor over a quarter century later, sitting ill-trained and outnumbered in an obsolete or obsolescent fighter. Even the introduction of higher-technology airplanes—for example, the Fokker D VII and Junkers D I—could not restore the *Luftstreitkräfte* to a position of primacy, as with the record of the German jets and the *Luftwaffe* in the Second World War. With air superiority lost after mid-1917, losses of all other aircraft types rose, and the German air service was increasingly unable to prevent the Allies from attacking German targets virtually at will, even in Germany itself.

If aviation was still clearly in its nascent stage, more often indicating future potential as opposed to contemporary ability, all this nevertheless spoke to capabilities, interest, and a rate of expansion that would have struck any of the pioneers of 1900–1909 as remarkable, if not impossible. After the war it formed the basis for the rapid introduction of commercial aircraft throughout Europe. In 1914 the airplane had still been largely an element of public entertainment and a questionable military investment, capable of at most a few hours flight. Five years later, in 1919, there were three flights across the North Atlantic: first by the Curtiss NC-4 seaplane that flew in stages from Newfoundland to England; next by a modified British Vickers Vimy bomber that flew nonstop from Newfoundland to Ireland, and then the British airship R 34 flew from England to America and back. A fourth flight that same year saw a Vimy piloted by an Australian crew fly the 11,000 miles from London to Darwin in 29 days. Commercial service between the European capitals, particularly Paris, Brussels, and London, began that same year; by the end of the year, more than a dozen small airlines equipped with ex–service

airplanes, maintained by ex–service mechanics, and flown by ex–service pilots had already sprung up.[66]

By the fall of 1919, ten years had passed since Reims's *Grande semaine,* marking the first full decade of European aeronautical supremacy. Europe still reigned supreme: another 15 years remained before American aviation would at last catch up and then speed by Great Britain and the Continent, its streamlined Boeing and Douglas airliners inaugurating an era of New World air-transport dominance lasting until the time of the Airbus. If nevertheless financially daunting, the prospects of commercial aviation using both airships and aircraft, particularly to meet the far-flung needs of empire, were generally bright. "Adam Smith's 'waggon way through the air,'" the *Spectator* perceptively intoned, "is about to be realized."[67]

A modified Friedrichshafen G IIIa bomber flown as a civil airliner in 1919–1920 by *Deutsche Luft Reederei (DLR).* DLR was a predecessor of today's *Lufthansa.*
AFMA

CHAPTER TWENTY

Reflections on the Beginning
of the Aerial Age

In 1927 Mark Sullivan authored *Our Times,* a remarkable and exhaustive reflection on American society after the first quarter of the twentieth century. "Of all the agencies that influenced men's minds, that made the average man of 1925 intellectually different from him of 1900," Sullivan wrote, "by far the greatest was the sight of a human being in an airplane."[1] In 1901 Sullivan had dined with telephone pioneer Alexander Graham Bell and Smithsonian Institution Secretary Samuel Langley at *Beinn Bhreagh,* Bell's Nova Scotia home. He listened in disbelief as the two men, bewhiskered and looking like latter-day prophets, discussed the possibilities of flight. Bell had even ventured, "You and I won't live to see it, Professor, but this young man will see the day when men will pick up a thousand pounds of brick and fly off in the air with it." Sullivan could envision many things, but this went too far. Telephone pioneer or not, the young writer thought, "I know he is talking plain nonsense."[2] A quarter century later, Sullivan good-naturedly could tell the story on himself as an example of how much the world had changed. He certainly hadn't been alone in his skepticism, and a far greater number of people—including leading representatives of the science and engineering communities, who should have known better—had felt the same way, or even more strongly.

Inventing flight took centuries, from the hunter-gatherers who crafted the first boomerangs to those who made the airplane a practical, useful reality by the middle of 1909. Along the way were some notable milestones: the kite ca. the second century B.C., the first rocket in the twelfth century (China), toy helicopters of the fourth to fourteenth century (China and Western Europe), crude hot-air and hydrogen balloons of the eighteenth century (Gusmão, the Montgolfiers, and Charles), model and "piloted" gliders in the nineteenth century (Cayley), demonstrations of powered winged flight, also in the nineteenth century (Pénaud's model of 1871), and the first powered, sustained, and controlled flights by airships and airplanes, in the nineteenth and twentieth centuries (Renard and Krebs, and the Wrights). America gave birth to the most significant one: the powered, sustained, and controlled airplane. If accomplishing flight took the better part of a millennium, the dream of flight went back a great deal further. And if the accomplishment of flight was largely the product of a European sensibility, certainly flight had been the stuff of global dreams from the Indian subcontinent to the barren vastness of Australia, the deserts and depths of Africa, the breadth of Asia, and the plains of North America. The aspirations, inspirations, and roots of flight, then, were global.

When humanity possessed the abilities, knowledge, resources, and materials to fly, events moved very swiftly and surprisingly consistently: roughly a century from aerostatic theory to the first balloon, roughly a century from aerodynamic theory to the first airplane. (Roughly a century—actually 120 years—separated the balloon and the airplane as well.) Once the first "technology demonstrators" of each had flown, events moved faster still, and again with surprising consistency, as demonstration gave way to practical use: the piloted balloon appeared in 1783 and first flew in warfare as an observation system in 1794, 11 years later. The piloted airplane first flew in 1903 and went to war in 1911, after just eight years. It is interesting how the nations that made both these revolutions eventually turned their back to them, and only returned to exploit them fully much later. France began the balloon revolution, but roughly two decades later had turned away from it except as an element of popular entertainment; only later would it regain official favor. America invented the airplane, but showed so little drive that, less than a decade later, it occupied last place among the world's industrial nations in exploiting its own invention. By mid-1909 America's lead over Europe had vanished, not to reemerge until the air transport revolution of the 1930s. In each of these cases, in hare-versus-tortoise fashion, the "fast seconds" had moved beyond the "slow firsts."

Questions . . .

Any number of questions can be asked regarding the development of flight and why things turned out as they did. Among the most intriguing are:

Why were the Wrights—and hence America—victorious in inventing the first successful airplane?

Why did Europe experience greater initial success in exploiting and developing the airplane more rapidly and more thoroughly than the United States?

Why did France in particular enjoy the success it did in leading this "post-Wright" aeronautical revolution through to the beginning of the First World War?

How did this experience affect the choices and decisions America made in the post–First World War era—in short, how did America respond?

Finally, what are the lessons learned from this experience?

At the outset one must recognize that had the Wrights never lived, the airplane would have been invented in Europe, in all likelihood France, by the year 1910. The success of the Wrights encouraged and goaded the Europeans to greater efforts and thus accelerated this process, but the people who made the first hopping flights, and then the first flights with greater authority, and then finally the great flights of 1909, the Farmans, Levavasseurs, Blériots, etc., would have worked at essentially the same pace as they did even if the Wrights had never existed. The invention of the airplane was thus not a singularity whereby the Wrights possessed unique knowledge that others had to tap or be given in order to achieve their own success. Rather, it was a race that the Wrights won. And it was but the first—albeit the most important—race in a larger international competitive technological "meet." The other events were for military utility, commercial market dominance, and rapid technological and industrial expansion. The winners here were the European nations in general and France in particular. And incidentally, the latest "heats" of that meet continue to the present day.

. . . and Answers

How, then, did the Wrights succeed, the Europeans advance beyond America, the French predominate, and America respond?

First, the Wright brothers succeeded because of their careful, methodical, logical, and insightful approach to flight, which separated them out from all their contemporaries seeking to invent the airplane. To a marked degree well beyond any of their predecessors and rivals—even such giants as a Cayley or a Lilienthal—they recognized the importance of blending theoretical understanding with experimentally derived information, and their own personal circumstances afforded them the necessary time and expertise to devote to first defining, then analyzing, and then overcoming the problem of heavier-than-air flight.

It might be said that they were the first to pass the "Billy Joel test of aeronautical sufficiency." Billy Joel, the great musician, was once asked, "What are the elements of a great song?" "Melody," he replied. "A song is meant to be sung. You can have all these great technical components but if it can't be sung, you ain't got nothing. *You know, it ain't an airplane until it flies.*"[3] Joel had it absolutely right. There were numerous individuals who sought to fly, and numerous claims have been put forth (and continue to be put forth) on their behalf because someone hopped, or someone tried to fly, or someone thought they flew, or someone thought someone flew . . . etc. And at best, all of these claims arrive at one point: *maybe* a person had sufficient abilities to create a design that *might possibly* have become airborne, at which point it *could have been* an unguided missile until it hit the ground . . . "could'a, should'a, would'a." That standard definition, *powered, sustained, and controlled flight,* separates out the Wrights from all the rest. As Tom Crouch has noted, these various claims "are fascinating and worthy of study. Their names, and the nature of their projects, deserve to be remembered. *But they did not invent the airplane.*"[4] (emphasis added)

Insight and acumen weren't enough. Equally important, the Wrights lived in society that prized invention and innovation, that had already enshrined a popular image of the Yankee inventor, and that had none of the restrictions of class, education, and social culture that would have mitigated against two middling mechanicians with a public-school background tackling a subject that had befuddled some of the most prosperous and best-educated minds in European science and technology. Certainly many people regarded their obsession with flight as odd, even foolish.

But the exuberantly buoyant and optimistic Gilded Age and Progressive Era culture that they grew up and flourished in more than compensated for any criticism they might have perceived and which, in different and more bleak circumstances, might have stifled their work or convinced them to give it up. As a result they had a roughly three-to-five year advantage over any potential rivals—not a great advantage, but one sufficient to ensure that the invention of the airplane would be an American triumph. It was *not* sufficient, however, to ensure that they would consolidate and secure that triumph into total American dominance in aeronautics.

Second, Europe seized upon the airplane and rapidly exploited it (as with the airship) because the pre-1914 European strategic and security environment demanded nothing less. Europe after 1870 was in a state of disarray. The Franco-Prussian War had created a new, unified German state, but at the expense of fatally fanning the traditional enmity between Germany and France into a white-hot heat. Pan-Slavic and transnational loyalties and identities destabilized central and eastern Europe. Alliances sprang up after the mid-1890s and complemented strong imperialistic rivalries to promote the growth of belligerency and accelerate an increasingly costly arms race that exploded in open and public competition (particularly the naval race between Britain and Germany) after 1907. After that time the advanced European militaries—France, Germany, and Britain—were particularly receptive to any new ideas that could transform their military forces for coming conflicts that most saw as unavoidable. Each already had a tradition of using military observation balloons, and the notion of advancing to using steerable airships or heavier-than-air "aeroplanes" seemed perfectly logical, even if the larger implications of the airplane—for example, its ability to profoundly influence surface operations far beyond "mere" reconnaissance—were generally collectively missed. The success of the Wrights offered Europe's would-be aviators a powerful goad, reinforcement of their beliefs, and a psychological stimulus, even if the "technology transfer" from the Wrights to the Europeans was actually less than has generally been supposed.

These same pressures did not exist in the United States, which, though taking a more prominent role in world affairs after its success in the "splendid little war" with Spain, still remained focused largely on its own hemisphere. It enjoyed a distancing from Europe, two oceans protecting it on the eastern and western coasts, and unthreatening nations on its northern and southern borders. This encouraged a mindset at once isolationist and unconcerned with massive and rapid rearmament on the scale that Europeans increasingly took for granted. The pace of military modernization in the United States, while respectable, was nowhere near as frantic nor as comprehensive as that of the European nations, awakening to the imminence of a general European war. Even as war drew closer in Europe, the American military and governmental structure supported aviation demonstrations, but it wasn't yet ready to build a robust combat-worthy aviation force within either the Army or Navy. Popular support was uneven as well: though flying demonstrations drew large crowds, local law sometimes limited what airmen could do. When Matilde Moisant, the vivacious flying sister of two pioneer aviators, went flying one Sunday in 1911, police detained her upon landing for breaking a Long Island ordnance against operating an airplane on the Sabbath. (The next morning a sympathetic sheriff refused to press charges: she had gone flying to prove to a skeptical visitor that she could indeed pilot an airplane, itself a commentary on the times.)[5]

There was a cultural driver for the European expansion in aeronautics as well: "Progress in aviation," David Hermann has written, "came to be a popular yardstick of national prowess."[6] In pre–First World War Europe, to a degree beyond that of the United States (again perhaps because of the perceived imminence of war), an aviation figure like Blériot or von Zeppelin commanded tremendous public respect and attention. That continued at an even greater level during the war itself, which elevated aviators to the status of cult figures. Public adulation of aviators continued long after the war, well into the middle of the century: one thinks of France and Jean Mermoz, Britain and Alan Cobham, Australia and Charles Kingsford Smith, and America and Charles Lindbergh, the latter the subject of the greatest adulation of all.

The related aspect of this—the association of aviation feats with a perception of modernity and societal advancement, caused totalitarian counties in the 1930s trying to sell their "progressive" nature, such as Stalin's Russia, Mussolini's Italy, and Hitler's Germany, to sponsor long-distance and other record flight attempts and make national heroes of their key airmen. Indeed, it reappeared in the midst of the Cold War in the Soviet Union's attempt to showcase itself before the Third World, via space feats such as orbiting cosmonauts, as more progressive, technologically capable, and future-oriented than the West. Each of these produced a public association between the leader and an aviator, an association carefully honed by state propaganda organs: Stalin–Valeriy Chkalov, Mussolini–Italo Balbo, Hitler–Ernst Udet, Khrushchev–Yuri Gagarin. To be fair, of course, during the Space Race of the late 1950s and 1960s, the United States responded in kind: witness the lavish attention accorded the first American astronauts, the Mercury Seven, and the special bond between John Kennedy and John Glenn, the Seven's "first among equals"—its undoubted leader.

Third, France advanced farthest of all because of some unique historical circumstances, established practices, and social and cultural conditions that encouraged it to do so. To understand the special advantages France possessed—and nearly threw away, as related earlier—it is necessary to examine why the two other major European powers, England and Germany, failed to either invent the airplane or exploit its development.

Safe behind the North Sea and the Dover Straits, and caught up in a succession of small imperial wars and interventions Britain's late-nineteenth-century military establishment saw little need to support aeronautical research on anything other than refinement of the existing paradigm—the tethered observation balloon. Some suggested man-lifting kites might be more flexible, and significant research was undertaken on them, but anything further than this received little attention until after the Wright brothers began to attract publicity in late 1902, a year before their success at Kitty Hawk. Beyond the military the outlook was not much better. The death of Lilienthal and the damning comments of Lord Kelvin gave proof, if any were needed, that Britain's powerful scientific establishment was at best dismissive or condescending towards those mechanicians who dabbled in the field of flight. Maxim's failure and Pilcher's death discouraged investment and experimentation, while at the same time, The Aeronautical Society was riven by internal bickering (Wenham left the organization for 17 years) until Baden-Powell put it right in 1899.

By that time the harm had been done, and Britain was behind not only America but France as well (and Germany, if one considered airships). To get ahead, it had to adopt the technology of America and France, as evidenced by the attempts at licensing agreements and partnerships with a range of American and French pioneers: the Wrights, Curtiss, Farman, Blériot, Niéport, etc. British frustration at its home-grown industry was perfectly captured by the editor of The Aeroplane, the ever-ascerbic Charles G. Grey, writing after the British military aircraft competition of 1912 which had been won by the Wright-influenced Samuel Cody, but with a tremendously good showing by a variety of French airplanes, including the Blériot, Nieuport, and Deperdussin monoplanes: "The Romans had to come and show us how to make roads. The Normans had to teach us how the keep the 'people' in order. The Flemings had to teach us to weave. The Germans had to teach us how to make a religion. The Italians had to teach us how to run a restaurant. The Americans had to teach us how to make watches, and boots, and bicycles. The French taught us what manners we have got, some appreciation of art, and how to build motor cars. Now the French and an Irish-American [Cody] are teaching us how to build aeroplanes. Let us be good children and learn our lessons willingly."[7]

Germany had a good shot at dominating European aviation, given the work of Lilienthal and later Parseval and Zeppelin. But Lilienthal's death removed the heart and soul of German work on heavier-than-air flight, while Zeppelin, Parseval, and other lighter-than-air partisans took German aviation down a very different path, emphasizing the large and small airship. Increasingly obsessed with the "englische Gefahr," (English danger) and fears of a "Copenhagen" strategy whereby the British fleet would someday annihilate the High Seas Fleet in harbor by a surprise attack à la Britain's savaging of Copenhagen in 1807 to deny the Danish fleet to the French, some of Germany's naval authorities perceptively looked to the long-range Zeppelin for the airborne early warning they would need to avoid such a disaster.[8]

Meantime the German army concentrated on maneuver strategies to offset the danger of a two-front war while ironically failing to recognize that any sort of successful military flying machine would offer an *inherent* maneuver advantage over the foe. So aside from an investment in airship technology, heavier-than-air flight stagnated in Germany, despite the work of Lilienthal—work that inspired French and American pioneers to seek the practical airplane. Only after the shock of Reims did Germany become serious about seeking heavier-than-air solutions and a balanced approach to flight. Thereafter it moved much more rapidly; nevertheless, at first it too initially had to swallow Teutonic pride and look abroad for its aircraft to America, France and Austria.

France had invented flight in 1783, had first incorporated it in warfare in 1794, and had a strong tradition of allying technology and the military together. This history offered a powerful rationale and appeal for continued French dominance in flight. Generally speaking, the scientific and technological elite supported such activity, as measured by the actions and pronouncements of the Académie des Sciences. Also it had a strong public education tradition and a very strong tradition of technological excellence in the education of engineers, mechanicians, and industrial workers. It had a growing sense of individual equality growing out of several bloody revolutions, chief of which was the great Revolution itself. And that in turn had spawned a sense of the mass-mobilized nation, the nation motivated by a fierce patriotism and beset by enemies on all sides. All this worked to build a cohesive nationalism supporting the activities of anyone or any group that offered to improve the lot of la France by some new scheme or idea. As the twentieth century dawned, "Patrie" had the same mystical connotation for the average Frenchman that "Volk" would for Hitler's Germany.

As measured by popular reaction to ballooning, airships, and early aircraft events, aviation clearly resonated with the French population in a very special way, different from that of the German and British populations. By the mid-nineteenth century the balloon as an iconic symbol had particularly seized the French imagination, inculcating arguably the most receptive mindset and strongest public support for flight and flying then existing worldwide. The experience of the Franco-Prussian War powerfully reaffirmed this attitude in two ways: first, the daring exploits of balloonists and the inability of the Prussians to prevent their flights constituted about the only bright spot in the war; secondly, it planted the thought that the French, vanquished on the ground, might yet be able to develop military advantage in the air.

It was this motivation that drove Clément Ader, who recognized the value of movement through the air in national security terms. France had lost Trafalgar, and thereby a sense of itself as a great and controlling maritime nation capable of rivaling Britain. It had lost at Sedan, and thereby lost the sense of itself as a powerful land power capable of confronting an ever-more-powerful German state. Ader promised control of the land and sea via the air; in modern terms, he enunciated an "asymmetric" strategy to offset potential enemies' investment in conventional weapons and power projection capabilities. For all his other deficiencies as an aircraft developer, in this he was correct, for once the practical airplane had been achieved, the pace of military affairs over the next century followed exactly his model. After 1870 the message from Ader and others that the air offered a chance to offset land and sea power had powerful appeal for potential aviation enthusiasts: one could work with the belief that the product of one's work would help the larger nation secure its own place back in the European forefront.

A series of regularly occurring events reinvigorated the public's interest in the air: Giffard's airship and the later airship of Renard and Krebs; Ader's *Éole;* the dirigible flights of Santos-Dumont; Ferdinand Ferber's gliding trials; the awareness that foreigners were investigating flight; the first hops of Santos, Voisin, Farman, and Blériot; the appearance of Wilbur Wright in 1908; Blériot's channel crossing; and finally, the clinching event, the great week at Reims.

Also there were other factors: France had perceptive leaders willing to support the activities of the country's aeronauts and aircraft developers, particularly as Germany evidenced a continuing and, indeed, growing threat. The French army, by and large, proved more supportive of military aviation in its early days—literally from de Freycinet and Ader through the first trials of aircraft in maneuvers—than that of any other European nation, something the German military leadership quickly recognized, to their dismay. (Though the French army, as noted, stumbled badly on the eve of the First World War by not procuring sufficient aircraft.)

Finally, goaded by clearly *not* having been the first to invent a powered airplane (the Ader camp's protestations aside) and facing a bellicose Germany, France's aviation enthusiasts worked continuously at "product improvement," refining their thinking about flight and airplane and engine design, building what would become the most powerful aeronautical-industrial complex of the First World War, a supplier of aircraft, engines, and skilled pilots not only to its own aviation service, but to that of the Allies as well. Every single Allied nation confronting the Central Powers flew at least some French aircraft or aircraft incorporating French manufactured, designed, or inspired components.

France's triumph, in short, was not the stuff of accident or luck. What *is* surprising, in view of its advantages, is why France was *not* the first to fly a powered airplane, for even the language of aviation showed this tremendous Gaullic influence, with words such as *fuselage, longeron, aileron, empennage, nacelle, monocoque, hangar, chandelle, renversement, volplane,* etc.—including the words *aviation* and *aviator* themselves.

What Happened in America

During the "war to end all wars," American airmen had acquitted themselves with a dedication, valor, and expertise matching the best of both foes and allies. Their accomplishments came at a high price, as one random example, the record of France's Lafayette Flying Corps, clearly indicates. Of the 269 who volunteered, young men from all walks of life, 69 died. Of these, 42 perished in combat, a 16 percent loss rate; overall the war claimed one of every four Lafayette volunteers, whose average age was 24. In 1917 their successors entered combat under the colors of the United States, writing their own heroic pages while flying from the North Sea and Western Front to Italy and the Adriatic. It was—and is—galling that these countrymen of the Wrights fought, and all too often died, in planes made in a foreign land. Thus, to air-minded Americans, the end of the war brought little comfort: there was too much embarrassment at not having had a robust wartime aeronautical industry of their own.[9]

At the outbreak of war in 1914, the belligerents fielded approximately 900 airplanes, slightly over 70 percent for armies and the rest for naval service. Of the major powers, Russia had 244, Germany had 232, France had 162, and Great Britain had 113. The United States possessed but 23 (indeed, in the years between 1909 and the outbreak of the war in 1914, the U.S. military had only purchased a total of 57 airplanes). In short, in 1914, the *birthplace* of heavier-than-air flight only accounted at best for 2 $\frac{1}{2}$ percent of the world's total military aircraft then in service.[10]

This situation triggered increasingly caustic commentary. In the midst of the war, former President Theodore Roosevelt had written to Augustus Post, the secretary of the Aero Club of America, "This country, which gave birth to aviation, has so far lagged behind that now, three years after the great war began, and six months after we were dragged into it, we still have not a single machine competent to fight the war machines of our enemies."[11] Roosevelt, who had flown as a passenger in 1910 with Wright pilot Arch Hoxsey in St. Louis, had a personal stake in the fight: his youngest son Quentin, who had seen La Grande Semaine d'Aviation at Reims in 1909, was an aspiring fighter pilot. (Sadly, he would become one of the 164 American airmen killed in action, his Nieuport 28 shot down in July 1918 in a single-handed dogfight with no less than seven German fighters; "His bravery was so notorious," Eddie Rickenbacker wrote after the war, "that we all knew he would either achieve some great spectacular success or be killed in the attempt").[12]

America's failure to adequately prepare for participation in the First World War stemmed from a fatal combination of uneven Presidential interest and support during the Roosevelt, Taft, and Wilson administrations; reluctant Congressional appropriators; an unresponsive military bureaucracy; a split over the relative merits of airships versus aircraft; the corrosive Wright-Curtiss patent feud; poor organization and mismanagement of training establishments (triggering, in one case, a highly publicized court-martial and some subsequent reassignments and resignations); and inarticulate and sometimes feuding service airmen loyal to the Wright or Curtiss camps (depending how they had been trained). An attempt in 1914 to use airplanes to help Brigadier General John J. "Black Jack" Pershing's punitive expedition hunt for Mexican guerrilla leader Pancho Villa ended disappointingly and highlighted some of the organizational and equipment problems. Though the Curtiss "Jennies" did locate *Villistas* and, in one notable case, pass the information to a cavalry patrol that subsequently attacked an encampment, inflicting heavy casualties (including wounding Villa himself and causing the death of one of his generals), mechanical reliability and operating problems eventually caused the loss of all of Pershing's airplanes. It was not a propitious sign.[13]

When the United States declared war on Germany in April 1917, it had barely 100 military airplanes: the Army had approximately 55 aircraft in service, most obsolete and the rest obsolescent, and the Navy had another 54, all trainers.[14] In June 1917 the newly formed Aircraft Production Board promised to darken the skies of Europe with clouds of American airplanes, fully 4,500 within the first year. Given the conditions within industry (still riven by the patent feud), government, and the military services, it was a staggering promise, and one that could not be fulfilled simply by throwing money at it, a whopping $640 million (approximately $11 *billion* at 2001 inflation rates), more than 45 times the highest previous yearly American appropriation for military aircraft. Confusion reigned, characterized by production orders placed and withdrawn. One day single-seat fighters were out; the next they were in. Differing kinds of aircraft competed for production monies, and outright cranks gained entry and funding to support notoriously unairworthy designs. Planners believed too readily that the methods of Henry Ford and the automotive industry could be immediately applied to aeronautics, with unskilled labor building advanced airplanes. Instead, as Roger Bilstein has noted, "Airplanes of the era were compounded of wood, glue, screws, fabric, and carefully adjusted bracing wires, all requiring the careful ministrations of workers who were more like craftsmen than unskilled laborers."[15] Despite its limitations American industry could take some pride it what it actually did accomplish. The

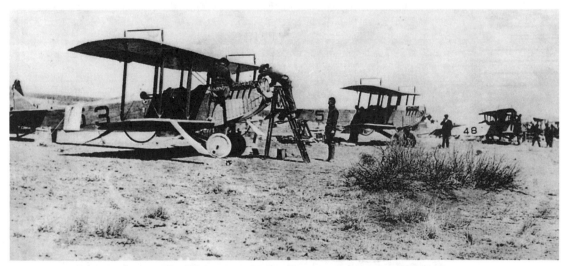

Airmen of the First Aero Squadron work on Curtiss JNs during Pershing's Punitive Expedition. Designed for Curtiss by émigré British Sopwith engineer B. Douglas Thomas, the JN borrowed heavily from European Sopwith, Avro, and Deperdussin—practice. USAF Enlisted Heritage Hall

29656

American airmen, foreign planes (I): Then First Lieutenant Edward V. "Eddie" Rickenbacker of the USAAS 94th Aero Squadron in his SPAD XIII fighter at Rembercourt, October 1918. America's "Ace of Aces" with 26 victories, he subsequently received the Medal of Honor. NARA

one great American success of the war was the Liberty engine, a fine and reliable over-400-horsepower power plant.

But a visitor to the United States in 1918 would never have assumed that just 15 years earlier America had *invented* the airplane. Aggregate numbers aside, aircraft production was quite something else. By the time of signing the armistice in November 1918, American contractors had delivered 11,754 aircraft to the Army, and the Navy had another 2,107 in service. But the vast majority were still trainers and other obsolete types; only 667 American built aircraft were overseas and almost all were of foreign, not indigenous American, design. America's combat aviators, aside from those few naval aviators crewing the excellent Curtiss flying boats, flew French, British, and Italian products. When Americans reading their morning newspapers followed the exploits of Eddie Rickenbacker, they saw him with a rugged SPAD. Doug Campbell leaned against a trim Nieuport. Eliot White Springs posed jauntily by an angular British S.E. 5a. Navy fighter ace Doug Ingalls

American airmen, foreign planes (II): USAAS Major Fiorello LaGuardia (left) before a Caproni Ca 3 bomber at San Pelagio, September 1918, with observer Major Negrotto Cambiaso (center), co-pilot Captain Federico Zapelloni, and gunner Airman Otello Firmani (sitting). AFMA

sat in a wicked little Sopwith Camel. New Yorkers saw feisty Fiorello LaGuardia standing in front of a huge Caproni bomber. America's home-grown equivalent was the dainty little Thomas-Morse Scout, an outdated rotary-engined biplane inspired by the early Nieuport and Sopwith designs, suitable only for Stateside training.[16]

So how did America respond? The long-overdue creation of an American aeronautical research organization constituted one immediate positive result of the outbreak of war. In the years between the Wright brothers' flight at Kitty Hawk and the outbreak of the First World War, European nations built ten wind tunnels to the United States's two—and one of the latter was itself a copy of a European design. Professor Albert Francis Zahm established the first true (if small) American aeronautical laboratory in April 1901 at the Catholic University of America, complete with a wind tunnel and sophisticated measurement system, but it closed several years thereafter when he ran out of research funds after the death of a patron. In 1911 Navy captain Washington Irving Chambers proposed creating a national laboratory but the idea failed to gain Congressional support. Not easily discouraged, Chambers turned to Zahm and Smithsonian Secretary Charles Walcott.[17]

In late 1912, on the Navy's recommendation, President William Howard Taft appointed a 19-member National Aerodynamical Laboratory Commission that drafted a pro-laboratory report, but the Congress failed to act before the Taft administration came to an end. Instead the Navy opened its own small laboratory at the Washington Navy Yard, and Walcott reopened Langley's old research shop as the Langley Aerodynamical Laboratory; its advisory board sent Zahm and Assistant Naval Constructor Jerome C. Hunsaker on a tour of European aeronautical laboratories in the summer of 1913. Their summary reports upon returning confirmed the backwardness of American aeronautical research organization. Then, because of the nuances of public law, Walcott had to close the Langley laboratory just as it started to produce research results.[18] Once again advocates turned to the Congress, and once again the legislative branch failed to act.

As 1914 passed into history, Walcott, armed with the growing evidence of the airplane's worth in war, persisted in his fight for a national laboratory, assisted by the aging Alexander Graham Bell. Suitably stirred, Senator Benjamin "Pitchfork Ben" Tillman introduced a joint resolution in January 1915 providing for creation of a national Advisory Committee for Aeronautics. Even here the European influence predominated, for the language consciously copied key passages from the creation of the British Advisory Committee for Aeronautics in 1909. Walcott and Bell submitted an appeal to defense preparedness, national pride, industrial efficiency, and scientific need and, aided by a strong endorsement from acting secretary of the Navy Franklin Roosevelt, the measure passed on March 3, 1915, with President Wilson signing it into law the next day. At its first meeting, held the next month, the committee prefixed the organization title with the word "National." The next year it took its first steps towards acquiring its first major research facility, which it opened in June 1920 at Hampton, Virginia, the Langley Memorial Aeronautical Laboratory. Over time the NACA became the world's most successful governmentally supported aeronautical research and development organization; in 1958 it evolved into the present-day National Aeronautics and Space Administration.[19]

Another response, as discussed earlier, was the end of the Wright patent dispute, thanks to industry intervention (assisted by the NACA). Freed from this burden, American industry at last began to move forward in substantial fashion to match what was happening in Europe, but it would take time and was far from easy. In 1923, on the twentieth anniversary of the first flight at Kitty Hawk, the Wrights' hometown paper, the *Dayton Daily News,* would editorialize, "The Old World, singularly enough, has utilized the airplane for many more purposes than America, though here in our country we invented it and first gave it to the world. Mail routes and transportation lines in France, England, Italy and Germany are commonplace elements in the lives of the people. *Here in America we have been a bit laggard about claiming for our own that to which we are entitled."*[20] (emphasis added)

America's military and commercial aviation remained through the mid-1920s in thrall to European technology. Army fighter pilots flew SPADs and American-built copies of the British S.E. 5a well into the 1920s; Charles Lindbergh trained on S.E. 5s as a student pilot before going on to fly D.H. 4s (another American-built copy of a British design) for a private airmail carrier. Navy pilots flew Sopwith Pups and Camels. Both flew American copies of the superlative British De Havilland D.H. 4, which formed as well the bulk of the Post Office's airmail fleet and the basis of the first American commercial aircraft operations. When the services and the government sought high technology, they generally went abroad: and Post Office acquired examples of the new Junkers all-metal monoplane transports, the military acquired examples of new Fokker fighters and transports, the foreign airships as well. Also, America looked abroad for scientific talent: the NACA hired the eminent (if tempestuous) German aerodynamicist Max Munk to direct its aerodynamics studies and future wind tunnel development, and the California Institute of Technology, at the behest of the Daniel Guggenheim Fund for the Promotion of Aeronautics, appointed Theodore von Kármán, a Hungarian aerodynamicist of courtly manner and even greater renown, to head GALCIT, its Guggenheim Aeronautical Laboratory.

Gradually a shift occurred. In 1919 the all-American NC-4 had first flown the Atlantic. In 1921, when Mitchell's airmen sank the *Ostfriesland,* they did so flying an all-American bomber built by Martin. In 1923 two Army airmen flew nonstop across the United States, and if they piloted a Dutch-built airplane, they nevertheless had an American engine. In 1924 Army airmen flew around the world in American-built Douglas biplanes. In 1925 an American pilot, Jimmy Doolittle, won the prestigious Schneider Trophy in a Curtiss racer, the first international speed contest won by an American airman and airplane since Curtiss won at Reims in 1909. Then, of course, in 1927 Charles Lindbergh flew solo across the North Atlantic in his all-American *Spirit of St. Louis,* as much a tribute to American aero engine design as it was to the airplane and to Lindbergh's own abilities. Arguably more significant were the institutional changes. Three acts in 1926—the Air Commerce Act, and the Army and Navy Five-Year Plans, stimulated research and development, freed the NACA to be more of a research organization than a mixed research-and-advisory body, and strengthened commercial aviation. The Daniel Guggenheim Fund for the Promotion of Aeronautics, between 1926 and 1930, spearheaded the growth of American professional aeronautical engineering education, key safety research on blind flying and low-speed flight, air-mindedness among Americans, and demonstrations of commercial air operations.

Hand in hand with this were some major technological developments that revolutionized propulsion, structures, aerodynamics, and safety. These were, mainly, more efficient liquid cooling, controllable pitch propellers, better exhaust-valve design permitting higher-power engines, new cowlings for air-cooled engines that

Charles Lindbergh and his *Spirit of St. Louis,* 1927. USAF

both improved cooling and reduced drag, advances in all-wooden and eventually all-metal monocoque and cantilever construction, wing slats and flaps, refinement of airfoil design, particularly the evolution of the so-called Clark Y airfoil and the beginnings of NACA's comprehensive program of airfoil design and overall studies of how to reduce aircraft drag, and comprehensive radio navigation and blind flying instrumentation. These innovations guaranteed that the American airplane would be fully as advanced as the best of its foreign competitors by the end of the 1920s, but, here, too, many of these developments had their origins or inspiration in European research and development, rather than purely indigenous work. By that time aircraft such as the Lockheed Vega and Northrop Alpha were already signaling the imminent advent of the practical, economical monoplane transport—which, when it appeared in the early 1930s, would place American aviation firmly ahead of Europe.[31] It had been a long, long recovery.

Echoes and Resonances

The invention of flight, specifically the invention of the airplane, offers a number of cautionary lessons. Clearly technological breakthroughs are not singular events in which achievement miraculously guarantees continued world-leading success. The Wrights believed that controlling their patents would in turn control the technology, buying them the long-term stability they needed as they continued to refine their basic concept and generate production machines. But this is impossible in the international business environment, both then and now, particularly when a development possesses both commercial and national security value. The technological dynamic itself takes hold, producing its own imperative. In any case specific developments always have a finite life that dramatically reduces their value, akin to the drop in an automobile's worth once it is driven off the sales lot. European aviation technology advanced so rapidly that the Wright concept of the airplane declined equally as fast, withering in the face of the more advanced and practical tractor monoplane and biplane. Some Europeans were thinking even further ahead: by 1912 French engineers had already conceptualized rocket-and-ramjet-powered high-speed jet airplanes (going so far as to produce reasonable designs for aircraft and engine concepts that would not appear for almost another 40 years), and both French and German engineers were well along the path to the

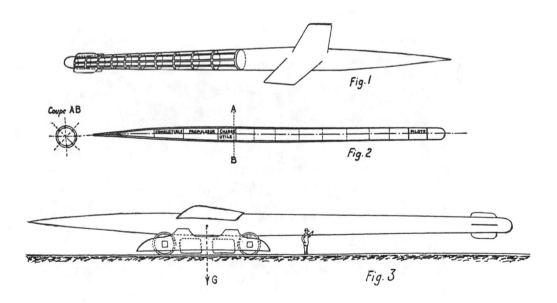

René Lorin's extraordinary trolley-launched reaction-powered aircraft of 1911 was a remarkable configuration anticipating ideas such as the Sänger-Bredt orbital boost-glider of 1944 and the supersonic aircraft of the early 1950s. Adapted from *L'Aérophile* (1911)

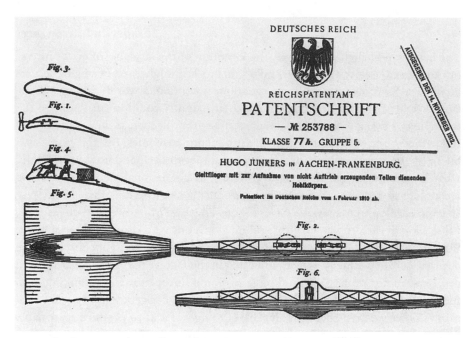

Hugo Junkers' 1912 patent for an all-metal flying wing, conceived in 1910, anticipated both the all-metal air transports of the 1930s and the unemcumbered aerodynamic efficiency of the pure flying wing, not attained until the advent of the Northrop B-2 almost eighty years later. From Reichspatentamt Patentschrift Nr. 253788, 14 Nov. 1912.

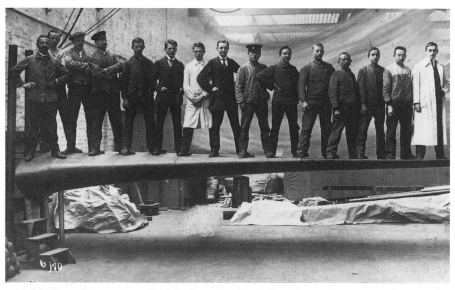

But first had to come more conventional airplanes. Here, technicians demonstrate the strength of one of Hugo Junkers' thick-section cantilever wings (though one hopes for the sake of the team leader on the end that the others did not all leap off at once!). Thick wings had better lifting properties than thin wings, and rapidly replaced them. USAF

all-metal streamlined cantilever monoplane.[22] Thus did Europe quickly match and then surpass the Wrights and thereby secure the lead in world aviation development for the better part of the next two decades.

So making a technological breakthrough is no guarantor of commercial success. One must remain actively engaged, scanning what is happening across a field, and above all being flexible and amenable to what one's prospective customers want. The Wrights had a clear vision and strong determination, and that sufficed to enable them to secure a goal that had eluded others for years: invention of the first successful airplane. But they had little idea of what to do *after* that point, and the basic technological layout of their concept—an unstable canard biplane—restricted its future development and success. As noted earlier, they knew how to make the world's first airplane—but they didn't know how to make its successors. Their great rival Curtiss did not, in all likelihood, possess their abilities as engineers and designers—but he possessed far stronger and perceptive business skills, and also a great deal more flexibility; in short, he thought and listened in terms of what his *customers* wanted—not just what *he* wanted. Thus Curtiss, not the Wrights, came to dominate American aviation.

Being a "fast second" can have its own advantages, as one has an opportunity to assess a breakthrough technology and then move well beyond it. This certainly benefited the Europeans after 1903, though as pointed out it would be both unfair and inaccurate to insist that they were dependent upon the Wrights for their own success in flight. As stated earlier, if the Wrights had never existed, the first flight would have taken place before 1910 in Europe, most likely France. The United States has benefited from being a "fast second" on numerous occasions, of which the following are just a few of the most notable: exploiting the turbojet revolution (both the development of military and commercial jet aircraft, each first pioneered in Europe), exploiting atomic physics (pioneered in Europe and then "industrialized" in the Manhattan Project to produce the first A-bomb); exploiting the liquid-fueled rocketry revolution (pioneered in America by Robert Goddard and made practical by Germany and then the Soviet Union).

However, this last point is also perhaps the most important of all: though being a "fast second" may have its advantages, it is not the way to lead one's life. Far better is to conceive, develop, refine, assess, adapt, and transform, always remaining at the peak of the "state of the possible," what one team of strategists and future planners call "winning in fast time." Conceived by John A. Warden, one of the key planners of the Gulf War air campaign, winning in fast time involves thinking strategically, focusing sharply on the key elements—the "centers of gravity"—that one must address, and then moving quickly to take advantage of circumstances.[23]

What is surprising is that subsequent American aviation history reveals numerous other occasions where national aeronautical development missed opportunities, at best only maintained pace with foreign initiatives, or occasionally lagged to the point where only chance prevented the kind of overwhelming inferiority experienced between 1909 and the end of the 1920s. In each case technological

Junkers' giant G 38 transport of 1929, immediately preceded the 1930s' "modern" airliners. Despite its all-metal structure, it still had a fixed landing gear and corrugated external skin, marking it as very much an interim design. American Institute of Aeronautics and Astronautics

American air transport primacy lasted until the early 1950s, when Great Britain introduced the De Havilland Comet, the world's first jet airliner. But a tragic series of accidents caused by a serious design flaw removed it from service, and so American dominance continued. BA

complacency or shortsightedness played a role. These include lagging in the development of liquid-fuel rockets despite having invented them first; ignoring the turbojet engine until exposure in 1941 to British turbojet work; missing the high-speed significance of the swept wing until the end of the Second World War; lagging in applying the jet engine to commercial aircraft until after the British, Canadians, French, and Russians had done so; lagging in launching an earth satellite (which could have been done in 1954) until the Soviet Union launched *Sputnik* in 1957. All of these threatened American competitiveness, and most, indeed, affected international security as well.

Transformations, Civil and Military

The invention of the airplane utterly transformed the world, yet even after the airplane flew, skepticism abounded as critics and supporters alike underestimated both its potential and its worth. In 1907 the chief of the U.S. Weather Service,

America surpassed the troubled Comet with the more advanced Boeing 707, which spawned the 727, 737, 747, 757, 767, and 777. The United States continued to dominate global air transport until the advent of the European Airbus, which generated its own string of successes. AA

Willis Moore, stated, "Commercially very little is to be expected from either balloons or flying machines. Carrying freight is out of the question and even profitable smuggling is doubtful. For passenger traffic the number carried will be so small and the cost so great that no competition is possible with existing modes of transit."[24] In 1908 Harvard astronomer William Pickering boldly stated, "It is doubtful if aeroplanes will ever cross the ocean, and despite the Wright success they offer little menace to warfare. The public has greatly over-estimated the possibilities of the aeroplane, imagining that in another generation they will be able to fly over to London in a day. This is manifestly impossible."[25] At the dawn of air transport, even airmen themselves could not agree as to its future; Britain's Mervyn O'Gorman dismally predicted, "From the commercial point of view, I see no prospect of large aeroplanes, carrying large numbers of passengers, competing either in price, convenience, safety or even in speed, with trains."[26] In 1915 a professor at the Massachusetts Institute of Technology advised a particularly enthusiastic student to stick with mechanical engineering, as "this airplane business will never amount to very much." The student was Donald Douglas, destined to spearhead a company whose "DC" designs would dominate the propeller-driven era of commercial flight. The professor was Jerome Hunsaker, a major player in creating the National Advisory Committee for Aeronautics, destined to chair the NACA during the fiftieth anniversary celebrations of the Wrights' first flights in 1953.[27] As novelist and science and technology commentator Michael Crichton has pointed out, even for the airplane's believers, "the sheer scale of their eventual use would have defied comprehension. One might have imagined an airplane—but 10,000 airplanes in the air at the same time would have been beyond imagining."[28]

Yet despite critics' negativity and lukewarm friends, commercial aviation advanced surprisingly rapidly. In 1914, just 11 years after Kitty Hawk (as previously discussed), a start-up American airline carried 1,200 passengers in three months. By that time DELAG, the German airship airline created in 1909, had *already* carried a total of 19,100 passengers on 881 flights.[29] In 1926, 5,800 passengers flew on short routes in the United States. Then, in 1927, Charles Lindbergh crossed the North Atlantic in the *Spirit of St. Louis,* triggering a tremendous wave of "airmindedness" among Americans. The next year, in 1928, 48,300 passengers took to the air in American skies. A decade later, in 1938 (despite the Great Depression), this had risen to 1.2 *million,* approximately a 25-fold increase; in 1952 it had risen again, reaching 25 million, with, for the first time, more people flying across the United States than taking a train. By the late 1950s, thanks to the turbojet revolution and the emergence of the economically viable jetliner, the airplane had become the dominant international "people mover," having swept past a century of accumulated railroad and maritime progress in less than 50 years of passenger operations. In 1981, 265.3 million passengers flew around the United States. Two decades later 610 million flew—over *half a billion* people per year, flying on nearly *nine million* flights: 1.67 million passengers per day, bound for various destinations on 24,600 flights, an average of 33,424 passengers per state. Worldwide in 2000 well over a billion passengers flew on international carriers, together with approximately 25 million tons of freight—equivalent in capacity to nearly 325,000 standard railroad boxcars.[30]

Today the major gateway, the major port of entry, to any big city is its airport. Atlanta's Hartsfield International Airport, the world's busiest, handled 80.2 million passengers in 2000. Next was Chicago's O'Hare, with 72.1 million. Then came LAX, Los Angeles International, which that same year witnessed a total of 67.3 million passengers pass through its terminals.[31] London's Heathrow airport greeted 64.6 million passengers; Frankfurt's Main 49.3 million; and Paris' Charles de Gaulle 48.2 million. As airplanes have replaced ships, so too international airport customs arrival halls have replaced harbors and dockside immigration offices. The Statue of Liberty lifts her lamp only rarely to arriving foreign visitors and émigrés, and far more often to camera-toting tourists who land at one of New York City's three major airports. So great had the international passenger flow become at the city's signature John F. Kennedy Airport ("the country's most important global gateway," in the words of *Time* magazine) that in 2001 the airport authority opened a 1.5-million-square-foot arrivals building, Terminal 4, capable of handling 3,200 arriving passengers per hour.[32]

So the airplane completely overturned a transportation and mobility model based exclusively on incremental improvements to roads and railroads. In less than six decades, the top speed of intercontinental transportation went from 20 miles per hour to 600 miles per hour, a 30-fold increase. On anything but the very shortest routes, the airplane quickly eclipsed the train, then the steamship, as a commercially viable means of long-distance business passenger travel, because of unprecedented affordability and ease of service. As of the summer of 2001, an Amtrak train ticket between Minneapolis and Los Angeles cost $254 and required a routing through Portland, Oregon. The proud owner of a Lincoln Navigator sports utility vehicle had to pay $206 in gas costs to drive between the two cities. Leaving the driving to Greyhound cost $124 for a bus ticket. A Northwest airline ticket for the four-hour, 1,530 mile flight from Minneapolis to LA cost $99, less than seven cents per mile.[33]

Then, of course, there is the military impact of flight. In the century since the Wright brothers, flight has become the arbiter of modern warfare and the heart of both deterrence and coercive strategies and doctrine. Already proven in the First World War, its steady maturation over time, aided by such technological developments as the jet engine, radar, aerial refueling, and advanced electronic systems and computers made it the centerpiece of the so-called revolution in military affairs that occurred after mid-century, and which utterly transformed notions of using force and projecting power in the modern world. Air superiority—indeed air supremacy—proved vitally important. "When the enemy had air superiority," defense analyst David Kirkpatrick has noted, "it was virtually impossible for any army to fight effectively since its movements were reported, its supplies were interdicted and its fortified positions were deluged with explosives."[34] Air-and-space-based surveillance and reconnaissance are the common currency of modern-day national security decision making, and global air mobility is the linchpin of coalition crisis response. Whether humanitarian interventions or combat operations, no spot on earth is beyond an approximately 15-hour flight. The innate characteristics of air power—its speed, range, flexibility, precision, and lethality—give it a unique blend of qualities that have, over the last century, reshaped military doctrine and thought.[35]

That reshaping became increasingly evident in the results of the four wars America fought in the decade after the onset of the Iraqi invasion of Kuwait in 1990: the Gulf, Bosnia, Kosovo, and most recently Afghanistan. All have showcased the asymmetric advantage air and space power offers over foes, what commentator Charles Krauthammer has called the ability to "drop thousand-pound bombs with the precision of a medieval archer."[36] It is the product of the synergistic interactions of land-and-carrier-based aircraft, precision munitions, cruise missiles, global mobility, aerial refueling, battlefield rocket artillery, attack and troop-lift helicopters, and atmospheric and space-based weather, navigation, communications, intelligence, surveillance, and reconnaissance systems, to name just a sampling of the more important facets of air and space power. But it reflects three very traditional military quests as well: seeking the triple advantages of *height, reach,* and *speed.* Height gives view: since before David and Goliath, combatants have desired to strike from the safety of distance; reach is quickest through the air and space medium.

Over the first century of winged flight, air and space power has both broken and forged a new relationship between air and surface forces. In classic Clausewitzian warfare, surface forces had to fight at great cost for the "right" to enter and subdue an occupied country. At first, as in the Great War, air power existed only in support of land and sea forces. But over time the balance shifted. By the midst of the Second World War, air attack coupled with submarine attack had become the dominant means of inflicting military casualties and destruction both on land and at sea.[37] It proved staggeringly and appallingly destructive when applied to urban areas from Rotterdam and London on to Hamburg, Berlin, Dresden, Tokyo, and Hiroshima-Nagasaki. In the postwar world, the Cold War revolved around developing, deploying, controlling, and (ultimately) limiting the products—the planes, aerial missiles, bombs, artillery rockets, and ballistic missiles—of the flight revolution. Today, in the era of ubiquitous joint-service air and space power, the swift and overwhelming use of precise force quickly shatters the morale and physical resources of an opponent, leading to rapid collapse. Circumstances obviously change and military planners must constantly prepare for warfare across the entire spectrum of conflict from "low" to "high," but whatever and wherever the scenario, joint service air and space forces coming from land and sea and drawing on systems orbiting the earth will undoubtedly continue to furnish the shock and awe that unhinges opponents and sets the stage for their rapid destruction, particularly in the emerging era of space-based, not just space-exploiting, weapons.[38]

Technology of Light or Technology of Darkness?
Considering Flight after 9/11/01

On the morning of September 11, 2001, the world witnessed the savagery of terrorism exploiting the technology of flight. The 9/11 attacks turned the promise of commercial aviation on its head. The twentieth century had witnessed the airliner bringing nations closer, reducing to hours journeys that previously had taken days or weeks. Now the hijacked airliner became the terrorist's cruise missile or bomber. Afterwards the editors of one highly respected aviation journal addressed what had happened:

> Not least among the grave injuries the world suffered on September 11 was the desecration of airliners. On that day, every advancement ever made in aviation—every piece of precision engineering, every tweak in performance and safety, all the worldwide, decades-long efforts made to improve air travel—was repudiated by the intent to destroy.
>
> Will we ever look at airplanes in the same way again? Will those of us who always looked up when we heard an airplane overhead, just for the pleasure of watching it for a few moments, still be able to do that without flashing back on the gruesome images of that day?
>
> Today aviation's future seems uncertain, but for comfort we need only look at its history: a hundred years of great struggle and almost incomprehensible progress. We don't believe the momentum has changed.[1]

Yet if the authors were in all other respects absolutely accurate, 9/11 *had* changed the momentum. The attacks disrupted what had been, up to that time, a remarkably cheap international system of transportation that most travelers had taken for granted, even as they had increasingly grumbled about delays, crowded flights, cattle-car seating, inconvenient hubs, and notoriously poor food. The economic health of the world's airlines took a dive, and some folded their wings. New orders for aircraft were put on hold. Desert boneyards filled with prematurely retired jetliners the airlines could no longer afford to fly. Utilization rates dropped and then began a slow climb back up. Citizens of major urban areas saw, once again, the skein of tangled contrails as fighters circled overhead, "on call" for wayward airplanes, something recollecting the Cold War, when fighters routinely guarded against the threat of Soviet nuclear-armed bombers. Demanding safety procedures and security checks seriously impacted travel schedules, forcing passengers to arrive even earlier at airports for their flights. Airliners not showing the proper codes, not following exact procedures, or with disruptive passengers faced diversion to emergency landings, with armed fighters following them down. It was analogous, but on a far broader scale, to reaction after the loss of the space shuttle *Challenger* in 1986. When *Challenger* exploded, it took with it the assumption that space flight was becoming so routine as to be virtually mundane and commonplace. As *Challenger* forced a rethinking of the pace and nature of America's national space program, so 9/11 has forced a rethinking of global air transport.

Never again will passengers and aircrew take the act of flying quite so casually: there will always be that lingering concern about the odd passenger in Seat 16A, or the whispering gentlemen in Row 12, or the unattended luggage by Gate 43, or the seemingly lax screener at Pier C . . . all the little corrosive uncertainties that undermine faith and trust. It reminds one of an old airman's joke: "There are two bad things that can happen to you, and one will: 1) One day you will walk out to an airplane knowing you are about to make your last flight; 2) One day you will walk out to an airplane *not* knowing you are about to make your last flight." It is that latter fear that bothers people. Undoubtedly air transport will continue to dominate both global and domestic travel, for nothing, certainly not even terrorist attacks, can turn back the clock on what has been accomplished over the last century. In time—in fact, probably even quickly—it will regain the momentum it has briefly (if significantly) lost. But it will be more inconvenient and overall even less pleasant than before 9/11, as passengers and crew alike confront the new uncertainties of flight in the age of terrorism.

So in the end, what does 9/11 say to us of flight? Actually, it says far more of *us* than of flight. It is the uses to which humans put their creations that make the difference.

Samuel Johnson recognized this in his 1759 novel *Rasselas*. His creative artisan tells the prince of Abyssinia that the secret of flight must be closely guarded: "If men were all virtuous, I should with great alacrity teach them all to fly. But what would be the security of the good if the bad could at pleasure invade them from the sky? Against an army sailing through the cloud neither walls, nor mountains, nor seas, could afford any security. A flight of northern savages might hover in the wind, and light at once with irresistible violence upon the capital of a fruitful region that was rolling under them. Even this valley, the retreat of princes, the bode of happiness, might be violated by the sudden descent of some of the naked nations that swarm on the coast of the southern sea."[2]

Today the prospective pilot who yearns to fly because of exposure to the writings of Saint-Exupéry, Richard Bach, or Ernest Gann—to feel the kinship with all who have flown and all who will fly, to gain the wonderful, all-encompassing perspective of the "third dimension"—may share a flight instructor with a student pilot who has adopted the twisted philosophy of individuals who have convinced him to learn to fly just so he can pilot a fuel-laden airplane filled with innocents into a building. And so it has become: the hands of a skilled airline crew exploiting the technology of the jetliner make possible journeys that bring pleasure, love, knowledge, and business, and the hands of hate-filled suicidal terrorists exploiting that same technology make possible journeys bringing monstrous injury, death, and destruction. Problems—and solutions—are never found within the technology; they are found within ourselves, and controlling ourselves has been a challenge since the days of the ancients. "Among all areas of human experience," historian William Green has noted, "the slowest to change is our system of values." Or, he might have added, the lack of them.[3]

Apocalyptic and military literature often envisioned urban destruction via aerial assault—witness Wells's *War in the Air*—though the horrific evil of what happened on September 11, 2001, certainly went well beyond any such fictional portrayals. (In the heyday of 1960s radicalism, New York members of the Weathermen entertained ideas of flying a radio-controlled model airplane into the descending ball dropping in Times Square on New Year's Eve as an attention-getting "guerrilla theater" publicity stunt to protest the bombing of North Vietnam, but 9/11 was the real thing.)[4] No pioneer, least of all the Wrights, looked to flight exclusively in beneficial terms. Nevertheless, when in 1908 and 1909 Orville Wright flew back and forth between Fort Myer and Alexandria, he could hardly have thought that his flight path would cross that taken by a team of madmen attacking the Pentagon almost a century later with a doomed plane full of hostages. When in 1910 he clattered over New York, he could likewise have little envisioned the skyscrapers that would dominate its airspace, or the image of two fully laden jetliners flying into the twin towers of the World Trade Center in an act of cataclysmic destruction. When Post Office pilots braved the treacherous weather of the "Hell Stretch" of the Pennsylvania Alleghenies in the early 1920s, they could have little conceived a modern jetliner flying high above them, much less one filled with courageous passengers battling terrorists to the death lest it be turned into a missile to kill their fellow countrymen. When Tony Jannus started the St. Petersburg-Tampa Airboat Line in 1914, he could have little imagined international terrorists hijacking airliners with box cutters or misfit zealots destroying airplanes with bombs in their shoes. Such has sadly become as much a reality of flight in the modern era as the ease of international travel that it makes possible.

But if few saw flight as a panacea, some nevertheless hoped it might be so. Harry Frank Guggenheim, First World War naval aviator, son of mining magnate Daniel Guggenheim, and co-architect of the great Guggenheim Fund for the Promotion of Aeronautics, which transformed American aviation, wrote in 1930: "The airplane gives to man a new freedom, eliminating the geographical barriers of river, sea, mountain and desert between him and his kind, and thus eliminating those prejudices and misunderstandings which have jeopardized human relations in the past."[5] If only it were so. . . . Not quite 15 years before, in the First World

War, he had trained as a bomber pilot. Not quite 15 years after writing these words, he would fly torpedo bombers on carrier air strikes in the Pacific.

Flight is utterly ubiquitous, pervasive in virtually all aspects of modern life, and recognized by the average individual—at least before 9/11/01, and hopefully now as well—for bringing unprecedented ease and freedom of communication, travel, and benefit to society and their lives: an undoubted triumph of the human spirit and capacity for invention and organization. In view of its extraordinary growth and influence, it should not surprise anyone that flight permanently transformed social culture and consciousness in ways both trivial and profound. Indications of its universal appeal may be seen in attendance figures for international air shows and aviation displays, and in the tremendous global popularity of aviation museums, chief among them the National Air and Space Museum of the Smithsonian Institution. On July 1, 2001, the NASM celebrated its twenty-fifth anniversary. Since its opening in 1976 at the time of the American bicentennial, it has become the world's most visited museum, with an attendance of 219 million visitors: an average of 8.76 million per year, 168,350 per week, just over 24,000 per visitors per day, most of whom have flown into one of Washington's three commercial airports.[6]

But no one would seriously suggest that the aerospace revolution has been free from negative consequences: every form of technology introduces its own nuances and forces its own accommodations upon society. Flight has always had, Janus-like, the twin faces of good and bad. The vehicles of flight all have had their

The DC-3 would itself exemplify the dual usage of transport technology for peace and war, excelling as both an airliner and as a combat transport. AA

Boeing's famed B-17 Flying Fortress drew heavily on the company's earlier airliner development, and, in fact, shared its wing and tail surfaces with the Boeing 307 Stratoliner airliner, developed in parallel with it. Boeing

Focke-Wulf's FW 200 Condor airliner, designed for 26 passengers, instead made its reputation in the Second World War as a deadly maritime patrol bomber, scourge of Atlantic convoys from North Cape to the Bay of Biscay. HC

dark uses. The black-powder rocket that illuminated the night sky with fantastic fireworks demonstrations served to panic horses and scatter troops in the midst of battle as well. (Its twentieth-century sibling would propel life-saving weather, communications, and navigation satellites and also savage cities and hold nations hostage in a prolonged nuclear standoff.) The balloon that enthralled fairgoers called down artillery fire on opposing troops.

Early aviators realized the airplane would be no different: in 1912 Jean Conneau, a naval officer and noted prewar international aviator who flew as "Andre Beaumont," wrote, "The light and graceful bird machine, cheered by all, may one day be a messenger of love or of hatred."[7] So it certainly was with the aircraft of the Great War: Sikorsky's *Il'ya Muromets,* the various Gothas and R-planes, the large Handley Pages, delivered passengers and dropped bombs with equal ease; the De Havilland D.H. 4 light bomber that served the Royal Flying Corps and American Air Service so faithfully in 1917–1918 formed the backbone of postwar civil aviation and postal air mail in both British and American skies well into the 1920s. Between the early 1930s and the end of 1945, France, Germany, Italy, Japan, Great Britain, the United States, and the Soviet Union built approximately *one million* airplanes—but the technology that produced the city-serving commercial airliners of the 1930s produced the city-destroying bombers of the 1940s as well.[8]

In 1932 Britain's Prime Minister Stanley Baldwin soberly warned the House of Commons that "it is well also for the man in the street to realize that there is no power on earth that can protect him from being bombed. Whatever people may tell him, the bomber will always get through"; three years later he would add morosely, "I wish for many reasons flying had never been invented. . . . Somehow we have got to Christianize it."[9] True enough: within the year Italian Caproni and Savoia-Marchetti bombers would routinely be saturating Ethiopian towns and tribesmen with bombs and mustard gas; in two years the Heinkels and Junkers of Germany's *Legion Condor* would flatten Guernica, inspiring Picasso's impassioned painting. In three years a British Airways Lockheed airliner would bring Neville Chamberlain from Munich back to England bearing a worthless promise of "peace in our time." In four years shrieking Stukas would introduce the world to Adolf Hitler's *Blitzkrieg,* enabling the forces of the Third Reich to enslave much of Europe in months. In five years the *Luftwaffe's* bombers would burn out great swaths of Rotterdam, London, and other cities. In six years the Imperial Japanese Navy would emphatically bring the supremacy of the dreadnought to an end in costly lessons over Hawaii and off Malaya. Charles Lindbergh, who had done so much to bring about the era of long-range commercial air transport, returned to his office one day, driving past the gigantic B-24 production plant at Willow Run after having come close to death during a particularly dangerous test flight in a new fighter. To him it was "a terrible giant's womb . . . a temple of the god of science at which we moderns worshipped. . . . I watched a steel door lift and an airplane roll outside; while, in reality, the walls of a cathedral fell and children died."[10]

But the airplane accomplished good as well: in 1940 Britain gained its national salvation from Hitler through a battle fought exclusively in the air and then launched an aerial second front against the Third Reich that in conjunction with the subsequent American bombing campaign set the stage for the cross-Channel invasion of Europe four years later. In 1942, off Midway, America's naval airmen fulfilled the eerily prophetic vision of "Capitaine Danrit," repaying the Japanese navy for Pearl Harbor in a battle that, fought entirely in the air, doomed Imperial Japan. In 1944, just after the Normandy invasion, supreme commander Dwight Eisenhower acknowledged what air power had contributed to the Allied cause, emphatically telling his newly commissioned son, "If I didn't have air supremacy, I wouldn't be here."[11] Nine months later, with the Third Reich just weeks from collapse, propaganda minister Joseph Goebbels morosely confided in his diary that he had met with Hitler and "again and again, we return to the starting-point of our conversation. *Our whole military predicament is due to enemy air superiority.*"[12] (emphasis added) Soon, after railing still further about the effects of allied air power, he stopped writing altogether. Shortly thereafter, and not a moment too soon, he followed his Führer into squalid suicide, even as, thousands of miles away, Japan's militarist leaders contemplated their own grim end under an unremitting aerial mining and bombing campaign that obviated the need for a costly and prolonged invasion of the Home Islands.[13] Thus did the airplane excel in furthering both the causes of darkness and of light, as it would later—and as it does today.

Product of our most noble qualities, created for the best and worst of purposes, servant to our finest and our most ignoble impulses, enabler of vast good and vast evil, tool of subjugation and tool of liberation, bringer of terror and bringer of joy: such has been, such is, such will be, the nature of flight, the legacy of its inventors.

ACKNOWLEDGMENTS

First come family. My late parents, Richard and Marie Hallion, encouraged my interest in aviation from an early age. My wife, Colonel Christine Hallion, USAF (ret.), our children Matt and Kate, and my sister, Dr. Marie Elizabeth Hallion, have been a constant source of support, advice, and insight.

A number of pioneer aviators and aviation personalities have influenced my thinking on some of the issues raised in this work, including Captain Walter Stuart Diehl, USN, General James "Jimmy" Doolittle, Brigadier General Harold Harris, Harold Hoekstra, Brigadier General Ben Kelsey, Helene Montgomery-Moore, Group Captain Paddy O'Sullivan, Jean Roché, and Major General Leigh Wade. Sadly, all have passed beyond.

Three notable historians (and good friends) deserve special thanks: the late Dr. Eugene M. Emme, the first historian of the National Aeronautics and Space Administration; the late Charles H. Gibbs-Smith, former keeper of the Victoria and Albert Museum and the first Lindbergh Professor of Aerospace History at the Smithsonian Institution; and Dr. Roger E. Bilstein, professor emeritus at the University of Houston at Clear Lake City.

The following assisted my research; (+) indicates individuals since deceased: *Aeroplane Monthly:* Philip Jarrett; *Baltimore and Ohio Railway Museum:* Matt Anderson; *Borough of Malmesbury:* Stan Hudson (+); *British Aerospace:* John Fozard (+), Graham Weller; *British Army:* Brigadier Jonathan Bailey; *Canadian Aviation Historical Society:* Timothy Dubé, Hugh Halliday; *Capital Pulmonary Internists:* Brian Turrisi; *Catholic University of America:* Rebecca Hurley, Timothy Meagher, William John Shepherd, Chris Wood; *Christ Church, Oxford:* Matthew Phillips; *College Park Airport Museum:* Catherine Allen; *The Dayton and Montgomery County Public Library:* Rhonda Brunn; *East Carolina University:* Mary Boccaccio; *The Huntington Library:* Erin Chase; *Imperial War Museum:* James Lucas, Janice Mullin, David Parry; *Joint Services Command and Staff College:* Chris Hobson, Nick Luft; *Library of Congress:* Len Bruno, Marvin McFarland (+), Arthur Renstrom (+), Ronald Wilkinson; *Lockheed-Martin Corporation:* Norm Augustine; *Martin Luther King*

Memorial Library (Washington, D.C.): Peggy Appleman; *Musée de l'Air et de l'Espace:* Philippe Gras, Stéphane Nicolaou, Christian Tilatti; *National Aeronautics and Space Administration:* Gene Emme (+), Frank Anderson (+), Lee Saegesser; *National Portrait Gallery:* Adam Grummitt; *New England Air Museum:* Michael Speciale, Bob Foster, Charles Stover, and Norm Wroble; *New York Public Library:* Stephan Saks; *Nieuport 17 (Tustin, California):* Bill Bettis; *Royal Aeronautical Society:* Brian Riddle; *Royal Air Force Historical Society:* Air Marshal Sir Frederick Sowrey, Air Commodore Henry Probert; *Royal Air Force Museum:* Michael Fopp, Peter Elliott; *Science Museum:* John Bagley, Brian Lacey, Peter Mann, David Thompson, Walter Tuck; *Smithsonian Institution:* Hal Andrews, Dana Bell, Dorothy Cochrane, Bill Cox, Tom Crouch, Phil Edwards, Farouk El-Baz, Walt Flint (+), Paul Garber (+), Dan Hagedorn, Kate Igoe, Peter Jakab, Allan Janus, Donald Lopez, Robert Meyer (+), Brian Nicklas, Mark Taylor, Frank Winter, Howard Wolko; *Society of World War I Aero Historians:* Lonnie Raidor (+); *Stanford University:* Nicholas Hoff (+); *United States Air Force:* General William Begert, Major General Thomas Fiscus, Major General Charles Metcalf (ret.); *United States Patent Office:* Ted Criares; *University of California at San Diego:* Howard Fisher; *University of Georgia:* Lee Kennett, John Morrow; *University of Hull:* Eric Grove; *University of Manchester:* John Ackroyd; *University of Maryland:* John Anderson, Wayne Cole, Mark Lewis, Keith Olson, Gordon Prange (+); *University of Notre Dame:* Charles Lamb; *Victoria and Albert Museum:* Martin Durrant; *Other Individuals:* Walt Bonney (+), Robert Dodd, Ray Fredette, Peter Grosz, Brigadier General Jay Hubbard, USMC, Jerome Lederer, Jim and Nancy McFeeters, Captain Chris Page, RN, Roger Pineau (+), Douglas Robinson, Kenny and Maggie Scheck, Charles Sterne, Barrett Tillman.

   Finally, I thank Andy Lambert and his family for graciously hosting me at their home in Devon for one wonderful weekend, despite chilly winds rattling windows, and mist and rain sweeping in from nearby Dartmoor. There I undertook the final review and tidying up of this study in a room built little more than a century after Eilmer's leap of faith from Malmesbury Abbey, as the sound of intercontinental jetliners passing overhead periodically punctured the cozy warmth, fellowship, good cheer, and stimulating conversation.

REFERENCES

INTRODUCTION

1. The search was made on www.google.com. Indeed, among aeronautical pioneers, the Wrights, at 391,000, have 9.4 times more citations than their nearest rival, Samuel Langley (41,400), and 32.3 times more than their bitter personal rival and business competitor, Glenn Curtiss (12,100). The precise figures (and pioneers) were: overall, 529,729, consisting of: Wright brothers 391,000 (including 85,100 for Wilbur Wright, and 60,700 for Orville Wright); Samuel Langley 41,400; Glenn Curtiss 12,100; Otto Lilienthal 11,600; Alberto Santos-Dumont 8,350; Gabriel Voisin 8,120; George Cayley 7,110; Louis Blériot 5,770; Igor Sikorsky 5,170; Joseph Montgolfier 4,210; Henry Farman 3,140; Charles Renard 2,940; Montgolfier brothers 2,690; Octave Chanute 2,650; Hiram Maxim 2,580; Étienne Montgolfier 2,440; Clément Ader 2,340; Ludwig Prandtl 2,050; Theodore von Kármán 2,040; Ferdinand Ferber 1,770; Percy Pilcher 1,640; Ferdinand von Zeppelin 1,620; Geoffrey de Havilland 1,570; Pilâtre de Rozier 1,280; Nikolai Joukovsky [Zhukovskiy] 747; Alphonse Pénaud 683; Henri Giffard 578; Martin Kutta 542; Samuel Cody 510; Robert Esnault-Pelterie 497; J. A. C. Charles 234; Arthur Krebs 209; Alliott Verdon Roe 78; Louis Bechereau 44; Dimitri Riabouchinsky 22; and Francis Wenham 5. These figures make for interesting comparison in relation to other personalities of the twentieth century: President John F. Kennedy 1,210,000; astronaut senator John Glenn 1,230,000; the Beatles 1,920,000; General George Patton 213,000.

2. William A. Green, *History, Historians, and the Dynamics of Change* (Westport, CT: Praeger, 1993), 210.

3. Carl L. Becker, *The Heavenly City of the Eighteenth-Century Philosophers* (New Haven: Yale University Press, 1932), 88.

4. Ibid., 22–23.

CHAPTER ONE

1. Theodore Ayrault Dodge, *Alexander: A History of the Origin and Growth of the Art of War from the Earliest Times to the Battle of Ipsus 301 BC, with a Detailed Account of the Campaigns of the Great Macedonian* (Boston: Houghton Mifflin, 1890), 500–502. I

thank Col. John A. Warden III, USAF (ret.), for bringing this anecdote to my attention. Sogdiana today is Bokhara, between the Jaxartes and Oxus rivers.

2. For an excellent and exhaustive survey of some of these myths, particularly those from China, see Berthold Laufer, *The Prehistory of Aviation*, Publication 253 in the *Anthropological Series*, v. 18, n. 1 (Chicago: Field Museum of Natural History, 1928), 7–30. See also Laurence Goldstein, *The Flying Machine and Modern Literature* (Bloomington: Indiana University Press, 1986), 5–6; Ernest Edward Walker, *Aviation: or Human Flight Through the Ages* (Washington, D.C.: Aeronautics Education Foundation, 1939), 4–19; and Charles C. Turner, *Aerial Navigation of Today* (London: Seeley & Company, Ltd., 1910), 17–20.

3. For the legend of Horus, see "The Hawk of Horus," *The Hawk: The Journal of the Royal Air Force Staff College*, v. 1, n. 1 (1928): 5–9.

4. O. R. Gurney, *The Hittites* (Harmondsworth, UK: Penguin Books, Ltd., 1954), 133–144, 148, 202–212.

5. As discussed subsequently in this chapter.

6. Robert Graves, *Greek Myths* (London: Book Club Associates, 1985), 100.

7. Laufer, 12–13; see also Goldstein, 21–22.

8. Laufer, 14–15. The reed-hat parachute version of this story is interesting, as the great historian of Chinese science, Joseph Needham, suggested that the kite may have been inspired by a hat riding on the end of a string.

9. Srikumar V. Gopalakrishna, "The Story of *Vimanas:* India's Tradition of Flying Machines," http://www.polycosmos.org/glxywest/vimanas.htm, pp. 1–3.

10. It is difficult to sort out whether these were physical attempts at flight, or drug-induced "trips" produced by a local hallucinogen called *ayahuasca*. If actual attempts, no reliable record exists, and given the dismal record of tower jumpers in other lands, one must conclude that the vast majority—and perhaps all—of such attempts would have ended in death or serious injury. For an interesting discussion of this in the context of modern myth, imagery, drugs, and mysticism, see Tahir Shah, *Trail of Feathers: In Search of the Birdmen of Peru* (New York: Arcade Publishing, 2002).

11. See Sam D. Gill and Irene F. Sullivan, *Dictionary of Native American Mythology* (New York: Oxford University Press, 1992), 77, 182–183; Diana Ferguson and Colin Taylor, *Native American Myths* (London: Collins & Brown, Ltd., 2001), 74–76; Heike Owusu, *Symbols of Native America* (New York: Sterling Publishing Co., Inc., 1999), 239; Tom Bahti and Mark Bahti, *Southwestern Indian Ceremonials* (Las Vegas, NV: Southwestern Indian Arts & Crafts and KC Publications, Inc., 1997), 24; and Tom Bahti and Mark Bahti, *Southwestern Indian Arts and Crafts* (Las Vegas, NV: Southwestern Indian Arts & Crafts and KC Publications, Inc., 1997), 48–50.

12. The best examples of these are at the British Museum, London, and the Metropolitan Museum of Art, New York City. See C. J. Gadd, *The Assyrian Sculptures* (London: British Museum, 1934), for general reference on these remarkable reliefs. Particularly good examples of these sculptures are an alabaster slab sculpture of a winged arm bearer for the Assyrian king at the Metropolitan Museum of Art, illustrated in Meyer Schapiro's essay, "On Some Problems in the Semiotics of Visual Art: Field and Vehicle in Image-Signs," in his *Theory and Philosophy of Art: Style, Artist, and Society: Selected Papers* (New York: George Braziller Inc., 1994), figure 10; 18; and a limestone human-headed winged lion (Cat. 32.243.2), also in the MMA collections.

13. See Chaim Herzog and Mordechai Gichon, *Battles of the Bible* (London: Greenhill Books, 1997 ed.), 35, 164–165, 166–167, 256–257.

14. Laufer (who spells the name Sin), 35. This story is a curious one. Some have suggested that Han Xin simply trailed a cord along the ground, but this cannot be accurate, as once the kite had crossed over enemy territory, the foe could simply have caught up the cord, confounding the plan and, indeed, bringing the kite to earth. Needham, who spent a lifetime studying Chinese science, stated, "Chinese mathematical thought was always deeply algebraic, not geometrical," and further, that "Euclidean geometry was probably brought to China in the Yüan period [c. 1200–1368]." See Joseph Needham, *Science in Traditional China: A Comparative Perspective* (Cambridge: Harvard University Press, 1981), 10, 15. Yet it is difficult to imagine how Han Sin could calculate the distance without reliance on Euclid's proposition (after Pythagoras) that for a right-angled triangle ABC having an enclosed right angle BAC, the square of BC (the hypotenuse—in this case Han Sin's kite string of known length) is equal to the sum of the squares of BA (the vertical height of the kite, which Han Sin needs to know) and AC (the ground distance to the palace, which Han Sin is seeking to know as the purpose of his inquiry). If the accuracy of both the story and Needham's conclusions is assumed, how Han Sin measured BA to solve for AC is uncertain—perhaps a guess, or perhaps he used the law of sines, since he would have known the length of one side and two angles. If Han Sin used Euclid, it would reveal a far more rapid proliferation of mathematical knowledge from Greece to Asia than is commonly accepted, as Euclid only published his elements less than a century before the Chinese kite flyer. See Euclid, *The Thirteen Books of Euclid's Elements,* translated by Sir Thomas Heath (Chicago: Encyclopedia Britannica, Inc., 1975 ed.), book 1, proposition 47: 28. The kite fishing anecdote is from Robert Temple, *The Genius of China: 3,000 Years of Science, Discovery, and Invention* (New York: Simon and Schuster, 1986), 174. Temple's book is a useful and popular distillation of Needham's larger studies of Chinese science and technology, and indeed, Needham wrote the foreword to the Temple work.

15. Laufer, 35–36. David Pelham, *The Penguin Book of Kites* (New York: Penguin Books, 1976) is a good survey history.

16. Temple, 175–177; see also Marco Polo, *The Description of the World,* v. 1 (London: George Routledge, 1938), 356–357; and Clive Hart, *The Dream of Flight: Aeronautics from Classical Times to the Renaissance* (New York: Winchester Press, 1972), 76, who notes "there appear to be no reports of man-lifters, either real or imaginary, before modern times."

17. Both the original and a reference facsimile of the Milemete manuscript are in the collections of the Library, Christ Church, Oxford, UK. The facsimile, available for researchers, is Montague Rhodes James, ed., *The Treatise of Walter de Milemete: De nobilitatibus, sapientiis, et prudentiis regum* (Oxford: Oxford University Press for the Roxburgh Club, 1913), folios f.77b and f.78a, 154–155, also xi-xiii, xx, xxii-xxiii. I thank Mr. Matthew Phillips, Assistant Librarian, Christ Church, for facilitating my research on this manuscript. The actual drawings were done by an unknown artist referred to as Artist I. This fascinating work shows as well early cannon and windmill concepts (see folios 70b, 74b, and 75a, pp. 140, and 148–149). See also Hart, *Dream,* 42–43; and Charles Gibbs-Smith, *Aviation: A Historical Survey from its Origins to the End of World War II* (London: HMSO, 1970), 7.

18. George Sarton, *A History of Science: Ancient Science Through the Golden Age of Greece* (Cambridge, MA: Harvard University Press, 1952), 440–441. See also Turner, 20, quoting Hatton Turnor, *Astra Castra* (London: Chapman and Hall, 1865); and

Walker, 17. For Archytas, see W. W. Rouse Ball's classic *A Short Account of the History of Mathematics* (London: Macmillan & Co., Ltd., 1912), 28–30; he assumed leadership of the Pythagorean school after Pythagoras perished at the hands of a mob incited by political rivals.

19. J. G. Landels, *Engineering in the Ancient World* (Berkeley: University of California Press, 1978), 28–30, 199–201; see also L. Sprague de Camp, *The Ancient Engineers* (Cambridge, MA: MIT Press, 1970), 98, 242–243.

20. Hart, *Dream,* 49–52 and 72, has an extensive discussion of Archytas and also offers the possibility that the bird's mechanism flapped its wings; see also his discussion on 53–61 of rocket-powered bird models *à la* Fontana.

21. Gopalakrishna, 3.

22. Dr. El-Baz, the former director of the Center for Earth and Planetary Sciences for the National Air and Space Museum, was instrumental in bringing this story to a truly global audience. He arranged for the copying of the model from the Egyptian National Museum, and then had it delivered to the three curators (of whom the author was one) of the Early Flight Gallery. I thank Mr. Brian Nicklas of the National Air and Space Museum Library for information regarding this important artifact. See also John H. Lienhard, *The Engines of Our Ingenuity: An Engineer Looks at Technology and Culture* (New York: Oxford University Press, 2000), 115–116.

23. For example, there is not the slightest shred of evidence, despite what some have said, that this was some sort of "design" or "model" of a full-size Egyptian aircraft, despite the wishful thinking of some to the contrary.

24. Walker, pp. 17–18. Ibn Firnas's attempt is more thoroughly discussed in Lynn White, Jr., "Eilmer of Malmesbury: An Eleventh Century Aviator: A Case Study of Technological Innovation, Its Context and Tradition," *Technology and Culture,* v. 2, n. 2 (Spring 1961).

25. For a discussion of the decline of Islamic science, see Howard R. Turner, *Science in Medieval Islam* (Austin: University of Texas Press, 1995), 202–207, 219–221; see also Ahmad al-Hassan and Donald R. Hill, *Islamic Technology: An Illustrated History* (Cambridge: Cambridge University Press, 1986).

26. James Reston, Jr., *The Last Apocalypse: Europe at the Year 1000 A.D.* (New York: Doubleday, 1998), 277; see also 6–7.

27. David Hackett Fischer, *The Great Wave: Price Revolutions and the Rhythm of History* (New York: Oxford University Press, Inc., 1996), 13; David C. Lindberg, *The Beginnings of Western Science: The European Scientific Tradition in Philosophical, Religious, and Institutional Context, 600 B.C. to A.D. 1450* (Chicago: The University of Chicago Press, 1992), 190–197.

28. Edward Grant, *God and Reason in the Middle Ages* (New York: Cambridge University Press, 2000), has an excellent discussion of the image versus the reality of the Middle Ages; see in particular pp. 17–30 and chapters 3–6. See also William A. Green, *History, Historians, and the Dynamics of Change* (Westport, CT: Praeger, 1993), 122–123; and H. R. Trevor-Roper's classic *The Rise of Christian Europe* (London: Thames and Hudson, 1965), passim. In the history of science field, at least some of this rampant secularism is due to the influence of England's William Whewell, France's Jules Michelet, and America's Andrew Dickson White in the nineteenth century, and more recently, the lingering effects of equally questionable works and interpretations by the late Havelock Ellis and particularly Robert K. Merton. Merton based at least a portion of his work on that of Ellis, whose own conclusions were refuted by the later scholarship of Jacques Barzun in his studies on racism and superstition. See

Grant, 283–355, and Nicholas Whyte, *Science, Colonialism, and Ireland* (Cork, Ire.: Cork University Press, 1999), 153–155.

29. Grant, 291. Earlier (18) he notes, "In a real sense Western Europe became a society obsessed with reason, which it consciously employed in many, if not most, of its activities. Nothing like it had ever been seen." See also Carl E. Schorske, "The Idea of the City in European Thought: Voltaire to Spengler," in his *Thinking with History: Explorations in the Passage to Modernism* (Princeton: Princeton University Press, 1998): 49–53

30. For example, see Lynn White, Jr., "Technology in the Middle Ages," in Melvin Kranzberg and Carroll W. Pursell, Jr., eds., *Technology in Western Civilization*, v. 1: *The Emergence of Modern Industrial Society: Earliest Times to 1900* (London: Oxford University Press, 1967), 68–69 (Hereafter Kranzberg and Pursell, 1 or 2); and Thomas Cahill's *How the Irish Saved Civilization: The Untold Story of Ireland's Heroic Role from the Fall of Rome to the Rise of Medieval Europe* (New York: Doubleday, 1995).

31. Winston S. Churchill, *The Birth of Britain*, v. 1 of *A History of the English-Speaking Peoples* (New York: Dodd, Mead & Company, 1956), xii.

32. Data computed from Lindberg, map 6, p. 207; the Cistercian comment is from the previously cited Green, *History*, 123. See also Rouse Ball, 139–143. See also Friedrich Heer, *The Medieval World: Europe, 1100–1350* (London: Weidenfeld & Nicholson/Orion, 1993 ed.), 190–226.

33. Indeed, God was often portrayed as a master craftsman, the architect of the universe. The classic example of such depictions is the thirteenth-cen. Latin MS, MS 2554, Folio Ir, in the Österreichische Nationalbibliothek, Vienna, depicting God with a compass, intently measuring His creation (it conveniently appears as the cover design of the paperback edition of the previously cited Grant and is likewise reproduced in Lindberg as figure 9.7, p. 199).

34. Lindberg, 158–159, 185, 188–190, 203; see also Richard Fletcher, *Moorish Spain* (Berkeley: University of California Press, 1992), 71, 148–49. For Gerbert's role in the evolution of mathematics, see Rouse Ball, 136–139.

35. Ibid., 23–24.

36. White, "Technology in the Middle Ages," 68.

37. There are two wonderful paintings depicting these themes in the collections of the Louvre in Paris. The first is Giotto's *St. Francis Receiving the Stigmata* (ca. 1300), and the second is a small painting (ca. 1350), *Master of the Rebel Angels*, which shows the victory of St. Michael and the loyal angels over Lucifer and his minions. At the top of the latter painting, directly below Christ and the Apostles, a heavenly "combat air patrol" of smoothly flying loyal angels with well-formed birdlike wings have clearly had no trouble securing "air superiority," driving the rebellious angels down totally out of control, as the doomed and repulsive spirits flap their inadequate (and almost insectlike) wings helplessly.

38. As depicted in medieval manuscripts; see Jean Gimpel, *The Medieval Machine: The Industrial Revolution of the Middle Ages* (New York: Penguin Books, 1977), 147.

39. For example, protecting Azariah and his companions from the fiery furnace of the Chaldeans, or rescuing the Apostle Peter from King Herod. See Daniel, chapter 3; and Acts, chapter 12.

40. There are excellent examples of this in Meyer Schapiro's brilliant "The Image of the Disappearing Christ: The Ascension in English Art Around the Year 1000," *Gazette des beaux-arts*, v. 23, series 6 (March 1943): 135–152, esp. 137–140. It was reprinted in a more readily available collection of his essays; see Meyer Schapiro, *Late Antiquity,*

Early Christian, and Mediaeval Art: Selected Papers (New York: George Braziller, Inc., 1979), 267–287.

41. Isaiah 19:1.

42. Psalm 103.

43. Psalm 18.

44. Psalm 55.

45. Psalm 91.

46. Exodus 19:4.

47. 1 Thessalonians 4:17.

48. 1 Thessalonians 5:21. I thank Monsignor William Dendinger, Maj. Gen., USAF (ret.), the former USAF chief of chaplains, for locating this passage from St. Paul.

49. Consider, for example, the motto of Britain's Empire Test Pilot School: "learn to test, test to learn," or that of the U.S. Air Force Flight Test Center, "towards the unknown."

50. Schapiro, 152, 135–138 and Figure 3; the Bury St. Edmunds psalter is Regina Manuscript 12, Folio 73, Vatican collections. See also White, "Eilmer of Malmesbury," 102, 97–111; and Goldstein, 17–23.

51. Visitors to the Louvre are invited to examine two sculptures that illustrate this: A beautiful winged ibex from fifth century B.C. Iran, probably used as a handle of a wine jar; and the Nike (winged Victory) of Samothrace from the second century B.C. Good images of these can also be seen in Alexandra Bonfante-Warren's *The Louvre* (New York: Art Resource/Hugh Lauter Levin Associates, Inc., 2000). Also, visitors to the Pergamum Museum in the former East Berlin can examine the depiction of Athena and Alcyoneus, on the Great Frieze, Altar of Zeus, ca. 180 B.C., again showing fully fledged winged creatures, but not the degree of accuracy or fidelity displayed by the contemporaneous Nike.

52. Krystyna Weinstein, *The Art of Medieval Manuscripts* (London: Hamlyn-Reed International Books, 1997), 74.

53. The detailing of the angel in the Annunciation depicted in the *Hastings Hours,* a notable Flemish manuscript (ca. 1480) offers a particularly fine example: see ibid., 91. Examples of all these artists can be found in leading European and American galleries. Good examples from the collections of the Victoria and Albert Museum, London, are, first, by an unknown artisan of northern France, *Angel of the Annunciation,* an oak, gilded, and polychromed figure, ca. 1415–1450, Cat. No. A. 10–1914; Michelozzo di Bartelommeo (1396–1472), *Adoring Angel,* a marble relief, Cat. No. 934–1904; and Andrea Della Robbia (1435–1525), two blue-and-white terra cotta wall hangings, *Cherub with a Label* and *Virgin and Child,* Cat. Nos. 72–1866 and 7547–1861. (I thank Martin Durrant of the V&A for facilitating my research into these works.) The Smithsonian's National Gallery of Art, Washington, D.C., contains its own notable examples, including: Simone Martini, *The Angel of the Annunciation,* tempera on panel, (ca. 1333, and thus an important early transitional work), Samuel H. Kress Collection, Cat. No. 1939.1.216; Andrea Della Robbia, *The Adoration of the Child,* glazed terra cotta, Kress Collection, Cat. No. 1961.1.21; Andrea Della Robbia, *Madonna and Child with Cherubim,* glazed terra cotta, Andrew W. Mellon Collection, Cat. No. 1937.1.122; workshop of Andrea Della Robbia, *Madonna and Child with God the Father and Cherubim,* glazed terra cotta, Mellon Collection, Cat. No. 1937.1.123; Petrus Christus, *The Nativity,* oil on panel, ca. 1444–1472, Mellon Collection, Cat. No. 1937.1.40; Fra Carnevale (Bartolomeo di Giovanni Corradini), *The Annunciation,* tem-

pera on panel, ca. 1448, Kress Collection, Cat. No. 1939.1.218. Another is Gerard David's *Virgin and Child with Four Angels,* oil on wood, ca. 1505, from the Bruges (Netherlandish) school, in the collections of the Metropolitan Museum of Art, Cat. No. 1977.1.1, depicting angels in the act of hovering with fully fledged and cambered high-aspect-ratio wings in various stages of the "power stroke" accompanying lift generation.

54. Lynn White, Jr., *Medieval Technology and Social Change* (London: Oxford University Press, 1969 ed.), 79–103; White's "Medieval Uses of Air," *Scientific American,* 270, n. 2 (Aug. 1970): 2–10, is an excellent and thought-provoking source on how medieval society regarded flight and flying. The de Milemete bee-hurler is in his *De nobilitatibus,* folios f.74b and f.75a, 148–49.

55. Grant, 356.

56. Churchill, *Birth,* 87. The history of Malmesbury is well covered in two works, Bernulf Hodge, *A History of Malmesbury* (Minety, Eng.: Taylor & Sons, 1976); and Stan Hudson's *A Hill Top Town: Fact and Legend* (Exeter, UK: Westprint, 1977).

57. William of Malmesbury, *The History of the Kings of England,* v. 3, part 1, of Rev. Joseph Stevenson, ed., *The Church Historians of England* (London: Seeleys, 1854), 212, §225. I thank the late Mr. Stan Hudson, three-term mayor of Malmesbury and a freeman of the Borough, the staff of the Athelstan Museum, and Air Commodore Andrew Lambert, RAF, for facilitating my research on Eilmer. For a good analysis of his gliding attempt, see Maxwell Woosnam, *Eilmer: Eleventh Century Monk of Malmesbury—The Flight and the Comet* (Malmesbury, UK: Friends of Malmesbury Abbey, 1986), 22–31. See also White, "Eilmer of Malmesbury," 98; and Schapiro, 144–145. Thanks to misreading of manuscripts by a later historian, Eilmer is sometimes incorrectly rendered as "Oliver."

58. In Latin, "Ipse ferebat causam ruinæ quod caudam in posteriori parte oblitus fuerit."

59. Over a quarter century ago, in my thirst for knowledge, I felt compelled to visit, refreshingly finding it well worth the effort; alas, on a recent trip I discovered that it is no more.

60. William of Malmesbury, Stevenson edition, 212, §225. The comet that Eilmer saw was, incidentally, the same whose periodic patterns were plotted later by Edmond Halley, the noted Royal Astronomer, for whom it is now named.

61. Needham, 30, 53.

62. See, for example, Lt. Col. Henry W. L. Hime, RA, *The Origins of Artillery* (London: Longmans, Green, and Co., 1915), 144. See also Willy Ley, *Rockets, Missiles, and Space Travel* (New York: The Viking Press, 1961 ed.), 52–53. As an aside, Ley, a genuine German rocket pioneer in his own right—but an anti-Nazi who fled the Third Reich and thus played no role in its development of terror weapons—was the first great historian of early rocketry, as well as a notable promoter of understanding of rockets and spaceflight.

63. Needham, 31–41. Ley, as previously cited, believed the ten paces referred to the circular blast area of a rocket's incendiary warhead; however, I think that Needham's interpretation is correct. I believe the ten paces refers to the length of the projected flame of the *huo ch'iang,* the fire lance itself, and thus must be considered the effective engagement range for the weapon.

64. Maj. Gen. J. F. C. Fuller, *Armament and History: A Study of the Influence of Armament on History from the Dawn of Classical Warfare to the Second World War* (New York:

Charles Scribner's Sons, 1945), 77–89. Regarding connections between the Chinese and Catholicism, see Needham 49–52. See also de Milemete, *De nobilitatibus,* folio f.70b, 140; and Lynn Montross, *War through the Ages* (New York: Harper & Row, third edition, 1960), 176–195.

65. Needham, 47–48; there is likewise a good discussion (with numerous illustrations) of these in Temple, 237–241.

66. Or as he was known at the time, Hsue-shen Tsien, a former professor at the California Institute of Technology. For his role in modern Chinese rocketry and missile development, see Iris Chang, *Thread of the Silkworm* (New York: Basic Books, 1995), and Joan Johnson-Freese, *The Chinese Space Program: A Mystery within a Maze* (Malabar, FL: Krieger Publishing Co., 1998) 44.

67. See David Baker's magnificent survey history, *The Rocket: The History and Development of Rocket and Missile Technology* (New York: Crown Publishers, Inc., 1978), 10–11. See also Ley, 53–54. The previously cited Hime discusses Bacon's work in detail, and deciphers his coded writings, 112–113. Bacon suggested a slow-burning mix of seven parts saltpeter, five parts charcoal, and five parts sulfur. Magnus suggested a more explosive mix of six parts saltpeter, two parts charcoal, and one part sulfur. See also Needham, 49–51.

68. Denys Forrest, *Tiger of Mysore: The Life and Death of Tipu Sultan* (London: Chatto & Windus, 1970), 140. Tipu Sultan's rockets had a range of approximately 1,000 yards, with explosive warheads or a sword blade. There is an excellent and detailed summary of Tipu's rockets and rocket forces in Frank H. Winter's *The First Golden Age of Rocketry: Congreve and Hale Rockets of the Nineteenth Century* (Washington, D.C.: Smithsonian Institution Press, 1990), 1–11. One of the British officers who both encountered Indian war rockets and played a significant role in the defeat of Tipu Sultan was a certain Anglo-Irish colonel destined for greater things, named Arthur Wellesley. See Christopher Hibbert, *Wellington: A Personal History* (Reading, MA: Perseus Books), 27–29, and Jac Weller, *Wellington in India* (London: Longman, 1972), 33–81. See also Baker, 12–14; Ley, 55–71; and Fuller, 157, 166, n. 45.

69. Quoted in Mike McCormack, "Historical Happenings: Icons of Independence," *The National Hibernian Digest,* v. 67, n. 3 (May-June 2000): 19. See also Winter, *Golden Age,* 15.

70. It is interesting to note that Emmet was the first of two nineteenth-century rocketeers executed by governing authorities, and a third followed in the twentieth century. The second was the Russian Nikolai Kibalchich (sometimes Kibaltchitch), one of six members of a terrorist cell called the Will of the People, that assassinated Tsar Alexander II with a bomb in March 1881. Kibalchich became a venerated figure in Marxist mythography surrounding the Soviet space program. See Ley, 89–91; and Walter A. McDougall, . . . *The Heavens and the Earth: A Political History of the Space Age* (New York: Basic Books, Inc., 1985), 17–18. The third was a not-so-well-known rocket-flight enthusiast who fell victim to the Nazis: the Polish cleric Maximilian Kolbe, murdered at Auschwitz after voluntarily substituting for a fellow inmate selected for death. Father Kolbe, incidentally, is now *Saint* Maximilian and so presumably has a special affection for astronauts and cosmonauts, something would-be space voyagers should keep in mind, as he might well become the St. Christopher of the space age.

71. Winter, *Golden Age,* 15–28. See also Maj. Gen. Sir William Congreve, *A Treatise on the General Principles, Powers, and Facility of Application of the Congreve Rocket System as Compared with Artillery* (London: Longman, Rees, Orme, Brown, and Green, 1827),

passim, copy in the archives of the National Air and Space Museum (hereafter NASM Archives), Smithsonian Institution, Washington, D.C. For an examination of Congreve's work, see Frank H. Winter, "Sir William Congreve, 1772–1828" in Ernst Steinhoff, ed., *The Eagle Has Returned*, pt. 2 of v. 45, *Science and Technology: A Supplement to Advances in the Astronautical Sciences* (San Diego: American Astronautical Society, 1976), 224–237.

72. Winter, *Golden Age*, 179–191. See also William Hale, *Treatise on the Comparative Merits of a Rifle Gun and Rotary Rocket Considered as a Mechanical Means of Ensuring a Correct Line of Flight to a Body Impelled through Space* (London: W. Mitchell, Military Bookseller, 1863); Great Britain, Public Record Office, British Patent A.D. 1844, No. 10,008, July 11, 1844, *Hale's Improvements in Rockets* (London: Eyre and Spottiswoode, 1854): 2–5; Brig. Gen. Stephen V. Bénet, U.S. Army, *A Collection of Annual Reports and Other Important Papers, Relating to the Ordnance Department*, v. 2, 1845 1860 (Washington, D.C.: Government Printing Office, 1880), 152–153, 212–213; and Richard P. Hallion, "The Evolution of William Hale's Spin-Stabilized War Rockets: A Patent Study in Nineteenth Century Rocket Technology," College Park: Department of History, University of Maryland, 18 May 1971, copies in the Hale Papers, NASM Archives.

73. For example see E. J. Hoffschmidt and W. H. Tantum IV, *German Combat Weapons* (Old Greenwich, CT: WE, Inc., 1968), 172, 209–211; and W. H. Tantum IV, and E. J. Hoffschmidt, *Japanese Combat Weapons* (Old Greenwich, CT: WE Inc., 1968), 171–172.

74. Temple, pp. 191–192; for the Flemish drawing, see Gibbs-Smith, *Aviation*, Fig. 1, xvi, 6; it is from a manuscript in the Royal Library in Copenhagen, n. 3384.8. Gibbs-Smith also shows a detail of the Virgin and Child painting (Plate I, a, after p. 16), but it is shown and discussed in much greater detail in Philippe Boulay's "L'hèlicoptére du Petit Jésus," *Le fana de l'aviation*, n. 365 (April 2000): 26–27. The actual painting is in the Muséc de Tessé, at Mans.

75. Laufer states that kites were introduced into Europe "not earlier than the end of the sixteenth century" (37). But the earliest depiction of a European kite actually dates to over 200 years earlier, in Walter de Milemete's *De nobilitatibus sapientiis et prudentiis regum* of 1326. See Hart, *Dream*, 42–43, for a reproduction of a plate from Milemete's treatise. For the aeronautical climate of this time, see Charles Gibbs-Smith, *The Invention of the Aeroplane, 1799–1909* (London: Faber & Faber, 1965).

76. The others being *flight by enclosed gas, stable winged gliding flight, winged flight under power*, and *powered, sustained, and controlled flight by inhabited airships and aircraft*.

CHAPTER TWO

1. Alan Palmer, *The Decline and Fall of the Ottoman Empire* (New York: Barnes & Noble Books, 1992), 1–2. See also Fuller, 82; Gimpel, 235; G. I. Brown, *The Big Bang: A History of Explosives* (Stroud, Eng.: Sutton Publishing, Ltd., 1998), 57–58; Fischer quote from his *Great Wave*, 57.

2. Introduction by Robert N. Linscott, in Leonardo da Vinci, trans. and edited by Edward MacCurdy and Linscott, *The Notebooks of Leonardo da Vinci* (New York: the Modern Library, 1957), vii (hereafter Leonardo).

3. Ibid., 233; see also Gimpel, 141–142.

4. Giorgio Vasari, *Lives of the Artists*, v. 1 (London: Penguin Books, 1987 ed.), 257.

5. Leonardo, 229; see also 226–228, and the previously cited Goldstein, *Flying Machine and Modern Literature*, 26–33.

6. Leonardo, 252.

7. For a good appreciation of Leonardo's place in the history of science and technology, see George Sarton's classic *Six Wings: Men of Science in the Renaissance* (Bloomington: Indiana University Press, 1957), 219–238. Charles Gibbs-Smith and Gareth Rees's *The Inventions of Leonardo da Vinci* (Oxford: Phaidon, 1978), 12–26, 39, has an excellent collection of drawings and photographs of Leonardo's aviation concepts; Clive Hart's *The Prehistory of Flight* (Berkeley: University of California Press, 1985), examines Leonardo's ornithopter designs in detail on 108–115 and subsequently those of others as well. See also Charles Dollfus and Henri Bouché, *Histoire de l'aéronautique* (Paris: l'Illustration, 1932), 5 (hereafter Dollfus and Bouché); and Ivor B. Hart, *The Mechanical Investigations of Leonardo da Vinci* (London: Chapman & Hall, Ltd., 1925), 143–193.

8. Vasari, 1: 268–269. For the notion that he might have actually constructed small model hot air balloons, see Leslie Gardiner, *Man in the Clouds: The Story of Vincenzo Lunardi* (Edinburgh: W. & R. Chambers Ltd., 1963), 16. The key seems to be how Vasari has been translated, for some have taken his words to mean hot air, and others ambient air, or breaths.

9. Leonardo, 226.

10. Hart, *Dream,* 138.

11. Gibbs-Smith and Rees, X; see also Linscott in Leonardo, xvii-xviii.

12. There is a provocative discussion in Goldstein on the bird as symbol and inspiration: see 1–3, 30–61; Hart, *Prehistory,* 28–107, has a thorough discussion on birds as symbolic and practical flying creatures.

13. Leonardo, 219–232. See also R. Giacomelli and E. Pistolesi, "Historical Sketch," in William F. Durand, ed., *Aerodynamic Theory: A General Review of Progress under a Grant from the Daniel Guggenheim Fund for the Promotion of Aeronautics,* v. 1 (Berlin: Julius Springer Verlag, 1934): 308; John D. Anderson, Jr., *A History of Aerodynamics and Its Impact on Flying Machines,* v. 8 in the *Cambridge Aerospace Series* (Cambridge: Cambridge University Press, 1997), 23.

14. For a fascinating examination of avian evolution that employs a broader perspective adapted from the history of mechanical flight, see anthropologist Pat Shipman's *Taking Wing: Archaeopteryx and the Evolution of Bird Flight* (New York: Simon & Schuster, 1998), 49–67, 139–169, 204–210, and 238–261.

15. See Curt Suplee, "Team's Model Demonstrates How Evolution Obeys Mathematical Laws," *Washington Post,* 7 April 1997. This general behavior has given rise to a variety of "three-quarter," "one-quarter," and "minus-one-quarter" laws to explain biological differences governing metabolic rate, life span, and heart rate differences both among and between species.

16. Interestingly, though, the differences do not match the relative differences in size. For example, the bird may be $1/10,000$ (10^{-4}) the size of the human, but its heart rate is only 10 times (10^1) as great.

17. Michael Segre, *In the Wake of Galileo* (New Brunswick, NJ: Rutgers University Press, 1991), 129–130. For more on Borelli, see 53–54 and 68; the Academy of Experiment in reality was far less supportive of empiricism than its name implied, as Segre amply shows: see 117–142.

18. Daniel J. Boorstin, *The Discoverers* (New York: Random House, 1983), 377.

19. Ibid., 378; Giovanni A. Borelli, *The Flight of Birds,* n. 6 of the *Aeronautical Classics* series (London: The Aeronautical Society of Great Britain and King, Sell & Olding,

Ltd., 1911), 36, 36–40. This is a translation of the section *De Volatu* of *De Motu Animalium*. I have examined a second edition dating to 1685 of *De Motu Animalium* in the rare book collection of the Royal Aeronautical Society, and I thank Mr. Brian Riddle, the RAeS librarian, for making it available for my use for comparative purposes. The quote in the original text is from part I, proposition 204. Incidentally, the 1911 translation of *De Volatu* is also available as a CD-ROM. See the Archive Britain Campaign, *Royal Aeronautical Society Archive Series*, v. 2: *Aeronautical Classics* (Portsmouth: Archive Britain, 2000). Archive Britain may be reached at www.archivebritain.com.

20. *Der Vogelflug als Grundlage der Fliegerkunst* (1889), published in English as *Bird Flight as the Basis of Aviation* (London: Longmans, Green, and Co., 1911). I have used "flying art" in place of "aviation" as I think it more accurately reflects the author's intent and the thrust of the book.

21. As discussed more fully subsequently.

22. Gibbs-Smith, *Aviation*, 27. And flapping still has its enthusiasts today. See, for example, Graham Chandler, "Ready, Set, Flap!" *Air and Space*, v. 16, n. 5 (Dec. 2001–Jan. 2002), 36–41.

23. Silvio A. Bedini and Derek J. De Solla Price, "Instrumentation," in Kranzberg and Pursell, v. 1: 178. See also Frederick L. Nussbaum, *The Triumph of Science and Reason, 1660–1685*, a volume in the *Rise of Modern Europe* series (New York: Harper & Row, 1953), 9, 11, 24, 121.

24. Archimedes, *On Floating Bodies*, translated by Sir Thomas Heath (Chicago: Encyclopedia Britannica, Inc., 1975 ed.), book I, postulate 1, propositions 5 and 6: 540; for more on Oresme and the tradition of the thought experiment, see the previously cited Grant, 153–182; and Lindberg, 54–55, 239, 241, 246, and 258–261; for medieval and Renaissance attitudes towards air and aether, see Hart, *Prehistory*, 1–27.

25. The larger folio work was his *Prodromo overo saggio di alcune inventioni nuove premesso all'Arte Maestra*, published in Brescia in 1670. The shorter work, chapter six of the larger volume, was entitled *La Nave Volante*. J. E. Hodgson in his *The History of Aeronautics in Great Britain: From the Earliest Times to the Latter Half of the Nineteenth Century* (London: Oxford University Press and Humphrey Milford, 1924) notes, (393) that this shorter volume was reissued in 1784 after the first flight of the Montgolfiers in Messina, Milan, and Rome. Then, in 1910, the Aeronautical Society of Great Britain (now the Royal Aeronautical Society) sponsored a larger extract, translating chapter 5 (on flying automata) and chapter 6, and issuing it as Francesco Lana [de] [Terzi], *The Aerial Ship*, n. 4 of the *Aeronautical Classics* series (London: The Aeronautical Society of Great Britain and King, Sell & Olding, Ltd., 1910). It is this later translation that I have used in this text; see also Laufer, 22.

26. Lana de Terzi, 22.

27. Ibid., 26–27.

28. Joseph Needham, *Science and Civilisation in China*, v. 4 (Cambridge: Cambridge University Press, 1965), 596; Temple, 184; and Charles Coulston Gillispie, *The Montgolfier Brothers and the Invention of Aviation, 1783–1784* (Princeton, NJ: Princeton University Press, 1983), 24.

29. See Col. Edgar Cardoso, "Bartolomeu de Gusmão," *air BP*, n. 53 (n.d.): 11–13; Jean Riverain, *Dictionnaire des aéronautes célèbres* (Paris: Librairie Larousse, 1970) 105; Baron de Teffe, "Congrès international d'Aeronautique de 1889," *L'aéronaute*, v. 23, n. 1 (Jan. 1890): 7; and Dollfus and Bouché, 8–9. There are also other useful materials in the Gusmão biographical file, National Air and Space Museum Library and

Archives, Washington, D.C., notably a letter from Sister Luz Maria Orozco (a Fulbright Scholar in England) to NASA Headquarters, 1971, passed to the Smithsonian by Les Gaver of the NASA audiovisual support staff. The Orozco letter has an attachment from the English *Evening Post,* n. 894 (23–25 Feb. 1710), carrying an announcement and description of Gusmão's work, which she located in the collections of the Bodleian Library, Oxford University.

30. Cardoso, 13. For two noted experts' interpretations of this design, one British and one Danish, see Gibbs-Smith, *Aviation,* 14; and Lennart Ege, *Balloons and Airships* (New York: Macmillan Publishing Company, 1974), 7. See also Douglas H. Robinson, M.D., *The Dangerous Sky: A History of Aviation Medicine* (Seattle: University of Washington Press, 1973), 1.

31. Cardoso, 11–12.

32. Ibid. See also the statements of Francisco de Carvalho citing the "chronicler [Salvador] Ferreira, who assisted in the ascension," and from Ferdinand Denis, in de Teffe, 7–8; and Riverain, 105.

33. Orozco letter and attachment.

34. Will and Ariel Durant, *The Lessons of History* (New York: Simon & Schuster, Inc., 1968), 45. Jacques Barzun, *From Dawn to Decadence: 500 Years of Western Cultural Life, 1500 to Present* (New York: HarperCollins, 2000), 35, 108–109, 194–195, and 271–272; see also Dava Sobel, *Galileo's Daughter: A Historical Memoir of Science, Faith, and Love* (New York: Walker & Company, 1999), 4–5, 76, 171, 275–278.

35. Cardoso, 13.

36. Statement of Ferdinand Denis in de Teffe, 7–8. See also Henry Kamen, *The Spanish Inquisition: A Historical Revision* (London: Weidenfeld & Nicolson, 1997), 103–136, 288–304.

37. That is, generating lift by shaping a wing to take advantage of the airflow.

38. That is, generating lift by reliance on the difference in weights between air and lifting gases such as hydrogen, helium, coal gas, or hot air.

39. For example, see Barzun, 190–207.

40. Nussbaum, 11–15; see also Grant, 108–113, 148–164; and Boorstin, *Discoverers,* 378.

41. See the previously cited Fischer, *Great Wave,* 17–45. See also Nussbaum, 1–20; Green, *History,* 66–77; White, "Technology in the Middle Ages," and Hall, "Cultural, Intellectual, and Social Foundations," 68–69, 107–109; and Robert S. Cohen and Marx W. Wartofsky, eds., *Hegel and the Sciences,* v. 64 in the *Boston Studies in the Philosophy of Science* series (Boston: D. Reidel Publishing Company, 1984), 195–239; see also Jacob Burckhardt's classic *The Civilization of the Renaissance in Italy* (New York: Modern Library, 1954 ed.), 153–157, 211–217.

42. A. Rupert Hall, "Cultural, Intellectual, and Social Foundations, 1600–1750," in Kranzberg and Pursell, v. 1:109.

43. Lindberg, 203–206, has an incisive discussion of this.

44. See Paul Kennedy, *The Rise and Fall of the Great Powers: Economic Change and Military Conflict from 1500 to 2000* (London: Fontana Press, 1989), 7–15; and Green, *History,* 199–204.

45. See Pervez Amir Ali Hoodbhoy, *Islam and Science: Religious Orthodoxy and the Battle for Rationality* (London: Zed Books Ltd., 1991), 97–133.

46. Lindberg, 174. Emphasis added. See also G. E. von Grunebaum, *Classical Islam: A History, 600–1258* (New York: Barnes & Noble Books, 1996), 91–92, 94–95, 130–131, 207.

47. Pervez Amir Ali Hoodbhoy, "How Islam Lost Its Way," *Washington Post,* 30 Dec. 2001, B4; see also his *Islam and Science,* 100–106, and von Grunebaum, 156–158, 187, 208; Lindberg, 180, and Karen Armstrong, "Was It Inevitable?: Islam Through History," in James F. Hoge, Jr., and Gideon Rose, *How Did This Happen?: Terrorism and the New War* (New York: Public Affairs, 2001), 64.

48. Hoodbhoy, "How Islam Lost Its Way." For the interrelationship between Greek, Hindu, and Islamic mathematics, see the previously cited Rouse Ball, 144–165; interestingly, he considered Islamic mathematics "as a whole, second-rate both in quantity and quality" to Greek and later European work.

49. Armstrong, "Was It Inevitable?" 65.

50. Hoodbhoy, "How Islam Lost Its Way."

51. Turner, *Science in Medieval Islam,* 203, 205 and the previously cited Green, *History,* 201. Such behavior resonates even to the present time, perhaps best exemplified by the wanton destruction of Buddhist statues by the Taliban in Afghanistan in the spring of 2001. See Molly Moore, "Taliban: Most Statues Destroyed," *Washington Post,* 4 March 2001, and Pamela Constable, "Buddhas' Rubble Marks a Turn for Taliban," *Washington Post,* 20 March 2001.

52. Lindberg, 166.

53. Ibn Khaldun, *The Muqaddima: An Introduction to History* (London: Routledge, 1978), 372–373; this example is related as well in Hoodbhoy, *Islam and Science,* 103–104.

54. Boorstin, *Discoverers,* 560.

55. Lindberg, 182, 203–206; see also Fletcher, *Moorish Spain,* 8, 133–134, 150–154.

56. Palmer, 6.

57. There is an excellent discussion of the Islamic world's attempt to respond to the West in Bernard Lewis, *What Went Wrong?: Western Impact and Middle Eastern Response* (New York: Oxford University Press, 2001), especially 7, 12, 72–81, 152–159.

58. After the Taliban abandoned Kabul in November 2001, the citizens celebrated by quickly raising kites aloft. For more on the reactionary response of Islamic fundamentalists to modern Muslim society, see Fischer, 230–231.

59. Needham, *Science in Traditional China,* 122. For an interesting perspective on this, see Derk Bodde, *Chinese Thought, Society, and Science: The Intellectual and Social Background of Science and Technology in Pre-modern China* (Honolulu: University of Hawaii Press, 1991), 158–172.

60. Kennedy, 7–9; Boorstin, *Discoverers,* 168–201.

61. Quote from Ricci's journals in Boorstin, *Discoverers,* 57. There is a good discussion of Chinese instrumentation and Ricci's reaction in Colonel Sir Henry Yule's *The Book of Ser [sic] Marco Polo the Venetian Concerning the Kingdoms and Marvels of the East,* v. 1 (London: John Murray, 1926 ed.), 448–456 n. 1

62. Quoted in Fergus Fleming, *Barrow's Boys* (New York: Grove Press, 1998), 4.

63. Boorstin, *Discoverers,* 201.

64. Kennedy, 14.

65. Palmer, 8–15.

66. Lewis Mumford, *Technics and Civilization* (New York: Harcourt, Brace, 1939), 14. See also A. Rupert Hall, "Early Modern Technology, to 1600," in Kranzberg and Pursell, I: 97–98.

67. Needham has an excellent discussion of the Su Sung clock in his *Science in Traditional China,* 15–22, together with some excellent drawings and reconstructions; see also Gimpel, 150–152; Boorstin, *Discoverers,* 56–78. I have benefited as well from con-

versations regarding Chinese and European clocks and their associated "feedback technology" with Dr. Otto Mayr at the University of Maryland in 1971.

68. Lewis, *What Went Wrong?*, 117–125.

69. Gimpel, 170, 153–169, and Heer, *Medieval World*, 46.

70. For examples involving Lord Kelvin, Simon Newcomb, Lord Rutherford, Vannevar Bush, Richard van der Riet Vooley, and Harry Wexler, see Letter, Kelvin to Baden-Powell, 8 December 1896, from the letters files, folder 13, in the Library, Royal Aeronautical Society, 4 Hamilton Place, London; Simon Newcomb, "The Outlook for the Flying Machine," *The Independent*, 22 Oct 1903, 2509; Testimony of Dr. Edward Teller, *Inquiry into Satellite and Missile Programs*, part I of *Hearings before the Preparedness Investigating Subcommittee of the Committee on Armed Services* (Washington, D.C.: United States Senate, 25 Nov 1957), 28; Testimony of Dr. Vannevar Bush, *Hearings on Atomic Energy* (Washington, D.C.: United States Senate, Special Committee on Atomic Energy, 27–30 Nov. and 3 Dec. 1945): 179–180; Arthur C. Clarke, *Profiles of the Future* (New York: Harper & Row, 1962), 8, and Arthur C. Clarke, *The Promise of Space* (New York: Harper & Row, 1968), 91. Lee D. Saegesser's "Quotes that Failed: A Chronology of Unhelpful Utterances," NASA publication HHN-112, June 1971, is a wonderful compilation containing many such pronouncements and is available through the NASA History Office, Washington, D.C.

71. Plato, *The Republic, in The Dialogues of Plato,* trans. by Benjamin Jowett, a volume in the *Great Books of the Western World* series (Chicago: Encyclopedia Britannica, Inc., 1975 ed.), 352, 398. The previously cited Landels, *Engineering in the Ancient World,* has an excellent and balanced discussion of this on 186–189.

72. Quote from Lindberg, 47.

73. Segre, 10.

74. Francis Bacon, *Novum Organum,* a volume in the *Great Books of the Western World* series (Chicago: Encyclopedia Britannica, Inc., 1952), 120, 125. See also Hall, "Cultural, Intellectual, and Social Foundations," 108–109.

75. Barzun, 204. For an example of the contrary view, see Stephen G. Brush, "Can Science Come Out of the Laboratory Now?", *The Bulletin of the Atomic Scientists*, v. 32, n. 4 (April 1976): 40–43. See also Benjamin Farrington's classic biography, *Francis Bacon: Philosopher of Industrial Science* (New York: Henry Schuman, 1949) 3–27, and the previously cited Lienhard, *The Engines of our Ingenuity*, 75–78.

76. Justus von Liebig, "On the Study of the Natural Sciences," in Wolfgang Schirmacher, *German Essays on Science in the Nineteenth Century*, v. 36 of *The German Library* (New York: Continuum Publishing Company, 1996), 53. See also Lorenz Oken's "On the Utility of Natural History," in the same work, 26.

77. Thomas Henry Huxley, "Science and Culture," in John J. Cadden and Patrick R. Brostowin, *Science and Literature: A Reader* (Boston: D.C. Heath and Company, 1964), 12.

78. Kendall A Birr, "Science in American Industry," in David D. Van Tassel and Michael G. Hall, eds., *Science and Society in the United States,* a volume in *The Dorsey Series in American History* (Homewood, Il: The Dorsey Press, 1966), 36. I am reminded of a story about the late John Fozard, a gifted British aircraft designer. Newly graduated, he told a distant relative he was an engineer; she looked at him in shock and disbelief: in her rural area, an "engineer" was a person who drained sewers and ditches (personally related to the author by John Fozard).

79. Plato, *The Republic,* 366; Aristotle, *Politics,* trans. by Benjamin Jowett, in *The Works of Aristotle,* v. 2, a volume in the *Great Books of the Western World* series (Chicago: Ency-

clopedia Britannica, Inc., 1952), 533; Archimedes' quote from Plutarch, "Marcellus," in *The Lives of the Noble Grecians and Romans*, Dryden translation, a volume in the *Great Books of the Western World* series (Chicago: Encyclopedia Britannica, Inc., 1952), 253; da Vinci quote from Gimpel, 143, who also notes "Leonardo's greatest problems were caused by the contempt in which he was held by the humanists" (142). For more on this, see Hall, "Cultural, Intellectual, and Social Foundations," Kranzberg and Pursell, v. 1: 107; Robert P. Multhauf, "The Scientist and the 'Improver' of Technology," *Technology and Culture*, v. 1, n. 1 (Winter 1959), passim; and Barzun, 190–207.

80. Arnold J. Toynbee, *A Study of History*, v. 1 (London: Oxford University Press and the Royal Institute of International Affairs, 1955 ed.): 3, n. 1. See also Derek J. De Solla Price, "Is Technology Historically Independent of Science? A Study in Statistical Historiography," and John Beer's "The Historical Relations of Science and Technology," both essays in *Technology and Culture*, v. 6, n. 4 (Fall 1965): 547–552, 553–568; for an excellent treatment on the engineering process as applied to aeronautics, see Walter G. Vincenti's *What Engineers Know and How They Know It* (Baltimore: John Hopkins University Press, 1990), a series of notable case studies.

81. Edwin Layton, "Mirror-Image Twins: The Communities of Science and Technology in Nineteenth-Century America," *Technology and Culture*, v. 11, n. 4 (Fall 1971): 562–580.

82. Wolfgang Schirmacher, *German Essays on Science in the Twentieth Century*, v. 82 of *The German Library* (New York Continuum Publishing Company, 1996), xii.

83. For various perspectives on the role of (and relationships among) technology, science, invention, and innovation, see Leo Marx, *The Machine in the Garden: Technology and the Pastoral Ideal in America* (New York: Oxford University Press, 1964), 145–169; George H. Daniels, *Science in American Society: A Social History* (New York: Alfred A. Knopf, 1971), 154–173, 255–256, 290–291; Peter F. Drucker's "Technological Trends in the Twentieth Century," in Kranzberg and Pursell, v. 2: *Technology in the Twentieth Century*, 10–22; and Paul Johnson, *The Birth of the Modern: World Society, 1815–1830* (London: Phoenix, 1992), 541–584.

CHAPTER THREE

1. Arthur Miller, "Death of a Salesman," in Edgar V. Roberts and Henry E. Jacobs, eds., *Literature: An Introduction to Reading and Writing* (Englewood Cliffs, NJ: Prentice-Hall, 1995 ed.), 1302.

2. John B. Rae, "Energy Conversion," in Kranzberg and Pursell, I. 341.

3. "La conquete des airs et le centenaire de Montgolfier," *L'astronomie*, n. 7 (July 1883): 237–247, copy in Montgolfier brothers' file, Musée de l'Air et de l'Espace (hereafter MAE), le Bourget Airport, Paris. I thank Christian Tilatti, le Conservateur, and Philippe Gras, le Chef du centre de documentation, for their assistance in my research on this and other aspects of early French aviation. Gillispie, 10–16. See chapters IV and V of Joseph Lecornu, *La navigation aérienne: Histoire documentaire et anecdotique* (Paris: Vuibert & Nony, Éditeurs, second edition, ca. 1905), for an excellent summary of the Montgolfiers work, and also Dollfus and Bouché, 10–15.

4. Marie-Hélène Reynaud, "Les Frères Montgolfier," in Antoine Dumas et al., eds., *Le temps des ballons* (Paris: Éditions de La Martinière and the Musée de l'Air et de l'Espace, 1995), 24. This latter is an excellent history of French ballooning and its impact, with a series of well-focused essays by noted experts across a variety of subjects. See also Gillispie, 17. The date of November 4 is from Roger Pineau, "Balloon-

ing in the United States: From Straw to Propane," in Eugene M. Emme, ed., *Two Hundred Years of Flight in America: A Bicentennial Survey,* v. I of the *American Astronautical Society History Series* (San Diego: American Astronautical Society, 1977), 41.

5. A. Rupert Hall, "Cultural, Intellectual, and Social Foundations, 1600–1750," in Kranzberg and Pursell, I, 114.

6. Bern Dibner, "The Beginning of Electricity," in Kranzberg and Pursell, I, 441; Gillespie, 21–22.

7. Turner, 25. Turner, incidentally, was a noted British balloonist who made a number of long-distance flights early in the twentieth century.

8. Reynaud, 28; Gillispie, 3–4, 21–24. See also Letter, Étienne Montgolfier to Barthélèmy Faujas de Saint-Fond, n.d., reprinted in J. Jobé, *The Romance of Ballooning: The Story of the Early Aeronauts* (New York: A Studio Book, Edita Lausanne and the Viking Press, 1971), 13. The latter is a remarkable compilation of illustrations and excerpts covering the entire history of ballooning.

9. Christian Bailleux, "Le rôle des physiciens au dix-huitième siècle: L'étude des gaz: l'hydrogène," in Dumas, 13; Gillispie, 23, 27–30. Cavallo's work with bubbles is from Turner, 25, and Gibbs-Smith, *Aviation,* 17.

10. Robert P. Multhauf, "Industrial Chemistry in the Nineteenth Century," Kranzberg and Pursell, I, 479; Bailleux, 13.

11. Bailleux, 12–13; Gillispie, 29–31; Turner, 26.

12. Quoted by Turner, 27.

13. Gen. Pierre Lissarrague, *Premiers envols* (Paris: Editions Joël Cuénot, 1982), 17; Tom D. Crouch, *The Eagle Aloft: Two Centuries of the Balloon in America* (Washington, D.C.: Smithsonian Institution Press, 1983), 14. Also see Pineau, 42, Donald Dale Jackson, *The Aeronauts,* a volume in the *Epic of Flight* series (Alexandria, VA: Time-Life Books, 1980), 14, and Gillispie, 52, for further slightly different versions of this oft-told anecdote.

14. Reprinted as Appendix C in E. Charles Vivian, *A History of Aeronautics* (London: W. Collins Sons & Co., Ltd., 1921), 502–503.

15. *Mercure de France,* n. 37 (13 Sept. 1783), reprinted in Jobé, 17.

16. Gillispie, 37.

17. Reynaud, 28–29; Gillispie, 39–43; Lecornu, chapter IV; see also Simon Schama, *Citizens: A Chronicle of the French Revolution* (New York: Alfred A. Knopf, 1989), 123; and Antonia Fraser, *Marie Antoinette: The Journey* (New York: Nan A. Talese/Doubleday, 2001), 208.

18. Reynaud, 29–30; Lissarrague, *Premiers envols,* 16; and Gillispie, plate VII, between 12–13 have excellent contemporary illustrations of the balloon.

19. Reynaud, 30; see also Dollfus and Bouché, 13–18.

20. From the *Journal de Paris,* 22 Nov. 1783, reprinted in Jobé, p. 20. See also Audouin Dollfus, "Premiers envols," in Dumas, 34–35; Gillispie, 44–56.

21. The marquis d'Arlandes, "The First Manned Flight," reprinted in Neville Duke and Edward Lanchbery, *The Saga of Flight: From Leonardo da Vinci to the Guided Missile* (New York: John Day, 1961), 42.

22. Quoted in Jackson, 24.

23. Gillispie, 56–58; see also Dollfus and Bouché, 19–23, and a good map of the flight on p. 20.

24. Quoted in Schieldrop, 22; see also A. Dollfus, 36–37.

25. Lecornu, 57–58.

26. James Glaisher, Camille Flammarion, W. de Fonville, and Gaston Tissandier, *Travels in the Air* (London: Richard Bentley, 1871), 6–7 (hereafter Glaisher et al.).

27. Ibid.; see also Robinson, *Dangerous Sky*, 3, Pineau, 42, and Richard P. Hallion, "Aerospace Medicine Nears the Millennium: Adaptation, Anticipation, and Advancement," Louis Bauer Memorial Lecture, Seventieth Annual Scientific Meeting of the Aerospace Medical Association, Detroit, Michigan, 17 May 1999, subsequently printed in *Aviation and Space Environmental Medicine,* v. 70, n. 11 (1999): 17–24.

28. Sir Walter Raleigh, *The War in the Air: Being the Story of the Part Played in the Great War by the Royal Air Force,* I (London: Hamish Hamilton, 1969 ed.) 32, 29–30.

29. Nelly Fouchet, "La mode 'au ballon,' la ballomanie," in Dumas, 42–62, is an excellent summary and is superbly illustrated, largely from the collections of the MAE; also there are excellent photographs of such items in Jackson, 36–41, Lissarrague, *Premiers envols,* 22–25; and Dollfus and Bouché, 28–30. Even before the balloon was a century old, people recognized how unique its contributions to cultural life had been. See Georges Lecocq, "La céramique et les aérostats," *L'aéronaute: Bulletin mensuel illustré de la navigation aérienne,* v. 10, n. 1 (Jan. 1877): 8–21 (hereafter editions of this journal are cited as *L'aéronaute*). See also the previously cited J. E. Hodgson, *The History of Aeronautics in Great Britain,* 215–217, and figures 68–69.

30. Walpole to Mann, 2 Dec. 1783, reprinted in Hodgson, 199–200.

31. F. M. Feldhaus, "Goethe und die Luftschiffahrt," *Illustrierte Aeronautische Mitteilungen,* v. 10, n. 9 (Sept. 1906), 298.

32. Quoted in Jackson, 12.

33. Letter, GW to Du Portail, 4 Apr. 1784, in John C. Fitzpatrick, ed., *The Writings of George Washington, from the Original Manuscript Sources, 1745–1799,* XXVII, June 11, 1783–November 28, 1784 (Washington, D.C.: Government Printing Office, 1938); 387.

34. Max Leher, "Lustige und traurige Episoden aus den ersten Zeiten der Luftschiff-Ära," *Illustrierte Aëronautische Mitteilungen,* v.9, n. 12 (Dec. 1905): 387–388; A. Dollfus, 38–39.

35. *Maryland Journal and Baltimore Advertiser* (25 June 1785), reprinted in Jeremiah Millbank, Jr., *The First Century of Flight in America: An Introductory Survey* (Princeton, NJ: Princeton University Press, 1943), 21–23. See also Pineau, 44, and Jobé, 41.

36. Victor Robinson, M.D., "Discovery of the Balloon," *Ciba Symposia,* v, n. 9 (Dec. 1943): 1622; see also Turner, 28–29, and Raleigh, 33–37. Lunardi, an appealing figure whose work was tragically brief (he died after a short and sudden illness) is the subject of a good biography, Leslie Gardiner's *Man in the Clouds: The Story of Vincenzo Lunardi* (Edinburgh: W. & R. Chambers Ltd., 1963); see particularly 4–5, and 39–64.

37. Samuel Johnson to Sir Joshua Reynolds, 18 Sept. 1784, in James Boswell, *Life of Johnson,* ed. by R. W. Chapman, a volume in *World's Classics* series (Oxford: Oxford University Press, 1980), 1353.

38. SJ to Dr. Richard Brocklesby, 6 Oct. 1784, Boswell, 1343.

39. SJ to Dr. Richard Brocklesby, 29 Sept. 1784, Boswell, 1342.

40. Ege, 103–104; Jeffries' letter describing the voyage is reprinted in Jobé, 48.

41. A. Dollfus, 40; Albert Francis Zahm, *Aërial Navigation: A Popular Treatise on the Growth of Air Craft and on Aëronautical Meteorology* (New York: D. Appleton and Company, 1911), 53.

42. Schama, 127.

43.   Quoted in Silvio A. Bedini, *Thomas Jefferson: Statesman of Science* (New York: Macmillan Publishing Company, 1990), 134. For Jefferson's interest in ballooning, see 122–123, 133–134, 141, 147, and 231.

44.   Robinson, "Discovery of the Balloon," 1620; Ege, 105–106.

CHAPTER FOUR

1.   Frederick Stansbury Haydon, *Aeronautics in the Union and Confederate Armies, with a Survey of Military Aeronautics Prior to 1861,* v. I (Baltimore: Johns Hopkins University Press, 1941), 2, n.6. Haydon's book is a remarkably detailed and insightful account, and easily ranks as one of the great works in aerospace historiography.

2.   Ibid., 2, n.7. The author of this work is generally considered to be William Cooke, but the identification of Cooke as the author is not completely certain.

3.   Ibid., 4, n.12.

4.   Letter, TJ to Philip Turpin, 28 Apr. 1784, reprinted in Millbank, 8–9.

5.   Quoted in the previously cited Bedini, 122.

6.   Haydon 3.

7.   Walpole to Mann, 2 Dec. 1783, in Hodgson, 200.

8.   Cowper to John Newton, Dec. 1783, in Hodgson, 205.

9.   Alain Dégardin and Francis Villadier, "Des ballons pour la République," in Dumas, 74–75, Montross, 450–453; Alan Forrest, "The Nation at Arms I: The French Wars," in Charles Townshend, ed., *The Oxford History of Modern War* (Oxford, United Kingdom: Oxford University Press, 2000): 55–56.

10.   John B. Rae, "The Invention of Invention," in Kranzberg and Pursell, I, 329; Haydon, 5, n. 15.

11.   Maurice Daumas, "Lighter-than-Air Craft: The First Steps," in Daumas, ed., *The Expansion of Mechanization, 1725–1860,* v. III of *A History of Technology and Invention: Progress through the Ages* (New York: Crown Publishers, 1979), 371–373.

12.   Ibid., 373. The characterization of Jourdan as a former apprentice is from Christopher Hibbert, *The Days of the French Revolution* (New York: Morrow Quill, 1981), 257.

13.   Daumas, "Lighter-than-Air Craft," 375; Dégardin and Villadier add further information on identities and total numbers; see 78–79.

14.   Alas, while it would be nice to report that the uniform color reflected the planned aerial mission of the unit, such was not the case. The basic French national guard uniform was blue, and the distinctive balloon company markings were colored red with black trim. For a translation of the instructions and organization of the balloon company, see Capt. Howard A. Scholle, USAS, "Military Balloons during the French Revolution," *U.S. Air Service,* v. 12 (May 1927): 41–42. For a summary history of ballooning in the French army at this time, see R. S. Waters, "Ballooning in the French Army During the Revolutionary Wars," *Army Quarterly,* v. 23 (1932): 327–340; and Dollfus and Bouché, 47–50.

15.   Dégardin and Villadier, 76. Increasingly Carnot was at odds with Robespierre over the conduct of the war. The first six months of 1794 represented the peak of Robespierre's excesses, with more than 2,000 dying under the blade (1,376 in six weeks alone, from 10 June to 27 July). Robespierre himself would perish as his fellow revolutionaries recognized the "us or them" nature of the revolution had increasingly changed into a dangerous "you or me," with Robespierre increasingly acting like an

ancient despot, including forming his own religion. For this and more background behind the war, see Alfred Cobban, *A History of Modern France, I: 1715–1799* (Baltimore, MD: Penguin Books, 1962), 228–234.

16. Jobé, 67; Jackson, 75–78; see also Lecornu, *La navigation,* 90–92.

17. Montross, 457.

18. Dégardin and Villadier, 76, Haydon, plate III, Gillispie, 134, Lecornu, fig. 58, all have good artistic impressions from a variety of perspectives of this battle. Contradicting Haydon, Gillispie states that there is no evidence the Montgolfiers "took any notice of [the balloon's] employment for military observation" at the battle of Fleurus, and, further, that there was no "Montgolfier participation in an effort to develop its wartime capabilities" (134). It is difficult to imagine that the brothers were ignorant of what occurred at Fleurus. If their comments are not simply lost to history one possible explanation may be that they didn't comment upon it because the Fleurus balloon was a closed-gas balloon of the Charles type, as opposed to their own rival hot-air concept. Haydon repeats in two places the claim that Joseph Montgolfier was a key advocate of using balloons as primitive bombers. Both Haydon and Gillispie's works are thoroughly researched, and thus the final answer may never be known. But I believe Haydon is more likely correct on Joseph Montgolfier's role in the Revolution's military aeronautics, even if Gillispie is correct in his conclusions regarding the brothers' lack of comment upon Fleurus. See also Lissarrague, *Premiers envols,* 27, and Lecornu, 91–92.

19. Ege, 106–107. See also Dégardin and Villadier, 77–78.

20. Haydon, 7–11, and in particular nn. 27 and 46; for Jourdan's flight see Schama, 839; Guglielmo Ferrero, *The Two French Revolutions, 1789–1796* (New York: Basic Books, Inc., 1968), 191. See also Lissarrague, *Premiers envols,* 27.

21. The quote is from Charles Christienne and Pierre Lissarague, trans. by Francis Kianka, *A History of French Military Aviation* (Washington, D.C.: Smithsonian Institution Press, 1986), 13; see also Ege, 107.

22. In the *Heeresgeschichtliches Museum,* the Army History Museum; it is complete with basket, netting, attachment cords, and envelope—a remarkable exhibit.

23. Dégardin and Villadier, 81–83; Haydon, 12–15; see also R. D. Layman, *Before the Aircraft Carrier: The Development of Aviation Vessels, 1849–1922* (Annapolis, Maryland: Naval Institute Press, 1989), 15; Christienne and Lissarrague, 12; Owen Connelly, *Blundering to Glory: Napoleon's Military Campaigns* (Wilmington, DE: Scholarly Resources, 1999), 52–56, and Ege, 107.

24. Haydon, 16–38; Lecornu, 190–191; Layman, 13; and Peter W. Brooks, *Zeppelin Rigid Airships, 1893–1940* (London: Putnam Aeronautical Books, 1992), 18.

25. Lowe's report on his Civil War activities (submitted to Secretary of War Edwin Stanton on 26 May 1863) is in Brig. Gen. Fred C. Ainsworth and Joseph W. Kirkley, eds., *The War of the Rebellion: A Compilation of the Official Records of the Union and Confederate Armies,* series III, volume III (Washington, D.C.: Government Printing Office, 1899), 252–319. For more on Lowe, see Millbank, 119–130. The ascension and passenger figure is from Pineau, 57. See also Ege, 114.

26. Letter, JH to Simon Cameron, 21 June 1861, in Ainsworth and Kirkley, eds., *The War of the Rebellion,* series III, volume I (Washington, D.C.: Government Printing Office, 1899), 283–284.

27. For the La Mountain ascension at Hampton Roads, see James Tertius de Kay, *Moni-*

tor: The Story of the Legendary Civil War Ironclad and the Man Whose Invention Changed the Course of History (New York: Ballantine Books, 1997), 80–85; see also Layman, 115–116.

28. See the messages reprinted in Lowe Report, in Ainsworth and Kirkley, eds., *The War of the Rebellion,* series III, volume III, 279–289. The many messages and the urgency of the Union command's need for reconnaissance information speak powerfully for the value of what Lowe was furnishing.

29. Quoted in Millbank, 126. See also T. S. C. Lowe, "Observation Balloons in the Battle of Fair Oaks," *Review of Reviews,* v. 43 (1911): 186–190.

30. Millbank, 123–124; Ege, 114.

31. Haydon, 216, 342.

32. Letter, JCP to brother, 25 Nov. 1863, Collection 58.5, Elizabeth Rudder Fearrington Croom Collection, file "Pass Correspondence, July-Dec. 1863," special collections, Joyner Library, East Carolina University.

33. Millbank, 126.

34. Quoted in Hennessy, 9–10.

35. For example see Ege, 114–115.

36. Letter, GBMcC to Mary Ellen McClellan, 11 April 1862, in Stephen W. Sears, ed., *The Civil War Papers of George B. McClellan: Selected Correspondence, 1860–1865* (New York: Ticknor & Fields, 1989), 235.

37. There is a reference to McClellan's flight by an eyewitness, Union Sgt. Jacob S. Kiester. See Letter, JSK to his father, 19 April 1862, Collection 72.1, Jacob S. Kiester Papers, diaries, in the special collections of the Joyner Library, East Carolina University, Greenville, N.C. I thank David Walton of the Joyner Library for facilitating my research. Kiester, sadly, was captured almost exactly two years later and died from illness while in captivity. McClellan, incidentally, thus became the first future presidential candidate to ever fly. See also Stephen W. Sears, *George B. McClellan: The Young Napoleon* (New York: Ticknor & Fields, 1988), 100.

38. Statement of GAC in John M. Carroll, ed., *Custer in the Civil War: His Unfinished Memoirs* (San Rafael, CA: Presidio Press, 1977), 144–150.

39. For example, in Beverly Kennon's "Phil in the Balloon Corps, or, A Fight Above the Clouds," *Red, White and Blue: A Patriotic Weekly Story Paper,* v. 1, n. 28 (15 May 1897), copy in the Gimbel collection, United States Air Force Archives Library.

40. See M. M. Hambourg, "Nadar: Ein Portrait," in Maria Morris Hambourg, Françoise Heilbrun, and Philippe Néagu, eds., *Nadar* (Munich: Schirmer/Mosel, 1994), 1–33; and André Rouillé, "Nadar, photographe et aéronaute: un aventurier de la modernité," in Dumas, 86–96; see also Dollfus and Bouché, 97–103, 107.

41. Ege, 116–117.

42. Alistair Horne, *The Fall of Paris: The Siege and the Commune, 1870–1* (London: Macmillan, 1965), 6–7; see also Edgar B. Schieldrop, *The Air,* a volume in the *Conquest of Space and Time* series (New York: Philosophical Library, 1958), 15.

43. Alfred Cobban, *A History of Modern France, II: 1799–1871* (Baltimore, MD: Penguin Books, 1968), 199–204.

44. Rouillé, 93, and Gérard Lhéritier, "Les ballons de la liberté, 1870–1871," in Dumas, 102–103.

45. Lhéritier, 106–107.

46. Horne, 85.

47. Rouillé, 93; Lhéritier, 106–107; and Horne, 84–85, 138–142, 240.

48. There is a detailed chronicle and log of the siege flights in the previously cited Glaisher et al. in an unnumbered section after the preface; see also Christienne and Lissarrague, 15–17; Lecornu, 190–243; Horne, 121–131.

49. Horne, 121. See also Dollfus and Bouché, 108; Ege, 119–121, has an excellent short summary of balloon operations out of Paris.

50. Crouch, *Eagle Aloft,* quoting von Zeppelin, 284.

51. See, for example, Raleigh, *War in the Air,* 147–155; Christienne and Lissarrague, 19–20; and "Japanische Militärluftschiffahrt während der Belagerung von Port-Arthur," *Illustrierte Aëronautische Mitteilungen,* v. 9, n. 10 (October 1905): 302–303.

52. Haydon, 13; Crouch, *Eagle Aloft,* 524–527; Patrick Facon, "L'armée française et l'aviation (1891–1914)," *Revue historique des armées,* 164, n. 3 (Sept. 1986): 78.

53. Extract from report reprinted in Jobé, 27. See also Dollfus and Bouché, 105.

54. Dollfus and Bouché, 51–52. There is an interesting postscript to the story: as Garnerin separated from the balloon, it rose rapidly upwards—and then exploded in flames, perhaps from static electricity as lines rubbed the fabric of the envelope. So Garnerin was perhaps luckier than he had any right to expect! Visitors to Paris can find the Parc de Monceau in the eighth *arrondissement,* off the Boulevard de Courcelles. There is a Metro stop at the park.

55. There is an excellent summary of early scientific ballooning in Glaisher et al., part II, 105–121.

56. From Paul Bert, *Barometric Pressure: Researches in Experimental Physiology* (Columbus, OH: College Book Co., 1943 ed.), 175–176. Bert was the most distinguished aeromedical researcher of his time and this is an American translation of his classic *La pression barométrique: Rescherches de physiologie Experimentale,* a volume in the *Libraire de l'académie de médecine series* (Paris: G. Masson, 1878); Jobé, 119.

57. Victor Robinson, M.D., "Origin of Aviation Medicine," *Ciba Symposia,* v, n. 9 (Dec. 1943): 1624–1626.

58. Daumas, 375.

59. Glaisher, et al., 33–58. See also William Marriott, "The Balloon Ascents Made by Mr. James Glaisher, F.R.S., for Scientific Purposes, 1862–69," *The Aeronautical Journal,* v. 8, n. 29 (January 1904): 19–22; Raleigh, 40; Robinson, *Dangerous Sky,* 17–18; Ege, 117–119.

60. V. Robinson, "Origin of Aviation Medicine," 1629. See also Robinson, *Dangerous Sky,* 18–21, and Lecornu, 250–254.

61. V. Robinson, "Origin of Aviation Medicine," 1630.

62. Ege, 123–124. See also Dollfus and Bouché, 113.

63. Robinson, *Dangerous Sky,* 22–23; V. Robertson, "Origin of Aviation Medicine," 1630–1632; Lissarrague, *Premiers envols,* 32–33.

64. "Monument commémoratif de la catastrophe du *Zénith,*" *L'aéronaute,* v. 10, n. 7 (July 1877): 187–189. See also Ege, 134–135.

65. Robinson, *Dangerous Sky,* 23–30.

66. Letter, TJ to Philip Turpin, 28 Apr. 1784, quoted in Millbank, 9.

67. Speculation continued over the summer of 1897 but quickly took a back seat to more current events; for example, on September 22, the leading newspaper in Christiania (now Oslo, Norway) ran a front-page article but gave far greater and prominent coverage to the opening of the city's newest hotel, the Grand (the front page is framed and on exhibit in the lobby of the hotel today); see "Andrée," *Orebladet,* v. 7, n. 246 (22 Sep. 1897); 1. The best account of the flight remains Edward Adams-Ray,

ed., *The Andrée Diaries: Being the Diaries and Records of S. A. Andrée, Nils Strindberg, and Knut Fraenkel, Written during Their Balloon Expedition to the North Pole in 1897 and Discovered on White Island in 1930. Together with a Complete Record of the Expedition and Discovery* (London: John Lane The Bodley Head Ltd., 1931); see esp. 1–17 (background), 42–53 (the balloon), 64–96 (the journey), 191–243 (on the ice), 244–267 (*Braatvag* expedition), 268–282 (*Isbjörn* expedition), 307–332 (recovery), and 339–346 (photo development). The noted polar aviator, early British jet test pilot, and historian John Grierson has an excellent summary of the flight in his *Challenge to the Poles: Highlights of Arctic and Antarctic Aviation* (London: G. T. Foulis & Co., Ltd., 1964) 27–40. See also Ege, 132–134.

68.   I thank Maj. Gen. Kjell M. Lutnes, Royal Norwegian Air Force (ret.), the Director of the Norsk Luftfartsmuseum in Bodø, for relating the details of the Frankel love story.

69.   Grierson, *Challenge,* 37. A small collection of recovered artifacts is in the possession of the Norsk Luftfartsmuseum.

70.   Grierson, *Challenge,* 40. A postscript: in 2000, the British explorer David Hempleman-Adams became the first balloonist to pass near the North Pole—passing within 12 miles of it, at an altitude of approximately 13,000 feet—in the modern Montgolfière, the *Britannic Challenger,* relying upon readings from navigation satellites for determining his final position. For an account of his (well-prepared) solo flight, see David Hempleman-Adams, *At the Mercy of the Winds* (London: Bantam, 2001).

CHAPTER FIVE

1.   SJ to Dr. Richard Brocklesby, 6 October 1784, Boswell, 1342–1343.

2.   Haydon has some excellent examples of this on 342–343.

3.   Horne, 126.

4.   A word on airship definitions. Airships are often called *dirigibles,* of which there are two major categories. A *blimp* is a small steerable airship having a streamlined shape; its envelope maintains shape due to the gas pressure within it. Blimps may be either *nonrigid* (i.e., no supporting internal framework whatsoever) or *semirigid* (i.e., having a small fixed keel to help distribute the loads of the gondola and its propulsion system more evenly across the entire envelope). *Rigid airships* have a structure of rings and longerons that maintain the shape. Their lifting gas is enclosed in separate cells (think of a stack of tuna fish cans) within the framework, and the framework is covered by an external fabric skin (although some experimental metal-skinned airships were flown as well). *Zeppelins* are rigid airships designed by Ferdinand von Zeppelin or the company that he founded and its American subsidiary. Thus all Zeppelins are rigids, but not all rigids are Zeppelins. All airships have control surfaces to change pitch attitude and direction. Increasingly modern airships also make use of small moveable thruster fans and pivoting engine installations for additional maneuver control.

5.   Lissarrague, *Premiers envols,* 46. See also "General Meusnier und die lenkbaren Balloons," *Illustrierte Aëronautische Mitteilungen,* v. 9, n. 12 (Dec. 1905): 373–387, and Fig. 4, p. 380.

6.   Turner, 53–54; Charles Dollfus, *Balloons* (New York: Orion Press, Inc., 1960), 78–79.

7.   Quote from Zahm, *Aerial,* 91; see also 88–91. See also Dollfus and Bouché, 77, 81–85; Raleigh, 76–77; Brooks, *Zeppelin,* 19–20; Ege, 112–113.

8.   Zahm, *Aerial,* 86–87; Crouch, *Eagle,* 316.

9. Ibid., 321–325. John Toland, *Ships in the Sky: The Story of the Great Dirigibles* (New York: Henry Holt and Co., 1957), 13–18.

10. Crouch, *Eagle*, 326;Toland, 19.

11. Crouch, *Eagle*, 327–329; Toland, 20–24.

12. Crouch, *Eagle*, 330–334. I wish to thank James and Nancy McFeeters of Monterey Dunes, California, for making me aware of the *Avitor* exhibit and the Hiller Museum. Since the dimensions of the *Avitor* are unknown, the word "replica" is used loosely. Some credit Marriott with coining the word "aeroplane," and he may have. But the Frenchman J. Pline used it in 1855 to describe a proposed hybrid airship-airplane. It was certainly used by the French pioneer Alphonse Pénaud in 1871–72, and featured in the title of an article of his in the French journal *L'aéronaute*, published in January 1872. See also Charles H. Gibbs-Smith, *The Aeroplane: A Historical Survey of its Origins and Development* (London: HMSO, 1960), 339.

13. Dolifus, *Balloons*, 79; see also Dollfus and Bouché, 110.

14. Ibid.; Zahm, *Aerial*, 91–93; Brooks, *Zeppelin*, 19; and Turner, 54.

15. "L'aérostat électrique dirigeable de MM. Tissandier frères," *L'illustration*, 4 Oct. 1884, in Renard and Krebs I file, MAE; see also Dollfus and Bouché, 130; and Ege, 125–126. Stéphane Nicolaou has prepared an excellent photographic record of this and other early French airships. See his *Les premiers dirigeables français* (Paris: Musée de l'Air et de l'Espace, 1997).

16. This is roughly equivalent to $80,000 in "then-year" monies (approximately $1,600,000 in 2001 dollars).

17. Vivian, 338; Dollfus, *Balloons*, 82; Lecornu, 285; Lissarrague, *Premiers envols*, 56–63. For Gambetta see Alfred Cobban, *A History of Modern France, III: 1871–1962* (Baltimore, MD: Penguin Books, 1968), 26–27, and David S. Bell, Douglas Johnson, and Peter Morris, eds., *Biographical Dictionary of French Political Leaders Since 1870* (New York: Association for the Study of Modern and Contemporary France / Simon & Schuster, 1990), 167–169.

18. Zahm, *Aerial*, 93.

19. Quote from Lecornu, 285. See also Dollfus and Bouché, 131–136, Charles Christienne and Pierre Lissarague, trans. by Francis Klanka, *A History of French Military Aviation* (Washington, D.C.: Smithsonian Institution Press, 1986), 18–23, Lissarrague, *Premiers envols*, 56–57, and Col. Charles Renard, "The First Flight of *la France*," reprinted from *The Airship*, II, n. 8 (Jan.-Mar. 1936): 63, and Dollfus, *Balloons*, 82.

20. Captain Charles Renard, *Le ballon dirigeable la France: Nouvelles expériences executs en 1885* (Paris: Gauthier-Villars, 1886), copy in Renard & Krebs I file, MAE; Lecornu, 288–289, and figure 228. See also Zahm, *Aerial*, 93–98.

21. "Colonel Charles Renard," *The Aeronautical Journal*, v. 9, n. 35 (July 1905), 53–54. See also Lecornu, 290; and Lissarrague, *Premiers envols*, 58–63.

22. Edouard Surcouf, "Le Colonel Charles Renard," *L'aérophile*, v. 13, n. 5 (May 1905): 83–85; G. Espitallier (trans. by H. Moedebeck), "Charles Renard," *Illustrierte Aëronautische Mitteilungen*, v. 9, n. 6 (June 1905): 169–72. See also Charles Dollfus, "L'oeuvre du Colonel Charles Renard," *Aviation français* (16 Jul. 1947); Jean Seillier, "Le Centenaire de Charles Renard"; and Génèral Lucien Robineau, "Le Colonel Charles Renard," *Air Actu*, n. 407 (June 1987), 44–49, all in Renard & Krebs I file, MAE. See also John H. Morrow, *The Great War in the Air: Military Aviation from 1909 to 1921* (Washington, D.C.: Smithsonian Institution Press, 1993), 3–4; and Christienne and Lissarrague, 23.

23. See Commandant Paul Renard, "Les Ancêtres: L'oeuvre du Colonel Renard," in Gustave Rives, *Rapport sur le Premier Salon de l'Aéronautique* (Paris:Librairie des Sciences Aéronautiques, Dec. 1908), 9–16. Copy in the library of the U.S. Army Military History Institute, Carlisle Barracks, PA (hereafter MHI). See also Section d'Arras, la Ligue Nationale Aérienne, "Le Colonel Charles Renard et son oeuvre," 9 June 1912, in Renard & Krebs file I, MAE. For purchase of the *Colonel Renard,* see John R. Cuneo, *The German Air Weapon, 1870–1914,* v. I of *Winged Mars* (Harrisburg, PA: Military Service Publishing Company, 1942), 149.

24. Christienne and Lissarrague, 23.

25. Vivian, pp. 339–340; Turner, 53–54; Brooks, *Zeppelin,* 20, Ege, 126–127; and Cuneo, I, 48.

26. Details of accident from Alfred Hildebrandt, *Airships Past and Present: Together with Chapters on the Use of Balloons in Connection with Meteorology, Photography and the Carrier Pigeon* (New York: D. Van Nostrand Company, 1908), 57–58; other sources claim a date of June 14, but I have accepted Hildebrandt as more authoritative since he was a captain and instructor in the Prussian balloon corps, based at Templehof. See also Zahm, *Aerial,* 99; Raleigh, 78; Vivian, 340; Botting, 22; Brooks, 20; fatality figures are from dedication page of Robertson, *Zeppelin in Combat,* v.

27. Alberto Santos-Dumont, *My Airships: The Story of My Life* (London: Grant Richards, 1904), 42–50. The best biography on him is Peter Wykeham's *Santos-Dumont: A Study in Obsession* (London: Putnam, 1962); for his youth, study in Paris, and his balloon *Brasil,* see 13–48, and 57–66. See also Michael Paris, *Winged Warfare: The Literature and Theory of Aerial Warfare in Britain, 1959–1917* (Manchester, UK: Manchester University Press, 1992), 25.

28. Santos-Dumont, pp. 74–81, and 282–302;Wykeham, pp. 67–71, 174–186. For another excellent photographic record of Santos-Dumont's work and flights, see Stéphane Nicolaou, *Santos-Dumont: Dandy et génie de l'aéronautique* (Paris: Musée de l'Air et de l'Espace, 1997).

29. During the time period covered by this work, one American dollar was worth approximately five francs: to convert "then-year" dollars to 2001 dollars, multiply the then-year dollar amount by 20.

30. Santos-Dumont., 153–204; Wykeham, 131–145. See also Dollfus and Bouché, 153–159, 168; Lecornu, 406–414; Vivian, 342–347; Botting, 22–29. Lt. Col. Fernando H. da Costa, *Alberto Santos-Dumont: The Father of Aviation* (Rio de Janeiro: Ministério da Aeronáutica, 1973), 7–27, 44–45; and Ege, 131–132.

31. As Raleigh wrote, "The accidents and perils that he survived in his many aerial adventures would have killed a cat" (79). See also Emmanuel Aimé, "Portraits d'aeronautes contemporains:Alberto Santos-Dumont," *L'aérophile,* v. 9, n. 4 (April 1901): 69–86; Charles Dollfus, "La vie aéronautique de Santos-Dumont," *Pionniers: Revue aéronautique trimestrielle des Vieilles Tigres,* v. 3, n. 11 (15 Jan. 1967): 13–23; Wykeham, 120–129; and Kenneth Munson, *Pioneer Aircraft 1903–1914* (New York: The Macmillan Company, 1969), 159.

32. Da Costa, 46.

33. Toland, 36.

34. Santos-Dumont, 316. He forecast airships dropping "dynamite arrows" on submarines, but the greatest value then and in the Second World War was in their serving as observation platforms rather than direct attack systems themselves.

35. This statistic is taken from a text panel in the exhibit "Twentieth Century

Seapower," at the National Maritime Museum, Greenwich, England; see also Christienne and Lissarrague, 64–7.

36. Dollfus and Bouché, 167; Zahm, *Aerial*, 115–16; Howard S. Wolko, *In the Cause of Flight: Technologists of Aeronautics and Astronautics*, n. 4 in the *Smithsonian Studies in Air and Space* series (Washington, D.C.: Smithsonian Institution Press, 1981), 13–14; Douglas Robinson, *Giants in the Sky: A History of the Rigid Airship* (Seattle, WA: University of Washington Press, 1973), 4. See also Dollfus, *Balloons*, 85; Ege, 140. Curiously, the Lebaudy's rubberized fabric envelope was manufactured by a German, not French, firm; Walter Wellman, *The Aerial Age: A Thousand Miles by Airship Over the Atlantic Ocean—Airship Voyages Over the Polar Sea; the Past, the Present, and the Future of Aerial Navigation* (New York: A. R. Keller & Company, 1911), 119–196; 276–367, esp. 318–334.

37. Wykeham, 237–260. See also Henry Serrano Villard, *Contact! The Story of the Early Birds* (New York: Thomas Y. Crowell Company, 1968), 247–248.

38. Wolko, *Cause*, 13; Toland, 244; da Costa, 56–57.

39. Crouch, *Eagle*, 284; Wolko, *Cause*, 14.

40. Hugo Eckener, *Count Zeppelin: The Man and his Work* (London: Massie Publishing Co., Ltd., 1938), 6–9, 33, 41–54 (Eckener, a former journalist turned airship captain-entrepreneur, became Zeppelin's closest confidant and the airship's most tireless and dedicated advocate after the count's death). See also "Zum Fünfzigstejährigen Militärjubiläum des Grafen Zeppelin," *Illustrierte Aeronautische Mitteilungen*, v. 12, n. 1 (Jan. 1908): 9–15; and Robinson, *Giants*, 9–11. Robinson's book remains the definitive English-language history of rigid airship development. See also his earlier *The Zeppelin in Combat: A History of the German Naval Airship Division* (Seattle: University of Washington Press, third ed., 1980).

41. There is controversy on this point, and some historians believe that von Zeppelin's interest only started later, after 1874. But it is undeniable that the count flew with Steiner, and that they discussed steerable balloons. Von Zeppelin himself, in 1915, stated that Steiner's conversation marked the beginning of his thinking about airships. Since as a rule elderly individuals hold very strongly to events and impressions of their youth, I believe this argues powerfully for the count's own account of how his interest in airships arose.

42. There is a photograph of the Kaiser wearing this weird getup in John S. D. Eisenhower, with Joanne Thompson Eisenhower, *Yanks: The Epic Story of the American Army in World War I* (New York: The Free Press, 2001), following 178. "This photograph," Eisenhower quite rightly writes, "shows why the Kaiser provided an ideal target for Allied and American propagandists."

43. Eckener, 109–121, and 142–148; "Zum Fünfzigstejährigen," 10–13; see also Henry Cord Meyer, *Airshipmen, Businessmen, and Politics, 1890–1940* (Washington: Smithsonian Institution Press, 1991), 26–29. Meyer offers a largely psychological interpretation of von Zeppelin's actions, which he sees as rooted in the "staggering blow," (29) "devastating career termination" (31), and "humiliation" (48) associated with his departure from the German army. Undoubtedly these expressions, as strong as they are, accurately describe what von Zeppelin must have felt. But as logical as such a "psychological cause" may seem in an age of casual diagnosis from afar and beyond the grave, I consider von Zeppelin's long-standing interest in airships and balloons predating his termination as the far more important factor in understanding his

energetic drive to build a large and useful airship, notwithstanding whatever trauma accompanied his separation from the military.

44. Quoted in Eckener, 175; see also 156–157. For more on de Freycinet, see chapter 7.

45. Militärgeschichtlichen Forschungsamt, *Die Militärluftfahrt bis zum Beginn des Weltkrieges 1914: Textband* (Frankfurt/Main: Verlag E. S. Mittler & Sohn GmbH, 1965), 25, 26. This is the narrative volume of a three-volume history first issued by the Nazi-era Luftwaffe. The other two volumes are the *Anlageband* (documents), and the *Technischer Band* (a developmental history of German army and navy aircraft). Hereafter, these three volumes are cited in abbreviated format, as *DMBW-T* or *DMBW-A* or *DMBW-TB*, followed by the page number. For more on Ganswindt, see Ley, 91–99; Brooks, *Zeppelin*, 26.

46. Von Zeppelin to Chef des Generalstabes der Armee, 14 Sept. 1893, *DMBW-A*, document 11: 14.

47. R. Giacomelli and E. Pistolesi, "Historical Sketch," in William F. Durand, ed., *Aerodynamic Theory: A General Review of Progress under a Grant from the Daniel Guggenheim Fund for the Promotion of Aeronautics*, v. I (Berlin, Ger.: Julius Springer Verlag, 1934), 306–334, 330–332; Theodore von Kármán, *Aerodynamics: Selected Topics in Light of Their Historical Development* (New York: McGraw-Hill, 1963), 34–40, 50–54, 68–72; John D. Anderson, Jr., *A History of Aerodynamics and its Impact on Flying Machines*, v. 8 in the *Cambridge Aerospace Series* (Cambridge, Cambridge University Press, 1997), 94–100, 245–246, 282–284. Von Helmholtz's own reputation soon entered terminal decline. The new physics, particularly quantum mechanics and relativity, swept aside his ideas of an "ether" governing the field of electrodynamics. Von Helmholtz, who might have contributed even more greatly to aeronautics had he not abandoned the field, died soon after the panel began its work, age 73. Incidentally, Joukovsky is more frequently spelled Joukowski, and less frequently appears as Zhukovskiy. I have used Joukovsky, as this is the spelling the Koutchino Institute that he helped create used.

48. Heinrich Müller-Breslau, et al., "Kommissionsbericht über die Prüfung der Entwürfe des Grafen Zeppelin," *DMBW-A*, document 14: 17–18. For a discussion of the committee's background and work, see *DMBW-T*, 28–30.

49. Zeppelin was not, as sometimes alleged, a witness to the Schwarz airship flight, though the Kaiser was. Reputedly he asked to ride in the vessel, though I personally find this very hard to accept. See Lee Kennett, *The First Air War, 1914–1918* (New York: The Free Press, 1991), 4; Hildebrandt, 58–60; Eckener, 210–211 and 158–209; Robertson, *Giants*, 22, and Brooks, *Zeppelin*, 27–29. For the second von Helmholtz report, see Richard Assdsmann, et al., "Kommissionsbericht über die Prüfung neuer Entwürfe des Grafen Zeppelin," *DMBW-A*, document 17: 24–26. There are likewise a good number of von Zeppelin's contentious letters and the war ministry's increasingly testy replies in this same volume; see esp. documents 19 and 20 (30–33). See also *DMBW-T*, 30–35; and Manfred Griehl and Joachim Dressel, *Zeppelin! The German Airship Story* (London: Arms and Armour Press, 1990), 23.

50. During this time period, one American dollar was roughly equivalent to four imperial German marks. Again, to determine approximate dollar amounts to 2001 equivalents, multiply then-year dollars by 20.

51. Details on construction from Ludwig Dürr (Zeppelin's chief engineer on all airships after the LZ-1), *Fünfundzwanzig Jahre Zeppelin-Luftschiffbau* (Berlin: VDI Verlag GmbH, 1925), especially chapter III, "Entwicklung der Z-Schiffe" and chapter IV,

"Konstructionsentwicklung der Z-Schiffe." There is a useful summary of airship specifications on 31. See also "The Zeppelin Air-Ship," *The Aeronautical Journal*, v. 3, n. 12 (Oct. 1899): 75–78.

52. *DMBW-T*, 35–36; Robertson, *Giants*, 23–28; and Brooks, *Zeppelin*, 32–33.

53. Quoted in Botting, 19 and 34.

54. For von Zeppelin's post-LZ-fund-raising activities, see Eckener, 220–221. There is an excellent summary of the structural evolution of von Zeppelin's designs from the LZ-1 onwards in the previously cited Dürr, 32–40. The structure began as a simple arrangement of rings and beams formed from T section girders joined and periodically cross-braced in an X pattern by ⌐ section cross strips. This gave a generalized I-beam-like cross section to the rings and beams, but this arrangement gave no protection against bending or compression loads. For his designs Dürr opted for more rigid, stiffer, and thicker rings and beams formed of Π and ⌐ longitudinal members continuously cross-braced in X fashion by O section tubular members, with the built-up rings and beams having a cross-sectional shape resembling a narrow Δ rather than the previous I shape. This structure sufficed for the LZ-2 through LZ-5, but later Dürr replaced the O members with modified U sections, added vertical cross-bracing between the longitudinal members in addition to the X cross-bracing giving the rings and beams a Pratt-truss appearance from the side, and opting for a thicker built-up Δ cross section. This structure at last furnished the Zeppelin with sufficient strength to be practicable, though further structural modifications were added to meet the needs of later wartime airships.

CHAPTER SIX

1. For the history or aerodynamics in this time period, see R. Giacomelli and E. Pistolesi, "Historical Sketch," in William F. Durand, ed., *Aerodynamic Theory: A General Review of Progress under a Grant from the Daniel Guggenheim Fund for the Promotion of Aeronautics* v.I (Berlin, Ger.: Julius Springer Verlag, 1934), 306–334, esp. 330–332; Theodore von Kármán, *Aerodynamics: Selected Topics in Light of Their Historical Development* (New York: McGraw-Hill, 1963), 34–40, 50–54, 68–72; John D. Anderson, Jr., *A History of Aerodynamics and Its Impact on Flying Machines*, v.8 in the *Cambridge Aerospace Series* (Cambridge: Cambridge University Press, 1997), 94–100, 245–246, 282–284.

2. See the previously cited Leonardo, *Notebooks*, 219, 317.

3. Ibid., 355.

4. The best survey of Leonardo's aerodynamic work is R. Giacomelli's "The Aerodynamics of Leonardo da Vinci," *The Journal of the Royal Aeronautical Society*, v. 34, n. 240 (Dec. 1930), passim. See also the previously cited Gibbs-Smith and Rees, 37 and 39; and Michael White, *Leonardo: The First Scientist* (New York: St. Martin's Press, 2000), 300–308.

5. For example, see the previously cited Grant, *God and Reason*, 180–181.

6. That is, R (R oc V^2,) where R is the resistance (the drag) and V is the velocity.

7. Expressed as $p_1 + \frac{1}{2}\rho V_1^2 = p_2 + \frac{1}{2}\rho V_2^2$ where p1, and p2, and V1 and V2 are, respectively, pressure and velocity measured at two points, and ρ is the density. Thus, as velocity increases, pressure decreases: the fundamental description of how a cambered wing produces lift by the acceleration of flow over the upper surface, which creates a low-pressure area "filled" by the wing being pushed upwards. For

the Bernoulli-Euler relationship, and their respective places in the history of mathematics, see the previously cited Rouse Ball, 377–378, 393–400.

8. Expressed as $R = \rho V^2 S \sin^2\alpha$ where R is the resistance (the drag), ρ the air density, V the velocity, S the area, and α the angle of attack. For the basic text for the derivation of the sine squared law see Issac Newton, proposition 34, theorem 28, and scholium, in section VII: "The Motion of Fluids and the Resistance Made to Projected Bodies," of book II: *The Motion of Bodies,* in *Mathematical Principles of Natural Philosophy,* trans. by Andrew Motte, revised by Florian Cajori, a volume in the *Great Books of the Western World* series (Chicago: Encyclopedia Britannica, Inc., 1952 ed.), 222–224.

9. Giacomelli and Pistolesi, 312–313; Anderson, 38–40; von Kármán, *Aerodynamics,* 9–10, 15, 17. See also J. A. D. Ackroyd, "The United Kingdom's Contribution to the Development of Aeronautics: Part I: From Antiquity to the Era of the Wrights," *The Aeronautical Journal,* v. 104, n. 1031 (Jan. 2000), 11–12. Curiously, while totally inappropriate for conventional aircraft, the sine-squared law *is* valid for very high-speed vehicles operating at hypersonic velocities (i.e., greater than five times the speed of sound) and is used to calculate hypersonic pressure distributions around blunt-nosed shapes—something researchers hardly could have foreseen in the seventeenth century!

10. There is an excellent model of one such machine in the collections of the Royal Artillery Museum, Woolwich, England. I thank Brigadier Jonathan B. A. Bailey, Director of Royal Artillery, for making me aware of this exhibit.

11. See von Kármán, 11, and Ackroyd 13.

12. That is, $R \propto V^3$.

13. See James Kip Finch, "Transportation and Construction, 1300–1800: The Rise of Modern Civil Engineering," in Kranzberg and Pursell, I, 194, 210–212.

14. From John Smeaton, *Experimental Inquiry concerning the Natural Powers of Wind and Water* (London: Royal Society, 1794), 38, quoted in N. H. Randers-Pehrson, "Pioneer Wind Tunnels," *Smithsonian Miscellaneous Collections,* v. 93, n. 4 (19 Jan. 1935): 1. See also Ackroyd Part I, 14.

15. Smeaton stated that the aerodynamic pressure on a flat plate perpendicular to the flow is expressed by the relationship $P = kSV^2$ where P is the pressure in pounds, k is a constant of 0.00492, S is the area in square feet, and V is the velocity in miles per hour. In fact, k was nearly twice as large as it should have been. Cayley calculated it more closely to the truth at 0.0038, Charles Renard at .00348, Samuel Langley at .00320, and in 1890 William Dines revised it to 0.0029. See Pritchard, 39–40, and Charles B. Hayward, *Practical Aviation: Understandable Presentation of Interesting and Essential Facts in Aeronautical Science* (Chicago: American Technical Society, 1919), 96.

16. Anderson, 447. See also Giacomelli and Pistolesi, "Historical Sketch," 334.

17. See, for example, Gibbs-Smith, *Aviation* 21–30, and also his *The Invention of the Aeroplane, 1799–1909,* 7–8, and his *Sir George Cayley, 1773–1857* (London: HMSO, 1968); J. E. Hodgson, "Some Notes on Sir George Cayley as a Pioneer of Aeronautics," *The Journal of the Royal Aeronautical Society,* v. 27, n. 152 (Aug. 1923), 371–380, and his book *History of Aeronautics in Great Britain,* 341–346; Anderson, 78–79; and also Ackroyd, part one, 15–19. The best Cayley biography remains J. Laurence Pritchard's excellent *Sir George Cayley: The Inventor of the Aeroplane* (London: Max Parrish, 1961), drawn from extensive correspondence and Cayley's own engineering notebooks, which are in the collections of the Royal Aeronautical Society, London. The finest most recent

treatment is J. A. D. Ackroyd's "Sir George Cayley: A Bicentennial Review," the forty-sixth Cayley Lecture of the Royal Aeronautical Society, presented to the Society on 19 April 2000. I thank Dr. Ackroyd for making a copy available to me.

18. Quoted in Gibbs-Smith, *Sir George Cayley*, 26.

19. Quoted in Pritchard, 34.

20. Dollfus and Bouché, 55–56. See also M. J. B. Davy, *Interpretive History of Flight: A Survey of the History and Development of Aeronautics with Particular Reference to Contemporary Influences and Conditions* (London: HMSO, 1948), 67.

21. This painting, Reg. No. 3977, is currently, regretfully, not on display; I thank Adam Grummitt of the NPG for greatly assisting my research on this work.

22. Johnson, *Birth of the Modern*, 198–199.

23. Ibid.; Hodgson, "Some Notes," 371; Pritchard, 1, 18.

24. Ibid.

25. See George Cayley, "On Aerial Navigation," part I, reprinted in James Means, ed., *The Aeronautical Annual for 1895* (Boston: W. B. Clarke & Co., 1894), 26; for ease of citation, these are hereafter cited as Means, year, Annual. See also Pritchard, 19–20. Cayley's notebooks are in the collections of the Royal Aeronautical Society, and a microfilm of volumes 1, 2, 3, and 5, covering the years 1795–1855, are in the holdings of the Science Museum (Catalog B246) at the Imperial College and Science Museum Libraries, London.

26. Cayley, 20. Means, a Bostonian, published three annuals, in 1895–1897, each an extraordinary compilation of information.

27. Ibid., 334–335; von Kármán, *Aerodynamics*, 7.

28. Peter Jakab, *Visions of a Flying Machine: The Wright Brothers and the Process of Invention* (Washington, D.C.: Smithsonian Institution Press, 1990), 32.

29. Anderson, 64.

30. Quoted in Theodore von Kármán, "Lanchester's Contributions to the Theory of Flight and Operational Research," *Journal of the Royal Aeronautical Society*, v. 62, n. 566 (Feb. 1958): 80–93.

31. Cayley, 2–22.

32. See also Giacomelli and Pistolesi, 312–313; and Anderson, 38–40. For an example of the lingering effects of this "law," see the statement of Joseph Le Conte, quoted in James Means, "Samuel Pierpont Langley," in Means, 1897, Annual, 9.

33. Von Kármán, *Aerodynamics*, 17.

34. For Wenham, see his "On Aerial Locomotion and the Laws by Which Heavenly Bodies Impelled through the Air are Sustained," reprinted in Means, 1895 Annual, 87; for Maxim, see his "Natural and Artificial Flight," reprinted in Means, 1896, Annual, 43. See also Pritchard, 39–40, and Anderson, 58–59, 76. It is surprising that Maxim, as late as 1895–1896, would have been unaware of the Dines recalculation of Smeaton's constant.

35. Pritchard, 39–40.

36. Quoted in Pritchard, 45. There is a discrepancy on whether the angle is 8 degrees (as printed by the Royal Aeronautical Society), or 18 degrees as printed in the Means, 1895, Annual, 25. I have accepted the 8 degrees figure because of its RAS origins. Incidentally, Octave Chanute detected this discrepancy and noted it in a letter to Orville Wright; see OC to OW, 16 Feb. 1905, in Marvin W. McFarland, ed., *The Papers of Wilbur and Orville Wright, Including the Chanute-Wright Letters and Other Papers of Octave Chanute*, v. I: *1899–1905* (New York: McGraw-Hill Book Company, Inc., 1953),

476 (hereafter cited as Wright Papers I or II). See also Ackroyd, "Sir George Cayley: A Bicentennial Review," 19, who has an interesting discussion of the "options" presented by this apparent typographical error.

37.   Ackroyd, "Sir George Cayley: A Bicentennial Review," 27.

38.   Cayley, "On Aerial Navigation," *Nicholson's Journal of Natural Philosophy, Chemistry, and the Arts,* v. 24 (November 1809): 164–174, v. 25, (February 1810): 81–87, and (March 1810): 161–169. These have since been reprinted four times, first as a part of the Royal Aeronautical Society's *Annual Report for 1876;* second by James Means in his *The Aeronautical Annual for 1895* (Boston: W. B. Clarke & Co., 1894) (the edition of Cayley's treatise I have used for this work); third by the Royal Aeronautical Society as *Aeronautical Classics,* n. 1 (London: RAS, 1910), and most recently by Charles Gibbs-Smith in his *Sir George Cayley's Aeronautics, 1796–1855* (London: HMSO, 1962), appendix 1, 213–237.

39.   Cayley, 21, fig. 2–3; 29, fig. 1–4; and 41, fig. 1–5. Fig. 5, 41, is the one most resembling the delta parawing, credited in large measure with creating the sport of hang gliding.

40.   Pritchard, 206–207. For Cayley's later work, see J. A. D. Ackroyd, "Sir George Cayley, The Father of Aeronautics: Part 2, Cayley's Aeroplanes," *Notes Rec. Royal Society London,* v. 56, n. 3 (2002), 338–348.

41.   J. S. Sproule, "Checking Up on Sir George," *Shell Aviation News,* n. 405 (1972); and Ackroyd, "Sir George Cayley: A Bicentennial Review," 30–31; Ackroyd, "Cayley's Aeroplanes," 346–347

42.   Hodgson, "Some Notes," 375.

43.   Ibid., 375.

44.   The hoax ran in a special edition of the *Sun* printed on 13 April, 1844. Widely reprinted since, it can be found in many Poe anthologies; the author used *The Complete Tales and Poems of Edgar Allan Poe* (New York: Vintage Books, 1975), 71–81: 81. Interestingly, Poe's story reveals that he understood much of what Cayley, Henson, and Stringfellow were doing, though he never really addressed aeronautics subsequently.

45.   Hodgson, "Some Notes," 379–380; Pritchard, 192–196; Gibbs-Smith, *Sir George Cayley,* 14–15.

46.   Gibbs-Smith, *Sir George Cayley,* 25.

47.   Ackroyd, part, 18.

48.   Aspect ratio is defined as the square of the wingspan divided by the planform area of the wing. For example, a wing having a span of 45 feet and an area of 500 square feet would have an aspect ratio of 4.05. If this same wing had a span of 70 feet, the aspect ratio would be 9.8. For a simple rectangular wing (that is, a wing having a constant chord length), the aspect ratio is defined as the span divided by the length of the chord. If, for example, the wing span is 36 feet, and the chord is 4 feet, the aspect ratio would be 9. Note that this is equivalent to squaring 36 (1,296), and dividing it by the area ($4 \times 36 = 144$): $1,296 \div 144 = 9$.

49.   Harald Penrose, *An Ancient Air: A Biography of John Stringfellow of Chard, the Victorian Aeronautical Pioneer* (Washington, D.C.: Smithsonian Institution Press, 1990), 70. For a good perspective on this project, from an astute and early observer of the aeronautical scene, see Octave Chanute, *Progress in Flying Machines* (Long Beach, CA: Lorenz & Herweg, Publishers, 1976 ed.), a facsimile reprint of the original 1894 edition, 83–87. See also Hodgson, *History of Aeronautics in Great Britain,* 355–367; and M. J. B. Davy's *Henson and Stringfellow: Their Work in Aeronautics* (London: HMSO, 1931), passim. There has been much commentary through the years on which of the two,

Henson or Stringfellow, was more influential on the design of the Aerial Steam Carriage, and the traditional view (not accepted by Penrose) is that Henson predominated. My personal belief is that it is inconclusive and, ultimately, pointless. Henson and Stringfellow both pursued the idea with great dedication, and after Henson married, gave up further work, and left for America, Stringfellow persisted, as did his son. There was dedication aplenty, obviously, by both men, and trying to sort it out is as pointless as trying to determine which Wright brother was the most "important." In both cases it is difficult to imagine that the team members could have succeeded as solo players.

50. Pritchard, 31.

51. Hodgson, "Some Notes," 377.

52. Lines 119–124. First published in 1842.

53. See Group Captain Peter W. Gray, RAF, "The Battle of Britain: So We Already Know the Story?" *Royal Air Force Air Power Review,* v. 3, n. 3 (Autumn 2000): 17–32, and Richard Overy's excellent *The Battle of Britain: The Myth and the Reality* (New York: W. W. Norton & Company, Inc., 2000).

54. Recollection of Cayley's granddaughter, in Pritchard, 207.

55. Victor Tatin, "Points d'histoire: L'aéroplane," *L'aérophile,* v. 15, n. 10 (Oct. 1907), 281.

56. The plaque anecdote is from Ackroyd, part I, p. 19, who adds, with the "most diplomatic of interpretations," that this might be considered equally "typical British understatement," or "base neglect." I consider it the latter.

57. Hodgson, "Some Notes," 373.

58. For example Pénaud paid tribute to Cayley and his research when commenting upon his own research; see his "Un brevet d'aéroplane," *L'aéronaute,* v. 10, n. 10 (Oct. 1877), and Wilbur Wright cited Cayley and Pénaud both in his original 1899 letter to the Smithsonian Institution requesting assistance in finding papers relating to aeronautical research. See WW to SI, 30 May 1899, Wright Papers I, 4.

59. Royal Aeronautical Society, *The Royal Aeronautical Society, 1866–1966: A Short History* (London: RAS, 1966), 1. The six were the Duke of Argyll (presiding), James Glaisher, Dr. Hugh W. Diamond, Francis Wenham, James Butler, and F. W. Brearey. In 1918 King George V granted the society the right to use the Royal prefix.

60. Ibid.

61. Hodgson, *History of Aeronautics in Great Britain,* 341–342.

62. For a good treatment of Wenham, see J. Laurence Pritchard, "Francis Herbert Wenham, Honorary Member, 1824–1908: An Appreciation of the First Lecturer to the Aeronautical Society," *Journal of the Royal Aeronautical Society,* v. 62 (Aug. 1958): 571–596; see also Ackroyd part I, 23–24.

63. There is a good discussion of this in Anderson, 115–117.

64. Randers-Pehrson, 1.

65. Ibid., 1–3; J. Lawrence Lee, "The Origin of the Wind Tunnel in Europe, 1871–1900," *Air Power History,* v. 45, n. 2 (Summer 1998): 6–9. See also Donald D. Baals and William R. Corliss, *Wind Tunnels of NASA,* SP-440 (Washington, D.C.: NASA, 1981), 1–7.

66. For Phillips see J. Laurence Pritchard, "The Dawn of Aerodynamics," *Journal of the Royal Aeronautical Society,* v. 61 (Mar. 1957): 149–180, and Randers-Pehrson, 3–4. Readers may recall a somewhat similar concept pioneered by William F. Gerhardt at McCook Field, Ohio, in the 1920s that has always been a source of some visual amusement: as it taxis along, the wings abruptly fail and collapse in a heap of tiny airfoil shards. Fortunately the failure took place on the ground, and not aloft.

CHAPTER SEVEN

1. As Montross writes, "Even in the final test of August 18 at Gravelotte-Saint Privat, the French cause was not lost except in the minds of leaders who had reached a state of moral bankruptcy" (648); Horne, 267–418.

2. Alphonse Pénaud, "Aéroplane Automoteur: Équilibre Automatique," *L'aéronaute,* v. 5, n. 1 (Jan. 1872): 5–6; see also 2–9 and figures 3 and 4.

3. See also Lecornu, *La navigation,* 264–265; Dollfus and Bouché, 115; Chanute, 117–118; and Gibbs-Smith, *Aviation,* 43. I have said "significant" because in 1845 and 1848 William Henson and John Stringfellow built and attempted to fly a steam-powered model of their Aerial Steam Carriage. The 1845 attempt was clearly unsuccessful, and afterwards Henson migrated to America. Of Stringfellow's 1848 attempt, historians are split in their judgment. The greatest of all historians of early aviation, the late Charles Gibbs-Smith, the Keeper of the Victoria and Albert Museum, rejected it, based on analysis by Captain J. Laurence Pritchard, the Secretary of the Royal Aeronautical Society (see Gibbs-Smith, *Aviation,* 29), but a more recent study by the late Harald Penrose, a pioneering British test pilot and popular historian of flight, concludes that the flight was, in fact, a success. See Penrose, *An Ancient Air,* 68, 73–75. My own conclusion is that the case for Stringfellow is, as the Scots' courts say, "not proven." Félix du Temple, a French naval officer, flew a clockwork (and later steam-powered) model in 1857–58, but without subsequent impact. In contrast to the Henson-Stringfellow-du Temple flight attempts, Pénaud's effort was widely witnessed, immediately publicized throughout Europe's aeronautical community, and his subsequent technical influence was great. Hence, Pénaud's flight was clearly the more significant.

4. Readers may find this power issue a bit much, but should keep in mind that the first powered, sustained, and controlled flight—by the Wrights, of course—lasted but 12 seconds. Further, at the beginning of the twenty-first century, NASA had an X-series program underway, the X-43 Hyper-X, with the goal of demonstrating sustained air-breathing hypersonic flight for *seven* seconds.

5. Dollfus and Bouché, 89.

6. Ibid., 97–103, 107; see the previously cited Rouillé, 91–92, Lhéritier, 102, and Gibbs-Smith, *Aviation* 36, 41. D'Esterno's work was more properly a booklet. See M. D'Esterno, *Du vol des oiseaux: Indication des sept lois du vol ramé et des huit lois du vol à voile* (Paris: Librairie Nouvelle, 1864). There is an original edition of d'Esterno's book (more properly a booklet) in the Colonel Richard Gimbel Aeronautical History collection at the U.S. Air Force Academy Library, Colorado Springs, Colorado. I thank archivist Duane Reed for his assistance in locating this and other resources from the Gimbel collection. Incidentally, despite his collaboration with Nadar, Jules Verne—just beginning his own career as a writer—did not see fit to include much on ballooning in his "lost novel," *Paris in the Twentieth Century (Paris au Vingtieme siècle,* first published in 1994), aside from a vague reference to armored balloons used to protect Paris from lighting strikes. See Jules Verne, *Paris in the Twentieth Century* (New York: Ballantine Books, 1997), 215. See also 24–25 for a prophetic discussion of how the Lenoir engine (an internal combustion engine) would radically reshape surface transportation, leading to the era of the automobile. Verne's interest in flight would come later, thanks to Nadar's own work, and the inspiration of the balloon post from Paris during the Franco-Prussian War.

7. Chanute, 119.

8. "Un brevet d' aéroplane," *L'aéronaute*, v. 10, n. 10 (Oct. 1877): 274–289, and figures 73, 74, and 75. See as well Dollfus and Bouché, 116–117; Lecornu, 268–269; Gibbs-Smith, *Aviation*, 43–44; Lissarrague, *Premiers envols*, 94–95; and Chanute, 119–122.

9. Chanute, 122.

10. Gibbs-Smith, *Aviation*, 43.

11. "Faits Divers," *L'aéronaute*, v. 13, n. 11 (Nov. 1880), 276; Dollfus and Bouché, 118; "Alphonse Pénaud (1850–1880): A Brilliant and Tragic Life," http://aerostories.free.fr/precurseurs/penaud/page2.html, 3.

12. Louis Mouillard, *L'empire de l'air: Essai d'ornithologie appliquée à l'aviation* (Paris: G. Masson/Libraire de l'Académie de Médecine, 1881), Gimbel collection, USAFA Library.

13. Victor Tatin, "Expériences sur le vol Mécanique," *L'aéronaute*, v. 10, n. 5 (May 1877): 141–145.

14. Victor Tatin, "Recherches et Expériences sur le Mécanisme du vol des oiseaux (1)" *L'aéronaute*, v. 13, n. 9 (Sep. 1880): 207–229, and fig. 38.

15. Ibid. See also Dollfus and Bouché, 119.

16. Tatin worked after the turn of the century with the expatriate Rumanian pioneer Trajan Vuia, the French balloonist Comte Henri de La Vaulx, and Louis Paulhan. He influenced Vuia's choice of the monoplane configuration and designed the propeller used on Vuia's first airplane of 1906, which, though no great success itself, inspired others to the monoplane planform, notably the French pioneer Louis Blériot. Vuia seems not to have been pleased with the Tatin prop; he continued his own work, designing another plane (equally unsuccessful) incorporating a different propeller by another manufacturer. Tatin also designed a monoplane (constructed for La Vaulx), but like Vuia's it was unsuccessful and abandoned following two very brief flights at Saint-Cyr. But Tatin's work with Louis Paulhan resulted in a very advanced and streamlined airplane for its time, the so-called *Aéro-torpille* ("aerial torpedo"). With this machine, Tatin finally achieved his potential. See Gibbs-Smith, *A Directory and Nomenclature of the First Aeroplanes, 1809–1909* (London: HMSO, 1966), 62, 77–78; and Gibbs-Smith, *Invention*, 108. See also Lissarrague, *Premiers envols*, 146, and "The Paulhan Torpedo," *The Aeroplane* (29 Dec. 1911): 709.

17. For the Goupil aircraft, see Dollfus and Bouché, 128; Lissarrague, *Premiers envols*, 103; Gibbs-Smith, *Aviation*, 53 and plate Ve; and Chanute, 154–156.

18. The two best and most exhaustive works that sum up the "pro" and "con" viewpoint are Pierre Lissarrague's highly laudatory *Clément Ader: Inventeur d'avions* (Toulouse: Bibliothèque historique Privat, 1990), and Gibbs-Smith's highly critical *Clément Ader: His Flight-Claims and his Place in History* (London: HMSO, 1968). For another example of the "true inventor" viewpoint, see Oliver Stewart's uncritical assessment in *Aviation: The Creative Ideas* (New York: Frederick A. Praeger, Publishers, 1966), 17–35. See also Dollfus and Bouché, 137–141.

19. Lissarrague, *Ader*, 19–29, 35–39.

20. Ibid., 44–45; see also Michel Ellenberger, *Les avions de Clément Ader* (Paris: Éditions Nathan, 1992), 21–22, 29–30.

21. See Clément Ader, *L'aviation militaire* (Paris: Berger-Levrault, Éditeurs, 1911), 2–32. I thank Lt. Col. Steven Rinaldi, USAF, for bringing this work to my attention, which was originally published in 1909, went through several editions, and then was reprinted and reissued by the *Service historique de l'armée de l'air*, Paris, in 1990. See also Lissarrague, *Ader*, 240–243.

22. Chanute, 212.

23. Lissarrague, *Ader*, 45–59, 272, 276–279; Dollfus and Bouché, 123; Ellenberger, 30–40.

24. Ibid., 58–59; see also Chanute, p. 213; and Ellenberger, 41–43.

25. The following technical discussion of the *Éole* is drawn from Ader's "L'aéroplane *Éole*," *Revue de l'aéronautique: Théorique et appeliquée*, v. 6, n. 4 (1893): 69–99 and plates 12 and 14. The illustrations to this essay offer the greatest possible evidence of the bat's influence on Ader's ideas.

26. Lissarrague, *Ader*, 61–96; and Dollfus and Bouché, 139. This latter is an important point, for two other pioneers, both naval officers, had, by this time, constructed crude steam-powered "airplanes" but launched them from inclines: France's Félix du Temple, in 1874, and the Russian Alexander Mozhaisky a decade later, in 1884. Neither of these machines constituted a true aircraft: their occupants more passengers than pilots, these attempts qualified more as ballistic excursions than exercises in lift and power overcoming drag and gravity, and they could not sustain level or climbing flight. (Indeed, Mozhaisky's craft used a ski-jump as its "runway.") See Gibbs-Smith, *Directory*, 12, 23. The Russian interpretation of Mozhaisky is captured in V. B. Shavrov's encyclopedic *History of Aircraft Construction in the USSR*, v. 1: *To 1938* (Moscow: Mechanical Engineering Publishers, 1978), [В. Б. Шавров, История Конструкции Самолетов b СССР до 1938 г. (Москва: Издательство «Машиностроение»)], pp. 11–23 (hereafter Shavrov I). For details of the more interesting of the two, the du Temple machine, see Félix du Temple, "L'appareil de locomotion aérienne," *L'aréonaute* v. 10, n. 8 (Aug. 1877): 223–234; and Dollfus and Bouché 89.

27. Chanute, 212.

28. Quoted in Alfred Bodemer, *De l'Éole à Hermès: Cent ans de moteurs dans le ciel* (Paris: Musée national des techniques / Conservatoire national des arts et métiers, 1990), 10.

29. The banker comments are from the previously cited Rouillé, 90–91. See Gibbs-Smith's previously cited *Clément Ader*. See also Lissarrague, *Ader*, 95–102, and 121; Ellenberger, 6–19; and Ader, vi. The *L'illustration* article appeared on June 20, 1891, and, unlike many such representations of early aircraft, was reasonably accurate, though it did not show the flatplate condenser and showed skids, rather than wheels, for the undercarriage.

30. Ader, vi; Vivian, 123; and Gibbs-Smith, *Director*, 6.

31. Ader, vi; see also Lecornu, 349–351; and the previously cited Rives, *Rapport sur le Premier salon de l'aéronautique*, 16–17.

32. Quote from Cobban, III, 22; also 72. See also Horne, 138–140; and the previously cited Bell, et al., *French Biographical Dictionary*, 163.

33. Quoted in Lissarrague, *Ader*, 127. De Freycinet used the expression *"éclairer et torpilleur"*: a scout and destroyer. Like many attempting to characterize early military airplanes, de Freycinet (not unreasonably) sought to relate existing army and naval terminology to describe them and their capabilities. A more appropriate term today would be light attack aircraft. See also Patrick Facon, *"L'armée française et l'aviation (1891–1914),"* *Revue historique des armées*, n. 164 (Sep. 1986): 78; Gibbs-Smith, *Clément Ader*, 15; and Lissarrague, *Premiers envols*, 97.

34. Lissarrague, *Ader*, quotes the contract on 134–135.

35. The site is easily accessible from central Paris, being a half block from the entrance to the Jasmin Metro stop, on the Pont de Sèvres-Mairie de Montreuil line.

36. Letter, SPL to OC, 2 Aug. 1892, in the Ader biographical file, NASM archives. (This

is a photocopy of a handwritten original in the Chanute Papers, Library of Congress Manuscript Division, Washington, D.C.).

37. Lissarrague, *Ader*, 132–169; Facon, *"L'armée,"* p. 78; Dollfus and Bouché, 140–141; Lissarrague, *Premiers envols*, 98; and Biruta Kresling, "Clément Ader's 'Bat,'" *La revue Musée des arts et métiers*, n. 13 (Dec. 1995): 23–31.

38. See David McCullough, *The Path Between the Seas: The Creation of the Panama Canal, 1870–1914* (New York: Touchstone/Simon and Schuster, 1977), 197–233. One of those implicated was Gustave Eiffel, the designer of the famous tower that has become Paris' signature attraction. Ironically, after the affair, Eiffel would leave construction completely, turning his attention to—aerodynamics and aviation! See von Kármán, *Aerodynamics*, 12–13; and Anderson, 268–271.

39. Cobban, III, 50–57. For a good survey of the Dreyfus affair, see Martin P. Johnson, *The Dreyfus Affair: Honor and Politics in the Belle Epoque* (New York: St. Martin's Press, 1999).

40. Ader, vii. See also Lissarrague, *Ader*, 171–179, which has excellent topographical reproductions of the site and the circular track.

41. Data taken from the Mensier report, which is reprinted in Vivian, 469–471, and also in Gibbs-Smith, *Clément Ader*, 19–23, and in Wilbur Wright's "What Clement Ader Did," *Aero-Club of America Bulletin* (May 1912), reprinted as Document 39 in Peter L. Jakab's and Rick Young's *The Published Writings of Wilbur and Orville Wright* (Washington, D.C.: Smithsonian Institution Press, 2000), 178–184 (hereafter Wright Writings). The French original is quoted at length in Lissarrague, *Ader*, 184–185, and 187–188. Perhaps most interestingly, Wilbur Wright used the Mensier report to bolster the brothers' case during their patent fights in Europe and America. The engines weighed a total of 42 kilograms, the firebox and boiler another 60 kilograms, and the condenser 15 kilograms, for a total weight of 117 kilograms; $117\text{kg} \times 2.2$ pounds/kilogram $= 257.4$ pounds.

42. Lissarrague, *Ader*, 180–187; see also Ellenberger, 60–63; Lissarrague, *Premiers envols*, 98; Vivian, 124–126, 474–475. The officers were Generals Mensier and Grillon, Lieutenant Binet, and professors Sarrau and Leaute. Mensier, Grillon, Sarrau, and Leaute were commission members. As chance would have it, the date of his flight attempt was almost 50 years to the hour before a pilot would first fly faster than sound.

43. Mensier report, Wright Writings, 180–181; also in Vivian, 476. See also Lissarrague, *Ader*, 188.

44. And indeed it was. Dreyfus came back for another trial in 1899, and though the *antidreyfusards* still prevailed, popular sentiment led to a presidential pardon, and, eventually, an inquiry that resulted in his complete exoneration and the discrediting of his foes.

45. Facon, 79.

46. "Ader's Flying Machine," *The Aeronautical Journal*, v. 2, n. 8 (October 1898): 73–74. See also the earlier "Ader's Flying Machine," *The Aeronautical Journal*, v. 2, n. 7 (July 1898): 67–68.

47. Lissarrague, *Ader*, 223–274.

48. Langley notes on visiting Ader workshop, 9 July, 1899, from Langley Papers, box 27, "Langley Correspondence in Reference to Aerodrome" folder, Smithsonian Institution Archives; copy in the Ader biographical file, NASM archives.

49. Indeed, the Blériot, the first plane to fly between two nations, and which forever ended Britain's isolation from the Continent, is downright shabby—in sadly deteriorated condition, tucked away in the rafters of the museum's *chapelle* and accessible

only by a shaky metal walkway and stairs. In contrast, the *Avion III,* restored by the Musée de l'Air et de l'Espace, is pristine, a great cocoa-colored bat bizarrely occupying pride of place over the museum's central staircase. See also Lissarrague, *Ader,* 227.

50.   Several example drawn from *L'aéronaute* suffice: Albert Bazin, "Observations sur les expériences aérodynamiques de M. Langley," and Jules Knockaert, "L'aéroplane Maxim et son moteur," both in v. 24, n. 10 (Oct. 1891): 219–222; Emile Simon, "Analyse de l'ouvrage de M. Otto Lilienthal," v. 25, n. 1 (Jan. 1892): 5–12; Edmond Henry, "Experiences d'aviation," v. 26, n. 7 (July 1893): 143–157 (on Phillips's steam injector tunnel and multiplane concepts); Otto Lilienthal, "L'homme volant," v. 27, n. 1 (Jan. 1894): 5–19; Wilfred de Fonville, "Les progrès de l'aéronautique en Allemagne," v. 27, n. 11 (Nov. 1894): 255–258; and Léopold Desmarest, "Les nouvelles experiences de M. Otto Lilienthal," v. 28, n. 2 (Feb. 1895): 23–39. See also M. P. Lauriol, "Les expériences de M. Lilienthal," *Revue de l'aéronautique,* v. 8, n. 1 (1895): 1–4.

51.   WW to OW, 31 Mar. 1911, Wright Papers II, 1022.

52.   WW, "What Clement Ader Did," in Wright Writings, 183.

53.   Ibid.

CHAPTER EIGHT

1.   Paul Charrier, *Gordon of Khartoum* (New York: Lancer Books, 1966), 7–14, 185–186.

2.   Winston S. Churchill, *The River War: An Account of the Reconquest of the Sudan* (New York: Award Books, 1964 ed.), 244.

3.   Charrier, 164–165.

4.   Ian J. Knight, "Needed Rounds Denied," *Military History,* v.4, n.3 (Dec. 1987): 43–50.

5.   Churchill, 274.

6.   Denis Judd, *Empire: The British Imperial Experience from 1765 to the Present* (New York: Basic Books, 1996), 99–101; Lawrence James, *The Rise and Fall of the British Empire* (London: Abacus, 2000 ed.), 282–283.

7.   See also Douglas Porch, "Imperial Wars," in Charles Townshend, ed., *The Oxford History of Modern War* (Oxford: Oxford University Press, 2000), 98–99, and the previously cited Fuller, *Armament in History,* 120, 137.

8.   The best sources on Maxim are his own biography *My Life* (London: Methuen & Co., Ltd., 1915), published just a year before his death; Iain McCallum, *Blood Brothers: Hiram and Hudson Maxim: Pioneers of Modern Warfare* (London: Chatham Publishing, 1999); and James E. Hamilton, *The Chronic Inventor: The Life and Work of Hiram Stevens Maxim* (London: Bexley Libraries & Museums, 1991).

9.   Maxim, *My Life,* 162–171; McCallum, 49–51.

10.   Reprinted in Chanute, 233–234. See also Ackroyd, pt. I, 26.

11.   Hiram S. Maxim, *Artificial and Natural Flight* (London: Whittaker & Co., 1908), v.

12.   Ibid., 31. There is uncertainty over his costs estimates, as in his autobiography, he states he told his questioners that it would cost £50,000. See Maxim, *My Life,* 291.

13.   Maxim, *My Life,* 291.

14.   For details of his work, see Maxim, *Artificial and Natural Flight,* especially 62–98, and appendix II, "Recapitulation of Early Experiments," 130–143. See also his "Natural and Artificial Flight," in Means, 1896, Annual, 26–55; and his "Screw-Propellers Working in Air," in Means, 1897, Annual, 142–144. See also Chanute, 234–247; Harald Penrose, *British Aviation, v. I: The Pioneer Years, 1903–1914* (London: Putnam & Company, Ltd., 1967), 21–40; and Gibbs-Smith, *Aviation,* 63. Opinion on Maxim is split,

with Gibbs-Smith (and most aviation historians) dismissing his work as a waste of his talent. Penrose is fulsome in praise, much as Stewart is for Ader. Chanute largely simply reported on Maxim's work. My own views are less enthusiastic than those of Penrose but more favorable than those of Gibbs-Smith; it is time to reassess Maxim and recognize that he had a more significant role in early aeronautics than is generally appreciated by the historical community.

15. Maxim, *Artificial and Natural Flight,* 77–98; see also Chanute, 237; Hamilton, 16–55; and McCallum, 98–120.

16. Maxim, *My Life,* 293. See also his *Artificial and Natural Flight,* appendix II, 138–139.

17. Ibid., 294.

18. Maxim, "Natural and Artificial Flight," 38–42 and fig. 6; Randers-Pehrson, 7–8. See also the previously cited Lee, "The Origin of the Wind Tunnel in Europe, 1871–1900," 12. I have also benefited from consulting an unpublished manuscript, "Man Flies," by Philip Jarrett, and thank him for making it available to me.

19. McCallum, 138–141. The best source of information on the tragic Pilcher is Philip Jarrett's masterful biography, *Another Icarus: Percy Pilcher and the Quest for Flight* (Washington, D.C.: Smithsonian Institution Press, 1987); see esp. 48–50, and 84–85 for the Pilcher-Maxim relationship.

20. For example, see Gibbs-Smith, *Aviation,* 62–63; Jakab, *Visions of a Flying Machine,* 26; and Crouch, 63.

21. See, for example, Jules Knockaert, "L'aéroplane Maxim et son moteur," *L'aéronaute,* v. 24, n. 10 (Oct. 1891), 219–222; the previously cited Means references; and J. H. Parkin, *Bell and Baldwin: Their Development of Aerodromes and Hydrodomes at Baddeck, Nova Scotia* (Toronto: University of Toronto Press, 1964), 134–135, 243, and 274–275.

22. WW to Charles L. Strobel, Wright Papers II, 27 Jan. 1911: 1018.

23. As expressed by Maxim in testimony before Britain's Secretary of State for War, Richard Haldane, as part of the deliberations of the Aerial Navigation Committee; for a transcript of his remarks, see Percy B. Walker, *Early Aviation at Farnborough: The History of the Royal Aircraft Establishment,* I: *The First Aeroplanes* (London: Macdonald, 1974), 320–321. Walker, incidentally, was the former head of the Aircraft Structures Department at the Royal Aircraft Establishment and the man credited with solving the riddle of the mysterious loss of three De Havilland Comet jetliners (from structural failure-induced explosive decompression) in the early 1950s.

24. McCallum, 204–205.

25. Originally known, fittingly enough, as Turkey Buzzard Point in colonial days, and then Greenleaf's Point after a prominent early landowner. It was the Washington Arsenal from 1803–1883. This is the current site of Fort Leslie J. McNair, home of the National Defense University. For more information on this historic site, see Phyllis I. McClellan, *Silent Sentinel on the Potomac: Ft. McNair, 1791–1991* (Bowie, MD: Heritage Books, 1993).

26. Juliette A. Hennessy, *The United States Army Air Arm, April 1861 to April 1917* (Washington, D.C.: Office of Air Force History, 1985), 20–21; Tom D. Crouch, *A Dream of Wings: Americans and the Airplane, 1875–1905* (New York: W. W. Norton & Company, 1981), 255–289.

27. This discussion is drawn largely from Samuel P. Langley, *Experiments in Aerodynamics* (Washington, D.C.: Smithsonian Institution, 1891), his "Experiments in Mechanical Flight," in Means, 1897, Annual, 11–25, and in particular (co-authored with Charles M. Manly) his *Langley Memoir on Mechanical Flight, pt. 1* (by Langley but

edited by Manly after Langley's death): *1887 to 1896,* and *pt. II* (by Manly): *1897–1903,* a study in the *Smithsonian Contributions to Knowledge* series, XXVII, n. 3 (1911) (hereafter *Langley Memoir* I or II). The latter folio work is definitive on Langley's thought, his work, the design of his Aerodromes, and the events of 1903. See also Norriss S. Hetherington, "The Langley and Wright Aero Accidents," in Roger D. Launius, ed., *Innovation and the Development of Flight* (College Station: Texas A&M University Press, 1999): 18–51.

28.   Letter, WW to Walcott, 23 Dec. 1910, Wright Papers II, 1009.

29.   Langley, *Experiments,* 63–67, 107; see also Means, "Langley's Law," 1895 Annual, 127–128.

30.   Anderson, pp. 179–181, has a thorough discussion of the test results and their implications, and I thank Professor Anderson for bringing it to my attention.

31.   See Crouch, *Dream,* 55, and Anderson, 108. Born John Strutt, Rayleigh worked across many scientific fields and won the Nobel Prize in 1904 for his discovery and isolation of argon; he died in 1919. As the first to conceptualize the problems associated with hypersonic (Mach > 5) flight, Rayleigh would undoubtedly take pleasure in knowing that argon is one of the key gases used in advanced hypersonic testing, as a testing medium in aeroballistic ranges and for rocket-propelled sleds.

32.   *Langley Memoir* I, 106.

33.   Ibid., 107. See also Robert B. Meyer Jr., "Langley *Aerodrome No. 5,*" in Claudia M. Oakes, ed., *Aircraft of the National Air and Space Museum* (Washington, D.C.: Smithsonian Institution Press, 1976), n.p. The *Aerodrome No. 5* is now on exhibit in the National Air and Space Museum, Smithsonian Institution.

34.   *Langley Memoir,* I, 107.

35.   Alexander Graham Bell, "The Aerodromes in Flight," in Means, 1897, Annual, 26–27.

36.   Parkin, 5. Langley had visited Bell at Beinn Bhreagh two years earlier.

37.   Octave Chanute, "Langley's Contributions to Aerial Navigation, in Chanute et al., "Samuel Pierpont Langley: Memorial Meeting, Dec. 3, 1996," *Smithsonian Miscellaneous Collections,* v. 49, special edition (1907), 33, copy in the Smithsonian Archives. I thank Mr. Bill Cox of the Smithsonian Archives staff for locating this for me. See also Mark Sullivan, *Our Times: The United States, 1900–1925, II: America Finding Herself* (New York: Charles Scribner's Sons, 1943), 557–558.

38.   Bell had been interested in flight for approximately twenty years by the time he first witnessed Langley's experiments in 1896; Parkin, 4–5. The "Mr. Laggle" characterization is from a letter, TR to Anna Roosevelt, 31 Dec. 1893, in Elting E. Morison, John M. Blum, and John J. Buckley, eds., *The Letters of Theodore Roosevelt, I: The Years of Preparation, 1868–1898* (Cambridge, MA: Harvard University Press, 1951), 344. See also Edmund Morris, *The Rise of Theodore Roosevelt* (New York: Ballantine Books, 1980), 608, and 840, n.76.

39.   Rigorous analysis has since suggested the probable cause as an undetected coal bunker fire that detonated a magazine.

40.   The *Naval War of 1812* (first published in 1882) illustrates his thorough grasp of, and interest in, technology. See Theodore Roosevelt, *The Naval War of 1812* (New York: Modern Library, 1999 ed.).

41.   Ltr, TR to Long, 25 March 1898, in Morison, Blum, and Buckley, eds., *Letters,* I, 799.

42.   For an excellent survey of this remarkable powerplant, see Robert Meyer, *Langley's Aero Engine of 1903,* a study in the *Smithsonian Annals of Flight* series (Washington, D.C.: Smithsonian Institution Press, 1971).

43. Langley notes on visiting Ader workshop, 9 July, 1899, from Langley Papers, box 27, "Langley Correspondence in Reference to Aerodrome," Smithsonian archives, copy in Ader biographical files, NASM.

44. As the author personally attests: as a curator at the Smithsonian's National Air and Space Museum, he did both to the restored *Aerodrome* to see the results: the plane jiggled for nearly half a minute.

45. Valerie Moolman, *The Road to Kitty Hawk,* a volume in the *Epic of Flight* series (Alexandria, VA: Time-Life Books, 1980), 133.

46. *Washington Post,* 8 Oct. 1903. See also Hetherington, 23–24.

47. *New York Times,* 9 Oct. 1903.

48. From a reply to Major B. F. S. Baden-Powell declining membership in the Aeronautical Society of Great Britain, 8 Dec. 1896, from the letters files, folder 13, in the library, Royal Aeronautical Society, 4 Hamilton Place, London. I thank the RAeS Librarian, Mr. Brian Riddle, for making this document available.

49. Parkin, *Bell and Baldwin,* 441.

50. Rear Admiral George W. Melville, USN, "The Engineer and the Problem of Aerial Navigation," *North American Review* (Dec. 1901): 820–821.

51. Simon Newcomb, "The Outlook for the Flying Machine," *The Independent,* 22 Oct. 1903, 2509; for sympathetic treatments of his background, see W. W. Campbell, "Biographical Memoir: Simon Newcomb, 1835–1909," and Raymond C. Archibald, "Simon Newcomb, 1835–1909: A Bibliography of his Life and Work," both in *Memoirs of the National Academy of Sciences,* v. 17 (1924): 1–69.

52. *Langley Memoir* II, 271.

53. I suspect that the poorly braced wings experienced asymmetric changes in center of pressure, resulting in wing flutter and flexing—the wings twisting both in angle of attack and dihedral angle, and thus producing the swaying motion that Manly experienced immediately before final catastrophe. Further, this kind of motion would produce exactly the diverging kind of structural loading necessary to destroy the *Great Aerodrome,* effectively replicating the loads pattern experienced by a modern airplane during a rolling dive pullout—the most demanding structural test that an aircraft can undergo.

54. *Langley Memoir* II, 272.

55. Ibid., 273.

56. Ibid.; see also Hetherington, 25.

57. *Langley Memoir* II, 273. This is discussed subsequently in relation to the Wright suits against Glenn Curtiss.

58. Sullivan, II, 567. There is a good discussion of the negative impact of Langley's accident upon popular and official opinion in Hetherington, 25–27.

59. *Langley Memoir* II, 278.

60. Quoted in Crouch, *Dream,* 292.

61. Quoted in Sullivan, II, 566. Nearly a quarter century later, retired in California and living near Santa Monica next to the Douglas plant—whose planes completed the first round-the-world flight in 1924—Robinson good-naturedly admitted to Sullivan, "I might considerably revise my original notion."

62. Hennessy, 21; I. B. Holley, Jr., *Ideas and Weapons* (Washington, D.C.: Air Force History and Museums Program, 1997 ed.), 26.

63. "The Progress of Science: Aerial Navigation," *Popular Science Monthly,* LXIV (1903–1904): 95–96.

64. "The Late Professor S. P. Langley," *The Aeronautical Journal*, v. 10, n. 42 (Apr. 1906): 19; see also 20–25.

65. Hermann W. L. Moedebeck, "Samuel P. Langley," *Illustrierte Aeronautische Mitteilungen*, v. 10, n. 5 (May 1906): 147–148.

66. WW to OC, 8 Nov. 1906, Wright Papers II, 737.

CHAPTER NINE

1. Peter Supf, *Das Buch der deutschen Fluggeschichte: Vorzeit, Wendezeit, Werdezeit*, I (Berlin: Verlagsanstalt Hermann Klemm AG, 1935), 107–108.

2. Karl Müllenhoff, "Otto Lilienthal: A Memorial Address delivered before the *Deutschen Verein zur Förderung der Luftschiffahrt*," 26 Nov. 1896, in Means, 1897 Annual, 82; Walter Zuerl, *Deutsche Flugzeugkonstrukteure: Werdegang und Erfolge unserer Flugzeug-und Flugmotorenbauer* (Munich: Curt Pechstein Verlag, 1938), 14–15; Supf, I, 107–108; and National Air and Space Museum, *Otto Lilienthal and Octave Chanute: Pioneers of Gliding* (Washington, D.C.: Smithsonian Institution, n.d.), 3. See also Wright Papers I, n. 9, 6.

3. Quote from Müllenhoff, 76. See also Gerhard Patt and Werner Schwipps, *Otto Lilienthal: 100 Jahre Menschenflug* (Munich: Gesellschaft zur Förderung der Geschichte der deutschen Luftfahrt, in association with the magazine *Flug Revue* and the Deutsches Museum and Deutschen Segelflugmuseum, 1991), 23, Anderson, 156, Supf, I, 81–83, and Zuerl, 7–15. Lilienthal's family background is enumerated in Helmuth Trischler, "Otto Lilienthal: Porträt eines Erfinderunternehmers," in Werner Heinzerling and Helmuth Trischler, eds., *Otto Lilienthal: Flugpionier, Ingenieur, Unternehmer—Dokumente und Objekte* (Munich: Deutsches Museum, 1991): 13–15, and Klaus Kopfermann, "Otto Lilienthal und seine Familie—Erinnerungen," in Heinserling and Trischler, 29–46; his early work as a mechanical engineer and a designer of steam signals is in Karl-Dieter Seifert, "Der Maschinenbauingenieur und Fabrikant Otto Lilienthal," in Heinzerling and Trischler, 55–82, and his various gliders are enumerated in Stephan Nitsch, "Otto Lilienthals Flugzeugkonstruktionen," in Heinzerling and Trischler, 83–100; and Gerhard Halle's older but still excellent *Otto Lilienthal und seine Flugzeug-Konstruktionen* (Munich: R. Oldenbourg Verlag, 1962); it is Halle who first catalogued the various Lilienthal designs. (As a teenager, incidentally, Halle witnessed Wilbur Wright's Berlin flights.) The best accounts of Lilienthal's life and work are K. D. Seifert, *Otto Lilienthal: Mensch und Werk* (Neuenhagen bei Berlin: Verlag Sport und Technik, 1961); and Werner Schwipps later *Lilienthal: Die Biographie des ersten Fliegers* (Munich: Aviatic Verlag Peter Pletschacher, 1979).

4. Walter Laqueur, *Weimar: A Cultural History, 1918–1933* (New York: G. P. Putnam's Sons, 1976), 3; Patt and Schwipps, 24. Both Brahm and Reinhardt were Jewish, born, respectively, as Otto Abrahamsohn, and Max Goldmann. For Berlin theater and its Jewish roots in this time period, see Peter Jelavich, "Performing High and Low: Jews in Modern Theater, Cabaret, Revue, and Film," in Emily D. Bilski, *Berlin Metropolis: Jews and the New Culture, 1890–1918* (Berkeley: University of California Press, the Jewish Museum/New York, under the auspices of the Jewish Theological Seminary of America, 1999): 209–213.

5. Zuerl, 8.

6. Otto Lilienthal, *Der Vogelflug als Grundlage der Fliegerkunst: Ein Beitrag zur Systematik der Flugtechnik* (Berlin: R. Gaertners Verlagsbuchhandlung, 1889), subsequently

printed in English as *Bird Flight as the Basis of Aviation* (London: Longmans, Green and Co., 1911). I have chosen the expression "flying art" because it is more consistent with both the original German and with the content and thrust of the book than the more general "aviation." A copy of the German original is in the Gimbel collection, USAFA Library.

7. For details, see Kopfermann, "Otto Lilienthal und seine Familie," and also the "Zeittafel," in Heinzerling and Trischler, 22–27.

8. Otto Lilienthal, "Practical Experiments for the Development of Human Flight," Means, 1896, Annual, 8–9.

9. See Nitsch, 83–99.

10. Ibid. Many accounts refer to various Lilienthal gliders by their "Type" numbers, such as the Type 11, Type 15, etc. These were not Lilienthal's own designations, but rather those of Gerhard Halle (1893–1966), a distinguished student of Lilienthal's work who published the first major directory and catalog of the glider pioneer's designs.

11. Wilbur Wright, "Some Aeronautical Experiments," 18 Sept. 1901, Wright Papers I, 100.

12. Müllenhoff, 81; Anderson, 158.

13. Otto Lilienthal, "At Rhinow," in Means, 1897, Annual, 92–93.

14. Supf, I, 107. Sadly, a photograph of the glider after its accident (108) dramatically illustrates just how lightly damaged, in fact, it was. By comparison the Wrights experienced far more serious accidents during their own flight test program, but having learned from the Lilienthal experience, suffered only rarely, and then minor scrapes and sprains.

15. Supf, I; Beylich quote from 107, and see also 108–109.

16. For example, see Léopold Desmarest, "La mort d'Otto Lilienthal," *L'aéronaute,* v. 29, n. 11 (November 1896): 239–245; and "The Death of Lilienthal," *The Aeronautical Journal,* v. 1, n. 1 (Jan. 1897): 11–12.

17. Jarrett, 129–133.

18. See James Means, "Editorial," 1895 Annual, 169. Maxim's statements were from the *Boston Transcript,* 8 Sept. 1894, and Lilienthal responded in *The American Engineer* (Dec. 1894): 576.

19. For further information, see the previously cited Nitsch, and two articles by Gerhard Filchner and Christian Piepenburg, "Der 'Normal-Segelapparat' von Otto Lilienthal im Deutschen Museum—eine Dokumentation," and Christian Piepenburg, "Die Rekonstruktion von Lilienthals 'kleinem Doppeldecker' im Deutschen Museum," in Heinzerling and Trischler, 101–123. The sole surviving American *Normal-Segelapparat,* sold to newspaper magnate William Randolph Hearst, is on exhibit in the Early Flight Gallery, National Air and Space Museum, Smithsonian Institution. The Bennett-Pilcher machine is on exhibit at the Science Museum, London, and Joukovsky's is on exhibit in Moscow. Another Lilienthal glider, the *Kleiner Doppeldecker,* is at the Deutsches Museum, Munich. Replicas abound, including an excellent *Schlagflügelapparat* at the San Diego Aero-Space Museum which previously hung in the bar at Boom Trenchard's Flare Path, a now-defunct aviation restaurant and watering hole at the San Diego airport, a favorite and fondly remembered haunt of '70s-era naval aviators and airline crews. The Norsk Luftfartsmuseum at Bodø has an excellent Lilienthal biplane replica. Sadly, Professor George Francis Fitzgerald's glider did not survive. Fitzgerald briefly toyed with it, and flew it as a kite, before dying of natural causes. For a while it hung in the dome of the New

Building at Trinity College, narrowly escaping being burned by a careless student (!). It was given to a certain Dr. MacCabe, who apparently flew it frequently, but a friend of MacCabe's then "smashed it to pieces," fortunately without injuring himself. See Maurice F. Fitzgerald, "Prof. Fitzgerald's Lilienthal Glider," *The Aeronautical Journal*, XV, n. 57 (Jan. 1911): 37 Gibbs-Smith, *Directory*, 17–21, and Jarrett, 96.

20. Wilbur Wright, "Some Aeronautical Experiments," 18 Sept. 1901, Wright Papers I, 103. This calculation would give an average glide of about nine seconds, consistent with Lilienthal's relatively high sink rate designs. There is an excellent appreciation of Lilienthal's work by Wilbur Wright, "Otto Lilienthal," *Aero-Club of America Bulletin* (Sept. 1912), published after its author's death from typhoid fever. It has been recently republished as document 40, Wright Writings.

21. Octave Chanute, "Recent Experiments in Gliding Flight," Means, 1897, Annual, 35.

22. Letter, Kelvin to Baden-Powell, 8 Dec. 1896, from the letters files, folder 13, in the library, Royal Aeronautical Society, 4 Hamilton Place, London.

23. See Otto Lilienthal, "Die Profile der Segelflächen und ihre Wirkung," *Zeitschrift für Luftschiffahrt und Physik der Atmosphäre*, n. 2 and 3 (Feb-March 1895): 42–47, esp. the table on 44.

24. Anderson, 155.

25. When confronted with glaring discrepancies between anticipated and actual performance with their 1901 glider, the Wrights immediately recognized they had to undertake their own comprehensive program of airfoil testing, and out of this came the 1902 machine, which formed the basis for the 1903 powered Kitty Hawk Flyer. See WW to Octave Chanute, 2 Nov. 1901; 1 Dec. 1901; and 19 Feb. 1902, in Wright Papers I, 145–148, 168–171; and 217–220. There are excellent and insightful discussions of this in the previously cited Jakab, *Visions of a Flying Machine*, 77–80, 143–152, and Anderson, 138–164. Like others before him, Lilienthal uncritically accepted the erroneous Smeaton constant, but detailed analysis by Professor John Anderson, a noted historian of aerodynamics, has indicated that (despite accounts to the contrary) this was not the source of his tabulated errors, as the method of presenting his results negated any impact by the Smeaton constant. But the Smeaton constant did cause serious problems for the Wrights; see Orville Wright to Maj. Harold S. Martin, 2 Dec. 1920, Wright Papers II, 1128–1129.

26. Otto Lilienthal, "Fliegesport und Fliegepraxis," *Prometheus: Illustrierte Wochenschrift über die Fortschritte in Gewerbe, Industrie und Wissenschaft*, v. 7, n. 323 (Nov. 1895): 172. For a complete description of his machine and its "workings," see Otto Lilienthal, *Flying Machine. No. 544816, Specification of Letters Patent*, application filed February 28, 1894, patented August 20, 1895 (Washington, D.C.: U.S. Patent Office, 1895), 1–4.

27. Chanute, "Recent Experiments," 34–35.

28. As enumerated in Halle's book, and also a letter in the files of the NASM; see Gerhard Halle to Kenneth Newland, 30 Aug. 1960, in Lilienthal biographical file, NASM.

29. See William B. Krissof, M.D., and Ben Eiseman, M.D., "Injuries Associated with Hang Gliding," *Journal of the American Medical Association*, v. 233, n. 2 (14 July 1975): 158–160, and private letter to the author from Douglas H. Robinson, M.D., on 10 October 1976. I thank Dr. Robinson for making this *JAMA* article and his views known to me.

30. Zuerl, 15; Supf, I, 109; see also Eugen Zabel, *Deutsche Luftfahrt: Rückblicke und Ausblicke* (Berlin: Verlag Gustav Braunbeck GmbH, 1918), 59–60, and Edward L. Homze, *Arming the Luftwaffe: The Reich Air Ministry and the German Aircraft Industry, 1919–39*

(Lincoln, NE: University of Nebraska Press, 1976), 210. For the origins and extent of the German gliding movement, see Homze, 13–15, but particularly Walter Georgii, "Ten Years' Gliding and Soaring in Germany," *The Journal of the Royal Aeronautical Society*, XXXIV, 237 (Sep. 1930): 725–752; and Alexander Lippisch, "The Development, Design and Construction of Gliders and Sailplanes," *The Journal of the Royal Aeronautical Society*, XXXV, 247 (Jul. 1931): 532–570.

31. McCullough, 119–120.

32. Wilbur Wright, "Octave Chanute's Work in Aviation," *Aeronautics*, VIII, 1 (Jan. 1911): 4.

33. "Octave Chanute," in Means, 1896, Annual, 56–59.

34. See the previously cited Wolko, *Cause*, 33–34.

35. See *Proceedings of the International Conference on Aerial Navigation* (New York: The American Engineer and Railroad Journal, 1894); the gas turbine paper is J. H. Dow's "The Elastic-Fluid Turbine: A Possible Motor for Aeronautical Use," 120–124. There is a good summary of the conference in the previously cited Crouch, *Dream*, 78–100.

36. *Proceedings of the International Conference*, 8–9.

37. Means's life and work are excellently and dispassionately treated in a surprisingly balanced biography written by his son; see James Howard Means, M.D., *James Means and the Problem of Manflight During the Period 1882–1920* (Washington, D.C.: Smithsonian Institution Press, 1964), 108 (hereafter cited as Means biography, to distinguish it from the father's aeronautical annuals).

38. Means biography, 17, citing an article by Means in the *Boston Transcript*, 21 Jan. 1893.

39. Fred Howard, *Wilbur and Orville: A Biography of the Wright Brothers* (New York: Alfred A. Knopf, 1987), 31.

40. Means biography, 9–37, 87–130, and esp. 101–104; quote from 131.

41. Octave Chanute, *Soaring-Machine. Specification Forming Part of Letters Patent No. 582718, dated May 18, 1897*, application filed December 7, 1895, serial no. 571366 (Washington, D.C.: U.S. Patent Office, 1897), 1–2.

42. For Lilienthal's views on wing design, see his "The Best Shape for Wings" in Means, 1897 Annual, 95–97.

43. For the Howe, Pratt, and Whipple trusses, see Carl W. Condit, "Buildings and Construction," in Kranzberg and Pursell, I, 373–374, 383–385.

44. See Chanute, "Recent Experiments," 30–53; there is a good summary of these trials in Crouch, *Dream*, 175–222.

45. Chanute, "Recent Experiments," 35–39, and Plate VII.

46. Ibid., 39–42.

47. Ibid., 42.

48. Unfortunately, the prickly Herring proved so difficult for the team to work with that despite his undoubted talent Chanute had little choice but to let him go, lest the entire team disintegrate. Herring continued his own work to less and less effect, though he eventually reconciled with Chanute. Wilbur Wright, reading of Herring's claims to have invented "everything that has been or will yet be discovered in flying," wrote to Chanute that he considered him "an amusing 'cuss.'" See WW to OC, 29 Mar. 1904, Wright Papers I, 426.

CHAPTER TEN

1. The best source of material on the Wrights and their thinking remains Marvin W. McFarland's indispensable two-volume *The Papers of Wilbur and Orville Wright* (New

York: McGraw-Hill, 1953), hereafter Wright Papers I or II; and the more recent Peter L. Jakab and Rick Young, eds., *The Published Writings of Wilbur and Orville Wright* (Washington, D.C.: Smithsonian Institution Press, 2000). Fred C. Kelly, ed., *Miracle at Kitty Hawk:The Letters of Wilbur and Orville Wright* (New York: Farrar, Straus, and Young, 1951), hereafter Kelly, *Miracle*, contains some materials not found in McFarland and Jakab-Young. The best short account of the Wrights and their significance is Charles H. Gibbs-Smith's *The Wright Brothers: A Brief Account of Their Work, 1899, 1911* (London: HMSO, 1978 ed.). The family history of the Wrights is related in Tom D. Crouch, *The Bishop's Boys: A Life of Wilbur and Orville Wright* (New York: W. W. Norton & Company; 1989). Several notable accounts cover the Wrights' work in great detail, notably Fred Kelly's dated but still-classic *The Wright Brothers* (New York: Bantam Books, 1983 ed. of a 1943 work authorized by Orville Wright)—hereafter Kelly, *TWB*; Fred E. C. Culick and Spencer Dunmore, *On Great White Wings: The Wright Brothers and the Race for Flight* (New York: Hyperion/Madison Press Books, 2001); Fred Howard, *Wilbur and Orville: A Biography of the the Wright Brothers* (New York: Alfred A. Knopf, 1987); Harry Combs with Martin Caidin, *Kill Devil Hill: Discovering the Secret of the Wright Brothers* (Boston: Houghton Mifflin, 1979); John E. Walsh, *One Day at Kitty Hawk: The Untold Story of the the Wright Brothers and the Airplane* (New York: Crowell, 1975); Howard Wolko, ed.,*The Wright Flyer: An Engineering Perspective* (Washington, D.C.: Smithsonian Institution Press, 1987); and Peter Jakab's previously cited *Visions of a Flying Machine: The Wright Brothers and the Process of Invention* (Washington, D.C.: Smithsonian Institution Press, 1990). The previously cited Hallion, ed., *The Wright Brothers: Heirs of Prometheus*, contains essays by recognized experts on the Wrights, as well as reprints of key documents. See also Charles A. Dempsey, "The Wright Brothers' Experience in the Evolution of Aircraft Design, Structures, and Materials," in Dayton-Cincinnati Section, American Institute of Aeronautics and Astronautics and Astronautics, *Evolution of Aircraft/Aerospace Structures and Materials Symposium* (Dayton, OH: Air Force Museum, April 1985): 1–1 to 1–13. Orville Wright left his own account of the first flight; see his "How We Made the First Flight," *Flying and the Aero Club of America Bulletin,* II (Dec. 1913): 10–12, 35–36. (Reprinted in Hallion, ed., *The Wright Brothers,* 101–109.) While much has been written of the Wrights, very little has been written about their engine maker. The best account of the 1903 Wright engine is H. R. DuFour and Peter J. Unitt's excellent *Charles E. Taylor: The Wright Brothers Mechanician* (Dayton, OH: Prime Printing, 1997), edited by David K. Vaughan. For an excellent survey of all Wright engines, see Leonard S. Hobbs, *The Wright Brothers' Engines and Their Design,* a study in the *Smithsonian Annals of Flight* series (Washington, D.C.: Smithsonian Institution Press, 1971), the latter written by a noted engine designer who himself received the prestigious Robert J. Collier Trophy for the design of the J57, the first jet engine used widely in both military and civilian applications.

2.   WW to OC, 15 Nov. 1904, Wright Papers I, 464.
3.   Crouch, *Boys,* 13–15, 48–65, 74–77, 93–95, 116–121, 482–483; Kelly, 1–15.
4.   Crouch, *Boys,* 91–99, 107–115; Kelly, 15–25.
5.   Deposition of Orville Wright in Regina C. Montgomery et. al. vs. the United States, 13 Jan. 1920, Wright Papers I, 3; Kelly, 3.
6.   "Orville Wright on the Wright Experiments of 1899," in Wright Papers I, 8.
7.   WW to SI, 30 May 1899, Wright Papers I, 4–5.
8.   "Darius Green and His Flying Machine," a mid-nineteenth-century tale on the fool-

ishness of trying to attempt flight (and by extension, the "impossible"). Even after the Wrights it remained a standard of children's literature; see John T. Trowbridge, *Darius Green and His Flying-Machine* (Boston: Houghton Mifflin Company, 1910), copy in the Gimbel collection, USAFA Library; and the previously cited Goldstein, *Flying Machines*, 6–7, and figure 1 for an evocative depiction of young Darius on the edge of disaster.

9. The biographical information is from the Rathbun Biographical File, Smithsonian Archives and in particular from Marcus Benjamin, "Richard Rathbun," *Science*, v. 48, n. 1236 (6 Sept. 1918): 231–235.

10. Wilbur and Orville Wright, "The Wright Brothers' Aeroplane," *Century Magazine*, v. 76 (Sept. 1908), 641–650.

11. Benjamin, 235.

12. Eugene S. Ferguson, "Expositions of Technology, 1851–1900," in Kranzberg and Pursell, I, 718–720; Thomas Parke Hughes, *American Genesis: A History of the American Genius for Invention* (New York: Penguin Putnam, Inc., 1990), 14–15.

13. Hughes, 2–3.

14. Daniel Boorstin, "Prologue: The Fertile Verge," xx. "American creativity," Boorstin avers, "has flourished on what I call the Fertile Verge. A verge is a place of encounter between something and something else" (xv). I thank Tamar Mehuron for bringing this work to my attention.

15. *Washington Post*, 31 Dec. 1901.

16. Ibid. And it is not too much, incidentally, to predict that the year 2100 might well witness routine 6,000–miles-per-hour transportation via hypersonic air transports, if current technological predictions hold true.

17. H. G. Wells, *Anticipations* (New York: Harper and Brothers, 1902), 208.

18. Le Corbusier, *Towards a New Architecture* (New York: Praeger Publishers, 1970 ed.), 101.

19. See also Donald J. Bush, *The Streamlined Decade* (New York: George Braziller, 1975), 39–44.

20. Le Corbusier, *Aircraft* (New York: Universe Books, 1988), 6.

21. Antoine de Saint-Exupéry, *Wind, Sand and Stars* (New York: Reynal & Hitchcock, 1942 ed.), 38–39. This translated text (by Lewis Galantière) is a "streamlined" and simplified adaptation of a more elaborate text in the author's original *Terre des hommes*. For the context of the original text, see Saint-Exupéry, *Terre des hommes* (Paris: Éditions Gallimard, 1939), 50–51. For a discussion of the symbolic significance of the airplane and flight, see Joseph J. Corn, *The Winged Gospel: America's Romance with Aviation, 1900–1950* (New York: Oxford University Press, 1983), 29–50.

22. See, for example, Donald J. Bush, *The Streamlined Decade*, 29–42.

23. Wilbur Wright, "Some Aeronautical Experiments," 18 Sept. 1901, Wright Papers I, 100.

24. Wilbur and Orville Wright, "The Wright Brothers' Aeroplane," *Century Magazine*, v. 76 (Sept. 1908): 641–650, reprinted in Hayward, 9–24.

25. Kelly, *TWB*, 27.

26. Wilbur Wright, "Die Wagerechte Lage Während des Gleitfluges," *Illustrierte Aeronautische Mitteilungen*, Band V (Jul. 1901): 108–109.

27. Kelly, *TWB*, 27.

28. Ibid., 28.

29. Wright Deposition, 13 Jan. 1920, Wright Papers I, 8–9.

30. WW to OC, 13 May 1900, Wright Papers I, 15.

31. WW to OC, 10 Aug. 1900, and OC to WW, 14 Aug. 1900, in Wright Papers I, 22–23.

32.   WW to OC, 16 Nov. 1900, Wright Papers I, 40–44.

33.   There is an excellent discussion of this in Frederick E. C. Culick, "The Wright Brothers: First Aeronautical Engineers and Test Pilots," in Society of Experimental Test Pilots, *2001 Report to the Aerospace Profession: Forty-fifth Symposium Proceedings* (Los Angeles: SETP, Sept. 2001): 280.

34.   Culick, "The Wright Brothers," 287–288; the aerodynamicists were Richard von Mises, and S. A. Tchaplygin; for the technically inclined, pitching moment is expressed as $M = \frac{1}{2}\,\rho V^2 S c C_m$ where M is the pitching moment, ρ is the air density, V is the velocity, S is the wing area, c is the wing chord, and Cm is the pitching-moment coefficient. See Ira H. Abbott and Albert E. von Doenhoff, *Theory of Wing Sections: Including a Summary of Airfoil Data* (New York: McGraw-Hill Book Company, Inc., 1949), 3–5, 19, 69.

35.   Ibid., 279–295.

36.   Samuel Eliot Morison, *The European Discovery of America: The Northern Voyages,* A.D. *500–1600* (New York: Oxford University Press, 1971), 295–299.

37.   Quote on map from William P. Cumming, *The Southeast in Early Maps* (Princeton, NJ: Princeton University Press, 1958), cited in "The Edward Moseley Map of North Carolina, 1733" a reference guide in the Special Collections department, Joyner Library, Eastern Carolina University. Only three original copies of the Moseley map exist, the best of which (the only American copy) is exhibited in the Special Collections archive, fourth floor, Joyner Library, Eastern Carolina University, Greenville, N.C. It should be noted that in later times cartographers "reassigned" the name Arcadia to the far northeast coast. Verrazano, "this valiant gentleman" (in the words of a contemporary) returned to the Americas in 1528, sailing down the Lesser Antilles; he mistook a party of warlike Carib tribesmen for gentle natives, waded ashore, and was instantly killed and eaten.

38.   OW to Alexander Klemin, 11 Apr. 1924, in Wright Papers I, 44, n. 8; see also OW to KW, 14 Oct. 1900, Wright Papers I, 29.

39.   WW to OC, 16 Nov. 1900, Wright Papers I, 43.

40.   See WW, "Some Aeronautical Experiments," Wright Papers I, 105–106.

41.   Ibid., 112.

42.   Ibid., 109–110; Excerpt from Chanute-Huffaker Diary, 8 Aug. 1901, Wright Papers I, 81. See also excerpt from Wilbur Wright's Diary A, 30 Jul. 1901, Wright Papers I, 77–78.

43.   Ibid., 108–109.

44.   Wilbur Wright speaking to the Aéro-Club de France, 5 Nov. 1908, Wright Papers II, 934. Recollection is a tricky thing, and in the official Wright biography, Orville recalled that his brother actually said that "Not within a thousand years would man ever fly!" (Kelly, *TWB,* 42). In any case, 50 or 1,000, the Wrights were pretty discouraged.

CHAPTER ELEVEN

1.   Quoted in Gibbs-Smith, *The Wright Brothers,* 5.

2.   But this was not, as has been alleged, the first wind tunnel in the United States. Alfred Wells built and employed the first tunnel in America at the Massachusetts Institute of Technology, Cambridge, Mass., in 1896 for the purpose of checking earlier whirling-arm results from Samuel Langley. Then, in 1901, Dr. Albert Zahm built a large tunnel at the Catholic University of America, Washington, D.C.

3. The actual Wright research methodology and their research results are presented (in great detail) in appendix II, "Wright Wind Tunnel, 1901," sections A-E, Wright Papers I, 547–593; additionally, there are excellent discussions of the Wrights' ground-based aerodynamic research in Jakab, 115–142; Anderson, 216–229; and Culick, 296.

4. WW to OC, 23 Dec. 1901, Wright Papers I, 187.

5. Crouch, *Bishop's Boys,* 215–218.

6. Wilbur Wright Notebook, 1, Sep. Oct. 1900, Wright Papers I, 34. The Wrights referred to this downturning of tips as "cathedral," which is more commonly called anhedral in the present day.

7. OW Diary B, 22 Sep. 1902, Wright Papers I, 258.

8. OW Diary B, 23 Sep. 1902, Wright Papers I, 260.

9. WW to MW, 2 Oct. 1902, in Kelly, *Miracle,* 79–80.

10. Note 4, Wright Papers II, 469–471.

11. Rating scale from TND 5153, National Aeronautics and Space Administration, n.d.

12. Wilbur Wright, "Experiments and Observations in Soaring Flight," 24 Jun. 1903, Wright Papers I, 323–324.

13. OW to KW, 23 Oct. 1902, Wright Papers I, 280.

14. Initially rejected as not being sufficiently understandable, this patent was reworked by the brothers using the services of a professional patent lawyer and refiled on March 23, 1903. The U.S. Patent Office granted it to the brothers on 22 May 1906. See Orville Wright and Wilbur Wright, *Flying Machine. No. 821,393, Specification of Letters Patent,* application filed March 23, 1903, patented May 22, 1906 (Washington, D.C.: U.S. Patent Office, 1906), 1–10.

15. Daniel Yergin, *The Prize: The Epic Quest for Oil, Money, and Power* (New York: Simon and Schuster, 1992), 25–29, 79–80, 171–172.

16. Lynwood Bryant, "The Beginnings of the Internal-Combustion Engine," in Kranzberg and Pursell, I, 648–653.

17. Ibid. The Wright engine had the same power to weight ratio. See H. R. DuFour and Peter J. Unitt's *Charles E. Taylor: The Wright Brothers Mechanician* (Dayton, OH: Prime Printing, 1997), 22. Actually, the 14 pounds per horsepower is only for the engine with all accessories attached. If just comparing the power to the finished engine, the ratio changes to 12.67 pounds per horsepower, an even greater tribute to Taylor's mechanical skills. This pales, however, in comparison with the phenomenal 1.15 pounds per horsepower achieved by the remarkable Manly-Balzer engine used on the ill-fated Langley *Great Aerodrome* of 1903. The comment on Daimler is based upon his "On the Novelty of My Patent Number 28022: A Reply," in the previously cited Schirmacher, *German Essays on Science in the 19th Century,* 275–276.

18. Wilbur Wright, "Experiments and Observations in Soaring Flight," 325. See also Letter, Wright Cycle Company to the Daimler Manufacturing Company, 3 Dec. 1902, Wright Papers I, 286–287, and Kelly, *TWB,* 41.

19. Excerpt from "Taylor-Webbert Nuptials," a newspaper article reproduced in DuFour, Unitt, and Vaughan, 12.

20. Ibid., 11–14.

21. Ibid., 15–22, 31–34; Hobbs, 13–28; Robert B. Meyer, Jr., "Three Famous Early Aero Engines," *Annual Report of the Smithsonian Institution* (Washington, D.C.: SI, 1961): 357–372; appendix V, "Aeroplanes and Motors," 1903 Motor, Wright Papers II, 1210–1214.

22. Hobbs, 10–12, has an excellent section on the engineering choices the Wrights made for their engine.

23. Or as Orville Wright put it, "an aeroplane [his term at the time for an airfoil] traveling in a spiral course." See his "How We Made the First Flight," *Flying and the Aero Club of America Bulletin,* II (Dec. 1913), reprinted in Hallion, ed., *The Wright Brothers,* 102.

24. Ibid. See appendix III, "The Wright Propellers," in Wright Papers I, 594–640, for an excellent summary discussion of Wright work on their propeller concepts. As yet another proof of the Wrights' excellent engineering, on December 2000, carefully fabricated reproductions of the Wrights' 1903 and 1904 propellers built for the Wright Experience® (a group dedicated to the reproduction of Wright Flyers and gliders) were tested in the NASA Langley Research Center Full Scale Tunnel; the test results plotting thrust coefficient versus rotational speed showed "very good to excellent agreement between the Wright brothers' measurements and the measurements taken during the current test series." See Robert L. Ash, Stanley J. Miley, Drew Landman, and Kenneth W. Hyde. "Evolution of Wright Flyer Propellers Between 1903 and 1912," Paper AIAA-2001–0309, 39th Aerospace Sciences Meeting and Exhibit, American Institute of Aeronautics and Astronautics, Reno, Nevada, 8–11 Jan. 2001.

25. See the previously cited Dempsey, "The Wright Brothers Experience," passim.

26. Appendix V, "Aeroplanes and Motors," 1903 Machine, Wright Papers II, 1187–1189; see also Culick, 291. There is an excellent summary of the Wrights' control system (and their later elaborations upon it) in Gibbs-Smith's previously cited *Invention of the Aeroplane,* 308–312, and also in a reference document in the holdings of the Science Museum, London, by Brian Lacey, Walter Tuck, and Gibbs-Smith, "The Wright Flyer I (1903): The Pilot and his Controls," (Sept. 1973): 1–3. I thank Messrs. Lacey, Tuck, and Gibbs-Smith for making it available to me.

27. WW to Chanute, 19 Sep. 1903; OW to KW, 18 Oct. 1903; OW Diary, 21 Oct. 1903, and 4 Nov. 1903, Wright Papers I, 354–376.

28. OW Diary, 3–28 Nov. and 11 Dec. 1903; OW to MW and KW, 15 Nov. 1903; OW to Charles E. Taylor, 23 Nov. 1903, Wright Papers I, 376–391.

29. WW to SI, 30 May 1899, Wright Papers I, 4–5.

30. OW to OC, 16 Oct. 1903, Wright Papers I, 364.

31. OW to MW and KW, 15 Nov. 1903, Wright Papers I, 381; the $100,000 would be equivalent to $2 million in 2001.

32. Telegram, WW to MW, 15 Oct. 1903, Wright Papers I, 393.

33. OW Diary, 17 Dec. 1903, Wright Papers I, 394–395.

34. For details of his actions in starting the plane, I have relied upon Lacy, Tuck, and Gibbs-Smith's "The Wright Flyer I (1903): The Pilot and his Controls."

35. OW Diary, 17 Dec. 1903, Wright Papers I, 395.

36. Telegram, OW to MW, 17 Dec. 1903, Wright Papers I, 397. The 57 seconds was incorrect, thanks to a transmission error, and Orville meant the wind was at least 21 miles per hour, not that 21 was the maximum.

37. Quoted in Crouch, *Bishop's Boys,* 270.

38. (Norfolk) *Virginian-Pilot,* 18 Dec. 1903. The article was almost entirely wrong in all details, not least of which was having the dour and reserved Wilbur allegedly shouting "Eureka!" See also Walter Lord, *The Good Years: From 1900 to the First World War* (New York: Bantam Books, 1962), 90.

39. "History of the Kramer Lumber Company of Elizabeth City, NC" (30 Oct. 1977): 35,

an oral history in Collection 347.1, Kramer Family Manuscript, Special Collections, Joyner Library, ECU.

40. *Washington Post,* 19 Dec. 1903. Like the *Virginian-Pilot,* much of the rest of the article was highly speculative and, particularly with regard to the design of the airplane, inaccurate.

41. Quoted in Penrose, *British Aviation: The Pioneer Years,* 48.

42. OC to WW, 27 Dec. 1903, and WW to OC, 28 Dec. 1903, Wright Papers I, 401.

43. Kelly, 74–75.

44. WW to OC, 8 Aug. 1904 and 28 Aug. 1908, and WW Diary, 7–15 Sep. 1904, Wright Papers I, 448–449, 452–455; Kelly, 76–77. It is important to note that this was the first use of a catapult by the Wrights; although they had a launching monorail at Kitty Hawk, it did not have any means of catapulting the Flyer into the air.

45. Amos I. Root, "Our Homes," *Gleanings in Bee Culture,* v. 33, n. 1 (1 Jan. 1905): 36–39. An original of the Root article is in the Gimbel collection, USAFA Library, and it is also reprinted in Hallion, ed., *The Wright Brothers,* 110–115.

46. From letter, H. M. Weaver to F. S. Lahm, 6 Dec. 1905, quoted in Mark Sullivan, *Our Times: The United States, 1900–1925,* v. II, *America Finding Herself* (New York: Charles Scribner's Sons, 1943), 597–598. The flight Stauffer witnessed occurred on Thursday, Oct. 5, 1905, as discussed subsequently in the text. See WW Diary, 5 Oct. 1905, Wright Papers I, 514.

47. WW Diary, 5 Oct. 1905, Wright Papers I, 514.

48. Culick, 313.

49. Hobbs, 61.

50. Culick, 321–323; see also Michael E. Ruane, "A New Race to be First in Flight," *Washington Post,* 17 Feb. 2002.

51. Statement of Bill Gates on the occasion of *Time Magazine's* honoring the 100 greatest individuals of the twentieth century.

CHAPTER TWELVE

1. Ernest Archdeacon, "Les progrés de l'Aviation," *L'aérophile,* v. 14, n. 1 (Jan. 1906): 9–14. There is a more literal translation of this passage in Gibbs-Smith, *Rebirth,* 173, but I believe the above is more consistent with the rest of Archdeacon's remarks.

2. Ernest Archdeacon in *La locomotion* (11 Apr. 1903): 225–227, reprinted, as "Mr. Chanute in Paris," Wright Papers I, 654–659, esp. 658 (also reprinted in Gibbs-Smith, *Rebirth,* 92, 357–358). For more on the Aéro-Club and the promotion of early French aviation, see Commission Histoire, Arts et Lettres de l'Aéro Club de France, *Cent ans avec l'Aéro-Club de France* (Paris: Addim, 1998), 65–70.

3. Victor Tatin, "L'analyse des expériences d'aviation," *L'aérophile,* v. 12, n. 2 (Feb. 1904): 31–32.

4. Archdeacon, "Les progrés. . . . "

5. Gibbs-Smith, *Rebirth,* 126–127.

6. Consider, for example, the statement "Die Brüder Wright wurden lange Zeit als 'Bluffer' angesehen," (for a long time the brothers Wright were seen as bluffers), in Raimund Nimführ, "Eindrücke und Erfahrungen auf einer aëronautischflugtechnischen Studienreise nach Paris," *Illustrierte Aeronautische Mitteilungen,* v. 12, n. 15 (29 July 1908): 509.

7. Quoted in Gibbs-Smith, *Rebirth*, 149–150; see also WW to OC, 12 Apr. 1905, Wright Papers I, 486, n. 6.

8. WW to OC, 12 Apr. 1905, Wright Papers I, 486–487.

9. OC to WW, 7 Mar. 1903, Wright Papers I, 299–300; Gibbs-Smith, *Invention*, 54; Alfred Gollin, *No Longer an Island: Britain and the Wright Brothers, 1902–1909* (Stanford: Stanford University Press, 1984), 19.

10. When Henri Farman would fly for nearly 45 minutes.

11. For tunnel building, see N. H. Randers-Pehrson, "Pioneer Wind Tunnels," *Smithsonian Miscellaneous Collections*, v. 93, n. 4 (19 Jan. 1935): 4–18, and Lee, "The Origin of the Wind Tunnel In Europe, 1871–1900," *Air Power History*, v. 45, n. 2 (Summer 1998): 11–14. There is an extraordinarily comprehensive discussion of European aeronautical laboratories in Ansbert Vorreiter's "Die Wissenschaftlichen lufttechnischen Institute," in *Jahrbuch der Luftfahrt, II: Jahrgang 1912* (Munich: J. F. Lehmanns Verlag, 1912), 359–397 (hereafter Vorreiter II). Albert F. Zahm, "Report on European Aeronautical Laboratories," *Smithsonian Miscellaneous Collections*, v. 62, n. 3 (27 July 1914): 1–23, is the best English-language reference. See also Zahm, "Advisory Committee on the Langley Aerodynamical Laboratory," *Smithsonian Miscellaneous Collections*, v. 62, n. 1 (17 July 1913): 1–5. Zahm, incidentally, had built the first genuine American laboratory (as defined by having a wind tunnel and a—for its time—sophisticated measurement system) at the Catholic University of American in Washington, D.C., in 1901.

12. B-P to OC, 27 Sep. 1902, in Gollin, *No Longer*, 19.

13. "The Experiments of the Brothers Wright," *The Aeronautical Journal*, v. 8, n. 30 (Apr. 1904): 37–42.

14. WW to OC, 15 Nov. 1904, Wright Papers I, 464.

15. The best single account of the Wright's attempt to secure production contracts is Phillip Jarrett's "Selling the First Aeroplane: Exploiting the Wright Flyer," *Air Enthusiast*, n. 62 (March-April 1996), pp. 34–40.

16. His first modified airplane—one of the world's oldest surviving aircraft—is now on exhibit at the Musée de l'Air et de l'Espace. See also Dollfus and Bouché, 180; Munson, 172–173; Penrose, *Pioneer Years*, 74–75; Gibbs-Smith, *Rebirth*, 207–208, 232, 236; Gibbs-Smith, *Directory*, 511; and Gibbs-Smith, *Invention*, 87–91.

17. WW to OC, 4 Dec. 1905, Wright Papers I, 530; Mark Sullivan has a reprint of the detailed text that followed in his *Our Times: The United States, 1900–1925, v. 2: America Finding Herself* (New York: Charles Scribner's Sons, 1943), 597–598.

18. "De tout autre que des frères Wright, les résultats announcés eussent ete considérés pour un simple bluff," in "Les frères Wright et leur aéroplane à moteur," *L'aérophile*, v. 13, n. 12 (Dec. 1905): 268; see also 264–272.

19. Victor Tatin, "Progrès possibles de l'aviation en France," *L'aérophile*, v. 14, n. 1 (Jan. 1906): 14–15. Researchers take what they wish to out of sources. Gibbs-Smith sees Tatin's essay as exhibiting what he termed (correctly) as the "chauffeur mindset"; an obsessive concern about lift and propulsion, and very little or no concern over controllability. While this is true, to me the most interesting aspect of this article is Tatin's status as France's most beloved and respected aeronautical pioneer (at this point), and his outright acceptance of the Wright claims at a time when many others refused to see the light. For Gibbs-Smith's interpretation, see his *Rebirth*, 201–203. See also, from the same issue of the journal, "L'aéroplane Wright," 18–23.

20. A. Cléry, "Dernier perfectionnements connus des machines volantes Wright," *L'aérophile*, v. 14, n. 1 (Jan. 1906): 23–26.

21. "Fliers or Liars," *New York Herald* (Paris ed.), 10 Feb. 1906.

22. L.-P. Cailletet, "Vers l'aviation," *L'aérophile*, v. 14, n. 8 (Aug. 1906): 156–157; and in the same issue, Bosquet de la Grye, L.-P. Cailletet, and E. Archdeacon, "Pour le succès de l'aviation Français," 157–158.

23. OW Diary, 17 Feb. 1904, and WW to OC, 1 March 1904, Wright Papers I, 421–422.

24. Gibbs-Smith, *Rebirth*, 353. I have also benefitted from Philip Jarrett's unpublished manuscript, "Man Flies," which revealed the connection between Hargrave and Wenham.

25. Ibid., 212, 218; see also his *Invention*, 87. Technical details are from G-S and from the previously cited Munson, 20 and 159–160.

26. A. de Masfrand, "Les progrès de l'aviation: L'essor de Santos-Dumont," *L'aérophile*, v. 14, n. 9 (Sep. 1906): 191–194. See also the previously cited Wykeham, *Santos-Dumont*, 207–225.

27. Recollection of C. G. Grunhold, "The Pioneers of Flight," in Claude Grahame-White and Harry Harper, eds., *The Aeroplane: Past, Present, and Future* (London: T. Werner Laurie, 1911), 10; see also Commission Histoire, *Cent ans*, 76.

28. F. Ferber, "La deuxième envolée de Santos-Dumont," *L'aérophile*, v. 14, n. 10 (Oct. 1906): 245–247. See also Dollfus and Bouché, 183–185.

29. Ibid. Emphasis added.

30. "Le banquet Santos-Dumont," *L'aérophile*, v. 14, n. 12 (Dec. 1906): 293–294. See also "Nouveau triomphe de Santos-Dumont," an article in the same issue, 291–293.

31. Gibbs-Smith, *Rebirth*, 224. See also Jacques May, "Sur Clément Ader," *L'aérophile*, v. 18, n. 9 (1 May 1910): 207–209.

32. For example, consider Gabriel Voisin's absurd comparison of the unsuccessful *Avion III* to Blériot's highly influential (and widely copied) channel-crossing monoplane: "One of them, the *Avion*, is a *highly developed* creation while the other [the Blériot] is an assembly, *carefully contrived but primitive*, owing its existence to improvisation." Gabriel Voisin, *Men, Women and 10,000 Kites* (London: Putnam, 1963), 101. (emphasis added)

33. See Lissarrague, *Ader*, 229–233, 274–275; for the etymology of the words *avion* and *aeroplane*, see Gibbs-Smith's "The History of Some Aeronautical Words," in his *Aeroplane*, 338–339, drawing upon the pioneering work of Svante Stubelius.

34. Again, to translate "then-year" francs into "now-year" dollars, divide the total amount of francs by 5 (to obtain "then-year" dollars), then multiply the result (the "then-year" dollars) by 20.

35. Northcliffe quote from Curtis Prendergast, *The First Aviators*, a volume in the Time-Life *Epic of Flight* series (Alexandria, VA: Time-Life Books, 1980), 27. See also Gollin, *No Longer*, 186–193; the *Daily Mail*, 194.

36. WW to OC, 2 Nov. 1906, Wright Papers II, 734–735.

37. WW to OC, 10 Oct. 1906, Wright Papers II, 729–730.

38. For further information on all of these, see the previously cited Parkin, *Bell and Baldwin*, 41–88; Louis S. Casey, *Curtiss: The Hammondsport Era, 1907–1915* (New York: Crown Publishers, Inc., 1981), 4–24; C. R. Roseberry, *Glenn Curtiss: Pioneer of Flight* (Garden City, NY: Doubleday & Company, 1972), 83–162; Penrose, *Pioneer Years*, 70–83, 99–143; Driver, *Birth of Military Aviation*, 188–193; Percy B. Walker, *Early Aviation at Farnborough: The History of the Royal Aircraft Establishment, v. 2: The First Aeroplanes* (London: MacDonald, 1974), xvi-xx; J. W. Dunne, "The Theory of the Dunne Aeroplane," *The Aeronautical Journal*, v. 17, n. 66 (April 1913): 83–87; Raimund Nimführ, "Der neue Motorgleitflieger von Etrich-Wels," *Illustrierte Aeronautische Mitteilungen*, v. 11, n. 4 (April 1907): 118–121; and Supf, *Deutschen Fluggeschichte*, I, 195–198.

39.   Gibbs-Smith, *Invention,* 205.

40.   Villard, 51–52.

41.   Ibid., 134–136.

42.   Brian A. Elliott, *Blériot: Herald of an Age* (Stroud, Eng.: Tempus Publishing Co., 2000), 8–25; Munson, 104; Villard, 44–45; Gibbs-Smith, *Directory,* 40, 69; and Gibbs-Smith, *Invention,* 71–72.

43.   Voisin, 100, and 142–143; Elliott, 29, 35.

44.   There are two remarkably good photographs of these trials by the noted French photographer Jacques Henri Lartigue, who was only *ten years old* when he took them. Lartigue, a gifted prodigy who took extraordinary photographs of airplanes, gliders, racing automobiles, and their operators (as well as some evocative portraits of French women and their fashions of the time) had a keen eye for composition and action. Also, his photograph of the Archdeacon-Voisin 1904 glider clearly reveals that it lacked any provision whatsoever for wing warping—indeed, the wing struts at the wingtips were rigidly braced in such a fashion that the wings would have been impossible to warp in any case. See plate 55 in Vicki Goldberg, ed., *Jacques Henri Lartigue: Photographer* (Boston: Bulfinch Press-Little, Brown and Company, 1998). Lartigue's photographs are held and administered by the Association des Amis de Jacques Henri Lartigue, in association with the French government's Ministry of Culture and Communication.

45.   Voisin, 137; Elliott, 35; Gibbs-Smith, *Directory,* 69. See also Michel Bénichou, "Pourquoi Louis Blériot a traversé la Manche," *La fana de l'aviation,* n. 356 (July 1999): 16–25, esp. 19–22.

46.   Gibbs-Smith, *Invention,* 103–106; Munson, 105.

47.   Consider his 1911 statement, "No aeroplane—however well it flies—is of any practical value unless it has an efficient system of either wheels or skids so that it may take its run along the ground safely before rising, and descend again equally successfully, with the undercarriage so constructed as to withstand, if necessary, quite a severe shock." In Blériot, "Sporting and Commercial Possibilities of the Aeroplane," Grahame-White and Harper, eds., 203.

48.   For the history of this particular design, see Tom D. Crouch's *Blériot XI: The Story of a Classic Aircraft* (Washington, D.C.: Smithsonian Institution Press, 1982), passim.

49.   Ivan Rendall, *The Chequered Flag: 100 Years of Motor Racing* (London: Weidenfeld and Nicholson, 1993), 35, 38, 41.

50.   Ernest Archdeacon, "Après le succès," *L'aérophile,* v. 16, n. 9 (1 May 1908): p. 169. See also "Les grandes étapes de l'aviation: Henri Farman vole près d'un kilomètre," *L'aérophile,* v. 15, n. 10 (Oct. 1907), 286–289. See also Gibbs-Smith, *Directory,* 69–72, and his *Rebirth,* 244–246, and 261–264.

51.   A. Cléry, "La première femme-aviateur," *L'aérophile,* v. 16, n. 16 (15 August 1908), cover.

52.   Gibbs-Smith, *Invention,* 350; Gibbs-Smith, *Directory,* 70–71.

53.   There is an excellent recollection of these flights by a former *New York Herald* journalist who witnessed them in the previously cited Sullivan, v. 2, 606–613.

54.   WW and OW to Gen. James Allen, 27 Jan. 1908; Milton Wright Diary, 8 Feb. 1908, and 15 Mar. 1908 inc. note 1; WW to OC, 8 Apr. 1908; WW Diary, 14 Apr. to 20 May 1908; and WW to OW, 20 May 1908, Wright Papers II, 856–883.

55.   See, for example, "Wilbur Wright à Paris," *L'aérophile,* v. 15, n. 6 (June 1907): 167–168. Wilbur arrived first, followed later by Orville.

56.   WW to OW, 17 June 1908, Wright Papers II, 900–901.

57. M. Degoul, "Les premiers vols de Wilbur Wright en France," *L'aérophile*, v. 16, n. 8 (15 Aug. 1908): 326–327; *The Times* (London), 10 August 1908; see also Villard, 54. It is interesting to note that the length of his demonstration is not at all inconsistent with the length of high-performance aircraft demonstrations at the Le Bourget air show today, nearly a century later! Finally, it is worth noting that three days after this amazing flight, which demonstrated to the Europeans that the problem of powered, controlled, winged flight had been solved, Francis Wenham died, age 84, probably unaware of the Hunaudières trials. In December 1905 he had written to Chanute congratulating the Wrights' success, stating it "removes me from the list of cranks who always stated I was advocating an *impossibility*." (emphasis in original) For their part the Wrights replied to Chanute that they regarded Wenham as "one of the ablest and most useful men who have labored in the cause of human flight." See OC to WW 23 Dec. 1905 and WW to OC, 27, 1905, and note 2, Wright Papers I, 539.

58. Griffith Brewer, "Wilbur Wright," *The Aeronautical Journal*, v. 16, n. 63 (July 1912): 149. See also Lt. Col. A. Ogilvie, "Some Aspects of Aeronautical Research," *The Aeronautical Journal*, v. 26, n. 142 (Oct. 1922): 381–382, for the recollections of another eyewitness to the Wright demonstrations.

59. Raimund Nimführ, "Eindrücke und Erfahrungen auf einer aëronautischflugtechnischen Studienreise nach Paris," *Illustrierte Aeronautische Mitteilungen*, v. 12, n. 15 (29 July 1908): 509–510. Note that despite the July date of this journal, the Nimführ article is signed and dated "Le Mans, 11. August 1908."

60. "Neue Flugversuche," *Illustrierte Aeronautische Mitteilungen*, v. 12, n. 15 (29 July 1908): 512.

61. *New York Herald* (Paris ed.), 6 Oct. 1908.

62. Degoul, "Les premiers," 324.

63. WW to OW, 15 Aug. 1908, Wright Papers II, 912.

64. Both quotes from Gibbs-Smith, *Invention*, 147.

CHAPTER THIRTEEN

1. WW to OC, 10 Nov. 1908, Wright Papers II, 935.

2. Wright to the *Aéro-Club de France*, 5 Nov. 1908, Wright Papers II, 934–935.

3. Time would show they endured, most touchingly in the tributes he would be given upon his death from typhoid fever, a mere four years in the future. For example see "Wilbur Wright," *Flugsport: Illustrierte technische Zeitschrift und Anzeiger für das gesamte "Flugwesen,"* v. 4, n. 12 (5 June 1912), 453–457, and the previously cited Brewer, "Wilbur Wright," *Aeronautical Journal*, 148–153.

4. Letter, Frank Lahm to his father, 27 August 1908, Cat. 167.601–25, in Lahm Correspondence, 06/10/07–31/05/10, Air Force Historical Research Agency, Maxwell AFB, AL (hereafter AFHRA).

5. The Fort Myer parade ground is still in existence, as are the buildings that flanked it at the time of his trials. His route took him near Quarters 7—now the home of the U.S. Air Force Chief of Staff, appropriately called "Air House" and fittingly sporting a brass Wright Flyer weathervane on its roof—across Arlington Cemetery, where so many military aviators are buried (including some Wright pupils), over what is now the Pentagon, the approach and departure paths for Ronald Reagan National Airport, and on down just west of downtown Alexandria to a low hill, now the site of a Masonic temple. Then he would reverse course and return to Fort Myer. Re the

bobbing and weaving: a stable airplane will hold a course "hands off." An unstable airplane will hold a course as long as the pilot actively keeps it in trim. If the pilot gets slightly "behind" or "ahead" of the airplane's motions (easily done due to a variety of factors, including control system lag and friction), he inadvertently creates a so-called pilot-induced oscillation (PIO). As shown by surviving film of its flights, the Flyer clearly had a lot of lag in its flight control system, and as a consequence the operator clearly was often either over or undercontrolling it, characterized by a "hunting" motion about all three axes. This is, of course, yet another argument in favor of the stable airplane. Today, in the era of computer-controlled flight, an inherently unstable design such as an F-16, F-117, or B-2 can be made to fly with no difficulty whatsoever. That option, of course, clearly did not exist in the early years of flight.

6. *Washington Post, New York Herald,* and *New York Times,* all 18 Sept. 1908. See also the previously cited de Kay, *Monitor,* 163; and Hetherington, "The Langley and Wright Aero Accidents," 40–45. The best accounts of the accident are Orville's letter to his brother, 14 Nov. 1908, Wright Papers II, 936–939; Frank Lahm's letter to his father, 2 Oct 1908, in the previously cited Lahm Correspondence, Maxwell AFB; letter, George A. Spratt to the Chief Signal Officer, U.S. Army, 19 February 1909, and Appendix No. 1, "Proceedings of the Aeronautical Board of the Signal Corps, by Maj. C. McK. Saltzman, Capt. Charles S. Wallace, and First Lieutenant Frank P. Lahm," Cat. 167.601–19, 17 Sept. 1908, AFHRA.

7. At that time, 5 francs FR = $1.00 US, making this a $4,000 prize (equivalent to nearly $76,000 at 2001 inflation rates).

8. Moore-Brabazon, 56.

9. Ibid., 58; the dog anecdote is from Sherwood Harris, *The First to Fly: Aviation's Pioneer Days* (New York: Simon and Schuster, 1970), 101, from a transcript of an oral history by Brabazon on file with the Columbia University Office of Oral History.

10. Gollin, *No Longer,* 445; see also Robert Wohl, *A Passion for Wings: Aviation and the Western Imagination, 1908–1918* (New Haven, CT: Yale University Press, 1994), 37–38, 42, 44–45.

11. It might be suggested he carried this too far, as he also died in the same year as Orville, 1948.

12. Milton Wright diary, 5 May 1909, 950. The 19,503 ton, 24–knot *Kronprinzessin Cecilie* avoided the sad fate of many liners sunk by or sunk as commerce raiders in the Great War. Designed so it could be converted into a commerce-raiding "auxiliary cruiser," the ship was returning across the Atlantic to Germany when the war broke out in 1914. Rather than risk the ship and its passengers, its captain put into Bar Harbor, Maine, and the vessel was interned. The *KC* had four stacks, giving it a close resemblance to the ill-fated *Titanic, Olympic, Empress of Ireland,* and *Lusitania.* See Paul Schmalenbach, *German Raiders: A History of Auxiliary Cruisers of the German Navy 1895–1945* (Cambridge, UK: Patrick Stephens, 1977), 26, 46. The celebrations accorded the Wrights are very well covered in Crouch, *Bishop's Boys,* 390–394.

13. Consider that in the 1930s, American commercial aviation raced ahead of the rest of the world, while military aviation lagged. Then, in the Second World War, military aviation rose to prominence. The aggressive high-speed research aircraft program of the late 1940s secured early American dominance of the transonic and supersonic regime, and after 1945 as well, commercial aviation would be dominated by American-built airplanes, up until the advent of Airbus as a serious competitor in the 1990s.

14. The cost figures are "then-year" 1909 amounts, from Gibbs-Smith, *Invention,* pp. 246, and 252. Smith quotes a lower figure of £1,100 for the Wright machine, but the definitive history of Shorts quotes a contract price of £8,400 for six aircraft, and I have used it. See C. H. Barnes, *Shorts Aircraft Since 1910* (London: Putnam, 1967), p. 35. In this time period, 25 francs FR = $5.00 US = £1 UK = 20 marks GER. Source for the cost comparison is the costing chart opposite the title page of Karl Badeker, *Paris and Environs: Handbook for Travellers* (Leipzig: Karl Baedeker, Publisher, 1907). $1.00 in 1908/09 = $18.93 in 2001.

15. For French and German examples, see Réne Gasnier, "L'aeroplane Wright décrit par un de ses passagers," *L'aérophile,* v. 16, n. 23 (1 Dec. 1908): 470–477; and Karl Dienstbach, "Die neue Epoche in der amerikanischen Luftschiffahrt," *Illustrierte Aeronautische Mitteilungen,* v. 12,n. 22 (4 Nov. 1908): 688–695. Regarding foreign flying, Henry Farman flew in Ghent and in Brighton Beach, New York, in May and July-August, 1908; and Delagrange in Italy in the early summer of 1908.

16. Geoffrey de Havilland, *Sky Fever: The Autobiography of Sir Geoffrey de Havilland, C.B.E* (Shrewsbury, Eng: Wrens Park Publishing, 1999 ed.), 47; see also 42.

17. Baudry de Saunier, "L'école américane," in the previously cited Gustave Rives, *Rapport sur le Premier salon de l'aéronautique* (Paris: Librairie des Sciences Aéronautiques, Dec. 1908): 37. Emphasis added.

18. But it had a happy ending, for within a year he created his own extremely successful aircraft company. The details can be found in Gibbs-Smith, *Directory,* 73, and Penrose, *Pioneer Years,* 160–161; in short, the Voisins sold an airplane that Farman had ordered and *paid for* to another pioneer, Britain's J. T. C. Moore-Brabazon (who did not know of Farman's involvement at the time he purchased the machine). Farman immediately wrote Moore-Brabazon, stating in part, "You can judge of [*sic*] my stupefaction to find that Voisin had given you *my* machine built according to *my* specifications" (Penrose, 160, emphasis in original). See also J. T. C. Moore-Brabazon's memoir, *The Brabazon Story* (London: William Heinemann Ltd., 1956), 53–56, and Villard, 38–43.

19. "The First Paris Aeronautical Salon," *Flight,* v. 1, n. 1 (2 Jan. 1909): 6. See also Jacques Lorisson, "Au Salon de l'aéronautique," a supplement to *La revue de l'aviation,* n. 26 (1 Jan. 1909): i-vi, and Rives, passim.

20. REP did not invent the word astronautics, thought he was present when it was invented, by André Louis-Hirsch, on December 26, 1927, during a meeting at Hirsch's mother's Paris home where the two men conceived the REP-Hirsch Prize, one of the major prizes in astronautics. REP corresponded with virtually all the major figures in the field and wrote the first major summary text on the subject, *L'astronautique.* Not content just with theory, he was very much a hands-on rocket experimenter, though a misjudgment while using a particularly nasty fuel cost him four fingers of one hand in 1931. See Frank H. Winter, *Prelude to the Space Age: The Rocket Societies: 1924–1940* (Washington, D.C.: National Air and Space Museum/ Smithsonian Institution Press), 1983), pp. 25, 77, and also the previously cited Bodemer, *De l'Éole à Hermès,* 43–44.

21. Lorisson, ii.

22. Ibid.

23. For details on these machines, see the previously cited Lorisson, ii-iv; Kenneth Munson, *Helicopters and Other Rotorcraft since 1907* (New York: The Macmillan Company, 1969), 24–26, 105–108; Paul Lambermont with Anthony Pirie, *Helicopters and Autogy-*

ros of the World (New York: A. S. Barnes and Company, 1970), 12–13, 38–40, 200–201; and Michael H. Gorn, *The Universal Man: Theodore von Kármán's Life in Aeronautics* (Washington, D.C.: Smithsonian Institution Press, 1992), 30.

24. For details, see "L'aéroplane Gastambide-Mengin," *L'aérophile,* v. 1 (renumbered), n. 17 (1 Sept. 1908): 336. The "Antoinette III" was actually a throwback, an unsuccessful biplane of Wright inspiration built to the specifications of Ferdinand Ferber, and better known as the Ferber IX; see "L'aéroplane Ferber IX" in the same issue, 336–337.

25. Quote from Lorisson, ii. Sources differ on the number of aircraft Blériot displayed at the show, but Lorisson is clear that there were four aircraft, three monoplanes and his biplane.

26. There is an excellent description and illustrations of his basic machine in "The Blériot Short-Span Monoplane: The Channel Flyer," *Flight,* v. 1, n. 31 (31 July 1909): 453–456; "Les aéroplanes L. Blériot," *La Revue Aérienne,* v. 2 (25 Nov. 1909): 692–699; Michael Gabriel, "Der neue Blériot-Viersitzer (Ein Besuch in den Ateliers Blériot)," *Zeitschrift für Flugtechnik und Motorluftschiffahrt,* v. 2,n. 7 (13 April 1911): 88–91 (which, despite its title, is about the entire Blériot "stable" of aircraft, and not just his abortive "flying bus"); and Gibbs-Smith, *Invention,* 252–258.

27. "The First Paris Aeronautical Salon," 7.

28. Vorreiter II, 366–370; See also Albert F. Zahm, "Report on European Aeronautical Laboratories," 3, 17–18, and Plate 6; "Aerotechnical Institute of the University of Paris," *The Aeronautical Journal,* v. 15, n. 59 (Jul. 1911): 120–122; von Kármán, *Aerodynamics,* 12–13; Anderson, 268–27; Hunsaker, "Forty Years," 242; Randers-Pehrson, 17–18; and Robert Schlaifer and S. D. Heron, *Development of Aircraft Engines and Fuels* (Boston: Graduate School of Business Administration, Harvard University, 1950), 328.

29. Among the engineering profession, Joukovsky is more frequently spelled *Joukowski,* and historians increasingly favor spelling his name *Zhukovskiy.* But I have used *Joukovsky,* as this is the spelling the Koutchino Institute used that he helped create. See Dimitri Riabouchinsky, *Institute aérodynamique de Koutchino, 1904–1914* (Moscow: Société J. N. Kouchnereff et Cie, 1914), 4–7. See also Dimitri P. Riabouchinsky, "Thirty Years of Theoretical and Experimental Research in Fluid Mechanics," Aeronautical Reprint No. 77 (London: Royal Aeronautical Society, 1935), 6; Vorreiter II, 368, 375–379, and figures 480–482; Lee, 11; Randers-Pehrson, 17; von Kármán, *Aerodynamics,* 14, 34–46; Jerome C. Hunsaker, "Forty Years of Aeronautical Research," *Smithsonian Report for 1955* (Washington, D.C.: Smithsonian Institution, 1956): 242; Von Hardesty, "Early Flight in Russia," in Robin Higham, John T. Greenwood and Von Hardesty, *Russian Aviation and Air Power in the Twentieth Century* (London: Frank Cass, 1998): 22.

30. Randers-Pehrson, 15; von Kármán, *Aerodynamics,* 14, 133, 147; Vorreiter II, 371–373.

31. The best treatment of Klein, Göttingen, and Prandtl is Paul A. Hanle's *Bringing Aerodynamics to America* (Cambridge, MA: MIT Press, 1982), 25–45. See also Vorreiter II, 381, 383, and 386–390; Anderson, 257–259; and von Kármán, *Aerodynamics,* 50–51.

32. Anderson, 88–93, 109–114; von Kármán, *Aerodynamics,* 73–82; and Ackroyd, pt. I, 20, 22–23.

33. Randers-Pehrson, 17; Hanle, 42–52; Fr. Ahlborn, "Die Widerstandserscheinungen in flüssigen Medien," *Illustrierte Aeronautische Mitteilungen,* v. 8, n. 6 (June 1904), 187–198; and G. Edward Pendray, *The Guggenheim Medalists: Architects of the Age of*

Flight (New York: Guggenheim Medal Board of Award of the United Engineering Trustees, Inc., 1964), 58–59.

34. F. W. Lanchester, *Aerodynamics: Constituting the First Volume of a Complete Work on Aerial Flight* (London: Archibald Constable & Company, Ltd., 1907), 151–178, and figure 86, 127, the latter his famous drawing of the now-classic "twisted rope" vortex showing its tendency to flow spanwise towards the tips and then trail in a widening pattern behind the wingtip. Lanchester also wrote a second volume devoted to stability and control, entitled *Aerodonetics: Constituting the Second Volume of a Complete Work on Aerial Flight* (London: Archibald Constable and Company, Ltd., 1910); see esp. 37–45, and 154–195. See also P. W. Kingsford, *F. W. Lanchester: The Life of an Engineer* (London: Edward Arnold Publishers, Ltd., 1960), 79–106; Giacomelli and Pistolesi, 341–345; Ludwig Prandtl, "The Generation of Vortices in Fluids of Small Viscosity," *The Journal of the Royal Aeronautical Society*, v. 21, n. 200 (Aug. 1927):720–741; and von Kármán, *Aerodynamics*, 48–53.

35. Statement of PM Herbert Asquith in *Hansard's Parliamentary Debates*, fifth series, v. IV (26 April-14 May, 1909): cols. 1047–1048. See also J. A. D. Ackroyd, "The United Kingdom's Contributions to the Development of Aeronautics: Part II: The Development of the Practical Aeroplane (1900–1920)," *The Aeronautical Journal*, v. 104, n. 1042 (Dec. 2000), 579–581; Hugh Driver, *The Birth of Military Aviation: Britain, 1903–1914*, a volume in the Royal Historical Society's *Studies in History* series (Bury St. Edmonds, UK: Boydell Press, 1997), 207–218; Richard B. Haldane, *Richard Burdon Haldane: An Autobiography* (London: Hodder and Stoughton, 1929), 232–234; Maj. Gen. Sir Frederick Maurice, *Haldane, 1915–1928: The Life of Viscount Haldane of Cloan, K.T., O.M.* (London: Faber and Faber, Ltd., 1939), 21–22; Raleigh, 158–159; Gollin, *No Longer*, 115–116, 168–169, 276, 400; Penrose, 166–167; Vorreiter II, 359–364; Randers-Pehrson, 18; see also J. C. Hunsaker, "The Wind Tunnel of the Massachusetts Institute of Technology," in J. C. Hunsaker, E. Buckingham, E. Rossell, D. W. Douglas, C. L. Brand, and E. B. Wilson, eds., "Reports on Wind Tunnel Experiments in Aerodynamics," *Smithsonian Miscellaneous Collections*, v. 62, n. 4 (15 Jan. 1916): 1–3; this tunnel was copied exactly from the NPL, from drawings sent by Glazebrook to MIT.

CHAPTER FOURTEEN

1. WW to OW, 18 Oct. 1908; and OW to WW, 14 Nov. 1908, Wright Papers II, 932, 938.

2. "Echos: La traversée de la Manche: Côté Latham," *La revue de l'aviation*, n. 33 (1 August 1909): 135. There is an excellent technical description of the Antoinette in "L'aéroplane Antoinette," *La revue aérienne*, v. 2 (25 Dec. 1909): 755–762; and L'Enseigne de Vasseau Lafon, "Le monoplan Antoinette," *Revue générale de l'aéronautique: Militaire théorique et pratique*, v. 1, n. 1 (Oct. 1911): 40–67. See also Gibbs-Smith, *Invention*, 259–265.

3. Elliott, 74–75, 87–94. See also Crouch, *Blériot XI*, 26.

4. Bernard S. Finn, "Electronic Communications," in Kranzberg and Pursell, II, 294–299.

5. Quoted in Owen S. Lieberg, *The First Air Race: The International Competition at Reims, 1909* (Garden City, NY: Doubleday & Company, Inc., 1974), 71. See also "Pour la traversée de la Manche," *L'aérophile*, v. 17, n. 15 (1 Aug. 1909), 345–346.

6. "Les grandes étapes de l'aviation," *L'aérophile*, v. 17, n. 15 (1 August 1909): 344–345.

7. In year-2001 terms, the total of these amounts represented approximately $225,000 in winnings and a loan of $95,000.

8. See Villard, 63–69.

9. Louis Blériot, "Comment j'ai traversé la Manche," *La revue de l'aviation*, n. 33 (1 August 1909): 134–135. I have relied primarily upon this memoir piece, supported by "La traversée de la Manche," *La revue aérienne*, v. 2 (10 August 1909): 458–461, A. de Masfrand, "Journée historique: De Calais à Douvres: Blériot s'envole triomphalement," *L'aérophile*, v. 17, n. 15 (1 August 1909); 350–351; and "Blériot's Cross-Channel Flight," *Flight*, v. 1, n. 31 (31 July 1909); 457–461. See also M. Bénichou, C. Fontaine, and R. Guérin, "Cette chose qui vint de la mer," *Le fana de l'aviation*, n. 368 (July 2000); 52–59; Villard, 69–72; Commission Histoire, *Cent ans*, 85–91; and Elliott, 109–115.

10. Blériot, "Comment j'ai traversé la Manche," 134.

11. Villard, 70.

12. This last point is interesting. The Model XI had a generally "well-protected" propeller shielded from excessive damage because of the size and robustness of the undercarriage (which resembled, from the front, a huge square and multibraced frame). Since the undercarriage failed, it is not surprising that the propeller was damaged as well. However, it is possible that the propeller was "inclined" to fail, that is—remember—it had hit and killed an unfortunate dog earlier. . . . Wooden propellers (then and now) are notoriously sensitive to damage. It is possible that the fatal blow also created a weakening—say, a steadily progressing crack—along the grain of the propeller, a flaw progressing slowly enough that it did not prevent Blériot from completing his flight. Then the final impact with the ground accomplished the rest. In that case Blériot might well have been far more lucky than he knew: had the flight been longer, and had the propeller shed a blade and become fully unbalanced, it could have wrenched the Anzani from its mountings, certainly destabilizing the airplane and causing an inevitable crash. And had it remained in place for a few more violent swings of the prop, it might have overstressed the Blériot's frail structure, breaking it up in the air. Either way Blériot probably would not have survived, because of either the fall or the plunge into the cold waters of la Manche.

13. The Latham quote is from "La traversée de la Manche," 461. All other quotes are from Blériot, "Comment j'ai traversé la Manche." See also Dollfus and Bouché, 211–214. How times change: in 1999, on the ninetieth anniversary, Swedish pilot Mikael Carlsson duplicated the flight, landing almost on the very spot, in an immaculate replica of Blériot's machine. The bobbies this time briefly detained him, having heard that a group of people had gathered on the cliffs to steal sheep! See Richard Paver, "No Longer an Island: The Ninetieth Anniversary Re-enactment of Blériot's Channel Crossing," *Aeroplane*, v. 27, n. 10 (1 Sept. 1999), 50–51.

14. Quotes are drawn from Gibbs-Smith, *Aviation*, 224. There is an excellent discussion of British reaction to the flight in Alfred Gollin, *The Impact of Air Power on the British People and their Government, 1909–14* (Stanford: Stanford University Press, 1989), 71–76.

15. Quoted in Gollin, *Impact*, 72, from a special article to the *Daily Mail*.

16. And clearly needing better care than it is receiving.

17. See the previously cited Wohl, 56–59.

18. "Cause gagnée," *La revue aérienne*, v. 2, n. 15 (10 August 1909), 453.

19. De Masfrand, "Journée historique," 350.

20. "The Channel as a Popular Educator," *Flight*, v. 1, n. 31 (31 July 1909): 452; Mussolini

quotes from R. J. B. Bosworth, *Mussolini* (New York: Oxford University Press, 2002) 71, 143.

21. Signal Corps diary, 20 July 1909, Wright Papers II, 959.

22. The airsickness comment is from a Letter, Frank Lahm to his father, 1 August 1909, in Lahm Correspondence, AFHRA. See also transcript of interview of Maj. Gen. Benjamin D. Foulois by Alfred Goldberg, Air Force History Program, Dec. 1965, Cat. K239.0512–766, copy 1, AFHRA, 13–14 (hereafter Foulois interview).

23. Bishop Wright diary, 30 July 1909, and note 1, Wright Papers II, 961. Also *Diary, The Wright Airplane, 17 June-1 Sept 1909*, Cat. 168.651–8 (June-Sept. 1909), AFHRA. See also Alfred F. Hurley and William C. Heimdahl, "The Roots of U.S. Military Aviation," in Bernard C. Nalty, ed., *Winged Shield, Winged Sword: A History of the United States Air Force, v. I: 1907–1950* (Washington, D.C.: Air Force History and Museums Program, 1997), 14. $1.00 in 1909 = $18.93 in 2001.

24. There are good writeups on Reims in "La Grande semaine d'aviation de la champagne," *L'aérophile*, v. 17, n. 17 (1 Sept. 1909): 386–394; the best coverage, interestingly, is in a series of articles in Britain's *Flight* magazine, which includes excellent tabulated data. See the series "Rheims Aviation Meeting," and H. Massac Buist, "The Flying Races at Rheims," in *Flight*, v. 1, n. 35–37 (28 Aug, 4 Sept, and 11 Sept. 1909): 518–523 (n. 35), 534–541 (n 36), and 551–552 (n 37) (hereafter RAM). Potions of these have been reprinted as appendix VII in the previously cited Gibbs-Smith, *Invention*, 319–340; see also 213–219. See as well Villard, 73–84; Wohl, 100–110; Prendergast, 60–71; Lieberg, passim; Dollfus and Bouché, 216; Commission histoire, *Cent ans*, 91–92; and Ferdinand C. W. Käsmann, *World Speed Record Aircraft: The Fastest Piston-Engined Landplanes Since 1903* (London: Putnam, 1990), 10–18.

25. Quote from Villard, 74. See also Thomas G. Foxworth, *The Speed Seekers* (New York: Doubleday & Company, Inc., 1974), 26–27.

26. Figures on attendance vary according to source, some suggesting a low of 250,000 (still impressive), and others 500,000 or above. I have accepted 500,000, as that is the figure in RAM, 537, is accepted by Gibbs-Smith, and is likewise the figure Villard uses, and Villard's account in all other respects is remarkably accurate. Further, in view of the lengthy program each day, and the total of eight days of flying, a figure of 500,000 equates to an average of approximately 8,000 visitors on scene each "working" hour, this is a most reasonable figure, since the grandstands alone could seat 5,000 and were literally packed during the event, with, as the reporter Buist noted, a "throng [that] stretched for miles and miles round the course."

27. Gibbs-Smith, *Invention*, 214–235. Again, 5 francs = $1.00 in 1909, and $1.00 in 1909 = $18.93 in 2001.

28. RAM, 518.

29. Ibid., 518–519. See also Lieberg, 8–13; and Villard, 77–78.

30. RAM, 551.

31. Ibid., 534–535; Lieberg, 126–134; Villard, 80–83.

32. RAM, 522–523, 534–535, 539–540.

33. Laurent Séguin, "Le development des moteurs spéciaux pour l'aviation et les débats du moteur rotatif," *La revue aérienne*, v. 2 (25 Dec. 1909), 750–754; and Étienne Taris, "Les moteurs d'aeroplanes: Le moteur Gnôme," *La revue aérienne*, v. 2 (10 May 1909), 257–265.

34. Bodemer, *De l'Éole à Hermés*, 13; see also 41–42.

35. Blériot, "Sporting and Commercial Possibilities of the Aeroplane," in Grahame-

White and Harper, 200; C. Fayette Taylor, *Aircraft Propulsion: A Review of the Evolution of Aircraft Piston Engines* (Washington, D.C.: Smithsonian Institution Press, 1971), 22–26; see also the previously cited Wolko, *In the Cause of Flight*, 63.

36.   There is an excellent cutaway drawing by John Batchelor of the Gnôme in Richard P. Hallion, *Designers and Test Pilots*, a volume in the Time-Life *Epic of Flight* series (Alexandria, VA: Time-Life Books, 1983), 30–31. For orders of the Gnôme by the U.S. after entry into the war, see Col. G. W. Mixter and Lt. H. H. Emmons, *United States Army Aircraft Production Facts* (Washington, D.C.: GPO, 1919), 13. Higher power requirements eventually forced the replacement of the rotary by the fixed radial engine, which became the standard propulsion system for most multiengine airplanes from the 1920s until the advent of the jet age.

37.   See "Tabulated Performance, etc. of Rheims Meeting," *Flight*, v. 1, n. 36 (4 Sept. 1909), 536.

38.   RAM, 516.

39.   Michael Paris, *Winged Warfare: The Literature and Theory of Aerial Warfare in Britain, 1859–1917*, a volume in the *War, Armed Forces, and Society* series (Manchester: Manchester University Press, 1992), 88.

40.   Gibbs-Smith, *Invention*, 213.

41.   Villard, 84.

42.   RAM, 533; Godfrey Hodgson, *Lloyd's of London* (New York: Viking, 1984), 75. By 1930 over 100 American companies wrote policies for airmen, though growth of this field remained relatively slow until after the Second World War. For particulars on the early years of American aviation insurance policy, see Ray A. Dunn, *Aviation and Life Insurance: A Study of the Death Rate and the Hazard of Flying in Relation to Policy Underwriting* (New York: The Daniel Guggenheim Fund for the Promotion of Aeronautics, 1930), 7–36, copy in box 5, Papers of the Daniel Guggenheim Fund for the Promotion of Aeronautics, Manuscript Division, Library of Congress, Washington, D.C.

43.   See the previously cited Facon, "L'armée française et l'aviation (1891–1914)," *Revue historique des armées*, n. 164 (Sept. 1986): 80–81.

44.   Quoted in Gibbs-Smith, *Invention*, 213. For more on George's response to Reims, see Gollin, *Impact*, 89–91.

45.   Quoted in the previously cited *DMBW-TB*, 22; see also *DMBW-T*, 118.

46.   "Paris Flight Show: First Impressions of an Artistic and fascinating Display," *Flight*, v. 1, n. 40 (2 Oct. 1909), 610.

47.   Dollfus and Bouché, 198; Gibbs-Smith, *Directory*, 76–77; See "Le capitaine Ferber (1862–1909)," and "La catastrophe de la "République," both in *La revue aérienne*, v. 2 (10 Oct. 1909): 596–602. See also Paul Renard, "Conclusions à tirer de la catastrophe de la "République," *La revue aérienne*, v. 2 (25 Nov. 1909): 685–691. Some sources maintain the *République* exploded, but in fact it is clear from photographs of the wreckage that it simply fell to earth.

48.   "Et nunc erudimini," *La revue aérienne*, v. 2 (10 Oct. 1909): 589.

49.   Mathilde Gräfin von Keller, *Vierzig Jahre im Dienst der Kaiserin: Ein Kulturbild aus den Jahren 1881–1921* (Leipzig: Verlegt bei Kocher & Amelang, 1935), 271. Von Keller uses the lower height of 160 meters in her text, but Wright is the source of the 172 figure; see OW Diary, 17 Sept. 1909, Wright Papers II, 964.

50.   See Milton Wright Diary, 8 Sept.–2 Oct 1909; OW diary, 15 Sept-14 Oct 1909, Wright Papers II, 964–967; Alfred Freund, "Wright-Flüge in Berlin," *Flugsport*, v. 1 n. 20 (17

Sept. 1909): 555–556; Eugene Zabel, *Deutsche Luftfahrt: Rückblicke und Ausblicke* (Berlin: Verlag Gustav Braunbeck G.m.b.H., 1918), 61–62; *DMBW-T*, 118–120; Supf, I, 264–266; John R. Cuneo, *Winged Mars, v. 1: The German Air Weapon, 1870–1914* (Harrisburg, PA: Military Service Publishing Company, 1942), 86–87.

51. See "Orville Wright und Wilbur Wright in Dayton (V.S.A.): Mit wagerectem Kopfruder und senkrechtem Schwanruder versehener Gleitflieger," *Flugsport*, v. 1, n. 22 (15 Oct. 1909): 662–665; and "Industrie et commerce aéronautiques: Le premier brevet Wright," in *La revue aérienne*, v. 2 (10 Nov. 1909): 678–682.

CHAPTER FIFTEEN

1. "Meeting of the International Commission for Aeronautical Maps," *The Aeronautical Journal*, v. 15, n. 59 (July 1911): 123–124. Clubs computed from adding the entries in the section "Aero Clubs and Societies," Aviation World Publishing Co., Ltd., *The Flying Book* (London: Longman, Green and Co., 1914), 21. The Clubs were the Aero Club of America, Aero Club Argentina, Österreichischer Aero Club, Aéro-Club de Belgique, Danske Aeronautiske Selskab, Aéro-Club d'Egypte, Aéro-Club de France, Deutscher Luftfahrer Verband, Royal Aero Club, Koninklijke Nederlandsche Vereeniging voot Luchtvaart, Fédération Aéronautique Hongroise, Aéro-Club d'Italia, Norsk Luftseiladsforening, Aéro-Club Imperial de Russie, Real Aero Club de Espana, Svenska Aeronautiska Saliskapet, and the Aéro Club Suisse. Great Britain and Ireland were lumped together as a single entity at this time, reflecting Ireland's pre-independence status.

2. Terry Gwynn-Jones, *Farther and Faster: Aviation's Adventuring Years, 1909–1939* (Washington, D.C.: Smithsonian Institution Press, 1991), 28.

3. See the previously cited Gollin, *No Longer*, and Driver, passim; John Howard Morrow, *Building German Airpower, 1909–1914* (Knoxville: University of Tennessee Press, 1976), 15–30; Piero Vergnano, *Origini dell' aviazione in Italia, 1783–1918* (Genoa: Edizioni Intyprint, 1964), 21–29; Rosario Abate, Gregory Alegi, and Giorgio Apostolo, *Aeroplani Caproni* (Trento: Museo Caproni, 1992), 7–17; Hardesty, "Early Flight in Russia," 19–22, 30–31; Lt. Col. B. Roustam-Bek, *Aerial Russia: The Romance of the Giant Aeroplane* (London: John Lane–The Bodley Head, 1916), 7–38.

4. Computed from adding the entries in the previously cited "Aero Clubs and Societies," *The Flying Book* (1914 ed.), 21–25. For background of Aerial League, see Gollin, *Impact*, 6–8.

5. See Penrose, *Pioneer Years*, 154.

6. Quoted in the previously cited Barnes, 51; see also 34–57, 76–79.

7. Ibid., 34–79.

8. Penrose, 154; De Havilland, 71–72; Sidney Hook, *The Hero in History: A Study in Limitation and Possibility* (Boston: Beacon Press, 1967 ed.), 154–157; Charles G. Grey, "The Death of S. F. Cody," *The Aeroplane* (14 Aug. 1913): 186–187; and "S. F. Cody—the Man and His Work," "A Cody Memorial," and "Armchair Reflections," in *Flight* (16 Aug. 1913): 905–907; R. Dallas Brett, *History of British Aviation, 1908–1914* (London: John Hamilton, Ltd., 1933), 27–28. The best and most comprehensive reference on Cody (born Cowdery) is Philip Jarrett's "Cody and His Aeroplanes," *Air Enthusiast*, n. 82 (July-Aug. 1999): 6–17. He was thus not, as alleged, a relative of Buffalo Bill Cody, though he clearly emulated the latter.

9. Conclusion 2 of the Report of the C.I.D. Sub-Committee on 'Aerial Navigation,' 28

January 1909, in Capt. S. W. Roskill, RN, ed., *Documents Relating to the Naval Air Service*, v. I: *1908–1918* (London: Spottiswoode, Ballantyne and Col., Ltd., in association with the Naval Records Society, 1969), 12. See also Walker, *Early Aviation at Farnborough,* II, xx-xxi, 273, 329–332; Gollin, *No Longer,* 167–168, 276, 300, 301; Gollin, *Impact,* 9–88; Driver, 188, 200–203. See also the following editorials from *The Aeroplane*: "The Government and Aerial Defence" (2 Nov. 1911): 507; "The Betrayal of British Industry" (9 Nov. 1911): 531; "What We Need" (16 Nov. 1911): 555; "In the Open" (23 Nov. 1911): 579; "The Government's Policy" (30 Nov. 1911): 603; "Lord Haldane and Military Aviation," (14 Dec. 1911): 651; "Matters of Moment" (18 April 1912): 363; "Matters of Moment" (1 Aug. 1912): 99; and "The Question of Flying on Duty" (19 Sept. 1912): 287.

10.   These quotes are in Gollin, *No Longer,* 276 (Haldane on airplanes), and Walker, II, 273, 329 (Haldane and PM on report).

11.   Moore-Brabazon, 15. See also R. Dallas Brett, *History of British Aviation, 1908–1914* (London: John Hamilton, Ltd., 1933), 27–28.

12.   Moore-Brabazon, 66. See also "The Bournemouth Catastrophe," *Flight* (July 16, 1910): 540; 546–547; "The Late Hon. Charles Stewart Rolls," *The Aeronautical Journal,* v. 14, n. 55 (July 1910): obit., 4; and Brett, pp. 29–31.

13.   See, for example, Captain F. H. Sykes, "Notes on Aviation in France," Nov. 1911, in the Frederick Sykes Papers, Collection AC 73/35, RAF Museum Archives, Hendon, Grahame Park Way, London, and his subsequent translation of a French report, "Aeronautics in France: Report of the Chamber of Deputies Budget Commission (M. Clémentel, *rapporteur*) upon the Aeronautical Section, French Budget, Published December 1911," *The Army Review* (Apr. 1912): 475–500.

14.   De Havilland, 72; "Witty Irishman" characterization from Penrose, *Pioneer Years,* 196; see also Gollin, *Impact,* 106–108; and Paul R. Hare, *The Royal Aircraft Factory* (London: Putnam, 1990), 22–35.

15.   Von Moltke to War Ministry, April 1912, in Erich Ludendorff, *The General Staff and its Problems: The History of the Relations Between the High Command and the German Imperial Government as Revealed by Official Documents,* v. 1 (New York: E. P. Dutton and Co., 1920), 35.

16.   This is told in great detail in *DMBW-TB,* 32–45; *DMBW-T,* 125–127; Paris, 89; and Cuneo, *The Air Weapon,* 89–109; Layman, *Before the Aircraft Carrier,* 22; Käsmann, *World Speed Record Aircraft,* 35; and R. D. Layman, *Naval Aviation in the First World War: Its Impact and Influence* (London: Chatham Publishing, 1996), 40. $1.00 in 1912 = $18.26 in 2001.

17.   "Der Parsevalsche Motorballon," *Illustrierte Aeronautische Mitteilungen,* v. 10, n. 8 (August 1906): 34; Zahm, *Aerial Navigation,* 138–144; "Army Airship Maneuvers, 1909," *Journal of the United States Artillery,* v. 33, n. 2 (March-April 1910): 171–172.

18.   Eckener, *Count Zeppelin,* 268.

19.   Quote from letter, R Z T (Jr.) to R Z-T (Sr.), 30 Nov. 1908, in Robert Zedlitz-Trützschler, *Twelve Years at the Imperial German Court* (London: Nisbet & Co., Ltd., 1951 ed.), 229. Zedlitz-Trützschler served as the imperial marshal at the Kaiser's court.

20.   Letter, Thomas Mann to Heinrich Mann, 1 April 1909, in Hans Wysling, ed., *Letters of Heinrich and Thomas Mann, 1900–1949* (Berkeley: University of California Press, 1998), 97.

21.   Eckener, *Count Zeppelin,* 224, and 226–267. See also Alfred Waldis, "Airship Station Lucerne: The Birth of Commercial Aviation in Switzerland," in William F. Trimble,

ed., *From Airships to Airbus: The History of Civil and Commercial Aviation, v. 2: Pioneers and Operations* (Washington, D.C.: Smithsonian Institution Press, 1995), 6–7. Peter Fritzsche, *A Nation of Fliers: German Aviation and the Popular Imagination* (Cambridge, MA: Harvard University Press, 1992), 17–18; see also 9–15. See also the following articles from *Illustrierte Aeronautische Mitteilungen*: "Die Aufstiege des Luftschiffes S. E. d. Grafen v. Zeppelin am 9. und 10. Oktober 1906," v. 10, n. 12 (Dec. 1906): 417–426; "Neue Versuche mit dem Zeppelinschen Luftschiff in Friedrichshafen," v. 11, n. 10–11 (Oct.-Nov. 1907): 367–372; "Graf v. Zeppelins Luftschiff. Modell IV," v. 12, n. 13 (1 July 1908): 354; Hugo Eckener, "Die Versuchsfahrten mit dem rekonstruierten dritten Zeppelinschen Luftschiff," v. 12, n. 22 (4 Nov. 1908): 698–701; Robinson, *Zeppelin in Combat*, 13–15; R. E. G Davies, *A History of the World's Airlines* (London: Oxford University Press, 1967 ed.), 5.

22. See von Keller, *Vierzig Jahre*, 270–271; 274; Morrow, *Building German Airpower*, 17, and the previously cited Meyer, *Airshipmen, Businessmen, and Politics*, 34–39.

23. Von Moltke to army chief of staff, 2 March 1911, in Ludendorff, *The General Staff and Its Problems*, v. 1, 32–33; the bomb issue is in von Moltke to Military Transport IG, 23 April 1912, 84; Robinson, *The Zeppelin in Combat*, 20; Supf, I, 397.

24. *DMBW-T*, 117, 119; Morrow, *Building German Airpower*, 23; Cuneo, *The Air Weapon*, 89. $1.00 in 1910 = 4 marks, and $1.00 in 1910 = $18.93 in 2001; thus the cost of this first aircraft was approximately $10,500 in 1910, $198,800 in 2001.

25. *DMBW-T*, 128–130; *DMBW-TB*, 198–202, 207–208; see also "Eindecker Etrich," *Flugsport*, v. 1, n. 19 (5 Oct. 1910): 602–603.

26. Kenneth Munson, *Fighters, Attack, and Training Aircraft, 1914–19* (New York: The Macmillan Company, 1968); 160–161; Hugo Hooftman, *Nederlandse militaire luchtvaart in beeld deel 1 (1913–1940)* (Zaltbommel, Neth.: Europese Bibliotheek, 1977), 1–9, I thank Gwynne Boeskool for bringing this to my attention; and Hans G. Andersson, *Saab Aircraft since 1937* (Washington, D.C.: Smithsonian Institution Press, 1989), 9–10.

27. There is a good exhibit on this at the Norsk Luftfartsmuseum, Bodø, and I thank Maj. Gen. Kjell Lutnes, the director, for bringing it to my attention; see Odd Arnesen and Einar Sem-Jacobsen, *Til viers på Norske vinger* (Oslo: Gyldendal Norsk Forlag, 1930), 47; see also 7–10, 19, 40–45; Odd Arnesen, *Mot blå horisonter* (Oslo: Forlagshuset, 1942), 30–42; Oberstløytnant Finn Lillevik, *Forsvarets luftflaade, 1912–1982: Beskrivelser av våre bevarte militaerefly* (Oslo: Forsvarsmuseet, 1984), 9. See also Olaf Riste, "No Strength in Unity: The Pre-History of the Royal Norwegian Air Force, 1912–1944," in Institute d'histoire des conflits contemporains, Service historique de l'armée de l'air, et Fondation pour les etudes de defense nationale, *Colloque air 1984* (Paris: École Militaire, Sep. 1984), 313–322. Rolv was called Rollo in England; for more on him, see the previously cited Reston, *The Last Apocalypse*, 81. The historic Rumpler Taube *Start* eventually was retired in 1922, probably the longest-flying Taube ever built. Today it is preserved at the Norwegian Armed Forces museum at Gardermoen, following transfer from the Norsk Teknisk Museum in Oslo. In May 2000, the Historischer Flugzeugbau Museum at Fürstenwalde Germany (southeast of Berlin) first flew a magnificent Taube reproduction, returning this distinctively shaped airplane to the sky.

28. Richard Charques, *The Twilight of Imperial Russia* (London: Oxford University Press, 1972 ed.), 130.

29. For Russia in this time period, see Charques, 11–61.

30. Riabouchinsky, *Institut aerodynamique*, 7. Forty-three years later, on October 4, 1957,

at 10:28 P.M. on a cool central Asian night, Russian Lieutenant Boris Chekunov would make the first step on that journey, pressing a launch button on his console in a bunker at Tyura-Tam that sent a modified Soviet R-7 missile rocketing upwards with *Sputnik*, the first earth satellite, ushering in the space age. Riabouchinsky himself lived to witness *Sputnik* and also the first human presence in space, having prudently left Russia for France in 1918, and eventually, in 1929, becoming associate director of the fluid mechanics laboratory at the University of Paris. For Chekunov and *Sputnik*, see Asif A. Siddiqi, *Challenge to Apollo: The Soviet Union and the Space Race, 1945–1974*, NASA SP-2000–4408 (Washington, D.C.: National Aeronautics and Space Administration, 2000), 166–167.

31.   Hardesty, "Early Flight in Russia," 24–31; see also Wohl, 144–153.

32.   For Sikorsky's and Shidlovskiy's work in this time period, I have relied upon Igor I. Sikorsky, *The Story of the Winged-S: An Autobiography* (New York: Dodd, Mead & Company, 1967 ed.), 69–117; K. N. Finne, with Carl J. Bobrow and Von Hardesty, eds., *Igor Sikorsky: The Russian Years* (Washington, D.C.: Smithsonian Institution Press), 55; Dorothy Cochrane, Von Hardesty, and Russell Lee's *The Aviation Careers of Igor Sikorsky* (Seattle: University of Washington Press in association with the National Air and Space Museum, 1989), 20–42; and the previously cited Hardesty, "Early Flight in Russia." Technical details and further information on Sikorsky's early aircraft are from the previously cited Shahrov I, 63–65.

33.   Shahrov I, 121–145, has an excellent discussion of this. See also Viktor Kulikov, "Aeroplanes of Lebedev's Factory," *Air Power History*, v. 48, n.4 (Winter 2001) 4–17.

34.   Sikorsky, 79–94; Finne, 25–46; and the previously cited Munson, *Pioneer Aircraft*, 165–166. The airplane began as the *Bolshoi Baltiskiy* [Большой Балтииский], the *Great Baltic*, a twin-engine tractor biplane, then evolved into a four-engine (two tractor, two pusher) version called *le Grand*. Out of this came the four-tractor-engine version called the *Russkiy vityaz* [Русский витязь]. The name *le Grand* has stuck as the "generic" for all of these. For details on this aircraft evolution, see Shahrov I, 85–88. See also Charques, 194–195.

35.   Katsu Kohri, Ikuo Komori, and Ichiro Naito, *The Fifty Years of Japanese Aviation, 1910–1960* (Tokyo: Kantosha Co., Ltd., 1961), v. 1, 1–10; and v. 2, 5–9; Herbert Chatley, "Aeronautics in China," and Alan Owston, "Aeronautics in Japan," *The Aeronautical Journal*, v. 15, n. 57 (Jan. 1911): 37–38; and "Aeronautics in Japan," *The Aeronautical Journal*, v. 16, n. 62 (Apr. 1912): 131.

36.   The best account of the development of aviation in Thailand is Edward M. Young's *Aerial Nationalism: A History of Aviation in Thailand* (Washington, D.C.: Smithsonian Institution Press, 1995), xxv-xxix, 1–11.

37.   For years pedestrians could walk up West Executive Avenue, but it is now closed to traffic for security reasons. In view of the trees, lights, and clutter, Grahame-White's flight was remarkably nervy. The State, War, and Navy Department is now called the Old Executive Office Building, on the southeast corner of Pennsylvania Avenue and Seventeenth Street N.W. Incidentally, as a young boy my late father both witnessed Grahame-White's Boston flights and met the airmen as well, leaving him with memories that he recounted with gusto to the end of his days.

38.   *Curtiss Flying Boats; Aeronautical Motors; Aeroplanes; Hydroaeroplanes* (Buffalo, NY: Curtiss Aeroplane Co., 1917), copy in Curtiss company file, NASM.

39.   Computed from data in tables 1 and 2 of Herbert A. Johnson's *Wingless Eagle: U.S.*

Army Aviation through World War I (Chapel Hill: University of North Carolina Press, 2001), 111.

40. Roseberry, 156–162. Curtiss had affiliated with Herring, believing the old Chanute collaborator's tales that he had patents that would invalidate the Wrights; but he did not, and the company fell apart at its first encounter with the courts in 1910. Curtiss followed with a highly successful company of his own that outlived him, but the brief Herring association continued to bring lingering grief, as Herring claimed he had been forced out unjustly. Herring and his family proved even more litigious than the Wrights and brought a series of actions against his one-time partner. Again, there is a strange irony that having joined with Herring to avoid the Wrights' suits, he affiliated himself with an individual and a surviving family who would hound him until his own death in 1930.

41. Parkin, 80. It was not, however, the first flight by a Canadian: F. W. "Casey" Baldwin had earned that distinction when he flew the *Red Wing* off the ice at Lake Keuka at Hammondsport, New York, on March 12, 1908. It was, incidentally, the first public flight anywhere in the Western Hemisphere. See Parkin, pp. 53–54. Walter T. Bonney, *The Heritage of Kitty Hawk* (New York: W. W. Norton & Company, Inc., 1962), 105, 130–137; William B. Harwood, *Raise Heaven and Earth: The Story of Martin Marietta People and Their Pioneering Achievements* (New York: Simon & Schuster, 1993), 43; I thank Dr. Norman Augustine for making me aware of this work. See also John R. Breihan, "When Did Glenn Martin First Fly?" *Journal of the American Aviation Historical Society,* v. 44, n. 2 (Summer 1999): 148–154; Grover L. Loening, *Takeoff Into Greatness: How the American Aircraft Industry Grew So Big So Fast* (New York: Putnam, 1968), 105–110; and Roger E. Bilstein, *The American Aerospace Industry: From Workshop to Global Enterprise,* n. 16 in the *Twayne's Evolution of Modern Business* series (New York: Twayne Publishers, 1996), 9–10. The latter is the finest summary history of the American aerospace industry prepared to date and was reissued in a revised edition by the Smithsonian Institution Press in 2001 under the title *The Enterprise of Flight.* The individuals were William Boeing, Donald Douglas, Lawrence Bell, and James "Dutch" Kindelberger, the companies being Boeing, Douglas, Bell, and North American; each made aircraft of profound significance to the subsequent history of aviation, of which the following are just a sampling: the Boeing 247 transport, B-17 and B-29 bombers and 707/727/747 jetliners; the Douglas World Cruiser, DC-3 airliner, and SBD dive bomber; the Bell X-1 supersonic research airplane; the North American P-51 and F-86 fighters, and the X-15 hypersonic research airplane. Martin, of course, built the Martin Bomber (which Billy Mitchell used to sink the *Ostfriesland*), some notable flying boats, and the wartime B-26 bomber. All as well would play a major role in the evolution of the national space program to the landing on the moon and on the present-day era of the space shuttle and the international space station.

42. Johnson, *Wingless Eagle*, pp. 96–115; I. B. Holley, Jr., *Ideas and Weapons* (Washington, D.C.: Air Force History and Museums Program, 1997), 32. The Guggenheim story is related in my *Legacy of Flight: The Guggenheim Contribution to American Aviation* (Washington, D.C.: University of Washington Press, 1977).

43. OW to WW, 10 Aug. 1909, Wright Papers II, 961–962, and note 3.

44. Wright Papers II, n. 6, 962–963.

45. See the previously cited Roseberry, *Glenn Curtiss*, 230.

46.   Crouch, *Bishop's Boys,* 415.

47.   OW to AB, 28 May 1911, Wright Papers II, 1023–1024. See also WW to Octave Chanute, 29 Aug. 1901, Wright Papers I, 85; see also 8–12. See as well OW to August Belmont, 28 May 1911, Wright Papers II, 1023–1024. Wrights to Editor, *Scientific American,* 14 March 1912, Wright Papers II, 1040–1041. See also Crouch, *Bishop's Boys,* 440–442, 466–467, 489–490.

48.   Ford quote from Daniel J. Boorstin, *The Americans: The Democratic Experience* (New York: Random House, 1973), 61. The automotive case was the so-called Selden patent which, if strictly interpreted, would have shut Ford out of the automobile industry entirely; see Boorstin, 59–61. There is a thorough discussion of the lawsuits in Crouch, *Bishop's Boys,* 402–467, and 484–490; Roseberry, *Glenn Curtiss,* 332–393; Seth Shulman, *Unlocking the Sky: Glenn Hammond Curtiss and the Race to Invent the Airplane* (New York: HarperCollins, 2002), 69–70, 175–176, 211–212 and Bruce D. Callander, "The Critical Twist," *Air Force Magazine* (Sept. 1989): 150–156.

49.   The full changes made to the aircraft were detailed in Charles G. Abbot, "The 1914 Tests of the Langley 'Aerodrome'," *Smithsonian Miscellaneous Collections,* v. 103, n. 8 (24 Oct. 1942): passim, and also reprinted as an appendix to Fred Kelly's authorized biography, the previously cited *The Wright Brothers,* 199–208. See also the previously cited Casey, *Curtiss: The Hammondsport Era,* 162–165; and Lorin Wright to OW, 4 June 1915; memorandum by Lorin Wright, 5 June 1915, and Wright Papers II, 1087–1097, n. 11.

50.   For photographs and more information on this strange craft, see Peter M. Bowers, *Curtiss Aircraft, 1907–1947* (London: Putnam, 1979), 87–88.

51.   Manufacturer's Aircraft Association, *Aircraft Year Book 1919* (New York: MAA, 1919), 32–41. Out of this agreement came the Manufacturers Aircraft Association, formed on July 24, 1917: its charter members consisted of the Aeromarine Plane and Motor Company, the Burgess Company, the Curtiss Aeroplane and Motor Corporation, the L.W.F. Engineering Company, the Standard Aircraft Corporation, the Sturtevant Aeroplane Company, the Thomas-Morse Aircraft Corporation, and the new Wright-Martin Aircraft Corporation.

52.   "A Patent Flight in America," *Flight,* v. 1, n. 35 (28 Aug. 1909): 523. The Ford quote is from the previously cited Roseberry, *Pioneer of Flight,* 357.

53.   The over-three-decade "negotiations" between Wright and the Smithsonian over the ultimate fate of the Kitty Hawk Flyer are related in Kelly, *TWB,* 186–207. Regarding the increasingly embittered relations between Wright and Curtiss, it appears that both men made some effort in later years to sort out their differences. Shulman suggests that in 1929, at the time of the Curtiss-Wright corporate merger, Curtiss penned a note to Wright offering to meet and set aside their acrimony, but that Orville Wright never replied to it (*Unlocking the Sky,* 229). Crouch relates how Ford and Wright eventually made their own separate peace, for, in one of the great oddities of the entire controversy, Ford later acquired the Wright's bicycle shop and home and moved it to his Greenfield Village theme park (*Bishop's Boys,* 507–510). Wright himself seems to have manfully tried (at least once) to reconcile his feelings for Curtiss: I recall an incident from the late 1970s, after a talk I gave on early flight. I was approached by a retired engineer (name regretfully unknown) who, as a teenager, had worked as a student aide at Wright Field during the Second World War. He related an apocryphal (if plausible) anecdote that he had met Orville Wright during the war when the two shared a small office space at "the Field," and

that, over time, they grew close enough to take their lunch breaks together. After the publication of the Kelly biography, he approached Wright and asked him about Glenn Curtiss. To his surprise Wright replied mildly that Curtiss was a great pioneer and due a great deal of credit, deferring further discussion until lunch. Then, he again began by stressing at the outset that Curtiss was a gifted and important contributor to aviation. But as the conversation (and his memories) unfolded over the next half-hour or so, he became more and more angry, finally clearly conveying his displeasure with Curtiss, an indication of just how bitter the legacy of the patent fight was.

CHAPTER SIXTEEN

1. Chanute, *Progress*, 269.

2. Robert Debs Heinl, Jr., *Dictionary of Military and Naval Quotations* (Annapolis, MD: United States Naval Institute, 1966), 161.

3. OC to WW, 26 Dec. 1904, Wright Papers I, 468–469. The $100,000 would be equivalent to $1,892,000 in 2001 monies.

4. WW to OC, 28 May 1905, Wright Papers I, 493.

5. See Russell J. Parkinson, "Aeronautics at the Hague Conference of 1899," *Airpower Historian*, v. 7, n. 2 (April 1960): passim, and Kennett, *First Air War*, 1–5. The best and most authoritative survey of the history of air warfare and the laws of war is W. Hays Parks' encyclopedic "Air War and the Law of War," The *Air Force Law Review*, v. 32, n. 1 (1990); readers desiring a shorter introduction are recommended to see his "Air War and the Law of War," in the Service Historique de l'Armee de l'Air, *Aviation militaire: Survol d'un siecle* (Paris: Ecole militaire and the Service Historique de l'Armee de l'Air, 2002), 295–300 (Hereafter cited as SHAA, *Aviation militaire*).

6. Quoted in I. F. Clarke, *Voices Prophesying War: Future Wars, 1763–3749* (Oxford: Oxford University Press, 1992), 79.

7. Quoted in Michael Paris, *Winged Warfare: The Literature and Theory of Aerial Warfare in Britain, 1859–1917*, a volume in the *War, Armed Forces, and Society* series (Manchester, UK: Manchester University Press, 1992), 190.

8. See Brigadier General Alfred F. Hurley, *Billy Mitchell: Crusader for Air Power* (Bloomington: Indiana University Press, 1975), 141–142, which excerpts Fullerton's pioneering paper; Gollin, *No Longer An Island*, 115–116, 168; and Penrose, *Pioneer Years*, 85, 91, 581.

9. For a good discussion of this and other pre–Great War speculative fiction, see the previously cited Clarke, *Prophesying*, 27–130; Goldstein, 63–74; Wohl, 69–94; Paris, 16–59; and also Oron J. Hale, *The Great Illusion, 1900–1914* (New York: Harper & Row, 1971), 261–261.

10. Published in English as *Master of the World*. For examples, see the Lancer Books edition (New York, 1968), 152–187. See also Paris, 21–23, and his shorter essay "Imagining War in the Air: The Early Literature of Aerial Warfare," in SHAA, *Aviation Militaire*, 301–307. As Paris notes in both his works, this change reflected Verne's increasing disillusionment with technology. In fact, as the recent publication of his dystopian "lost" novel *Paris in the Twentieth Century* reveals, Verne had serious reservations about technology and its societal impact since the early 1860s. See the previously cited Jules Verne, *Paris in the Twentieth Century* (New York: Ballantine Books, 1997), passim. None of his novels are quite so enthusiastic about technology as they might first appear.

11. For example his trilogy *La guerre de demain,* but more particularly, two works that explicitly discuss heavier-than-air flight: *L'aviateur du Pacifique* (Paris: Librairie E. Flammarion, 1909); and *Au-dessus du continent noir* (Paris, Librairie E. Flammarion, 1911). See also Clarke, *Prophesying,* 76–77, 101–108, and Wohl, 81–94. Driant, a French army officer who died at Verdun, hit uncomfortably close to home. The former work predicted a gigantic naval battle between Japan and America at Midway Island, and the latter a retaliatory French air raid against a despotic ruler, something the French air force undertook in Chad in 1987. For the latter, see Yvon Goutx, "Cachés par les 'Mirage', les 'Jaguar' attaquent," *Le fana de l'aviation,* n. 369 (August 2000): 18–27.

12. Rudolf Martin, *Berlin-Baghdad* (Stuttgart: Deutsche Verlagsanstalt, 1907). See also Paris, 127–128 and Gollin, *No Longer an Island,* 332–336.

13. Charles Carrington, *Rudyard Kipling: His Life and Work* (London: Macmillan & Co., Ltd., 1955), 374–375, 453.

14. Paris, 27–28, and 49–50; see also Goldstein, 38 and 72. The Hollywood version of Wells' *The Shape of Things to Come* (New York: The Macmillan Company, 1936), featured Ralph Bellamy as the enlightened one-world air leader.

15. Paris, "Imagining War in the Air," 306.

16. H. G. Wells, *The War in the Air* (London: George Bell & Sons, 1908). I have utilized an electronic version of this work, at: www.literature.org/authors/wells-herbert-george/the-war-in-the-air/chapter-01.html. The quotation is from Chapter 1. See also Paris, 33–39; and the previously cited Goldstein, 63–74.

17. Charles De Forest Chandler and Frank P. Lahm, *How Our Army Grew Wings: Airmen and Aircraft Before 1914* (New York: The Ronald Press Company, 1943), 162–165, 193–205, 225–227; William Edward Fischer Jr., *The Development of Military Night Aviation to 1919* (Maxwell AFB, AL: Air University Press, Dec. 1998), 13–14.

18. For details, see Hennessy, 39–54; Hurley and Heimdahl, "Roots," 14–25.

19. Flint O. DuPre, *Hap Arnold: Architect of American Air Power* (New York: The Macmillan Company, 1972), 20. See also Dik Alan Daso, *Hap Arnold and the Evolution of American Airpower* (Washington, D.C.: Smithsonian Institution Press, 2000), 48–50.

20. OW to William Kabitzke, 19 June 1912, Wright Papers II, 107.

21. James Lea Cate, "Development of United States Air Doctrine, 1917–41," a paper presented at the annual meeting of the Mississippi Valley Historical Association, Columbus, Ohio, 24 Apr. 1947, reprinted in Eugene M. Emme, ed., *The Impact of Air Power: National Security and World Politics* (New York: D. Van Nostrand, 1959), 190.

22. *Washington Post,* 10 Oct. 1911. Most sources state the tests took place on the tenth, but the *Post* article, in a morning newspaper published that date, is clear that the test occurred on the afternoon of the day before, which would be 9 October. Further, the fact that the ninth was a work day and not a weekend day (as is the tenth) argues powerfully for the test to have been done on the ninth. Therefore I have accepted the ninth as accurate.

23. Chandler and Lahm, 207; equivalent, in 2001, to $91,300. Overall, Michelin put up $30,000 in prizes, equivalent in 2001 to $547,800.

24. Stephen L. McFarland, *America's Pursuit of Precision Bombing, 1910–1945* (Washington, D.C.: Smithsonian Institution Press, 1995), 9–10. See also Hurley and Heimdahl, "Roots," 22; Hennessy, 54; Johnson, *Wingless Eagle,* 69–72; and Paris, 160.

25. Ibid., 22; Chandler and Lahm, pp. 222–225; Harry Woodman, *Early Aircraft Armament: The Aeroplane and the Gun up to 1918* (Washington, D.C.: Smithsonian Institu-

tion Press, 1989), 11–13; Christienne and Lissarrague, 49–50; Johnson, *Wingless Eagle,* 49; Paris, 177–178.

26. See the previously cited Ader, *L'aviation militaire,* 260–268; see also Maud Jarry, "L'aéronautique navale naquit avec la *Foudre,*" *Le fana de l'aviation,* n. 377 (April 2001): 16–26.

27. Terms of Reference of the C.I.D. Sub-Committee on 'Aerial Navigation,' 23 Oct. 1908, in Roskill, ed., *Documents Relating to the Naval Air Service,* v. 1, 8–9; see also 3–5.

28. Details on Fabre from Kenneth Munson, *Flying Boats and Seaplanes Since 1910* (New York: The Macmillan Company, 1971), 17, 97. See also Jarry, "L'aéronautique navale naquit avec la *Foudre,*" 23–26, and Lissarrague, *Premiers envols,* 144–145; and Layman, *Before the Aircraft Carrier,* 17–18.

29. Robert L. Lawson, ed., *The History of U.S. Naval Air Power* (New York. Military Press, 1985), 10.

30. C. G. Grey, "Practical Naval Aviation," *The Aeroplane* (18 Jan. 1912): 51; and "Launching of Acroplanes from Warships," and "Aeroplanes in Naval War," both in *The Aeroplane* (3 Oct. 1912): 344; see also Layman, 17, 31, 107–108. See also Christina Baron, "Du *Béarn* au *Charles de Gaulle,*" in Michel Bez, ed., *Porte-avions Charles de Gaulle* (Paris: Éditions du Chêne-Hachette Livre, 1998), 68.

31. The story of these flight attempts is told in greater detail in Richard P. Hallion, *Test Pilots: The Frontiersmen of Flight* (Washington, D.C.: Smithsonian Institution Press, 1988 ed.), 38–40; see also Layman, 107–110.

32. Equivalent then to $50,000 and, in 2001, to $860,500.

33. Ibid., 40–43; Harris, *First to Fly,* 232; Bowers, *Curtiss Aircraft,* 44–54; Captain Richard C. Knott, USN *The American Flying Boat: An Illustrated History* (Annapolis, MD: Naval Institute Press, 1979), 6–57; the story of the "Nancy" boats is thoroughly told in Richard K. Smith's *First Across! The U.S. Navy's Transatlantic Flight of 1919* (Annapolis, MD: Naval Institute Press, 1973).

34. David G. Herrmann, *The Arming of Europe and the Making of the First World War* (Princeton, NJ: Princeton University Press, 1996), 75. The French only built one rigid airship, the *Spiess.*

35. Gollin, *Impact,* 49–63; see also Paris, 130–131, 169–177.

36. George Dangerfield, *The Strange Death of Liberal England* (New York: Capricorn Books, 1961 ed.), 123; see also 120–122.

37. Gollin, *Impact,* 230–260.

38. Costs from Supf, I, 397.

39. Admiral Sir R. H. Bacon, *The Life of John Rusworth the Earl Jellicoe* (London: Cassell and Company, Ltd., 1936), 183, 187; Robin Higham, *The British Rigid Airship, 1908–1930: A Study in Weapons Policy* (London: G. T. Foulis & Co., Ltd., 1961), 40–53; Robinson, *Giants,* 144–151. See also Vice Admiral Sir Arthur Hezlet, *Aircraft and Sea Power* (New York: Stein and Day, Publishers, 1970), 5–10.

40. Winston S. Churchill, *The World Crisis: 1911–1914* (London: Thornton Butterworth Ltd., 1923), 313; Hezlet, 10.

41. Admiral of the Fleet Lord Fisher, *Memories* (London: Hodder and Stoughton, 1919), 125. (emphasis in original)

42. See Robinson, *The Zeppelin in Combat,* 26–27. See also Ege, *Balloons and Airships,* 143.

43. Lieutenant F. E. Humphreys, "The Wright Flyer and Its Possible Uses in War," *Journal of the United States Artillery,* v. 33, n. 2 (March-April 1910): 144–145.

44. Patrick Facon, "L'armée française et l'aviation (1891–1914)," *Revue historique des*

armées, n. 164 (Sept. 1986): 77. Some sources suggest he said instead, "That's good sport, but for the army the plane is of no use," while others allege he stated, "Aviation is fine as sport. I even wish officers would practice the sport, as it accustoms them to risk. But, as an instrument of war, it is worthless." The latter quote is also attributed to March 1913. It is not unreasonable to assume that he expressed all these sentiments over the years from 1910 through mid-1914, but I have stuck with the 1910 attribution because it makes particularly good sense given the state of aviation technology and military interest in aviation at that time than the later suggested date. Foch, as will be noted, completely changed his views to a pro-aviation position by the middle of the war. See Michael Dewar, ed. *An Anthology of Military Quotations* (London: Robert Hale, 1990), 25; Morrow, *Great War in the Air,* p. 35; and Henry Serrano Villard, *Contact! The Story of the Early Birds* (New York: Thomas Y. Crowell Company, 1968), 98.

45. See Holley, 10–15; and also Jack Snyder's excellent *The Ideology of the Offensive: Military Decision Making and the Disasters of 1914* (Ithaca, NY: Cornell University Press, 1984).

46. Facon, "L'armée française et l'aviation," 83–84.

47. Raleigh, 137–139, 142; Christienne and Lissarrague, 40–48; Vivian, 210; Cuneo, *The Air Weapon,* 95; Hardesty, "Early Flight in Russia," 24–31; Hennessy, 39–40; Morrow, *The Great War in the Air,* 24; and N. D. G. James, *Gunners at Larkhill: A History of the Royal School of Artillery* (Henley-on-Thames, UK: Gresham Books in association with The Royal Artillery Institution), 26; see also 24–29. I thank Brigadier Jonathan Bailey, Director Royal Artillery, for bringing this work to my attention, and also for arranging a visit to the Larkhill hangars, which are to this author's knowledge the oldest aeronautical buildings extant in Great Britain.

48. Norman Macmillan, *Sir Sefton Brancker* (London: William Heinemann Ltd., 1935), 15–18; Basil Collier, *Heavenly Adventurer: Sefton Brancker and the Dawn of British Aviation* (London: Secker and Warburg, 1959), 11–13. Out of this experience, Brancker determined to make his own future in the air, and he did so with brilliant distinction, before perishing tragically in the crash of the R-101 airship in France in 1930.

49. John Terraine, *Douglas Haig: The Educated Soldier* (London: Cassell & C., 1963), 53–54; Raleigh, *War in the Air,* 242–244.

50. Quote on air superiority in "Major F. H. Sykes on Military Aviation," *The Aeroplane* (6 March 1913): 286; quote on revolutionizing warfare from John Terraine, "Land/Air Cooperation," in Derek Wood, ed., *The End of the Beginning: A Symposium on the Land/Air Co-operation in the Mediterranean War 1940–43,* n. 3 in the *Bracknell Paper* series (Bracknell, UK: Royal Air Force Historical Society and the Royal Air Force Staff College, 20 March 1992), 5.

51. Address to officers and men of RFC, 23 Sept. 1912, 1, in Sykes Papers, RAF Museum; see also Major General Sir Frederick Sykes, *From Many Angles: An Autobiography* (London: George G. Harrap & Co., 1942), 103–105; and Lt. Col. Eric Ash, *Sir Frederick Sykes and the Air Revolution, 1912–1918* (London: Frank Cass, 1999), 22–23, 25, 29–30.

52. W. E. de B. Whittaker, "Aeroplanes and the Manoeuvres," *The Aeroplane* (26 Sept. 1912): 316.

53. Von Moltke to Chief of Army Staff, 3 Dec. 1912, in the previously cited Ludendorff, *The General Staff and Its Problems,* v. 1, p. 48; DMBW-TB, 39–40.

54. Quoted in Lieutenant Henry H. Arnold, "America and Military Aviation: U.S. Weakest of Powers," *Aerial Age,* v. 1, n. 6 (Nov. 1912): 2; see also Christienne and Lissarrague, 51.

55. For an excellent discussion of the changes in warfare accruing from adaptation of key lessons at this time, see Brigadier Jonathan Bailey's *The First World War and the Birth of the Modern Style of Warfare,* n. 22 of the *Occasional Papers* series (Camberley, UK: Strategic & Combat Studies Institute, 1996).

56. See two clippings in the Sykes papers, RAF Museum: "Aerial War of the Future" (for Sykes quote), and "Sir John French on Aircraft in Warfare," *The Morning Post* (Feb. 1913); see also the previously cited "Major F. H. Sykes on Military Aviation," *The Aeroplane* (6 March 1913): 286–288.

57. Quoted in Sykes, *From Many Angles,* p. 105; see also Maj. Gen. A. S. H. Irwin and Lt. Col. D. C. Eccles, "How Close Are We to the Long-Awaited Demise of the Main Battle Tank?", *British Army Review: The House Journal of the Army,* n. 117 (Dec. 1997): 3.

58. Douhet quote from Lieutenant Colonel Frank P. Donnini, "Douhet, Caproni and Early Air Power," *Air Power History,* v. 37, n. 2 (Summer 1990): 45. See also Capitano Giulio Douhet, "Le possibilità dell'aereonavigazione," *Revista delle communicazioni,* v. 3, n. 8 (1910): 758–770, copy in the Gimbel collection, USAFA Library; Claudio G. Segre, "Douhet in Italy: Prophet Without Honor?" *Aerospace Historian,* v. 26 (June 1979): 69–80; Colonel Phillip S. Meilinger, "Giulio Douhet and the Origins of Air-power Theory," in Meilinger, ed., *The Paths of Heaven: The Evolution of Airpower Theory* (Montgomery, AL: Air University Press, 1997), 1–4; and Baldassare Catalanotto and Hugo Pratt, *Once Upon a Sky: Seventy Years of Italian Air Force* (Rome: Lizard edizioni s.r.l., 1994), 11.

59. For Libya experience, see B. Melli, *La guerra Italo-Turca* (Rome: Enrico Voghera Editore, 1914), 55, 75, 132; Piero Vergnano, *Origini dell'aviazione in Italia, 1783–1918* (Genoa: Edizioni Intyprint, 1964), 21–29, 40–42; W. E. de B. Whittaker, "Aviation in the Italian Army," *The Aeroplane* (4 Jan. 1912): 12; "Turks Capture an Italian Airman," *Flight* (21 Sep. 1912): 861; Paris, 107–109, 112–115; Catalanotto and Pratt, 12–14; Cuneo, *The Air Weapon,* 264; and the previously cited Palmer, *Decline and Fall of the Ottoman Empire,* 214–215.

60. Gerald Silk, "*Aeropittura* and Italian Futurism," in John F. Fleischauer, et al., *1998 National Aerospace Conference Proceedings* (Dayton, OH: Wright State University, 30 Apr. 1999): 46–48; see also Goldstein, 8, 32–33. The *Aeropittura* Movement eventually inspired a number of artists including Alfredo Gauro Ambrosa, Barbara (Olga Biglieri Scurto), Benedetta (Benedetta Cappa Marinetti), Armando Dal Bianco, Ivanhoe Gambini, Giovanni Korompay, Sante Monaschesi, Osvaldo Peruzzi, and Thayaht (Ernesto Michalhelles) who produced works of varying quality (and influence). There is an excellent sampling of their art (among that of others) in Bruno Mantura's *Volo e Pittura: Dipinti inediti poco e mal noti raffiguranti il volo* (Rome: Edizioni de Luca, 1994), particularly Plates 25, 35–37, 50–58, and 109.

61. Sykes, "Notes on Aviation in France," 2; see also Paris, 190.

62. Samuel S. Pierce, "Aeroplanes on Service: A Study on the Spot," *The Aeroplane* (26 Aug and 2 Sept. 1914): 196–197, 218; Christienne and Lissarrague, 39; Paris, 112–114.

63. "On Aerial Defence in General," *The Aeroplane* (5 Dec. 1912): 555.

64. "Aviation in War," *Flight* (25 Jan. 1913): 89.

65. "With the Bulgarian Air Corps," *The Aeroplane* (6 Feb. 1913): 130.

66. Roustam-Bek, *Aerial Russia,* 77.

67. Christienne and Lissarrague, 39; Paris, 112.

68. Lawrence D. Taylor, "Pancho Villa's Aerial Corps: Foreign Aviators in the Division del Norte, 1914–1915," *Air Power History,* v. 43, n. 3 (Fall 1996): 31–43. I have discounted

the long-cherished account of the first dogfight in aviation history having taken place in the Mexican civil war between opposing pistol-armed mercenary pilots, as it is now generally considered to have been a "crooked fight" one of the participants conceding that both airmen went through the motions with at least a tacit understanding between them that no serious attempt would be made to score on the opponent.

CHAPTER SEVENTEEN

1. The analysis is based on speed (in miles per hour) × distance (in miles) × power (in horsepower) divided by flight time in hours, with the 1909 figure [(47) × (12.4) × (50)] / (.264) = 110378.78 normalized to 1.000 [that is, (110378.78) / (110378.78) = 1.000]. The results are then: 1910 = 3.366, 1911 = 5.497, 1912 = 13.986, and 1913 = 22.445. The last figure is produced by taking the 1913 results [(124.5) × (124) × (160)] / (.997)] / (110378.78) = 22.445. The "raw data" for making this comparison is from appendix 2 of the previously cited Foxworth, *The Speed Seekers,* p. 428, though one figure in his tabulation is incorrect; the 1912 Deperdussin had a 140–horsepower, not a 160–horsepower, engine.

2. See Dollfus and Bouché, 236, and Munson, *Pioneer Aircraft,* 151.

3. See the series "The French Army Aeroplane Trials," in *The Aeroplane,* (12, 19, and 26 Oct., and 2, 9, and 30 Nov., 1912): 443–445, 462, 486, 512, 534, 608; see also Wolko, *In the Cause of Flight,* 78, and Foxworth, 91–92.

4. The best survey reference on shell structures in aeronautical development is Nicholas J. Hoff's classic paper, "Thin Shells in Aerospace Structures," the fourth von Kármán Lecture, presented at the third American Institute of Aeronautics and Astronautics annual meeting, and printed in *Astronautics and Aeronautics* (Feb. 1967): 26–45; see also Hugo Junkers, "Metal Aeroplane Construction," *The Journal of the Royal Aeronautical Society,* v. 27, n. 153 (Sept. 1923): 406–449. The author owes a debt of gratitude to the late Professor Hoff, a pioneer in flight structures, for his support and insights.

5. "Fatal Accident to Ruchonnet," *Flight* (20 Jan. 1912): 62; Ruchonnet obituary, *Weiner Luftschiffer-Zeitung,* n. 3 (Jan. 1912): 47; Swiss Aero Club obituary notice, Ruchonnet biographical file, NASM archives.

6. See "The 100–horsepower Deperdussin Racing Monoplane," *Flight* (10 Feb. 1912): 119–120; and the previously cited Käsmann, *World Speed Record Aircraft,* 27–29.

7. See Henri Mirguet, "Le 'Monocoque' Deperdussin," *L'aérophile,* v. 20, n. 18 (15 Sept. 1912): 410–411.

8. James G. Robins, *The Wooden Wonder: A Short History of the Wooden Aeroplane* (Great Britain: privately published, n.d., but ca. 1976), 20–21, copy in the library of the NASM; Käsmann, 29–30.

9. See "How about America in 1913?" *Aerial Age,* v. 1, n. 5 (Oct. 1912): 9; and the previously cited Casey, *Curtiss,* 82–83.

10. "How about America in 1913?", 9; see also Don Vorderman, *The Great Air Races* (Garden City, NY: Doubleday, 1969), 39–42.

11. Recollection of Fred E. Weick; see Fred E. Weick and James R. Hansen, *From the Ground Up: The Autobiography of an Aeronautical Engineer* (Washington, D.C.: Smithsonian Institution Press, 1988), 7.

12. "How about America in 1913?", 9; For details on the Model D, see the Wright Papers, II, 1203.

13. "The New Aerial Regulations," *The Aeroplane* (13 March 1913): 314–315.

14. Lissarrague, *Premiers envols*, 148–149; Dollfus and Bouché, 256–263; Gwynn-Jones, 52–58.

15. Lissarrague, 150–151; Dollfus and Bouché, 263; Gwynn-Jones, 54–55; Foxworth, 92–93.

16. Davies, *History of the World's Airlines*, 5–6; Kenneth Munson, *Flying Boats and Seaplanes Since 1910* (New York: The Macmillan Company, 1971), 100; Oliver E. Allen, *The Airline Builders*, a volume in the *Epic of Flight* series (Alexandria, VA: Time-Life Books, 1981) 17; Richard P. Hallion, "Commercial Aviation, 1919–1976," in Eugene M. Emme, ed., *Two Hundred Years of Flight in America: A Bicentennial Survey*, v. 1 of the *AAS History Series* (San Diego: American Astronautical Society, 1977), 156.

17. Kohri, et al., *Fifty Years of Japanese Aviation*, book, II, 13.

18. See the previously cited Hughes, *American Genesis*, 16–17, 67–69, 126–130. Lawrence was lost at sea while crossing the Channel in a light aircraft in 1923.

19. Villard, 228–229.

20. Sikorsky, *Winged-S*, 98–99. For technical details on the *Muromets*, see the previously cited Shahrov I, particularly 187–203.

21. Sikorsky, *Winged-S*, 100.

22. Ibid., 102–103.

23. Ibid., 108. Finne, *Sikorsky: The Russian Years*, 49, asserts that it was the *left* inboard engine that fractured its fuel line and caught fire, but I have relied on Sikorsky's own account, which states that it was the right inboard engine.

24. Sikorsky, *Winged-S*, 108; for Guggenheim Fund work on instruments for blind flying (called "Fog Flying" in the 1920's), see Guggenheim Full Flight Laboratory, *Equipment Used in Experiments to Solve the Problem of Fog Flying: A Record of the Instruments and Experience of the Fund's Full Flight Laboratory* (New York: The Daniel Guggenheim Fund for the Promotion of Aeronautics, Inc., March 1930), 18, 42–53.

25. A. E. Berriman, "Parke's Dive," *Flight* (31 Aug. 1912): passim. See also Constance Babington-Smith, *Testing Time* (New York: Harper & Brothers, 1961), 52–54; de Havilland, *Sky Fever*, 65; and Dunstan Hadley, *Only Seconds to Live: Pilots' Tales of the Stall and Spin* (Shrewsbury, UK: Airlife, 1997), 17–24.

26. Sikorsky, *Winged-S*, 110–111.

27. Ibid., 113.

28. Ibid., 115.

CHAPTER EIGHTEEN

1. The newspaper was the *New York Tribune*. See Walter Lord's previously cited *The Good Years*, 243.

2. British minister of trade Alan Clark's evocative reflection upon seeing a photograph of the young assassin in the Princip museum, Sarajevo, in October 1986. He added, "Something between Seventies CND and Baader-Meinhof." CND refers to the leftist anti-nuclear Campaign for Nuclear Disarmament, and Baader-Meinhof is a reference to one of the more murderous leftist terrorist organizations of the late Cold War. Alan Clark, *Diaries* (London: Phoenix, 1993), 146.

3. There is an excellent summary of the events leading to assassination in Edward

Crankshaw's *The Fall of the House of Habsburg* (New York: Popular Library, 1963 ed.), 402–406. Earlier in the day, Franz Ferdinand himself had to deflect a potentially fatal hand grenade hurled at his car; enormously (if foolishly) brave, he pressed on with the visit, and was in the second car of the motorcade, which was forced to halt and back up when the mayor's car made a wrong right-hand turn. "Security precautions," Crankshaw has rightly concluded, "were practically nil" (403).

4. Knut Hoff, "Først over Nordsjøen," *Luftposten: Organ for Bodø Luftfartshistoriske Forening*, n. 4 (2000), 9; see also the previously cited Arnesen and Sem-Jacobsen, *Til viers på Norske vinger*, 70–74.

5. "Deutsche Flieger!" *Flugsport*, v. 6, n. 16 (5 August 1914): 1; "Kriegsflieger," and "1870–1914," *Flugsport*, v. 6, n. 18 (2 Sept. 1914): 732–733.

6. "War!" *The Aeroplane* (5 August 1914): 127.

7. Quote from Dangerfield, 424; see also Hale, *Great Illusion*, 285–314; and Montross, *War Through the Ages*, 685.

8. Quote from Clark, *Diaries*, 146.

9. Dangerfield, 439.

10. Quoted in Morrow, *Great War in the Air*, 87.

11. There is an excellent case study on Moltke the Younger in Correlli Barnett, *The Swordbearers: Studies in Supreme Command in the First World War* (London: Eyre & Spottiswoode, 1963); for an incisive look at his predecessor, see Lt. Col. Kenneth M. Nesbitt, "Strategy and Technology in Transition: Moltke and the Prussian General Staff," in Allan D. English, ed., *The Changing Face of War: Learning from History* (Kingston: Royal Military College of Canada and McGill–Queen's University Press, 1998), 33–49.

12. Cyril Falls, *The Great War* (New York: Capricorn Books, 1959), 35.

13. Jack Snyder, *The Ideology of the Offensive: Military Decision Making and the Disasters of 1914* (Ithaca, NY: Cornell University Press, 1984), 54.

14. Alistair Horne, "Marshal Philippe Pétain," in Field Marshal Sir Michael Carver, ed., *The War Lords: Military Commanders of the Twentieth Century* (Boston: Little, Brown and Company, 1976), 57.

15. Numbers rarely agree, and force structure at the outbreak of the war is no exception. I have accepted the figure of 232 German aircraft, from General der Kavallerie Ernst von Hoeppner, *Deutschlands Krieg in der Luft: Ein Rückblick auf die Entwicklung und die Leistungen unserer Heeres-Luftstreitkräfte im Weltkriege* (Leipzig: Verlag von K. F. Koehler, 1921), 7, as he presumably had the best access to reliable data, and have also relied upon the Kriegswissenschaftlichen Abteilung der Luftwaffe, *Mobelmachung, Aufmarsch und erster Einsatz der deutschen Luftstreitkräfte im August 1914* (Berlin: Ernst Siegfried Mittler und Sohn, 1939), 8–9, and table 3, 106 (a copy of the latter work is in the library of the Air University, Maxwell AFB, Alabama) (hereafter KAL, *Mobelmachung*). There is surprising agreement on Russian figures. See Morrow, *Great War in the Air*, 39 and 47; Hardesty, "Early Flight in Russia," 30–33.

16. Data from KAL, *Mobelmachung*, tables 3 and 11, 106, 115. I have assumed a mission capability rate of approximately 70 percent. See also von Hoeppner, 15–16, 24.

17. Alexander Solzhenitsyn, *August 1914: The Red Wheel/Knot 1* (New York: Farrar, Straus and Giroux, 1989), 112; A word for readers aware this is a "novel": Solzhenitsyn's book, like Tolstoy's *War and Peace* on Borodino, is extraordinarily well researched, and arguably presents a more compelling and accurate analysis of the battle of Tannenberg from the Russian side than any existing overtly "historical" work.

18. Quote from Cuneo, *The Air Weapon,* 129; see also Hew Strachan, *The First World War,* v. 1: *To Arms* (Oxford: Oxford University Press, 2001), 327; Solzhenitsyn, 112; in fairness to Martos, Solzhenitsyn believes strongly that the general was a superb combat commander once the "close battle" actually began, noting "The Fifteenth Corps, led by the brilliant General Martos, attacked, and attacked successfully, from first to last" (841; see also 323 and 393–394).

19. Alan Clark, *The Eastern Front 1914–1918: Suicide of the Empires* (Moreton-in-Marsh, UK: The Windrush Press, 1999 ed.), 35–36; see also Morrow, *Great War,* 82.

20. Dennis E. Showalter, *Tannenberg: Clash of Empires* (New York: Archon Books, 1991), 152–153; Cuneo, *The Air Weapon,* 110–111; Robinson, *Giants,* 84–85.

21. Von Hoeppner, 15; Clark, *Eastern Front,* 26–30; Showalter, 169, 189, 192; Cuneo, *The Air Weapon,* 112–116; Strachan, 322–324.

22. Clark, *Eastern Front,* 39; Showalter, 193–194, 266–267, 300–301, 310–313, 323–325; Cuneo, 117–130. In light of Showalter's research, I do not accept Cuneo's argument that communications intercepts alone would have sufficed to generate the victory. As Showalter demonstrates, this is one of the more persistent myths of Tannenberg.

23. Roger Chickering, *Imperial Germany and the Great War, 1914–1918* (Cambridge, UK: Cambridge University Press, 1998), 26.

24. Charques, *Twilight of Imperial Russia,* 215.

25. Showalter, 324.

26. Georg Paul Neumann, *Die deutschen Luftstreitkräfte im Weltkriege* (Berlin: Ernst Siegfried Mittler und Sohn, 1920), 462; see also 463.

27. Von Hoeppner, 10.

28. Captain Paul-Louis Weiller, "L'Aviation Française de Reconnaissance," in Maurice de Brunoff, ed., *L'Aéronautique pendant la Guerre Mondiale, 1914–1918* (Paris: Maurice de Brunoff, 1919), 63; and Christienne and Lissarrague, 59.

29. Von Hoeppner, 7–9; KAL, *Mobelmachung,* 9.

30. Wing Commander P. J. Daybell, "The March Retreat of 1918: The Last Battle of the Royal Flying Corps," *Royal Air Force Historical Society Journal,* n. 32 (2000): 108.

31. Raleigh, *War in the Air,* 294; see also 282–301; see also Sykes, *From Many Angles,* 125–126.

32. This period is covered extensively: I have relied upon Barnett, Strachan, 213–233; Sykes, *From Many Angles,* 125–139; Terraine, *Haig,* 81–89; John Terraine, *Mons: The Retreat to Victory* (London: B. T. Batsford, Ltd., 1960); Marshal Joseph Joffre, trans. by Col. T. Bentley Mott and Lt. Col. S. J. Lowe, *The Memoirs of Marshal Joffre,* v. I (London: Geoffrey Bles, 1932); Field Marshal Sir John French, *1914* (London: Constable and Company, Ltd., 1919); Brig. Gen. E. L. Spears, *Liaison, 1914: A Narrative of the Great Retreat* (Garden City, NY: Doubleday, Doran & Company, Inc., 1931); Brig. Gen. J. E. Edmonds, *Military Operations: France and Belgium, 1914,* a volume in the *History of the Great War* series (London: Historical Section of the Committee of Imperial Defence and Macmillan and Co., Ltd., 1922); Georges Blond, *The Marne* (New York: Pyramid, 1967); and General André Beaufre, "Marshal Joseph Joffre," in Carver, 13–22.

33. The quote is from Terraine, *Haig,* 88; see also 82, 89–90; Terraine, *Mons,* 61–62, 125, 150, 193, 195; Raleigh, *War in the Air,* 302–304.

34. Barnett, 71–73.

35. Ibid., 73–74.

36. Christienne and Lissarrague, 78; Joffre, *Memoirs,* 224–225.

37. See the previously cited Whittaker, "Aeroplanes and the Manoeuvers," 316; and Blond, 42, 45.

38. Barnett, 77.

39. Christienne and Lissarrague, 78–80; Sykes, *From Many Angles*, 136–137; Ash, 54–58; Edmonds, *Military Operations*, 256, 273–274, 277–279, 281, 288; Raleigh, *The War in the Air*, 315–322; Robert B. Asprey, *The First Battle of the Marne*, a volume in the *Great Battles* series (London: Weidenfeld & Nicholson, 1962), passim; French, *1914*, 104–111; Cuneo, *The Air Weapon*, 66–73.

40. See von Hoeppner, 13; Strachan, 254; and Cuneo, *The Air Weapon*, 90–93. The delayed German staff officer was *Oberstleutnant* von Hentsch, chief of the Foreign Armies Section of the General Staff; see Falls, *Great War*, 68.

41. Barnett, 101–102, and Alistair Horne, "Field-Marshal Erich von Falkenhayn," in Carver, ed., 113.

42. Spears, 416.

43. Quote from 3, chapter IV, of the "Life of Sir David Henderson," an unpublished manuscript in the David Henderson Papers, AC 71/4/2, RAF Museum; see also Sykes, *From Many Angles*, 138–139.

44. Letter, Field Marshal John D. P. French to the Secretary, War Office, Oct. 17, 1914, copy in the Frederick Sykes Papers, Collection AC 73/35, RAF Museum.

CHAPTER NINETEEN

1. David Lloyd George, *War Memoirs of David Lloyd George*, v. 2 (London: Odhams Press Ltd., 1938 ed.): the first half of the quote is from 1095, but the final two sentences are from 1588.

2. Quoted in Maj. Gen. A. S. H. Irwin and Lt. Col. D. C. Eccles, "How Close Are We to the Long-Awaited Demise of the Main Battle Tank?" *British Army Review: The House Journal of the Army*, n. 117 (Dec. 1997): 3.

3. Quoted in David Jordan, "The Battle for the Skies: Sir Hugh Trenchard as Commander of the Royal Flying Corps," in Matthew Hughes and Matthew Seligmann, eds., *Leadership in Conflict, 1914–1918* (London: Leo Cooper, 2000). I thank Brigadier Jonathan Bailey, director, Royal Artillery, for bringing this to my attention.

4. Patrick Facon, "L' armée française et l'aviation (1891–1914)," *Revue historique des armées*, n. 164 (Sept. 1986): 77.

5. Foch to Commander, troisième bureau, no. 6145, 23 Nov. 1916, reprinted in Bernard Pujo, "*L'evolution de la pensée du général Foch sur l'emploi de l'aviation en 1915–1916*," Institute d'histoire des conflits contemporains, Service historique de l'armée de l'air, et Fondation pour les études de defense nationale, *Colloque air 1984* (Paris: École Militaire, Sep. 1984), 221.

6. Maj. Gen. Heinz Guderian, "*Achtung—Panzer!*" *The Development of Armoured Forces, Their Tactics and Operational Potential* (London: Arms and Armour Press, 1996 ed.), 128.

7. Von Hoeppner, 25–26; Doc. 53, Report of Attack on Düsseldorf and Cologne, in Roskill, *Documents Relating to the Naval Air Service*, v. I, 180–181. Note that von Hoeppner refers to only three lost, but this refers only to those on the Western Front, and does not include the Z V shot down over Mlawa on August 28; see Robinson, *Giants*, 85. See also Lt. Cmdr. P. K. Kemp, *Fleet Air Arm* (London: Herbert Jenkins, 1954), 27–28.

8. Letter, DH to Lady OM, 9 Sept. 1915, in Harry T. Moore, ed., *The Collected Letters of*

D. H. Lawrence, v. 1 (New York: The Viking Press, 1962), 366; details on the raid are from Robinson, *Zeppelin in Combat,* 107–109; ironically, D. H. Lawrence's wife was Frieda von Richthofen, a cousin of Germany's most successful fighter pilot, the Red Baron, Rittmeister Manfred von Richthofen.

9. Grand Admiral Alfred von Tirpitz, *My Memoirs,* v. 2 (London: Hurst & Blackett Ltd., n.d.), 487.

10. From Robinson, *Giants,* 92.

11. Overall, Germany lost 443 army and navy Zeppelin crewman, with another 170 taken prisoner. The dead included 89 officers, 264 NCOs, and 90 enlisted personnel. See the previously cited Griehl and Dressel, *Zeppelin,* 103; Robinson, *Zeppelin in Combat,* 194–196.

12. Statement of British pilot C. S. Iron, quoted in Robinson, *Zeppelin in Combat,* 331; see also 330–339, and 352–353; see also Meyer, *Airshipmen,* 46.

13. For a retrospective look that also examines the current possibilities of the Zeppelin, see Douglas Botting, *Dr. Eckener's Dream Machine: The Great Zeppelin and the Dawn of Air Travel* (New York: Holt, 2001). See also Daniel Michaels, "Zeppelin-Crazy Town Is Floating on Air Over a Shiny New One," *The Wall Street Journal,* 20 Feb. 2001.

14. The literature of First World War aviation is voluminous: herewith, in addition to those already cited in this text, are several works illuminating some of these aspects of the first war in the air. Dominick A. Pisano, Thomas J. Dietz, Joanne M. Gernstein, and Karl S. Schneide's *Legend, Memory, and the Great War in the Air* (Seattle: University of Washington Press/National Air and Space Museum, 1992) is a useful introduction to the air war; the best "mission area" surveys are Lee Kennett's *The First Air War, 1914–1918* (New York: The Free Press, 1991) and John Buckley's *Air Power in the Age of Total War,* a volume in the *Warfare and History* series (London: UCL Press, 1999), chapter 3, 42–69; Raymond H. Fredette's *The Sky on Fire: The First Battle of Britain, 1917–1918* (Washington, D.C.: Smithsonian Institution Press, 1991 ed.) is a classic; Paul G. Halpern's *A Naval History of World War I* (Annapolis: U.S. Naval Institute, 1994) does a good job placing maritime aviation in the larger naval war context; Guy Hartcup's *The War of Invention: Scientific Developments, 1914–18* (London: Brassey's Defence Publishers, 1988), is a good survey of appropriate technical developments and the air war; and John Ferris, ed., *The British Army and Signals Intelligence During the First World War* (London: Army Records Society and Alan Sutton, 1992) is an important survey of the early days linking communications intercepts to air operations.

15. The previously cited Strachan, *The First World War, v. 1: To Arms,* details much of this usage; see particularly, 211, 213, 218, 232–233, 244, 251, 254, 322, 324, 327, 463, 550, 567, 589, 738, 748, 764. See also Maud Jarry, "Les missions secrètes de la première guerre mondiale," *Le fana de l'aviation,* n. 360 (Nov. 1999): 13–22; Kemp, 46–47; Layman, *Naval Aviation,* 128–137.

16. Dollfus and Bouché, 256, 272. For the technical development and employment of the fighter in this time period, see Richard P. Hallion, *Rise of the Fighter Aircraft, 1914–1918* (Baltimore: Nautical and Aviation Publishing Company of America, 1984), esp. 44–51, and 112–114. Samples of these generations are: first, Morane Saulnier Type L Parasol; second, Nieuport Bébé; third, Albatros D II; fourth, S.E. 5a; fifth, Junkers D I.

17. Col. George G. Nasmith, *On the Fringe of the Great Fight* (Toronto: McClelland, Goodchild, and Stewart, 1917), 237. I thank Hugh Halliday of the Ottawa Chapter, Canadian Aviation Historical Society, for bringing this quote to my attention.

18. From MvR letter to a friend, 18 July 1917; I wish to thank Peter Grosz for making this correspondence available to me from his archive; it is quoted in greater detail in my previously cited *Rise of the Fighter,* 114, 116. Professor John Morrow has an extensive discussion of von Richthofen's subsequent efforts to strengthen the German fighter force with newer designs; see his *German Airpower in World War I* (Lincoln, NE: Univ. of Nebraska Press, 1982), 115.

19. Goldstein, 87. Lloyd George noted, "They fight the foe high up and they fight him low down; they skim like armed swallows, hanging over trenches full of armed men, wrecking convoys, scattering infantry, attacking battalions on the march."

20. He left an evocative memoir illustrated by his paintings; see Lieutenant Henry [sic] Farré, *Sky Fighters of France: Aerial Warfare, 1914–1918* (Boston: Houghton Mifflin Company, 1919). For a good portrait of one group of remarkable individuals who joined the European air war, see Dennis Gordon, *The Lafayette Flying Corps: The American Volunteers in the French Air Service in World War One* (Atglen, PA: Schiffer Military History, 2000).

21. Quoted in Joseph Blotner, *Faulkner: A Biography* (New York: Vintage Books, 1991 ed.), 60, drawing upon *The Faulkner Reader* (New York: Modern Library, 1959), p. viii. Faulkner wrote one novel about flying, *Pylon,* and it figured prominently in many of his stories and in his interaction with various friends and acquaintances.

22. Hallion, *Fighter,* 72, 142–145; Wohl, *Passion,* 203–250; see also Denis Winter, *The First of the Few: Fighter Pilots of the First World War* (London: Allen Lane, 1982); casualty data from H. A. Jones, *The War in the Air,* v. 6: *Appendices* (Oxford: Clarendon Press, 1937), appendix 37, "Comparison, By Months, of British Flying Casualties (Killed and Missing) and Hours Flown: Western Front, July 1916 to July 1918"; and the Gulf War statistics are from the Gulf War Air Power Survey, v. 5, *A Statistical Compendium and Chronology* (Washington, D.C.: USAF, 1993), Table 205, 651. For the record, a combat sortie is a single combat flight by a single airplane. For samples of some of the better English language First World War pilot memoirs, see: Captain Edward V. Rickenbacker (edited by W. David Lewis), *Fighting the Flying Circus* (Chicago: The Lakeside Press/H. R. Donnelley & Sons. Co., Dec. 1997); Charles J. Biddle, *Fighting Airman* (Garden City, NY: Doubleday, 1968); William Bishop, *Winged Warfare* (Garden City, NY: Doubleday, 1967); Raymond Collishaw, *Air Command: A Fighter Pilot's Story* (London: William Kimber Limited, 1973); Willy Coppens, *Flying in Flanders* (New York: Ace Books, 1971); Frank Courtney, *The Eighth Sea* (Garden City, NY: Doubleday, 1972); Marshal of the RAF Sir William Sholto-Douglas, *Combat and Command* (New York: Simon and Schuster, 1966); René Fonck, *Ace of Aces* (Garden City, NY: Doubleday, 1967); Duncan Grinnell-Milne, *Wind in the Wires* (Garden City, NY: Doubleday, 1968); Harold Hartney, *Up and At 'Em* (New York: Ace Books, 1971); Bill Lambert, *Combat Report* (London: Corgi Books, 1975); Arthur Gould Lee, *No Parachute: A Fighter Pilot in World War I* (New York: Pocket Books, 1971); Cecil Lewis, *Sagittarius Rising* (New York: Collier Books, 1970); James McCudden, *Flying Fury: Five Years in the Royal Flying Corps* (Garden City, NY: Doubleday, 1969); Cecil Montgomery Moore and Peter Kilduff, *"That's My Bloody Plane"* (Chester, CT: The Pequot Press, 1975); Manfred von Richthofen, *The Red Baron* (New York: Ace Books, 1969), (a translation of *Der rote Kampfflieger*); Marshal of the RAF Sir John Slessor, *The Central Blue* (New York: Frederick A. Praeger, 1957); Louis Strange, *Recollections of an Airman* (London: John Hamilton, Ltd., 1933); Sir Gordon Taylor, *Sopwith Scout*

7309 (London: Cassell & Co., Ltd., 1968); and Ernst Udet, *Ace of the Iron Cross* (Garden City, NY: Doubleday, 1970).

23. Charles Nordhoff and James Norman Hall, *Falcons of France* (Derby, CT: Monarch Books, Inc., 1959 ed.), 31. Nordhoff and Hall, both veteran airmen, put these words in the mouth of Selden, their biographical character in this novel, which is an homage to the Lafayette flying corps.

24. Sir Robert Saundby, *Early Aviation: Man Conquers the Air* (London: Macdonald, 1971), 76. See Robert Graves, *Good-Bye to All That: An Autobiography* (New York: Jonathan Cape & Harrison Smith, 1930), 78–79; and the previously cited Sholto-Douglas, 139.

25. Hardesty, "Early Flight in Russia," 33–34; Finne, *Sikorsky: The Russian Years,* passim; Kenneth Munson, *Bombers, Patrol, and Reconnaissance Aircraft, 1914–1918* (London: Blandford Press, 1972), 160–161.

26. See the previously cited Donnini, "Douhet, Caproni, and Early Air Power," 48. Caproni popularized this thought via the Italian journalist Nino Salvaneschi, in the booklet *Let Us Kill the War, Let Us Aim at the Heart of the Enemy,* which included the memorable line "A bomber is mainly a means to deliver a payload on a target that a gun cannot reach." See also the previously cited Abate, et al., *Aeroplani Caproni,* 36; Munson, *Bombers,* 155–158; and A. D. Harvey, "Bombing and the Italian Front, 1915–1918," *Air Power History,* v. 47, n. 3 (Fall 2000): 34–39. For an interesting memoir of flying the Caproni, see General Harold R. Harris, *The First 80 Years,* Twenty-First Wings Club 'Sight' Lecture (New York: The Wings Club, 1984), 23–26.

27. For information on the G I, see Peter M. Grosz, *Gotha G I,* n. 83 in the *Windsock Datafile* series (Berkhamsted, UK: Albatros Productions Ltd., 2000).

28. Falls, *Great War,* p. 366; Admiral (Major General) Mark Kerr, *Land, Sea, and Air: Reminiscences* (London: Longmans, Green and Co., Ltd., 1927), 287.

29. "*Raum-m*" quote from Nordhoff and Hall, p. 51; Stimson quote from Elting E. Morison, *Turmoil and Tradition: A Study of the Life and Times of Henry L. Stimson* (New York: Atheneum, 1964), 191.

30. James Redding Rives II, diary for 1917–1918, 36–42, in Collection 487.1, Rives Papers, Special Collections, Joyner Library, East Carolina University. The airplane was a so-called R XIV, the R 43, the victory credited to Captain A. B. Yuille of 151 Squadron. For more on the R-planes, see G. W. Haddow and Peter M. Grosz, *The German Giants: The Story of the R Planes, 1914–1918* (London: Putnam, 1962).

31. Kerr, pp. 287–293; Jones, *War in the Air, v. 6: Appendices,* appendix 44, "Summary Statistics of German Air Raids on Great Britain, 1914–18." The best account of the Gotha raids and their impact is Raymond H. Fredette's classic *The Sky on Fire: The First Battle of Britain 1917–1918 and the Birth of the Royal Air Force* (Washington, D.C.: Smithsonian Institution Press, 1992 ed.), passim. For the impact of both the bombing and air defense mindset on interwar planning, see H. Montgomery Hyde's brilliant *British Air Policy Between the Wars, 1918–1939* (London: Heinemann, 1976), particularly 28–35, 405–413, and 482–489; and Brian Bond's army-oriented *British Military Policy Between the Two World Wars* (Oxford: Clarendon Press, 1980), 260–263, 322, 336–337.

32. Tami Davis Biddle, "British and American Approaches to Strategic Bombing: Their Origins and Implementation in the World War II Combined Bomber Offensive," *The Journal of Strategic Studies,* v. 18, n. 1 (March 1995): 93; George K. Williams, *Biplanes and Bombsights: British Bombing in World War I* (Maxwell AFB, AL: Air University Press, May 1999): 135–137, 161–162.

33.   Kerr, 294.

34.   Monte Duane Wright, *Most Probable Position: A History of Aerial Navigation to 1941* (Lawrence: The University Press of Kansas, 1972), 65.

35.   Despatch, Maj. Gen. Hugh Trenchard to Secretary of State for Air (Lord Weir), *The London Gazette,* Tenth Supplement, 31 Dec. 1918, 133–138, copy in the library, Joint Services Staff College, UK. I thank Chris Hobson for locating this document. See also Munson, *Bombers,* 150–153; Neville Jones, *The Origins of Strategic Bombing: A Study of the Development of British Air Strategic Thought and Practice Up to 1918* (London: William Kimber Ltd., 1973); and the previously cited Williams, *Biplanes and Bombsights.*

36.   See T. E. Lawrence, *Seven Pillars of Wisdom* (Ware, UK: Wordsworth Editions Limited, 1997 ed.), 616–617. For details on the Palestine campaign, see Richard P. Hallion, *Strike from the Sky: The History of Battlefield Air Attack, 1911–1945* (Washington, D.C.: Smithsonian Institution Press, 1989), 29–36.

37.   Despatch, General Charles Monro to Secretary to the Indian Government (Army Department), *The London* Gazette, Second Supplement, 12 March 1920, pp. 3271–3286, JSCSC Library. I am indebted to Mr. Sebastian Cox, the head, Air Historical Branch, Royal Air Force, for other materials on this raid; see also David E. Omissi, *Air Power and Colonial Control: The Royal Air Force, 1919–1939,* a volume in the *Studies in Imperialism* series (Manchester, UK: Manchester University Press, 1990), 10–11; Group Captain Robert "Jock" Halley, "The Kabul Raid," *Aeroplane Monthly,* v. 7, n. 8 (Aug. 1979): 437–441. Halley was the aircraft commander on the mission.

38.   This data is from an independent assessment of raids against Germany, made by the intelligence section (G-2), General Headquarters, American Expeditionary Force and reprinted as "Part II: U.S. Bombing Survey," in Maurer Maurer, ed., *The U.S. Air Service in World War I, v. 4: Postwar Review* (Washington D.C.: Office of Air Force History, 1979), 500; see also 363–503.

39.   See, for example, David Nevin, *The Pathfinders,* a volume in the Time-Life *Epic of Flight* series (Alexandria, VA: Time-Life Books, 1980), 26–39, 109–114.

40.   J. B. A. Bailey, *Field Artillery and Firepower,* v. 1 of the *Combined Arms Library* (New York: The Military Press/Oxford, 1989), 127, fig. 3.

41.   David T. Zabecki, *Steel Wind: Colonel Georg Bruchmüller and the Birth of Modern Artillery,* a volume in the *Military Profession* series (Westport, CT: Praeger, 1994), 13, 38–42, 48, 56, 89–95, 108, 113, 127, 143; see also Bailey, *Field Artillery and Firepower,* 60; 141–145; 161. It is interesting to compare Bruchmüller's philosophy of attack with the notion of "effects-based warfare" of the early 1990s that the U.S. Air Force pursued during the Gulf War. In the planning for that conflict, planners (chiefly then-Lieutenant Colonel David Deptula) confronted with a paucity of precision-strike stealthy attack aircraft and a large target set emphasized temporarily neutralizing Iraqi defenses by wide-ranging stealth aircraft attacks that damaged numerous targets quickly rather than totally destroying a smaller number. While these facilities were disrupted, follow-on opportunistic (and nonstealthy) attackers were able to exploit the disruption of the Iraqi air defense to cripple its military machine. By dawn the next morning, the outcome of the war was, frankly, already without doubt. Bruchmüller recognized perceptively that one could achieve similar effects during the First World War by emphasizing surprise and overwhelming firepower rather than the sometimes weeks- (or even months-) long artillery preparation that had predominated in the early years of the war.

42. Falls, *Great War*, 68. The officer was Oberstleutnant Hentsch, the chief of the foreign armies section of the general staff; "It took him the better part of five hours to cover 37 miles" (ibid.).

43. Much of this discussion and that which follows is drawn from the author's *Strike from the Sky: The History of Battlefield Air Attack, 1911–1945* (Washington, D.C.: Smithsonian Institution Press, 1989), 13–41.

44. See, for example, Brevet-Colonel J. F. C. Fuller, *Tanks in the Great War, 1914–1918* (London: John Murray, 1920), 242–249; Jones, *The War in the Air*, v. 3: 371–379; v. 4: 129–130, 163–180, 245–246; Neumann, 74, 90–93; Johannes Hohmann, "Wir Schlachtflieger," in Walter von Eberhardt, *Unserer Luftstreitkräfte, 1914–1918* (Berlin: Vaterlandischer Verlag C. A. Weller, 1930), 249–258; Brereton Greenhous, "Close Support Aircraft in World War I: The Counter Anti-Tank Role," *Aerospace Historian*, v. 21, n. 2 (Summer 1974): 92–93. See also Patrick Facon, "Marie Charles Duval et le Breguet XIV, artisans méconnus de la victoire de 1918," *Le fana de l'aviation*, n. 348 (Nov. 1998): 12–19; Christienne and Lissarrague, 128; and Falls, *Great War*, 369.

45. See the previously cited Eisenhower, *Yanks*, 264; and 188–189. The official report on St. Mihiel is in Maurer, ed., *The U.S. Air Service in World War I*, v. 3, *The Battle of St. Mihiel* (Washington, D.C.: Office of Air Force History, 1979), passim; and Brigadier General William Mitchell, *Memoirs of World War I: From Start to Finish of Our Greatest War* (New York: Random House, 1960 ed.), 258–260; and the previously cited Hurley, *Billy Mitchell*, 34–37.

46. General Liman von Sanders, *Fünf Jahre Turkei* (Berlin: Verlag von August Scherl, 1919), 364–365; see also Jones, *The War in the Air*, v. 6: 224–227, 231–235, and Falls, *The Great War*, 400.

47. Data tabulated from Layman, *Naval Aviation*, appendix 1; 206–208.

48. Grossadmiral Erich Raeder, *My Life* (Annapolis, MD: United States Naval Institute, 1960), 40; Robinson, *Zeppelin in Combat*, 81–94, 139–164; Hezlet, 54–55; Layman, *Naval Aviation*, 172–180.

49. Raeder, 49; see also Layman, *Naval Aviation*, 41.

50. Paul G. Halpern, *A Naval History of World War I* (London: University College London Press, 1994), 43; Kemp, 54–55.

51. Doc. 150, Memo, Capt. Murray F. Sueter, RN, "Policy to be Followed as Regards Development and Use of Torpedo-Carrying Seaplanes," 20 Dec. 1916, in Roskill, *Documents*, pt. II, 435; see also Paris, 193; and Sykes, *From Many Angles*, 174 (Sykes was an eyewitness to the attacks).

52. Doc. 189, letter, Adm. Sir David Beatty to Admiralty re "Considerations of an Attack by Torpedo Planes on the High Sea Fleet," 17 Aug. 1917, in Roskill, *Documents*, Pt. II, 541–543.

53. Doc. 261, Beatty to Admiralty, 30 July 1918, in Roskill, *Documents*, pt. II, 686.

54. Quote from Flight Lieutenant W. F. Dickson, one of the pilots, in "HMS 'Furious' with the Grand Fleet, 1918," *The Hawk: The Annual Journal of the Royal Air Force Staff College*, v. 1, n. 1 (1928): 108; Halpern, 443; Ronald H. Spector, *At War at Sea: Sailors and Naval Combat in the Twentieth Century* (New York: Penguin Books, 2001), 122–125; see also Kemp, 84–85.

55. Quote from Halpern, 444. For example, in the Second World War, total of 1,475 German surface vessels (representing 1,654,670 tons of shipping) sank at sea or were destroyed in port by RAF attack, constituting 51 percent of the total German losses of 2,885 ships (totaling 4,693,836 tons) destroyed by Allied sea and air action, cap-

tured, or scuttled from 1939 through 1945. For an excellent analysis of the RAF's anti-shipping war, see Christina J. M. Goulter, *A Forgotten Offensive: Royal Air Force Coastal Command's Anti-shipping Campaign, 1940–1945*, a volume in the *Studies in Air Power* series (London: Frank Cass, 1995). In the Pacific American submarines were responsible for sinking 48 percent (1,314) of the total ships lost by Japan, but aircraft were responsible for sinking by direct attack or with mines 45 percent (1,232). Further, in concert with other attackers, they sank an additional 2 percent (46 ships). Therefore, air power forces, directly, indirectly, or partnered with other attackers, were responsible for sinking 47 percent of Japan's maritime losses, a tonnage value of 4,066,380 tons. See the Joint Army-Navy Assessment Committee, *Japanese Naval and Merchant Shipping Losses During World War II by All Causes* (Washington, D.C.: GPO, Feb. 1947), table II, vii; for other British carrier developments, see Hezlet, 66–68.

56.   Christienne and Lissarrague, p. 66, and data from the exhibit "Twentieth Century Seapower" at the National Maritime Museum, Greenwich, England; Kennett, p. 205.

57.   The U-boat commander's remark is from John Buckley, *The RAF and Trade Defence, 1919–1945: Constant Endeavor* (Keele, UK: Ryburn Publishing-Keele University Press, 1995), 17; see also Hezlet, 85–103; Layman, *Naval Aviation*, 157–171; Kennet, 197; Lawson, 14; Paul Kemp, *U Boats Destroyed: German Submarine Losses in the World Wars* (Annapolis, MD: Naval Institute Press, 1997), 35; see also 20 and 55; Clay Blair, *Hitler's U-Boat War*, v. II: The *Hunted, 1942–1945* (New York: Random House, 1998), 710–711.

58.   Roy Alexander, *The Cruise of the Raider "Wolf"* (New Haven, CT: Yale University Press, 1939), 5; and the previously cited Schmalenbach, *German Raiders*, 67.

59.   Layman, *Naval Aviation*, appendix 2; 209–211.

60.   Quoted in Hezlet, 103. Robinson, *Giants*, 125–138; Saunders, *Per Ardua*, 129, 194–203; see also Layman, *Naval Aviation*, 59

61.   Brigadier General William Mitchell, "America in the Air: The Future of Airplane and Airship, Economically and as Factors in National Defense," *National Geographic Magazine*, v. 39, n. 3 (March 1921) 347.

62.   Hurley, *Billy Mitchell*, 66–68; for an interesting perspective from the naval censor assigned to the trials, see the memoir of Captain Jules James, "Planes vs. Battleships" (22 Mar. 1938), in Collection 223.9.a, James Papers, "Articles by Jules James" file, Special Collections, Joyner Library, ECU, 1–6. There is a succinct and amusing account of the Mitchell trials in Robert L. O'Connell's irreverent *Sacred Vessels: The Cult of the Battleship and the Rise of the U.S. Navy* (Boulder, CO: Westview Press, 1991), 257–260. See also Hezlett, 132–135.

63.   Colonel the Master of Sempill [Sir William Forbes-Sempill], "The British Aviation Mission to the Imperial Japanese Navy," *The Journal of the Royal Aeronautical Society*, v. 28, n. 165 (Sept. 1924): 553–581; Stephen Roskill, *Naval Policy Between the Wars, v. 1: The Period of Anglo-American Antagonism, 1919–1929* (London: Collins, 1968), 245, 529–530; and Martin Middlebrook and Patrick Mahoney, *Battleship: The Loss of the Prince of Wales and the Repulse* (Harmondsworth, UK: Penguin Books Ltd., 1977), 290, 329–330.

64.   Production followed a general curve defined by the equation $y = x^2$; see Commandant Guignard, "Les fabrications de l'aviation militaire pendant la guerre mondiale," in Brunoff, 385, 394–395, 397–399. I have also had to refine the figures in this work by incorporating information from Col. G. W. Mixter and Lt. H. H. Emmons, *United States Army Aircraft Production Facts* (Washington, DC: GPO, 1919), 29–30, 57; and H. A. Jones, *The War in the Air, v. 6: Appendices* (Oxford: Clarendon Press, 1937), appendix

31, "British Aircraft Produced and Labour Employed August 1914 to November 1918," 154; Catalanotto and Pratt, 31; and the previously cited Bilstein, *The American Aerospace Industry,* table I, 225.

65. These figures are extracted and computed based upon information in J. M. Spaight's *The Beginnings of Organized Air Power: A Historical Study* (London: Longmans, Green and Co., Ltd., 1927), 270–293, a remarkable and indispensable reference for the period.

66. For details on these, see the previously cited Smith, *First Across!;* John Alcock and Arthur Whitten Brown, *Our Transatlantic Flight* (London: William Kimber Limited, 1969 ed.); Wallace Graham, *The Flight of Alcock and Brown, 14–15 June 1919* (London: Putnam, 1955); Edward M. Maitland, *The Log of H.M.A. R 34: Journey to America and Back* (London: Hodder & Stoughton, 1920); and Sir Ross Smith, "A Personal Narrative of the First Aerial Voyage Half Around the World—From London to Australia by Aeroplane," *National Geographic Magazine,* v. 39, n. 3 (March 1921): 229–339. For an interesting comparison with the latter, see Peter McMillan, "The Vimy Flies Again: Reliving the First Aerial Voyage From England to Australia," *National Geographic,* v. 187, n. 5. (May 1995): 2–43. David Beaty's *The Water Jump: The Story of Transatlantic Flight* (New York: Harper & Row, Publishers, 1976) is a solid history; see in particular 11–35; see also Robert Boname, "Les grandes traversées de l'Atlantique nord," *Icare: Revue de l'aviation française,* n. 150 (1994), 9–121, a superb survey from an early French airline pioneer. For the airline story, see the previously cited Davies, *History of the World's Airlines,* 8–20.

67. Quote is from Robert Graves and Alan Hodge, *The Long Week-End: A Social History of Great Britain 1919–1939* (New York: W. W. Norton & Company Inc., 1963 ed.), 84, citing a January 1919 issue of the *Spectator.*

CHAPTER TWENTY

1. Mark Sullivan, *Our Times: The United States, 1900–1925,* IV: *The War Begins* (New York: Charles Scribner's Sons, 1937), 215. Sullivan had carefully considered those words, going so far as to have an associate, William Shea, circulate his manuscript to the surviving brother who started it all, Orville Wright. See Letter, OW to William E. Shea, 28 Jun. 1927, Wright Papers II: 1142–1143 n. 1.

2. Mark Sullivan, *Our Times: The United States, 1900–1925,* II: *America Finding Herself* (New York: Charles Scribner's Sons, 1943 ed.), 558 n. 1.

3. Billy Joel, "Pop Quiz," *People Weekly,* v. 55, n. 25 (25 June 2001), p. 22.

4. Tom D. Crouch, "First Flight? Says Who?" in John F. Fleischauer, et al., *1998 National Aerospace Conference Proceedings* (Dayton, OH: Wright State University, 30 Apr. 1999): 119. This is the best summary survey of all the various claimants for first flights. I am thinking in particular of the many claims put forth on behalf of Gustav Whitehead (Weisskopf), who allegedly "flew" in 1901 and 1902 near Bridgeport, Connecticut, and then over Long Island Sound. None stand up under scrutiny. Whitehead was thoroughly investigated by the late Charles Gibbs-Smith, particularly in his "Reflections on the Whitehead Claims to Powered Flight in 1901 and 1902," a manuscript of record in the collections of both the National Air and Space Museum, Smithsonian Institution, and the Science Museum, London. I thank the late Professor Gibbs-Smith for making a copy of this study available to me for my research.

5. For example, see Hale, 252–275; Charles A. Fisher, "The Changing Dimensions of Europe," in Walter Laqueur and George L. Mosse, eds., *1914: The Coming of the First World War* (New York: Harper & Row, 1966), 3–20; René Albrecht-Carrié, *The Meaning of the First World War* (Englewood Cliffs, NJ: Prentice Hall, Inc., 1965) 3–36; and John Keegan, *The Price of Admiralty: The Evolution of Naval Warfare* (New York: Penguin Books, 1990), 111–128; the Moisant story is from Harris, *First to Fly,* 239–247, based on an oral history interview of Moisant in the Columbia University Oral History Office.

6. David G. Herman, *The Arming of Europe and the Making of the First World War* (Princeton, NJ: Princeton University Press, 1996), 75; see also 76–79, 138–145, 158–159, and 203.

7. "The Results of the Military Aeroplane Competition," *The Aeroplane* (5 Sept. 1912): 238.

8. For the roots of this fear, see Jonathan Steinberg, "The Copenhagen Complex," in Laqueur and Mosse, 21–44.

9. Gordon, *Lafayette,* 9.

10. As discussed earlier, numbers rarely agree; as a reminder to readers, I have accepted the figure of 232 German aircraft from von Hoeppner, 7, as he presumably had the best access to reliable data, and the KAL, *Mobelmachung,* 8–9, and Table 3, 106; there is general agreement on Russian figures, from Morrow, *Great War in the Air,* 39 and 47, and Hardesty, "Early Flight in Russia," 30–33; French figures are from Captain Paul-Louis Weiller, "L'aviation française de reconnaissance," in Maurice de Brunoff, ed., *L'aéronautique pendant la guerre mondiale, 1914–1918* (Paris: Maurice de Brunoff, 1919), 63, and Christienne and Lissarrague, 59; British figures are computed from Gollin, *Impact,* 307; and the American from Hunsaker, "Forty Years," 243. Hunsaker's European figures (1,400 French airplanes, 1,000 German, 800 Russian, and 400 British), however, are clearly wrong; they are drawn from testimony during the war, when reliable data on non-U.S. numbers was nonexistent. The production figures are drawn from the previously cited Johnson, *Wingless Eagle,* 112, Table 4; the precise Army-Navy breakdown is 640 Army aircraft (71.2 percent), and 260 naval aircraft (28.8 percent).

11. TR to AG, 27 July 1917, in Elting E. Morison et al., *The Letters of Theodore Roosevelt,* v. 8 (Cambridge, MA: Harvard University Press, 1954), 1214.

12. James J. Hudson, *Hostile Skies: A Combat History of the American Air Service in World War I* (Syracuse, NY: Syracuse University Press, 1968), 97–98.; and the previously cited Rickenbacker (with Lewis), *Fighting the Flying Circus,* 229.

13. See the previously cited Holley, *Ideas and Weapons,* 29–38; Johnson, *Wingless Eagle,* 52–54, 70–86, 101–112, 116–139, and 162–174.

14. Numbers from Mixter and Emmons, 5; Holley, 37n. 34, Layman, *Naval Aviation,* Table I, 207.

15. Bilstein, *The American Aerospace Industry,* 19; see also Jacob A. Vander Meulen, *The Politics of Aircraft: Building an American Military Industry* (Lawrence, KS: University Press of Kansas, 1991), 28–40. The most compelling example, perhaps, being the story of Dr. (M.D.) William Christmas and his awful "Christmas Bullet," which killed two pilots in accidents before program cancellation. See Robert Casari, "A Christmas Fantasy: The Incredible Story of the Bullet," *Air Enthusiast,* v. 5, n. 6 (Dec. 1973): 293–295, 303; and Dean C. Smith, *By the Seat of My Pants* (Boston: Little, Brown, 1961); 102–103.

16. Mixter and Emmons, 57–58; Daniel R. Mortensen, "The Air Service in the Great War," in Nalty, ed., *Winged Shield, Winged Sword,* v. I, 44–47; Lawson, 16; Holley, 118–146.

17. See J. Lawrence Lee, "Parallel Winds: The Emergence of Three American Aerody-
     namical Laboratories," in John F. Fleischauer et al., *1998 National Aerospace Conference
     Proceedings* (Dayton, OH: Wright State University, 30 Apr. 1999), 189. See J. C. Hun-
     saker, "The Wind Tunnel of the Massachusetts Institute of Technology," in J. C.
     Hunsaker, E. Buckingham, E. Rossell, D. W. Douglas, C. L. Brand, and E. B. Wilson,
     eds., "Reports on Wind Tunnel Experiments in Aerodynamics," *Smithsonian Miscel-
     laneous Collections*, v. 62, n. 4 (15 Jan. 1916), 1–3; this tunnel was copied from drawings
     sent from Britain's National Physical Laboratory to MIT. The debate over creation
     of an American laboratory is discussed in Richard P. Hallion, "To Study the Prob-
     lem of Flight: The Creation of the National Advisory Committee for Aeronautics,
     1911–1915" (Washington, D.C.: National Air and Space Museum Dept. of Science and
     Technology, 1976), an unpublished manuscript (copies are in the archives of the
     National Air and Space Museum library and the History Office of the National
     Aeronautics and Space Administration, Washington, D.C.), see also Alex Roland,
     Model Research: The National Advisory Committee for Aeronautics, 1915–1958, NASA SP
     4103 (Washington, D.C.: National Aeronautics and Space Administration, 1985), 2–5.
     See also Zahm biographical file, Catholic University of America Archives, including:
     letter and attachment, Zahm to Rt. Rev. D. J. O'Connell, 19 Apr. 1906; "New Meth-
     ods of Experimentation in Aerodynamics," paper submitted to the American Asso-
     ciation for the Advancement of Science, June 1902; "A Crisis in Aeroplane
     Litigation," *Popular Mechanics* (June 1912); "Air Pioneer 70 Today," *The Evening Star*
     (Jan. 5, 1932); Louis H. Crook, "The Department of Aeronautical Engineering,"
     Catholic University Bulletin, v. 19, n. 1 (October 1951): 2–3; and Gabriel D. Boehler,
     "From Aeronautics to Space Sciences," *Catholic University Bulletin* (July 1963): 5–7. I
     thank Timothy Meagher, Rebecca Hurley, William John Shepherd, and Chris Wood
     for their assistance to my research. See also Randers-Pehrson, 10–11; Letter, George
     v. L. Meyer to Chambers, 13 March 1911, Washington I. Chambers Papers, Box 4,
     Library of Congress Manuscript Division. See also J. C. Hunsaker, "Forty Years of
     Aeronautical Research," *Smithsonian Report for 1955*, Publication 4237 (Washington,
     D.C.: Smithsonian Institution, 1956), 242; Archibald D. Turnbull and Clifford L.
     Lord, *History of United States Naval Aviation* (New Haven, CT: Yale University Press,
     1949), 7–8.

18. There is a complete set of letters and other documents covering this activity in the
     Chambers papers, Boxes 4, 7, and 18. See also U.S. Congress, *Congressional Record*,
     Sixty-second Congress, Third Session (1913), 1258, 1396, 1479, 1481, 1725, 2508–2509,
     2682, 2783; and U.S. Congress, *Congressional Record*, Sixty-third Congress, First Ses-
     sion, 81, 194, 306. "Minutes of the First Meeting on the Advisory Committee of the
     Langley Aerodynamical Laboratories," *Smithsonian Miscellaneous Collections*, v. 62, n.
     1 (17 July 1913): 4–5. See the previously cited Zahm, "Report on European Aeronauti-
     cal Laboratories," 4–23; Hunsaker, "Forty Years," 245; and Jerome Hunsaker,
     "Europe's Facilities for Aeronautical Research," *Flying*, v. 3, n. 3 (April 1914): 75, 93;
     and n. 4 (May 1914): 108–109; and Lee, "Parallel Winds," 190; and the previously cited
     Hunsaker et al., "Reports on Wind Tunnel Experiments in Aerodynamics"; and
     Holden C. Richardson, "Hydromechanic Experiments with Flying Boat Hulls,"
     Smithsonian Miscellaneous Collections, v. 62, n. 2 (20 April 1914): passim.

19. There is extensive correspondence in the Walcott papers, boxes 327 and 339A. See
     also "Proceedings of the Board of Regents of the Smithsonian Institution at the
     Annual Meeting held December 10, 1914," in *Proceedings, Board of Regents, Smithson-*

ian Institution, a bound volume covering the years 1907–1919, 296, 306–310, Smithsonian Archives; Tillman to Walcott, 30 Jan. 1915, and statement of Walcott before the House Committee on Naval Affairs, in *A Documentary History of National Advisory Committee for Aeronautics,* 40, 56–61, 64, and 1219–1229, mss. on file in the History Office, National Aeronautics and Space Administration, Washington, D.C.; U.S. Congress, Senate Joint Resolution 229, sixty-third Congress, third Session (1915), 2–3; the previously cited Asquith Parliamentary testimony in *Hansard's Parliamentary Debates,* fifth series, v. IV (26 April-14 May, 1909), cols. 1047–1048; *Memorial on the Need of a National Advisory Committee for Aeronautics,* House Document 1549, sixty-third Congress, third Session, 1; *Congressional Record,* sixty-third Congress, third Session, (1915), 2656–2657, 2827, 3153, 4601, 4713, 4716, 1869, 5137, 5209–5216, 5232, 5237–38, 5251, 5459, 5461, 5523. See also Roosevelt to Padgett, 12 Feb. 1915, in *National Advisory Committee for Aeronautics Report,* House Report 1423, sixty-third Congress, third Session, 2–3; see also, 1–2. The bill became Public No. 271, sixty-third Congress third Session, H.R. 20975.

20. There are a number of works on aviation in the 1920s that survey key developments. Of particular value are Roger E. Bilstein's *Flight Patterns: Trends of Aeronautical Development in the United States, 1918–1929* (Athens: The University of Georgia Press, 1983); William M. Leary's *Aviation's Golden Age: Portraits from the 1920s and 1930s* (Iowa City: University of Iowa Press, 1989); Pamela E. Mack, ed., *From Engineering Science to Big Science: The NACA and NASA Collier Trophy Research Project Winners,* SP-4219 (Washington, D.C.: NASA, 1998); the previously cited Hallion, *Legacy of Flight;* Ronald Miller and David Sawers, *The Technical Development of Modern Aviation* (New York: Praeger Publishers, 1970); Brig. Gen. Benjamin S. Kelsey, *The Dragon's Teeth? The Creation of United States Air Power for World War II* (Washington, D.C.: Smithsonian Institution Press, 1982); Jeffery S. Underwood, *The Wings of Democracy: The Influence of Air Power on the Roosevelt Administration, 1933–1941* (College Station: Texas A&M University, 1991); and Fred E. Weick and James R. Hansen, *From the Ground Up: The Autobiography of an Aeronautical Engineer* (Washington, D.C.: Smithsonian Institution Press, 1988).

21. This evolution is very well traced in Peter W. Brooks's masterful *The Modern Airliner* (London: Putnam, 1961) and the previously cited Miller and Sawers, *Technical Development of Modern Aviation,* both excellent works deserving updating covering the last 40 years.

22. See René Lorin in *L'aérophile,* v. 1, n. 17 (1 Sept. 1908), 332–336; Lorin, "La sécurité par la vitesse," *L'aérophile,* v. 19, n. 17 (1 Sept. 1911), 409–412; see also Jean Lacroze and Philippe Ricco, *René Leduc: Pionnier de la propulsion à réaction* (Clichy: Docavia Editions Larivière, 2000), 34–37.

23. John A. Warden III and Leland A. Russell, *Winning in Fast Time* (Montgomery, AL: Venturist Publishing, 2001).

24. Lee D. Saegesser, "Quotes that Failed. A Chronology of Unhelpful Utterances," NASA draft publication HHN-112, June 1971, 36; copy in the archives of the NASA History Office, Washington, D.C.

25. Quoted in John E. Allen and Joan Bruce, eds., *The Future of Aeronautics* (London: Hutchinson, 1970), 21.

26. Quoted in Claude Graham-White and Harry Harper, *The Aeroplane: Past, Present, and Future* (London: T. Werner Laurie, 1911), 310.

27. Quoted in the previously cited Bilstein, "The Airplane, the Wrights, and the American Public," in Hallion, ed., *The Wright Brothers,* 50. For Hunsaker's career, see William Trimble, *Jerome C. Hunsaker and the Rise of American Aeronautics* (Washington, D.C.: Smithsonian Institution Press, 2002). "Jerry" Hunsaker became a major force in American aeronautics, but advising Douglas wasn't the last time he would miss out on the significance of some future development. Before the Second World War, he turned MIT away from rocketry, remarking to Caltech's Theodore von Kármán, "You can have the Buck Rogers job." The eager von Kármán was more than happy to oblige: out of that decision eventually sprang the Jet Propulsion Laboratory. Despite his formidable nature, some remained unintimidated: on one occasion, when Hunsaker was chairman of the NACA, John Victory, the agency's long-serving executive secretary (and first employee), was observed backing out of Hunsaker's office, snarling, "Your initials may be JC, but they don't stand for Jesus Christ!" (anecdote from Frank W. Anderson, the deputy NASA Historian, in a conversation with the author, 1970).

28. Michael Crichton, *Timeline* (New York: Ballantine Books, 2000), x.

29. R. E. G. Davies, *A History of the World's Airlines* (London: Oxford University Press, 1967 ed.), 5–6.

30. Statistics from Rudolf Modley and Thomas J. Cawley, eds., *Aviation Facts and Figures 1953* (Washington, D.C.: Aircraft Industries Association of America, Inc., and the Lincoln Press, Inc., 1953), table 6–7, "Domestic Scheduled Airlines Passenger Service, 1926–1952," 126–127; Economic Data Service, Aerospace Industries Association of America, Inc., *Aerospace Facts and Figures, 1996/1997* (Washington, D.C.: AIA, 1996), 83; the capacity of a standard Association of American Railroads Class XM boxcar is 154,000 lbs. I thank Matt Anderson, the archivist of the Hays T. Watkins Research Library, Baltimore and Ohio Railroad Museum, for furnishing this information.

31. Marilyn Vos Savant, "Ask Marilyn," *Parade* (17 June 2001); and data from telecons with Ms. Nancy Castle, Los Angeles International Airport Public Information Office, 8 August 2001; and Mr. Dan Curtin, O'Hare International Airport Media Relations office, 13 Nov. 2001.

32. "Grounded Again," *The Economist* (7–13 July 2001): 75–76; see also Sally B. Donnelly, "Terminal Envy," *Time* (20 Aug. 2001) Y12; and Jennie James, "Stuck in Traffic," *Time* (16 July 2001): 52.

33. Conversation with Amtrak ticket agent, a Northwest airline ticket agent, and a Lincoln-Mercury salesman, Aug. 2001. The train fare can be as high as $441. The basic stats are from "Numbers," *Time Magazine* (28 May 2001): 28.

34. David Kirkpatrick, "Revolutions in Military Technology, and Their Consequences," *Royal United Services Institute Journal,* v. 146, n. 4 (Aug. 2001): 70. I am aware that critics might take issue with this statement using the case of Vietnam, but I would suggest that the Vietnam experience was far less about the *limits* of air power, and far more about the *limitations imposed upon* air power: contrast, for example, *Rolling Thunder* with *Linebacker I* and *II*; further, throughout the war, tactical air power over the south earned generally high marks from friend and foe alike.

35. For perspectives on these, see Air Commodore Andrew G. B. Vallance, *The Air Weapon: Doctrines of Air Power Strategy and Operational Art* (New York: St. Martin's Press, Inc., 1996); Group Captain Andrew Lambert and Arthur C. Williamson, eds., *The Dynamics of Air Power* (Bracknell, UK: Royal Air Force Staff College, 1996);

Richard P. Hallion, ed., *Air Power Confronts an Unstable World* (London: Brassey's, 1997); Peter W. Gray, ed., *Air Power 21: Challenges for the New Century* (London: Ministry of Defence, 2000); Benjamin S. Lambeth, *The Transformation of American Air Power* (Ithaca, NY: Cornell University Press, 2000); and two collections edited by Major John Andreas Olsen, *From Manoeuvre Warfare to Kosovo?* (Trondheim: Royal Norwegian Air Force Academy, 2001), and *A Second Aerospace Century: Choices for the Smaller Nations* (Trondheim: The Combined Air Operations Centre 3 and the Royal Norwegian Air Force Academy, 2001). See also Fareed Zakaria, "Face the Facts: Bombing Works," *Newsweek* (3 Dec. 2001). For lingering traditionalist viewpoints, see Lieutenant Colonel Thomas R. Rozman and Lt. Col. William A. Saunders, "The Expansible Army," *Military Review*, v. 70, n. 11 (Nov. 1990): esp. 31, published just two months before Saddam Hussein's military machine would be shattered by coalition air attack, and Daryl G. Press, "The Myth of Air Power in the Persian Gulf War and the Future of Warfare," *International Security*, v. 26, n. 2 (Fall 2001): 43, published even as air attack pounded the Taliban regime in Afghanistan out of power.

36. Charles Krauthammer, "We Don't Peacekeep," *The Washington Post*, 18 Dec. 2001.

37. I realize that this is a controversial point and not likely to be accepted at first glance by many readers. Further, I stress that I am discussing *military* casualties so as not to conflate casualties at the fighting fronts with the occasionally massive civilian casualties inflicted in both the Allied and Axis bombing campaigns. My statement is based on the postwar Joint Army-Navy Assessment Committee, which examined the sinking of the Japanese navy and merchant fleet, and on the interrogations of Generalleutnant (Professor Doctor) Siegfried Handloser, the Wehrmacht's director of medical services, made immediately after the Second World War by Allied investigators of the United States Strategic Bombing Survey. While submarines were responsible for sinking 48 percent (1,314) of the total ships lost by Japan, aircraft were responsible for sinking by direct attack or with mines 45 percent (1,232). Further, in concert with other attackers, they sank an additional 2 percent (46 ships). Therefore, air power forces, directly, indirectly, or partnered with other attackers were responsible for sinking 47 percent of Japan's maritime losses, a tonnage value of 4,066,380 tons. Dr. Handloser had responsibility for all medical services furnished to the Wehrmacht, giving him a unique perspective on German casualties. He stated that through mid-1943 infantry weapons had caused most casualties, followed by artillery, and then air attack. Late in the year, air attack assumed preeminence: by 1945 Allied air power was "far ahead of either artillery or infantry weapons as a cause of casualties in the German armed forces," and significantly deadlier as well—casualties shifted from an 8:1 wounded-to-killed ratio at the time of the Blitzkrieg in 1939–41, to 3:1 wounded-to-killed in 1945, which he "attributed entirely to the devastating effect of aerial warfare." Handloser summarized Germany's overall Wehrmacht casualties as 2,030,000 killed, 5,000,000 wounded, and 2,000,000 missing, and speculated that fully 50 percent of all German missing in action casualties were attributable to air attack. Thus, by the end of 1945 centuries of previous military patterns of destruction, death, and injury had been overturned by air attack, both at sea and over land. See the Joint Army-Navy Assessment Committee, *Japanese Naval and Merchant Shipping Losses During World War II by All Causes* (Washington, D.C.: Government Printing Office, Feb. 1947), table II, p. vii; and Group Captain A.P.N. Lambert, *The Psychology of Air Power*, RUSI Whitehall Paper Series 1994 (Lon-

don: Royal United Services Institute for Defence Studies, 1995), p. 13. I thank now–Air Commodore Lambert for making me aware of the Handloser testimony, which can be found in the following two documents: United States Strategic Bombing Survey (USSBS), *The Impact of the Allied Air Effort on German Logistics* (Washington, D.C.: USSBS, Military Analysis Division, Jan. 1947 ed.), chapter VI, and "Medical," para. 216, 105, on Air Force Historical Research Agency Microfilm Roll A1128, Frame 1099, call number 137.306–7; USSBS Interview #75, "Interview with Professor Doctor Siegfried Handloser, Lt. Gen., Chief Medical Officer, *OKW*," by Lt. Col. Richard L. Meiling, MC, Chief, Morale Division, USSBS, on 27 July 1945, reprinted as appendix 2 of the USSBS, *Consolidated Report of the Medical Sciences Branch* (Washington, D.C.: USSBS Morale Division, 1945), available on Air Force Historical Research Agency Microfilm Roll A1128, Frames 1974–1985, call number 137.307–1.

38. I recognize that this latter point is controversial, but we have already crossed the frontier with ballistic missile assault and satellite-guided munitions, as well as the whole range of space-supported services, such as intelligence, communications, weather, and navigation. Some argue that weapons in space would be unacceptable to civilized sensibilities, but, in an era in which popular culture endorses a space future reflected in such entertainment as the *Star Trek* family of shows (and numerous knock-offs) and the *Star Wars* series, such an argument seems unsound. In any case, for pure destructiveness and dreadfulness, it is hard to imagine what space-based weapon could be more awful than the unfortunate range of "traditional" systems now available in the world's arsenals—or a terrorist-controlled jetliner flown into a skyscraper.

AFTERWORD

1. *Air and Space,* v. 16, n. 5 (Dec. 2001–Jan. 2002): 3.
2. Samuel Johnson, *Rasselas,* chapter 6, "A Dissertation on the Art of Flying," paragraph 9. I have used the Jack Lynch edited edition from http://newark.rutgers.edu/njlynch/Texts/rasselas.html.
3. Green, *History, Historians, and the Dynamics of Change,* 77.
4. Jonathan Lerner, "I was a Terrorist," *Washington Post Magazine* (24 Feb. 2002), 27.
5. Harry F. Guggenheim, *The Seven Skies* (New York: Putnam, 1930), 12.
6. Jacqueline Trescott, "The Museum That Took Off," *Washington Post* (30 June 2001).
7. "Andre Beaumont" [J. Conneau], *My Three Big Flights* (London: Eveleigh Nash, 1912), 153–154.
8. Computed from tables 29 and 34 in previously cited Kennedy, *Rise and Fall of Great Powers,* 419, 455.
9. Quoted in G. M. Young, *Stanley Baldwin* (London: Rupert Hart-Davis, 1952), 144; see also H. Montgomery Hyde, *Baldwin: The Unexpected Prime Minister* (London: Hart-Davis, MacGibbon, 1973), 354; and the *Times* (London), 24 March 1935.
10. Charles A. Lindbergh, *Of Flight and Life* (New York: Charles Scribner's Sons, 1948), 10.
11. John S. D. Eisenhower, *Strictly Personal* (Garden City, NY: Doubleday, 1974), 72.
12. Goebbels Diary, 21 March 1945. It was all the more bitter for Goebbels, as he had gone out of his way to publicize the achievements of leading *Luftwaffe* pilots when things were going far better for the Reich earlier in the war. Incidentally, Allied air

attacks destroyed his own home—on *Herman Goering* Strasse! See Ralf Georg Reuth, *Goebbels* (New York: Harcourt Brace & Company, 1993), 285, 320, 325, 326, 349.

13. Again, a potentially controversial comment. At the end of the war, Premier Kantaro Suzuki stated, "It seemed to me unavoidable that in the long run Japan would be almost destroyed by air attack *so that merely on the basis of the B-29s alone I was convinced that Japan should sue for peace.* On top of the B-29 raids came the atomic bomb . . . which was just one additional reason for giving in. . . . I myself, *on the basis of the B-29 raids,* felt that the cause was hopeless." (emphasis added) See James Lea Cate and Wesley Frank Craven, "Victory," in Craven and Cate, eds., *The Army Air Forces in World War II, v. 5: The Pacific: Matterhorn to Nagasaki, June 1944 to August 1945* (Chicago: University of Chicago Press, 1953), 756.

INDEX

Page numbers in *italic* refer to illustrations.